2025

Social Psychology

Steven Penrod
University of Wisconsin

Psych

PRENTICE-HALL, INC.

Sociology

Englewood Cliffs, New Jersey

To Joan Dobrof Penrod and Rachel

Library of Congress Cataloging in Publication Data

Penrod, Steven.
  Social psychology.

  Bibliography: pp. 639–668
  Includes indexes.
  1. Social psychology.   I. Title.   [DNLM:
1. Psychology, Social.   HM 251 P417s]
HM251.P416   1983   302   82–20422
ISBN 0-13-817924-7

© 1983 by Prentice-Hall, Inc., Englewood Cliffs, N.J.

Printed in the United States of America.

10 9 8 7 6 5 4 3 2 1

Prentice-Hall International, Inc., *London*
Prentice-Hall of Australia, Pty. Ltd., *Sydney*
Editora Prentice-Hall do Brasil Ltda., *Rio de Janeiro*
Prentice-Hall Canada, Inc., *Toronto*
Prentice-Hall of India Private Limited, *New Delhi*
Prentice-Hall of Japan, Inc., *Tokyo*
Prentice-Hall of Southeast Asia Pte. Ltd., *Singapore*
Whitehall Books Limited, *Wellington, New Zealand*

Art Director: Florence Dara Silverman; **Development Editor:** Marjorie P. K. Weiser;
Production Editor: Madalyn Stone; **Production Assistant:** Niels Aaboe; **Page Layout:** Otto
Barz/Publishing Synthesis; **Cover Designer:** Diana Hrisinko; **Cover Art:** Arshile Gorky,
Water of the Flowery Mill. The Metropolitan Museum of Art, George A. Hearn Fund, 1956;
Line Art: Danmark & Michaels, Inc.; **Manufacturing Buyer:** Ray Keating

Credits for chapter opening photos: 1, Marc Anderson; 2, Louis Fernandez; 3, Jan Lukas,
Photo Researchers, Inc.; 4, Kenneth Josephson, *Matthew*, The Metropolitan Museum of Art,
Warner Communications, Inc. Purchase Fund and National Endowment for the Arts, 1981
(1981.1045); 5, Mark W. Berghash, *Serial Portrait of Thomasina Webb, Artist, from the
series Aspects of the True Self*, The Metropolitan Museum of Art, Warner Communications,
Inc. Purchase Fund, 1981 (1981. 1173.1–6); 6, Brassai, *Couple d'amoureux dans un petit
cafe, quartier Italie*, The Metropolitan Museum of Art, Warner Communications, Inc.
Purchase Fund and National Endowment for the Arts, 1980 (1980.1023.5); 7, A.T. & T. Photo
Center; 8, Louis Fernandez; 9, Marc Anderson; 10, Ken Karp; 11, Arthur Tress, Photo
Researchers, Inc.; 12, copyright 1967 Jacksonville *Journal*, Rocco Morabito; 13, Edward C.
Topple, New York Stock Exchange; 14, John Isaac, United Nations; 15, UPI; 16, Hella
Hammid, Rapho/Photo Researchers, Inc.

ISBN 0-13-817924-7

Contents

V

Chapter 2

Research in Social Psychology   39

2

SOCIAL COGNITION: EXPERIENCING OURSELVES AND OTHERS   81

Chapter 3

Development of the Self   83

3

COMMUNICATION, ATTITUDES, AND SOCIAL INFLUENCE   249

Chapter 10

Conformity, Compliance, and Prejudice   365

4

ANTI- AND PROSOCIAL BEHAVIOR   399

Chapter 11

Aggression and Violence   401

Chapter 12

Prosocial Behavior   439

5

APPLYING SOCIAL PSYCHOLOGY   473

Chapter 13

Groups, Leadership, and Organizations   475

Chapter 14

Environmental Influences on Social Behavior   515

Chapter 15

Social Psychology and the Law   553

Chapter 16

Social Psychology and the Quality of Life   593

Preface

If you were to write a social psychology textbook, where would you begin and end? When I first considered it I was confronted both by the sense that social psychology did not need yet another textbook *and* by the various complaints I have heard about them in recent years. It was easy to see the challenge in writing a new social psychology text. But, of course, avoiding the pitfalls that have trapped others is not an easy matter. Even though I started with a blemish-free vision of the final product, I learned that there are inevitably compromises to be made when writing a textbook. It cannot be as exhaustive, as thoughtful, as contemporary, or as forward-looking as one would like. But it can be engaging, informative, sometimes challenging and thought-provoking—as I hope this volume is.

My vision of what a social psychology text ought to be has been profoundly shaped by my own experiences as a student. I think my vision of social psychology is broader than that encountered in many social psychology texts. I came to social psychology late in my student career. My undergraduate major was in political science (in a department with a strong behavioral orientation) and before completing my PhD in social psychology I managed to squeeze in a law degree and some practical legal experience. Part of social psychology's attraction for me was that it offered theories and methods of inquiry that could help to answer many of the questions raised in political science and law. As a college student of the late 1960s I was immersed in calls for "relevance," and in social psychology I found much more relevance than I had encountered in any other discipline.

I found in my meanderings through other disciplines that much of social psychology had already been "given away"—one need only look at research on political behavior, communication, advertising, law, medicine, and many other topics to realize the profound influence social psychological theories and methods have had. When I think about the "applications" discussed in this book, I think not only about the applied research being done within the traditional boundaries of social psychology, but also about research being conducted in other disciplines by people who may not even consider themselves social psychologists.

Despite the attention to applied issues, I have tried not to sacrifice basic theory and research. The text covers most of the topics encountered in other social psychology texts, and the familiar—and important—classics are presented also. However, I have avoided the temptation to be encyclopedic. While a large number of interesting and theoretically significant studies of recent vintage are presented, they have been selected carefully to produce a sensible balance between new and old, basic and applied, theoretical and straightforwardly empirical.

Being a student for nearly a quarter of a century has sensitized me to the problems encountered by students. It is no fun reading turgid prose, and while the Socratic method may be fine in some settings, it has no place in introductory texts. The emphasis in this volume is on clear and engaging presentations of basic concepts and research findings.

About This Book

Social Psychology is intended for use as a text for a first course in social psychology. It provides an introduction to research methods, theories (and the research upon which they are based), and applications, and can be used in a one-term course.

Features   The distinguishing features of this book include:

1. Balanced coverage. Classic studies are emphasized in order to place the major themes of social psychology in historical perspective. Throughout, research that has advanced theory and given birth to further research is noted. In an effort to show where today's interests lie, recent research is also stressed. Thus, emerging areas such as social cognition, the "self," and applications are given more attention, while relatively dormant areas such as cognitive dissonance and group dynamics receive somewhat less attention than in traditional texts. This text emphasizes key modern views (behaviorist and cognitivist) to illustrate the role of theory in research, without idealizing the scientific method.

2. Scientific foundations and research methods. Special emphasis is placed on the fact that social psychology is a science—albeit a young one that has not yet realized its full potential. I have tried to convey the importance of research and show how it is conducted, and also to evaluate the strengths and weaknesses of the varied methods used by social psychologists. Indeed, chapter 2 is more informative on these matters than most such chapters; I wrote it in the hope that instructors will use it to stimulate further discussion of the role of research. In addition, each chapter has a box highlighting research in which one or more studies are examined in some detail. My goal, especially in the first two chapters, was to provide a thorough introduction to the scientific world-view of contemporary social psychology and to underscore the advantages of systematic observation and study.

3. Social implications. This text, although not an "applied" volume, aspires to one extra step of relevance beyond that of traditional texts. Throughout, an effort has been made to illustrate the applications of traditional theories and research findings to the real world. In each chapter there is a box highlighting applied aspects of some theory or finding discussed in the main body of the text. In every chapter there are also boxes discussing controversial issues, within social psychology as a discipline, or within the larger society in which we all live. In addition the final section of the book is largely devoted to applied topics.

4. Readability and aids to learning. The goal in writing has been clarity. Each chapter is preceded by a summary outline of its content, and a few "Questions about . . ." the subject under discussion, which was designed to get students to start considering relevant issues even before they begin reading an assignment. These questions are answered at the end of each chapter, where a chapter summary and a list of Suggested Additional Reading can also be found. Within each chapter descriptive heads guide the reader from topic to topic; generous use of tables and figures graphically supplements text discussion; and photographs and a cartoon provide additional illustrative comment on the relevance of the chapter content. The writing tends to be personal—the text was written for students and is meant to speak to them. I have tried to spice it with examples that they can relate to, and to steer a sensible course on the use of jargon, selecting and defining those terms that are central to the discipline and avoiding those that are merely pedantic. In every chapter, key terms are boldfaced and defined in context. These terms appear again in the extensive Glossary at the back of the book.

Organization   This text is organized in a logical sequence that is adaptable to most instructors' course organizations. We start in part 1 by examining the historical framework and guiding principles of social psychology, and describing its scientific foundations and means of operation. Chapter 2 is devoted to a description of the research methods employed in social psychology.

The remainder of the text moves from the micro or personal level outward to the macro perspective of society as a whole. In part 2 the individual is the focus, as we look at the social cognition of the self and others and at interactions between individuals. Part 3 explores the effects of society on the individual, while in part 4 we examine the development of anti- and prosocial behaviors. Finally, in part 5, we look at people's roles and behaviors in the real world, examining such applied areas for social psychological insights as organizational behavior, environmental psychology, psychology and the law, and psychology and the quality of life in key areas. The sequence used is sufficiently flexible to allow the chapters to be assigned in any order, and to omit or assign as supplementary reading only those topics that lie beyond the purview of a particular course. The rich project suggestions as well as additional readings to be found in the *Instructor's Manual*, on the other hand, make possible the expansion of a given topic for fuller emphasis where this might be desirable. The *Instructor's Manual* also includes the *Test Item File*, which is made up of multiple choice questions and an answer key.

Acknowledgments

This book represents a collaboration of the best talent I could find. Initial drafts of manuscript chapters were provided by professional writers working under explicit instructions from my graduate students and myself. I want particularly to acknowledge the assistance of all those whose efforts made this book possible. First, I would like to thank four graduate students who labored long and hard to organize and assemble this book: Daniel Linz (who worked on chapters 7, 8, 9, 11, 12, 15 and 16), Sarah Tanford (chapters 5, 13 and 15), Michael Atkinson (now at the University of Western Ontario, chapters 1, 4, 7 and 10) and Carol Krafka (chapters 3, 6 and 14). In every instance, many of the strengths of these chapters can be attributed to their diligent efforts.

Lisa Thrush must receive credit for coordinating the activities of the throngs of people at the University of Wisconsin (including me) who worked on the book. Scott Broetzmann managed herculean efforts at the university library and Patricia Klitzke somehow produced typed manuscripts from scribbled drafts. James Coward, Hope Hunter, and Leslie Manke helped to tie up loose ends.

At Prentice-Hall, Marjorie P. K. Weiser must receive credit for somehow keeping all the bits and pieces of the text in sensible and working order, editing and rewriting, for exercising sound judgment on organization and where to cut and expand, for providing invaluable assistance on the basics of writing a book, for providing encouragement when I was discouraged, and for steering me back to the task when I had a tendency to wander.

Thanks must also be extended to many other people at Prentice-Hall: Ed Stanford and John Isley, who entrusted this project to those of us here at the University of Wisconsin; Marilyn Coco, editorial assistant; Bill Webber, marketing manager; and JoAnn Petrullo, market researcher. I especially want to thank Madalyn Stone, who oversaw production of the text, for her diligence, expertise, and perseverance; Cecil Yarbrough, who read draft chapters and provided very thoughtful feedback; Florence Silverman for caring about the book's appearance; and Anita Duncan for locating precisely the right photos for every chapter. I am grateful also to Toni Goldfarb, Alice Harvey, Robert Mony, Jerry Ralya, and Henry Weinfeld for their writing skills and professional assistance in the preparation of the manuscript; to Peter Rooney for preparing the index; and to Sara Lewis for her intelligent preparation of the glossary.

A number of reviewers provided guidance along the way; I am grateful for the thoughtful comments of: Robert Arkin, University of Missouri; Eugene Borgida, University of Minnesota; Robert Buckhout, Center for Responsive Psychology, Brooklyn College; John T. Cacioppo, University of Iowa; Shepard B. Gorman, Nassau Community College; Charles M. Judd, University of Colorado, Boulder; Rosemary H. Lowe, Louisiana State University; Melvin Mark, Pennsylvania State University; Elaine C. Nocks, Furman University; Richard Reardon, University of Oklahoma, Norman; R. Lance Shotland, Pennsylvania State University; Garold Stasser, Miami University, Oxford, Ohio; Warren R. Street, Central Washington State College; Philip Tetlock, University of California, Berkeley; Charles J. Walker, Saint Bonaventure University; and Stephen G. West, Arizona State University.

Finally, I would like to extend my sincere thanks to all those social psychologists (both cited and uncited) whose research efforts produced the body of knowledge represented in this text.

Social Psychology

THE WHYS AND HOWS OF SOCIAL PSYCHOLOGY

1

UNDERSTANDING SOCIAL PSYCHOLOGY

Questions about Human Behavior

1. How does social psychology differ from commonsense observation?
2. Why is it impossible to explain all human behavior by a single, unified theory?
3. What are the scientific objectives of social psychology?
4. Is social psychology really a science, or is it merely the study of history and culture?
5. Does human behavior reflect physiological needs or environmental influences?
6. Do people spontaneously react to external stimuli or do they pause to think before they act?

"Alert! Alert! Alert! Everyone to the pavilion." The Reverend Jim Jones was on the loudspeaker, summoning members of his Peoples Temple to their last communion. . . . In 1974, the followers of Jim Jones (had) heeded his call to build a Christian, socialist commune in the wilds of Guyana. They planted their crops and built substantial, if plain, housing. They established medical facilities that were advanced by Guyanese standards. There was little racial friction. Children seemed especially happy. . . . Then . . . life at Jonestown began to change. Meat, served twice a day at first, was served once, then not at all. The workday increased from eight hours to eleven. The commune's security forces began to impose harsher discipline. Jones himself seemed to deteriorate physically. . . . In Jonestown's final months, (meetings) became a nightly ritual that often lasted from 7:30 until 3 A.M. Jones would ramble on for hours. . . . To (him), everyone—including the cult members themselves—was a potential enemy. . . . Announcing that the commune was on the verge of being destroyed, Jones ordered his medical team to bring out "the potion," a battered tub of strawberry Flavor-aide, laced with tranquilizers and cyanide. "Everyone has to die," said Jones. "If you love me as much as I love you, we must all die or be destroyed from the outside. . . . Bring the babies first," he commanded.

At the fringe of the huge crowd, armed guards fingered guns and bows and arrows. Some families edged forward voluntarily. Others held their ground. The guards moved in, grabbing babies from recalcitrant mothers and holding them up to let 'nurses' spray the poison down their throats with hypodermics. . . . "It is time to die with dignity," said Jones on the loudspeaker. . . . The apocalyptic end of Reverend Jones and his Peoples Temple left more than 900 people dead.*

What Is Social Psychology?

In the wake of such a grisly episode, we search for answers. By what magic did the charismatic Jones maintain his hold on his flock? How did the idealism go astray? How could so many people give up control of their own lives?

Dramatic, out-of-the-ordinary episodes raise disturbing questions. We fumble to make some sense of extraordinary and disturbing events. We search our historical memories for analogies, but find few that are relevant. Mass suicides have been few: the ancient Hebrews at Masada, in the face of certain defeat at the hands of Roman invaders; a battalion of Japanese on a Pacific island overrun by American troops in World War II. Other cult leaders have commanded fanatic obedience from their followers: Joan of Arc, Hitler, Gandhi, a group of gurus in our own day. What makes a successful cult leader? What perverts the idealism of some of these figures so that their names live on for the evil they have caused?

Raising questions about human behavior is something that most of us do every day, not only when a tragedy on a grand scale has occurred. We wonder why our neighbor was making so much noise early in the morning, whether the young couple were quarreling about their feelings for one another or something less important, and how we should respond when a stranger approaches. What makes a child unhappy enough to run away from home? What makes a marriage last lovingly for a half-century and more? Why do some people face trouble with equanimity, while others grumble even when they have good fortune? Why does one person find success and another cannot seem to make a go of anything?

A Commonsense Look at Human Behavior

When we search for answers to our questions about the small dramas taking place in the lives around us, we often find them. Commonsense observations about everyday human nature have been recorded by writers and philosophers since ancient times. The loves and hates, greeds and delights of the old Greek tragedies are no different from the passions and predicaments of today's television soap operas; the political intrigues of Old Testament kings and Roman emperors echo in modern Watergates and Abscams.

Social psychology is the discipline that tries to analyze and understand human interactions, the extraordinary as well as the everyday. Many human interactions are familiar and predictable; this makes life easier for us all. It is helpful to know, for example, that a handshake and greeting—"My name is Susan Smith; I'm General Manager at Ajax Industries"—will be returned by the expected, "Nice to meet you, Susan. I'm Mike Brown, from Acme Products." Driving a car is much safer because everyone stays on the right side of the road. Group discussions are more productive because people wait their turn to speak, rather than shouting out all at once. The examples are endless.

"What could Sharon see in Glenn? They are so different," someone might ask. "Why, opposites attract," might be your answer. When Glenn moves to another town and Sharon quickly shifts her attentions to someone else, "Out of sight, out of mind," you would probably think. That is common sense.

Dick Hanley, Photo Researchers, Inc.

"As long as the fighting continued, men were more eager to be returned to the States than they were after the German surrender." Or so most soldiers during the Second World War, such as these troops on their way home, believed, according to an attitude survey by Lazarsfeld (1949). But the true attitude of American fighting men was the very opposite.

If much of social behavior is so predictable, and our commonsense answers serve our purposes, is there really a need for scholarly study? That thought has crossed the minds of many social scientists who have tried to discover whether the proverbial "man on the street" (or student at the university) really needs help to understand social interactions. During the Second World War, for example, an attitude survey of American soldiers found that they generally knew some commonsense "truths" about their fellow fighting men, including:

Men from rural backgrounds were usually in better spirits during their Army life than soldiers from city backgrounds.
Southern soldiers were better able to stand the climate in the hot South Sea Islands than Northern soldiers.

As long as the fighting continued, men were more eager to be returned to the States than they were after the German surrender (Lazarsfeld, 1949, p. 380).

More recently, Vaughan (1977) asked students in introductory psychology courses about other aspects of human behavior. She, too, found wide agreement on such observations as:

Fortunately for babies, human beings have a strong maternal instinct.
The more highly motivated you are, the better you will do at solving a complex problem.
Boys and girls exhibit no behavioral differences until environmental influences begin to produce such differences.
To change people's behavior toward members of ethnic minority groups, we must first change their attitudes. (p. 139)

If these facts are so obvious, even to untrained observers, how can social psychologists justify tremendous expenditures of time and money just to reaffirm what everyone knows already? (Indeed, many members of Congress ask this same question as they debate budgetary priorities; see box.) Wouldn't it be more valuable to focus our scientific efforts to prevent the Jonestowns and other social disasters?

There is one basic flaw to this argument: Although commonsense observations are often correct, they are just as likely to be mistaken. For example, every one of the previously mentioned widely accepted statements cited by Lazarsfeld and by Vaughan is simply not true. Rural men do not adjust to army life any better than city men. Southerners do not withstand hot climates better than northerners. Most human maternal behaviors are not instinctive, they are learned. And so on. How many statements did you question?

In fact, had we listed the opposite views first:

Soldiers were more eager to return to the United States after the German surrender than they were while the war was still going on.
Unlike lower animals whose maternal behavior is instinctive, most human maternal behaviors are learned;

you might have accepted these "truths" just as quickly. And, returning to our "proverbial" observations about Sharon and Glenn, if Sharon and Glenn had been quite similar rather than entirely opposite, you might have concluded that "birds of a feather flock together." Or, if Glenn's departure had strengthened and not disrupted their relationship, well, everyone knows that "absence makes the heart grow fonder."

There is only one good, knowledge, and one evil, ignorance.
Socrates

As these examples show, our commonsense knowledge about social behavior is incomplete. If commonsense expectations were always contradictory or incorrect, they would obviously be discarded. But we often continue to hold incorrect expectations because they are never proved completely right or wrong. If southern-born soldiers were sent to hot climates on the basis of commonsense expectations, and they won every battle, commanders would continue to use only southerners and would never learn that northern-born soldiers can be just as effective in hot climates. Only by planned, controlled experiments can facts be separated from commonsense opinions.

Defining Social Psychology

Social psychology is a systematic approach to social behavior. One of the tasks of the discipline is to determine when our commonsense knowledge about human interactions is correct, and when it is not. As we will see in chapter 2, social scientists often start with popularly accepted observations as a guide to formulating research ideas. This type of research can appear almost trivial, because it seeks to explain what everyone apparently knows already. However, much of what we "know" is not the whole story. And when our commonsense knowledge is incorrect, it is important to discover the real explanations for what is taking place. And even if our commonsense verdict is accurate, we can still learn more about what makes us—and our fellow human beings—"tick."

The life which is unexamined is not worth living.
Plato

Social psychology is a broad discipline that is concerned with more than our everyday interactions and social relationships. It is, in the words of Allport, "an attempt to understand . . . how the thought, feeling, and behavior of the individuals are influenced by the actual, imagined, or implied presence of others" (1968, p. 3). Allport's definition emphasizes that social psychology is concerned not only with a person's behavior, but also with the influence of others, including the groups a person belongs to, on that person's behavior. The definition emphasizes also that social psychologists are interested in people's thoughts and feelings, an aspect of social interaction that may not be expressed overtly in their acts or deeds.

Even the name "social psychology" reflects a unique position with respect to the major disciplines of psychology and sociology. Unlike sociology, which studies the forms, customs, behavior patterns, and functions of human groups, social psychology is concerned with the behavior and attitudes of individuals themselves and of individuals within groups. Much of social psychology is based on experimental research in which an investigator systematically changes (manipulates) key factors in a particular social situation, and then observes the effects on specific behaviors. In contrast, sociology and its related disciplines of anthropology and political science emphasize observation rather than manipulation, and group processes rather than individuals' behavior.

Although social psychology differs from other disciplines in its emphasis on individual behavior and experimentation, the distinction between disciplines is by no means clear-cut. As you can see from the table of contents of this textbook, social psychology is a wide-ranging field of study. Social psychologists conduct research on such diverse topics as loneliness (chapter 6), communication (chapter 7), attitude change (chapter 8), environmental influences on human interaction (chapter 14), and psychology and the law (chapter 15). Not surprisingly, social communication and attitude researchers are sometimes more at home in university departments of communication than in psychology departments. And researchers of social issues sometimes work in political science and sociology departments. In fact, researchers who regard themselves as social psychologists are found in academic departments of communication arts, education, criminal justice, computer science, athletics, anthropology, and even in medical schools and law schools. But in whatever department social psychologists teach, all agree that their interests generally lie within the definition offered by Allport. Social psychologists are united in their perspective that the social aspects of human behavior can be understood through systematic (scientific) inquiry and study.

The Development of Social Psychology

Social psychology is a young discipline, but the goals and frustrations of trying to analyze human interactions are not new. The earliest social psychologists were the ancient philosophers. Plato (427–347 B.C.), the most prominent among them, reflected on the social nature of human beings in *The Republic*. He believed that social interactions develop because no individual is self-sufficient. Needing the help of many others to get through life, people form states (governments).

A likely impossibility is always preferable to an unconvincing possibility.
Aristotle

In contrast to Plato's utilitarian view of the state, Aristotle (384–322 B.C.) viewed people as "political animals," gregarious by instinct. Aristotle believed that social interaction was necessary for the normal development of human beings. It is their inborn gregariousness that leads humans to affiliate with others. Both Aristotle and Plato agreed that individuals differ in their abilities. Some are innately disposed to leadership; others to following.

Other great minds have added to these early explanations. Auguste Comte (1790–1857), sometimes called the "founder" of social psychology, believed that individuals, like society and like science itself, pass through three important stages of development: (1) the theological stage, in which events are explained in terms of personified "gods"; (2) the metaphysical stage, in which phenomena are explained by impersonal powers and laws of science; and (3) the positive stage, in which phenomena are explained by their invariableness or constancy (Sahakian, 1974). In Comte's hierarchy of sciences, this third and highest stage would be a hybrid of biology and sociology called *la morale*. This "true final science" would be concerned with the individuality of human beings as it develops out of their biological nature and within their social and cultural context (Allport, 1968). (See Figure 1–1.)

Where Comte saw human behavior as an interaction of biological and social forces, most early views of human nature sought one unified explanation. For example, Jeremy Bentham's (1789) "Principle of Utility" or **hedonism** proposed that people act solely to gain pleasure and to avoid pain. Similarly, Thomas Hobbes (1651) believed that the basic motive of human beings is **egoism,** the desire for power. Other unified approaches attributed human behavior to motivations of *sympathy* (love and trust for others, as exemplified by the mother–child relationship), *gregariousness* (an innate "herd instinct" to affiliate with others), and *suggestion* (the hypnotic power that Mesmer called "animal magnetism" and LeBon called "the group mind," which can be responsible for normal agreement at one extreme and "mob hysteria" at the other extreme).

The theories of these philosophers underscore the fact that humans have long inquired about the causes of their behavior. As we shall see in this chapter, one of the unique contributions of social psychology to this inquiry is the use of scientific research methods—in particular, the use of experiments.

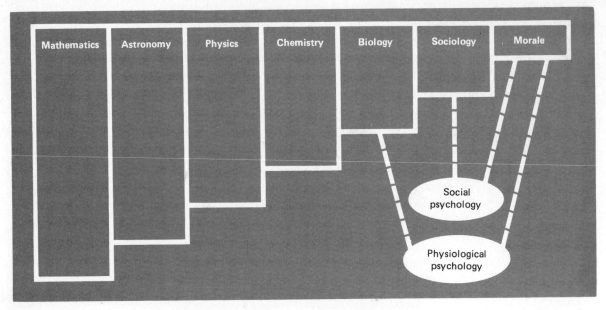

FIGURE 1-1.   Comte's Hierarchy of the Sciences

Source: *From "The Historical Background of Modern Social Psychology" by G. Allport. In G. Lindzey and E. Aronson (Eds.),* The Handbook of Social Psychology *(Vol. 1), Reading, Mass.: Addison-Wesley, 1968.*

The Discipline Develops   The first laboratory experiment in social psychology was performed by Norman Tripplett in 1897. Tripplett had observed that bicycle riders rode faster with a pacer (another rider) than when they rode alone. To investigate this observation, he brought children into the laboratory and asked them, while alone and in groups, to wind fishing reels. The groups produced faster winding times than the individuals winding alone. This phenomenon, known as *social facilitation*, is still being investigated today.

The first two textbooks devoted to social psychology both appeared in 1908. In one, William McDougall, a psychologist, emphasized a variety of instincts (innate drives) as the controlling forces behind human behavior, and thus suggested that plural, not single, factors might be at work. In the other, sociologist E. A. Ross stressed imitation and suggestion as controlling forces, but, like McDougall, agreed that these forces are instinctive.

Like all unified explanations, though, neither instinct nor suggestion could account for the tremendous diversity of human behavior. Nor could instinct or suggestion successfully predict behavior; both were explanations describing what had already taken place. In addition, neither of these concepts was observable, and social psychology had already begun to stimulate additional research based on empirical measurement. By 1924, when Floyd Allport's *Social Psychology* appeared, its contents leaned heavily on experimental findings. Allport's primary concern was the influence of the group on individual behavior. His book marked the beginning of social psychology as we know it today.

Ken Karp

In the first social psychology experiment ever performed, Triplett found that bicycle riders increased their rate of speed when they rode with others; contrary to popular wisdom, they travel less swiftly who travel alone.

Nothing endures but change.
Heraclitus

The Discipline Matures Following the introduction of Allport's text, social psychology entered a period of rapid growth. In 1927, L. L. Thurstone published sophisticated statistical methods for measuring attitudes. In 1934, J. C. Moreno developed a system of sociometrics, used for coding individual–group interactions. Public opinion polling was introduced in 1936 by George Gallup. Kurt Lewin, after fleeing Nazi Germany, initiated studies of leadership style and social climate in 1939. At the same time, social psychologists created their own professional journals to report this growing body of experimental research. The first to appear was the *Journal of Abnormal and Social Psychology*, introduced by editor Morton Prince in 1921 as an expansion of the *Journal of Abnormal Psychology*.

In each succeeding decade of the twentieth century, research interests continued to change and expand (see box). During the 1940s and 1950s, largely due to the influence of Kurt Lewin and the pressures of World War II, research in social psychology concentrated on group influences, attitudes, and attitude change. In 1952, Solomon Asch reported that individuals tend to conform to the opinions of a majority, even when those opinions are blatantly incorrect. Also in the 1950s, Carl Hovland's Yale University research group produced many studies and books on the topic of group persuasion. In 1954, Leon Festinger published his social comparison theory, which suggests that people evaluate their own performance by comparing themselves with others of similar abilities.

Research: Milestones in Understanding Social Behavior

Date	Milestone	Date	Milestone
400 B.C.	Plato suggests that human beings have a basic instinct to form groups (states).	1924	Floyd Allport publishes his *Social Psychology* text.
19th Century	Simple theories of human behavior begin to develop: Jeremy Bentham's hedonism; Thomas Hobbes's egoism.	1927	L. L. Thurstone demonstrates that attitudes can be measured using scaling techniques.
1830–1842	Auguste Comte develops his hierarchy of the sciences, with *la morale* at the pinnacle.	1929	Carl Murchison and John Dewey found the *Journal of Social Psychology*.
1859	Charles Darwin publishes *On the Origin of Species*.	1934	George Herbert Mead, a symbolic interactionist, publishes his work on the self.
1878	Wilhelm Wundt establishes first psychological laboratory.		R. T. LaPierre demonstrates that attitudes and behavior are not consistent.
1890	William James publishes *Principles of Psychology*.		J. C. Moreno develops a system for coding individual–group interactions.
1895	Gustave LeBon studies the behavior of *The Crowd*.	1935	Muzafer Sherif uses the autokinetic effect to study social norms.
1897	Norman Tripplett conducts the first social psychological experiment on *social facilitation*.	1936	George Gallup develops methods for public opinion polling.
1902	C. H. Cooley publishes his influential volume on *Human Nature and the Social Order*.	1937	J. C. Moreno founds *Sociometry*, a journal devoted to studies of group processes.
1908	William McDougall and E. H. Ross independently publish the first social psychology texts.	1939	Kurt Lewin et al. investigate the effect of leadership styles on group performance.
1913	Thorndike proposes the Law of Effect: people will continue to engage in behavior that they are rewarded for, and will cease behavior that results in punishment.	1946	Solomon Asch demonstrates the influence of cognitive set in impression formation.
1918	W. I. Thomas and F. Znaniechi begin their work on attitudes.	1948	David Krech and Richard S. Crutchfield publish a social psychology text, reviewing much of the experimental work of the past two decades.
1921	Morton Prince founds the *Journal of Abnormal Psychology* (which later becomes the *Journal of Abnormal and Social Psychology*).	1952	Solomon Asch demonstrates that individuals will conform to a majority when their beliefs are questioned.

Date	Milestone
1953	The Yale Group under Carl Hovland publishes its findings on persuasion and attitude change.
1954	Leon Festinger formulates his Social Comparison Theory, suggesting that individuals compare themselves to equivalent others in order to gain information about their own abilities and beliefs.
1957	Leon Festinger proposes a Theory of Cognitive Dissonance, a model of attitude change based on the principle that individuals strive for consistency.
1958	Fritz Heider offers another consistency model in his book, *The Psychology of Interpersonal Relations*, which lays the foundation for Attribution Theory.
1959	Leon Festinger and Merrill Carlsmith demonstrate that individuals are more likely to change their attitudes when they have insufficient justification for their behavior.
1962	Stanley Schachter and Jerome Singer publish research on the social psychological determinants of emotional states.
1963	Stanley Milgram reports the first in a series of studies on obedience to authority.
1964	Leonard Berkowitz launches an influential series of edited books: *Advances in Experimental Social Psychology*.

Date	Milestone
1967	Harold H. Kelley publishes "Attribution Theory in Social Psychology"—one of the earliest works on attribution theory. Attribution research is a dominant theme of the 1970s.
1968	Bibb Latané and John Darley first report on their research on bystander intervention.
1969	Alan Wicker challenges social psychologists to provide a better demonstration of the relationship between attitudes and behavior.
1970s	Calls for "relevance" in social psychology begin to bear fruit as social psychologists increasingly apply their skills and theories to problems in medicine, law, the environment, education, and other aspects of social life.
1970	Philip Zimbardo and his associates conduct the famous prison simulation study in the basement of Stanford University's psychology department.
1972	*Attribution: Perceiving the Causes of Behavior*, an influential collection of papers on attribution theory, is published and further fuels the 1970s emphasis on attribution research.
1980s	Attribution theory gives way to a new emphasis on the "cognitive" aspects of social behavior, and applied social psychology continues to grow in importance.

Contemporary Trends   Perhaps the greatest change in social psychology in recent years is a shift toward *applied research,* or toward a wide range of relevant social concerns. In part, this trend reflects the fact that theories of social psychology are now developed enough to be applied to important social issues. Another impetus for change has been an increasing push toward "relevance" in the social sciences.

Another significant change is an expansion of the theoretical base of social psychology into a large, comprehensive framework of integrated theories encompassing many factors. This expansive trend is also reflected in the choice of subject matter, which has shifted away from *intra*personal behavior (that is, the behavior of separate individuals) toward increasing emphasis upon *inter*personal behavior in the larger context of the group. Parallel to this shift, the development of computer data processing has given researchers a powerful new tool for analyzing large quantities of information about human behaviors, clarifying statistical relationships and suggesting new avenues to explore. And at the same time, the research approach of social psychology has expanded to include non-experimental, everyday situations, and away from artificial laboratory settings.

These trends, however, do not mean that all or even most social psychologists have abandoned their laboratories or that every published study has clear and immediate applications. As new trends and concerns arise in society, we can expect new directions in research interests and techniques to emerge.

The Perspective of Social Psychology

Social psychologists are interested in behaviors on three levels: individual, interactive, and group. To understand and clarify these three analytical approaches, let us consider how each would be used in the example of interpersonal attraction, which will be discussed fully in chapter 6. Why do you almost instantly like some people and dislike others? What causes the intense personal attraction we know as love? Do "opposites attract," or do "birds of a feather flock together"?

1. At the individual level, social psychologists are concerned with what makes one person attractive to another. Within this approach there are three fruitful areas of inquiry: The genetic or sociobiological focus would look at the genetically determined role of factors—in this case gender—on the behaviors of individuals, and the constraints posed by such factors as physical appearance and sexual orientation. The physiological approach might study the roles of such biochemical substances as pheromones, which generate sexually attractive odors, as well as hormones and other body secretions that control a person's sexual and intellectual excitability. Cognitive studies, on the other hand, analyze the information that people perceive in their environment, and how they process that information to form judgments about the social attractiveness of others. Cognitive analyses might also focus on a person's past social learning experiences, which determine his or her future behavior toward other people.
2. At the interactive level, the focus turns to processes that control attraction between people. In this area, too, we can take several approaches. We can look at the kinds of interactions that may influence attraction—for example,

going out on dates, participating in sports, or even sitting next to someone in class. Or we can turn this approach around and discover how high or low levels of attraction between people affect their behavior during various kinds of interaction—on the job, at a party, in a class. Since social learning is another determinant of interactive responses, we can examine childhood experiences with parents and peers that may affect later attraction behaviors.

3. At the group level, concern is for differences in relevant behavior according to group membership. We can consider men and women as distinct groups in order to discover differences in their sexual behavior or judgments of attractiveness. For example, many men are attracted to women who wear sexy clothes, but what do other women think of female flashy dressers? The influence of cultural, ethnic, and age groups as determinants of interpersonal attraction could also be studied. We could, for example, compare the dating habits of people born in the 1920s and those born in the 1960s, or the sexual mores of Protestants with those of Catholics, Muslims, or Jews.

As these examples show, it is possible to examine a particular social behavior from a variety of perspectives. And social psychologists do just that, as we will see throughout this book. Each of the different perspectives and theoretical approaches provides another insight into the multifaceted social behaviors of human beings in our society.

Social Psychology as a Science

What does it mean to say that social psychology is a science? A science is an organized body of knowledge derived from objective observation and systematic testing. The term *science* refers not to one particular subject matter, but to all areas that can be systematically and objectively studied.

The work of science can be performed by sitting in a field and watching the clouds pass by (if the watcher collects and records those observations objectively and systematically, and relates them to existing knowledge), or sitting on a college campus and interviewing students who pass by (again, only if the interviewer fulfills the requirements of objectivity and systematic observation).

The **natural sciences,** which include botany, biology, chemistry, physics, and zoology, attempt to explain observations about nature and the physical world. The **behavioral sciences,** which include anthropology, ethology, psychology, and sociology, deal with observations about the activities, including the mental operations and motor responses, of animals and humans. The term **social science** refers to those behavioral sciences and related disciplines—economics, political science—concerned with the activities of people within human communities. **Psychology** is concerned with human and animal behavior and mental and emotional processes. And, narrowing our focus even further, **social psychology** invesigates the actions of individuals and of individuals within groups. Social psychology, then, is both a behavioral and a social science; the terms are often

Interviews for the purpose of collecting scientific data can be conducted in any location where subjects exist, as long as the subjects are appropriately and randomly chosen and the data are recorded accurately.

used interchangeably. Although, like its parent discipline, psychology, it is not a natural science, social psychology draws on developments in human biology whenever appropriate.

The Methods of Science

When scientists collect observations, they follow certain established rules of operation. These rules, collectively known as the **scientific method,** specify how observations should be made, recorded, and tested. The scientific method involves: systematic observation, the development of theories that explain those observations, the use of theories to generate predictions about future observations and the revision of theories when predictions are not accurate. This process insures that all participants in a discipline are "speaking the same language."

Observations made according to the scientific method are much more precise than nonscientific, commonsense information-gathering. The difference can be illustrated through the proverbial observation that "birds of a feather flock together." People who associate with one another resemble one another in many ways. From such everyday perceptions people develop a loosely knit concept of one way the world operates.

What differentiates this everyday concept from a scientific theory? First, everyday observations are far from orderly. Random observation of the environment can produce many examples of how birds of a feather flock together, but a determined searcher might also uncover examples of the converse adage that "opposites attract." Secondly, nonscientific observers may not keep good records of the information they collect; relying on scattered memories may lead to faulty recall of data.

Theory Building, Theory Testing

Next, science requires facts, not just observations. What is the difference? Facts are explained observations. In other words, we need explanations—**theories**—to help us interpret what we observe. We produce a theory when we form general rules on the basis of the specific observations we make. The progression from specific observations to general rules or theories is known as *logical induction*. It was through a process of induction that Isaac Newton devised his theory of gravity from his observations of falling objects.

They travel swiftest who travel alone.

In science, facts remain constant, but their interpretation can vary considerably, depending upon the theory that is used to explain them:

> There's a common myth that facts are more important in science than theories, so much so that a theory must collapse as soon as contradicted by a single experimental observation. In practice it doesn't work that way. It's not facts that topple theories, but other theories. You don't abandon a boat in a stormy sea just because it has a leak—you wait for another boat to come along.
>
>   Theories are never lightly abandoned. They, after all, explain the world, whereas facts merely describe it (Wade, 1982).

Thus, more than one theory can explain the same set of facts. The goal of science is to test many theories to determine which one provides the most meaningful understanding of any phenomenon. It is not necessary to prove that a theory is correct. Even respected theories in chemistry and physics are not considered to be 100 percent certain. Theories are explanations of facts, not facts themselves. As long as the explanations work, or fit the known facts, the theory is considered *valid*.

The need for scientific testing makes considerable demands on a theory. It must be based on objective observations, so that other scientists can recheck the originator's perceptions about what has been observed. If repeated observations produce new facts that cannot be accounted for by the theory, then the theory must be changed.

Observations and Predictions   A theory must also make testable predictions. Theories are formulated to explain prior observations. If the theory is good, it should also explain new observations in the same category and suggest new observations that can be used to test the theory. The theorist should be able to use deductive logic to make predictions about phenomena that will take place if the theory is correct. A good theory of gravity should predict the falling behavior of apples, other kinds of fruit, meteors, baseballs, and so on. In other words, the theory should generate predictions—hypotheses that can be tested. Given the theory that "birds of a feather flock together," which is based on prior observations that people with similar traits choose to associate with one another, what could you predict? If you predicted that like-minded individuals, who had never met before, would be attracted to each other, and they were, you would think your theory was pretty good. On the other hand, if you found that many people who seemed alike failed to get along, you would have to change your theory. You

It is for wisdom that people travel together.
African proverb

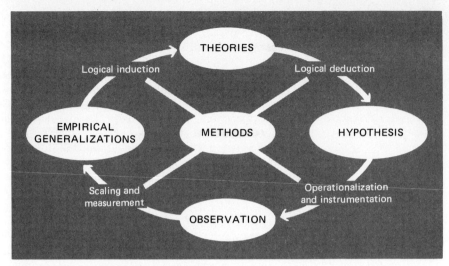

FIGURE 1-2.   Components of the Scientific Process

Source: *Adapted from Walter Wallace (ed.),* Sociological Theory, *1969, p. ix. Reprinted with permission of Aldine Publishing Company.*

would have to make new observations and new tests to develop a revised explanation that could provide a more meaningful understanding of the facts.

Haste in every business brings failure.
Herodotus

This constant and cyclical process of theory development and theory testing (see Figure 1-2) underlies all scientific disciplines. That is why science constantly grows and changes. In social psychology, a discipline that evolved in the last 50 years, research questions, methods, and theories are continually undergoing major revisions. Unlike the so-called "hard sciences," such as physics and chemistry, which have evolved over centuries, the young science of social psychology has been marked by the rapid building and testing of theories.

What Makes a "Good" Theory?   Nevertheless, a number of general theories are recognized and accepted by most social psychologists. We will discuss some of them later in this chapter, as well as throughout this book. What makes these theories "good" is not that they have not been disproved, but that they follow several important scientific rules:

1.   A theory should logically and consistently account for all observed facts.
2.   A theory should be consistent with other existing, generally accepted theories.
3.   A theory should produce predictions that are confirmed by future observations.
4.   A theory should be parsimonious, that is, built on the fewest concepts necessary to explain the observed facts.
5.   A theory should be heuristic, that is, it should stimulate further research and development.

Scientific Assumptions of Social Psychology All scientists, social psychologists included, share certain assumptions about the scientific method of research (see box). These key assumptions are:

1. **Empiricism.** The empirical approach rests on the belief that direct observation and experience provide the only firm basis for understanding natural events. Unlike "rational" thinkers who analyze events through reason and intuition—these are the so-called "armchair philosophers" who conduct research in the comfort of a quiet study—empiricists rely on the gathering of data to confirm or disprove the predictions made by social theories.
2. **Determinism.** Nature—including human nature—proceeds in an orderly and systematic (determined) manner. One event has an impact on other events. Determinism implies that nothing happens by chance. If we understand the causal relationships underlying human behavior, we could predict *all* human actions.
3. **Invariance.** The concept of invariance implies that causal relationships between the same events do not change over time or over location. In other words, observations made today will follow the same rules as observations made last year. The concept of invariance provides a lasting foundation on which to base scientific theories, but it is easier to apply to physics, chemistry, and the other hard sciences than to the behavioral sciences. Whereas atoms and molecules follow fixed laws, human beings are subject to frequent changes produced by social experiences and learning. However, this in itself is an example of invariance: Humans today, tomorrow, and 10 years from now will invariably remain susceptible to learning and experience. When social psychologists speak of invariance, therefore, they mean the general relationships governing human behavior remain constant, providing that observations are made under the same conditions. If, for example, a recent study found that American women are attracted to men who have a strong sense of humor, whereas Chinese women are attracted to more serious men, we would expect that a follow-up study 10 years from now would reach the same general conclusions, as long as relevant conditions had not changed radically in either country.
4. **Operationalism.** Theories must be described accurately and precisely so they can be tested objectively. Operationalism demands that predictions be phrased so researchers can perform tests that will either confirm or disprove those predictions. When psychologists talk about interpersonal attraction, for example, they do not say that people who are attracted to each other will "fall in love." What is love? How can it be measured? As you will read in chapter 6, social psychologists have translated "love" into quantifiable, operational terms, such as the amount of time two people spend in direct eye contact, or the physical distance (or lack of it) that separates them when they sit together. Although these terms may be less enchanting than love and romance, they are measurable. (We shall have more to say about operational definitions in chapter 2.)
5. **Objectivity.** As a science, social psychology attempts to be objective in its approach to human interactions. What this means is that researchers strive to collect data, develop theories, and make predictions fairly and impartially in

a way that other investigators can understand and agree upon. We would be remiss, however, if we pretended that social psychology is fully objective. Our subject matter exists within a social context and is investigated by researchers who also have been socialized within that context. Try as they might for objectivity, social psychologists are humans, susceptible to human failings. However, their training and professional detachment helps to assure the highest possible objectivity in observations and theories. In the next chapter, we will discuss some of the pitfalls that threaten objectivity, and ways to overcome them.

Controversy: Is Social Research A "Golden Fleece"?

In these tight budget times, would you pay. anyone $1,325 to study why bowlers, hockey fans, and pedestrians smile? A division of the National Institute for Mental Health (NIMH) did just that, and Wisconsin Senator William Proxmire did not think it was anything to smile about. He angrily gave the grant recipients his "Golden Fleece" award for the month's "most ridiculous waste of the taxpayers' money" (Smith, 1980).

Although the NIMH claimed that the study might be useful to therapists, teachers, policemen, judges, and political leaders interested in judging "the genuineness of people's messages," Proxmire questioned why the hard-pressed taxpayer should be asked to pay for what he called "an academic version of *Bowling for Dollars*."

Bowling was not Proxmire's only target. Another Golden Fleece award went to two social psychologists from the University of Wisconsin for research on sociological aspects of love and affection. Proxmire explained that he, as a taxpayer, did not want to know the answers to the questions being posed by the researchers and that therefore it was a waste of public money. Research on aggressive behavior, including studies of teeth-clenching in monkeys, also earned an award from Proxmire, but the social psychologist responsible for that project turned the tables and successfully sued Proxmire for libel.

What makes some social research valuable, and some a taxpayer's Golden Fleece? Obviously, opinions vary. The U.S. Office of Naval Research, which paid for some of the teeth-clenching studies, believes that its findings can help identify individuals who have a high tolerance for aggressive stimulation, particularly those who might work in submarines and patrol planes. Even if possible applications were not so clear, most social psychologists would defend this research topic on the basis of pure scientific interest. Other objections that are raised point out that such research is merely uncovering what we have always known—commonsense information—about human behavior. But, as we have seen, our commonsense knowledge is often flawed. Moreover, it is the application of scientific methods to these human problems that gives social science research its values. As research funds diminish, though, and taxpayers grow testier, social psychologists realize that justify they must to obtain research awards, rather than Golden Fleece awards. It is easy to appreciate the scientific wisdom of investigations that turn up the unexpected, but researchers do not know in advance if their results will be startling or mundane. What justifies both kinds of studies are the underlying theories, assumptions, and objectives that make social psychology a science.

Scientific Objectives of Social Psychology

So far, we have described theory development, theory testing, and the basic assumptions that underlie social psychological research. This set of procedures for data collection and hypothesis testing exists to achieve four basic objectives: description, explanation, prediction, and control.

The first objective of social research is to *describe* the phenomena that are observed. Descriptions flow naturally from the systematic collection of facts and observations about any phenomenon. For example, observations about heterosexual and homosexual attraction might start with a list of a number of observed people who showed attraction to members of the same sex, and the number who showed attraction to members of the opposite sex. Then researchers would attempt to describe the characteristics of individuals showing heterosexual as compared with homosexual attraction, and to pinpoint specific situations that elicited one type of attraction more than the other.

It is one thing to describe patterns of heterosexual and homosexual attraction, and an entirely different matter to transcend description and develop theories that *explain* what has been observed. Explanation, the second major objective of social psychology, involves identification of the causal relationships that produce particular behaviors. For instance, if in the group of people we observed significantly more tall men than short men exhibited homosexual behavior, we might try to explain this observation by theorizing that physical growth could be a factor in causing male homosexuality.

But our theory may be wrong. As we mentioned before, the best measure of a theory is its ability to make accurate predictions. *Prediction*, the third major objective of social psychology, is perhaps the most difficult to obtain. Social psychology is not as advanced as the older material sciences and, as a result, it is rarely possible to predict the behavior of any one individual with complete accuracy. Generally, the best psychologists can do is to specify the *probability* that any one individual will engage in a particular kind of behavior. However, it is easier to predict patterns of behavior common to individuals in general, or to collections of individuals (groups). When government agencies predict inflation or unemployment, for example, they are not guessing what is going to happen to Robert Adler, Juan Brown, and Karen Chin. Rather, they are predicting that an average of 10 people out of any 100 will be out of work this year. Similarly, social psychologists would not predict from your observations that your tall friend definitely will be attracted to other men, but they might theorize that a significant number of tall men show attraction to other men. If this prediction is not supported by later observations, however, the theory will have to be discarded, or revised. (In this case, of course, observation of a different set of individuals would likely demonstrate that the correlation of tallness and homosexuality was merely coincidental.)

Theories and predictions help us understand why behavioral phenomena occur. The fourth objective of social psychology is *control* over when or whether behavioral phenomena occur. "Control" can be an alarming word, prompting images of a society like that in Huxley's *Brave New World*. But scientific control is vastly different from manipulating behavior for evil or personal gains.

Later in this chapter, we discuss ways psychologists help to solve social problems. In that context, the objective of control or management of events be-

Application: Eyewitness Reliability

You are sitting in the classroom of Professor von Liszt, a famous criminologist at the University Seminary in Berlin. The year is 1902. Professor von Liszt has just finished discussing a book, and one of your fellow students suddenly shouts:

"I wanted to throw light on the matter from the standpoint of Christian morality!" Another student throws in, "I cannot stand that!" The first starts up, exclaiming, "You have insulted me!" The second clenches his fist and cries, "If you say another word. . . ." The first draws a revolver. The second rushes madly upon him. The Professor steps between them and, as he grasps the man's arm, the revolver goes off.

You have been an eyewitness to a horrifying crime. Can you describe it in detail for the police investigators?

According to Hugo Munsterberg, who reported this incident in 1908, not one of the students who was present could provide an accurate account of what had happened. In the most accurate report, 25 percent of the details were in-

correct. In poorer reports, up to 80 percent of all statements were mistaken. Words were put into the mouths of men who had never spoken. Actions were incorrectly attributed to the chief participants. Essential details were completely forgotten.

Fortunately, the entire scene was a tragicomedy carefully planned and rehearsed by student actors to test observers' ability to recall and describe emotionally charged events. Immediately after the described events, Professor von Liszt established order in the lecture hall and asked some students to write an exact account. The remaining students were asked to give their accounts at later dates.

This early experiment in social psychology laid the basis for research that is still continuing today. It illustrates the value of simulations that are designed to mimic everyday social conditions. Although the results have strong bearings on perception and memory, their greatest implication is in the field of criminal justice. Based on Munsterberg's study, would you trust the report of an eyewitness to a crime?

comes meaningful and desirable. For instance, most people agree that reducing the number of deaths from automobile accidents is desirable. Since studies have proved that people who wear seat belts are less likely to be seriously injured in a car accident, we might want to motivate more people to use seat belts.

To achieve this, we need studies to identify the social psychological reasons that encourage people to use seat belts. This requires a description of the people who use their belts, and the circumstances under which they are most likely to "buckle up." Next, we develop a theory to explain our observations. For example, we might theorize that people whose cars sound an alarm when seat belts are not buckled are most likely to wear their belts. For our next step, prediction, we hypothesize that equipping more cars with seat belt alarm systems increases seat belt use. If subsequent observations prove this to be correct, social psychologists might recommend a law mandating the installation of alarm systems in all newly manufactured cars. And, if auto fatalities subsequently declined, we could conclude that this action had helped to control the death rate from auto accidents.

Is Social Psychology Really a Science?

Formal scientific objectives guide researchers in their work, but realistically we know that even trained social psychologists do not follow every rule precisely. We have already mentioned social factors that can threaten social scientists' objectivity, but those factors are minor when compared with the social influences that affect experimental subjects.

Think how you would behave if you were a research subject. You would probably be a bit nervous at first, hoping you would not say or do something foolish. You would try to understand what the experiment was about, so that you could answer questions and perform tasks correctly. And, rather than being entirely truthful, you would probably avoid any confessions that might be embarrassing, or try to give answers that you think would be distinctive. Unlike the elements and compounds under a chemist's microscope, you would hardly be a passive participant. Your responses would be personal and individualistic—possibly different from those of most other students from your own campus, from other universities, in the country as a whole, or in different countries.

Given all these "human factors," how can social psychology claim to be a scientific enterprise? Even within the discipline of social psychology, many researchers have raised this question. Gergen (1973) and others have argued, for example, that social psychology is more a study of "historical circumstances" than of unchanging, theoretical principles because social phenomena are inconstant and subject to infinite influences. It is charged also that the communication of research goals and findings immediately causes subjects to change their behavior. The circulation of research findings in the news media may even cause entire populations to change their social behavior. For instance, if you read that subjects in an important research study callously disregarded a cry for help, you might become more aware of your own behavior and thus more likely to help a stranger in distress.

That such charges have validity is no reason to abandon all hope of analyzing, predicting, or controlling human interactions. Most social psychologists set their sights toward a realistic middle ground in which findings are expressed in terms that recognize the limits of their universality (Schlenker, 1974), and that take into account the limitations of cultural and historical contexts (Hendrick, 1976).

Theoretical Perspectives in Social Psychology

Human behavior is complex. Although social psychology has been working toward comprehensive theories, no single theory can be expected to include every relevant factor. Behavior is determined by many factors. Consequently, multiple theories have arisen.

Six major theories of human interaction (see Table 1–1) are prominent in social psychology: (1) physiological theory is concerned with innate genetic predispositions; (2) sociobiological theory holds that social behavior traits evolve

TABLE 1–1.

Six Key Theories in Social Psychology

Theory	Major Proponents	Concepts and Focus	Individual Involvement	Causes of Behavior	Impact on Social Psychology
Physiological	McDougall Lorenz	Innate predispositions, drives, or instincts	Passive	Internal	Low
Sociobiology	Wilson	Behavior traits subject to natural selection	Passive	Internal	Low
Learning	Skinner Pavlov Miller & Dollard Bandura & Walters	Conditioning Reinforcement Imitation	Passive	External	High
Cognitive	Koffka Koller Asch Heider Kelley	Interpretation and meaning of events Assimilation–contrast Field Synergy	Active	Both	High
Psychoanalytic	Freud Adler Horney	Psychosexual stages of development Ego, id, superego Identification	Passive	Internal	Moderate
Symbolic Interactionism	Mead Merton Goffman Sarbin	Social interaction and communication	Active	Both	Moderate

through a process of natural selection; (3) learning theory postulates a stimulus–response relationship between the environment and social behavior; (4) cognitive theory states that people perceive and interpret stimuli in their environment, rather than reacting passively to those stimuli; (5) psychoanalytic theory describes internal drives that must be satisfied through social relationships; and (6) symbolic interactionism emphasizes social interaction and communication between people.

Each of these theories provides a different view of how people function in their environment. Each represents a different perspective on social behavior. No one theory is sufficient to explain all human social phenomena. But together, these six approaches reflect the diversity of human interactions.

The Physiological Approach

Physiological theories postulate that inborn, genetically transmitted characteristics control human behavior. McDougall (1908) was an early proponent of this view, believing that each behavior trait was controlled by a corresponding instinct. For example, mothers and fathers interacted with their children in certain ways because of a parental instinct. People fought with one another because of the instinct of pugnacity. People sought out each other's company because of the gregarious instinct, and so forth. Unfortunately, McDougall's concept of instincts had little predictive power. Given any type of behavior, one could always postulate an instinct that might be controlling it, but naming instincts is not the same as providing an empirical explanation of the behavior.

Nevertheless, some advocates of social instincts still exist. A contemporary exponent of this position is Lorenz, who suggested (1966) that aggression is an instinctive behavior, that is, humans are born with an aggressive drive, a need to engage in fighting. Aggressive energy builds up within the human nervous system, and when it reaches a high level, an appropriate external stimulus (the *releaser*) triggers an aggressive response. On an optimistic note, Lorenz also explained that aggressive energy can be expended in harmless ways, as through athletic competition, thus avoiding active combat.

Lorenz's theory, and indeed most physiologically based theories, can be criticized as overly simplistic (as it is in chapter 11). Human behavior is too complex to be explained solely by innate mechanisms. People fight with friends and with enemies, when they are frustrated and when they are well-adjusted, when they are hungry and when they are well-fed. Other factors, apart from specific instincts and specific releasers, must be at work. Nevertheless, the existence of innate, hereditary, physiological differences is too important to ignore.

Sociobiological Theory

Sociobiology is a hybrid discipline, combining the physiological and the sociological approaches to human behavior. E. O. Wilson, the main proponent of sociobiology, believes that behavior is genetically determined, but that it has evolved by the natural selection of particular sets of genes. In other words, Wilson concludes that the same genetic selection process Darwin described for physical characteristics also operates for behavioral characteristics:

> If the possession of certain genes predisposes individuals toward a particular trait, say a certain kind of social response, and the trait in turn conveys superior fitness, the genes will gain an increased representation in the next generation. (Wilson, 1978, pp. 19–20)

Wilson believes, for example, that aggressive behavior is necessary for human survival, and that altruistic behavior (helping others, even at the expense of oneself) aids survival of the group, but not of the altruistic individual. According to Wilson, "genes hold culture on a leash" (1978). In other words, human behavior is capable of wide variation, but only as wide as our genetic makeup permits. This idea has been criticized by psychologists who think that individual differences are too great to be explained by heredity alone. For example, Dugger (1981 a,b,) argues that even genetically determined behaviors are shaped by cultural and environmental factors. Consider human infancy, which is genetically programmed to last many years. Nevertheless, youngsters in various cultures spend vastly different time spans in infancy and childhood. Whereas an Eskimo male may show every trait of adulthood by age 12, an American male may take up to age 25 (Dugger, 1981a).

The sociobiological approach shares many of the same assets and liabilities of the physiological approach. Both are supported by irrefutable facts of biology, but neither grants sufficient credit to the social determinants of human behavior.

Theories of Learning and Socialization

A significant part of human behavior is acquired through instruction and by observation and imitation of other people's behavior. Even behaviors with strong innate components—eating, drinking, having sex—have forms of expression that are typically learned (acquired). For example, all humans have an innate hunger drive, but the ways they satisfy that drive vary considerably. Some humans dig roots and eat them raw; others purchase their food at large supermarkets, cook it according to elaborate recipes, and eat it with silver knives and forks at a formal dining table. The drive is the same; the learned behavior is vastly different.

Learning theorists believe that human social responses are also acquired by imitating (copying) the responses of others (Bandura & Walters, 1963; Miller & Dollard, 1941) and by interacting with others who reward certain behaviors, which consequently increase in frequency (Homans, 1961).

Drive, responses, rewards—these are the familiar terms of learning theory. As you may recall from an introductory psychology course, classical conditioning proposes that learning occurs when a particular response (any behavior) is paired with a conditioned (previously neutral) stimulus. In contrast, operant conditioning theories propose that randomly occurring behaviors become attached to a specific stimulus when an appropriate reinforcement (reward or punishment) follows the stimulus–response pairing.

Whichever description you use, the results are the same: New behaviors are acquired. Children, for example, learn to speak because their parents selectively reinforce (shape) utterances that resemble words, using reinforcers such as smiles, hugs, and cookies. Conversely, behaviors that the child emits that are not desirable to others—drooling, screaming, hitting—are followed by negative reinforcers such as frowns, spankings, and harsh words. Gradually, the child learns which behaviors are acceptable and which are unacceptable. Learning theorists call this the **socialization process.**

Learning theories are often criticized for having a "black box" orientation to human behavior. The emphasis is on what enters the box (the stimulus) and what leaves the box (the response), but little concern is given to what actually goes on inside the box. Those inside elements—emotions and cognitions—are the prime concern of cognitive theorists. Their omission from learning theories of socialization has been a serious drawback. Although learning theories have had a significant impact in experimental, physiological, clinical, and other branches of psychology, social psychologists have long criticized them on this humanistic basis, and also on scientific grounds. One valid criticism is that reinforcers that work for one individual do not always work for others. Similarly, it can be difficult to predict in advance how an individual will respond to the consequences of his or her own behavior; some social behaviors (courtship is a good example) will be repeated even in the absence of positive reinforcement.

"Anything wrong?"

Learning theorists are beginning to take note of these criticisms. As a result, their studies are applied more frequently to child-rearing, the modification of socially undesirable behaviors, and to other significant social problems.

Cognitive Theories

In the early 1900s, a group of German psychologists suggested that human behavior is not passive and automatic, as the learning theorists had stated. Each individual is not a simple black box that lets stimuli in and responses out. Instead, according to these cognitive theorists, people actively perceive and interpret stimuli, organize their perceptions, and impose meaning on the environment. The behaviors that result represent more than conditioned responses. They reflect thought, emotion, philosophy—a "total whole nature" that the German theorists called a gestalt.

Basic to this gestalt approach is the concept that the whole can be greater than the sum of its parts. A library is more than a collection of books, a group is more than a set of individuals. Unlike the empirical principles of learning theory, this gestalt principle seems nonoperational and unscientific. After all, how is it possible to measure a mysterious "something more" that arises from subjective thoughts and emotions?

Interestingly, gestalt psychologists did not try to bypass this criticism. They sought proof of their ideas in rigidly controlled experimental investigations, and they found that proof. For example, the concept that the whole is greater than the sum of its parts was experimentally verified in studies of what is known as synergy, or closure, a notion that has been applied in many disciplines outside of psychology. The concept of synergy explains why a 350° arc is perceived as a circle, although it is incomplete. Similarly, a dotted or broken outline of an object is interpreted as the whole object. (See Figure 1–3.)

Gestalt theorists also argued that psychological responses should not be viewed in isolation, but as part of a *field*, a coexisting system of perceptions, past experiences, and innate tendencies. This idea of stimulus perception in relation to an individual's physical, mental, and environmental "surroundings" has been called the *principle of assimilation and contrast*. It, too, has been proved experimentally, in visual perception tests of figure–ground relationships (see Figure 1–4) and by commonsense observations. For example, we all recognize that $20 is a large amount of money to a child who receives a $1 weekly allowance, but it is perceived as "small change" by a business executive.

In contrast to these purely experimental studies, later research in gestalt and cognitive theory focused more directly on everyday social processes. Studies by Asch and by Heider, which you will read about in later chapters, demonstrated that people organize their observations of social experience to make them meaningful and coherent. In other words, they look beneath the surface at

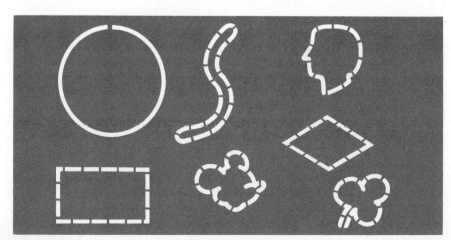

FIGURE 1–3. Visual Representations of Synergy

Synergy is the concept that the whole is greater than the sum of its parts. It is synergy that enables you to read the 350° arc (left) as a circle, and to recognize the familiar—and even unfamiliar—forms shown in incomplete dotted outlines.

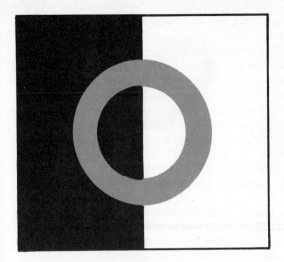

FIGURE 1-4. Assimilation and Contrast

The principle of assimilation and contrast derives from Koffka's (1935) statement that "either as little or as much as possible will happen." In visual terms, this means that an object is perceived to blend with (be assimilated to) its background when differences between object and background are at a low level. Conversely, an object is perceived to stand out sharply from (contrast with) its background when differences between them are great. In the figure, the ring is seen as a uniform gray, with each half assimilated to the other half, when it is viewed as a whole. However, if you place a pencil along the vertical boundary between the black and white backgrounds, contrast operates to make the left half of the ring on the black ground appear brighter than the right half on the white ground.

Source: *After D. Krech and R. S. Crutchfield.* Elements of Psychology. *New York: Alfred A. Knopf, Inc., 1958.*

the person who produced the behavior, at possible motives and attitudes, and at the social context in which the event occurred. (For example, somebody steps on your toe in a crowded elevator; the culprit is your best friend; did he do it on purpose?)

Leon Festinger, another influential theorist whose studies will be discussed in later chapters, also examined the social context in which responses occur. If, for example, you believe two independent facts—Festinger called them *cognitions*—(Jim is your friend; Jim stepped on your toe) that seem to be inconsistent or what Festinger termed *dissonant* (Why would your friend step on your toe?), you will strive to reduce that dissonance by altering one of those cognitions. (The fact that Jim is your friend is unalterable—you have known each other for years—however, he would not step on your toe purposely, so he must have been pushed.)

Psychoanalytic Theory

If cognitive theories can be criticized because their hypothetical constructs are difficult to measure, then psychoanalytic theories—which focus almost entirely on internal forces—should be open to even greater criticism. Nevertheless, Sigmund Freud, the father of psychoanalysis, is perhaps the most influential name in psychology, and a powerful force in social psychology as well.

He who knows others is wise; He who knows himself is enlightened.
Lao Tzu

Everyone has heard of psychoanalysis. Even before you studied psychology, you probably knew about Freud, his psychosexual stages of development, and his three-part structure of personality (ego, id, and superego). But psychoanalytic theory is more than sex and personality. Did you know that Freud's major concern was physiology? Based on his training in medicine, Freud believed that even the most abstract emotional behaviors—dreams, slips-of-the-tongue, humor, religious beliefs, artistic expression—are rigidly determined by lawful, biological processes. Although he did not dissect the human brain to discover those biological processes (physiological psychologists would attempt to do that many years later), Freud definitely believed that his hypothetical constructs reflected measurable, physiological events.

The applications of Freud's ideas are found not only in psychiatry and clinical psychology, but also in developmental psychology and social psychology. Freud's ideas about the incest taboo and other social prohibitions are still used to explain the bonding between parents and children. Modern explanations of group cohesiveness also rely on Freud's theories, particularly on his concept of identification (that is, people are bound together in groups because they have given allegiance to the same leader, identified with that leader, and consequently identified themselves with one another). Freud also postulated that humans have an innate aggressiveness that is one of the chief destructive forces in society, and which society must control if it is to survive. This idea, too, has stimulated much current research.

Any attempt to understand human interactions must recognize the social, psychological, and biological processes that control our behavior. This, in fact, is just what Freud and his followers attempted to do. However, their best-known theories describe hypothetical biological or behavioral processes that have not been measured or validated. Nevertheless, psychoanalytic theory is a useful tool for explaining the complexities of human interaction.

Symbolic Interactionism

Apart from some of the gestalt field theories, the other theoretical approaches of psychology focus mainly on the individual. In contrast, the theory of symbolic interactionism hypothesizes that an individual's self-development is directly controlled by interpersonal interactions and communications. Therefore, symbolic interactionism is more of a sociological than a psychological approach.

Role theory, one example of the symbolic interactionism approach, focuses on the many parts (roles) each individual plays in society: child to one's mother and father, friend to one's peers, lover to one's mate, student at school, citizen in the community, and so on. Which role we occupy at any particular time depends upon our expectations for that particular setting or social group. For example, at the doctor's office, role expectations demand that people act as patients are required to act (wait in the outer office, answer questions, undress when asked to do so). Obviously, these actions would be inappropriate in the classroom, where people are expected to act like students.

Humans learn most of their social roles by imitation. Children imitate their parents; adults imitate other adults. This learning process often focuses on communication. People who speak the same language can interact effectively. They can agree on the meaning of words used to describe and interpret events. This shared meaning builds social bonds. In addition, it helps to explain similarities within cultural or social groups, and differences between those groups.

The Perspectives Compared

This short overview of the six major theories of social interaction presents only a small part of their contributions to the field of social psychology. Even before

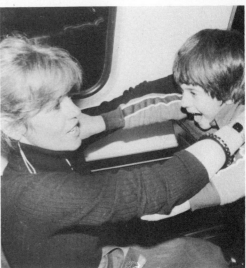

A woman of many faces . . . mother . . . political activist . . . wife . . . film actress . . . daughter . . . entrepreneur. Who is the real Jane Fonda? Role theory focuses on the many parts played by every person. Here, clockwise from left, Jane Fonda practices cattle-roping on location for a Western film; works out in her own exercise salon as Mike Douglas, partially visible behind her, prepares to tape a television interview with her; with her father, actor Henry Fonda; horsing around with her son Troy Hayden during a train trip; and at an anti-nuclear rally, joining her husband Tom Hayden in an appearance before a 1000-person crowd near the Three Mile Island nuclear plant.
All: United Press International Photo.

reading the more detailed discussions in the following chapters, you may wonder why so many theories are needed. Wouldn't one all-encompassing theory do just as well? Yes, but the diverse practitioners of social psychology cannot agree on one comprehensive explanation for all the varieties of social phenomena they have observed.

However, a few of the six major theories do show signs of displacing their competitors. Learning and cognitive theories, for example, have grown increasingly influential because of their extensive applications for testing, prediction, and control of social behavior. Symbolic interaction theories also have gained influence because of a growing interest in language and communication as the prime controlling factors in modern society.

All of the currently popular theories have been supported by numerous research studies, and criticized by many others. Until more decisive findings become available, each theory must be considered as a viable explanation for some social behaviors.

Social Psychology as a Course and a Career

Social psychology asks questions. Because these questions can reflect many perspectives—as you have read in this chapter—this course will help you to view human behavior from perspectives you may not have recognized before. As you explore our growing knowledge of social phenomena, your own expanding perspective will make you a better observer of the social interactions in your own life.

This Course and This Text

This preliminary chapter has given you a general survey of what lies ahead. Chapter 2 describes the many research techniques psychologists have devised to examine social phenomena objectively. Following part I, we will begin our examination of "what makes people tick" at the three levels described earlier in this chapter: individual, interactive, and group. We will look first at the development and behavior of the individual (part II) and then at the social influences that determine an individual's attitudes and behavior toward others (part III). In part IV we look at the fabric of the social community, first at the antisocial forces of aggression and violence, and then at the prosocial forces of altruism and cooperation. Part V, our closing section, explains how the overall perspective of social psychology can be applied to some major concerns of our society today.

As we discuss human interactions from the various perspectives of social psychology, though, we will not ignore the special perspectives contributed by the other sciences concerned with the physiology and behaviors of our species. Consider one of the most important social problems of modern society: *crime.* This issue knows no scientific boundaries. *Biologists*, for example, have tried to identify genetic factors, biochemical influences (hormonal changes, nutritional deficiencies), and physiological functions (stress reactions, arousal levels) that might explain criminal behavior. *Anthropologists* have looked to other cultures to discover why the same kinds of violent behavior that are tolerated and even encouraged by some societies are discouraged and punished by others, and why there are some societies in which "crime" as we know it is virtually nonexistent.

Sociologists have studied the "alienation" of individuals from social institutions (the home, the church, the schools, the government) as a possible way to explain deviant behavior. *Political science*, in studies of the effects of legislation, or the workings of the legal system and the courts (including the Supreme Court and its rulings on the handling of criminal evidence and the rights of criminal suspects), also has addressed the ways in which government institutions can affect criminality. Similarly, *economists* explore relationships that may exist between economic factors (unemployment, inflation, economic inequalities between social groups) and patterns of crime.

What does the organization of this course tell you about the perspective of social psychology on crime? How will our approach to this issue differ from those described for the other social sciences?

Our chapter headings provide the answer. Social psychologists would look at the *social development* of criminals as compared with noncriminals (see part II). How do they differ? What do they think of themselves? How do they account for their own behavior? They would also want to know about the *attitudes* of criminals and noncriminals (see part III). Do criminals view their acts as appropriate responses to the social environment? Would a change in their attitudes lead to more socially acceptable behavior? What social forces account for their deviance from societal norms?

Part IV suggests additional concerns about the *social forces* that produce antisocial behaviors such as aggression and violence, and prosocial behaviors such as altruism. Part V discusses the influence of *groups* (social classes, family groups, peer groups—including gangs) and *environments* (cities versus suburban or rural areas, crowded conditions versus open space). These topics also raise questions about crime. Why are crime rates higher in cities? Why are they higher in some cities than in others? Is there anything we can do to the environment—rather than to the criminals—that might reduce criminal behavior? As you will read in chapters 15 and 16, these social psychological issues have broad implications for legal, governmental, and economic policy.

Careers and Research in Social Psychology

Due to their differing research interests and theoretical approaches, social psychologists find themselves not only in many different university departments, but also in diverse job settings. About 66 percent of recent social psychology doctoral program graduates remain in academic settings as teachers and researchers after completing 4 to 5 years of graduate studies and writing an original research thesis. About 25 percent find jobs in business, government, and private organizations, where most still perform research, but on work-related (applied) rather than theoretical problems. Some social psychologists find employment in hospitals, clinics, and private practice (Stapp et al., 1981; Stapp & Fulcher, 1981).

TABLE 1–2.
Social Psychology Research Publications by Topic, 1979

Topic	Number of Publications	Topic	Number of Publications
Achievement and Task Performance	19	Law and Crime-Related Research	12
Aggression	24	Life Satisfaction	5
Attitudes and Attitude Change	50	Locus of Control	6
Attraction and Affiliation	31	Methodological Issues	19
Attribution	55	Nonverbal Communication	21
Bargaining and Coalition Formation	12	Personality and Individual Differences	39
Cognitive Processes	41	Person Perception	15
Conformity and Compliance	11	Racial and Ethnic Issues	9
Cross-Cultural Research	8	Self-Awareness	13
Crowding and Interpersonal Distance	16	Self-Presentation	8
Disciplinary Concerns	16	Sex Roles and Sex Differences	26
Dissonance	7	Social and Personality Development	44
Environmental and Population Psychology	10	Social Comparison	4
Equity, Distributive Justice, and		Social Influence	13
Social Exchange	14	Social Interaction	15
Group Processes	23	Stress, Emotion, and Arousal	17
Helping	24	Victims	5
Issues in Personality Research	11	Total	642

Source: Adapted from Stevens S. Smith, Deborah Richardson, and Clyde Hendrick, *Bibliography of Journal Articles in Personality and Social Psychology:* 1979, *Personality and Social Psychology Bulletin,* Vol. *6,* No. 4, Dec. 1980, pp. 606–636.

The beginning is the most important part of the work.
Greek proverb

Any description of the work of social psychologists must include the wide range of research carried out in both academic and nonacademic settings. For example, a survey of publications in major social psychological journals in 1979 alone (Smith et al., 1980), showed that social psychologists published 55 studies on the subject of attribution—how people perceive the causes of others' behavior. Another 50 publications described attitudes and attitude change. Over 40 studies reported findings in social development and personality development. Other popular topics included individual differences, sex roles and sex differences, aggression, interpersonal attraction, cognitive processes, helping behavior, nonverbal communication, conformity and compliance, crowding and interpersonal distance, group processes, law and crime, person perception, self-awareness, social influence, stress, and emotion. (See Table 1–2.)

As you will learn in later chapters, the range of topics for social research is growing even larger. In this textbook we have tried to maintain a broad perspective on what constitutes social psychology and to pay special attention to emerging areas of research. As research and applications expand, new opportunities arise for social psychology graduates, who are finding their ways into increasingly diverse careers.

Although social psychologists recognize the existence of a broad perspective, their research interests often focus on only a narrow part of it. Each of the following chapters provides a narrow focus on specific aspects of social interaction. Nevertheless, with careful study, it will be possible for you to acquire a broad perspective on social psychology—to have a social psychological gestalt!

Answering Questions about Understanding Social Psychology

1. Although social psychology often draws from commonsense observations about the world, social psychologists go one step further and use scientific methods to test and explore those observations. Thus, social psychology offers a method both for resolving inconsistencies in "commonsense knowledge" of the world and for explaining why people behave as they do.

2. Social psychology is a very young science—hundreds of years younger than physical sciences such as chemistry and physics. One result is that social psychology still has a variety of theories, each stressing a different aspect of social behavior, for example: physiological theories, learning theories, cognitive theories, and theories of symbolic interaction. Of course, the search for a unified theory continues, but social behavior is a very complex phenomenon that defies simple explanation.

3. As with any science, social psychology seeks first to systematically collect facts and observations in order to *describe* accurately social behavior. Through careful study of those observations, social psychologists next attempt to develop theories that will tie together and *explain* the causes of social behavior. A third scientific objective is to use theories to make *predictions* about social behavior. These predictions can then be tested to evaluate the theories. Finally, scientific social psychology seeks well-developed theories that will allow *control* of the social environment. The objective is not to construct an environment like that depicted in Orwell's *1984*, but to use our scientific knowledge to reduce social ills.

4. A few social psychologists have argued that we cannot build a science of social behavior because such behavior changes over time (and is even influenced by the insights into such behavior). Others argue that a science is possible even within the confines of "historical circumstances." And some have even argued that the circumstances of history can and should become a part of the science of social psychology.

5. Social behavior undoubtedly reflects the influence of both physiological and environmental factors. Among social psychologists, however, the greatest emphasis has been placed on theories and research on environmental influences. Of course, one of the most important environmental influences is other people, and social psychology particularly focuses on the interactions between and among people.

6. One old question in social psychology concerns the extent to which people behave in a thoughtful and reflective manner as opposed to simply and mindlessly reacting to their environment. There is no easy answer to this question and it is one to which we will return several times in the remainder

of this text. You might try to formulate your own answer to this question and test your theories against the research findings reported in later chapters.

Summary

Social psychology starts with commonsense observations of social interactions and attempts to study and analyze them, to formulate a more complete and objective explanation of the rules that govern human behavior. The discipline can be defined as an attempt to understand how the thoughts, feelings, and behaviors of individuals are influenced by the actual, imagined, or implied presence of others (Allport, 1968, p. 3).

Some social psychologists focus on individual traits that affect social interactions; others focus on interactive influences or on group influences. Within each of these approaches, specific research interests range from genetics and physiology to cognition and learning. Due to this variety of perspectives, social psychologists are employed in a variety of academic settings (in departments of psychology, sociology, education, political science, and others), business (industry, government, hospitals, private practice), and government settings.

Social psychology is a young discipline—established within this century—but its roots can be found in the philosophical writings of Plato, Aristotle, and other ancient thinkers who tried to explain the nature of human interactions. In the early 1800s, Auguste Comte, the "founder" of social psychology, formulated "la morale," a hybrid of biology and sociology, which included many of the concerns of today's social psychology.

Early theories and research studies in social psychology emphasized single or unified explanations of human behavior such as **hedonism** (acting solely to gain pleasure and to avoid pain), **egoism** (behavior determined completely by the desire for power), and such other human motivations as *sympathy, gregariousness*, and *animal magnetism*. Contemporary research emphasizes broader, more integrated theories and applied research topics that are relevant to everyday social issues.

Social psychology is both a behavioral and a social science. It is accepted as a science because it meets all requirements of the **scientific method**: systematic description, explanation, prediction, and control. Scientific descriptions are collected to form **theories**, which help to explain social phenomena that have been observed. Many theories can be used to explain a particular set of facts. A good theory is one whose predictions can be tested.

Social psychologists, like all scientists, follow five basic assumptions: (a) **empiricism** (reliance on data gathering and observation to prove or disprove predictions); (b) **determinism** (belief that human behavior proceeds in an orderly, systematic manner, and not by chance); (c) **invariance** (belief that causal relations between events do not change over time or over location); (d) **operationalism** (agreement that theoretical terms must be objective and measurable); and (e) **objectivity** (data collection, theory development, and prediction that is fair, impartial, and capable of replication by other investigators).

However, social scientists recognize that their discipline differs in significant ways from the so-called "hard" sciences. Human behavior does not remain unaffected by being studied; it can be influenced and altered by numerous situational (historical) factors.

Six major theories of human interaction have evolved from research in social psychology: (a) **physiological theory** focuses on genetic predispositions; (b) **sociobiological theory** believes that social behavior traits evolve through a process of natural selection; (c) **learning theory** postulates a stimulus–response relationship between the environment and social behavior; (d) **cognitive theory** states that humans actively perceive and interpret stimuli in their environment to create meaning in their social interactions; (e) **psychoanalytic theory** stresses internal drives that must be satisfied through social relationships; and (f) **symbolic interactionism** views self-development as directly controlled by social interaction and communication with others. Each theory represents a different view of human behavior. Together, these approaches reflect the diversity of social interaction and the many ways we can examine human behavior.

Suggested Additional Reading

Allport, G. W. This historical background of modern social psychology. In G. Lindzey & E. Aronson (Eds.), *The handbook of social psychology* (Vol. 1) (2nd ed.). Reading, Ma: Addison-Wesley, 1968, 1–80.

Boring, E. G. *A history of experimental psychology.* 2nd ed. New York: Appleton Century Crofts, 1950.

Deutsch, M., & Krauss, R. M. *Theories in social psychology.* New York: Basic Books, 1965.

Gilmour, R. & Duck, S. (Eds.). *The development of social psychology.* New York: Academic Press, 1980.

Jones E. E. History of social psychology. In G. Kimball & K. Schlesinger (Eds.), *History of modern psychology.* New York: Wiley, 1978.

Lewin, K. *Field theory in social science.* New York: Harper & Row, 1951.

McDougall, W. *An introduction to social psychology.* London: Methuen, 1908.

Shaw, M. E., & Costanzo, P. R. *Theories of social psychology.* New York: McGraw-Hill, 1970.

Watson, J. B. Psychology as a behaviorist views it. *Psychological Review*, 1913, *20*, 158–177.

2

RESEARCH IN
SOCIAL PSYCHOLOGY

Questions about Research in Social Psychology

1. Suppose you are a social psychologist interested in the relationship between physical attractiveness and liking. How do you go about proving your hypothesis that physically attractive people are better liked?
2. In the real world, how do researchers test for causal relationships? That is, how can we be sure that phenomenon X causes phenomenon Y?
3. What are the primary differences between laboratory experiments and field experiments?
4. What is randomness and what is its role in research?
5. What does it mean to say that the results of an experiment are significant?
6. Researchers in medicine are often confronted with difficult ethical issues. For example, is it ethical to withhold a new and potentially effective drug from sick patients in order to test the drug? What are some of the ethical concerns faced by social psychology researchers?

I n the early morning hours in a quiet neighborhood in New York City in 1964, apartment dwellers heard someone in the street screaming for help and calling for the police. Those who looked out of their windows later reported seeing a young woman fighting off an attacker. The cries stopped after more than a half-hour. The woman was found dead with multiple stab wounds. Thirty-eight people had looked down on this scene from the safety of their apartments, but not one had come to her rescue or had even called the police. When questioned, many said they had not responded because they were not sure whether the woman was actually being attacked or was merely involved in a lovers' quarrel.

A jetliner took off from a metropolitan airport in a large city in early 1982 just after a midwinter snowstorm. Minutes later it crashed into the ice covered river that runs through the city. Helicopters hovered over the wreckage, lowering ropes to survivors. Police and firefighters tossed lifelines from shore. Onlookers jumped into the icy water and dragged some survivors to safety. One survivor repeatedly refused help and remained in the water, passing the helicopter rope to others. When the helicopter returned for him, he had drowned.

You may recognize the first story as the infamous case of Kitty Genovese. You may remember that the onlooker who performed the heroic rescue in the Washington air crash was decorated for his deed. What causes people to ignore one another's troubles, and thus contribute to disaster? What causes people to go out of their way to help one another? "It's human nature," we may say of both. But such real life incidents have aroused social psychologists and others concerned with human behavior to investigate the occasions and motivations for altruistic behavior—behavior that involves helping others simply for the satisfaction of having done a good deed, and not from self-interest or expectation of gain. These investigations aim to uncover some general truths about human behavior. Will people respond automatically with helping behavior in some situations but not in others, or only when it is safe to do so?

Lack of knowledge is darker than the night.
Hausa proverb

Much research in social psychology begins with questions like these about the factors that determine specific behaviors. For the social scientist, as we saw in chapter 1, questions about human behavior have to be approached in a systematic way. You may believe that people help others only when it is safe for them to do so. If someone challenges your belief, how can you convince that person that your idea is valid? How can you yourself be sure that it represents a general truth about human behavior that will stand up at all times, in all places, in all circumstances? By itself, your belief is not sufficient; to convince another person of your belief you need a large body of evidence to support it. In this chapter we shall present some of the tools social psychologists use to answer such challenges. Before we do, however, we shall have to consider whether the question itself has been posed in the right way.

Basic Research Concepts

You may not realize it, but your idea about helping behavior is really a theory. It is one of the many thoughts and hunches you have for explaining the way people behave. As we observed in chapter 1, everyone has theories about human behavior. Theories are statements about the real world that try to explain events and behavior in a coherent way. They help us predict future events such as election returns, or the kind of greeting we can expect when we meet an old friend. They enlarge our understanding of human social behavior by discovering and explaining cause-and-effect relationships. However, no theory in social psychology is the final word on human behavior. By its very nature, even the best theory is tentative, a temporary explanation that will have to do until a more thorough one comes along. No theory can ever be completely verified; it can only be supported or disproved by facts. To be supported or disproved, a theory must be rigorously tested and retested in a variety of situations. In this chapter we shall discuss some of the major experimental and nonexperimental research methods that are the tools with which social psychologists test theories.

Formulating Hypotheses

Assertion is no proof.
German proverb

Theories are general statements about the real world, general in that they are difficult to support in their totality. Your theory of altruism might be stated as, "People are automatically helpful to each other most of the time." A hard-boiled social psychologist would listen to your theory and then ask you how you know this. Did you get it from reading the Bible story about the Good Samaritan? From Greek philosophy? From a "feeling" about human nature? Or have you actually observed so many instances of helping behavior in the real world that you cannot avoid concluding that most people are truly altruistic? The social psychologist would force you to break your theory down into more limited statements that could be tested. One such limited statement might be: "People in crowded public places are more (or less) apt to help others than when they are alone." Or "People of the same race are more likely to help each other than people of different races." Now you have formulated hypotheses. You have made the theory much more specific, and you can more easily test whether it is valid. But the first question is whether your hypothesis has grown out of a theory or out of your general observations of the world.

Many social psychologists begin with a large theory and then form hypotheses to assess how it operates in the world. For example, Piliavin, Rodin, and Piliavin (1969) believed that people are genuinely altruistic, but they wanted to know just how and in what situations. They formed a series of hypotheses about altruism and designed an experiment to test them. They chose Good Samaritanism as one possible form of altruistic behavior, and they decided to see how it would operate in a large impersonal environment like New York City's subway system. Some of their hypotheses included those just mentioned: People are more apt to help a person if they first see someone else come forward to help. People are more likely to help a victim who is ill than one who is drunk. As we shall see later in the chapter, in the course of a field experiment, some of these hypotheses were confirmed.

It more often happens, however, that hypotheses in social psychology come not from theories but from outside sources. Many hypotheses have sprung from observations in the real world, as researchers, out of concern for social problems or from curiosity, noticed patterns and similarities in human behavior and then later constructed hypotheses to explain them.

Other hypotheses arise from debates over social policy: Does the negative income tax work? Is remedial education effective? Evaluation research attempts to find out whether a particular program has worked. It is applied directly to problems in the real world, and it has immediate effects: Programs continue or are halted; money is given or withdrawn. As such, evaluation research is a kind of applied research. It is used to formulate new social policies, compare alternative programs, and solve practical problems. It addresses such questions as the effects of abolishing the draft on army enlistments, the effect that "cracking down" on drunken drivers might have on accident rates, the impact of no-fault divorce laws on the number of divorces initiated, and so on.

Basic Research, on the other hand, is conducted to acquire new knowledge for its own sake. Studies such as the subway altruism experiment or those that explore the effects of staring on passersby (Ellsworth et al., 1972) are confined to isolated bits of behavior. Their results may or may not have any immediate practical application. These experiments are conducted because some researchers feel that certain aspects of human behavior are worth studying in their own right and because the long-range issues might be of social importance.

Selecting a Research Design

Whatever the source of a hypothesis, researchers must design an appropriate test for it. Just as they must formulate a hypothesis carefully, so must they be equally careful in choosing their research strategy. Much of this chapter will be devoted to a discussion of possible research strategies. Sometimes researchers use several strategies to investigate a hypothesis; however, they are more likely to tailor a particular design to the hypothesis. The design of a research procedure is a major challenge in social psychology.

Experimental vs. Nonexperimental Methods   There are two kinds of research in social psychology: (1) **Experimental studies** attempt to explain some aspect of behavior by testing a hypothesis about it and discovering causal relationships; and (2) **nonexperimental observations** describe some aspect of naturally occurring behavior by collecting data that may result in a theory or hypothesis to explain the observations.

You may not realize it, but you conduct experiments continually in your daily life. For example, you might want to test the truth of the proposition: "I would get more done if I got up earlier in the morning." Instead of waiting passively for mornings in which you automatically woke up earlier, you would instead *create your own conditions.* You would deliberately get up two hours earlier for a number of mornings and at the end of a week see how much more you got done than you had before. Experimenters in social psychology similarly create their own conditions to test the truth of other propositions. In this way they can study only those factors they choose, manipulating conditions to test the effect of each manipulation on the behavior being studied. In order to tell whether a given manipulation has any effect at all, experimenters must compare its effects on one group of subjects that experiences the manipulation to another group of subjects that does not. Of all research methods, only an experiment allows researchers to say with certainty, "This factor was the cause of that observation."

For ethical and practical reasons, however, some conditions cannot be tested on human subjects. For example, researchers cannot allow a test group of subjects to become addicted to morphine in order to study drug addiction and personality change. Nor can researchers create volcanic eruptions, hurricanes, or no-fault divorce laws to study how people react to natural disasters and social legislation. Instead, researchers must be ready to observe and describe the spontaneous events of real life and the naturally occurring behavior that results. They must use *nonexperimental techniques* such as content analyses, field studies, and surveys. These techniques allow them to describe the characteristics of the people under study, but not to control the events in those people's lives.

Whether they are conducting experiments or using nonexperimental techniques, researchers are studying qualities, characteristics, and attributes called **variables.** Variables include subjects' weight, skin color, consumer behavior, political attitudes, hostile impulses, helping behavior, and more. In any group of people, these qualities will vary in strength or degree from person to person. However, any one person will show only one value of the variable in question— that is, a person cannot at the same time have two different weights, or eye colors, vote for two candidates for the same office, or be both aggressive and friendly to the same person. Thus, while any variable can have two or more values, no one person can possess or express the range of values that exists in a single variable.

The variables that social psychologists test represent **constructs.** These qualities, characteristics, and attributes are abstractions to which we have given descriptive names. Intelligence, hostility, bias, and affection are not things that exist in reality; they cannot be touched or seen. We infer their existence indirectly from behaviors. These constructs must be translated into specific events such as IQ scores, thermometer readings, answers to questions, or any other concrete measurements of behavior. When the constructs we want to test have been translated into measurable behaviors, we can say that they have been **operationally defined.**

For example, to investigate the expression of racial prejudice among a group of people, researchers would have to consider the specific ways in which prejudice is shown in behavior, ways that can be observed and measured. They could then design a questionnaire to probe racial attitudes in specific ways by asking such questions as, "What would you do if your sister married a man of a different race?" or, "How would you feel if a black family moved in next door?"

Causal Inference   The problem with nonexperimental studies is that they do not allow researchers to draw conclusions about causality. Only controlled experiments do that. At best, nonexperimental studies—often called **correlational studies**—allow researchers to observe the relationships between variables. They may find that when one variable increases so does another, or that one variable decreases while another increases, or that there is no clear relationship between the variables. Variables that change at the same rate are co-related. Correlations occur everywhere in daily life: As young people grow taller, they also grow heavier (a **positive correlation**—as height increases so does weight). As the air temperature rises, the amount of clothing worn decreases (a **negative correlation**). Some people who drink six cups of coffee a day have blue eyes (no correlation).

If a poor man eats a chicken, either he is sick or the chicken is.
Yiddish proverb

It is a great temptation to look at the results of a correlational study and say, "There is such a close relationship between these two variables, one must be the cause of the other." You might be right, but you might just as easily be wrong. When one variable *causes* another, they are always correlated, but correlation alone is never sufficient proof of causality. Suppose you found, for example, that both ice cream sales and the crime rate rise in June. Would that mean that eating ice cream causes criminal behavior in some people? Or that criminals have an innate liking for ice cream? Closer analysis would show the relationship to be *spurious*—that is, although crime rate and ice cream sales co-vary, they are not correlated. Each may be, however, related to an unknown, unmeasured third variable—in this case, rising air temperature. As the temperature rises so do both ice cream sales and the crime rate, but neither ice cream sales nor the crime rate have any effect on each other (Kasarda, 1976).

Manipulation of Variables   In the study of social phenomena, there are many extraneous variables operating that might explain the presence of an attitude or cause a particular behavior to occur. To isolate the forces and events (**independent variables**) that actually cause behavior (**dependent variables**) and to control the influence of such extraneous variables, researchers must employ an experimental design. Such a design allows them to definitely say that "This *independent variable* causes that *dependent variable*" or "This *stimulus* causes that *response*." They can say any of these things because they have satisfied the **three conditions for causality:**

1. The independent variable and the dependent variable are correlated—that is, they vary together.
2. The independent variable occurs *before* the dependent variable.
3. Nothing else explains the relationship between the two (Cook & Campbell, 1979).

In an ideal experiment, researchers have complete control over the independent variable. They can vary it and manipulate it at will, creating situations where it appears and others where it does not. Researchers manipulate the independent variable in this way not only to see what effect it has (or its absence has) on the dependent variable, but to be sure that the independent variable, and it alone, is causing the dependent variable.

Better twice measured than once wrong.
Danish proverb

Researchers conducting a true experiment would never administer an independent variable or stimulus to just one group of subjects. The experimental method demands that two groups be used: one that experiences the effects of the independent variable and one that does not. The group that does not experience the effects of the independent variable is called the control group; and its purpose is to rule out the effects of the experiment itself, to provide an untreated base against which to compare the effects of the experimental treatment. Both groups must be similar to be sure that results are due to the experimental treatment and not to characteristics of the subjects. Similarity is achieved by randomly assigning subjects to experimental and control groups.

The Role of Randomness in Research

There are many potential sources of error in an experiment. One frequent problem comes from subject variables such as gender, age, self-esteem, intelligence, and visual acuity. These qualities, which the researcher cannot control and does not want to study, inevitably accompany subjects. Subject variables can become *confounded* or mixed up with the experimental variable. A subject group that is predominantly male or female, young or old, bright or dull, normal seeing or near-sighted, can bias the results of an experiment. In the control group, a majority of one characteristic or another would not provide a fair comparison against which to test the treatment group. In either case, researchers would be unable to determine whether the effects they observed were due to the manipulation of the independent variables or to the differences in the makeup of the test and the control groups.

The best way of assuring that both groups are absolutely equal and that no characteristic is more likely to occur in one group or the other before treatment begins is by random assignment. This is accomplished either by drawing names out of a hat, giving numbers to all the subjects and assigning even numbers to the experimental group and odd numbers to the control group, or by using a table of random numbers. It ensures that any given subject has an equal chance of being placed in the test or in the control group.

Random assignment should not be confused with random sampling (although researchers might use random sampling to select the subjects for their experiment before they randomly assigned them to experimental or control groups). Random sampling assures that the subjects are representative of a larger population. Thus, instead of drawing only college students for their experiment, researchers would go outside the college and randomly select subjects from a vastly wider group of people. They might, for example, select every tenth person in a phone directory, or the first five people to enter a shopping mall every hour on the hour. Random sampling procedures assure that every person in the larger population has an equal chance of being selected for the study, and thus that results observed in the sample will represent what might have been observed if researchers could test the entire population.

Reliability

Reliability is a characteristic of good research designs. Research results that are reliable will be repeatedly demonstrated. There are three kinds of reliability in social psychology research: intrapersonal, interpersonal, and replication.

Intrapersonal reliability applies mostly to the measurement of long-lasting, stable characteristics such as intelligence in one subject. On such measures, a research subject should give the same responses when tested again at a later time. An IQ test would be considered reliable if it were consistent over time—that is, if the same subjects took the test again and received almost the same scores months or years after they took the test the first time.

Interpersonal reliability is demonstrated when two observers record or rate an event in the same way. It is a gauge of how accurately a dependent variable has been translated into a behavior that can be easily measured by observers. For example, a study of obedience in children might measure obedience by the number of blocks a child picks up when asked to, or by the amount of time that elapses after the child is asked to pick up the blocks and when he or she actually begins to do so. Observers can easily count the blocks or record the elapsed time. The designers of the experiment have translated the dependent variable, obedience, into a simple behavior that can be measured or recorded by anyone.

The third form of reliability occurs when an experiment is replicated—repeated—and produces the same results. If the obedience experiment were repeated at another time and place with different subjects but with the same procedures and methods of scoring, and produced the same findings, it would be considered to be highly reliable. But will the results of that experiment still hold if the experimental conditions are changed? Researchers may want to see if they can replicate the findings of one experiment by conducting a second experiment in another place using different people and procedures. If they succeed, they will have demonstrated that their findings apply not only to the subjects of these particular experiments, but are very likely to be true for people generally.

Validity

Researchers are interested in being able to generalize their findings to other situations and people. They want to arrive at general truths that apply to large numbers of people. For this reason, *external validity* is a crucial factor in any social psychological research, and we shall have more to say about it shortly. There is, however, another kind of validity that has to do with the experiment itself, and the amount of control a researcher has over it.

In a study that has **internal validity**, researchers' findings are solely a result of their manipulation of the independent variable. There will be no other unmeasured or uncontrolled variables to confuse the results. Presumably, the researchers have already taken precautions against extraneous subject variables by randomly assigning people to experimental and control groups. A study with internal validity will accurately reflect the manipulations of the experiment itself. But rival variables and other internal explanations may affect the behavior being studied and threaten internal validity (see box).

Internal validity can be threatened by other factors as well. Is the independent variable capable of producing the effect being tested for? For example, if researchers plan to show subjects erotic pictures to test sexual arousal under various conditions, first they want to be sure that the pictures they are using really do arouse normal subjects. They would confirm this by showing the pictures to a test group and measuring such physiological states as genital changes, hormone levels, pulse rates, and blood pressure. Or, if indirect questions are used to get at complex or sensitive attitudes or behaviors, is it possible that subjects will not understand what is being asked? Researchers can protect against this by asking a variety of questions to test each variable.

If the results of a study can be generalized to the larger population, the study will have **external validity**. When researchers examine the results of an experiment they must take a critical look at their findings. Would they have obtained the same results if they had used different subjects? If they used different measures of the independent variables? If they tested different independent variables? The issue of external validity is especially important to social psychologists who conduct studies using undergraduates as subjects. Undergraduates may differ from the larger society in key respects—they are usually younger, do not have long employment histories, are not supporting a family, and so on—and thus may not be representative of the general population. The results of some studies may therefore not be generalizable to the larger society; they are said to lack external validity.

If you want an expert to identify a bird, do not remove its feathers.
Ashanti proverb

Another threat to external validity arises from the nature of the experimental situation itself. Laboratory research has been criticized for lacking **experimental realism**—the conditions of the experiment have no real impact on the subjects' lives. They do not believe in the reality of the test situation, they do not take it seriously, or they may suspect the purpose of the research. They will not be giving authentic responses to the test situation and as a result the test findings will not apply to any other group of people or be representative of naturally occurring processes.

Laboratory research has also been criticized for lacking **mundane realism**. The laboratory setting is seen to be artificial, and events that occur there have little resemblance to those in the real world. To compensate, some researchers go to some trouble to make their laboratory settings as realistic as possible.

The only way to assure external validity is to perform the experiment with as many subject populations as possible, in a variety of situations, and with many

Research: Eight Threats to Internal Validity

A number of unforeseen threats to an experiment's internal validity may arise from the subjects themselves, the outside world, or the testing process itself. Following is a list of some of the most serious threats (Campbell & Stanley, 1969; Judd & Kenny, 1981).

1. Selection. Selection problems occur whenever subjects are not assigned to experimental and control groups on a random basis. One study, for example, attempted to show that living in interracial housing projects reduces prejudice and discriminatory behavior to a greater degree than living in more segregated housing. But critics pointed out that people who decided to live in such projects were more tolerant to begin with—that is, the greater racial tolerance observed in interracial projects was a product of choice—a self-selected group of unprejudiced people had chosen to live there. Therefore, no valid conclusions could be drawn about the effects on prejudice of living in desegregated housing.

2. Maturation. At the end of some experiments, it may be difficult to determine whether the differences in subject behavior were caused by the effects of the experiment or were due to the fact that people change in subtle ways over time. In long-term experiments, subjects in both control and test groups grow older and perhaps wiser, regardless of what is done to them. In short-term experiments, they may become hungry, tired, bored, or sleepy, and thus, in addition to the treatment itself, their posttest performance may reflect these changes.

3. History. Events in the outside world can also bias the results of an experiment. A sharp increase in the price of alcohol, for example, during a study of the effects of alcohol education on drinking patterns might cause subjects to drink less (Judd & Kenny, 1981). Babbie cites the example of the assassination of a popular black leader during the course of a study on racial prejudice. This event would likely cause subjects in both test and control groups to reexamine their attitudes toward blacks and thus reduce the overall level of prejudice (1979).

4. Mortality. When subjects drop out of an experiment, the composition of the remaining group may differ from that of the original group in a number of unknown ways. A long-term study of the effects of unemployment in an industrial city might lose subjects who move to another location to find employment. Those that remain might have characteristics—such as home ownership, less motivation, or employed spouses—that would make them different from the subjects who left. The results of the study would erro-

different procedures. The independent variable should be presented in as many different ways as the researcher can devise, and the dependent variable should be given a wide range of response possibilities.

Collecting and Analyzing Data

The theories and hypotheses of social psychology stand or fall on the data—the observations, factual information, or other direct sensory evidence—that can be gathered to support them. But the data are only as useful as they are accurate. Everything depends on how social psychologists collect and interpret data. They

neously show a continued low level of reemployment, since those who dropped out could no longer be questioned.

5. *Testing.* The process of testing and retesting may change subjects' opinions or behavior and thus bias experimental results. Babbie's prejudice experiment involved a pretest that probed racial feelings, a test treatment consisting of viewing a film on blacks' contributions to American history, and a posttest on racial attitudes. It was found that the pretest and the film were enough to "sensitize most subjects to the issue of prejudice," so that on the posttest they became "more thoughtful in their answers" (Babbie, 1979, p. 278).

6. *Regression to the mean (regression artifact).* Subjects who stand at an extreme in some behavior or attitude on a pretest often prove to be in a less extreme position on the posttest. Researchers could mistakenly conclude that the change was due to experimental treatment. But this effect has been observed among controls who have not been exposed to the treatment at all. Such subjects demonstrate the statistical effect called *regression toward the mean.* The scores of extremely poor math students are bound to improve somewhat, not because of a new teaching method but simply because they

are already at the bottom and there is nowhere for them to go but up. Similarly, high scorers may have a "bad day" on the next test.

7. *Instrumentation.* This refers to problems in the test measures or researchers themselves. Experimenters must guard against the possibility that their pretests and posttests may contain different operational definitions of a behavior or attitude. They may see less prejudice in posttest responses because their posttest measures are less sensitive than those in the pretest (Babbie, 1979). Another possibility is that the scoring criteria or the standards of the experimenters themselves have changed during the experiment. They may have become more alert to certain behavior traits, or less sensitive to certain responses, and thus miss small but important changes.

8. *Selection–maturation interactions.* Sometimes two or more of these problems of internal validity may interact to produce more subtle errors in the outcome of a study. Groups that are self-selected or selected by the experimenter may differ also in their maturation rates. Compensatory education programs administered to a selected group of low achievers may seem to be ineffective not because of the program's inadequacies but because of the inherent slow growth rate of the low achievers themselves.

must decide what data to seek, how to measure it, where to obtain it, what instruments or techniques to use in collecting it, who should collect it, when to collect it, and how to record it. Once they have collected their data, they must analyze it to see if it adequately tests the hypothesis under study. We shall consider some of the units of measurement social psychologists use in collecting data, then discuss some basic methods of statistical analysis.

Units of Analysis   Units of analysis fall into two broad categories: They can be measures of population or of behavior. Individuals, groups, or organizations are most often measured in order to present a composite picture of a population. Behavior is used as a unit of analysis when researchers want to study the social processes within groups of people. Dependent variables must be operationally defined or translated into specific behaviors such as smiling, eye contact, amount of talking, body postures, or eyebrow raising. Behaviors can be measured in terms of *frequency* (how often bowlers smile when they get a strike), *rate* (how many movies the average student sees in one week), or *intensity* (length of eye contact between dating couples who have made self-reports of being in love (Kidder, 1981, p. 264). The kind of behavior being measured is limited only by the researcher's imagination, and as we shall see in later chapters, social psychologists can be very imaginative.

Having gathered such data, researchers must make sure that it adequately tests the hypothesis. It is often helpful to have more than one operational definition of a dependent variable. If there is only one, we have no way of knowing if it adequately reflects what the study intends to measure.

The Null Hypothesis   In order to increase our confidence that the manipulated variable was responsible for any observed differences between the test and control groups, researchers must first consider two standard hypotheses: 1. The **null hypothesis** (from the Latin for "not any") states that the groups are equal and that any differences between the two are due to chance and not to experimental manipulation, and 2. the **research hypothesis,** which states that the systematic cause (that is, the independent variable) did have an effect on the subjects and that the differences are not due to chance. Before researchers can accept the research hypothesis they must be able to show that the null hypothesis is wrong.

Kidder (1981, pp. 334–335) has compared the process of testing the null hypothesis to a criminal trial. A defendant—the research hypothesis—is accused of having committed a crime (that is, the independent variable did have an effect). A jury must decide whether the defendant is guilty, but must first presume that the defendant is innocent (that is, they must presume that the null hypothesis is true). Researchers are like prosecutors who must try to prove to the jury that the defendant is guilty "beyond a reasonable doubt." To do so, they must collect enough data and evidence to prove that the null hypothesis is incorrect, that the defendant is not innocent, and that the independent variable is responsible for the effect.

Statistical Significance   To remove any traces of reasonable doubt, researchers must show that there is a very low probability that the differences between the two groups are due to chance. Consider the following simple experiment: Suppose we wanted to test whether people's impressions of strangers are affected by the temperature of the room in which they meet. According to the null hypothesis, any effects would be due to chance. Our research hypothesis states that room temperature does affect people's impressions. In our experiment subjects are to spend 5 minutes getting to know a research confederate, that is, another student who was working in cooperation with the researcher. We would randomly assign subjects either to the control group in a room whose temperature is 68°F, or a test group in a room whose temperature is 85°.

After the 5-minute exchanges, we ask subjects to rate how much they liked the confederate, and we find that subjects in the cool room liked the confederate more than those in the hot room. Are the differences statistically significant?

Could the difference have arisen by chance alone? The null hypothesis states that it has, and after all it is possible that heat has absolutely no effect on liking. Rather, it is conceivable that a number of very friendly people were assigned by chance to the cool room, and a number of unfriendly people were assigned by chance to the hot room. Whenever people are randomly assigned to experimental conditions, there is always a chance that the people in the test and control groups will have different characteristics. The null hypothesis is the researcher's way of saying that even though the test and control groups differ, the difference may have happened by chance and not as a result of the manipulation.

It is possible to calculate the probability that the difference did occur by chance. As a matter of convention, scientists say that results are statistically significant if the difference between the two groups would occur by chance in less than 5 cases out of 100, or less than 5 percent. We can express this as $p < .05$; that is, probability is less than 5/100. If the differences observed in our experiment were at this level, we would be inclined to reject the null hypothesis. If the differences arise in less than 1 out of 100 chances ($p < .01$), we would be even more inclined to reject the null hypothesis. The figures .05 and .01 are levels of statistical significance.

Correlation Coefficients Psychologists frequently report the results of non-experimental studies as a correlation coefficient. A correlation coefficient (symbolized by r) is an index of how strongly two variables are related to one another. Suppose a researcher was interested in finding out if the most attractive people are the best liked by others. In collecting data, the researcher would make two sets of observations for each subject—one for attractiveness and one for liking. This would produce two scores, one for each variable. The researcher would test the degree of the relationship mathematically to obtain their correlation coefficient, or r. Correlation coefficients can range in value from $+1.00$ to -1.00. The $+$ and $-$ signs indicate positive and negative relationships. A perfect positive relationship ($r = +1.00$) indicates that as one variable increases by a constant amount or rate, so does the other; a perfect negative relationship ($r = -1.00$) indicates that as one variable increases at a constant rate, the other decreases. And if $r = 0$, there is no relationship between the two variables being measured. The value of r indicates the strength of the relationship; as r approaches 1.00 (either $+$ or $-$), the stronger the relationship. If $r = \pm 1.00$ (plus or minus 1.00), a perfect correlation has been reached (see Figure 2–1a). As a correlation between two variables approaches ± 1.00, researchers are able to predict with increasing accuracy the exact value of one variable simply by knowing the value of the other. As the correlation approaches 0.00, from either the $+$ or $-$ side, the less the two variables are related, and "knowing the value of one variable will tell a researcher nothing about the value of the other" (Carlsmith et al., 1976, p. 28; see Figures 2–1b and c). In social psychology, correlations between 0.00 and 0.2 would generally be interpreted as weak, correlations between 0.2 and 0.5 are of moderate strength, and correlations over 0.5 are strong. In the physical sciences, where theories and causal relationships are much more reliable, a correlation of less than 0.95 might be considered weak. Thus, the interpretation of correlations depends in part on the nature of the phenomena being observed. As we stated earlier, the fact that two variables are strongly correlated does not mean that one may be causing the other.

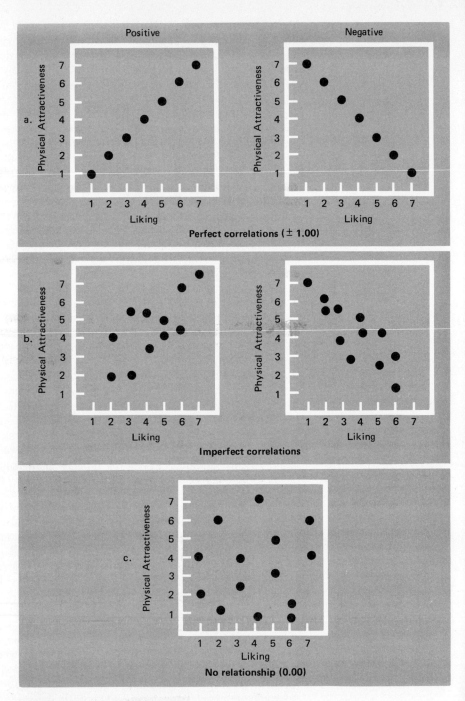

FIGURE 2–1. Types of Correlation

Source: *Adapted from* Methods in Behavioral Research, *2nd ed., by P. C. Cozby, Palo Alto, California: Mayfield Publishing Co., 1981, 82–83.*

Main Effects and Interaction   Recall the experiment on the effects of room temperature on liking for the research confederate. Suppose we found a statistically significant difference between the liking behavior of the two groups, those in the cool room and those in the hot room. We could therefore conclude that the independent variable, room temperature, did have an effect on the dependent variable, liking. We would then say that the room temperature has a **main effect** on liking behavior (see Figure 2–2a). But what if, in addition to room temperature, we had used a second independent variable by having the confederate praise subjects in both the cool and the hot conditions? We are interested in seeing what effect the combination of these independent variables has on the dependent variable, liking. We would then have an experimental design in which half the subjects would be praised and half criticized, some when the room was cool and some when the room was hot. We would therefore have four different conditions to which subjects could be randomly assigned: cool praise, cool criticism, hot praise, and hot criticism.

At the end of this experiment, we would be likely to find an *interaction* between room temperature and feedback. For example, those who were praised in a hot room might actually like the confederate more than those who were praised in the cool room. But those who were criticized in a hot room might show a far lower level of liking for the confederate than those subjects who were criticized in the cool room (see Figure 2–2b).

The combination of room temperature and feedback has thus yielded a more pronounced effect than that of either variable alone. In this case praise magnified the effect of room temperature on liking. This is called the **interaction effect**. It is an important aspect of many social psychology studies because researchers must often study the effects of two or more independent variables on behavior or attitudes.

FIGURE 2–2.
The Interaction Effect

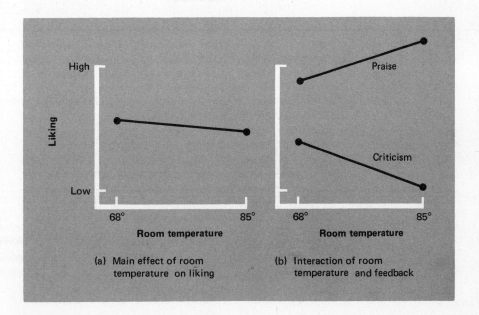

(a) Main effect of room temperature on liking

(b) Interaction of room temperature and feedback

Interpreting and Reporting the Results

Researchers who have carefully constructed their research hypotheses and gathered data that adequately tests those hypotheses will have few problems in analyzing the data and reporting the results. Unfortunately, it is all too easy to formulate hypotheses and collect data that do not provide clear answers about the validity of the hypothesis. Sometimes the problem lies in formulating the hypothesis, sometimes in the kinds of data that have been collected. Sometimes in spite of a carefully formulated hypothesis and scrupulously analyzed data, the researcher still does not have clear results and it is not clear whether the hypothesis has been supported or disproved. Since social psychology is a scientifically conservative enterprise, researchers must be very careful not to read too much into the results or overreach those results when they draw conclusions.

One head cannot go into consultation.
Ashanti proverb

Having reached our conclusions, as researchers we have an obligation to share our results with our colleagues. Other researchers may be tackling similar problems and our findings may help them avoid pitfalls, may indicate new approaches that should be explored, or may alter the nature of the problem entirely. Just as the components of research follow a generally agreed upon pattern, so does the content of a report on research. As you will see when you read research reports during this course, a written report has the following parts:

1. Summary or abstract. A brief summary of points 2–5.
2. Introduction. What problem were you investigating and why?
3. Method. What procedures did you employ?
4. Results. What did you find?
5. Discussion. What do your findings mean? Where do we go from here?
6. References. An alphabetical list of books and articles cited in the report.
7. Appendix (optional). Copies of questionnaires, scales, or stimulus materials used in the research or tables of data too extensive or too peripheral to include in the body of the report (After Kidder, 1981, p. 344).

Nonexperimental Research Techniques

So far we have been discussing nonexperimental and experimental research techniques in general. In this section and in the next one, we will discuss in more specific detail the various research techniques used in social psychology, and the particular strengths and weaknesses of each method. How do social psychologists decide which variables to investigate? How do they determine the best experimental design to use for a given problem?

We begin with descriptions of nonexperimental research designs. These have one thing in common: The researchers have no direct control over the independent variable. Instead, they must observe its operation as it occurs naturally in real-life situations and record its effects on people's attitudes and behavior. Researchers cannot, for example, study the relationship between economic conditions and mental health in a laboratory. To confirm or disprove a hypothesis that mental health suffers in a period of inflation and high unemployment, researchers must either go into the field or consult data that already exist in public records. Existing data can provide information for the intensive study of individuals and groups, and of historical trends; they are the sources for such methods as content analyses, archival studies, and case histories. Sometimes, however, researchers must go into the field to collect data. Here they can observe behavior as it occurs naturally, or obtain it by asking people to fill out questionnaires, or by interviewing them face to face. Finally, by using simulation and role-playing techniques, they can recreate environments in the laboratory that would otherwise be unavailable for study. In this section we will first examine nonexperimental techniques that use existing data, and then we will look at various kinds of field studies.

Content Analyses

To see is to know.

Often, the problems that social psychologists want to investigate have already occurred. Especially in our well documented society, there exists a multitude of sources of information about human behavior that are just waiting to be analyzed and interpreted. For example, rich sources of data can be found in statistical records kept by insurance companies and governments; written documents such as poems, diaries, and letters; the mass media such as newspapers, television, and magazines; and many cultural artifacts such as paintings, photo albums, and popular songs. Any of these existing data can be systematically and objectively studied for specific characteristics in a process called **content analysis** (Holsti, 1969). Content analyses allow researchers to draw conclusions about human attitudes and behavior, social conditions, and cultural traits. For example, researchers could study television programs over a 30-year period for what they reveal about sexual attitudes.

In performing content analyses, researchers have four major concerns: (1) They must choose a unit of analysis that accurately reflects the phenomenon they are studying; (2) they must find the best available sources of data on the phenomenon; (3) they must devise a way of coding the data; and (4) they must choose a sampling procedure that will provide enough representative data to test the hypothesis.

An interesting example of content analysis was that performed by Mosteller and Wallace (1964, 1972), who set out to decide a long-standing historical dispute concerning the authorship of a number of *The Federalist Papers. The Federalist* consists of 85 papers written in 1787–1788 to advocate ratification of the United States Constitution. It had been generally agreed that 51 of the papers were written by Alexander Hamilton, 14 by James Madison, and 5 by John Jay. Authorship of the remaining 15 papers was in dispute. Were they written by Hamilton, by Madison, or as a collaborative effort of the two men?

To resolve this dispute, Mosteller and Wallace examined the frequency with which common words such as *upon, by, from,* and *to* were used in the papers acknowledged to have been written by Hamilton and Madison. The frequency of such words reflects certain characteristics of a writing style peculiar to an author and has been found to be consistent throughout the works of an individual. Since the two writers used these words at different rates (e.g., Hamilton used *upon* 3.24

times in every 1000 words, while Madison used *upon* only 0.23 times per 1000) it was possible to examine the disputed papers to see whether they were more consistent with authorship by Hamilton or by Madison. The researchers concluded that Hamilton was the likely author of all the disputed papers.

Content analyses permit researchers to study historical trends (as do archival studies; see the next section). They are both *unobtrusive* and *nonreactive*— that is, they do not require cooperation or any effort on the part of the individuals being studied nor can they influence subjects' behavior, as an interview might. At their best, content analyses allow us to examine and make *qualitative* judgments about the materials being analyzed. The research on *The Federalist Papers* helped to establish authorship without looking at the political ideas in the writings. Similarly, the fairness of televised news broadcasts might be assessed by testing whether democratic and republican candidates are given equal coverage. Unlike surveys, content analyses do not require special equipment or large staffs, and are therefore relatively economical.

Content analyses have some disadvantages, however. They tend to be limited to written (or graphic) records, which may or may not be reliable indicators of what actually happens in the real world because they depend on decisions made by the people who compile the records. It is also possible that the coding categories chosen by the researcher may be too vague or generalized, and thus not be accurate measures of the behavior under study.

Archival Studies

Like content analysis, **archival studies** allow the researcher to observe real world events and their consequences. In contrast to content analyses, however, archival studies typically examine *quantitative* aspects of behavior. Buried public and private documents are raw data researchers can use to discern the natural patterns of occurrence and assess the social impact of such phenomena as suicide, urban riots, economic recessions, and earthquakes. Among the most useful archival records are the statistics published by the United States Census Bureau. Here the researcher can find regularly collected data on social conditions, including crime rates, family size, and employment rates; and health statistics such as birth and death rates, major causes of death, and hospital admissions. Other government agencies regularly publish data on weather, agricultural and industrial production, unemployment, wages, absenteeism, and strikes. Researchers can find statistics for these and other subjects for other parts of the world in publications by the United Nations, as well as in the files and publications of numerous international organizations. In addition, private organizations such as Gallup Polls, local chambers of commerce, Common Cause, and specialized magazines and journals publish monthly and yearly reports on public opinion, business conditions, and consumer issues.

Archival material can present researchers with an enormous mass of data, as well as with contradictory information from different sources. Fortunately, modern statistical procedures and data processing technology make it possible for researchers to probe the raw data carefully to detect the underlying meanings and patterns.

Archival studies allow us to search through existing records to find data relevant to social psychological analysis. Here a researcher is examining records from several years in a community health center.

Ken Karp

Researchers benefit from using archival data in many ways. As with content analyses, the data already exist—the researcher does not have to go out and collect it. And again as with content analyses, the measures used are unobtrusive and nonreactive. The behavior registered in the data has occurred naturally with no outside interference from researchers. Since most archival data have been collected repeatedly over the years, historical trends can be observed in a way that is impossible to do with other methods.

Archival studies have a number of disadvantages, however. One serious danger is drawing false conclusions from correlations; recall our earlier example of the spurious relationship between ice cream sales and June crime rates. Another problem is that research in archival data can be tedious and time-consuming. In a study to determine whether there was a relationship between urban riots and weather conditions, for example, Carlsmith and Anderson (1979) found that collecting 57,000 and more temperature readings was "an unending task" (p. 337). Sometimes even wider searches are necessary to collect the needed data.

Researchers may encounter other problems. Sometimes they cannot find the right kind of data to answer particular questions. It may be difficult to translate some information into meaningful units of measure, or to make the measures used in one data source compatible with those used in another. Systematic errors of various kinds often creep into archival reports. Japanese birth statistics, for example, are sometimes unreliable because they report an inaccurate year of birth for many thousands of individuals born in a year that is regarded as unlucky (Babbie, 1979). Reported suicide rates are notoriously unreliable in Catholic countries, where suicide is considered a mortal sin and so is usually reported as death by accident or misadventure.

Case Studies

Sometimes the intensive study of a single individual, group, incident, or event will shed new light on aspects of human behavior. In recent years, a number of "psychohistories" or "psychobiographies" have appeared. These have used psychological insights to reinterpret the lives and careers of outstanding individuals such as Luther, Gandhi, Hitler, and Nixon. The close study of isolated groups has been a specialty of anthropologists and sociologists for many decades. Anthropologists may focus on an individual to illustrate the features of an entire society, or may focus on a society to illustrate a larger point about group behavior. Sociologists and social psychologists using *one-shot case studies* have intensely researched unusual groups such as "doomsday" cults (those who believe that the end of the world is near) and victims of natural disasters. However, case studies are not very common in social psychology.

Case studies provide a rich and versatile area for researchers to work in. They enable researchers to lavish much attention on unusual groups and to use numerous research methods. Some case studies have generated vast amounts of information.

One-time case studies are often the only means of studying events that happen suddenly or only once in a lifetime. Because they are unique, they cannot be applied or generalized to a larger population. By definition case studies do not use a control group against which to compare the group under study. Although the results may well be applicable to other groups or situations, we cannot make a clear generalization from a case study.

Field Studies and Observational Techniques

The term **field studies** applies to a variety of research techniques, all of which share the same purpose: to examine social behavior in its natural setting. Some field studies are similar to experiments in that data are gathered systematically and some naturally occurring group serves as a control. But field studies generally differ from experiments in that researchers are not able to manipulate the behavior being observed or the factors that may be causing it (that is, the dependent and independent variables). The field researcher's task is to observe naturally occurring behavior and to make accurate records of the subjects' responses to events.

Observation is the fundamental characteristic of field studies. Ideally, the researcher interferes as little as possible with the behavior as it occurs, with its setting, or with the event that stimulates it—and in most field studies little interference is possible. As we shall see, observers in natural settings can be involved to various degrees with various effects on the subjects' behavior. Some field research consists of observation alone, and there is no specific hypothesis or theory for which the observer is gathering evidence. In fact, field research itself is often the source of new theories. It may result in the discovery of new relationships or new forms of behavior. It may uncover subtle nuances of attitude, behavior, or communication that have gone unnoticed until now. On the other hand, a good deal of field research is undertaken to confirm the results of laboratory findings or to substantiate a hypothesis or theory about human behavior and social processes.

There are three broad dimensions to most field research: natural behavior, natural setting, and natural treatment (Tunnell, 1977). An ideal field study would observe behavior while it is occurring. *Natural behavior* refers to behavior that would occur if no researcher were present.

Field studies focus on behavior that occurs in *natural settings*; the behavior is observed under conditions that are not manipulated by an experimenter. Field studies concern behavior that occurs as the result of a *natural event*. A natural event is one that would have happened whether or not the researcher was present.

The role of the field researcher affects the kind of data gathered and the quality of the study. Field researchers may have to assume the role of a totally unobtrusive outsider, or they may participate to varying degrees in the behavior being studied. As detached observers, field researchers simply observe behavior without in any way becoming a part of the behavior they are studying. They are unobtrusive; the subjects are usually not aware of being studied. An example of this is observers watching a trial as it takes place in a courtroom. When people know they are being observed, they may change their behavior. This problem is called *reactivity*, and it may reduce the quality of the data being collected.

Participant observers take part in the situation along with the natural subjects. This technique was developed and is used most by anthropologists who go out into the field and live—usually for a year or more—with the groups they are observing. From time to time social psychologists serve as jurors; they may later report (as scientifically as they can) their experiences as participant observers.

One well known participant–observation study involved an investigation of conditions in several mental hospitals (Rosenhan, 1973). The only way the researchers could conduct a sufficiently detailed study was to become complete participants in the situation. They decided to feign insanity, and presented themselves at the admissions desks of the various hospitals claiming to hear voices. All were admitted, and all but one were diagnosed as schizophrenic. Once inside, the "patients" reverted to normal behavior and, indeed, were quickly identified as normal by the real patients. They set about collecting data and then tried to get discharged. However, although they displayed no symptoms of mental illness, the hospital staffs continued to treat them as if they were disturbed. Much of their normal behavior was labeled deviant, and they were given a total of over 2,000 pills to alleviate their "symptoms." It was not easy to get discharged; the average stay was 19 days, and one of the "patients" was retained for 52 days.

While field research such as this allows researchers to observe naturally occurring behavior with all its rich and varied characteristics, the technique has its disadvantages. Field studies may lack reliability because there is only one observer. In addition, the observer may be biased, and may have trouble sorting out facts from impressions, which can affect the validity of the data collected.

Surveys

Another field method, the **survey,** is the form of social psychological research best known to the general public. Surveys examine such naturally occurring behavior as voting preferences among a certain population. While participant–observation studies allow researchers to study complex interactions among people, survey methods allow researchers to focus on measurable characteristics of natural populations. Surveys reveal how these characteristics are distributed, how frequently they occur, and how they are related.

You will encounter the results of survey research throughout the rest of this book. In order to evaluate them, it is important to understand some of the techniques used in collecting survey data, and to define some important terms.

A **population** is the group of people to whom we wish to generalize our findings. Theoretically it could include everyone in the world, or we could limit it by giving it definite characteristics. In a broad question such as "What is the frequency of sexual intercourse among unmarried couples?" the population might be all the unmarried people in the United States. A survey based on this population would entail canvassing several million single adults. We could narrow it down considerably by asking what the frequency of sexual intercourse is among unmarried couples at your college. We would probably not want to ask everybody, either in the total population or this smaller college population, about their behavior. We would be satisfied to ask our questions of a smaller **sample**. We would want this sample to be *representative*; its characteristics should be the same as, or very similar to, those of the larger population. This will help to assure that the answers we receive will accurately reflect the answers we would have received had we contacted every eligible member of the population.

Sampling Methods   Having decided what the representative sample will be, we must decide how to obtain it. The only way of getting a representative sample is to use a *probability sampling* plan. Such a plan ensures that every member of a cohabiting couple at the college has an equal chance (or at least a *known* chance) of being selected. Perhaps seniors are the most numerous category of cohabiting students. We might be tempted to sample only seniors. However, we would be leaving out a significant number of other eligible students. Since we want our sample to be truly representative, we would want it to include members of other classes in the same proportion as they occur in the larger population. To assure this we would use *random sampling* methods.

First, we would assign every individual in the population a number, beginning with 1 and continuing in sequence. Then we would select our sample by using a random number table. Since this method is very time-consuming, we might use a simpler one called *systematic sampling*. Here we would choose every *n*th name on our list. If we wanted to draw a sample of 200 out of a list of 1000 names, we would go down the list and select every 5th name. Systematic sampling is much more convenient than random sampling, and the results are generally the same.

We would of course want to make sure that, through some computer quirk, every fifth name on our list did not happen to be a senior, for our sample would no longer be representative; it would be biased toward seniors. Such hidden patterns in the data are one source of **sampling error**.

The dangers of biases in sampling are clearly shown in a survey that was conducted during the presidential race of 1936 between Franklin D. Roosevelt and Alfred M. Landon (Babbie, 1979). From the results of a poll, a magazine called *Literary Digest* predicted that Landon would win in a landslide. Of course, Roosevelt won in a landslide with over 60 percent of the vote. The magazine had drawn its sample of 2 million voters from telephone directories and automobile registration lists, a procedure that had given it accurate results in polls in the 1920s. However, it had not taken into account the effects of the depression. A great many people in those years, many of them democrats, could not afford telephones or automobiles; telephone directories and automobile registration lists disproportionately contained the names of republicans who voted for Landon.

The sample was not truly random, and could not be safely used to generalize to the entire voting population.

Interviews and Questionnaires   In survey techniques, and particularly in interviews and questionnaires, the data come from respondents' *self-reports*. In questionnaires, respondents provide written answers to a carefully assembled series of questions; in interviews, they give oral answers that are then coded or written down by the interviewer. Self-reports, however, can be very unreliable sources of information. People may give the wrong information because the truth is too embarrassing, because they forget unpleasant events, because they wish to appear respectable, or to amuse the interviewer. Sometimes they cannot report their feelings and beliefs on some issue because they do not know what their feelings are or have never learned how to verbalize them. People have a tendency to fall into what are called *response sets*; they may systematically agree or disagree with statements in questions; they may give extreme responses too often (such as "strongly agree" or "strongly disagree"), or they may give answers that never waver from the middle of the scale.

Interviewing calls for a great deal of skill and tact if it is to yield reliable and valid data. Even with the best of intentions, however, systematic errors, or biases, can distort the results of a survey. Such biases arise as a result of how interviewers and respondents perceive each other. Respondents answering sensitive questions about sexual behavior, for example, will give different answers depending on the sex or age of the interviewer. For their part, interviewers themselves can be unconsciously biased in their perceptions of respondents. An interviewer may expect housewives to have "no opinion" on some issues, and thus fail to interview in depth on that issue.

Simulation and Role-Playing Techniques

Survey methods allow researchers to measure the attitudes and behavior of natural populations in natural settings. But some behaviors and attitudes can only be tapped accurately by means of other techniques. It is very difficult, for example, to study crime as it occurs naturally. Indeed, criminals behave in ways deliberately calculated to avoid detection. Similarly, as we shall see in chapter 15, it is legally impossible for social psychologists to study actual jury decision-making. Some environments, such as prisons, are also extremely difficult to study in real life. However, it is possible to construct a sufficiently realistic mock prison that will allow researchers a large measure of control over physical conditions and an opportunity to observe the behavior that occurs spontaneously within them. But as we have seen, subjects will often not behave spontaneously if they know they are being observed.

Simulation, or role-playing, techniques provide one solution to this problem. Here the purposes of the experiment are explained to the subject in advance, and subjects are then asked to behave "as if the situation were real . . . or as if they did not know the purpose of the research" (Carlsmith et al., 1976, p. 125). Many role-playing studies ask subjects to *predict* how they would behave in a given situation. However, like self-reports, this approach has serious difficulties.

In a simulation experiment conducted at Stanford University, subjects were randomly assigned to be guards or prisoners, and confined to a mock prison built for purposes of the study. Here the "guards" have lined up the "prisoners" against a corridor wall and are keeping them there for an indefinite period.

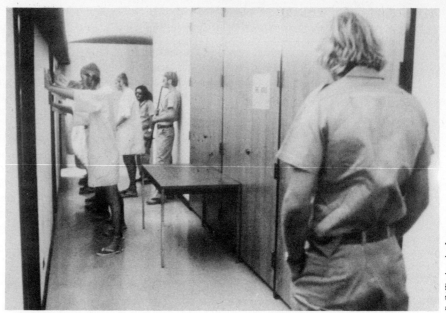

People cannot always predict accurately how they would behave in certain situations—at best they can only guess. And even if they are able to guess accurately, they may be reluctant to reveal such behavior to researchers. On one hand, they may not want to appear to be too conventional and thus distort their true reactions with bizarre behavior or attitudes. On the other hand, they may want to be "cooperative" and behave in a way they think the researcher expects, or they may want to "look good" and "conform to the image of a healthy, intelligent, mature person" (Carlsmith et al., 1976, pp. 127–128).

One famous simulation that avoided many of these pitfalls was conducted at Stanford University in 1973 by Haney, Banks, and Zimbardo. The study was undertaken to investigate the extent to which the violence and human degradation found in most prisons are due to the characters of inmates and their custodians as opposed to the prison situation. It was thought that the prison itself might "distort and rechannel the behavior of essentially normal individuals" (p. 90).

Because the researchers could not ethically place normal individuals inside an actual prison, they decided to simulate prison conditions. Naturally, they had to inform their subjects beforehand of the purpose of the study and get their consent. Twenty-four men between the ages of 17 and 30 were randomly assigned to be "prisoners" and "guards," and confined to a mock prison built in the basement of the Stanford University psychology building. The results of this study showed that simulations can produce powerful, realistic, psychological effects. This one demonstrated that normal, stable individuals are capable of pathological behavior when put into an environment that promotes it. Given this reaction on the part of normal people in response to simulated conditions, it is no surprise that real prisons are the scenes of so much indiscriminate violence and brutality. (For more on the Stanford prison study, see chapter 15.)

Experimental Research Techniques

In the kinds of studies we have discussed so far, researchers are limited to observing the influence of natural events on human behavior. In this section, we shall examine experimental methods that allow researchers increasing degrees of control over both independent and dependent variables. We begin with the simplest one-group preexperimental and quasi-experimental designs, where the researcher has little control over the events but can measure the resulting behavior. Field experiments, the next group, use naturally occurring populations, but allow researchers greater control over independent variables, giving these studies strong external validity. Evaluation research uses the experimental point of view to assess the results of social programs. In the last type of technique to be discussed, laboratory experiments, researchers have total control over independent variables. Here they can create their own conditions and can randomly assign subjects to test groups or to control groups, thus insuring that the resulting behavior is a product of experimental manipulation and is not due to some preexisting difference between the groups. In each of these four techniques, design problems can threaten internal or external validity, and we shall discuss a number of these problems as they appear.

As we have noted several times, it is often impossible for researchers to use true experimental methods in studying the effects of large-scale social interactions or natural events. Only rarely is it possible to assign tens of thousands of people at random to test and control groups (although in a number of medical studies it has been done). Nor can such large-scale events or interventions be controlled at will. Instead, researchers must be content to compare the characteristics of the same group of people before and after an event, or compare two groups that are merely similar but not strictly equivalent. In the following section we shall look briefly at some simple preexperimental designs and at more complex quasi-experimental designs. These are study designs that do not strictly meet all the requirements of true experiments.

Preexperiments

Suppose you wanted to test the hypothesis that studying while drinking beer will improve exam scores. One method you could use would be a case study in which you find students who drink while studying and ask them about their school performance. This **one-time case study design** can be represented as

X   0

where X signifies that your subjects drink and study at the same time and 0 is your assessment of their school performance. This design is quite weak, since your subjects have been specifically selected, and it does not compare their performance to that of students who study without the benefit of alcohol.

Now let us suppose you decide to compare the performance of a set of students on one exam (without beer) to their performance on a second exam (with beer). This **one-group pretest-posttest design** can be represented by

$$O_1 \qquad X \qquad O_2$$

where O_1 is the pretest, X is the beer-drinking "treatment," and O_2 is the posttest.

Let us further suppose that a dozen of your friends (who are enrolled with you in a theoretical physics course) have agreed to be subjects in your study—since you are providing the beer. As luck would have it, you get the idea for this study after the first exam in the course has been given, so you already have a pretest measure. The evening before the second exam your friends come to your room to drink and study. When you compare the pretest (O_1) and the posttest—that is, the second exam (O_2)—you find that everyone's score went down.

You are discouraged by these results (remember, you want to prove drinking beer will improve exam scores), but your friends (who are taking physics as a pass/fail course and enjoy your beer) point out several threats to internal validity. Do you see any alternative explanations for your results? (Hint: Perhaps everyone's performance deteriorates as the semester goes on—maturation. Maybe the second exam was tougher—instrumentation. Possibly there is something unusual about your friends; after all, they volunteered for this study and maybe they then decided to "let up" after the first exam—history. You can probably think of other threats, and may want to refer back to the box on page 48.)

One friend detects a serious threat to external validity and suggests that you remedy the problem by rerunning the study using her favorite imported premium beer. All agree that you should run the study again with a better design. What are some of the possibilities?

If you decide to compare your friends' posttest scores (the O_1 "treatment" group) with the scores of other members of the class (the O_2 "control" group) you would have a **static-group comparison design:**

Friends	X	O_1
Other Class Members	—	O_2

This design would help rule out history, maturation, and instrumentation effects. But you still would not know whether your friends as a group differ in some way from the other members of the class (a selection problem), because your control group is not necessarily equivalent to your treatment group. This problem will remain until you randomly assign people to your treatment (beer drinking) group; random assignment is, of course, what distinguishes true experimental from preexperimental designs.

Quasi-Experimental Designs

There are other simple experimental designs—called quasi-experimental designs—that can help to rule out some threats to validity. An **interrupted time-series design**

$$O_1 \qquad O_2 \qquad O_3 \qquad XO_4 \qquad XO_5 \qquad XO_6$$

is an extension of the one-group pretest-posttest design and helps to rule out maturation effects. In this design, any patterns of change can be detected in the many pretests (0_1, 0_2, and 0_3) and posttests ($X0_4$, $X0_5$, $X0_6$) you administer to your subjects.

Interrupted time-series designs can be used to investigate whether a particular social measure causes permanent long-term behavior change. One such study (Mazur-Hart & Berman, 1977) examined the effects of a no-fault divorce law in Nebraska. Critics of no-fault laws claimed that eliminating the idea of fault in divorce litigation would make divorce too easy to obtain; the divorce rate would soar. To see whether this was true, the researchers examined monthly divorce trends in archival data over a 5-year period from 1969, beginning 3 years before Nebraska passed its no-fault divorce law and continuing for 2 years afterward. If critics were right, there should have been a steep increase in the number of divorces after July 1972, when the law went into effect. The researchers found that the number of divorces had been systematically increasing long before the law went into effect and continued to increase at the same rate afterward. There was therefore no basis for attributing the increase to no-fault divorce laws; it was clearly due to a preexisting trend.

As we can see, because it measures data at many points before and after an event, the interrupted time-series design allows researchers to be far more certain about the effects of social innovations than a simple pretest-posttest design. Time-series designs can be strengthened, however, by the addition of a control group that does not experience the event or social measure. This would rule out any threats to validity from historical events. For example, an alternative design for the Nebraska study might have compared Nebraska's divorce rate before and after no-fault laws with divorce rates in one or more similar states that did not have no-fault laws. A pretest-posttest nonequivalent control group design such as the one below

| Nebraska (treatment) | 0_1 | X | 0_2 |
| Other states (control) | 0_3 | | 0_4 |

combines the static-group and one-group pretest-posttest designs. This makes it possible to compare the treatment (Nebraska) and control group (Iowa) scores both before (0_1 and 0_3) and after (0_2 and 0_4) the no-fault divorce law goes into effect in Nebraska. Although this design is still not as sound as a true experiment (where states would be randomly assigned to the no-fault treatment), it allows us to examine any preexisting differences between our groups or states.

Experimental Designs

An okra's seeds cannot be seen through its skin.
Ashanti proverb

Now that we have noted the threats to validity that arise with preexperimental and quasi-experimental designs, let us look at the ways in which true experimental designs can reduce and eliminate those threats. (For a summary of the experimental designs we have been discussing, see Figure 2–3.) The key to experimental research is the random assignment of subjects to treatment and to control groups.

FIGURE 2–3. Summary
of Experimental Designs

Key:
X: Experimental treatment
Y: Second variable
O: Subjects
R: Random selection

Type of Design	Diagram
Pre-experiments:	
One-time Case Study	$X \quad O$
One-Group Pretest-Posttest	$O_1 \quad X \quad O_2$
Static-Group Comparison	Treatment $\quad X \quad O_1$ Control $\quad O_2$
Quasi-experiments:	
Interrupted Time-Series	$O_1 \quad O_2 \quad O_3 \quad XO_4 \quad XO_5 \quad XO_6$
Pretest-Posttest Nonequivalent Control Group	Treatment $\quad O_1 \quad X \quad O_2$ Control $\quad O_3 \quad O_4$
True Experiments:	
Randomized Two-Group	Treatment $\quad X \quad O_1$ R Control $\quad O_2$
Before-After Two-Group	Treatment $\quad O_1 \quad X \quad O_2$ R Control $\quad O_3 \quad O_4$

If everyone in your physics class had agreed in advance to participate in your study, before the first exam you might have randomly assigned each student to either the beer (treatment) or no beer (control) condition—perhaps by flipping a coin. We can represent this by

$$\text{Treatment} \quad \quad X \quad O_1$$
$$R$$
$$\text{Control} \quad \quad \quad O_2$$

where R means random assignment. This randomized two-group design allows us to rule out problems of selection (since the subjects were randomly assigned).

We need not worry about maturation since both groups were tested at the same time and would have "matured" at the same rate. History may be ruled out for similar reasons. Since the groups were tested under the same conditions instrumentation is not a threat. To test the effect of beer drinking we can simply compare the average scores of the treatment groups and the control groups on the exam.

If you wanted to assure that your randomization procedure produced comparable treatment and control groups, or if you were afraid that your treatment would have only a small impact (but a real one nonetheless), you might want to pretest both groups. The resulting **before-after two-group design** looks like this:

Treatment	R	O_1	X	O_2
Control		O_3		O_4

This design allows us to compare the posttest exam scores for the treatment and control groups (i.e., compare O_2 to O_4), and to compare pretest and posttest scores within each (the treatment and the control) group. In fact, all subjects can serve as their own comparison, yielding very precise assessments of the impact of the treatment.

Field Experiments

Experiments can be run in field or laboratory settings. In **field experiments,** the subjects are the people researchers find by chance on street corners, in department stores, subways, courtrooms; ideally these subjects are *nonreactive*—they are frequently not aware that an experiment is taking place. Random assignment can work naturally in these situations. The chosen neighborhood or location, however, may have a certain amount of selective force over who experiences the treatment—that is, upper-middle-class people are more likely than lower-middle-class people to be subjects in a field experiment that takes place in some sub-

To find out what people's attitudes are, ask them! This psychology student at left is taking an opinion survey of young people in a suburban shopping mall. Social psychologists might also videotape a public event, as these graduate students are doing, so that they can later stop individual frames to analyze such aspects of human interaction as distance between people, eye contact, and posture.

urbs. Otherwise, chance determines who walks into a store, subway car, and courtroom, or who pulls up to an intersection.

Another reason for using field experiments is their strong external validity. As we shall see in the next section, a major disadvantage of laboratory experiments is their artificiality. The behavior that occurs in them is often not representative of what might occur in the real world. Field experiments allow researchers to observe naturally occurring, spontaneous responses.

Let us briefly examine a classic field experiment that takes up the issue of social responsibility. The researchers (Piliavin et al., 1969) wanted to study the ways "good Samaritan" (helping, altruistic) behavior occurs in public places. The independent variable, or stimulus event, was a victim (actually a male research confederate) who apparently collapsed in a subway car traveling between two stations. The dependent variable was helping behavior, and the subjects were the random assortment of people who happened to be in the car at any given time. The researchers manipulated the independent variable in various ways. Sometimes the victim collapsed in cars with only a few people, sometimes in cars with many. Sometimes another research confederate posing as a passenger would help the victim after a certain amount of time; sometimes this confederate simply observed what other passengers did. Some victims were black, some white; some feigned illness, some drunkenness. The researchers wanted to find out whether these different aspects of the independent variable would have different effects on bystander helping behavior. Would people of the same race be more likely to help each other? Were people more likely to help an ill victim than a drunk victim? Finally, they wanted to see if the *diffusion of responsibility* effect held true. This effect assumes that a person in a large group tends to believe that others will always come to the rescue. Is a person who is part of a large group less likely to help a victim than one who is alone or is part of a small group?

After 40 days of trials involving about 4,450 men and women as unwitting subjects and 4 teams of researchers, the study found that people were slightly more likely to help an ill victim of the same race, and considerably more likely to help if the victim was not drunk. In fact, ill victims of either race were more likely to be helped than drunken victims. Apparently people see drunks as more responsible for their behavior than ill victims and thus have less sympathy for them. There is also a risk in coming to the aid of a drunk victim; drunks can be capable of sudden violence or can act in embarrassing ways. The researchers were surprised to find that the diffusion of responsibility effect did not occur. Instead, people who were part of a large group were considerably more likely to help a victim, and to act more quickly than those who were part of a small group or who were alone.

There are a number of difficulties in conducting field experiments. First, many kinds of events occur in the natural world that cannot be controlled by the researcher—events that can contaminate the independent variable being manipulated. Perhaps a big city subway is an environment that discourages helping behavior because passengers have heard too many stories about subway crime. And field experiments often have practical problems. In the subway study, it was always possible that some cars might remain empty, that the train would stall, or that a police officer would intervene to help or arrest the "victim." Or another, "real," victim might appear.

The measurement of dependent variables can also present practical problems in field experiments. As they counted the number of passengers who came to the aid of the victims, researchers might have missed a number who moved away from the victim, or went into another car to avoid the situation. Finally, there is the problem of research ethics. People who are subjects in field experiments usually are not aware that they are participating in an experiment. Researchers must therefore be very careful about what situations they create for naive subjects. They must always avoid placing subjects in unnecessarily uncomfortable positions or forcing them into unsettling behavior.

Evaluation Research

Many social reform programs are a form of field research. Social planners identify specific social problems and then devise treatments for them. Such treatments are really independent variables directed at the problems of particular groups of people (Campbell, 1969). Beginning with the New Deal programs in the 1930s, federal agencies have sponsored experimental programs for the treatment of alcoholism, drug addiction, low educational achievement, juvenile delinquency, mental illness, poverty, and many other social problems (Perloff et al., 1976). At some point the legislators and administrators responsible for such programs want to know how effective they are. Many social intervention programs therefore are periodically assessed to determine their effectiveness and to help legislators decide whether to continue funding them. These assessment studies are called **evaluation research,** a form of applied research.

Evaluation research deals with practical issues in the real world; decisions reached on the basis of evaluative studies can affect the lives of many thousands of people and involve billions of dollars. Researchers may be asked to evaluate the effectiveness of social programs such as preschool education, the negative income tax, and job training, or of specific treatments such as home care for dialysis patients, behavioral techniques for obesity, or drug addiction programs.

Evaluation studies raise several philosophical and ethical problems. Social reform programs such as Head Start and income maintenance are usually intended to have a long-range effect; that is, the desired effects may not be immediately apparent, and in some cases may not appear for 20 years or more after the inception of the program. Nevertheless, researchers are often asked to evaluate them shortly after they have begun.

Another problem is that most social reform programs are not philosophically or politically neutral; almost all of them embody one social philosophy or another. Social psychologists who conduct evaluation research are therefore forced to play some complicated roles. They must fill the role of experts insofar as they possess the skills necessary to evaluate programs; at the same time, however, they are often collaborators in that they help plan solutions to social problems; and finally they are advocates in that they use the results of their research to argue on behalf of particular solutions (Ornstein, 1975).

When evaluation researchers recommend discarding an ineffective program, they often encounter much resistance. Program administrators whose income and prestige may depend on the continuation of ineffective programs will challenge any reports that threaten their existence. Researchers may also encounter ethical problems in conducting evaluation research. For instance, when a new medical treatment is being evaluated, those who already believe it to be effective may object to withholding it from a control group who might benefit from its use.

Laboratory Experiments

As we saw earlier in the chapter, a true experiment is the only research design that will permit researchers to say with confidence that a particular treatment causes a particular effect. This is because, in a true experiment, researchers have complete control over the independent variable. They can systematically vary it from one test situation to another and thereby influence the resulting behavior in very precise ways. Many kinds of social behavior have been explored by this means, and we will see many examples of experimental research throughout the remaining chapters of the book.

You already have an idea about how an experiment is set up. A recent experiment by Tanford and Penrod (in press) illustrates experimental methods. The experiment addressed a legal issue called "joinder": If a defendant in a criminal case is charged with several offenses (let us call them A, B, and C), is the defendant more likely to be convicted of a particular offense if the offenses are "joined" together in a single trial (ABC) or if each offense is tried separately? In part of the laboratory study, undergraduate students who played the role of jurors were randomly assigned to read a trial summary and decide a case. One group of subjects read about a defendant charged with a single offense (B); a sec-

Application: Evaluation Research and the *Head Start* Program

Begun in 1964–1965, the Head Start program provides enriched education opportunities to children between the ages of 3 and 5 from low-income families. The program developers felt that such children were disadvantaged by a "culture of poverty" that discouraged them from becoming self-supporting, achievement oriented adults. To correct this, the Head Start program provides a wide range of educational, nutritional, health, and social services, with special emphasis on the development of verbal skills, inquisitiveness, and self-confidence. The full effects of the program would be realized when the children reached young adulthood. In the meantime, evaluators measured the program's short-term effectiveness in terms of children's academic achievement in elementary school.

Early evaluative studies produced generally negative conclusions; more recent ones have reported much more positive results. The first evaluation was the Westinghouse study conducted in 1968–1969 (Rein & White, 1977). Head Start children in elementary school were tested on academic achievement and "self-concepts," and the results were compared with those of similar groups of children from the same schools who had not been in Head Start. This study concluded that the Head Start program was ineffective. Children in summer Head Start programs had made no lasting academic or psychological gains, while those from 1-year programs had made only slight gains and were below the national average in academic achievement and language ability. As a result, federal officials ended the summer programs while continuing the year-long ones.

Critics of the Westinghouse study pointed out that it had not randomly assigned children to test groups and to control groups. Children in the control groups were suspected of possessing many hidden advantages such as having educated grandparents and access to books in the home; any comparison between them and the Head Start children was inherently unfair. Other critics accused the study of unduly concentrating on emotional and mental development and overlooking health and nutritional benefits.

Fifteen years later, with many of the first Head Start children in their early twenties, the effects of the program can be more accurately evaluated. One recent study (Deutsch et al., 1981) has shown, for example, that the Head Start program produced some long-lasting, tangible benefits—at least for boys. Over 150 young men and women who had grown up in Harlem in the 1960s were assessed in 1980 for academic and occupational achievement. Half had participated in an experimental forerunner program of Head Start; an otherwise matched group had no compensatory training and thus served as a control group. The study found boys to be more successful than girls in school and in the job market. Of the Head Start boys, 32 percent had gone on to college, compared with only 20 percent of the control group; 57 percent were employed full- or part-time, as against 44 percent of the control group. Many girls, however, had become pregnant and dropped out of school or were unemployed. Researchers believe that the cause of the disparity between the girls and the boys may lie in the sex stereotyping characteristic of elementary schools. The Head Start program had emphasized self-assertiveness and curiosity for both boys and girls. While these qualities served the boys well in later years, they raised difficulties for the girls. Elementary school teachers consistently punished girls and rewarded boys for self-assertive behavior and for asking questions. As a result, many girls lost interest in school work and dropped out of school. However, their early Head Start training seems to have had some effect: Head Start girls who dropped out of school when they became pregnant are more likely than those not in the program to return to finish their high school education. The demonstrated success of Head Start has given its partisans ammunition to resist budget cuts and other threats.

TABLE 2-1.
Summary of Research Design Strengths and Weaknesses

	Internal Validity	External Validity	Experimenter Control	Resistance to Experimenter Bias	Ethical Problems	Ease of Conducting Study
Content Analysis	moderate	moderate	weak	moderate	few	very easy
Archival Studies	weak	moderate	weak	strong	few	very easy
Case Studies	weak	weak	weak	weak	many	moderate
Field Observations	weak	weak	weak	weak	many	moderate
Surveys	moderate	moderate	moderate	moderate	some	moderate
Simulations	moderate	moderate	strong	moderate	many	moderate
Quasi-Experiments	strong	moderate	moderate	moderate	few	most difficult
Lab Experiments	strong	moderate	strong	moderate	some	moderate
Field Experiments	moderate	strong	strong	moderate	some	most difficult

ond group read about two offenses joined together (AB); and the third group read about a case with three offenses joined together (ABC).

When the trial consisted of only the single offense (B), the students convicted the defendant 6 percent of the time. When there were two offenses, 6 percent of the students still convicted the defendant on charge B and 7 percent convicted the defendant on charge A. But when the defendant was charged with all three offenses in a single trial, the defendant was convicted by 29 percent of the students on charge B, by 29 percent of the students on charge A, and by 25 percent of the students on charge C.

Although joinder of the three offenses did significantly increase the likelihood of conviction on both offenses B and A, a laboratory demonstration that higher conviction rates may occur as a result of joinder is certainly not proof that this happens in real trials (especially since real judges admonish jurors to exercise great care in their decision-making). Nonetheless, these results do make one wonder what does happen in real trials. Can you think of research designs that might increase the external validity of this laboratory study? The strengths and weaknesses of the various research designs we have examined are summarized in Table 2-1.

Issues in Experimental Research

The very nature of experimental research has produced a number of problems concerning bias and ethics. Experimental results can be rendered useless if biases are introduced by subjects, by the experimental situation, or by the experimenters themselves. Other kinds of problems are raised by the fact that researchers are manipulating the behavior of other human beings. To conclude our survey of research methods, we will look closely at the need for obtaining informed consent from subjects, the practices of deception and debriefing, the invasion of subjects' privacy, and the use of research findings.

Threats to Experimental Research

Researchers encounter a number of pitfalls in conducting experimental studies. Sometimes the experimental situation gives subjects clues about what kind of behavior is expected. Sometimes the characteristics of research subjects threaten the validity of the results of a study, and sometimes the threat to a study's validity comes from the behavior and biases of the experimenters themselves.

Demand Characteristics   Certain aspects of the experimental situation may suggest to the subjects the expected or appropriate behavioral response. The subjects generally know they are participating in an experiment. They know the researchers are watching them and expecting them to behave in a certain way. They know a certain hypothesis is being tested, and they may spend some time trying to guess what it is. They may also want to appear in a favorable light to the researchers and to impress the researchers that they are well intentioned, cooperative individuals (Weber & Cook, 1972). They could want to help the cause of science, and in particular help support the hypothesis under study by emitting the right kind of behavior. (Others, out of resentment or hostility, may try to undermine the hypothesis by deliberately giving contradictory answers or behaving inappropriately.) Efforts by some subjects to confirm researchers' hypotheses prevent researchers from observing the true effects of the independent variable under study.

Researchers have developed a number of techniques to combat these demand characteristics. They can deceive subjects about the purpose of the experiment by giving them a plausible but false hypothesis. The subjects' attempts to support this hypothesis should then not affect the behavior that is being studied under the true hypothesis. Another technique is to measure the subjects' responses at a time and place other than where the independent variable was given.

Researchers have still other methods to keep subjects from guessing the true hypothesis of an experiment. They can disguise experimental conditions to prevent subjects from realizing that they are participating in an experiment. They can use subjects' actual behavior instead of verbal replies as a measure of the dependent variable. (People are more apt to demonstrate their true feelings and beliefs by what they do than by what they say.)

Volunteer Subjects   Subjects can undermine the validity of experiments in other ways, some of which may be beyond researchers' present means of control. Research subjects who *volunteer* to participate in experiments are a self-selected group of people (Rosenthal & Rosnow, 1969, 1975). Studies of volunteer subjects have found them to have personal qualities that are highly unrepresentative of

Experimenter behavior can affect the results of a study. Here a consumer panel is being led through a discussion of product desirability, while researchers watch behind a one-way glass. The researchers, who cannot be seen by the panel members, also have a video monitor and can hear the discussion. Do you think that the all female panel will respond to the male discussion leader in the same way as to a female leader?

the general population. Compared to nonvolunteers, volunteer subjects generally are better educated, work in higher status occupations, are more intelligent, and also tend to be younger and more unconventional.

The research situation itself may attract a biased sample of subjects: those who have a particular interest in the topic under study or are more knowledgeable about it; those who expect to be evaluated favorably on the behavior being studied; and those who perceive the research project to be newsworthy in some way. Among the means suggested to reduce the effects of volunteer bias is to make the appeal for volunteers as interesting as possible in order to attract a wider range of participants (Rosenthal & Rosnow, 1975).

Experimenter Effects   The behavior, biases, and personal qualities of the researchers themselves can significantly affect the outcome of experiments. Researchers' behavior may have biasing effects—for example, male researchers may smile only at female subjects. Because of their biases, two or more researchers may come to contradictory conclusions about the results of the same experiment. Their biases can also alter their perceptions of a subject's behavior, especially if that behavior is ambiguous. Finally, without intending to, researchers may send out very subtle cues to subjects about what response they expect (Rosenthal & Rosnow, 1969).

Several techniques have been proposed to keep researcher bias to a minimum. One technique is to keep research assistants ignorant of the hypothesis being tested. One problem with this technique is that, like subjects, research assistants will try to discover the hypothesis anyway. Another solution is to tell the research assistants what the hypothesis is, but not to indicate whether the subjects they are working with are a test or a control group. This eliminates the possibility that the assistant will communicate any performance expectations to the subjects and thus distort the performance results. Other methods of eliminating researcher bias include using tape recordings or closed-circuit television to instruct subjects. Bias can be further reduced by having more than one observer record behavioral data.

Ethical Concerns

Researchers' elaborate—and often ingenious—attempts to conceal the purposes of their research from subjects create a number of ethical problems. Is it ethically right for researchers not to tell subjects what is being studied, or to mislead subjects by giving them a false hypothesis? Once we raise these questions a host of others spring up. Do researchers in the name of science have a right to manipulate the emotions of other human beings? Does the gain in knowledge of human behavior justify creating anxiety, shame, or self-doubt in subjects during an experimental manipulation? And will these negative emotions, once aroused, persist long after the experiment has ended?

These and similar questions have led to a serious concern about the rights of subjects. As a consequence, scientific organizations and government agencies have issued codes of ethics for research. Sometimes a project that might have made an important contribution to the knowledge of human behavior has been terminated because it involved too great a violation of human rights. Researchers must weigh the potential benefits of their study against the potential harm to their subjects. (The ethical issues facing social psychological researchers are summarized in Table 2-2.)

Informed Consent and Deception   In many social psychological studies, subjects are never aware of being observed or participating in a study, especially in

---

TABLE 2-2.
Major Ethical Issues in Social Psychological Research

1. Should researchers study people without their knowledge or consent?
2. Should researchers coerce subjects into participation?
3. Should researchers conceal research objectives from subjects?
4. Should researchers actively deceive subjects?
5. Should researchers induce subjects to perform behaviors that reduce their self-respect?
6. Should research that may have a long-term effect on subjects' attitudes be conducted?
7. Should research procedures place subjects under stress?
8. Should research invade subjects' privacy?
9. Should subjects in control conditions receive the benefits given to subjects in experimental conditions?
10. Are there any conditions under which researchers may not treat subjects with respect?

Source: Adapted from "Ethical Issues in the Conduct of Research in Social Relations," by S. W. Cook. In C. Selltiz, L. C. Wrightsman, & S. W. Cook (Eds.), *Research Methods in Social Relations* (3rd ed.). New York: Holt, Rinehart & Winston, 1976. Reprinted by permission.

observational and field studies. In many cases, informing them of the nature of the study would cause them to alter their behavior to such an extent that it would no longer be natural. How far can researchers go before their manipulations constitute an invasion of privacy or harassment?

Wilson and Donnerstein (1976) surveyed a large sample of people for their

Controversy: The Questionable Uses of Research Findings

In a recent study, sociologist Coleman, Hoffer, and Kilgore (1981) cited evidence that private schools do a better job of educating children than do public schools. Children in private schools score higher on tests of reading, vocabulary, and mathematics than do those in public schools. Since private schools provide a superior education, they could help equalize the educational disparities between children from high- and low-income families. As the way to accomplish this, Coleman advocated giving every family in the country $1,000 in the form of vouchers or tuition tax credits. More black and Hispanic families would then send their children to private schools. In addition, the integration of private schools would be given a large boost.

Coleman's study was based on a sample of 59,000 students in 1,000 high schools. Children from every income level, low to high, were represented, and whatever their background Coleman's conclusion was that children make more cognitive gains in private than in public schools.

A number of critics have questioned Coleman's findings. Arthur Goldberger and Glen Cain (1982) pointed to what they regarded as flaws in Coleman's analysis. For one thing, he noted that Coleman's report did not state what specific tests had been administered to the students in his study. Coleman said only that the mathematics questions were "all rather elementary, involving basic arithmetic operations, fractions, and only a few hints of algebra and geometry" (p. 159). Because mathematics at this level is routinely taught prior to high school, Goldberger speculated that student achievement on such

tests would reflect the effectiveness of their elementary schools, not their present ones.

Goldberger also pointed out that Coleman compared private school students, who are virtually all in pre-college programs, with public school students in general and vocational as well as college tracks. In other words, he may not have been comparing similar students or programs. Another criticism centered on Coleman's statement that private school students of all socioeconomic levels performed better than public school students of the same socioeconomic level. Goldberger observed that the data on family income had come from a questionnaire answered by the students themselves, and not by their parents. Since students are frequently unaware of their household income, it was possible that the income information was inaccurate.

Whatever the merits or deficiencies of the Coleman study, the danger is that public opinion is often formed and public policy is often formulated on the basis of questionable research findings. Social scientists are constantly on the lookout for flaws in research methodology and analysis. The publication of research studies allows for comment from the scientific community and leads to further research. Social policy is too important and the implementation of new policies is too cumbersome and too costly to be undertaken on the basis of inadequate evidence. Fortunately, the democratic process that allows for ample public discussion and contains its own (inadvertent) inefficiencies often helps us to avoid costly and ineffective mistakes. High quality research is of course the best safeguard.

reactions to field studies that involved unaware participants. Examples of such studies included disguised researchers asking passersby on the street for money and noting their reactions; knocking on the doors of houses in various neighborhoods and asking to use the telephone; the remote filming of what passersby do to abandoned automobiles; visiting shoe stores, asking to be shown shoes, systematically rejecting whatever the salesman brings, and observing his behavior; and the subway car study discussed earlier.

The survey subjects were asked to put themselves in the place of the experimental subjects and say whether they would have felt annoyed or harassed, whether their privacy would have been invaded, whether such studies contribute significantly to the knowledge of human behavior, and whether such deception is morally acceptable. Most of those questioned did not object to the use of such research methods. While they agreed that some studies—especially those that involved asking passersby for money and staging subway collapses—did harass their subjects, they felt that none invaded privacy to a serious degree, and only one used unethical procedures. Most of the people surveyed felt that such research should continue. However, about one third of the respondents disapproved of these techniques and felt that social scientists should stop using deceptive methods on unaware subjects. Given the size of this minority, Wilson and Donnerstein recommend that researchers use deception with caution.

Some degree of deception, however, may be crucial to the validity of study results. Researchers can warn prospective subjects that they may experience some psychological discomfort, even though the true nature of an experiment cannot be fully revealed. Subjects who then decide to participate would give their *informed consent* to the researchers to proceed as planned. This was done, for example, in Milgram's controversial 1963 study exploring obedience to authority (see chapter 11).

Debriefing   In debriefing sessions after experiments, researchers usually describe how awkward and uncomfortable it was for them to have to deceive the subjects in order to obtain the data, but that the results add significantly to our knowledge of human behavior. Moreover, since most people do not like to feel that they have been fooled, researchers usually explain in some detail why it was necessary to deceive the subjects, how much trouble it was for them to construct an experimental situation that would convince anyone, and that they, the subjects, were not to go away thinking they have been overly gullible.

Answering Questions about Research in Social Psychology

1.   One of the most important research tools available to social psychologists is the experiment. In an experiment, researchers can manipulate one (or perhaps a few) independent variables that are hypothesized to produce certain effects. It is then possible to determine whether the manipulation(s) caused the hypothesized effects. For example, a simple experiment can test your hypothesis that greater physical attractiveness leads to greater liking. You can use photographs in which individuals are made up to look attractive and to

look unattractive. You would then ask strangers to view the photos and indicate how much they like the individual shown in each one. The ratings of the (experimentally manipulated) attractive and unattractive photographs could then be compared to see whether the differences in appearance influenced the "liking" rating.

2. This is almost a trick question: Remember that hypotheses about how the world works can never be proven absolutely true because it is impossible to examine every circumstance to which the hypothesis applies. Hypotheses (and the theories to which they are linked) can, however, be disproved if they fail to predict or account for the results we observe. Once a hypothesis or theory fails, we should use the new results together with the results from the previous studies to generate a new theory that is consistent with all the known facts. The new theory may yield new and testable hypotheses.

3. Generally, the same types of questions can be examined in both laboratory and field settings. In the laboratory it is easier for a researcher to achieve internal validity by maintaining tight control over all the extraneous variables that might influence or disturb the experimental result. This control makes it easier to assess the impact of the experimental manipulation. But the laboratory study may not generalize to the real world because it lacks external validity. Field experiments are often more difficult to conduct than laboratory studies because the researcher is constrained by real world events. The researcher typically has less control over extraneous variables, but may achieve better insight into how the experimental manipulations influence real world events.

4. Randomness, which implies an absence of a systematic relationship or unpredictability, appears in two forms in research: In the *random assignment* of subjects to experimental and control groups (e.g., by flipping a coin), the researcher tries to assure that any differences between the groups are a result of the experimental treatment. In *random sampling* (e.g., every tenth person checking out in a supermarket) a researcher attempts to assure that the group of subjects for study is fully representative of the larger population (e.g., all supermarket customers).

5. Although all researchers would like to believe that their research has practical and/or theoretical significance, when researchers talk about significance they are more likely to be concerned with the statistical variety. When a study has statistical significance, the differences between the experimental group and a control group are due to the experimental manipulation and not to chance. For example, if the researcher has manipulated attractiveness (the independent variable) and finds differences in liking (the dependent variable), tests of statistical significance will reveal whether the difference could have arisen as a result of chance (e.g., despite the random assignment of subjects the two groups will, by chance alone, be different in some ways) or as a result of the experimental manipulation.

6. Two of the primary ethical concerns confronted by social psychologists involve the deception and the debriefing of subjects. Most researchers try to keep deception to a minimum so that subjects can truly give informed consent. Other ethical concerns can sometimes arise: Does a study invade a subject's privacy? Will the research procedures have long-term effects on the subjects? Does the research place subjects under undue stress?

Summary

Social psychologists, like all social scientists, study human behavior systematically. The systematic study of human behavior begins with **theories**, general explanations or statements that may, or may not, be proved correct through research. In order to test a theory, it must be broken down into more limited statements or **hypotheses**. Each hypothesis must be tested through an appropriate **research design**.

Research may be **experimental**, an attempt to explain some aspect of behavior by determining causal relationships, or it may be **nonexperimental**, a description of naturally occurring behavior. Nonexperimental techniques are used when practical or ethical considerations make a true experiment impossible. The factors studied by social psychologists—features of behavior, character traits, or other qualities and attributes—are known as **variables**.

Nonexperimental studies, often called **correlational studies**, observe the relationships between variables. When variables change at the same rate, they are said to be **co-related**. When variables change in the same direction (both increasing, for example), there is a **positive correlation**; when they change in opposite directions (one increasing while the other is decreasing) there is a **negative correlation**. The existence of a correlation does not mean that one variable has caused the other. Instead, both may be affected by still another outside variable.

In a true experiment, researchers manipulate one factor, the **independent variable**, in order to determine its effect on another factor, the **dependent variable**. **Causality** is proved when a correlation is shown to exist between the independent and dependent variables; when the independent variable occurs before the dependent variable; and when there is no other explanation for the relationship between the two. The variables must be translated into measurable items in order to be tested and scored; when they are redefined as test scores, questionnaire items, or other measures, we can say they have been **operationally defined**.

In order to tell whether a given manipulation has had an effect, researchers use a **control group** of subjects that does not experience the manipulation. The best way of assuring that the test group and the control group are equal is to use **random assignment**, in which each subject has an equal chance of being assigned to either group. **Random sampling** insures that the subjects will be representative of a larger population.

Research results that are **reliable** will be repeatedly demonstrated. Research results that have **internal validity** will be an accurate reflection of the experimental manipulation, and will not be influenced by other variables or by a flaw in the research design. **External validity** exists if the results can be generalized to the larger population.

A theory or hypothesis is only as good as the **data** that can be gathered in its support. Researchers must make sure that the results observed in their experiments are not the result of **chance**. To do this, they must first disprove the **null hypothesis**, which states that any differences in the results between the test and control groups are due to chance and not to the experimental manipulation. Researchers prove the null hypothesis wrong by clearly showing, through the collection of high quality data, that their findings have **statistical significance** beyond that that would result from random error. Then the researchers can assert the **research hypothesis, which states that manipulation** of the independent variable was indeed responsible for the observed results. The statistical correlation determined by research is often expressed as a **correlation coefficient,** r. When $r = \pm 1.0$, there is a perfect correlation; when $r = 0$ there is no correlation at all.

In nonexperimental research designs, researchers observe changes that have actually occurred in the real world. Existing data, such as government records and personal diaries, can be used for such methods as **content analysis, archival studies,** and **case histories.** In **field research,** information is obtained by **observation, surveys, questionnaires,** or **interviews. Simulation** and **role-playing** can recreate a real-life situation in the laboratory.

Weak experimental research designs can be as simple as **one-group pre-experimental** and **quasi-experimental** designs, in which the researchers introduce a manipulation and determine its effects in a real-life situation. Strong experimental designs include **field experiments** in which researchers introduce the independent variable into a naturally occurring population. **Evaluation research** assesses the results of policies that have, in effect, already introduced an independent variable to a naturally occurring population. Finally, in **laboratory experiments,** researchers have total control over independent variables and can create complex research designs to test a number of related factors.

Experimental research is subject to contamination from the experimental situation itself. Experimental research may give subjects a hint of the expected behavior; or it may be affected by a particular characteristic of the subjects or by the behavior or biases of the researchers themselves. In addition, ethical concerns affect research design. Subjects are often given false or misleading statements about the purpose of the research. Should such behavior variables like emotions or moral judgments be manipulated at all? How can researchers make sure that the conditions of an experiment do not have long-term negative consequences for subjects? Subjects should be told before an experiment that they may experience some psychological discomfort so they can give their **informed consent** to participate. Subjects should also be given full explanations, or **debriefed,** afterward.

Suggested Additional Reading

Adair, J. G. *The human subject: The social psychology of the psychological experiment.* Boston: Little, Brown, 1973.

Carlsmith, J. M., Ellsworth, P. C., & Aronson, E. *Methods of research in social psychology.* Reading, Mass.: Addison Wesley, 1976.

Cozby, P. C. *Methods in behavioral research* (2nd ed.). Palo Alto, Calif.: Mayfield Publishing, 1981.

Judd, C. M. and Kenny D. A. *Estimating the effects of social intervention.* Cambridge, England:

Cambridge University Press, 1981.

Kidder, L. Ethical issues in the conduct of research in social relations. In C. Sellitz, L. C. Wrightsman, & S. W. Cook (Eds.), *Research methods in social relations* (3rd ed.). New York: Holt, Rinehart & Winston, 1981.

Stern, P. C. *Evaluating social science research.* New York: Oxford University Press, 1979.

Webb, E. J., et al. *Nonreactive measures in the social sciences.* Boston: Houghton Mifflin, 1981.

SOCIAL COGNITION: EXPERIENCING OURSELVES AND OTHERS

3

DEVELOPMENT OF THE SELF

Questions about Development of the Self

1. What would happen to a child deprived of contact with adult members of society?
2. Which is more important in the development of a child—inherited characteristics or the social environment into which it is born? Do you think either factor can overcome the effects of the other?
3. How do the actions of other people help shape your own behavior?
4. How does a person become "moral"? Can morality be taught?
5. What was the role of your family in determining the kind of person you are? What influences did your peers and education have on you?
6. What do you believe to be proper roles for women and men? Where did you get those expectations?

Social psychology is concerned with human social behavior. We usually take social behavior for granted, since we are all active participants in a complex, everyday social reality. But our ability to participate in the world—indeed, the very existence of that social world—depends on the fact that people develop the skills necessary to maintain a successful social environment. Newborns clearly do not possess these skills. Thus, we may ask: How does a helpless infant become a fully socialized adult? Given such basic provisions as food and shelter, the passage of a certain amount of time will permit the physical growth from baby to adult. But what accounts for the growth of social behavior?

Many theories have been proposed to explain the socialization process. In this chapter we will examine some of them. The first half of this chapter is devoted to the elaboration of the main theoretical perspectives on social development, while the second half reports the results of the relevant empirical research. We will also look more closely at a few key aspects of socialization: how a sense of morality is produced; the influences exerted by parents, peers, and others on the growing child; and the development of sexual identity and sex-role behavior.

Before reading the chapter you might consider your own moral development and your attitudes about the appropriate roles for males and females in our society. Where have your values and attitudes come from? Who were the most important influences in your life? Can you think of any profound changes in your values that have occurred since you started college? How did these changes come about?

Theories of Becoming a Social Being

Human beings are innately capable of a variety of behaviors and responses. The socialization process teaches people which behaviors their community considers socially important and acceptable; it shows the developing individual which responses conform to its standards. Parents generally act as agents for the community in transmitting this knowledge, but their socializing efforts are supplemented by input from other adults in the community and from the person's own peers as well. The socialization process is important not only for the survival and well-being of the social group, but also for the survival and well-being of the person being socialized.

The importance of socialization is stressed by the rare documented cases of feral (wild) children—humans who have not been socialized. One well-known case was that of Anna, a 5-year-old child found tied to a chair in a dark room in a Pennsylvania farmhouse (Davis, 1940). A more recent case was that of Genie, a 13-year-old girl who was kept harnessed to a potty seat in a small room in a house in California. Genie's mother, who was partially blind, had kept the child secluded to avoid angering her husband, who hated children. Genie was fed only milk and baby food. She lived in virtual silence, being beaten by her father if she made any noise. She had virtually no human contact—and no socialization. Her mother did not train, speak to, or caress Genie. In 1970 Genie's mother ran away with Genie after a violent fight with her husband, and sought the help of a social worker. By then Genie was severely malnourished. She could not chew, walk, move her arms, cry, control her bodily functions, or talk. She salivated and spat a great deal, and recognized only her own name and the word *sorry*.

Placed in a children's hospital, her physical condition improved somewhat and she also developed some human responses: She learned to recognize words and began to speak one- and two-word phrases. She showed interest in places she was taken to, such as supermarkets. However, despite intensive training she never learned to ask questions or to speak normally (that is, she did not grasp the structure of the language; see chapter 7). However, she creatively used gestures to make herself understood and learned sign language. On a battery of developmental tests, she did well in an IQ performance test, raising her score from 38 in 1971 to 74 in 1977. The following year, though, her mother removed her from the hospital and from the researchers who had been working with her (Curtiss, 1977; Pines, 1981). By then it was quite clear despite all the personal attention she had received, Genie's original isolation from human contact and from the socialization process had prevented much—though not all—of her mental capacity from being developed.

The Nature–Nurture Controversy

The story of Genie demonstrates the powerful effect of the absence of human contact. But the reported facts leave many questions unanswered. Perhaps Genie did not have the potential for further development. To what extent is human social behavior controlled by factors and experiences in the environment (nurture)? What role do genetic inheritance and instincts (nature) play? Are people born the way they are? Or do they become the way they are? This is the nature–nurture controversy.

Making Assumptions about Human Nature   The nature–nurture controversy, and the theories that address it, revolve around these basic questions:

1. Is human social behavior controlled by genetic inheritance and instincts, or by factors and experiences in the environment? Or—to take a middle position—is human nature a byproduct of the interaction between instincts and environment?
2. Are human beings by nature good or evil? Or do both aspects contribute to the truth?
3. Do human beings play active or passive roles in their own socialization? Do we simply receive whatever stimuli are brought to us by our environment, letting ourselves be acted upon? Or do we actively seek out specific stimuli, have control over our responses, and process and organize our experiences?

Stage Theories of Human Development   These questions about human nature are answered in diverse ways by the theories we will examine. The theories

Theory: Philosophical and Historical Assumptions

From antiquity, thinkers have taken sides on the nature–nurture issue (Lerner, 1976). Plato held that the human soul exists before birth in a "realm of ideas," and becomes entrapped by the body during life. And beliefs that an individual's nature, and perhaps destiny, are determined before birth led many early societies to view children as adults in miniature, and to treat them accordingly. In line with the idea that nature is the key to behavior, many religions subscribed to the doctrine of original sin: We are sinful at birth.

Eighteenth-century British philosopher Thomas Hobbes, in *Leviathan*, held that the purpose of society is to tame the selfish and self-serving impulses of people. While not denying nature, this position ascribes a strong role to nurture. John Locke, another eighteenth-century British philosopher, held that children are born with their minds a blank slate—a *tabula rasa*—

and acquire knowledge solely through nurture, or experience. In the same period, Jean Jacques Rousseau in France and Immanuel Kant in Germany argued that human beings are basically good—the "noble savage"—and that an interaction occurs between the innate qualities of the individual and the environment.

Social scientists and biologists today are in general agreement that nature and nurture interact throughout the development—indeed, the life—of the individual. Nature provides the potential and the limitations; nurture determines how or whether they will be realized. In contemporary research, the issue is no longer the old philosophical either/or debate. The issue is, rather, to identify the relative contribution of each factor, and to understand the interplay between them. The argument, although still heard, is ultimately futile: All people are inevitably influenced both by nature and nurture.

themselves take two approaches: **Stage theories** claim that development occurs in successive but distinct steps or stages. The child goes through a spurt of development, reaches a steady, unchanging period, goes through another spurt of development, reaches another plateau, and so on. The specific stages proposed by one theorist differ from those proposed by another: Sigmund Freud, Erik Erikson, and Jean Piaget all offer stage theories, but they describe different kinds of stages, as we shall see.

The developmental spurt leading to the plateau of a given stage provides children with new abilities. Once on the plateau, children can try out and perfect these new abilities before the next spurt of development occurs. Children are not interested in what new developments will bring, and are also unprepared for them. Similarly, they lose interest in the skills they acquired and perfected during earlier stages. They focus on the present stage, exploring its potential in full, until they are ready for another spurt (Brophy, 1977).

Continuous Process Theories of Development   Although stage theorists disagree about the stages and about the breaks between them, they all differ fundamentally from **continuous process theories**. Believing that human beings are largely the product of their environment, continuous process theorists do not see why development should wait at certain points. In this view, the learning process itself, independent of any timetable or maturational sequence, determines the course of development.

In the next few sections we will consider several prominent theories of human development—psychoanalytic, cognitive developmental, and social learning. First we will examine the basic assumptions and concepts behind each theory. We will then apply each of these theories in turn to the problem of moral development to illustrate how researchers working within each framework approach a common problem. Although each of these major theories has its adherents, it is safe to say that the social learning approach is the dominant theoretical perspective in social psychology today. In the second half of this chapter we will examine social development largely from that perspective.

Freud and the Psychoanalytic Approach

Modern theories that explain socialization begin with the proposals of Sigmund Freud (1856–1939), a physician who specialized in treating nervous disorders. Freud had studied with the famous French neurologist Jean Martin Charcot, who used hypnosis to investigate "hysteria" or neurosis. Freud was also influenced by Josef Breuer, who advanced a theory of "talking cures" for neuroses. Freud worked with Breuer until Breuer became upset at the emphasis Freud gave to sex in his theories. Freud then developed the talking cures technique on his own, discarding hypnosis in favor of *free association*. He found that by letting his patients freely speak about whatever came into their minds, they were able to recall events they had "forgotten" or *repressed*.

Freud's patients would recount their life histories, which he would then analyze and reinterpret in terms of key childhood experiences and traumas. Just before the turn of the century, due to his father's death and the defection of Breuer, Freud himself fell into a deep depression and began analyzing his own dreams. *The Interpretation of Dreams* (1900) was the product, and it marked the start of psychoanalysis as we know it today.

Although Freud's influence on psychology and psychiatry cannot be disputed, recent critics have questioned the extent of his contribution (Sulloway, 1979). There is also growing awareness that many of his concepts sprang from conditions in the repressed Victorian society of his day, and that these concepts may not be equally applicable to human experience in other times and places. Despite this and other criticisms, Freud's theory of personality development laid the foundation for a new and significant way of looking at human nature, and remains influential today.

The Id, the Ego, and the Superego   According to Freud, the human personality is divided into three parts: the id, the ego, and the superego. The id contains inherited psychological elements, such as the instincts, as well as the psychic energy that powers the other two systems. When the energy of the id, due to external stimulation or internal impulses, increases beyond a tolerable level, the id acts to reduce the resultant tension by immediate discharge of the excess energy. This tension-reduction is experienced as pleasurable, and fulfills a basic human need, which Freud called the **pleasure principle** (see Figure 3–1).

The **superego** enforces the moral code a person learned in the socialization process. Parental authority is internalized in the superego, which strives for an ideal perfection that is directly opposed to the more basic concerns of the id.

Mediating between the id and the superego is the **ego,** the executive branch of the mind. The ego must control both the id and superego in order to deal with the real world. For instance, the ego prevents the id from its immediate discharge of energy until it finds an appropriate object that satisfies the need; this postponement is called the **reality principle**. The ego, through problem solving or thinking, discovers plans of action that fit reality (Hall & Lindzey, 1970). Both the ego and superego are partially conscious and partially unconscious in the mind; the id is fully unconscious.

Identification and Internalization   Identification is a strong attachment to an object or person. In the identification process, an individual accepts and internalizes the values and needs of someone else, making them a part of his or her own personality. Freud described two key identification mechanisms: First is identification, usually with a parent, that grows out of love and deepens as the child moves toward independence and experiences or fears loss of love. Second, and very different, is identification that grows out of fear of an aggressor. In both cases, the object is to reduce tension through internalizing the values and wishes of the person identified with. By patterning behavior after this model, things will go more smoothly (Bronfenbrenner, 1960).

As the twig is bent, so's the tree inclined.

Thus, to avoid punishment—when simple escape is impossible—a victim can identify with the aggressor. The aggressor's demands become the victim's own; the victim creates aggression against the very impulses that would normally operate against the aggressor. When a father punishes a child, the child identifies with the father in his role as "punisher." The child learns that the transgression deserves punishment. The father's authority then becomes internalized in the child's superego, which will subsequently punish the ego (guilt) whenever it is

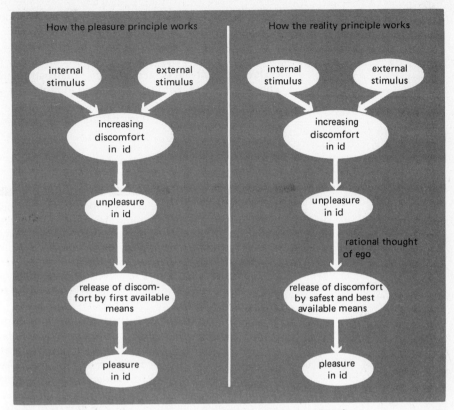

FIGURE 3-1. The Pleasure Principle and the Reality Principle of Freud

disobedient (Hall, 1979). Some extreme forms of identification with an aggressor have occurred when people are placed under unusual pressures (see box).

Psychosexual Stages   Freud's theory of human development is a stage theory. Successful passage through each stage is essential for entering the next one, and for later mental health.

1. The *oral stage*. Up until about age 1, the infant derives pleasure from activities involving the mouth, such as sucking and biting.
2. The *anal stage*. Following the oral stage and continuing up until about age 3, children learn to regulate the instinctual impulses of elimination. This is, in a sense, the infant's first experience in directly controlling the environment.
3. The *phallic stage*. Between ages 3 and 5, children connect sexual and aggressive feelings with their genitals, and experience sexual attraction to the opposite-sexed parent.
4. The *latency stage*. From about 5 years of age until the start of puberty, the libido is inactive and psychosexual development temporarily halts.

5. The *genital stage.* At about age 12 (with marked variations among individuals), sexual development and interest resurface. The genitally based sexual activities of adulthood begin.

Development can be arrested through frustrations or problems encountered at any of the stages. For instance, Freud thought that adults who were greedy, insecure, or still seeking oral gratification such as smoking had been frustrated in satisfying their oral needs during their first year of life.

Erikson and the Psychosocial Approach

Erik H. Erikson (1963) elaborated on the Freudian stages by including psychosocial events that he feels are as important as the biological events emphasized by Freud, and also by extending the stages into adulthood. Like Freud's theory, Erikson's theory is a stage theory, but the later stages concentrate on adaptive

Controversy: A Hostage Internalizes

"Finally, the only person who really knows tells what really happened," says the ad. But that's precisely what Patricia Campbell Hearst's autobiography doesn't do, because Patty Hearst, to this day, either doesn't know or doesn't want to tell what really happened.

Oh, she knows the series of events—her kidnapping in Berkeley, Calif., in 1974; her confinement in a closet for 57 days by a group of gun-happy misfits who called themselves the Symbionese Liberation Army, though the entire army consisted of one black man, two white men, and five white women; her decision to join the group as her only means of survival; her emergence as Tania, the urban guerilla, who helped stick up a bank; her apparent conversion to the aims of the group; her subsequent acts, which included another bank robbery and setting bombs under parked police cars; and her eventual arrest, conviction and release.

All this is told with close to total recall, but one element is still missing: Why on the occasions when she was left alone and could have escaped, did she stay with her captors?

After the group's leader and five of his "soldiers" were killed, Patty was left with the Har-

rises, William and Emily. . . . Instead of abandoning the Harrises, whom she hated for their bullying manner, Patty saved them from arrest. When they were caught shoplifting in a sporting goods store, Patty, waiting outside in their van, fired a submachine gun, which allowed them to escape. Why had she acted against her own self-interest? "The only answer I could find that satisfies *me*," Patty Hearst writes, "which later was bolstered and reaffirmed by expert opinion on the subject, was that I acted instinctively, because I had been trained and drilled to do just that, to react to a situation without thinking. . . . By the time they had finished with me I was, in fact, a soldier in the Symbionese Liberation Army."

This was the defense used at her trial. She was brainwashed, the experts affirmed; she was part of a growing aggregate of victims of mind bending, from Jozsef Cardinal Mindszenty, who signed a written confession after only 35 days of imprisonment in Communist Hungary, to those American prisoners in Korea and Vietnam who cooperated with their jailers and sometimes remained behind when the war was over. . . .

As Patty describes herself . . . she was by na-

and reality-oriented aspects of personality rather than on sexual drives. And also like Freud's theory, each stage contains both a positive and negative component; problems encountered while working through conflicts at any one stage may result in impairments that will affect the individual throughout life. Erikson's eight stages of development are summarized in Table 3–1 on the next page.

The Cognitive-Developmental Approach

The stage theories we have discussed so far—those of Freud and Erikson—were concerned with the total process of becoming a social being. In this section, we will consider the leading contemporary authority on cognitive development (how we learn to think), Jean Piaget.

Jean Piaget   Jean Piaget's concepts and basic concerns differ greatly from those of Freud, the other major theorist on child development. Piaget first

---

ture too submissive and obedient. Brought up by strict parents, she was made to go to schools she didn't like and to conform to a rigorous code of behavior. In college, she lived with Steven Weed, her high-school math instructor, substituting the authority figure of a former teacher for her parents. She began to dislike Weed because he was not respectful to *his* parents. But she went along with wedding plans, choosing silver patterns while resenting her fiancé. . . .

At first, Patty complied with her captors out of fear and an instinct to survive, but after a while she says she did so willingly. She could have called her parents or gone home, but she did neither. Was she brainwashed, or had she simply adapted her normal pattern of behavior to a new setting, transferring those qualities of submissiveness she had already shown toward her parents and her fiancé to the Symbionese Liberation Army? Just as she had been an obedient daughter, returning the extra dollar the grocer gave her in change, just as she had been an obedient fiancée, agreeing to marry a man she disliked, she now developed a kind of allegiance to her kidnappers. "I felt I owed them something," she writes, "something like loyalty." This

was after a woman had been killed in a bank robbery in which Patty was driving the getaway van. She was "upset," but not enough to leave the aimlessly violent group—not because she believed in what the group was doing, and not because she was indoctrinated by lectures on Maoism, but because she had been made a member of the team and wanted to perform as a team player. She was obeying her mother's favorite saying: If you start something, you must finish it.

Also, she was conforming to the principles of her father's corporate world: If you work hard, you get promoted, you rise in the organization. When she was picked to conduct gun classes for the other women, she felt a great sense of accomplishment. "For once," she writes, "I was not the know-nothing idiot in the group; for once I was contributing something; for once I was receiving praise from my sisters." It seems to me that if Patty Hearst was brainwashed, she was brainwashed from birth.

Source: © 1982 by The New York Times Company. Reprinted by permission.

TABLE 3–1.
Erikson's Eight Stages of Development

Stage	Basic Conflict
1. Oral-Sensory	Trust vs. mistrust
2. Anal-Muscular	Autonomy vs. shame
3. Genital-Locomotor	Initiative vs. guilt
4. Latency	Industry vs. inferiority
5. Puberty and Adolescence	Identity vs. diffusion
6. Young Adulthood	Intimacy vs. isolation
7. Adulthood	Generativity vs. stagnation
8. Maturity	Ego integrity vs. despair

studied the development of knowledge in his own children. He believed that children are born with "innate schema." A *schema* is an organized behavior sequence that involves (1) recognition of a sensory stimulus from the environment and (2) some motor (physical) activity in response.

Piaget stresses that learning is an active and interactive process. For example, as an infant interacts with objects—chews them, bangs into them, throws them around, and so on—knowledge is gained, not only through the infant's own actions or the properties of the objects alone, but through a necessary interaction between the two and the consequent links between actions and objects.

To Piaget, cognitive development aids the human organism in adapting to the environment. This adaptation consists of two component processes: *assimilation*, the incorporation of new knowledge into existing schemas, and *accommodation*, the modification of existing schemas as a result of new information that does not fit into them. These processes are complementary.

We can illustrate these concepts by means of Rubik's cube, one of the newest fads of our civilization. The first time you pick up one of these toys, you randomly twist the sections around to get an idea of how it works. Your existing *schema* (unless you are a genius!) is probably incapable of solving the puzzle. With a little practice, however, you can probably figure out the necessary moves to get one side a solid color. This demonstrates *accommodation*, or modification of the previously random schema for solving the puzzle.

But suppose your interest has been aroused enough for you to read one of the books that explains the strategy to achieve a complete solution. If you practice the strategy to a level of proficiency, you have once again accommodated a previously existing schema, refining it to yet a higher level. But if you get to the point where familiarity with the solution to Rubik's cube helps you to create a strategy to solve a different puzzle, *assimilation* has occurred.

According to Piaget, human cognitive development proceeds through the following four stages (Piaget, 1926):

1.   The *sensorimotor stage*. This stage covers the years from birth to age 2. The first activities of an infant are reflexive. Knowledge is gained through using the senses and through reaching, touching, walking, and otherwise interacting with the environment. The child develops motor habits and expands the innate schemas.

2. The *preoperational stage*. During this stage, which lasts from about ages 2 to 7, children develop the ability to represent schemes in their heads, and this leads to symbolic problem-solving capabilities. Language develops, which clearly demonstrates the use of more complex mental schemes. This stage also witnesses the development of symbolic play.

3. The *concrete operational stage*. In the third developmental stage, which spans ages 7 to 11, children begin to think logically about concrete objects and events. They recognize that properties can remain constant even though appearances change (as, for instance, when water from a short, fat glass is poured into a tall, thin one). Numerical thought, classification of objects, and the construction of mental images of complex actions commence during this stage. The child's capacity to deal with the real world is extended, because the child can think about objects and mentally perform actions on them without having the objects in hand.

4. The *formal operational stage*. In this stage, which begins at about age 12 and continues throughout adulthood, full logical thought is achieved. The child is now able to think abstractly and hypothetically. It is possible, for instance, to think *about* one's own thoughts, to reason about the future, and to entertain propositions that are contrary to fact.

Social Learning Theory

Unlike the stage development theorists, Albert Bandura views development as a continuous process of learning rather than as a series of stages. Bandura's social learning theory is a behavioral approach that differs in key respects from that of the other behavioral theorists. For example, B. F. Skinner assumes that a response must be performed and reinforced before it can be considered to have been learned. Bandura, on the other hand, believes that learning can occur vicariously as well, in the form of observations. In this way actual learning takes place before it is demonstrated in behaviors. This combines a cognitive viewpoint—that people are capable of thinking about their experiences, and do so—with elements of behaviorism.

Learning, according to Bandura (1977), occurs in a four-step sequence:

1. *Attention* is paid by watching or listening to a "model" perform the behavior to be learned. The degree of attention is enhanced if the model exaggerates key features of the behavior being taught—for instance, a singing instructor might exaggerate and prolong the mouth movements necessary to produce a certain sound. Attention is also enhanced by means of rewards and by the use of attention-directing remarks.

2. *Retention* of the behavior occurs in memory. If the subject is too young to remember things verbally, the behavior is retained as pictorial symbols or images. A subject with verbal skills remembers images in addition to verbal descriptions. Verbal symbols are better remembered than sensory symbols.

3. *Motor reproduction* of the behavior converts the symbols stored in memory into the appropriate act itself. This involves adjusting the behavior to fit the memory of what was taught, and using feedback which may, for example, include the helpful comments of observers.

4. *Motivation for performance* of the act persuades the subject not just to show that he or she *can* do it, but to get on with actually doing it—for instance, not just to sing the note successfully once, but to do so correctly each time it comes up in the song. Rewards can be direct (a pat on the back, a better grade) or indirect (watching the instructor smile). Punishments can also be direct or indirect.

The emphasis in Bandura's theory is on the ability to learn behavior without the need to reproduce it, and on the retention and manipulation of symbols. Bandura's approach implies that human beings are self-regulators of behaviors—they can plan behavior, set goals for themselves, and reward or punish themselves. Rewards and punishments are an important influence on behavior, and can have effects on immediate behavior. Moreover, according to social learning theorists, for learned behaviors to persist, "secondary reinforcements" are necessary—for example, receiving both a cookie and the mother's smile as a reward, several times, until the smile alone becomes sufficient as a secondary reinforcer. Parental behavior itself can take on reinforcing properties. In a nurturant environment, parents' behavior, if it is attached to sufficient past rewards, can become reinforcing to the child: The child then finds it rewarding to act as the parents do (Sears et al., 1957).

Comparing Theories of Development

Thus far in chapter 3 we have examined the three major theoretical models of human development: the psychoanalytic approach (both Freud's psychosexual version and Erikson's psychosocial version); the cognitive-developmental approach (Piaget); and social learning theory (Bandura). All share some assumptions about the socialization process—the developing individual must achieve certain abilities before progressing further, for example. Social learning theory holds that social growth takes place continuously, while psychoanalytic and cognitive-developmental theories assert that social growth occurs in age-related stages. Each strikes a different balance on the nature–nurture issue, as many philosophers did even prior to the existence of psychology as a field of study in its own right.

The psychoanalytic approach focuses on the nonrational parts of human behavior, and on conflicts inherent in human nature. The cognitive-developmental approach emphasizes an unfolding of the mind, giving equal emphasis to both environmental and cognitive forces as shapers of the infant and child. In social learning theory, the focus is almost exclusively on the environment and experience.

Each approach has its own utility, as well as its own limitations, in explaining human behavior. In fact, the existence of three different and yet related approaches side-by-side provides a comment on the complexities of the developmental process and the difficulties inherent in studying human beings. In the pages that follow we examine these approaches in terms of what they can tell us about the development of moral judgment and behavior.

Development of Moral Behavior

Why should a person follow the path of most resistance, instead of the path of least resistance? Why have saints been obsessed with their guilt rather than content with their virtues? Great social thinkers have asked such questions throughout recorded history. American psychology, in its early stages, also asked them, and then seemed to conclude that most moral behavior depended on the situation. In 1958, however, Harvard psychologist Lawrence Kohlberg reawakened interest in the subject.

Moral behavior follows a system of rules regarding the reciprocal obligations and rights of the individuals in a society. The rules, which exist independently of the people themselves, may be explicit or implicit, depending on the society. Even in a society where many rules are written, most interpersonal behavior is still implicit, unwritten, but understood by virtually all the members of the society. Understanding these rules can help us, as social psychologists, to better understand human beings and their interactions (Hogan, 1973).

The child is father of the man.

In most societies, rules for moral behavior exist for the following: the need for safety, physical health of the society, respect for property, control of aggression, control of sex, contribution to group support, keeping promises, and respect for authority. Rules for moral behavior are accepted by members of a society because the rules are felt to be "right" and "proper" in and of themselves, and because by following known rules, a member of society can win the valued respect of others (Maccoby, 1980).

In our society, most people apparently do not view the moral norms as external or coercively imposed. In any society, when the norms are first learned, they are often in conflict with personal desires; eventually the norms become built into the individual's own scheme of the way things should be, and moral behavior persists even when external authority is absent (Hoffman, 1979). In this section we will consider, from the points of view of the three theoretical approaches outlined earlier in the chapter, how such a development takes place.

Freud's Theory of Morality

According to Freudian theory, moral behavior is the responsibility of the superego. The superego is in effect the conscience, and it serves to censor the more primitive urges of the id and to help the person behave as the kind of person he or she would ideally like to be. The superego is the ideal; the ego, however, puts the ideal into practice. The result is of necessity not quite so perfect as the superego would have it, because reality can only approach, but never really attain, an ideal.

The superego develops under the influence of parents, teachers, siblings, peers, and others who dictate prohibitions that are necessary restraints on the child. According to Freud, children are essentially amoral, and follow moral prohibitions because of parental power. At around age 6, however, when the process of identification with the parents occurs, the child internalizes parental standards. In this way the superego develops so that children will then produce moral behavior on their own.

Freud thought that most of the organization of the personality—and especially those aspects that affect moral development—occurred in early childhood. Some subsequent psychoanalytic theorists such as Erik Erikson disagree, arguing that development takes place throughout the life span of the individual.

Cognitive Developmental Theories

The cognitive-developmental approach, as expounded by both Piaget and Kohlberg, views moral behavior as developing hand-in-hand with the ability to think. This approach attempts to describe the specifics of the process, rather than taking refuge in the more vivid but less precise images of psychoanalysis.

Jean Piaget According to Piaget, the evolution of moral judgment in children occurs in two basic stages. In the first stage, which takes place between the ages of 4 and 7, moral rules are objective, concrete, and stem from higher authority, such as the child's parents or God. In this stage children exhibit what Piaget terms "heteronomous morality" (meaning that the rules come from others—"hetero") or the "morality of constraint." Children at this age lack the ability to empathize with others, which means that morality must be externally imposed.

The second stage begins at about age 7, when children shift to "autonomous morality" or the "morality of cooperation." Children free themselves from adult supervision and interact as equals with their peers. At this age children understand that acts have a purpose, and they see rules as relative. They can empathize with others, putting themselves in another's place to judge intentions and feelings. They begin to comprehend that rules represent accepted social agreements that form a basis for cooperative action (Maccoby, 1980).

Piaget bases his theory on his experiences in telling children pairs of stories that involve damage done by children. To help illustrate his two-stage theory, here is one story pair (Piaget, 1932, p. 118):

> A: A little boy who is called John is in his room. He is called to dinner. He goes into the dining room. But behind the door there was a chair, and on the chair there was a tray with 15 cups on it. John couldn't have known that there was all this behind the door. He goes in, the door knocks against the tray, bang go the 15 cups and they all get broken!

> B: Once there was a little boy whose name was Henry. One day when his mother was out he tried to get some jam out of the cupboard. He climbed up onto a chair and stretched out his arm. But the jam was too high up and he couldn't reach it and have any. But while he was trying to get down he knocked over a cup. The cup fell down and broke.

After hearing the two stories, children were asked if the boy was naughtier in story A or in story B. Younger children—in Piaget's first stage—thought John (of story A) was naughtier, because he broke more cups, 15 instead of 1. The fact that John was not to blame for breaking anything, since he was merely opening a door, did not figure into the younger children's reasoning. Instead, their focus was on the quantity of damage done. Older children, however, considered the motive accompanying the deed. John was judged innocent because his intentions were blameless; it was another matter with Henry, who tried to reach jam presumably placed intentionally out of his reach. This made Henry the naughty party. Although he did not actually intend to break a cup, he did intend to do something he shouldn't.

Research has shown, however, that in at least some instances younger children understand intention and *can* take it into account (Constanzo et al., 1973; Schultz et al., 1980). These studies and the experiences of many parents and teachers, would call into question the distinction made between Piaget's two stages.

Lawrence Kohlberg   Accepting most of Piaget's findings on cognitive development, but extending Piaget's scheme of moral development, Lawrence Kohlberg believes that moral reasoning occurs at three different levels. Within each level, moral development is further subdivided into stages (see Figure 3–2):

1. Level 1, *Preconventional Morality.* Behavior is governed by individual punishments and rewards.
   a. In the *punishment stage*, children defer to power in order to avoid punishment. They do not yet understand that there is a basic need for rules

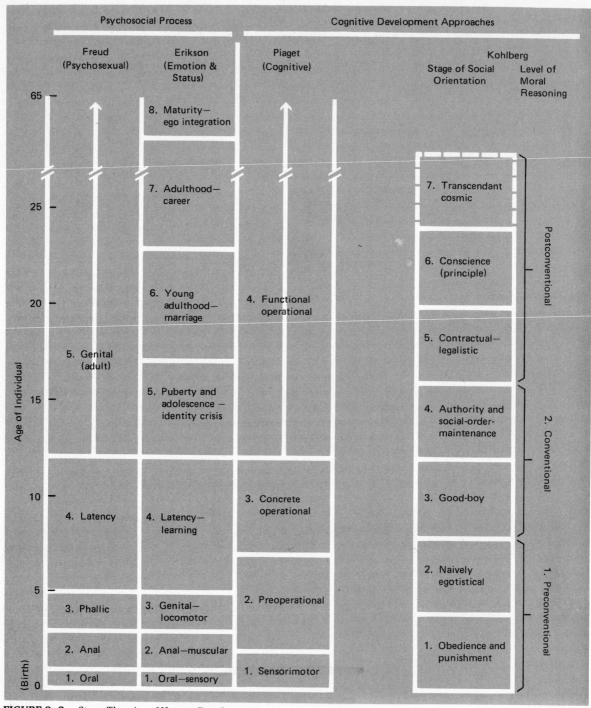

FIGURE 3–2.   Stage Theories of Human Development

in a social system; they obey rules simply because they are weak and must obey the strong. [Stage 1]

    b. In the *satisfaction stage*, children do what they are told in order to get what they want. For example, a child might deliberately behave well during a shopping trip to a supermarket, because she knows this will increase the odds of having some treat bought for her at the checkout line. There is still no sense that society has a need for rules. [Stage 2]

2.   Level 2, *Conventional Morality*. Behavior is based on the observance of rules.

    c. In the *interpersonal agreement stage*, children try to win the approval of others by acting like a "good girl" or "good boy." The intention of actions is important. A "nice person" tries to do the right thing. [Stage 3]

    d. When and if children reach the *law and order stage*, they become keenly aware of society's needs for rules and regulations in order to function smoothly. Rules are obeyed for their own sake, because they represent the wisdom of established authority. [Stage 4]

3.   Level 3, *Postconventional Morality*. Behavior is based on universal ethical principles that can take precedence over explicit laws.

    e. Adolescents who reach the *social contract stage* recognize that rules and laws represent correct actions according to society, but believe that such rules and laws are relative, and are therefore subject to change. A stage-5 person obeys laws but, encountering a bad one, works through established societal mechanisms to change it. [Stage 5]

    f. Those persons, fairly few in number, who attain the *conscience stage* have developed self-chosen ethical principles. These aim at comprehensiveness and are applied equally to the actions of everyone. Martin Luther King operated at this level, not hesitating to disobey laws that came into conflict with his higher ethical principles. [Stage 6]

    g. The *transcendence stage* was only recently added by Kohlberg (1981) to the previous 6-stage model. This stage is characterized by a "cosmic" perspective, seldom attained, in which even the ethical principles of stage 6 are seen as part of a larger totality. A stage-7 person views moral issues in religious or metaphysical terms, seeing all human actions, ethics, and rules as a part of the all-encompassing cosmos. [Stage 7]

Kohlberg's theory is a stage theory, in that one stage must be reached and mastered before a person can pass on to the next. However, people can apply reasoning from several stages simultaneously, according to the situation. Most never reach the higher stages, and the average person operates at stage 4 most of the time. Indeed, Kohlberg has observed that only 15 percent of Americans function at stage 5, and only 6 percent at stage 6 (1975).

Like Piaget, Kohlberg bases his theory primarily on responses given to questions about a story that poses a moral dilemma (Kohlberg, 1963). Criticism of Kohlberg's theory has centered around the subjective nature of the "moral dilemma" stories and of the methods of scoring data so obtained. In scoring, much discretion is left to the persons conducting the research. This subjective element does raise questions about the reliability of Kohlberg's findings (Froming, 1978;

Haan et al., 1968; Kurtines & Greif, 1974). Simpson (1974) has also pointed out that Kohlberg's model should not be considered universally applicable. Because of the content of the stories and the types of subjects tested, these stages are ethnocentric and the scoring is culturally biased.

Bandura's Theory of Morality

Where Freud, Piaget, and Kohlberg look at the development of moral *thinking* in the growing person, Albert Bandura's approach examines moral *behavior* as well. Social learning theorists are concerned with how the understanding of moral rules translates into moral action. Early studies conducted by social learning theorists concentrated on the influence of behavior models, the external shapers or reinforcers of behavior (Bandura & McDonald, 1963; Berger, 1971; Rosenkoetter, 1973). Other researchers looked at how punishment affects the individual's ability to resist temptation (Cheyne & Walters, 1970). Aronfreed (1968) found that children who were given an explanation for the punishment they received were more resistant to later temptation than those who were not given explanations. These studies stressed the importance of cognitive processes in moral behavior. Identification with the behavior model was also shown to be important. For example, children were found to donate more to charity when they identified with the model (Yinon & Kipper, 1978).

Also, in contrast to the other approaches, social learning theorists do not argue that moral reasoning and moral behavior are unified concepts. Instead, it is recognized that people are responding to complex situational forces, integrating the information from those sources, evaluating previous experiences with the same or similar situations, reaching a moral decision, and, finally, acting on it. Certain aspects of the situation will naturally receive more weight than others. For example, it has been shown that what a model practices is more influential than what a model preaches (Bryan & Walbek, 1970a; Bryan & Walbek, 1970b). Bandura (1977) suggests that children are capable of *abstract modeling*; they are able to formulate or abstract rules from the observation of others' behavior.

At first, social learning theory assumed that children would copy exactly the behaviors of a model. In Bandura's later writings, however, he asserts that after people observe a fixed number of situations involving moral behavior, they derive moral guidelines from them that fit a wider range of situations (1977). This extension of social learning theory not only emphasizes the role of the external environment—the behavior models, reinforcements, and even the nature of the act itself—but takes into account human capabilities for reasoned thought and self-regulation.

Social Influences on the Self

Now that we have examined and compared the major theories of social development, let us turn to the empirical side of the coin. What do we know about social development in areas other than moral behavior? What is the role of the family in socialization? What happens when children begin to spend a great deal of time with their peers when they start attending school?

Socialization refers to the total upbringing that prepares the child for full adult participation in society. Parents and family are the most important socializers of the child, but they are not the only ones. Peers, schools, teachers, and the media are among the other significant socializing influences during these years.

We begin this section by emphasizing the importance of early social influences to development, and thus to later life. We will then consider social development research in two important areas—sex differences and sex role socialization.

Think back, if you can, to your early childhood. Can you recall any events that seem to have helped to make you what you are today? Were there any people besides your parents whose influence was crucial to your development?

Birth Order and Family Size

Do you recall if your siblings were an important influence on you? If you had any, they probably were. Studies have shown that the number of children there are in a family, and the order in which they were born, can affect achievement in later life. The older children in a family have been shown to perform best, with the intellectual performance of each subsequent child declining relative to its predecessor (Belmont & Marolla, 1973; Zajonc & Markus, 1975). Children from smaller families also outperform those with more siblings (see Figure 3–3). The difference is presumably due to the greater amount of attention parents are able to devote to their first-born child or to fewer children. It may also be due to the amount of interaction younger children have with their older siblings.

These findings, however, have been disputed by other researchers. Olneck and Bills found that birth order effects were insignificant, but that family size was the most important factor in intelligence and achievement (1979). Interestingly, the family's socioeconomic status does not seem to affect achievement beyond the fact that families of higher socioeconomic position generally have fewer children (Belmont & Marolla, 1973; Olneck & Bills, 1979; Zajonc & Markus, 1975).

Interactions between Parents and Children

We will now look at the general interactions between parents and children that occur during socialization. We will first examine aspects of parent–child interactions and consider what may happen if children are not able to become attached to a parent. Then we will discuss two topics that are currently the subjects of research attention as well as public concern: interactions between children and their fathers, and the effects of day-care on children's adjustment.

A child tells in the street what its mother and father say in the home.
The Talmud

The Interaction System Interaction between parent and child is a two-way system. Hartup and Lempers (1973) point to a number of parent–child interactions—gazing, touching, game-playing, and imitation—that involve reciprocal behaviors. Child and parent are stimuli for one another, and each responds to the other's responses. The result is an extended chain of coordinated interactions in

FIGURE 3–3. Effects of Birth Order and Family Size on Intellectual Development

Findings by Belmont and Marolla (1973). For this analysis, the scores of the actual test administered to the subjects have been adapted so that the average score of the only child equals 100. Numbers within graph represent total number of children per family.

Source: *Adapted from "Birth Order and Intellectual Development" by R. B. Zajonc and G. B. Markus,* Psychological Review, *1975, 82, 75.*

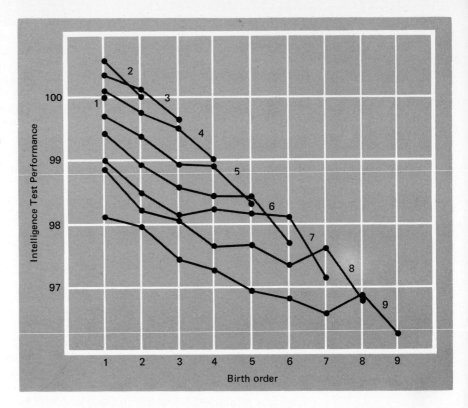

which it is sometimes difficult to determine if the parent or the child has initiated a given act, or who is responding (Beckwith, 1972). Mother and child exhibit a "dialogue of exquisite precision in its patterning" (Schaffer, 1977; see also Stern, 1974).

Parents can also affect children's social behavior by rewarding and punishing different behaviors. For instance, Baumrind (1967) found that parents of children she described as "energetic–friendly" were more nurturing, used positive reinforcement rather than punishment, and offered their children ample support and attention. These parents did not yield when children cried or nagged to get their way, but encouraged their children to base demands on logical arguments. Baumrind called these parents of children with the most social competence "authoritative," because they allowed their children to express themselves while remaining firm, instead of being "authoritarian" or rigidly overbearing.

Attachment and the Influence of Deprivation   Attachment is the effort made by an infant to maintain physical closeness with a parent. Dependency is the reliance of an infant on a parent for satisfaction of its needs. Both psychoanalytic theory and social learning theory hold that attachment results from the prolonged physical dependency of the human child. Research on attachment is particularly difficult because attachment must be inferred from the infant's behavior, as the infant cannot yet speak.

John Bowlby (1969) has described three distinct phases in the development of attachment:

1. From about 8 to 12 weeks of age, the infant shows an indiscriminate responsiveness to all individuals. Infants follow nearby figures with their eyes; they smile, vocalize, and grasp at all people.
2. From about 3 to 6 months of age, infants show a preference for the mother while remaining responsive to others.
3. From about 6 months to 2½ years, infants show an active attachment to the mother, and to a few subsidiary figures, along with a wariness toward others.

It has been found that mothers who have more contact with their newborn infants than modern hospitals generally allow develop a stronger attachment to their babies. They pick up their babies more often when they cry, and spend more time at home with them (Kennell et al., 1974). At the other extreme, if early handling by the mother is prevented—as, for example, when a premature baby must be kept in an incubator—attachment-formation seems to be inhibited. Parke and Collmer (1975) found that premature infants were more likely to be abused than normal full-term babies. Another study found that mothers of premature babies smiled less often at them, and were less likely to hold them in a position permitting eye contact than mothers of full-term infants (Leifer et al., 1972).

Many researchers believe that human beings, as well as other primates, are "programmed" for the formation of attachments: that is, the tendency to form attachments is inherited and has survival value for the species. Apparently, though, infants must have a minimum amount of social contact before they can form attachments (Pawlby, 1981). By studying primates as well as actual instances of human children separated from their parents early in life, we can see what happens when these social experiences are lacking.

In one study of social deprivation, Harlow (1958) gave baby monkeys a soft cloth "dummy mother" to which they seemed to become attached. When they were placed with monkeys raised by real mothers, they became aggressive or withdrawn. Later they had difficulty mating and raising their own infants. They would sit on them, hold them upside down, and even attack them. However, these deficient mothers showed much more competence with a second infant.

Studies such as Harlow's support the contention that mothers and infants, human as well as other primates, are equipped with instinctive abilities and patterns of reactions that support the formation of attachment. Clearly infants benefit from the formation of attachment, and may suffer in their later years if they lack it. This does not mean, however, that they will suffer permanently if they do not remain with their first attachment figure throughout childhood. Primates are socially resilient creatures: Monkeys reared with surrogate mothers and in isolation from other monkeys for only 3 months, and then placed together with normally parented age-mates, recouped their losses in social abilities in about 1 month (Harlow & Harlow, 1970; Suomi & Harlow, 1972). Research has shown that human children can recover from separations provided the new situations are socially adequate and offer the possibility of meaningful attachment relationships with the new caregiver(s) (Maccoby, 1980).

In a series of experiments, young monkeys raised with padded dummies instead of real mothers showed a variety of social deficits. This young monkey is clinging to one such surrogate mother.

Photo courtesy of Harry F. Harlow, University of Wisconsin Primate Laboratory

Fathering   In the past, the role of the father in the socialization of children was not emphasized. Developmental research concentrated on early infancy, where the father was traditionally less involved than the mother. When researchers did attempt to study fathers too, they encountered substantial difficulty in both locating them and gaining their cooperation. Indeed, the largest body of research has studied how the *absence* of the father influences personality. Considerable evidence exists about the importance of the relationship with a father upon his son's social and masculine development. Boys from homes where the father was absent have been found to be less well-adjusted and socially more inept than those raised in the presence of a father. They have also been found to be less masculine, or to exhibit exaggerated masculine behavior (Biller, 1970).

Glueck (1950) found that among delinquent boys, 40 percent had absent fathers, as compared to 25 percent for nondelinquent boys. The usual explanation for this is that a boy has difficulty in forming an appropriate same-sex identification, since the male role model is missing. However, this explanation may not be entirely adequate. Rutter (1971) reports that parental conflict, rather than the absence of the father, accounts for findings of antisocial behavior such as those reported by Glueck. Although delinquency is twice as likely for boys from broken homes, there is no difference in the rate of delinquency between boys from homes where the father is present and boys from homes where the father is absent as a result of death (instead of desertion or divorce). It appears then that the presence or absence of the father is only part of the issue; the reasons for the father's absence, and the mother's ability to cope with the situation, may be equally important factors.

It turns out that fathers may be more significant than mothers in fostering achievement motivation in both girls and boys. Many high-achieving women had a close relationship with their fathers, who encouraged them to develop independence and provided motivation toward achievement (Hoffman, 1977). More recent developmental studies have shown that babies turn either to their fathers or to their mothers for comfort when they are upset, depending on which parent usually takes care of them. Also, children whose fathers are especially warm and involved in their care seem to cope more successfully with stressful situations and to adapt more readily to strangers (Kotelchuk, 1976). Fathering style differs from mothering, though; it has been found that fathers engage in more physically active play even with young infants, and smile less at them, than do mothers (Parke, 1981). Lamb and Bronson (1980) emphasize that there is a difference in the father's role as the male parent and his "gender-irrelevant role as one of the child's parents and as a major socializing agent" (p. 339). The research thus far indicates that fathers can parent as well as mothers, but that a parent or suitable surrogate of each sex facilitates sex-role socialization (see below).

The Effects of Day-Care on Attachment   In the early 1980s in the United States, over 40 percent of the mothers of preschoolers were employed outside the home (Hoffman, 1979). While their parents work, it has become increasingly common for infants to be placed in group-care situations.

Day-care centers vary significantly in the quality of attention they give to children. Given the frequently documented negative effects of institutionalization upon early childhood development—as in orphanages and hospitals—many people have expressed concern for the future mental health of children of working mothers. Recommendations that mothers should not work, however, fail to take an important fact into consideration: Children of mothers who work are not treated like children raised in institutions. Although separation does occur each morning when the children are left at the day-care center, most centers provide substantial adult contact and attention (as well as peer interaction). In addition, children of working parents do have daily extended contact with their parents during their nonworking hours. The types of social deprivation previously described are distinctly different from the experiences of children in day-care centers. (See Figure 3–4 on the next page.)

What effects does day-care have on attachment and emotional stability? Despite extensive day-care experience, the attachment bond to the mother seems to remain intact and primary (Farran & Ramey, 1977). In fact, even at the age when the vital attachment to the major caretaker is being formed—from 6 to 10 months—and when we would expect separation to have the worst consequences, the actual consequences were shown to be minimal (McCutcheon & Calhoun, 1976).

Some researchers also report that day-care can have beneficial side effects. For example, Ramey and Smith (1976) found better performance on IQ tests for day-care raised infants than for those raised at home. The results were particularly striking for infants from lower socioeconomic backgrounds.

FIGURE 3-4. Distress Shown by Day-Care and Home-Care Children in Response to Separation

Source: *Kagan, J. Emergent themes in human development.* American Scientist, 1976, *64,* 186-196.

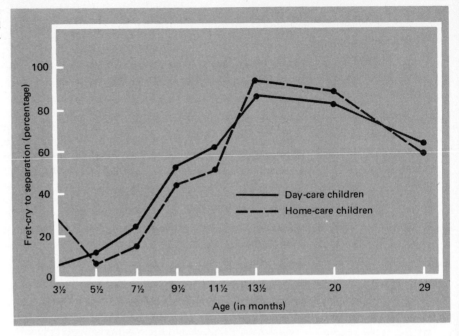

Other Social Influences on the Self

So far in our study of social influences on the self we have discussed primary caregivers in general, mothers and fathers in particular, and substitute caregivers. Strong socializing influences outside this immediate realm include those of peer groups, schools, and the media, which all become more influential as children mature and have experiences outside the home (Devereaux, 1970). (We will discuss media influences in greater detail in chapters 7 and 10.)

The Peer Group Behavior is a result of both parental and peer influence. Siman (1977) suggests that parental influence is filtered through peer influence. Those parental norms that successfully pass through the peer group become even more meaningful to the individual. Peers may introduce new attitudes and values, or they may reinforce those that a person already has. For example, Youniss (1980) found that peers with the same moral standards act to bolster an individual's own moral attitudes.

At every age, peers are also an important source of beliefs about the self. Most people form their self-concepts—at least in part—by internalizing the way other people behave toward them (Mannheim, 1966; Reeder, 1960). This was shown in a study of the self-concepts of the members of two college fraternities and two sororities. Each member rated himself or herself for intelligence, self-confidence, physical attractiveness, and likeability. Each member also rated every other member of the sorority or fraternity for these same attributes. In addition, each person predicted how every other person would rate him or her, and also how *most* people would. Results showed that the self-ratings corresponded very closely to those of peers, suggesting that self-concept does seem to stem from an interactional process (Miyamoto & Dornbusch, 1956). (In the next chapter we discuss the development of the self-concept in greater detail.)

The School Environment   Most people regard schools and teachers as important socializing agents with respect to achievement and occupational aspirations. Teachers have traditionally served as role models, especially for children of working-class backgrounds who were inspired by a teacher's example to achieve higher academic levels. Solid evidence exists that teachers' expectations can substantially alter the performance of students. A teacher who believes that a particular student is bright or dull will, somehow, not only communicate that opinion but also influence the child's performance to conform to it.

To study this "self-fulfilling prophecy" effect, Robert Rosenthal visited an elementary school that had three classrooms for each grade level, divided into below-average, average, and above-average ability. After administering an IQ test to all the children, Rosenthal randomly selected 20 percent of those at each level. He labeled all of them "intellectual bloomers" and gave their teachers their names, along with the hint that they could be expected to show marked progress in the course of the school year. Shortly before the end of the school year he retested the children. Those who had been arbitrarily designated as "intellectual bloomers" did in fact bloom, gaining an average of 4 points in total IQ points and achieving a reasoning IQ score an average 7 points higher than that of the other children. This was true regardless if the children were in the low-ability or high-ability classrooms. The probable explanation is that teachers taught better to those they expected to learn best (Rosenthal, 1973).

Sex-Role Socialization

When it comes to the development of the sexual self, it is not always possible to distinguish socializing influences from physiologically based differences. That boys and girls are distinctively different at very early ages, though, has been demonstrated many times. Jacklin and Maccoby (1978) studied the play behaviors of children only 33 months old. Two by two,

> previously unacquainted children were brought into a laboratory playroom—some were same-sex pairs, others were mixed-sex pairs. . . . An observer dictated a running account of the children's actions, and this record was used to determine frequency of solitary play versus socially directed play. . . . Both boys and girls directed more social behavior toward partners of their own sex. . . . Boy–boy pairs were more likely to engage in a tug-of-war over a toy than girl–girl or boy–girl pairs. While both boys and girls were somewhat more likely to cry or retreat toward their mothers (who were quietly seated in the room) when playing with a boy partner, girls were particularly affected by a male partner and tended to retreat or stand quietly watching the boy play with the toys. Girls with female partners rarely exhibited such behavior. (See Figure 3–5.) (Maccoby, 1980, pp. 214–215)

FIGURE 3–5. Sex Preferences of Toddlers' Playmates

At 33 months of age, both boys and girls direct more social behavior toward playmates of the same sex.

Source: *From* Social Development: Psychological Growth and the Parent-Child Relationship *by E. E. Maccoby, New York: Harcourt, Brace, Jovanovich, Inc., 1980.* © The Society for Research in Child Development, Inc. Reprinted by permission.

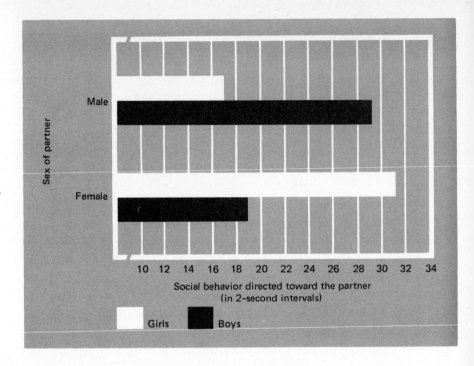

Differences in Male and Female Behavior

If human awareness of sex-based differences begins at such an early age, by adulthood these differences overwhelmingly influence our consciousness and our behavior. Are these differences in men's and women's behavior only due to physiological differences? What behaviors, if any, are conditioned by society? And what exactly are the differences between male and female behavior in our society? As we examine these issues, we will look first at some problems with research in this area, examine sex differences in cognition, and then discuss the behaviors of males and females.

Research Bias The investigation of sex differences can easily lead to biased research results. Studies of behavior that rely on subjective *ratings* (for example, rating how "dependent" someone is) "find" larger sex differences than studies that use more objective procedures (such as counting behaviors). The problems of subjective ratings are illustrated by an experiment in which college students watched a videotape of a 9-month-old infant and rated the infant's behavior in terms of pleasure, anger, and fear. Before watching the tape, some students were told that the infant was a boy, while others were told that it was a girl. The tape showed the baby playing with a teddy bear, a jack-in-the-box, a buzzer, and a doll. The students who thought the infant was a boy rated it as showing more anger, more pleasure, and less fear than students who thought the infant was a girl. The bias arose from "knowing" the sex of the child. There were no actual behavior differences—it was always the same tape showing the same child—but the students perceived behavior differences (Condry & Condry, 1976).

Another bias in measuring sex differences is due to the techniques used to assess those differences, as well as to the prevalent stereotypes about what "should be" obtained. Rating scales (even self-ratings) are not to be completely trusted, since the subjective perceptions and possible bias of the person doing the rating intrudes (Frieze et al., 1978). In chapter 2 we touched on some of the problems with rating scales, and saw that one problem with self-rating is that people often do not want to present themselves as too extreme. The problem is compounded when it comes to self-ratings in the area of sex differences. For example, few men are comfortable rating themselves as "never aggressive," even if they know this to be objectively true.

Even when statistically reliable sex differences are obtained in a study, this does not mean that males and females differ radically. Consider, for instance, Figure 3–6, which shows how the scores on a test of spatial skills are distributed. Boys as a group and girls as a group received different scores. But the overwhelming majority of both boys and girls earned scores in the same range (Frieze et al., 1978). In other words, if the difficulties in conducting unbiased research are surmounted, the striking feature of the research is not the differences between the sexes, but the similarities. (See Table 3–2 on the next page.)

Cognitive Differences   Research to date indicates that there are no overall differences between males and females in intellectual ability, whether measured by IQ tests or tests of aptitude, creativity, or general problem-solving ability. However, there are some differences for specific abilities.

In the areas of quantitative and spatial skills, for example, males generally have a slight edge over females, an advantage that begins at puberty. This sex difference may be due to cultural and environmental influences, as parents and

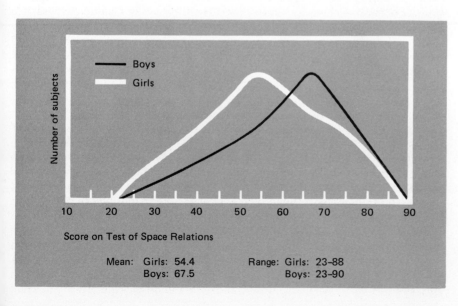

FIGURE 3–6. Score Distribution by Sex for Spatial Skills*

* The means and ranges are taken from Sherman's study, and the distribution curves are assumed.

Source: *Sherman (1974) as cited in* Women and Sex Roles: A Social-Psychological Perspective *by I. Frieze, J. Parsons, P. Johnson, D. Ruble, and G. Zellman, New York: W. W. Norton, 1978.*

TABLE 3–2.

Comparison of Sex Stereotypes with Actual Findings

	Stereotype*	Strength of Finding
Aggression	Males aggressive; females not at all aggressive.	1. Strong consistent differences in physical aggression. 2. Inconsistent findings with indirect aggression.
Dependency	Females submissive and dependent; males dominant and not at all dependent.	Weak differences, which are more consistent for adults than for children.
Nurturance	Females tactful, gentle, and aware of feelings of others; males blunt, rough, and not at all aware of feelings of others.	Moderate differences on some measures. Overall, findings are inconclusive.
Emotionality	Females emotional and very excitable in a minor crisis; males not at all emotional nor excitable in a minor crisis.	Moderate differences on paper-and-pencil measures. Overall, findings are inconclusive.
Verbal skills	Females very talkative; males not at all talkative.	Moderate differences on some measures, especially for young children.
Math skills	Males like math and science very much; females dislike math and science very much.	Moderate differences on problem-solving tests, especially after adolescence.

* Note: Source for stereotypes: Broverman, et al., 1972.

Source: Adapted from *Women and Sex Roles: A Social-Psychological Perspective* by I. Frieze, J. Parsons, P. Johnson, D. Ruble, & G. Zellman, New York: W. W. Norton, 1978.

teachers covertly, as well as overtly, steer girls away from mathematic and science activities. Females have been shown to have superior verbal skills, a linguistic advantage that appears as early as 17 months and persists at least through adolescence. This too may be a product of social experience. A study by Cherry and Lewis (1976) reached this conclusion, finding that mothers talked more to their 2-year-old daughters than to their 2-year-old sons, used longer sentences with their daughters, and asked more questions. Cross-cultural evidence similarly underscores the importance of socialization. Female superiority in reading skill, the predominant pattern in the United States, is reversed in England and Germany, where males excel in reading achievement. And in the Eskimo culture, women are more adept than men at spatial tasks (Nash, 1979).

Waber (1977), pointing out that girls mature earlier than boys, has suggested a possible biological explanation for differences in quantitative, spatial, and verbal abilities. Early maturation appears to strengthen the dominance of the left hemisphere of the brain, where language abilities are centered. If the left hemisphere is dominant, the right hemisphere, which controls quantitative and spatial abilities, will be less influential. Waber theorizes that early maturers of either sex will perform verbal tasks better than spatial tasks, while the reverse will be true for late maturers. Research has begun to bear this out (Buffery & Gray, 1979; Waber, 1979).

The fact that cognitive gender differences have been "well established" in the three areas mentioned—verbal ability, quantitative ability, and spatial skills—is often taken to mean that the differences are extreme. For example, in vocational counseling the temptation may exist to advise men not to choose occupations that require language ability, or to advise women to steer clear of professions that require quantitative and spatial skills, such as engineering. But this reasoning misses the point altogether. These well established differences are nothing more than statistical differences (Hyde, 1981).

Differences in Social Behavior

Pause for a moment. We have just concluded that there are some cognitive differences between males and females (although both are clearly more alike than they are different). But what about social *behavior*? What differences between males and females do you see and experience? Are these differences major or minor? Are they obvious or subtle? How different are *you* from an average member of the opposite sex? Assuming the differences you detect are real, where might they have come from?

Now we will examine comparisons between male and female social behavior. We will consider aggressiveness, conformity, dependency, social orientation, and achievement.

From father to son, so it goes on.
Ashanti proverb

Aggressiveness   One of the most firmly established distinctions in behavior is that men are more aggressive than women. Frieze et al. (1978) reviewed 48 studies and found them in agreement on this point. In almost all of the world's cultures, men appear to be—in fact, are *expected* to be—aggressive (Whiting & Edwards, 1973). Generally, women are both physically and verbally less aggressive. In our own society, though, while men are generally more aggressive, this is not true in all situations, nor are all men equally aggressive (Maccoby, 1980). While women are more likely than men to emphathize with the victims of aggression, it is unclear if the ability to empathize with victims acts as a strong deterrent to aggression (Frodi et al., 1977).

The basis for this difference in aggressiveness is to some extent biological. Other primates exhibit the same sex-based characteristic, and these differences have been ascribed to the effects of hormones (Maccoby & Jacklin, 1974; Phoenix, 1974).

But human females are not always less aggressive than males. Culture has a distinct influence on the extent of aggressiveness displayed by both sexes, and the situations in which it is appropriate. In our society, when situations arise where aggression is perceived as the right and positive response, women can be just as aggressive as men (as their increased presence in the military and in local police forces is proving). The lack of aggressiveness displayed by women as compared to men in most instances may be due to the fact that in our society women consider aggression inappropriate in the situations in which men consider it appropriate (Frodi et al., 1977). Among the Pueblo Indians in the southwestern United States, however, aggressiveness is not considered desirable for either men or women, and the situations in which it is acceptable are very few.

Aggression is a virtually universal male behavior. In most of the world's societies, men are expected to defend the community and hunt for animal sources of food. This traditional male role is exemplified by the Arunta tribesman of Australia shown here, boomerang in hand, preparing to hurl a throwing spear.

Courtesy of the American Museum of Natural History

Like mother, like daughter.

Conformity The thesis that women are more easily influenced than men—more conforming—is often stated in social psychology textbooks and studies. Alice Eagly (1978) conducted an extensive review of the research literature on conformity and largely rejected this hypothesis. She found that differences in apparent conformity disappear when the tasks given to males and females are equal in terms of their familiarity to the two sexes. Research that found otherwise has often involved mathematical or perceptual tasks in which, as we discussed under "Cognitive Differences," males sometimes have an advantage. Eagly also found that the spirit of the period in which research is conducted makes a difference in the findings: Studies reporting that females are more suggestible were more prevalent before 1970 than after.

Dependency Defined here as wanting to be near one's parents, dependency does not seem to be more common to one sex than to the other. In a number of studies that observed children's behavior, 50 percent found no difference between the sexes, and the remaining 50 percent divided evenly in finding that either sex was more dependent (Maccoby & Jacklin, 1974; Oetzel, 1966). When research is conducted using *ratings* by teachers, parents, and peers, however, girls are judged as more dependent (Frieze et al., 1978). Because of the bias that naturally occurs in ratings (as we saw before), these data should not be given undue weight. No firm evidence exists that either sex is inherently more dependent than the other. Dependency in adulthood, a more complex issue involving relationships with partners, children, and friends as well as parents, is a product of individual life experiences; the differences between male and female dependency in adulthood remain to be studied.

Social Orientation　Social orientation involves being near others, helping others, expressing empathy, and so on. Most studies that address these areas from the point of view of sex differences have been of older children or adults, and studies in the past ranked females as exhibiting a stronger social orientation than males. These studies supported the traditional stereotype of women as being more nurturant than men, needing more affiliation, and showing more interest in others.

Most recent studies have found no differences in social orientation behavior, or have found very specific indicators of social orientation (Frieze et al., 1978). For example, the ability to empathize may be greater in women (Hoffman, 1977). Women *are* better encoders and decoders of nonverbal behavior (Hall, 1980); that is, they tune in to unspoken cues about emotional states more often and more accurately than do men.

Achievement　As a group, women have not been as successful as men in entering high prestige occupations, earning high salaries, or reaching positions of political power (see Tables 3–3 and 3–4). Society's barriers to a high level of achievement by women have often been noted in recent years. Employers' expectations have restricted the positions available to women as well as their promotion opportunities. Women have generally not been expected to perform as successfully on the job as men.

But within women themselves are there internal blocks to high achievement? Atkinson (1957) found that achievement motivation was a function of both desire for success and fear of failure. Horner (1972) found that women did fear the social rejection and loss of traditional feminine attributes if they became too successful. Later studies, however, have found that men too fear success (Condry & Dyer, 1976). Women score higher than men on anxiety scales (great anxiety has a detrimental effect on achievement), and have lower expectations of success and higher expectations of failure. But, as with the other studies of behavioral differences, many findings of women's inadequate preparation for achievement date from a period prior to the mid-1970s and, because they involve ratings, are therefore subject to some bias (Frieze et al., 1978). It is already apparent that

TABLE 3–3.

Distribution of Scientists and Engineers in the U.S. by Sex, 1976 and 1978*

	1976	1978								
	Total	Engineers	Physical Scientists	Mathematical Specialists	Computer Specialists	Environmental Scientists	Life Scientists	Psychologists	Social Scientists	Total
Total.....	2,706,000	1,396,000	255,000	108,000	238,000	81,000	328,000	132,000	205,000	2,741,000
Percent distribution										
Male	90.8	98.4	91.0	81.6	82.0	89.4	78.0	72.7	79.4	90.3
Female	9.2	1.6	9.0	18.4	18.0	10.6	22.0	27.3	20.6	9.7

* Note:　Represents the total science and engineering population in the United States.

Source:　National Science Foundation, *U.S. Scientists and Engineers: 1978* (NSF 80-304), Washington, D.C., 1980.

TABLE 3-4.

Women in Political Life, 1975 and 1979

	State and Local Government						U.S. Congress	
	State Judiciary	State Legislature	County Commission	Mayoralty	Townships and Local Councils	Total	House of Representatives	U.S. Senate
Number of women in 1975	92	610	456	566	5,365	7,089	19	0
Number of women in 1979	177	770	958	998	11,461	14,364	16	1
Percent of all office holders in 1979	3	10	5	10		9	–	–

Source: Center for the American Woman and Politics, The Eagleton Institute of Politics, Rutgers University, New Brunswick, N.J. National Information Bank on Women in Public Office. Adapted from Statistical Abstract, 1980, Table 843, p. 510 (U.S. Congress) and Table 850, p. 515 (State and Local Office).

both men's and women's attitudes toward women's achievement have changed radically in only a few years, and the wave of research now under way will tell us much more.

Sexual Identification

From early childhood children realize that they belong to a particular sex. Girls realize that they are girls, and boys realize that they are boys. At first this is merely a matter of self-labeling. Later children understand that the label designates a group that they belong to, and that they will continue to belong to throughout their lives. This process of labeling, of realizing that a group shares the label, and that the designation is permanent, is sexual identification.

Although the biology of sex and the socialization necessary for sexual identification almost always coincide, sometimes they do not. Interestingly, in these cases biology does not seem to be the overriding factor. Some babies are born with incomplete or ambiguous sexual organs and require surgery for their organs to develop according to one sex or the other. Today it is possible to analyze a child's chromosome composition to determine its genetic sex, and to restructure the organs accordingly. But in the past, parents and/or the doctor often decided arbitrarily what sex the child should be. One investigation of what happened in later life to 100 children whose sex was arbitrarily chosen at birth concluded that the children and the parents most comfortably accepted the assigned sexual identity if it matched the child's genetic sex. Before about 2½ years of age, sexual identity can apparently be changed without causing psychological problems. Parents can rename the child, dress him or her appropriately, and perhaps change the hairstyle. Appropriate reactions from both parents will soon help the chosen sexual identity to become firmly established. Changes in sexual identity at later ages, however, can be damaging (Money et al., 1975).

Thus, the socialization process is very important in establishing sexual identification, and biological makeup is not always the deciding factor. The rare case of transsexuals—people who wish to take on the sexual identification of the opposite sex in contradiction to their own biological sex—lends further weight to the contention that biology is not the key factor in establishing sexual identification (Maccoby, 1980).

Development of Sex Roles

Sex roles are the outgrowth of sexual identification. Sex roles are the appropriate behaviors of a person of a given sex—*which* sex is established during sexual identification. In this section we will discuss the development of sex roles through the socialization process, and the impact of sex-role stereotypes on real life.

Learning Sex Roles   As early as age 5, boys and girls select "sex-typed" toys—trucks for a boy or dolls for a girl—from a collection to play with. Children of this age also identify men's and women's clothing and occupations (Garrett et al., 1977; Masters & Wilkinson, 1976). Sex-role socialization is already well under way.

Earlier in this chapter we looked at three major theoretical approaches to development. Each of these has a different explanation for the acquisition of sex roles in children. According to Freudian theory, innate or biological drives are very important; children are motivated to reduce anxiety by learning sex-appropriate behavior. They learn sex roles primarily from their parents or other caregivers, and sex-role behavior, once learned, cannot be modified or reversed.

Cognitive-developmental theory, less concerned with biological factors, starts from the premise that sexual identification and appropriate sex-role behavior can take place only when the child reaches a critical stage of cognitive development. Parents, the entire social system, and the child's own growing cognitive system are the sources of sex-role socialization. Because children desire to be competent, they are motivated to acquire sex-role behaviors. Once the schema for sex-role behavior is established, it can still be changed to some extent.

Social learning theory ignores biological factors, and assigns the socialization function both to parents and the larger social system. In this view, reinforcement is the motivation for learning sex roles; and role behavior is permanent if it is maintained by reinforcement, but is otherwise subject to modification.

The importance of parents in sex-role acquisition evidently transcends these theoretical viewpoints. In a study by Hetherington and Deur (1972), adolescent boys who lost their fathers before the age of 5 were found to be less masculine in their behavior than those who lost their fathers later in life or those who grew up with fathers present. During the course of adolescence, however, the differences decreased. In another study (Hetherington, 1972), girls who lost their fathers showed no effect until they reached adolescence, at which time they showed apprehension and inadequate social skills around males. Girls seem to acquire the social skills that are necessary to interact with males from their fathers. Siblings also affect sex-role behavior. Sutton-Smith and Rosenberg (1970) found that boys with older sisters showed a weaker preference for traditionally masculine behaviors than boys with older brothers or with no brothers at all.

Sex Role Stereotypes   Stereotyping, as we shall see in chapter 5, can serve to provide us with a useful organizing system. Stereotypes are based on an abstracted or oversimplified version of reality, but they can be fairly accurate. The problem with stereotyping is that it does not take individual differences into account, and that decisions made on the basis of stereotypes may be inaccurate and unfair.

Sex roles differ from *sex role stereotypes*. Sex roles are the actual activities and behaviors of girls and women, boys and men. Sex role stereotypes, on the other hand, reflect people's expectations about the behaviors and traits that males and females possess. Like other stereotypes, these are often inaccurate, but they perpetuate themselves. Stereotyped beliefs about sex roles have, in this way, restricted both men and women to traditional activities, and encouraged discrimination against those who differed. (See box.)

Broverman and her associates had subjects rate the typical male and the typical female on a number of dimensions, such as "very emotional" to "not at all emotional." She also asked them to indicate which end of the dimension was desirable. This yielded a list of stereotyped male and female traits, and indicated which traits were positive and negative. The researchers identified two clusters of traits: a competency cluster that rated "masculine" traits as more desirable, and a warmth-expressiveness cluster that favored "feminine" traits (Broverman et al., 1972). (See Table 3–5.) Some research by Korabik (1972) supports this view. Other research suggests that the desirability of the masculine stereotype results from the stereotype's "active" connotations, whereas the female stereotype is less positively valued because it is "passive" (Best, Williams, & Briggs, 1980).

A study by Helmreich and Stapp (1975) came up with a slightly different set of masculine and feminine traits. They found that desirable attributes for one sex were usually desirable for the other, with some exceptions. For instance, independence and ambition were thought of as typical of men, but desirable for both sexes; gentleness and kindness were thought of as typical of women, but desirable for both sexes. Aggressiveness and dominance were thought of as appropriate primarily for men; being home-oriented and requiring security were thought of as appropriate primarily for women. These stereotypes are obviously not etched in stone. Where do they come from?

Reinforcement of Stereotypes   Sex role stereotypes are learned early through the cumulative effect of statements made by parents and peers or by observations of actual behavior. Two other powerful sources that perpetuate sex role stereotypes are schools and the media. Schools reinforce stereotyping in several ways. First, administrators and teachers have expectations of how boys and girls should behave. These result in self-fulfilling prophesies like those mentioned previously. Secondly, the teaching materials have stereotypic content. For instance, basic readers and textbooks that were widely used from kindergarten to the third grade were found to contain more male than female characters. Boys

TABLE 3–5. Stereotyping Sex-Role Items
(Responses from 74 College Men and 80 College Women)

Competency Cluster: Masculine Pole is More Desirable	
Feminine	**Masculine**
Not at all aggressive	Very aggressive
Not at all independent	Very independent
Very emotional	Not at all emotional
Does not hide emotions at all	Almost always hides emotions
Very subjective	Very objective
Very easily influenced	Not at all easily influenced
Very submissive	Very dominant
Dislikes math and science very much	Likes math and science very much
Very excitable in a minor crisis	Not at all excitable in a minor crisis
Very passive	Very active
Not at all competitive	Very competitive
Very illogical	Very logical
Very home oriented	Very worldly
Not at all skilled in business	Very skilled in business
Very sneaky	Very direct
Does not know the way of the world	Knows the way of the world
Feelings easily hurt	Feelings not easily hurt
Not at all adventurous	Very adventurous
Has difficulty making decisions	Can make decisions easily
Cries very easily	Never cries
Almost never acts as a leader	Almost always acts as a leader
Not at all self-confident	Very self-confident
Very uncomfortable about being aggressive	Not at all uncomfortable about being aggressive
Not at all ambitious	Very ambitious
Unable to separate feelings from ideas	Easily able to separate feelings from ideas
Very dependent	Not at all dependent
Very conceited about appearance	Never conceited about appearance
Thinks women are always superior to men	Thinks men are always superior to women
Does not talk freely about sex with men	Talks freely about sex with men

Warmth-Expressive Cluster: Feminine Pole is More Desirable	
Feminine	**Masculine**
Doesn't use harsh language at all	Uses very harsh language
Very talkative	Not at all talkative
Very tactful	Very blunt
Very gentle	Very rough
Very aware of feelings of others	Not at all aware of feelings of others
Very religious	Not at all religious
Very interested in own appearance	Not at all interested in own appearance
Very neat in habits	Very sloppy in habits
Very quiet	Very loud
Very strong need for security	Very little need for security
Enjoys art and literature	Does not enjoy art and literature at all
Easily expresses tender feelings	Does not express tender feelings at all easily

Source: From "Sex-Role Stereotypes: A Current Appraisal" by I.K. Broverman, S. R. Vogel, D. M. Broverman, F. E. Clarkson, & P. S. Rosenkrantz, *Journal of Social Issues*, 1972, *28*, 63. Used by permission of Plenum Publishing Corporation.

Traditional sex-role stereotyping has not lost its influence on the majority of girls today. A call to audition for the cheering squad seldom goes unanswered in American high schools. These girls are showing off their costumes at a Saint Patrick's Day parade.

Marc Anderson

were generally active in the story situation; they were shown as more outgoing, engaged in physical activity, and more often the problem solvers. Girls were generally portrayed to be in a world of fantasy, doing what other people said, and making statements about themselves (both positive and negative). When good things happened to female characters, it was generally due to chance or to someone else's efforts; when good things happened to male characters, however, it was through their own efforts. Stereotyped sex-role differences were so emphasized, in fact, that a basic truth about human males and females was ignored: They are more alike than different in their behavior (Saario et al., 1973). As a result of this study and others, parents, teachers, and the publishing community have made efforts to correct the imbalance. Unfortunately, cosmetic changes such as increasing the number of female characters have been the easiest to implement. The roles assigned to these characters are still largely expressive, insignificant, and stereotyped (Kolbe & LaVoie, 1980).

Television, too, perpetuates sex-role stereotypes. Sponsors determine what is shown on television, and *their* concern is not to offend viewers, who then might be disinclined to buy the sponsor's product. Hence, it is extremely rare for the characters or situations of television shows to diverge from the realm of stereotypes. (This is as true of ethnic, racial, and socioeconomic stereotyping as it is of sex-role stereotyping.) When a character who does *not* fit the usual stereotype—such as a single father or a woman who has a successful career—does reach the television screen, it is long after the majority of the viewing audience has accepted such a role—and assigned it a new stereotype.

It might be argued that television sponsors and producers, and textbook editors and authors, only mirror reality; it is not their job to provide a false picture of what everyone else knows to be true. Unfortunately, the situation is reversed. The reality of what women do in society has changed, but our stereotypes have not

Application: Sex-Role Stereotyping and Career Choices Today

Both of the following episodes actually happened within the last 10 years.

A teenage boy enjoyed his stenography class so much that he seriously considered attending secretarial school after graduation. When he learned that the most prestigious secretarial school was sending a representative to his high school, he hastened to his guidance counselor to sign up for an interview. "Surely you're kidding," the guidance counselor responded. Hopelessly embarrassed, the young man fled from the room.

Interestingly, the first stenographers and secretaries were men; a century ago, women choosing such a career were given such advice as "be ladylike in your office" and not to "accept gifts or other attentions from your employer unless he has introduced you to the members of his family and you have been received on a basis of social equality by them." Today, 1 percent of American secretaries are male.

Source: From Marjorie P. K. Weiser and Jean S. Arbeiter, *Womanlist.* Copyright © 1980 Marjorie P. K. Weiser and Jean S. Arbeiter (New York: Atheneum, 1980). Reprinted with the permission of Atheneum Publishers.

The woman in the employment office had left her last full-time job 12 years earlier, on the day her first child was born. Since then she had continued her career as a writer and editor on a free-lance basis. Now she was hoping to return to full-time employment. The director of the personnel agency agreed that she was, if anything, over-qualified for the position that had been advertised. "But I can't refer you for that job," she told the applicant, "I have men who are unemployed who need it more." Six months later, the still unemployed job applicant was separated from her husband and responsible for the support of her two school-age children.

Forty-three percent of those women who are living with their husbands and have children under 6 years and 59 percent of those whose children are between 6 and 17 years are employed or looking for work. Of women who are divorced, the corresponding figures are 69 and 83 percent respectively. Overall, nearly 16 million women who work have pre-school or school-age children.

Source: Personal communication; statistics from U.S. Bureau of Labor Statistics, Special Labor Force Report, No. 198, and *Monthly Labor Review,* April 1980.

kept pace. Children with working mothers, or those from a single-parent home, cannot recognize their world in the idealized and unrealistic one shown in many textbooks and television programs.

"It's only a story," people often say. But McArthur and Eisen (1976) found that impressions received through stories readily spill over into behavior. In their study, preschoolers were read a single brief story depicting achievement behavior by a male or by a female. Girls showed considerably more task persistence in their activities following the story in which the female had shown such behavior than when they heard a story about male activity. The direct opposite was true with boys. If one brief story had such an effect, what can we say about all the influences children are exposed to? In the course of growing up, they read hundreds of stories and spend thousands of hours in front of the television set!

Changes in Stereotypes   There are some indications that sex-role stereotypes—or the way people interpret them—may be changing. For example, especially among young adults, there seems to be a trend toward valuing emotional expressiveness in males and competence in females. In a study of college students, although men and women still held traditional stereotypes, women's attitudes had changed. Stereotypically feminine traits that were earlier viewed negatively were now considered positively (Der-Karabetian & Smith, 1977).

Other researchers have observed that a new female stereotype of the independent woman has joined the more traditional ones of housewife and sex object. This stereotype consists of such traits as "active, aggressive, hardworking, alert, confident, ambitious, competitive, persistent, and independent." These adjectives were used by both men and women to describe career women, club women, and women athletes, which seem to be the new categories of the new stereotype (Clifton, McGrath, & Wick, 1976).

Sex Roles in Transition

As we have seen, sex roles are not immutable. They have already changed in significant ways, and their evolution continues. As men's and women's roles in society alter, society must alter its view of what behavior is appropriate for them; thus future generations will be raised under the influence of a new set of sex-role socialization pressures. In this incremental manner, change begets change. Studying recent changes in sex-role attitudes of both men and women, Cherlin and Walters (1981) found that attitudes held in the late 1970s were significantly less traditional than in 1972. Almost all of the change, however, had already occurred by 1975. They also observed that the attitudes of men and women became more similar at the same time, and that the climate favoring sex-role equality did not regress even though the nation as a whole became politically and socially more conservative in the late 1970s. At the same time, the goals of male and female college students appear to be converging. Females in one survey emphasized career goals as much as their male counterparts; males were as interested in the social aspects of their college experience as were females (Goldberg & Shiflett, 1981).

Women's Roles   To what extent are women's views of their own roles in society changing? A recent study of women's attitudes toward sex roles since the early 1960s was concerned with who makes decisions in the home, with women working outside the home, and with sharing housework. Those women who showed the most change toward equality were younger women, women with more education, with better-educated husbands, and those who had been working in the early 1960s. Those who showed the least change in attitude were mothers of large families or fundamentalist Protestants (Thornton & Freedman, 1979).

Komarovsky (1973) has compared women's attitudes toward their own intellectual abilities and found that, where nearly three-fourths of college-age women in a 1950 study were reluctant to show their true intellectual competence, about half of the women in 1970 and 1971 classes were self-confident enough to act as smart as they were. (Full comparison is shown in Table 3–6.)

The proposed Equal Rights Amendment would have made denial of equal

TABLE 3–6.
Readiness of Women to Play Down Intellectual Abilities

	Wallin* 1950 (N = 163)	Sociology Class 1970** (N = 33)	Advanced Sociology Class 1971** (N = 55)
	Percent Responses		
When on dates how often have you pretended to be intellectually inferior to the man?			
Very often, often, or several times	32	21	15
Once or twice	26	36	30
Never	42	43	55
In general, do you have any hesitation about revealing your equality or superiority to men in intellectual competence?			
Have considerable or some hesitation	35	21	13
Very little hesitation	39	33	32
None at all	26	46	55

* Paul Wallin, "Cultural Contradictions and Sex Roles: A Repeat Study," *American Sociological Review, 15* (April, 1950): 288–293.

** Mirra Komarovsky, unpublished study.

Source: From "Cultural Contradictions and Sex Roles: The Masculine Case" by M. Komarovsky, The University of Chicago Press, *American Journal of Sociology*, 1973, *78*, 878.

rights on the basis of sex illegal. Some existing civil rights legislation has been interpreted by the courts as providing such protection, but a constitutional guarantee of equality would have emphatically established its legal basis and changed the ways women deal with discrimination. However, the climate of governmental opinion and the mood of some segments of the country became more conservative after the mid-1970s, when the ERA was passed by Congress and also ratified by most states. The campaigns that resulted in its defeat seem to have slowed the pace of this change toward equality. The women's movement, however, in fighting this social backlash in attitudes, may arrive at a new plateau of influence and power.

Another force pushing for the redefinition of roles results from changes in women's childbearing patterns. Effective contraception techniques are now widely used, giving women far more control over their fertility than in the past. As a result, women are marrying later, postponing childbearing, and having fewer children (Hoffman, 1977). The number of divorces has also skyrocketed, and the number of unmarried couples living together almost tripled from 1970 to 1980 (still constituting, however, only 3 percent of all couples living together). Family size hit a new low of fewer than two children in 1980 (U.S. Bureau of the Census Current Population Reports, 1981).

Economic necessity is another factor that brings about redefinition of sex roles. Many families today cannot possibly pay the bills unless both wife and husband work. With the United States economy in the early 1980s taking its sharpest

Pressure from women has opened up higher-paying, traditionally male occupations to them. Among the traditional argument used to keep women from such jobs was their delicacy and need for protection. This woman needs no bodyguard as she performs her job of collecting money deposited in a pay phone.

A.T.&T. Co. Photo/Graphics Center

downturn since the Great Depression of the 1930s, and with government taxation and spending policies that penalize the lower and middle socioeconomic groups, the necessity for the two-paycheck household has seldom been stronger. In addition, about one-fifth of all children in 1980 were living in a single-parent home, the vast majority with their mothers. There is a strong necessity to work (when circumstances permit leaving the children) for these women.

All of these factors that work toward a change in women's sex roles interact with one another. For instance, marrying later and postponing children allows women the freedom to stay in school longer, or to pursue a career where family responsibilities do not act as a restrictive factor. Attitude changes accepting of women who work outside the home, combined with the economic necessity to do so, remove many women from the traditional role of mother and housewife. It is likely that these pressures will mount as time goes by, and we will probably see even more changes in women's roles and their perceptions of those roles.

Men's Roles   As women's roles have changed, so have those of men. This is in-evitable, since the relationship between the two sexes is complementary.

Komarovsky (1973) investigated the effects of women's changing roles on men. She found that men exhibited inconsistencies in their attitudes toward women's changing roles, and showed some stressful effects. Although most male college seniors did not feel insecure when dating female college students of equal or superior intelligence, nearly a third of them did. Presumably the major-ity of the men no longer considered male intellectual superiority a necessary component of a relationship, nor perceived intelligent women as unfeminine. But a sizable minority had trouble making this role transition, and many who agreed in principle that their wives should work hedged their "pseudo-feminism" with numerous qualifications.

It has been found too that the definition of masculinity has been changing, both in how men regard themselves and in how women regard men. The "macho" traits of physical strength and aggressiveness were not important to subjects in one study (a self-reporting sample of readers of *Psychology Today*, probably better educated and somewhat more progressive than the average person). Instead, qualities desirable in a man included self-confidence, being warm and gentle, sticking up for beliefs, and being able to love (Tavris, 1977).

Another area of changing men's roles concerns raising children. Men today expect to be more involved in childrearing, and they often are. This would seem to result from necessity as well as from newer, more equal attitudes on the part of men. Many more women work than in the past, making new child-care arrangements necessary; and the number of fathers who are single parents is increasing. In 1980, nearly one million children under 18 lived with their fathers in single-parent homes (U.S. Bureau of the Census, 1981).

Androgyny   Traditionally, masculinity and femininity have been regarded as opposite ends of a single scale. In this view a person can be either masculine or feminine, but not both. Such a polar approach has been used in studies of individual traits or personality; on each listed attribute, a person is rated as more masculine or more feminine.

Androgyny means having both traditionally male and female characteristics simultaneously. Two basic models of androgyny exist. The first, a "balance" model originally proposed by Sandra Bem (1974), postulates that androgyny is a state in which a person's "masculine" and "feminine" tendencies are fairly balanced. Using a list of traits (see the Bem Sex-Role Inventory, Table 3–7), Bem found that characteristics of masculinity and femininity were independent of one

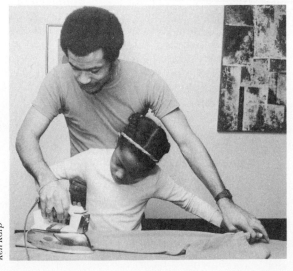

Ken Karp

Male roles are changing today, too. Men are, increasingly, performing tasks formerly done only by women. This father in a single-parent family does the shopping, cooking, and laundry—and teaches his 10-year-old daughter that there is nothing "male" or "female" about household tasks.

TABLE 3–7.

Sample of Selected Items from the Bem Sex-Role Inventory

Items on the Masculinity, Femininity, and Social Desirability Scales of the BSRI		
Masculine Items	**Feminine Items**	**Neutral Items**
49. Acts as a leader	11. Affectionate	51. Adaptable
22. Analytical	50. Childlike	36. Conceited
55. Competitive	32. Compassionate	60. Conventional
34. Self-sufficient	53. Does not use harsh language	45. Friendly

Note: The number preceding each item reflects the position of each adjective as it actually appears on the Inventory. For each item on the list, the respondent completes a 7-point scale ranging from "never or almost never true of me" (1) to "always or almost always true of me" (7).

Source: Reproduced by special permission from the Bem Sex Role Inventory, by Sandra Bem, PhD, copyright 1978, published by Consulting Psychologists Press, Inc.

another. That is, the same individual could display traits that were associated with both sexes. Bem's balance model of androgyny also suggests that androgynous people can learn more readily from interactions with members of the opposite sex, giving them creative and intellectual advantages and greater flexibility in problem-solving (Harrington & Andersen, 1981).

The second model of androgyny is that of Spence, Helmreich, and Stapp (1975). It is an "additive" model that views only those individuals who score fairly high in both masculine and feminine characteristics as androgynous. People who are low in masculinity and femininity are considered undifferentiated or unclassifiable. This model also suggests that creativity benefits from androgyny. Creativity has been linked to such "masculine" characteristics as independence and self-sufficiency, and such "feminine" characteristics as sensitivity and aesthetic interests (Barron & Harrington, 1981). This model also suggests that androgynous people can learn more readily from cross-sex situations (Harrington & Andersen, 1981).

What support is there for these conceptions? LaFrance and Carmen (1980) found that androgynous men and women both showed more flexibility in behavior, probably due to their larger behavioral repertoire. The researchers suggested that androgynous people add opposite-sex traits to their repertoire and omit some traditional same-sex traits. Sex-typed individuals, in contrast, apparently concentrate on traits traditionally associated with their sex and avoid acquisition of cross-sex characteristics. Korabik (1982) finds evidence that androgynous people are less likely to view others in terms of sex-role stereotypes.

Androgynous people also seem to have higher self-esteem (Orlofsky, 1977), are less likely to respond to another person based primarily on physical attractiveness (Andersen & Bem, 1981), and are generally more flexible in dealing with members of the opposite sex (Ickes & Barnes, 1978). One recent study found that androgynous people were better liked and better adjusted; their "masculine" behaviors were seen as highly goal-oriented, and their feminine behaviors as highly expressive (Major et al., 1981).

Androgyny scales have been accused of measuring personality traits that were only slightly related to sex-role behavior (Helmreich et al., 1979; Spence &

Helmreich, 1980). The Bem Inventory in particular has been criticized as measuring sex stereotypes and ignoring the fact that, in the real world, traditional masculine traits are more highly valued than feminine ones (Locksley & Colten, 1979). Thus, society apparently rewards androgyny in women in general (and in the working world in particular), but does not particularly encourage it in men. It appears, however, that androgyny in men may have greater adaptive value today than in the past, as men's social roles change. Possession of androgynous characteristics may help men in the personal arena too, allowing them to relate better to today's women and to assume a more active share of homemaking responsibilities.

Answering Questions about Development of the Self

1. Children who are deprived of contact with adults do not learn the rules and behaviors expected in human society. Their behavior usually seems animallike. They may respond to and learn from their environment, but their mental functioning never develops fully. Attempts to socialize such children have never successfully overcome the effects of their past.

2. Individual differences are due to so complex an interaction of biological and social factors that it is difficult to separate their influence. Deficits in environment and heredity usually occur together. While an enriched social environment can often compensate for a deficient inheritance, debate continues over the role of environment in specific areas such as intelligence test results. Hereditary and environmental factors probably work in tandem: Heredity determines the upper and lower limits of potential development, while social environment shapes the position reached by an individual within those bounds.

3. People can influence your behavior in a variety of ways. They may be able to punish or reward your actions, increasing the likelihood that your behavior will (or will not) be repeated. You can learn new behaviors by observing the behavior of others; whether you use what you have learned is another matter. Finally, the behavior of people toward you can have a reciprocal influence on your behavior toward them: If someone smiles at you, you will respond in kind.

4. A sense of morality develops through contact with others; it is not present at birth. Three models describe this process: The psychoanalytic model emphasizes the internalization of rules as the child identifies with the parent. The social learning model stresses reward, punishment, and imitation, and finds morality specific to a situation. Finally, cognitive–developmental theories stress the importance of cognitive functioning and successive stages in moral thinking. Despite differences, these theories share the assumption that standards of morality evolve in part through the socialization process.

5. Family and schools are potent socializers of young children. They contribute to attitudes and values, self-esteem, the need for achievement, social effec-

tiveness, and various personality factors. As children get older, they depend more on friends to shape the kind of people they will become.

6. Your beliefs about the proper roles of men and women derive largely from what you have been told and what you have actually seen. Sex roles often reflect stereotypes, but changes are taking place in our images of what is appropriate for men and women to do.

Summary

The self develops as a result of the interaction between genetic inheritance and instincts (nature) on the one hand, and factors and experiences in the environment (nurture) on the other. Nurture includes **socialization,** the process by which individuals learn what their community considers socially important and acceptable behavior. The socialization process is fundamental to the survival and well-being of individuals as well as to society itself.

Psychologists address human development from various perspectives. Freud offered a three-part mental model containing the **id, ego,** and **superego.** Human development, according to the founder of psychoanalysis, consists of attaining a successful balance between the inherited, subconscious instincts of the id and the ideals of the superego through the mediation of the ego as the link to the outside world. Erik Erikson extended Freud's developmental model to encompass the entire human life span and to include psychosocial as well as psychosexual events. Another approach is that of Jean Piaget, who stresses interaction with the environment and the development of cognitive (thinking) processes in the growing individual.

Freud, Erikson, and Piaget all offer **stage theories,** which view human development as proceeding in spurts from plateau to plateau in a fixed sequence. The social learning theory of Albert Bandura, on the other hand, is a **continuous process theory.** It views development as determined by the learning process itself independent of any timetable or maturational sequence. Bandura's focus is almost exclusively on the environment and experience as the sources of development.

Moral behavior, which might be dubbed the path of most resistance, is accounted for in different ways by key theorists. Freud considers moral behavior as a function of the successful development and functioning of the superego. Piaget stresses the development of cognitive processes that permit moral judgments to be made. Lawrence Kohlberg offers an elaborate seven-stage theory of moral development grouped into three levels: preconventional, conventional, and postconventional morality. Kohlberg's higher stages are seldom attained. Bandura focuses on moral behavior as a function of the learning process.

Parent–child interactions are a prime social influence on the development of the self. An effective interaction system between infant and parent permits the infant to form an attachment relationship. Placing an infant in day-care does not seem to interfere with this attachment. Other social influences on development of the self include peers, school, and the media.

Sex role stereotypes—the behavior and traits that many people in society think, often incorrectly, are appropriate for one sex or the other—are acquired during socialization. Both the stereotypes and the ways that people interpret them are changing today.

Studies of male and female behavior have found no difference in intellectual ability. Minimal differences have been found in verbal, quantitative, and spatial skills, but even on these points most males and most females share more similarities than differences. Research on sex differences, in addition to being an emotionally charged issue, is subject to unintended bias in construction of research tools and subjective interpretation of behavior. The only difference in social behavior between the sexes that has been consistently shown is aggressiveness, which is almost universally characteristic of males but not females.

Sex-role behavior is the outgrowth of sexual identification, and is acquired during the socialization process that begins in early childhood. Sex roles have considerable impact on career options, with women encountering substantial societal barriers toward equal opportunity. Due to changes in the attitudes of both sexes, the increasing tendency to delay marriage and children, and economic factors, both women's and men's sex roles are currently undergoing fundamental change.

Suggested Additional Reading

Bandura, A. Social learning theory. Englewood Cliffs, N.J.: Prentice-Hall, 1977.

Bowlby, J. Attachment and loss. (Vol. 1). New York: Basic Books, 1969.

Erickson, E. Identity, youth, and crisis. New York: Norton, 1968.

Erickson, E. Childhood and society (2nd ed.). New York: Norton, 1963.

Frieze, I. H., et al. Women and sex roles: A social psychological perspective. New York: W. W. Norton & Company, 1978.

Kohlberg, L. Stage and sequence: The developmental approach to moralization. New York: Holt, 1969.

Maccoby, E. E. & Jacklin, C.N. The psychology of sex differences. Stanford: Stanford University Press, 1974.

Piaget, J. The moral judgment of the child. New York: Free Press, 1965.

Schaffer, R. Mothering. Cambridge, Mass.: Harvard University Press, 1977.

4

SELF-PERCEPTION AND PRESENTATION

Questions about Self-Perception and Presentation

1. Can you describe yourself in 25 words or less? Would others describe you in the same way?
2. The "self" is not a singular, unified being. We possess multiple selves—as many as the different groups of people with which we interact. How many selves do you have?
3. How would you complete the sentence "I am _____"? Think for a minute before you answer. Now think about your answer. Does it reflect something that makes you "stand out" from other people?
4. The last time you went to the supermarket and purchased a quart of milk, you probably picked up the container and put it in your shopping cart. But why did you choose one container instead of another? Indeed, can you explain how you have made any of your decisions in the past month?
5. Sometimes, as when we look into a mirror, we become acutely aware of our own existence. How does this awareness influence the way we think of ourselves?
6. Do you put salt (or pepper) on your food before or after you taste it?
7. You and a friend are betting on the outcome of a coin toss. You toss 5 "heads" in a row, winning your bet each time. Would you say that you were just lucky, or was there some skill involved?

W hen you gaze into the mirror, who looks back? Is the person peering back always the same, or do changes take place in the person you see? Is the individual facing you the same person your friends encounter? Do your parents relate to that "you" or to a different one? How would you describe yourself? Would you describe yourself the same way to a potential employer and to a new friend who is trying to know you better? Why? How do you know who you are? Indeed—who are you?

In chapter 3, we talked about the development of the self. Now we turn to the perception of that self—how we come to understand who we are, how we experience ourselves, how we present ourselves to others, and how we maintain our opinions of ourselves. We usually take for granted the familiar phrases about the "self." Such expressions as, "To thine own self be true," "Just be yourself," are commonplace. Whether literary origin or folk wisdom, they represent a subjective approach. People interested in exploring the matter scientifically, however, have taken a more systematic approach.

Who Am I? Concepts of Self-Identity

William James (1890) distinguished between the *me* (the self as an object of experience) and the *I* (the self as an active agent in the environment). James's concept of the "me" contained three distinct entities: The spiritual self is the inner core of identity, including the person's goals, ambitions, and beliefs; the material self is the person's physical attributes; the social self is the personal identity as it is known by others. According to James, the self extended beyond the physical body and included a person's possessions, reputation, and family and social ties. A change in any of these changes a person's self-perception.

Since James's time, psychologists have tried several ways to find out how we see ourselves. Gordon (1968) presented subjects with the task of answering the question, "Who am I?" 15 times in 6 or 7 minutes. Participants were instructed to write their answers freely, at home, as though talking to themselves, and not to arrange them in any order. One student replied that she was "5 feet 5 inches tall," "a Negro," "not conceited," "Catholic," "sometimes easy to get angry," "now feeling very depressed," "interested in people in general," "honest," and "interested in sports." Answers to the question covered a wide area, but Gordon reported that the first few answers tended to reflect social categories, such as sex and occupation or ethnic group, whereas later responses referred to more personal atributes, such as sensitivity, intelligence, and special interests.

Schemas for the Self

We refer to our view of ourselves as our **self-concept**. It is our understanding of what we are or, in Roger Brown's words (1965), a "theory of one's life." One's life theory is similar to other theories in science: It is based on some data (life experience), contains certain assumptions, and enables us to make predictions about ourselves.

Our life theories are **schemas** for understanding ourselves. (Schemas are also discussed in chapter 5.) A schema is a set of cognitions or information about an object, person, or situation. Schemas create a framework within which we can fit new experiences. They help us to organize incoming information, and to process and react to new information quickly. Schemas help us to make sense of the events that take place in our world, and to anticipate events as well.

Social psychologists believe that we have schemas about ourselves in the same way we have them about other people. Epstein (1973) states that "the self-concept is a self-theory." He holds that it is a theory built unconsciously by the individual as part of the larger life theory people create about important experiences. Epstein believes that self-theories help people derive more pleasure than pain in their lives, maintain their self-esteem, and arrange information about their experiences in a way they can cope with.

Our Multiple Selves

Do I contradict myself?
Very well then I contradict
*   myself,*
(I am large, I contain
*   multitudes.)*
Walt Whitman, Leaves of Grass,
Song of Myself

We probably think of ourselves as single (and singular) entities—individual, uni-fied beings. A bit of reflection will reveal, however, that we all contain a number of "selves." James (1890) wrote, "A man has as many social selves as there are individuals who recognize him and carry an image of him in their mind" (p. 294). There is the self that attends classes, the one that argues politics, the one that goes to a club or disco, the one that communicates with parents, and many more. The self we present to the outside world changes, depending on who inhabits that world.

Goffman (1959) explains that we manage impressions of ourselves at all times, presenting the "self" we think others want to see. For example, you may wear jeans, speak casually, and display the same social behaviors as your fellow students when you are in school. When being interviewed by a corporate re-cruiter, however, you present a different self altogether, dressing more formally and choosing the ideas you express more carefully. In a sense, we are like actors on a stage, playing various roles to different audiences.

Switching the roles we play can create a problem for our self-concept. How is the self-concept affected by our multiple selves? Turner (1968) makes a dis-tinction between self-image and self-concept. The self-image is momentary and

In a series of photos in chapter 1 we examined some of the real-life roles of Jane Fonda—wife, mother, daughter, political activist, entrepreneur, and actress. As an actress, she is professionally trained to handle multiple roles. Here she relaxes in a Las Vegas hotel suite after filming a confrontation scene for the 1979 film *The Electric Horseman.*

may change frequently in a short time; we can also have several self-images at the same time. For example, you know you are being perceived differently by a friend, a competitor, and a stranger as you skillfully and gracefully ski down a steep slope. These different perceptions of ourselves by others create different self-images, which, as we see in this case, all exist simultaneously. But according to Turner, the self-concept is the picture of oneself that is accompanied by the

Research: The Uses of Self-Schemas

Self-schemas are thoughtful generalizations we have formed from watching ourselves in the past. We use these generalizations to help ourselves make sense of what pertains to us in our experiences with other people.

Young women, students in introductory psychology classes, were asked by a questionnaire to rate themselves on several dimensions of personal behavior. Markus (1977) interpreted their responses according to whether they had schemas of themselves as independent or dependent people, or had no schemas of themselves at all. She divided them into 3 groups of 16 students on this basis. Several weeks later, the 48 women performed 3 different tasks designed to measure the impact of self-schemas on self-perceptions. In the first task, the subjects indicated whether descriptive words—related to independence or dependence—applied to them. In the second task, they chose adjectives they felt described themselves and then provided accounts of their behavior that supported their choices. In the last task, the women predicted their likely behavior in various situations.

Markus found that the subjects who had schemas of themselves as independent chose more independent words to describe themselves than those who thought of themselves as dependent. Similarly, those who had schemas of themselves as dependent chose more dependent words. Students who did not have schemas of themselves also chose more dependent descriptive words than independent words. However, they took longer to make decisions about which words described them than either the depen-

dent-schema or independent-schema subjects. In predicting their behavior in the third task, students without schemas chose independent behaviors as often as dependent behaviors. Markus inferred that the aschematic women were just as likely to think of themselves as being independent as dependent. She found that those women who had schemas of themselves could make judgments related to their self-concept more quickly than those who did not have such schemas.

Schemas about the self may help us to organize not only preexisting information but also new data that are relevant to the self-concept. Rogers (1977) conducted experiments dealing with statements reflecting opinions about various matters, such as, "I would like to travel freely from country to country." Subjects (30 undergraduates) read 60 such statements. They were then exposed to 120 statements, in no particular order, some of them new and some they had seen before. They were asked to indicate which statements they had read before and which ones they were seeing for the first time. Later, 18 of the 30 students reported that they had decided they had already seen the items by applying the statements to themselves and deciding whether the statements were personally relevant. In a second experiment, when Rogers's (1977) subjects were told to remember only those test items that described themselves, their responses were signifcantly speedier and more accurate. Reference to a self-schema, then, enabled the subjects to decide quickly which statements applied to them and which did not.

feeling of "the real me," which remains stable. Turner believes that the self-concept and a steady stream of self-images interact with each other. If a self-image threatens the self-concept, the self-image will be changed as necessary to maintain the stability of the self-concept.

In contrast, Kenneth J. Gergen (1968) believes that the self can change according to the situation in which it is operating. According to Gergen, people are often inconsistent, even in such important personal dimensions as self-esteem. Gergen advocates a theory of multiple selves and a process of self-conception rather than the self-concept.

If the self is not a single structure but a process, that process can be understood in terms of the self-schema. We can think of the self-schema as a collection of sub-schemas, each reflecting our beliefs and behaviors with regard to people, situations, and events. Our self-conception dictates our choice of sub-schema in a particular situation. Our self-concept might be, for example, that we are sensitive to role requirements; therefore we choose a sub-schema that has us wear tattered blue jeans when we visit a friend but a tailored suit for a job interview. On a surface level it might seem that the same person could not dress in two different fashions, and yet both are consistent with our self-concept as one who fits easily into a given role. Thus we can consider the self, although divided into sub-schemas, unified as a process.

Taking the Role of the Other: Who Are You?

The idea of the self as a social entity was expressed as early as 1890 by James. In 1922 C. H. Cooley theorized that our self-concept emerges from our interactions with other people. His phrase, "the looking-glass self," expresses the idea that the self-concept is a reflection of how we believe other people perceive us. According to Cooley, there are three main elements of this looking-glass self: how we think we appear to another person; how we think the other person judges that appearance; and how we react—with pleasure or shame, for example—to what we think that judgment is.

Oh wad some power the giftie gie us
To see oursels as others see us!
Robert Burns, To a Louse

G. H. Mead (1934) expressed a similar view. He believed that we develop our own self-concept only when we become aware of being the *object* of other people's perceptions. This awareness emerges as we learn to anticipate how others will react to our actions. In Mead's perspective, an important aspect of self-concept is our ability to take the role of others—to see ourselves as others see us.

McGuire and Padawer-Singer (1976) showed that this awareness develops quite early. They asked sixth graders in a classroom situation to write responses to the statements, "Tell us about yourself" and "Describe what you look like." A more formal questionnaire then asked specific questions about physical appearance, demographic information, and the composition of their families. The responses of the three sections were analyzed together to see if, for example, the children who were tallest among their classmates mentioned their height in their self-descriptions. The researchers found that the children were more aware of those aspects of themselves that made them stand out among their classmates. For example, only 6 percent of the children who had been born in the same area they now lived in mentioned that fact spontaneously; but 22 percent of those who had been born elsewhere mentioned their birthplace as part of "telling about themselves." Among children born in foreign countries, 44 percent wrote down their birthplaces, whereas only 7 percent of the American-born children did so.

The children frequently reported their activities—hobbies, sports, books read—important other people (and pets) in their lives, and their attitudes in response to the question, "Tell us about yourself." Of the spontaneous responses of all the children, self-evaluations comprised only 7 percent of the total. Thus it seemed that the children did perceive themselves in light of what "stood out," or was salient, in their lives. What mattered to them most was how they spent their time, the people they lived with or studied with, how they felt, and what they hoped for. These topics were more important for them than self-evaluations of a moral, physical, intellectual, or emotional nature (see Table 4–1). The researchers concluded that our sense of self consists of the "spontaneous self-concept." By this they mean the self that becomes most salient, most noticeable or distinctive in a given situation.

TABLE 4–1.
Categorizing of Sixth Graders' Responses to "Tell Us About Yourself"

Category	Percent of Children	Category	Percent of Children
Own activities		School (excluding	
Hobbies, amusements	48	teachers	71
Sports	43	Miscellaneous	5
Daily schedule	43	Demographic	
Places lived	5	Age, birthdate	25
Skills	8	Name	19
TV	10	Residence	16
Books	6	Birthplace	11
Jobs	3	Health	11
Miscellaneous		Sex	10
experience	6	Race, ethnic	5
Significant others		Religion	3
Family	38	Self-evaluation	
Friends	43	Moral	20
Pets	22	Physical	15
Teachers	16	Intellectual	10
Public figures	0	Emotional	2
Attitudes		Physical characteristics	
Likes and dislikes	52	Hair color	13
Vocational	18	Weight	11
Hopes and desires	12	Height	10
		Eye color	11

Note: Percentage column indicates percentage of the 252 children who gave at least one response in that category.

Source: Adapted from "Trait Salience in the Spontaneous Self-Concept" by W. J. McGuire and A. Padawer-Singer, *Journal of Personality and Social Psychology,* 1976, *33,* 748.

TABLE 4–2.
Number of Children Spontaneously Mentioning Their Gender As a
Function of Household Sex Composition

Sex	Spontaneous Mention	Females in Majority	Equal Numbers of Each Sex	Males in Majority	Over-all Total
Boys	Mention	13	5	4	22
	No mention	81	81	93	255
Girls	Mention	6	7	18	31
	No mention	85	68	93	246
Total		185	161	208	554

Source: Adapted from "Effects of Household Sex Composition on the Salience of One's Gender in the Spontaneous Self-Concept" by W. J. McGuire, C. V. McGuire, and W. Winton, *Journal of Experimental Social Psychology*, 1979, *15*, 86.

In a similar study, McGuire, McGuire, and Winton (1979) asked first, third, seventh, and eleventh grade children to "Tell us about yourself." The children were much more likely to mention their sex spontaneously when most of the people in their family were of the opposite sex (see Table 4–2).

Thinking about the Self

The children in these studies were making highly selective judgments about themselves, and about how to present themselves to outsiders. Can you remember how your self-concept developed in your early years? What about your self-concept today? In this section we will discuss how we seek knowledge about the self, and what happens as a result or the consequences of finding out about ourselves.

Self-Awareness

Social psychologists often ask people to give their opinions on a particular topic (construction of a nuclear power plant, the definition of sexual responsibility) or to explain why they engage in a particular behavior (smoking marijuana or using a deodorant). Essentially, these questions ask people to report on their internal mental states. The "Who am I" questionnaire mentioned earlier requests just this kind of information. Recently, however, some cognitive psychologists suggested that people really cannot provide accurate answers to such questions. Neisser (1967) theorizes that people do not have direct access to their higher order mental states, and thus cannot give true accounts of the more complex aspects of their thinking.

Reporting on Mental Processes—The Question of Self-Awareness   The issue of our awareness of our own mental processes will also be examined in later chapters. Although the problem is an old one in philosophy, it has recently generated some controversy in social psychology as a result of research by Nisbett and Wilson (1977), Nisbett and Bellows (1977), and Wilson, Hull, and Johnson (1981). These and other researchers argue that people are often unaware of changes in their own cognitive processing. When people do apparently report internal processes correctly, they often resort to cause-and-effect theories such as we all employ to explain behavior. That is, they rely on explanations that are familiar to them, rather than engaging in introspective awareness.

Wilson (1975) demonstrated subjects' low awareness in a two-sided listening experiment. Subjects using earphones heard a human voice through one ear while tone sequences were played on the other channel. Afterward they reported that they had not heard anything on the tone channel. When subjects later listened with both ears to some new tone sequences and some that had been played for them before, they were unable to distinguish the new tone sequences from those they had previously heard. However, a mere exposure effect (Zajonc, 1968) was evident. That is, subjects liked tone sequences they had heard before better than those they were hearing for the first time. Apparently, their attitudes toward the sounds they heard were influenced by having heard some of these sounds before, but the subjects remained unaware of being influenced in that way.

Nisbett and Wilson (1977) report several studies demonstrating that subjects' attitudes and behavior seemed to be influenced by factors of which they (the subjects) were unaware. For example, they asked randomly selected shoppers to evaluate the quality of clothing in a store. Four identical nightgowns were used in one case; four identical pairs of nylon hose in another. Subjects were asked to choose which nightgown (or pair of hose) was of the best quality. After they made their choice, they were asked why they had chosen that particular article. Subjects chose the article on their right-hand side most frequently—even though all were identical. Yet when they were asked why they had chosen that garment, not one mentioned its position as a reason. When they were directly questioned about the possible effect of the garment's position on their choice, they not only denied this as a reason, but showed through a nonverbal gesture that perhaps they had misunderstood the question or that the questioner was a "madman."

Does this mean that we don't know what's going on in our own heads? That clearly overstates the case. In fact, Smith and Miller (1978) suggest other explanations for this seeming lack of cognitive awareness. Subjects may report their thought processes inaccurately, may forget information, or they may distort material. White (1980) and Adair and Spinner (1981) have also criticized Nisbett and Wilson's (1977) work on methodological grounds. One common criticism is that the self-awareness studies fail to examine individual explanations and awareness of individual behavior, but instead look at responses from groups of subjects. The group method of analysis may conceal the fact that many individuals actually are aware of the causes of their behavior. Kraut and Lewis (1982) have also challenged the low self-awareness theory by demonstrating that subjects who rated the intelligence, friendliness, and deceptiveness of people being interviewed were moderately accurate in explaining the bases of their judgments—

although they were also clearly influenced by conventional theories about what factors should influence their judgments.

Also, several of these studies have used such relatively trivial test tasks as remembering tone sequences or choosing nylon hose. As a rule, people pay more attention to information and tasks that are important and interesting. Thus, if we ask people about such important matters as their own self-descriptions, we expect them to pay more attention and to perform that task more accurately (Shiffrin & Schneider, 1977). In fact, probably all of us have had experiences in which we have been acutely aware of ourselves.

Objective Self-Awareness   It is the first day of the semester. Your social psychology instructor has asked the students to announce their names and to explain briefly why they are in this class. Your classmates in turn tell their names, and each gives a good account of him- or herself. Now it is your turn. Should you tell them that this was the only course still open for registration that began later than 8 A.M., or that you really want to learn something about social psychology? All eyes are on you. Why is the young woman in the next row staring directly at your left elbow? (You know you should have worn a different shirt today, but you put off doing the laundry.) Why is the young man in front of you doodling as you prepare to start? Such situations evoke a state of self-consciousness, sometimes even acute self-consciousness. You are in a state of objective self-awareness. You are aware of yourself as an object of other people's perceptions.

Duval and Wicklund (1972) point out that we can focus our attention outward toward the environment or inward toward ourselves. Objective self-awareness is the result of directing our attention inward. When we do so, we become aware of our own values and standards and evaluate our behavior to see if we are living up to those standards. It is human nature to fail to reach some standards, especially when they are very high; when that happens, though, we become self-critical and very aware of our own shortcomings.

Ickes, Wicklund, and Ferris (1973) conducted an experiment in which 32 undergraduate men from introductory psychology classes at the University of Texas were told by a female experimenter that they had scored either high or low on a bogus trait called "surgency." They then filled out 15-item questionnaires rating themselves on 11 familiar personal traits (items that measured self-esteem), "surgency," and 3 filler items that were intentionally unfamiliar. The students filled out the questionnaires alone in a cubicle while facing a mirror (high self-awareness), or while seeing only the back of the mirror and not seeing themselves (low self-awareness). Of the subjects who received negative feedback on their "surgency" test, those who were facing the mirror rated themselves lower in self-esteem when they answered the questionnaire than those who were not forced to face the mirror while answering the questionnaire. The experimenters theorized that the mirror created a high self-awareness condition by directing the subjects' attention toward themselves, causing them to make more critical self-judgments.

Unlike the students confronting a mirror-image, sometimes we can avoid self-criticism by physically avoiding a situation (Duval, Wicklund, & Fine, 1972), or by distracting ourselves and focusing our attention outward toward some aspect of the environment (Duval & Wicklund, 1972; Wicklund, 1975).

Fortunately, our behavior does not always fail to meet our standards; sometimes we even exceed our ideals. When we do better than we expected, we may engage in self-praise. In the experiment just discussed (Ickes et al., 1973), the students who were told they scored high in "surgency" (that is, those who received positive feedback) rated themselves higher in self-esteem in general—even when they filled out the questionnaire in front of the mirror—than those who did not receive positive feedback.

It appears that when we are in a state of objective self-awareness, our standards and values become important or salient. We then evaluate our behavior, our appearance, and so on against those standards and values. For those students called upon to give an account of themselves before their classmates, standards of appearance and academic seriousness became salient through one of the elements of Cooley's (1922) looking-glass self: how we think other people judge us.

It seems, then, that in helping us "put our best foot forward," self-awareness serves a practical purpose. Carver, Blaney, and Scheier (1979) have shown that subjects who failed a first task and were made self-aware worked longer on a second task when they expected to be able to improve their performance. (See also Steenbergen & Alderman, 1979.) In another series of experiments, subjects in a hypothetical car-accident situation took more blame in a self-aware condition; and self-aware students also took more credit for getting an "A" in a hypothetical term-paper situation (Duval & Wicklund, 1973). These findings indicate objective self-awareness enhances responsibility for positive and negative behaviors.

If I am not for myself, who will be for me? If I am not for others, who am I for? And if not now, when?
Rabbi Hillel, The Talmud

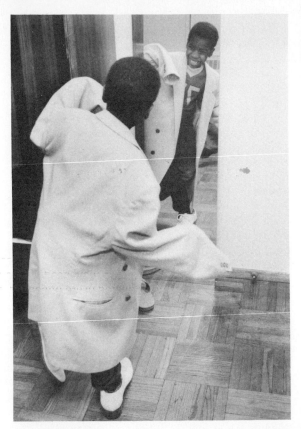

When we gaze at ourselves in a mirror, we are in a state of objective self-awareness: we look at ourselves as others might. The young lad at left tries on an adult role along with his father's jacket. The aspiring ballet dancers below must see how they will look to an audience.

Deindividuation   The research just described has focused on situations in which self-awareness is accentuated. Are there situations in which people lose their sense of self-awareness? Consider the presidential nominating conventions held every 4 years. Television reveals thousands of delegates wearing buttons and odd hats, crowding together, pushing each other, waving frantically, screaming the names of candidates in raucous confusion, and probably not at all looking as they do in their everyday lives. Emotions are highly charged. Inhibitions are lowered. These people seem, at least for the moment, to have lost their self-awareness. They are so strongly focused outward—on the world outside themselves, including the other people in it—that they lose themselves, in a sense, in the masses. They are, in the words of Zimbardo (1969) and Diener (1979), **deindividuated:** They become members of a kind of group-being, a mob-thing, instead of distinctive human beings.

Some of Zimbardo's research has emphasized such aspects of deindividuation as anonymity, sensory overload, involvement in group activity, and group size. (Recall the discussion of Zimbardo's prison studies in chapter 2.) One of his studies (1969) was an electric shock experiment using college women as subjects. Zimbardo created an environment where these subjects were either deindividuated (they wore hoods over their heads, were impossible to identify, and sat in a dark room) or individuated (were unhooded, were clearly identified with large name tags, and sat in a bright room). The subjects were told that the experiment involved empathy and responses to strangers, and that their group would be given an opportunity to deliver electric shocks to a woman who was not in the group. The subjects were encouraged (through the use of a bogus tape-recorded interview between the "victim" and the experimenter) either to think kindly of their future "victim" or to dislike her. That is, the "victim" was depicted as sweet, socially responsible, and altruistic, or as obnoxious, self-centered, and critical. The subjects who had been deindividuated administered longer shocks to the "victim," even when she was depicted as a likable person, than did the individuated subjects.

Diener (1979) had subjects in several groups participate in discussions of sexuality. In a low self-awareness condition, confederates discussed pornography, bestiality, and other controversial topics in an interesting and lively manner; confederates in a high self-awareness condition discussed the same topics in a repetitious and boring way. For both conditions, confederates in some groups behaved in an uninhibited manner, using sexual slang, cursing, and telling explicitly sexual stories, while confederates in other groups avoided explicit content and told boring tales in a dull, unenthusiastic way. The sessions were tape-recorded, and the behavior of the true subjects was analyzed. Results indicated that subjects in the low self-awareness condition were more responsive to the uninhibited confederates, and thus showed more evidence of deindividuation than those in the high self-awareness condition.

Thus deindividuation (as illustrated by these studies) results in a lowering of objective self-awareness: We become less concerned about the consequences of our behavior or about taking responsibility for our actions. And directing our attention away from ourselves results in deindividuation: We behave as the group behaves, getting caught up in its activity and losing our individuality.

Self-Esteem

What is **self-esteem**? The word **esteem** comes from a Middle English word *estemen*, meaning to estimate or appraise. Thus, self-esteem is the appraisal we make of ourselves, an evaluation of what we have become. Our self-esteem includes both positive and negative aspects. Most of us like to think well of ourselves; indeed, we spend considerable amounts of time and money trying to raise our self-esteem, trying to become what we aspire to be. We like to think we are good, decent, and reasonable people, but that may not always be the case.

Truly be what you would be thought to be.
French proverb

There have been many measures of self-esteem, but probably the most popular is the scale devised by Rosenberg (1965). (See Table 4–3.) Using a 5-point scale, subjects were asked to indicate whether they agreed or disagreed with each of 10 statements. According to Rosenberg, the combined scores in this scale are predictive of subjects' emotions and behaviors. For example, when the test was administered to patients in psychiatric hospitals, those who scored low in self-esteem were also unhappy and discouraged. The self-esteem scores corresponded with professional views too: Nurses rated as depressed those patients who scored low in self-esteem.

Self-esteem affects our behavior and the way we present ourselves to others. Individuals with high self-esteem are more optimistic and less depressed. They get involved in life and may become leaders. In classroom settings, students with low self-esteem are less likely to be involved in class discussions and in formal groups; they are usually not group leaders. People with low self-esteem are unhappy and see themselves as failures. Since they foresee failure in the future as well, they are unlikely to attempt difficult tasks, and quickly abandon undertakings that present obstacles (Coopersmith, 1968; Ickes & Layden, 1978; Rosenberg, 1965).

People with low self-esteem also assume that other people will not like them. Anticipating rejection at every encounter, they are awkward and fearful in social situations. In extreme cases, their awkwardness may even make people around them uncomfortable, creating a self-fulfilling prophecy. People with low self-

---

TABLE 4–3.
The Rosenberg Scale for Measuring Self-Esteem

1. On the whole, I am satisfied with myself.
2. At times I think I am no good at all.
3. I feel that I have a number of good qualities.
4. I am able to do things as well as most other people.
5. I feel I do not have much to be proud of.
6. I certainly feel useless at times.
7. I feel that I am a person of worth, at least on an equal plane with others.
8. I wish I could have more respect for myself.
9. All in all, I am inclined to feel that I am a failure.
10. I take a positive attitude toward myself.

Source: From M. Rosenberg, *Society and The Adolescent Self-Image.* Copyright © 1965 by Princeton University Press; Princeton Paperback, 1968. Extracts totaling 102 words, pp. 17–18, reprinted by permission of Princeton University Press.

esteem often experience an abiding sense of regret, as though their very existence was an offense.

Can such people be helped? Is it possible to raise self-esteem? Is it possible to change people so that they do not habitually attribute responsibility for failure to themselves and do not blame themselves all the time? Attempts at changing these attributional styles have had some success (Ickes & Layden, 1978; Layden, 1981).

Ickes and Layden (1978) selected 60 subjects who had previously demonstrated a low self-esteem attributional style, that is, they attributed unfortunate happenings to themselves but would not take credit for positive occurrences. In a series of experimental manipulations, these subjects were asked to "practice" using attributional styles other than those common to people with low self-esteem. Although no *significant* change in attributional style resulted, those who did manage to change even a little in the direction common to high self-esteem subjects increased their self-esteem significantly more than those who retained the low self-esteem attributional style. (See also Layden, 1981.)

Maintaining Self-Esteem

Self-esteem, then, is important to successful human functioning, and people generally are eager to maintain a positive self-image. What happens when they engage in some behavior or hold some view that is inconsistent with their "good" self-image? Aronson (1969) has argued that such a situation creates *cognitive dissonance.* (Cognitive dissonance is discussed in detail in chapter 8.)

If a girl doesn't know how to dance, then she says the band doesn't know how to play.
Yiddish proverb

Festinger (1957), the first to discuss cognitive dissonance, referred to it as a state of tension that results when people hold cognitions, such as attitudes, beliefs, or opinions, that contradict each other. When people sense there is a contradiction between their cognitions, sometimes without even being conscious of it, they become uncomfortable. They feel the need to do something to relieve the discomfort and resolve the contradiction. For example, perhaps you believe that nuclear power is dangerous and undesirable. Then you learn that the electricity in your own home is being generated by a nuclear power plant. What do you do? You might turn off the stereo, the TV, even the lights. However, that is a difficult alternative. Instead, you might change your attitude toward nuclear power, deciding that it really is not all that bad. The authorities are careful, after all; they have safety guidelines and the plant is regularly inspected. Such an attitude change would make your attitude and your behavior consistent. You can continue to play the stereo, watch TV, and keep pizzas in the freezer.

Aronson (1978) argues that we are most likely to engage in attitude change to reduce dissonance when a cognition is inconsistent with some part of our self-concept. People have several techniques for managing their self-images, as we will see in the following sections.

Insufficient Justification In 1959 Festinger and Carlsmith discussed an experiment conducted with young men in an introductory psychology class at Stanford University. The subjects performed 2 tasks, each for 30 minutes. For the first 30 minutes they put spools in a tray, emptied it, refilled it, and so forth. For the second 30 minutes, they turned pegs clockwise in a board a quarter of the way, then another quarter of the way, and so on. The subjects were then asked to lie to a woman confederate, telling her that the task was interesting and enjoyable. Some of the subjects were paid $1 to lie; others were paid $20. Finally, the subjects were asked to tell how much they had really enjoyed the task.

Put yourself in their place. How would payment affect your attitude? If you received $20, would you say the task was more enjoyable than if you received $1? Elms and Janis (1965) predicted that you would. But, in fact, just the opposite was true. The subjects who were paid $1 evaluated the task as more enjoyable than the subjects who were paid $20. This follows logically from the premise of dissonance theory: Apparently, $1 was *insufficient justification* for the men to lie to the confederate about a boring task. They experienced cognitive dissonance, and had to convince themselves that they had enjoyed the task and would not lie for so trivial a reward as $1. However, the subjects who were paid $20 had sufficient external justification to lie to the young woman. When it came time for them to tell the experimenter what they thought of the tasks, they rated them nearly as negatively as some control subjects who had not been asked to lie and who had not been paid. This basic phenomenon has been replicated many times using other experimental variables (Brehm & Cohen, 1962; Nel, Helmreich, & Aronson, 1969).

Overjustification and Intrinsic Motivation   It is possible that the subjects moving spools and turning pegs in Festinger and Carlsmith's (1959) experiment were overjustified in telling a small lie when they received $20 for completing the task.

Examples of overjustification occur every day. Automobile manufacturers are encouraging people to buy their products by offering large rebates. "Get a car, get a check," is a resounding cry. The advertising agencies and manufacturers expect that such rewards will increase sales now and in the future. It is possible, however, that such rewards will provide an overjustification to the buyer; that is, they may buy a new Farnsworth (or Elwoodmobile) this year because the maker will give them $1,000 to do it. But when they want to buy a new car in the future and that rebate is no longer in effect, they may well decide on a different model. A Farnsworth purchase is no longer justified; its outstanding feature was the accompanying rebate. A consumer survey in Chicago obtained exactly this result (Dodson, Tybout, & Steinthal, 1978).

Lepper, Greene, and Nisbett (1973) tested the overjustification hypothesis in a study of intrinsic and extrinsic motivation in children. Preschool children were given the opportunity to draw whatever they wanted on artist's paper with felt-tipped markers. The children were then divided into three groups: those who were told that for more drawing activity they would receive a "Good Player" certificate with a gold seal and a ribbon; those who received that reward for more drawing activity but were not told to expect it; and those children who were told of no reward and received none. In accord with a theory of intrinsic motivation (Deci, 1971, 1975; Lepper, 1981), the children who expected and received the certificate as a reward (extrinsic motivator) subsequently spent less time playing with the art paper and markers than either the children to whom the certificate was a surprise or the children who received no reward at all. Apparently, the children to whom the certificate was secondary and the children who received none at all were intrinsically motivated to play with the art materials for the

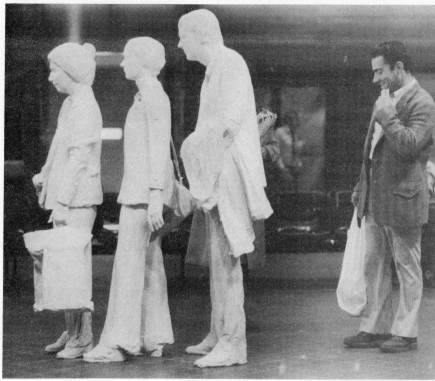

Marilynn K. Yee / The New York Times

Sculptor George Segal captured the essence of the patient commuter in these figures standing in line at New York City's Port Authority Bus Terminal. Several real commuters added themselves to the line. As one of them said, "The line seemed to be moving at a normal pace." Was that person maintaining self-esteem by overjustification, or simply being ironic?

pleasure of the activity itself. But like the people who bought the Farnsworth buggy for the $1,000 rebate instead of for the vehicle itself, the children who were motivated by the promise of a reward extrinsic to the activity lost interest in the activity.

The overjustification effect can be understood in terms of self-perception. Individuals who are promised a reward for engaging in a particular behavior infer that they lack intrinsic motivation. They see the desired behavior as a means to reach a goal rather than as a worthwile activity in its own right.

Several authors (e.g., Pittman, Cooper, & Smith, 1977; Ross, 1975) have argued that the overjustification effect is tempered by stimulus salience. When a reward is offered (an extrinsic cue) it is perceived as more important (salient) than the task or behavior demanded (an intrinsic cue). Consequently, if intrinsic cues can be made more salient than extrinsic cues, we might be able to eliminate the overjustification effect. Fazio (1981) reported exactly this result. Children who were promised a reward for their drawing, but were reminded of their initial intrinsic interest in the task (they were shown a photograph of their earlier behavior) played with the drawing materials as much as control subjects who were not promised a reward. Thus, the children used the salient intrinsic cues to explain their behavior and did not engage in overjustification. (See also Boggiano, Ruble & Pittman, 1982.)

Effort Justification   A corollary of over- and under-justification is effort justification. Effort justification research indicates that the harder we work on something, the better we like it. Aronson and Mills (1959) conducted an experiment in which college women underwent severe, moderate, or no initiation in order to participate in a discussion group. The women in the severe initiation group had to read aloud sexual slang and vivid descriptions of sexual behavior to the experimenter; those in the mild initiation condition read words related to sex but not those usually reserved for graffiti and curses. The control subjects, of course, became members of the discussion group without undergoing any initiation. The group in which all subjects later participated was exceedingly dull; its confederate members did their best to be banal, inarticulate, and uninteresting.

Results indicated that, as predicted, the women who underwent severe initiation to become members of this group rated its members and their discussion more favorably than did those subjects who had a mild initiation or no initiation at all.

Gaining Self-Knowledge

The self-concept is not stable; it changes as we interact with other people and gain experience in new situations. Our self-concept changes because of the addition of new information, information that can come from our own behavior as well as from the evaluations of other people.

Information from Our Own Behavior

Earlier, we talked about maintaining consistency between what we believe and what we do. When a conflict exists, we can alter either our attitude or our behavior and thus reduce dissonance. Sometimes we do something and then, thinking about it, wonder why we did it. We may discover that we have no attitude toward a particular behavior and might, as a result, infer what our attitude is from what we have done. For example, first-time voters who voted for Jimmy Carter might infer that they are democrats even though they had not really thought before about being a democrat or a republican.

Self-Perception Theory   The theory of self-perception (Bem, 1965, 1972) explains that people learn about their own attitudes, emotions, and other inner states by inferring them from their own behavior. According to Bem, we don't have any advantage over an outsider when it comes to understanding what we feel or what we believe. We use the same external cues as an outside observer would—our behavior—to infer our own internal state.

The so-called Cartoon Experiment (1965) illustrates Bem's theory of self-perception. Subjects were taught to use a colored light as a cue to accuracy. They were told to tell the truth in answering questions about themselves when the light was amber and to lie when it turned green. Thus, they learned to believe themselves when the light was amber but not to accept their own answers when the light was green. Later, asked to decide whether magazine cartoons were "very funny" or "very unfunny," their opinions were found to be influenced by whether the "truth" light (amber) or the "lying" light (green) was on at the time. They apparently judged their "real" attitude about the cartoons according to the cue provided by the light. They perceived their own behavior as an outsider might have done. Perceiving the amber light as a cue to telling the truth, they decided that they must be doing so.

Self-perception theory can also explain the results of insufficient justification experiments. Recall the men who were paid $1 or $20 to lie to the confederate about their feelings toward the boring tasks. According to dissonance theory, they changed their attitudes toward the tasks in order to resolve the dissonance they were experiencing. According to self-perception theory, however, they witnessed their own behavior and its surrounding conditions; then, the $20 subjects decided that the condition of being paid $20 was what had caused their lying; thus, they attributed that behavior to the $20. The $1 subjects, on the other hand, inferred that they must really have enjoyed the tasks since what they had witnessed themselves do, and the conditions under which they did it, offered no other logical explanation.

Self-perception theory is more parsimonious (see chapter 2) than dissonance theory—it requires us to make fewer assumptions. It does not presuppose the existence of a negative drive state arising from inconsistencies between attitudes and behavior. According to Bem and self-perception theory, people simply try to find an explanation for their behavior. They look first at the environment to see if it contains sufficient cause (for example, the $20 payment); if they find such a cause, their behavior is explained (or justified), and everything is fine. If sufficient justification is not evident, however, they look inward for an attitude or opinion that would justify their behavior. If no such attitude or opinion is evident, they infer one from the behavior under observation (see Figure 4–1).

Mis-Attribution to the Self   Much research has been devoted to distinguishing between self-perception theory and dissonance theory. Several researchers have reported some evidence of a negative drive state, or negative arousal, in dissonance situations (e.g., Kiesler & Pallak, 1976; Pallak & Pittman, 1972; Zanna & Cooper, 1974). When do we engage in self-perception and when do we experience dissonance? Fazio, Zanna, and Cooper (1976) believe that when behavior is congruent with one's attitudes, it is more appropriately explained by self-perception theory than by dissonance theory. On the other hand, when people are trying to understand something they have done that is in conflict with their attitudes, dissonance theory helps explain their behavior more appropriately. (See also Fazio, Zanna, & Cooper, 1979.) Attribution is discussed in detail in the following chapter. It is included here, too, to show that self-perception theory is a special case of attribution theory. When we make an attribution, we explain something by giving its cause. If you decide that your behavior at a party arose from a shyness you feel around people you do not know, you have attributed your behavior to that shyness. As we will see in chapter 5, there are a number of conditions that lead people to attribute causation to themselves.

Some research results of self-attribution theory indicate that people do not

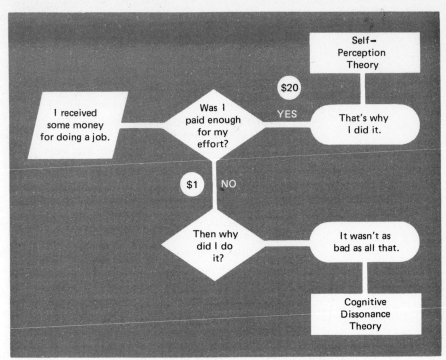

FIGURE 4-1.   Self-Perception Theory and Cognitive Dissonance Theory.

always identify the causes of their own behavior correctly. An experiment by Valins (1966) illustrates this point. Subjects looked at 10 erotic slides while hearing sounds that they were told were their own heartbeats, although the sounds were actually prerecorded and had nothing to do with their heart rates. Some subjects heard their alleged heartbeats speed up while watching 5 of the slides but remain steady while they viewed the other 5. The remaining subjects heard their heartbeats slow down while they looked at 5 of the slides but remain steady in response to the other slides. In both groups, most subjects judged the slides they were looking at while their supposed heartbeats changed as significantly more attractive than those they viewed while the sound remained stable. False feedback (the phony heartbeat sounds) led subjects to misattribute their own responses.

Storms and Nisbett (1970) used a *placebo* to create misattribution. Placebos are chemically inert substances, usually in the form of a pill, that do not have any physiological effects. The experimenters told their subjects (all light sleepers) that they would be participating in a dream research project. Some subjects were told that the placebo would make them more wakeful, while others were told that it would relax them. The experimenters believed that subjects who were told that the pill would arouse them would now be able to attribute their usual wakefulness to an outside source—the pill—and thus be freed of an emotional involvement in their wakefulness and fall asleep more quickly than usual. They expected those who were told the placebo would relax them to be more emotionally reactive than usual and thus to have more trouble falling asleep than usual. These expectations were confirmed. Subjects who could attribute their normal arousal to the pill fell alseep about 12 minutes sooner than usual; while those who had to attribute their wakefulness to themselves, despite having taken a pill that they expected to relax them, took 15 minutes longer than usual to fall asleep.

In this experiment a negative placebo effect was seen. In other studies, though, subjects who are told that a placebo will relax them do indeed experience relaxation (e.g., Bootzin, Herman, & Nicassio, 1976; Kellogg & Baron, 1975). This, too, of course, is misattribution. These and other studies hint that misattribution techniques may be useful in treating sleep disturbances and other similar problems.

Information from Other People

There have been cases where people were labeled incorrectly (and tragically)—for example, as mentally retarded when, in fact, they were deaf. Placed in institutions for the mentally retarded and labeled as belonging to that category, they grew up believing they were retarded, imitated the behavior and speech patterns of the truly retarded people around them, and missed the opportunity to develop their abilities to the fullest.

Labeling Theory   Labeling theory began as a sociological perspective to explain some aspects of deviance (see Becker, 1963). In general, labeling theory argues that, as a society, we pin "labels" on people we regard as deviant: criminals, the mentally ill, and so on. Such negative labels are applied primarily to members of the lowest classes in society—precisely those people without enough power to defend themselves against such labels. The label is assumed to have great power. Once labeled, people find themselves stuck with the self-image indicated by the label. Other people treat them as though they are deviant; soon the labeled people even believe they are. They infer their own nature from the reactions of those around them; they accept the definition of self that other people provide them.

It is perhaps obvious that labeling theory does not lend itself to laboratory research methods. There have, however, been field studies of labeling. Farrington (1979) did a field study of 400 English youths. Over a 4-year period he tested their beliefs and behavior in regard to delinquency three separate times. Those who were subsequently convicted on criminal charges had scored higher in delinquency both on the test and as shown by their behavior than a population of young men who had had the same delinquency scores as the convicted group at the beginning of the study. That is, in 4 years those who had been convicted increased in deviance compared to those who were not convicted, even though both groups essentially had held the same attitudes and exhibited the same behaviors at the start of the study.

While labeling theory has been criticized by some (Gove, 1975), it need not only have negative consequences; they can be positive as well. A child who is loved and wanted will be labeled as more attractive, more desirable, perhaps even more intelligent by parents than a child with similar attributes who is born into a family that is unprepared to care for it. Positive labels seem to stick, too,

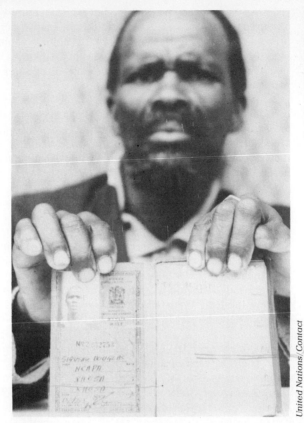

The man holding this identity card may be a community leader, husband, father, and hard worker—but under the laws of apartheid in South Africa he has been labeled a black man, and that is all that matters. When derogatory labels are pinned on people, deindividuation and low self-esteem inevitably follow.

United Nations/Contact

and it will probably be easier for the child who is regarded (and labeled) as attractive to attain self-esteem and to accept and believe in the love of others, than it will be for the child who grows up without such labels.

But even positive labeling is not without its drawbacks. When positive labeling is applied unrealistically, the labeled person may be disappointed by the response of a world that makes judgments based on performance rather than on labels. For example, if a child hears from a parent whose appraisal is unrealistic that she is an extremely talented athlete, she will be unprepared for rejection by the varsity team or the Olympic selection committee when her ability, not just a label, is being assessed.

Social Comparisons   In addition to getting information about ourselves directly from other people, including the labels they affix to us, we also use other people as a source of comparison to shape our self-concept. Am I more adept than Henry? Better looking than Joanne? Not as talented as Kim? Comparisons help us to evaluate ourselves, identify what our distinctive (or salient) characteristics are, and to construct our identity. Much of our self-knowledge is obtained by comparing ourselves with other people during social interactions. When we lack an objective standard (such as a test performance), we measure our own showing against the performance of other people (Festinger, 1954). Research suggests, however, that people do not compare themselves to just anyone. The person with whom we compare ourselves must be similar to us in some relevant ways. Zanna, Goethals, and Hill (1975) gave 60 college students (30 women, 30 men) false tests of logical reasoning or verbal acuity. They also told the students that men (or women) performed better on each of the tests. Later, most of the students (all but 2, in fact) first chose to compare their test scores with those of other subjects of the same sex. When they made second comparisons, most chose to compare their performance with the standard setters when the standard setters were of the opposite sex. Presumably, after comparing themselves with those most like themselves on the obvious, and reassuring, aspect of gender, they chose to compare their performance with those who excelled in general. It seems we choose to evaluate ourselves against people whose performance we expect to be similar to ours, and then against those who perform the best. (Also see Suls & Gastorf, 1978.)

Goethals and Darley (1977) argue that we cannot observe the ability of another directly; we must infer it from factors such as their performance informa-

We are constantly comparing ourselves to relevant others but seldom do our faces betray us in the act as much as the face of this young woman does.

tion and from characteristics such as physical size, weight, education, socio-economic status, and so forth. To make an accurate assessment of our own ability, we must consider all the relevant performance-related attributes of other people. The "best" social comparisons will be with people who are similar to us on all relevant dimensions.

Judging Ourselves by the Behavior of Others   In addition, Schachter and Singer (1962) demonstrated that other people can provide us with an explanation for our own feelings *through their behavior.* In other words, when we are confronted with an internal state for which we have no prior explanation—one that is unexpected and that we do not understand—we often interpret our own feelings by picking up on the behavior of other people. In their experiment, subjects, under the guise of testing a vitamin compound's effects on vision, were given either a drug that produced physiological arousal or a placebo. Those who received the actual drug were told either what its effects would be, that it would cause some side effects—but were not told the true ones—or that it would have no side effects. Those given the placebo were told there would be no side effects. Prior to the bogus vision tests, while each subject waited for the "vitamin" to take effect, an experimental confederate entered the room. The confederate was represented as being another vision test subject. The newcomer then proceeded to behave in either a euphoric way—playing wastebasket basketball, flying paper airplanes, twirling a hula hoop, and generally encouraging the true subject to join in—or in an angry fashion, declaiming that the test was unfair, and that the questionnaire they had filled out was too long, too personal, unreasonable, and insulting. The confederate eventually left the room in a huff.

After the confederate had finished his antics, subjects were asked how happy or angry they felt, and whether they had had any heart palpitations or tremors in their limbs. Those who had been misinformed about the drug's effects, and those who had been told that it would have no effects on them seemed to have "absorbed" the confederate's mood, whether euphoric or angry, and behaved likewise more often than those who had been accurately forewarned of how the drug would make them feel. That is, all experienced physiological arousal, but they variously labeled their feelings as happiness or anger according to the expressed mood of the confederate who had been with them (see also Schachter, 1964).

Schachter's work has been criticized on both methodological and theoretical grounds so, unfortunately, the conclusions to be drawn may not be as clear-cut as they appear. For example, Leventhal (1974) notes that many subjects who received the placebo also expressed the emotion (especially the anger) demonstrated by the confederate. The placebo subjects did not, of course, experience any drug-induced arousal that required explanation on their part. Therefore, their experience of emotion cannot be explained simply by using the label of physiological arousal, as Schachter and Singer (1962) suggest. Leventhal (1974) argues for a more social psychological approach to the phenomenon of emotion. This includes the belief that the onset of emotion is critically affected by external situations and how we interpret them. Thus, other people's behavior provides us with cues that we may use to interpret our feelings, but not just because we feel a need to explain arousal. (See also Berkowitz, 1978.)

Presentation of the Self

"All the world's a stage" wrote Shakespeare in *As You Like It*, "And one man in his time plays many parts." And, like it or not, we do play many parts and have many selves. Each self is real in its own right. In the first part of this chapter, we mentioned Goffman's (1959) conviction that we are constantly presenting one self or another; we are managing an impression of ourselves all the time. Goffman's (1959) conception has been called a dramaturgic model, and its basic point is that, like actors, we change our behavior to play various kinds of roles and to present various selves. We do this to manage the impression that we make on other people (Brown, 1970; Modigliani, 1968).

Impression Management

A number of studies indicate that, depending on the situation, we choose which images to present to others. Newtson and Czerlinsky (1974) demonstrated, for example, that politically moderate college students expressed more conservative attitudes when they thought they were communicating to a conservative audience and more liberal attitudes when they thought they were communicating to a liberal audience. Gergen and Wishnov (1965) examined how people manage their impressions using "self-descriptions" from hypothetical partners. Subjects read paragraphs and self-evaluations supposed to have been written by experimental partners who were presented as egotistical and self-centered, as self-demeaning and self-effacing, or as "average." The subjects then filled out the same forms about themselves. Those who had read descriptions from the boastful partner rated themselves more positively; those in contact with depressed partners rated themselves more negatively. Those describing themselves for an "average" partner stressed negative characteristics more often when they thought they would actually meet the partner. That is, all presented an impression of themselves in accord with how their partners had first presented themselves.

In 1975, Zanna and Pack performed an experiment with the help of 80 women attending Princeton University. The women rated themselves on traditional sex role attitudes—for example, independence/dependence, aggressiveness/passiveness, sentimentality/lack of sentimentality, and career orientation/lack of desire for a career. About three weeks later the subjects returned, allegedly to meet their male "partners." They were given questionnaires supposedly representing the "opinion on women" of those partners. Along with those opinions the women read descriptions of the partners, depicting them as highly desirable or undesirable (according to stereotypes of male desirability). Later the women filled out additional attitude questionnaires, supposedly to be given to the men, which repeated 11 items on sex role stereotypes from the first questionnaire. In general, the women who received descriptions of a desirable partner who preferred independent women presented themselves as significantly less conventional than when they filled out their initial attitude questionnaire. Those who had been presented with a desirable partner who held stereotypical expectations of women presented themselves as much more conventional in their attitudes the second time around. And the undesirable male partners did not have any significant effect on the self-presentations of the women.

The women conformed, at least in their written presentations, to the expectations of the attractive male partner, whether his expectations coincided with their initial descriptions of themselves or not. Thus, when they had reason to desire further contact, they altered the "self" they presented to the other person (even though the other was imaginary) in accordance with what they believed that person wanted. Moreover, in another part of the experiment, women who were expecting to interact with a desirable man who held unconventional views of what was desirable in a woman performed better in an anagram test (billed as a test of intellectual ability that the partner would see) than women who expected to meet an undesirable man. Thus, in this study, not only written attitudes but also real performance was altered by the women's expectation that those attitudes and that performance would be presented for appraisal to a desirable, eligible male.

In a similar study, Von Baeyer, Sherk, and Zanna (1979) demonstrated that female subjects dressed in ways designed to convey an impression of themselves as traditional or liberated, according to what they had been led to believe interviewers wanted.

It appears that at times we may even serve as the audience for our own performances. For example, Jones, Gergen, and Davis (1962) demonstrated that people can be persuaded not only to change their self-presentations according to what is expected of them; they can also be persuaded to believe their own "press," so to speak. Having presented themselves in a flattering way to interviewers, subjects who were commended (in the form of personal approval) rated their self-flattery as more accurate and honest than did those who did not receive the positive feedback.

Self-Disclosure

As we manage the impressions we make on others, we also reveal information about ourselves to them. This is self-disclosure. Jourard (1964) observed that self-disclosure also enables us to learn more about ourselves, and that people who disclose too much or too little may have problems in social adjustment.

In a study involving 40 liberal arts college and nursing-school students, evenly distributed by race and sex, Jourard and Lasakow (1971) found that women revealed more about themselves in general than men, and that whites disclosed more than blacks. This group disclosed most to their mothers and progressively less to, in decreasing order, fathers, male friends, and female friends. (See Figure 4–2.) The information that was most readily disclosed concerned subjects' tastes and interests, attitudes and opinions, and work. Low-disclosure topics included money, personality, and their bodies.

Married and single subjects showed no difference in the total amount of information they revealed about themselves. However, single subjects revealed more than married ones to their parents and to their same-sex friends. Not surprisingly, married subjects let their spouses know more about themselves than

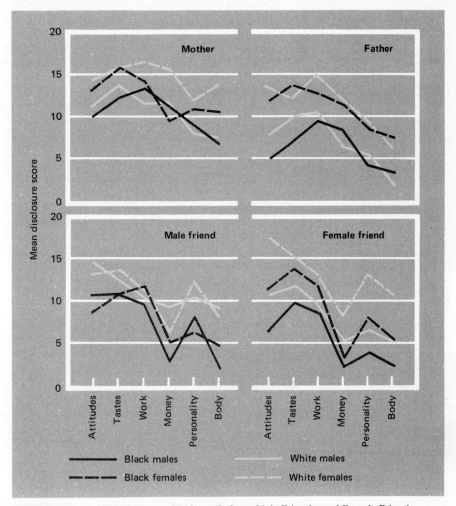

FIGURE 4–2.   Self-Disclosure to Mothers, Fathers, Male Friends, and Female Friends.

Average number of disclosures on six key topics by white and black male and female subjects.

Source: *Adapted from "A Research Approach to Self-Disclosure," by S. M. Jourard and P. Lasakow,* Journal of Abnormal Psychology, *1958*, 56, *220.*

anyone else, and revealed more than single subjects showed to anyone else. Similar research by Stokes, Fuehrer and Childs indicates that men are less willing than women to disclose to intimate friends, but more willing to disclose to strangers and acquaintances (1980).

What impact does self-disclosure have on other people's impressions of us? There is evidence that people like others who reveal themselves (Worthy, Gary, & Kahn, 1969), unless their disclosures are so intimate as to be discomforting (Cozby, 1972).

Self-Monitoring

We have discussed how people manage their impressions and that they disclose more or less of their "real" selves to others, depending on who the others are and what relationships they have. Another aspect of self-presentation is self-monitoring—measuring how we "come off" to those around us. Some people have many social skills in presenting themselves; others are relatively inept at the process.

According to Snyder (1974, 1979), people differ in their awareness of how their behavior appears to others. He believes that some people are high self-monitors. High self-monitors are concerned with what is socially appropriate, and are particularly sensitive to how others express and present themselves in social settings. Observing others closely, they use the behavior they see as a guideline for presenting and expressing themselves. High self-monitors are skillful at expressing their emotions and are usually situationally controlled; they behave more in accord with what is appropriate to the situation than with their true feelings.

Application: Do You Salt Before You Taste?

Have you ever noticed that some people salt the food they are about to eat before they taste it? McGee and Snyder (1975) reasoned that people who respond to a situation (high self-monitors) would taste food to see if it really needed salt before reaching for the shaker. To test this hypothesis, they noted whether people in a restaurant salted their food before tasting, or tasted it first to see if it really required salt. An experimenter later approached these restaurant patrons and asked them to cooperate with a course project by answering a questionnaire. They were asked to indicate which adjective in each of 20 pairs of trait descriptions described themselves. They could also choose the phrase, "It depends on the situation," instead of a descriptive adjective. High self-monitors, of course, would be more likely to choose the "It depends" option than a specific adjective to describe themselves.

McGee and Snyder's hypothesis was confirmed by the results: Those people who salted their food first and tasted it later (low self-monitors) chose an average 14.87 self-descriptive adjectives, while the salt-after-tasting subjects chose less than half as many (6.9), marking "It depends" most of the time.

In a related experiment, the subjects were asked why they salted their food. The experimenters hypothesized that the salt-before-tasting people would say something like "I like salt," while the salt-after-tasting people would say something like "The food needed salt." The former explanation is *dispositional*, arising out of the individual, while the latter is *situational*. Again, the hypothesis was confirmed. Of 12 subjects who salted afterward, 10 used situational explanations, and of the 12 who salted first, 10 used dispositional explanations.

Do *you* salt before you taste? Now you know whether you are a high or low self-monitor. Look around you the next time you dine with your friends. Are they high or low self-monitors? Do you think salt is a good test?

Low self-monitors are less concerned than high self-monitors are about the impressions they make on other people. Low self-monitors seem less likely and less able to alter their behavior in different situations. They tend to act out their feelings and ignore situational cues that indicate other behavior might be more appropriate.

TABLE 4–4.
Self-Monitoring Scale Items

1. I find it hard to imitate the behavior of other people. (F)
2. My behavior is usually an expression of my true inner feelings, attitudes, and beliefs. (F)
3. At parties and social gatherings, I do not attempt to do and say things that others will like. (F)
4. I can only argue for ideas that I already believe. (F)
5. I can make impromptu speeches even on topics about which I have almost no information. (T)
6. I guess I put on a show to impress or entertain people. (T)
7. When I am uncertain how to act in a social situation, I look to the behavior of others for cues. (T)
8. I would probably make a good actor. (T)
9. I rarely need the advice of my friends to choose movies, books, or music. (F)
10. I sometimes appear to others to be experiencing deeper emotions than I actually am. (T)
11. I laugh more when I watch a comedy with others than when alone. (T)
12. In a group of people I am rarely the center of attention. (F)
13. In different situations and with different people, I often act like very different persons. (T)
14. I am not particularly good at making other people like me. (F)
15. Even if I am not enjoying myself, I often pretend to be having a good time. (T)
16. I'm not always the person I appear to be. (T)
17. I would not change my opinions (or the way I do things) in order to please someone else or win their favor. (F)
18. I have considered being an entertainer. (T)
19. In order to get along and be liked, I tend to be what people expect me to be rather than anything else. (T)
20. I have never been good at games like charades or improvisional acting. (F)
21. I have trouble changing my behavior to suit different people and different situations. (F)
22. At a party I let others keep the jokes and stories going. (F)
23. I feel a bit awkward in company and do not show up quite so well as I should. (F)
24. I can look anyone in the eye and tell a lie with a straight face (if for a right end). (T)
25. I may deceive people by being friendly when I really dislike them. (T)

Note: The letters in parentheses (T, true, or F, false) represent the responses of a high self-monitor.

Source: From "The Self-Monitoring of Expressive Behavior" M. Snyder, *Journal of Personality and Social Psychology*, 1974, *30*, 531.

Snyder (1974) constructed a Self-Monitoring Scale of 25 items that measure an individual's sensitivity to the social appropriateness of his or her self-presenting behaviors. (See Table 4–4 on page 157.) High self-monitors are more skillful at conveying emotions and are more attentive to social cues in situations that are ambiguous. In one study using this scale, Snyder demonstrated that professional actors were higher self-monitors than a group of undergraduates at Stanford University. Geizer, Rarick, and Soldow (1977) administered the Self-Monitoring Scale to subjects before showing them videotapes of the television program *To Tell the Truth*. They found that the high self-monitors were more accurate at telling "the real person" from the imposters than the low self-monitors.

High self-monitors take the initiative in social settings more often than low self-monitors. High self-monitoring women are more expressive (in terms of gestures, gazes, and the like) than low self-monitoring women. With men, however, the opposite seems to be true (Ickes & Barnes, 1977). High self-monitors are also less likely to carry through with previously expressed intentions than low self-monitors (Ajzen, Timko, & White, 1982). That is, low self-monitors show more consistency between their attitudes and behavior than high self-monitors, who tend to change their behavior to suit the situation.

Maintenance of Self-Image

Imagine that you, an intelligent, maturing person, with some understanding of what democracy means, with an appreciation of a society that aims—in its best moments—to provide equality for all its citizens, were suddenly revealed to yourself as one of the most loathsome creatures around—a bigot, as bad as Archie Bunker, but in real life! What would you do? How would you square yourself with yourself?

That is just about what happened to some of the 80 white college students in an experiment by Dutton and Lake (1973). Subjects first rated themselves on, among other things, how prejudiced they were and how high a value they put on equality. Then the students watched slides of social scenes and were convinced by false physiological feedback that they were prejudiced against black people. As the subjects left the laboratory and made their way across campus, they encountered a panhandler (actually an experimental confederate) asking for directions and for whatever money they could spare. Some of the panhandlers were black, some white. Those subjects who had been told that their feedback results indicated prejudice against black people gave, on the average, 47¼ cents to black panhandlers but only 16¾ cents to white panhandlers. The phenomenon of reverse discrimination was at work—discrimination *in favor* of a particular group instead of against it. The subjects had thought they were unprejudiced (and, in all probability, were so); being told that they were prejudiced by authoritative test results made them so uncomfortable that they made an extra effort to overcome the affront to their self-image, to prove to themselves who they really were.

Self-Control

Why do people work so hard to make their behavior fit their notion of themselves? Our self-concept partly depends on evaluations and comparisons with other people, as we have already seen. We like other people to be predictable so we can have an accurate (and reliable) idea of what their evaluations of us are going to be. Indeed, Heider (1958) argued that because we prefer people to behave in a predictable way, when uncertainty exists in social situations we are motivated to reduce it and thereby regain predictability. We desire predictability because it gives us a sense of having some control over the environment.

However, it is perceived, rather than actual, control that is important in our view of ourselves. There is evidence that people who think they have control (even though, in fact, they do not) are better adjusted than those who have no control and are aware of it. Sherrod, Hage, Halpern, and Moore (1977) exposed subjects to unpleasant noise while they were performing tasks involving detail (such as proofreading and matching numbers). Some subjects were able to control whether the noise started at all. Some could shut it off if they chose. Others could control both the starting and the stopping of the noise. Subjects with the greatest degree of control over the noise were the most accurate in their tasks. Subjects with the least degree of control made the most mistakes. And after the noise stopped, those subjects who had previously had the greatest degree of control demonstrated the most persistence in a puzzle task that tested their frustration tolerance.

But what if these subjects had only perceived they had control over the noise? Glass and Singer (1972) exposed subjects to an unpredictable noise and told some of them they could stop the noise by pressing a button. Although in actuality the button had no effect on the noise itself, those subjects who thought they could stop the noise rated it as less disruptive than those who believed they had no control.

The illusion of control, then, is sufficient to influence our attitudes and behavior (see chapter 8). Langer and Roth (1975) found that subjects who were led to believe that they correctly predicted the toss of a coin also believed that their prediction accuracy had something to do with skill. It seems, then, that the need to perceive events as being controllable is so powerful that people are ready to believe they can control a coin toss, a matter commonly known to depend on chance.

Rotter (1966) has suggested that the illusion of control is subject to personality or individual differences in the ways in which people give credit to the "moving force" they perceive as responsible for outcomes. Some people are *internalizers*; they generally attribute rewards and positive outcomes to their own behavior. *Externalizers*, on the other hand, attribute good outcomes to chance or luck rather than to their own actions.

The control over negative outcomes (failures) represents a different matter entirely. If people internalized failure, it might damage their self-concept. They would have to admit that they lacked the ability to perform the tasks they tried. If they blame failure on outside causes, such as bad luck, however, they can maintain a positive self-image. The failure was not their fault; it was a "bad break." Next time their luck will improve, and they will succeed.

We can take responsibility for a failure (make an **internal attribution),** but can attribute that failure to a temporary source, such as a lack of effort (something that can be remedied by a resolution to do better next time). Or we can attribute a failure to interference by an enemy (an **external attribution**) and decide that the source of interference is stable, or unchanging. We can thus resign ourselves to lifelong failure without letting it threaten our self-image (Weiner, 1972). These are the key features of Weiner's model of attribution, which is discussed in the next chapter.

Learned Helplessness

If, as we have seen, attributing failure to a lack of ability (an internal attribution) can damage the self-concept, is such damage serious? Can it be overcome?

Overmeier and Seligman (1967) conducted an experiment in which dogs who had been electrically shocked in conditions that prevented them from escaping the shocks later failed to make responses that would have ended the shocks.

Controversy: Learned Helplessness and Depression in Women

"We women can't go in search of adventures—to find out the North–West Passage or the source of the Nile, or to hunt tigers in the East. We must stay where we grow, or where the gardeners like to transplant us. We are brought up like the flowers, to look as pretty as we can, and be dull without complaining. That is my notion about the plants: they are often bored, and that is the reason why some of them have got poisonous. What do you think?"

George Eliot, *Daniel Deronda*

The concept of learned helplessness has been applied to the traditional sex-role conditioning of women. Until very recently, women were taught, sometimes subtly and sometimes blatantly, that being "helpless" was "feminine." When baby boys took their first steps, dad proudly encouraged his son, gesturing him to "Come ahead, try out those new legs." When girl babies made their first moves, however, all sorts of cautions were expressed: "Be careful, don't fall," and even "don't get dirty."

Later in life, women were told that work in many professional and occupational areas was "too hard" for them. The socially acceptable traits of being "feminine" conflicted with being successful. In the social arena, too, learning that it was "unfeminine" to be competent or effective encouraged many women to perceive themselves as unable to take action except in a limited sphere.

The rate of depression for women is significantly greater than for men, so perhaps Seligman's (1975) theory is accurate. To grow up in a world where you are trained not only to accept any inadequacies you might have, but to magnify them to achieve social acceptability and popularity as a woman is to grow up in nearly constant conflict.

Even when the experimenter actually lifted the dogs from the enclosure, demonstrating that escape was possible, the dogs still failed to help themselves. The dogs appeared to have learned that they could not alter the situation, and therefore they didn't try.

Seligman (1975) called this phenomenon **learned helplessness,** and hypothesized that in humans it may result in clinical symptoms of depression. "Helpless" people seem to lack motivation, have difficulty coping with problems, and appear overwhelmingly sad. They say things like "Nothing will help" or "It won't do any good." Helplessness is closely related to the perception of control; it is the perception that behavior cannot influence outcomes that creates a state of helplessness. People who have learned to be helpless have learned to be ineffective. They have learned that their actions cannot help them achieve their goals.

Abramson, Seligman, and Teasdale (1978) have reformulated the original theory of learned helplessness and put it in attributional terms. First, they distinguished between situations in which all people are helpless (universal helplessness) and those in which only some people are helpless (personal helplessness). They argue that when people believe that outcomes do not depend on their behavior, they attribute the fact of their helplessness to a causative factor that may be stable/unstable, global/specific, and internal/external.

Global attributions for failure are easier to deal with than specific ones. Unstable causes are not damaging to self-esteeem, but stable causes may indeed harm the self-image. For example, after failing a psychology test you may decide that the reason for your failure was simply that you were tired out from studying all night. You have made an internal (something about yourself), global (something that can happen to anyone), unstable (something that can change) attribution. Similarly, deciding that the test was unfair or too difficult would be an external, specific, stable attribution. (See Table 4–5.)

The kind of attribution made by a person can determine the scope of helplessness and its effects, or lack of them, on his or her self-esteem. Abramson et al. (1978) suggest that internal, stable attributions result in a feeling of personal

TABLE 4–5.

Some Possible Reasons for Failing a Psychology Test

	Internal		External	
	Stable	**Unstable**	**Stable**	**Unstable**
Global	Lack of intelligence	Exhaustion	University gives unfair tests	Today is Friday the 13th
Specific	Lack of psychological ability	Fed up with psychology	This test was unfair	This is the 13th test I've taken

Source: Adapted from "Learned Helplessness in Humans: Critique and Reformulation," by L. Y. Abramson, M. E. P. Seligman, and J. D. Teasdale, *Journal of Abnormal Psychology*, 1978, *87*, 57.

helplessness, while external, stable attributions produce universal helplessness. Furthermore, global attributions yield chronic helplessness, and specific attributions yield acute helplessness. The most devastating situation results when an individual makes an internal, stable, and global attribution ("I'm just not smart enough"). This person perceives the self as a failure—as a person who is and has been ineffective and lacks the ability to do anything about it.

Can anything be done to alleviate feelings of helplessness? Helplessness does take some time to set in. Wortman and Brehm (1975) report that people try very hard to regain control in their initial exposures to outcomes that are uncontrollable. It is only over time, when they learn that even increased effort is unsuccessful, that they finally give up. But before that final surrender, intervention may be successful. Langer and Rodin (1976) performed an experiment in which elderly residents in a nursing home were either encouraged to take some responsibility for their own welfare, given plants to care for, and given decision-making freedom; or they were cared for as they had been previously, with no intervention made to give them some control over their own lives. Those given choices, freedom, and responsibility improved to a significant degree in happiness, activity, and a sense of well-being. This points to opportunities for unlearning helplessness and bolstering self-esteem at any age.

Answering Questions about Self-Perception and Presentation

1. Only you, of course, can answer the first series of questions at the beginning of this chapter. Very rarely do we stop and think about the "self." What is it that makes each individual unique as a person? James (1891) pointed out that we can think about the self on several levels—spiritual, social, and so on—and that these levels define different aspects of the "self."

2. We really have many selves, and are able to choose a different one to present, depending on the social situation. As James (1891) observed, we often have as many selves as there are separate groups of people with whom we identify. Our self is a child to our parents, a peer to our classmates, an employee in the workplace, and so on, and we change our behavior accordingly. This does not imply that we are inconsistent. Indeed, our self-concept is best thought of as a process or a schema. We choose various images or sub-schemas for different interactions, but all are consistent with our self-concept.

3. McGuire and his colleagues have suggested that we define ourselves in terms of salient attributes, those qualities that make us different from other people and thus emphasize our individuality. Such characteristics are typically given first in completing the phrase "I am _____." Only after we have listed our most salient attributes do we add evaluation descriptions (e.g., intelligent, hardworking, etc.).

4. Did you know that most people have a "right preference"? That is, other things being equal, people are most likely to choose the object, entrance, or path on the right more often than the one on the left. But when we make de-

cisions about choosing a carton of milk or a doorway are we aware of this preference? Nisbett and Wilson (1977) have argued that we are not. Indeed, they even suggest that people are not consciously aware of their higher order mental processes. This may well be true for relatively simple or trivial tasks such as buying milk, but for more complex and important issues it is likely that we are aware of our thought processes.

5. When we look into a mirror, we are able to see ourself as another person would; we become the object of our own perception. According to Duval and Wicklund (1972), being in such a state of objective self-awareness makes us acutely conscious of social responsibilities and standards. We may conclude that we are either not living up to those standards, or we may find that we are actually exceeding them. These observations can influence both our self-esteem and our behavior.

6. Some people are very sensitive to the situations they find themselves in and alter their behavior accordingly. Others behave more or less consistently in every situation. Snyder (1974, 1979) has referred to these two types of people as high and low self-monitors, respectively. High self-monitors are more likely to examine the situation (to see if the food needs salt before reaching for the shaker), while low self-monitors ignore situational variables (they always salt their food and this time is no exception).

7. We prefer to have control and predictability in our lives, to be the masters of our fates. This desire is so strong that we will often take responsibility for purely random events, as in the coin toss example. Skill is more predictable than luck, and more dependable. When we lose control over important life events we may become depressed and exhibit the effects of learned helplessness.

Summary

Self-perception refers to the ways in which we come to understand who we are, and self-presentation refers to the aspects of ourselves that we show to others. Our self-concept is our own understanding of who we are. It is our own theory of our life, and provides us with a schema for understanding ourself. Although we think of ourselves as a unified person, we all contain a number of different "selves" or sub-schemas, each showing itself in a different situation.

We can make a distinction, then, between the self-image, which reflects our different selves (or different roles in the world) and is therefore constantly changing, and our self-concept, which contains all of our different aspects. Turner (1968) believes that when a self-image is in conflict with the self-concept, it is the image that gets altered so that the concept remains stable.

We are in a state of objective self-awareness when we become consciously aware of being an object of other people's observation. In this state our attention is directed inward, to ourselves. We attempt to look and act our best, become aware of our standards and values, and are highly conscious of our individual identity. However, in a crowd or under certain other conditions, we can lose our individuality, get caught up in the group's actions, and become deindividuated.

In this condition objective self-awareness is lowered, and we may even act in ways that are contrary to our personal values.

Self-esteem is our own evaluation of ourself. Low self-esteem has been found to correlate with unhappiness and lack of leadership; severely low self-esteem is characteristic of those who are depressed. Most people try to maintain a positive self-image, and thus try to keep their self-esteem fairly high. When a situation occurs that conflicts with a "good" self-image, people may experience **cognitive dissonance** and attempt to resolve it.

According to Bem's (1965, 1972) **theory of self-perception**, we learn about our attitudes, emotions, and other inner states by inferring them from our own behavior. We also learn about ourselves through information from other people. **Labeling theory** provides one example of how this happens: An individual may become identified with a particular characteristic and given a label—clever, silly, clumsy—that sticks for life. Because labels do not easily change, people act in accord with them, and may overlook more realistic aspects of themselves.

We also learn about ourselves through comparisons with others who are similar to us in relevant ways, by observing the ways in which others behave toward us, and from our own responses to various situations and to other people.

When we present ourselves to others, we choose the self or image that we show. Through **impression management** we try to make ourselves likable and attempt to fit the preconceived notions of others. We also manage our **self-disclosures,** carefully choosing to whom we reveal most about our lives and opinions. Problems in social adjustment are associated with either too little or too much self-disclosure.

Self-monitoring (Snyder 1974, 1979) refers to our awareness of how we appear to others. **High self-monitors** are particularly sensitive to the ways in which they are viewed by others, and watch others closely for clues to appropriate behavior. **Low self-monitors** guard their emotions less carefully, act more impulsively, and are not skilled at altering their behavior to suit varied occasions.

We work at maintaining our self-images because we desire predictability in our world, and like to believe we can control events. We try to avoid a negative self-image by ascribing our failures to sources over which we have no control, an **external attribution**, rather than to our own actions, an **internal attribution**. When people believe that their efforts are unable to improve the outcome of a situation, or that whatever they do is bound to come out wrong, they are experiencing **learned helplessness:** They have learned to be ineffective in life (Bandura, 1977). Learned helplessness may be reversed when people have the opportunity to take responsibilities and act with effectiveness.

Suggested Additional Reading

Abramson, L. Y., Teasdale, J. D., & Seligman, M. E. P. Learned helplessness in humans: Critique and reformulation. *Journal of Abnormal Psychology*, 1978, *87*, 49–74.

Carver, C. S., & Scheier, M. F. *Attention and self-regulation: A control-theory approach to human behavior.* Secaucus, N.J.: Springer-Verlag, 1981.

Cooley, C. H. *Human nature and the social order* (rev. ed.). New York: Scribner's, 1922 (Originally published 1902.)

Duval, S. & Wicklund, R. A. *A theory of objective self-awareness.* New York: Academic Press, 1972.

Goffman, E. *The presentation of self in everyday life.* Garden City, N.Y.: Doubleday Anchor, 1959.

Rosenberg, M., & Kaplan, H. B. *Social psychology of the self-concept.* Arlington Heights, IL: Harlan Davidson, Inc., 1982.

Schachter, S. The interaction of cognitive and physiological determinants of emotional states. In L. Berkowitz (Ed.), *Advances in experimental social psychology* (Vol. 1). New York: Academic Press, 1979.

Snyder, M. Self-monitoring processes. In L. Berkowitz (Ed.), *Advances in experimental social psychology* (Vol. 12). New York: Academic Press, 1979, 85–128.

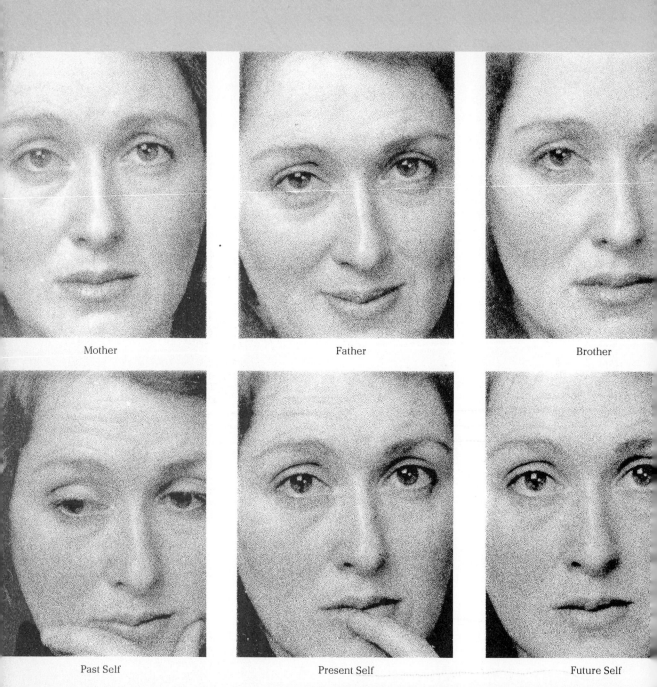

Mother   Father   Brother

Past Self   Present Self   Future Self

5

PERSON PERCEPTION AND ATTRIBUTION

Photographer Mark Berghash attempts to illustrate through multiple portraits the concept that a person's character and destiny are formed by the closest family members. "The complete portrait is made up of a series of expressions evoked by asking the subject to think about his/her mother, father, siblings, children, self in the past, present, and future. I give the subject control of the shutter and leave the room . . . [to allow the subject to] recollect his/her thoughts without being self-conscious. When the subject feels that the person . . . is strong in the mind's eye . . . he/she releases the shutter. I then enter the room, change the film holder, and ask the subject to think about the next person on the list."
Serial Portrait of Thomasina Webb, Artist, from the series Aspects of the True Self.

Questions about Person Perception and Attribution

1. How do we combine the different things we know about a person in order to form an overall impression of him or her?
2. Do we evaluate people in the same way we evaluate automobiles? Do you think that organizing information about people is similar to organizing information about objects?
3. How accurate are we in assessing the causes of other people's behavior?
4. What factors do we take into account when we attribute behavior to various causes?
5. People are not computers, and relatively few of us are statisticians or fortune-tellers. Nevertheless, we are constantly called upon to predict events and the behavior of others. How well do we perform?
6. When you ride a bicycle, you don't have to think constantly about how to peddle, how to steer, and how to maintain your balance. These activities are relatively "mindless." How much of your social behavior is similarly mindless?

U nless you are a hermit, you live in a world surrounded by other people. You must deal with these other people every day and at various levels of interaction. Ordinary chores like going to the store, standing in line for a movie, or buying a newspaper require social exchanges that involve perceptions of and judgments about other people.

Perhaps you feel that you understand the behavior of others. But do you know how you have arrived at your understanding? Probably, like most of us, you are sometimes surprised by the way others behave. Have you ever considered how your behavior appears to others, and how they judge you?

On the first day of this class, what kind of impression did your new instructor make on you? Do you know what led you to decide he or she was self-assured or nervous, experienced or new, forceful or reticent? Did your classmates get the same impression?

Also consider your first day on campus. How did you react to all the new people you met? How did they react to you? If you made a good impression, did you know why? What made you aware of it? If you felt that someone you just met did not like you, did you know the possible reasons for this dislike?

These questions form the basis for the study of person perception. In this chapter, we will consider how we form impressions of other people, the ways we organize those impressions, and the reasons why we may reach wrong conclusions about the people and events in our world.

168

Impression Formation

You are introduced to someone at a party who immediately begins to tell you about her accomplishments. This new acquaintance is obviously intelligent, yet her conversation is completely self-centered. Later, perhaps, she shows some interest in you and your accomplishments. But by then it is too late and you are no longer interested in her. You have formed an impression of her as a highly self-involved personality.

Although further observation may alter or refute our first impressions, they are usually quite difficult to erase. And we all form first impressions of the people we meet, often with considerable ease and speed and without even thinking about it. We are aware, however, that we perceive an individual not as a set of disconnected traits but as a unit: When we talk about someone's "personality" we include the entire range of characteristics belonging to that individual.

Asch (1946) conducted many experiments on impression formation. In one experiment, lists of character traits were read to two groups of students. The lists were identical except that the trait *warm* appeared on one list and *cold* on the other. When the students were asked to write character sketches of the individuals defined by those traits, those who were given the list with the *warm* trait were more favorably disposed to the hypothetical person than those given the list with the *cold* trait. (See Table 5-1.) Furthermore, the *warm* trait not only added a

TABLE 5-1.

Asch's Central Trait Theory Experiment

Person	Trait List[a]	Typical Description
A	Intelligent Skillful Industrious Warm Determined Practical Cautious	A person who believes certain things to be right, wants others to see his point, would be sincere in an argument and would like to see his point won.
B	Intelligent Skillful Industrious Cold Determined Practical Cautious	A rather snobbish person who feels that his success and intelligence set him apart from the run-of-the-mill individual. Calculating and unsympathetic.

[a] Subjects were presented with lists of traits that were identical except for one key trait, and asked to write a description of the person to whom the traits belonged. It was found that differences in only one trait in the list were sufficient to elicit very different personality descriptions.

Source: Adapted from "Forming impressions of personality" by S. Asch, *Journal of Abnormal and Social Psychology*, 1946, *41*, 262–263.

new quality to the overall personality being described, but actually transformed some of the other characteristics. For example, a person perceived as *warm* and *determined* might be judged as earnest and hardworking, while the *cold* and *determined* individual might be seen as pushy and ruthless.

Central Trait Theory

Asch concluded that the warm–cold characteristic was a major factor in impression formation, and that a change in a single key characteristic can significantly affect the entire impression made by a person. These findings are the basis of central trait theory, which holds that certain personality characteristics are of particular importance in determining how we perceive other individuals, and that the significance of a trait depends on its context. Our everyday experience corroborates Asch's theory: We tend to describe people in terms of relatively few but highly distinctive characteristics.

In another series of experiments, Asch sought to determine if the order in which we learn about personality traits affects impression formation. Again, two lists of characteristics were read to two groups of students. Those students who first heard the subject described in positive terms (intelligent, industrious, impulsive, critical, stubborn, envious) judged that person as competent despite shortcomings, and even excused the negative characteristics ("That he is stubborn and impulsive may be due to the fact that he knows what he is saying and what he means"). On the other hand, those who heard the same list in reverse order saw the person's negative qualities as overshadowing the positive ones. Furthermore, certain qualities such as impulsiveness and criticalness were interpreted favorably when they followed positive qualities on a list, but were considered unfavorable when they followed negative qualities.

Implicit Personality Theories

We all have expectations about how characterisics are related to each other in the personalities of other people. Most of these expectations are not fully articulated, that is, most of us do not go around saying, "That overweight person must be lazy." Yet connections exist in our minds and are activated when we encounter new people. Bruner and Tagiuri (1954) were the first to examine this tendency to intuitively associate groups of personality characteristics with one another. It is often discussed in terms of implicit personality theories.

Methods of Study   Social psychologists are interested in the traits people group together. They use three methods to study trait relationships:

1. Ratings of similarity. Subjects are asked to identify the similarity or difference between paired traits.
2. Likelihood of co-occurrence. Subjects are asked, "If a person has trait *x*, how likely is it that he or she also has trait *y*?"
3. Trait sorting. Subjects are asked to divide a list of personality traits into separate groups, each representing a complete person (Schneider, 1973).

Milton Rogovin / Photo Researchers, Inc.

Does this man fit your implicit personality theory for an alcoholic? Why or why not?

Identifying Components   Once personality trait ratings have been obtained, they are analyzed using one of two methods. In factor analysis, the researcher attempts to find the traits that generally co-vary, or fit together. How often, for example, is *curious* associated with *intelligent*? *Suspicious* with *timid*? By identifying predictable trait associations, factor analysis reduces a large number of personality characteristics to a smaller set of connected traits that are more readily interpreted.

Multidimensional scaling similarly clarifies relationships among various traits and thus reduces the number of individual characteristics that comprise a total personality. In multidimensional scaling, trait associations are graphically plotted to provide a "picture" of the distance between individual traits. (See Figure 5–1 on the next page.)

Supporting Evidence for Implicit Personality Theories   In real life, do we actually make associations between personality traits when we form our first impressions of people? And how accurate are our first impressions? Passini and Norman (1966) tested the existence and validity of implicit personality theories. They asked students at a large university to rate one another for character traits during the first class meeting of the semester. Although these subjects did not know one another, there was remarkable agreement about themselves in terms of opposing trait pairs such as *talkative–silent*, *sociable–reclusive*, and *good-natured–irritable*. Moreover, the associations of traits were similar to those in earlier studies in which subjects had rated one another after considerable acquaintance and interaction (Norman, 1963). In both studies, the same groupings of traits were linked regardless of the length of time the subjects had known one another. These studies confirm not only the use we make of implicit personality theories, but the consistency of our judgments about people.

In thy face I see the map of honor, truth, and loyalty.
Henry VI, Part 2, III, 1
William Shakespeare

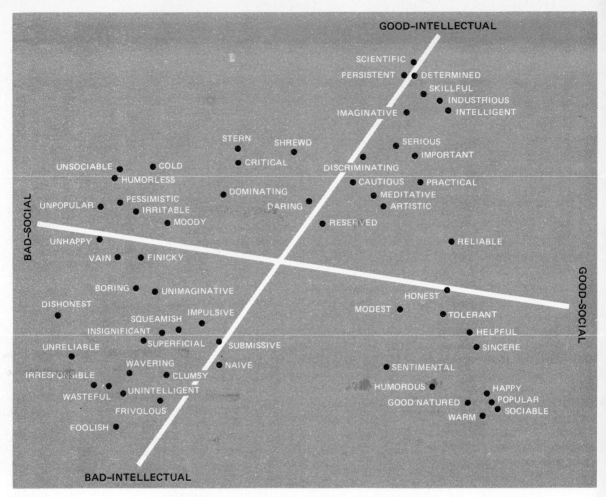

FIGURE 5–1.

A two-dimensional graphic configuration of 60 character traits on which have been superimposed the best-fitting axes representing social desirability and intellectual desirability.

Source: *From "A Multidimensional Approach to the Structure of Personality Impressions," by S. Rosenberg, C. Nelson, and P. S. Vivekananthan,* Journal of Personality and Social Psychology, *1968, 9, 289.*

Identification of implicit personality theories and studies to confirm them are relatively recent. One aspect of such theories, however, was described over half a century ago by Thorndike (1920), who coined the term **halo effect**. This term refers to our tendency to infer other positive (or negative) characteristics from our observation of a single, but major, positive (or negative) trait. In an early study on the halo effect, Kelley (1950) found that different subjects responded differently to the same individuals, depending upon what they had been led to believe about them. Subjects registered more favorable first impressions of the individuals when they had been previously told they would be "very warm" than of those same individuals when they expected them to be "rather cold." This study also corroborated Asch's (1946) findings, described earlier, that *warm–cold* appears to be a central or key personality trait. A more recent study (Nisbett & Wilson, 1977) also showed the halo effect of a warm personality.

Individual Differences   Our dependence on implicit personality theories, then, seems to be supported by research, which also indicates a remarkable consensus of opinion about which personality traits generally seem related. Nevertheless, we know that our views of people and the world we live in are not always shared by others. Kelley (1955) accounts for these differences by explaining that people differ in the systems they devise for understanding the events in their lives. All of us have our own individual organizing system or **personal construct,** which is the result of our unique background, experience, and set of values. For each of us, it serves as a framework to make sense out of the world we inhabit. No two people view an event precisely the same way; in a situation that involves us, we perceive ourselves as the central figure and perceive everyone else as external figures. In other words, we see ourselves as the "hero" of our own story, while other people are inevitably supporting players, judged and perceived by us according to their relationship to our own interests and activities.

Finding a Personal Construct   In the personality research methods just described, the researcher provided the list of character traits that the subject responded to. More revealing of personal constructs, however, are **free response data,** where subjects choose their own terms to describe individuals. Rosenberg and Jones (1972) used literary sources to identify the implicit personality theory

Daniel Linz

What do you think you know about this person? What is your implicit personality theory about a stern-looking, well-dressed individual standing in front of a blackboard?

of a popular American author, analyzing the descriptions of characters in Theodore Dreiser's *A Gallery of Women*. Published in 1929, these 15 short stories are based on the lives of women whom Dreiser had known.

The researchers noted every personal characteristic mentioned in the book that was associated with each male and female figure, and grouped these traits into related categories. The 99 most frequently occurring trait groups were identified in terms of their co-occurrence and analyzed in a variety of ways: for association with male or female or young or old characters, as bad or good characteristics, as dominant or submissive, as conforming or nonconforming, and so on.

You don't judge a book by its cover.

Rosenberg and Jones found that some female characters in *A Gallery of Women* were described as "attractive," "sensual," and "physically alluring," while others were described by "reads," "defiant," and "intelligent." Men were often described as "great," "poetic," "sincere," and "genius." Associated with nonconforming characters were such descriptions as "sad," "suffering," "lonely," and "troubled" (pp. 383–385). Then the resulting trait associations were compared against the known biographical data about the author.

Dreiser, whose sexually liberated life-style was unusual for his time, struggled as a man and as an artist against the standards of his society; his writings were severely edited by his wife and the other women in his life to make them publishable and popular. Thus, the trait associations in this author's writing reflected his personal experiences very clearly: Women were either alluring sex-objects or determined intellectuals, and social rebels clearly suffered.

Integrating Information about Others

Given that we all have notions about others' personality characteristics, how do we process this information? Do we simply add each new piece of information as we perceive it to our previous observations of an individual? Does each observed item of information have the same weight and importance in our perceptions?

Anderson (1968) has proposed a model for information integration. According to this model, our impressions are formed through a kind of averaging process. We start with (1) our own personal tendency to evaluate people in a positive or negative fashion, and (2) mentally "add" all positive information about the person with each item weighted according to its relative importance, and (3) "subtract" all negative information about the person, again weighted according to its importance, and finally (4) "divide" by the total number of items, or take an average, in order to form an overall impression of the person. Suppose, for example, we are told a person is friendly, intelligent, stubborn, and lazy. Figure 5–2 illustrates how we might combine this information to form an overall impression.

Anderson's averaging model has been the basis for some recent studies that show that certain aspects of character traits affect the model in varying ways. In one experiment, subjects were given two neutral traits (that is, a trait that seems to have no bearing on likableness, such as *tall* or *athletic*) and one polarized trait (*trustworthy* or *untrustworthy*) and were asked to evaluate the character of this individual. The subjects who were given the negative characteristic scored the individual low on a likability scale. These subjects were also more convinced of the unlikability of their individual than were the other subjects convinced of

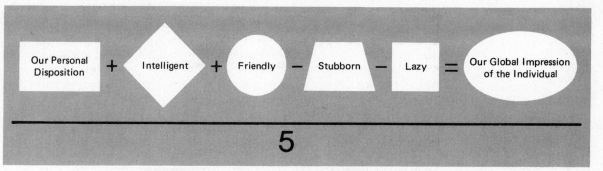

FIGURE 5-2. Anderson's Averaging Model of Information Integration in Impression Formation.

Source: *From "Averaging Versus Adding as a Stimulus–Combination Rule in Impression Formation,"* *by N. H. Anderson*, Journal of Experimental Psychology, *1965, 70, 394–400.*

the likableness of their person (Hamilton & Zanna, 1972). This and other studies indicate that a **negativity effect** is weighted more heavily in impression integration, although Kaplan (1975) has shown that some people emphasize favorable information in forming impressions, while others take a more sour view of their fellow human beings.

There is an important **contextual effect** as well. The same word can have both positive (*daring* and *adventurous*) and negative (*daring* and *foolhardy*) overtones (Zanna & Hamilton, 1977). Also, certain traits in combination are seen more negatively than they would be perceived separately. The role *father* has a positive connotation, while the trait *irresponsible* is usually perceived in a negative way. Rokeach and Rothman (1965), however, observed that the combination of the two—*irresponsible father*—had a far more negative impact than the word *irresponsible* alone. Thus, they determined that a characteristic with a negative evaluation may be judged more negatively when it is combined with a positive word than when it stands alone—perhaps because of the expectations aroused by association with a positive role or trait. This **interaction effect** has a converse side: A trait viewed positively alone, such as *compassionate*, becomes more positive when associated with a negative attribute. Thus, a *compassionate bureaucrat* evokes a positive evaluation because of our expectations that bureaucrats are not compassionate.

Order Effects in Impression Formation

Although the research into implicit personality theories indicates that people generally have a shared view of human personality, this discussion of information integration implies that the way in which we form impressions is neither straightforward nor a one-time process. Exactly how do we go about considering information about, for example, a new acquaintance? We have already seen that the perceived order of positive and negative traits strongly influences our overall impressions (Asch, 1946). Why is this so? Asch theorized that "when the subject hears the first term, a broad, uncrystallized but directed impression is born. The second characteristic comes not as a separate item but is related to the established direction" (Asch, 1946, pp. 271–272). Thus, if we are told that the woman we met at the party last weekend is bright, we are quite prepared to learn that she is also quick-witted and successful. If, however, we later learn that she is unsuccessful, we will not consider her any less intelligent; instead, we may try to find ways to account for this new information.

Primacy Effect   This theory—that the first information received is the most influential—is known as the **primacy effect**. When the information about a person that we receive first influences the meaning we attach to later information, a **change-of-meaning effect** is taking place. An **attention decrement** occurs when, after paying close attention to the information they receive first, people lose interest and pay less attention to subsequent information. Often, too, people discount subsequent information that does not agree with the previous data; this is referred to as the **discounting hypothesis**.

To test the existence of the primacy effect, Luchins (1957) used two paragraphs describing a fictitious person named Jim. In the first paragraph (called paragraph *E* for extrovert), Jim was described as outgoing and extroverted. The second paragraph (called paragraph *I* for introvert) described Jim as withdrawn, introverted, and a bit of a loner. Four groups of students were given these para-

What do you think you know about this person? What is your implicit personality theory about a casually dressed, open-handed individual seated at a table with a bottle of beer? Did you realize that this is the same person whose picture appears on page 173? What would you have thought if you saw this picture first? (To find out who this person really is, turn to page 568.)

TABLE 5-2.

Luchins' Primacy Effects Experiment

Group Reading Paragraph	Percent Extrovert (E) Responses	Percent Introvert (I) Responses
E only	95	3
E before I	78	11
I before E	18	63
I only	3	86

Note: Percentages may not add up to 100 because some subjects failed to respond or gave "both" answers.

Source: Adapted from "Primacy-Recency in Impression Formation" by A. Luchins in C. Houland, et al., *The Order of Presentation in Persuasion*, New Haven: Yale University Press, 1957, 33–61.

graphs and were asked to evaluate Jim as friendly or unfriendly. The groups that saw only one paragraph responded as you might expect—those who were given the *E* paragraph rated Jim as friendly, while those given the *I* paragraph viewed him as unfriendly. But when the two paragraphs were presented together, the group seeing the extroverted material first overwhelmingly rated Jim as friendly, while the group that had the paragraphs in reverse order found Jim to be essentially unfriendly or shy. (See Table 5–2.)

Recency Effects   Some research, however, indicates that later impressions may have a greater impact on our overall judgments. In particular, recency effects occur when subjects are asked to make a separate evaluation after each new piece of information has been presented (Stewart, 1965). Also, when subjects are forewarned to avoid making hasty impressions, the recency effect takes precedence and reduces the primacy effect. If, before meeting a young woman at a party, you had been told that the person you were about to meet doesn't always show her best side to new acquaintances, you would probably be wary about making a judgment. Instead, you might try to see her on other occasions and assume that the later information you acquired was a more accurate picture of her personality. Primacy is also weakened when there is a significant time lag between the presentation of initial trait information and the final judgment (Luchins, 1957).

Organization of Person Perception

We have just examined the variety of factors that contribute to impression formation. How do we put these implicit personality theories and personal constructs to work for us? How do we organize and use the mass of distinct impressions we form?

Schemas

In chapter 4 we introduced the idea of self-schemas. The schema notion can also be applied to our perceptions of others to help us understand how we organize our impressions. Our multiple perceptions of other people constitute the raw data from which, like a complex computer program, we sort and analyze impressions in order to generate usable information. The human mind is a highly sophisticated information processing system, constantly

> scanning the environment, selecting items to attend to, taking in information about those items and either storing it in some form, so that it can be retrieved later for consideration, or using it as a basis for action. (Taylor & Crocker, 1981, pp. 2–3)

We need some basic guidelines to select and store the information that is relevant to our needs. **Schemas** are the categories into which we mentally sort our accumulated information on a given topic. A schema may be defined as a cognitive structure containing our knowledge about some specific domain and its attributes, allowing us to categorize and interpret new information related to that domain (Taylor & Crocker, 1981). Our schema for furniture, for example, might include such separate and distinct items as chairs, lamps, beds, and tables, but might exclude items such as pictures, rugs, and ashtrays, which we perhaps assign to another schema, decorative accessories. Thus a schema can

Does this scene fit your schema for a pediatric examination? Why or why not?

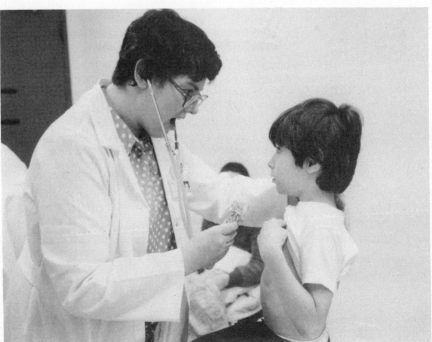

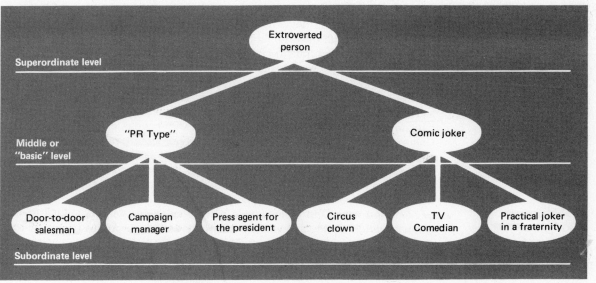

FIGURE 5–3. The "Extrovert" Prototypes for "PR Type" and "Comic Joker."
Source: *From "Prototypes in Person Perception," by N. Cantor and W. Mischel, L. Berkowitz (Ed.),
Advances in Experimental Social Psychology (Vol. 12). New York: Academic Press, 1979, 17.*

be a broad and abstract category (furniture), or it can be more specific (livingroom chair).

Taylor and Crocker (1979) describe three categories of social schemas: for individuals (Mary Jane, my mother), for roles (instructor, parent) or groups (working women), and for events (office party, counseling meeting). Whenever we encounter a person or situation, we use our schemas to predict additional characteristics of the individual or situation so that we can respond or behave appropriately (p. 4).

Our basic schemas for person perception may include **prototypes**. A prototype is a type of schema—one that may represent the "typical" instance of a person or object. For instance, while we might have a general schema for people we categorize as extroverted, we may have a very specific prototype for identifying a "PR Type," (public relations type) which, in turn, greatly differs from the prototype that we associate with a "Comic Joker." Studies using hierarchies of objects and persons (as in Figure 5–3) have shown that people generally use the middle level of specificity to meet their classifying needs. This level allows for both richness of description and differentiation of persons or things.

Cantor and Mischel (1977) studied the ways prototypes function to organize person perceptions. Subjects were given lists of traits representing a specific individual. In some lists the traits were mainly characteristics of an extrovert, in some mainly characteristics of an introvert, and in some the traits were inconsistent. When subjects were asked to recall the traits after a time lapse, they were more successful in recalling them when the pattern was consistent with a prototype than when both extroverted and introverted traits were included. Moreover, when subjects were presented with new, additional traits and were asked if they had been listed, they tended to think that they were when the new traits were consistent with the original trait list. For instance, those subjects who saw the list of extroverted traits might assume that *bold* was on it, because bold behavior was consistent with their prototype for an extroverted person.

Effects of Schemas   Even though we may be unaware of their existence, our schemas influence us in many ways. They enable us to organize and to fill in the gaps in our information in initial encounters with people, objects, or situations. One example of this is found with scripts, which are a type of schema that describes the series of steps one goes through during a particular event. (See Table 5–3.) Bower, Black, and Turner (1979) found that subjects who were given incomplete scripts, with some steps left out, would later "remember" this information as having been included when it actually was not.

Schemas also help us anticipate how other people will act toward us in a given situation. Zadny and Gerard (1974) showed three groups of subjects the identical videotaped skit, but with different introductions. The skit involved two students in the apartment of a third, and contained references to theft, drugs, and waiting for the absent friend. Group 1 was told the two students were there to burglarize the apartment of the third; Group 2 was told the two students knew the third had drugs and were afraid his apartment would be raided; and Group 3 was told that the two students were waiting for the third to return. When quizzed later about what they had seen on the videotape, the subjects assigned specific intentions to the actors who were related to the purpose they had been given. That is, Group 1 saw the actors' behavior as consistently reflecting their intention to rob the apartment even though some of the behavior could just as easily have been attributed to simple boredom or concern for a possible "drug bust." Thus, the activated schema for how the actors would behave influenced the perceptions of how they were behaving.

Schemas also influence the information we recall about people we have met. In one experiment, all participants first read an extensive case history about a woman designated as Betty K. One week later, some subjects were told that Betty was now living with a lesbian partner, a second group was told that she was living with a heterosexual partner, while a third group was not given any further information about Betty's sexual life-style. All were then asked to recall her case history in answering a number of questions that were largely related to sexual preference. For instance, one of the questions was: In high school, Betty (1) occasionally dated men; (2) never went out with men; (3) went steady; (4) no information provided.

Although many of the questions had no basis in the actual case history, a number of answers were influenced by the schemas that were evoked by the information about Betty's sexual preferences. Thus, participants who had been told of Betty's lesbian relationship reconstructed her life based on prototypical beliefs about lesbians. Similarly, those told of Betty's heterosexual relationship "remembered" information that bolstered their schema for that life-style, and forgot or overlooked information that contradicted that schema (Snyder & Uranowitz, 1978). A recent study by Clark and Woll (1981), however, failed to replicate some of Snyder and Uranowitz's results, suggesting that some caution is necessary in generalizing their findings.

TABLE 5–3.
Script* for Restaurant

Name: Restaurant

Props: Tables	*Roles:* Customer
Menu	Waiter
Food	Cook
Bill	Cashier
Money	Owner
Tip	
Entry Conditions: Customer hungry	*Results:* Customer has less money
Customer has money	Owner has more money
	Customer is not hungry

Scene 1: Entering	*Scene 3: Eating*
Customer enters restaurant	Cook gives food to waitress
Customer looks for table	Waitress brings food to customer
Customer decides where to sit	Customer eats food
Customer goes to table	
Customer sits down	
Scene 2: Ordering	*Scene 4: Exiting*
Customer picks up menu	Waitress writes bill
Customer looks at menu	Waitress goes over to customer
Customer decides on food	Waitress gives bill to customer
Customer signals waitress	Customer gives tip to waitress
Waitress comes to table	Customer goes to cashier
Customer orders food	Customer gives money to cashier
Waitress goes to cook	Customer leaves restaurant
Waitress gives food order to cook	
Cook prepares food	

*A script is a kind of schema, which describes the series of steps one must go through during a particular event.

Source: From "Scripts in Meaning for Text" by G. Bower, J. Black, and T. Turner, *Cognitive Psychology*, 1979, *11*, 177–220. Adapted from Schank & Abelson, 1977.

Stereotypes

Thus, at the same time that our schemas complete our scanty store of information, they are also colored by our biases and may lead to erroneous conclusions. A number of studies have supported this (see, e.g., Taylor & Crocker, 1978). A potentially negative aspect of schemas is **stereotyping**. Stereotyping involves reaching conclusions about a person because of that person's membership in a particular social group (Hamilton, 1979). We usually think of stereotypes that are based on ethnic or racial group membership, but it is common for people to hold stereotypes about members of other groups as well: all athletes are dumb, all students are social activists, and so forth. The causes and effects of stereotyping have been studied by social psychologists for a long time. Psychodynamic research studied the value of stereotyping in reassuring the perceiver of his or her own social groupings. Other research saw stereotypes arising from the sociocultural background and experiences of the perceiver. Recently, however, emphasis has shifted to the cognitive bases underlying stereotypes. Does the information-processing method itself cause us to reach biased conclusions about others?

Why Does Stereotyping Occur? According to some research, stereotypes occur when:

1. We recall perceptions in terms of a group rather than in terms of that group's constituent individuals; and
2. We remember exceptional individuals more strongly than those with less distinctive personality traits (Rothbart et al., 1978).

Three interrelated mental processes seem to produce stereotyping effects. First, we process information for mental storage more efficiently in terms of

Stereotypes help us to organize information about our surroundings—but also limit our perceptions.

groups than in terms of individuals, and, second, we reach judgments more readily in terms of group than individual characteristics. Also, third, the greater our memory load and the more demands made on our mental organization systems, the more likely we are to use group categories as a shortcut for identifying and making judgments about people (Rothbart et al., 1978).

Although many stereotypes are based on valid perceptions of individuals that have been generalized to a group, numerous stereotypes are without factual basis. These are derived by illusory correlation, erroneous inferences that are made about associations between traits without any real experience of a relationship (Crocker, 1981). Illusory correlation was undoubtedly responsible, for example, for Shakespeare's portrayal of Shylock in *The Merchant of Venice* as a shrewd, greedy Jewish moneylender—at a time when there had been no Jews in England for several hundred years.

Hamilton and Gifford (1976) showed that even in the absence of relevant information subjects shown two sets of individuals perceived them as being different from each other by the mere fact that they belonged to one of two distinct groups. They concluded that because of the ways social information is processed, group differences are highlighted as a result. Hamilton has also shown that stereotypes persist because of their usefulness in reducing the complexity of our world (1979).

Attribution Models: Theory and Research

Rush-hour commuters hurried by the well-dressed, middle-aged man who was propped, eyes half shut, against the wall in the railroad station. Was he an urban bum who had seen better days, now passing the time idly? Had he been injured in a mugging, or stricken by sudden pain and unable to seek help? Finally one woman stopped to inquire, determined that the situation was merely a matter of a few drinks too many, and helped him on his way.

The ambiguous cues in this actual situation led most viewers to avoid the loiterer. Yet one onlooker correctly recognized the possibility that the man's condition could be attributed to a cause that might require assistance. Attribution is a person's perception of the reasons for other people's behavior. Our responses to other people depend on the attributions or inferences we make about their actions and intentions. If our attributions are accurate, our responses will be appropriate. In the remainder of this chapter we examine research and theories about the attribution process. First we examine the general rules that govern the ways in which we make attributions and then we assess the extent to which these rules serve as accurate guides to our understanding of the social world.

Causality and Naive Psychology

Appearances can be deceitful. The first person to study attributions systematically was Fritz Heider, a professor of psychology at Smith College. In one early experiment, students saw a short animated film in which geometric shapes—a large triangle, a small triangle, and a circle—come together, separate, and move in and out of a rectangle when one of its sides is partially open (see Figure 5-4). Although the shapes were clearly not figures, nearly all viewers interpreted them as people, describing scenes in which the two "males" "fight" over the "female," "chase" one another, try to open the "door" of the "house," and so on. Thus, though the subjects *saw* only geometric shapes in apparent motion, they *attributed* human qualities and moti-

Research: Racial Stereotyping in the 1930s

More than half a century ago, 100 Princeton students were asked to select from a list of 84 adjectives those traits they felt were most typical of each of 10 ethnic or racial groups: Germans, Italians, Negroes, Irish, Chinese, English, Jews, Americans, Japanese, and Turks. This classic study by Daniel Katz and Kenneth Braly found a remarkable uniformity of opinion among the subjects. For instance, 78 percent of the students agreed that Germans were "scientifically minded," 53 percent described Italians as "artistic," 79 percent considered Jews to be "shrewd," and 47 percent believed Turks to be "cruel." Characteristics described by the students for Negroes were consistent with the then popular portrayal of blacks as "superstitious" (84 percent) and "lazy" (75 percent) (Katz & Braly, 1932). (See table on next page.)

Clearly, the exceptional agreement among the students was not the result of personal acquaintance with members of most of these groups, since Princeton students at that time were overwhelmingly white Protestant males. Katz and Braly felt that the racial stereotyping they identified was, in fact, the result of a lack of contact, and that any personal contact with members of these groups was so rare that it actually reinforced generally held stereotypes. They described the mechanism by which this occurs:

> By thus omitting cases which contradict the stereotype, the individual becomes convinced from association with a race that its members are just the kind of people he always thought they were. In this manner

almost any characteristic can become attached to any race and stick there with scarcely any factual basis. (p. 288)

Of course, the makeup of the Princeton student body has changed greatly since the 1930s, and so has the content of racial and ethnic stereotypes. Katz and Braly's study of 1932 was replicated at Princeton in 1951 by Gilbert and again in 1967 by Karlins, Coffman, and Walters. In both instances, the results indicated that many of these stereotypes had changed. For example, in 1967 only 13 percent of the subjects said blacks were superstitious and 26 percent described them as lazy. The ratings for the Japanese demonstrate the influence of the Second World War. In 1951, 17 percent of the subjects rated the Japanese as "treacherous." But these hostilities did not persist: in 1967 only 1 percent used that label. Nevertheless, stereotypes do persist, even though their content may change. In 1967, 47 percent of all subjects rated blacks as "musical," a stereotype that actually increased in frequency over the years.

Do you think that stereotypes have changed since the most recent data in the table were collected? Make your own judgment about the characteristics listed for each ethnic group. Would you agree with more than a quarter of the 1967 respondents that blacks are "happy-go-lucky" or Italians "artistic"? Consider those items that seem to have changed the most. Are these changes due to something the ethnic group has done, or are they in part a reflection of world events? Do you think today's stereotypes are more valid than those of half a century ago?

vations to them (Heider & Simmel, 1944). Heider concluded that the processes involved in perceiving objects are similar to those involved in perceiving people. Thus, viewers attributed human motivations and even emotions to the geometric shapes in the film. Heider believed that we try to discover ordinary or commonsense reasons for behavior—causality—in order to understand and predict events and to feel in control of our environment (1944). Heider referred to this tendency to make commonsense attributions as naive psychology (1958).

Comparison of Stereotype Trait Frequencies for Selected Ethnic Groups

Trait	Percent Checking Trait			Trait	Percent Checking Trait		
	1933	1951	1967		1933	1951	1967
Americans				**Italians**			
Industrious	48	30	23	Artistic	53	28	30
Intelligent	47	32	20	Impulsive	44	19	28
Materialistic	33	37	67	Passionate	37	25	44
Progressive	27	5	17	Musical	32	22	9
Aggressive	20	8	15	Imaginative	30	20	7
Sportsmanlike	19	—	9	Revengeful	17	—	0
Germans				**Japanese**			
Scientifically minded	78	62	47	Intelligent	45	11	20
Industrious	65	50	59	Industrious	43	12	57
Intelligent	32	32	19	Progressive	24	2	17
Methodical	31	20	21	Sly	20	21	3
Extremely nationalistic	24	50	43	Imitative	17	24	22
Efficient	16	—	46	Treacherous	13	17	1
Chinese				**Blacks**			
Superstitious	34	18	8	Superstitious	84	41	13
Sly	29	4	6	Lazy	75	31	26
Conservative	29	14	15	Happy-go-lucky	38	17	27
Tradition-loving	26	26	32	Ignorant	38	24	11
Loyal to family ties	22	35	50	Musical	26	33	47
Deceitful	14	—	5	Very religious	24	17	8
English				**Jews**			
Sportsmanlike	53	21	22	Shrewd	79	47	30
Intelligent	46	29	23	Mercenary	49	28	15
Tradition-loving	31	42	21	Industrious	48	29	33
Conservative	30	22	53	Grasping	34	17	17
Sophisticated	27	37	47	Intelligent	29	37	37
Courteous	21	17	17	Ambitious	21	28	48

Source: Adapted from "On the Fading of Social Stereotypes: Studies in Three Generations of College Students," by M. Karlins, T. L. Coffman, and G. Walters, *Journal of Personality and Social Psychology*, 1969, *13*, No. 1, pp. 4–5.

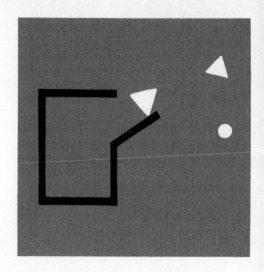

FIGURE 5–4.

Objects in a scene from Heider's animated film: large triangle, small triangle, circle, and rectangle in open position. Only one subject wrote: "A large solid triangle is shown entering a rectangle." Nearly all subjects saw a "dominating" or "powerful male" entering "his house."

Source: *From "An Experimental Study of Apparent Behavior," by F. Heider and M. Simmel,* American Journal of Psychology, *1944, 50, 243–259. Published by the University of Illinois Press. Copyright © by the Board of Trustees of the University of Illinois. Copyright renewed 1977. Reprinted by permission.*

Correspondent Inferences

When we observe another's behavior, we infer meaning from it or attribute intentions to it. When an action and its underlying behavior are both described from an inference, the action and the inference are in correspondence. For instance, suppose you are watching two people painting a poster. You see one giving orders to the other, expressing disapproval of her work and continually remarking on her lack of progress. You might infer that the first person is bossy and domineering. That would be a **correspondent inference,** since your perception would correspond to the observed behavior.

The amount of correspondence varies with the context of the action. If you knew that the first person was assigned responsibility for this task, and that the second person was designated to assist her, you would be less inclined to infer that the first person had an underlying disposition to bossiness. In this case, you would correctly infer that the first person was fulfilling her obligations, and there would be greater correspondence between the observed action and its underlying causes.

The more information one possesses about an action and its causes, therefore, the greater the degree of correspondence all inferences made about that action will have. The more unusual a person's behavior is, the greater correspondence there will be in observers' inferences or explanations for that behavior (Jones & Davis, 1965).

Correspondent inferences are influenced by three factors:

1. *Noncommon effects.* Noncommon effects are elements of the chosen pattern of action that are not shared with alternative patterns of action. If, for instance, a student gets up from her chair, closes a window, and puts on a sweater, we may infer that she is chilly. By itself, though, the action of closing the window could also indicate that she wished to shut out noise from

outside. But the noncommon effect of putting on a sweater allows us to infer that the actions result from the underlying condition of chilliness.

2. *Social desirability.* If there is a perceived social desirability to the actions we are observing, it is far more difficult to infer intentions from behavior. In this situation it is presumed that the person we are observing is making an attempt to be seen favorably. For instance, if you meet a candidate for political office who speaks to you at great length about your own interests it would be difficult to determine if the interest was genuine, because this social behavior may well be an attempt to make a positive impression and gain votes. On the other hand, the *social undesirability* of actions seems to be a good indicator of underlying intentions, precisely because under most circumstances most people avoid creating an unfavorable impression. If the political candidate spoke rudely or lost his temper, you would be likely to decide that those were true aspects of his character (Miller, 1976).

3. *Freedom of choice.* Behaviors that are a product of free choice tend to yield correspondent inferences, whereas behaviors that are a result of constrained or limited choice do not. This was demonstrated in a study by Jones and Harris (1967) where people were asked to read speeches that were either pro-Castro or anti-Castro. Subjects in a condition of choice could choose which of those positions they themselves would agree to speak for; those in a no-choice condition were assigned positions to defend. When subjects were asked to determine the actual beliefs of the person who had written the speech, those who read it under a free-choice condition were more likely to judge that the speech reflected the writer's true attitude.

Correspondent inferences are not necessarily accurate perceptions. They reflect only the information we have about an individual. In making inferences in the absence of detailed information, we tend to rely on whatever information we do have, however limited it may be.

The Covariation Principle

When we seek the causes and effects of actions and events, we are seeking a consistent way to attribute meaning. We assume that cause and effect go together, and that a changed cause will have an altered effect. We assume, then, that causes and effects will co-vary. However, a given effect is usually the result of interaction among a number of causes. According to the **covariation principle**, people look for covariation in three areas: stimulus objects, people, and context. Suppose you went with friends to see a movie, and you laughed loudly throughout. Someone observing you might wonder: Did every viewer find the film so hilarious? Do you always laugh loudly at the movies? Would you have enjoyed the film as much if you saw it at a different time or if you had been alone? Accurate attribution by the observer would depend on factors inherent in the stimulus object (the film), the person (yourself), and the context (time and company).

Kelley's (1967) covariation model asserts that attribution to one of these components (the film, yourself, or the time and company) depends on three aspects of behavior. The value of each of these three behavior variables can be either high or low. Attributions are made either to internal factors (the person) or external factors (the object or the situation), depending on the relative levels of these three variables. These behavior variables are:

1. **Distinctiveness.** A behavior can be accurately attributed to some cause if it occurs only when that cause is present and does not occur when that cause is absent (high distinctiveness).
2. **Consistency.** Whenever the cause is present, the behavior is the same or nearly the same (high consistency).
3. **Consensus.** Others behave in the same manner toward the same entity (high consensus).

In one test of Kelley's model, McArthur (1972) prepared a questionnaire with a number of items reporting the actions of an individual ("George translates the sentence incorrectly"). For each item, subjects were presented with statements representing one of eight possible combinations of consensus, distinctiveness, and consistency information ("Almost everyone translates the sentence incorrectly," or "Hardly anyone translates the sentence incorrectly, etc."). Subjects were asked to choose among the different causes for the behavior noted in the statements. The subjects most often attributed the cause (George's performance) to the stimulus (the difficulty or easiness of the sentence) when high consensus and high distinctiveness information was provided ("Nearly everyone translates this sentence incorrectly"). However, when there was low consensus and low distinctiveness ("No one else translates this sentence incorrectly," or "George generally has trouble translating sentences"), the cause was widely attributed to the person. McArthur's findings are summarized in Table 5–4.

TABLE 5–4.

Covariation of Consensus, Distinctiveness, and Consistency in Leading to Various Attributions

Type of Attribution	Information about the Behavior		
	Consensus	Distinctiveness	Consistency
Person	Low	Low	High
Stimulus	High	High	High
Person–stimulus	High	No significant effect	High
Circumstance	No significant effect	High	Low

Note: Taking the text's example ("George translates the sentence incorrectly"), if the remaining information was low consensus ("Everyone else translates the sentence correctly"); low distinctiveness ("George translates many other sentences incorrectly"); and high consistency ("George almost always translates sentences incorrectly"); then a person attribution would be made.

Source: From "The Know and What of Why: Some Determinants and Consequences of Causal Attribution," by L. A. McArthur, *Journal of Personality and Social Psychology*, 1972, *22*, 171–193.

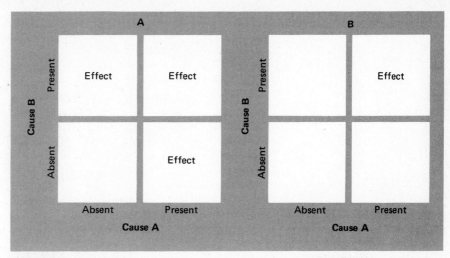

FIGURE 5-5.   A. Causal schema for multiple sufficient causes.   B. Causal schema for multiple necessary causes.

In case A, the event could take place if (1) cause B were present but cause A were absent; (2) if both causes A and B were present; or (3) if cause A were present but cause B were absent. Any of these conditions could be a sufficient cause for the event. In case B, we see that the event could not take place unless both causes A and B were present; both were necessary causes of the event.

Source: *Adapted from "Causal Schemata and the Attribution Process," by Harold H. Kelley. © 1972 General Learning Corporation. Reprinted by permission of Silver Burdett Company.*

Inferring Causes of Behavior or Events

The covariation model is useful for considering patterns of action about which we have some information. However, it does not help us make attributions for isolated actions. How do we judge behavior when we have no information about consistency, distinctiveness, and consensus? To fill this gap, Kelley (1972) proposed a **causal schemata model,** which is "a general conception the person has about how certain kinds of causes interact to produce a specific kind of effect" (pp. 1, 2). Each schema consists of the person's understanding of how various factors might have interacted to produce a particular effect.

When we consider an action or event, we are trying to figure out of a number of possible causes which is the true cause. Kelley observed that in most cases, **multiple sufficient causes** exist that could lead to a given outcome. Some situations, though, by their very nature require specific preconditions or **multiple necessary causes**; in that case, the situation itself tells us some of what we need to know. (See Figure 5-5.) When we try to determine which of the possible sufficient causes is the most likely, we tend to pass over or discount those that are the least plausible; Kelley referred to this as the **discounting principle.**

How do these principles work? Suppose we hear that some young men we knew were hospitalized following an accident: Their car hit a lamppost. Among

It would not be easy to make an accurate attribution for this scene unless one had more information. We can tell you that the place is a university campus in a large city. The occasion is Women's Day. Do you think these two young men are being chastised for a sexist remark? Are they "trying on" a female mask to see what being in a woman's position might feel like? Can you think of any other explanations for this episode?

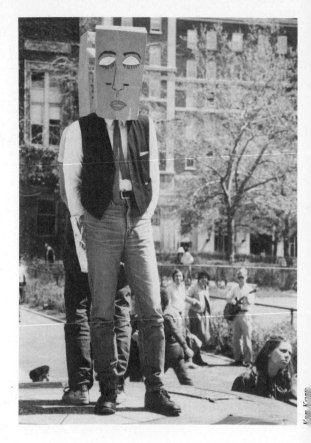

the necessary causes that can readily be determined are that the car was moving, that it had left the roadway, and that its speed was significant. We hear also that the men had been celebrating the coming wedding that night of the driver, that it was rainy, and that the accident took place at some distance from where the men lived. This leads us to think of numerous sufficient causes: low visibility, unfamiliar territory, being "high," or simply not paying attention. If we also know that the accident occurred before the celebration, and that the driver was familiar with the area, we can then discount two of the possible causes (unfamiliar territory, being "high"), and we might well conclude that extremely low visibility was the most likely cause of the accident.

Attributions of Success and Failure

In real life, we must often determine the reasons for success and failure—of our own efforts and of those of others. Why did we do well on an exam, fail to complete the marathon, feel well-liked in a social gathering? Was the result due to a cause in ourselves or to some environmental or outside factor? If the reason is in

Shallow men believe in luck.
Ralph Waldo Emerson

ourselves or in another person whose achievement we are judging, was the outcome a result of ability ("I always test well") or of effort ("I didn't train long enough")? If the result was external, did it relate to the ease or difficulty of the task itself ("It's not possible to run well on such a hot day") or to favorable circumstances ("Everybody was in a mood to enjoy a party just before school started, and a funny thing really did happen to me on the way to the dorm")?

Weiner and his associates (1972) group these causal attributes according to internal or external factors, and to stable or unstable factors. Luck, for example, is an external and unstable factor, since circumstances are highly subject to chance, while ability is internal and (relatively) stable. (See Table 5–5.)

Frieze and Weiner (1971) studied the ways we attribute success or failure. Subjects were given information about an individual's success (or failure) at a particular task, and at similar tasks. They were also given data about the past success (failure) rates of other individuals at that task. They then had to answer a questionnaire about the roles of the internal factors of ability and effort and about the role of the external factors of task difficulty and luck in the success (or failure) story they had read. Table 5–5 summarizes the Frieze and Weiner findings. Subjects were more likely to attribute the successful outcomes than the failures to internal factors. Task ease or difficulty was most frequently attributed to the tasks of those individuals who had a consistent record of previous success or failure at the task. When an individual's performance was consistent with that of others, then outcomes were widely attributed to the nature of the task itself, a stable factor, while an outcome that differed from that experienced by others was sometimes attributed to the stable factor of ability *and* sometimes to the unstable factors of effort and luck. Consistent performance of the same and similar tasks by the same person was attributed overwhelmingly to both stable factors, ability and task difficulty, while inconsistent performance was strongly attributed to both unstable factors, effort and luck.

Actor–Observer Differences in Attribution

Confronted by the same information, do two people arrive at the same conclusions? Nisbett and his colleagues (1973) decided to find out. They asked male students to answer these questions: Why do you like the person you are dating? How would your best friend describe his reasons for liking his current girl-

TABLE 5–5.
Perceived Determinants of Success and Failure

	Internal	External
Stable	Ability	Task difficulty
Unstable	Effort (trying)	Circumstances (luck)

Source: Adapted from "Causal Ascriptions and Achievement Behavior: A Conceptual Analysis of Locus of Control," by B. Weiner, et al., *Journal of Personality and Social Psychology,* 1972, *21,* 239–248

friend? Why did you choose your major subject? Why did your best friend choose his major? The researchers found that different answers were given for the men's own choices and for the choices made by their friends. In answering for themselves, they described their choice in terms of characteristics inherent in their girlfriends or majors ("She's fun-loving and pretty," "It will aid my career"). But when answering for a close friend, the students attributed behavior to qualities in that other person ("He needs someone he can relax with," or "He wants to make a lot of money") (1973).

These findings agree with the hypothesis proposed by Jones and Nisbett (1972) that actors attribute their actions to situational factors, while observers attribute the same actions to personal dispositions (p. 80). It is not surprising that there should be a difference in the attributions made by a participant or actor in an event, and by an outsider or observer. Actors and observers view events from different perspectives, have different motivations, and have different information about the event and its participants as well (Jones & Nisbett, 1971). For one thing, as actors we have information about our own past behaviors and motivations, while as observers we do not know that much about the history of other people's behavior. Would there be less difference in actor–observer perceptions if observers understood more of the background of the situation? One study found that additional information did increase the situational attributions made by observers (Eisen, 1979; see also Monson & Snyder, 1977; Small & Peterson, 1981).

Other experiments have succeeded in altering the actor–observer discrepancy by focusing subjects' attention on the points of view of participants in an event. In one study, observers of a videotaped "get-acquainted" conversation were asked to either view the conversation objectively or to empathize with one of the actors. Observers with an empathetic perspective made fewer attributions to character aspects of the actors and more to situational factors than those who viewed the action objectively (Regan & Totten, 1975).

Attribution Biases

Actor–observer differences in perceptions, like the halo effect that we discussed earlier, indicate that our perceptions follow certain patterns, and that our attributions are not always accurate. To the extent that we perceive inaccurately, our judgments will be biased. A **bias** is a distortion in perception or judgment. Biases can be favorable as well as unfavorable. A bias is quite subjective, and is not based on a fair evaluation.

Beauty is in the eye of the beholder.

Social psychologists have studied the biases in the ways we attribute causes to our own behaviors and to those of others. They generally distinguish between *motivational biases*, which are in some way self-serving, and **cognitive biases**, which arise from the methods people use to process perception-related information. (Some theorists, however, argue that motivational biases arise from cognitive processes, and that attribution errors should not be divided into two categories; see, for example, Miller & Ross, 1975; Nisbett & Ross, 1980).

Motivational Biases

A **motivational bias** is a coloring of perspective that takes place to fulfill a need of the perceiver. One widespread motivation is to enhance ourselves and our efforts in order to increase our self-esteem. As a result, *ego-enhancing biases* have received a great deal of attention.

The subjects of one experiment were experienced classroom teachers. They were asked to teach two prepared arithmetic concepts by using a microphone to speak to students who were allegedly in an adjoining room. After presenting each part of the lesson, the teachers received workbook tests supposedly completed by the "students," and then answered a questionnaire evaluating the students and their own presentations. Student A scored well on his first test while Student B did poorly. At this point in the experiment, the teacher-subjects generally attributed the test results to differing characteristics of the two students. On a second "test," some teachers were shown continued poor work by Student B, while others were shown work indicating that B had improved and was as good as Student A, who continued to perform well. Those subjects who were told that B's performance continued to be poor blamed B, while subjects told that B's performance had improved credited themselves as teachers (Johnson, Feigenbaum, & Weiby, 1964; for other examples of the self-serving bias in operation see Bradley, 1978; Carver, DeGregorio, & Gillis, 1980; Sicoly & Ross, 1977; and Zuckerman, 1979).

It has also been shown (Miller, 1975) that the self-serving bias can be even stronger when the situation is especially ego-involving. In particular, ego-enhancing attributions are more likely to be made when the person performs a task in public, or when the individual is able to choose elements of the task and feel a greater involvement with the outcome (Arkin et al., 1976).

Modesty, however, may override ego. People avoid boasting about their successes, at least in public (Arkin, Appelbaum, & Burger, 1980), but may be less self-effacing in private (Schopler & Layton, 1972).

Illusion of Control Another motivational bias is the belief that we control events when in reality many of the events in our lives are likely to be determined by chance and external causes. Indeed, when we examine the events in our lives it is striking how many might have turned out differently if even one factor had been changed. We acknowledge this all the time: "Being in the right place at the right time" is the way to get a good job; and something favorable happened when "it was my lucky day." Sometimes we ponder a chance event that had a positive outcome: "What if I had taken the other road instead?" And, too often, we find ourselves reflecting on a less happy chance outcome and still assuming responsibility: "If only I hadn't." We desperately want to feel that we control our own lives, but this reflects wishful thinking as much as it reflects reality.

For instance, dice players believe they can control the dice by the way they toss them or by talking to them (Henslin, 1967). Langer (1975) hypothesized that people feel in control when they believe a factor of skill is involved in a chance situation. In one lottery experiment, half the subjects were allowed to choose their own tickets, while the others were given theirs. On the day of the lottery, subjects were individually pressured to resell their tickets. Those who had selected their own demanded higher prices than those who had been given tickets;

Controversy: Why Do We Boost Our Egos? Motivation vs. Cognition

Before an exam, students in an introductory social psychology course were asked to predict their test grades. They were also asked to rate the extent four factors—ability, effort, the test itself, and luck—would influence their performance. When they received their actual test scores, the students were asked to identify which of the four factors had really been responsible for the results. A clear ego-enhancing effect was demonstrated: Students who received A and B scores attributed their success to ability and effort, while those receiving C, D, or F grades blamed test difficulty and bad luck. Seems like a pure and simple case of self-serving bias, but . . .

At the beginning of the semester the students had had unrealistically high expectations of their test scores. On subsequent tests, however, they became more accurate in guessing their grades. And when they did make accurate estimates, the amount of studying they did was cited as the most influential factor. Naturally, those students who had studied a lot expected to do well and, if they succeeded, attributed their success to internal causes; the results met their expectations. Students who did not study a great deal and expected that they would not do well, however, also achieved results that met their expectations and realistically attributed the outcome to their (lack of) effort. Only those who were surprised by the outcome blamed test difficulty or luck (Bernstein, Stephan, & Davis, 1979).

The question arises: Do we claim responsibility only when an outcome meets with our expectations? According to Miller and Ross (1975), success–failure attributions involve this kind of cognitive, but not self-serving, bias. They suggest that people will not claim responsibility when an outcome is unexpected because they do not see a direct relationship between their efforts and the results. People expect success, not failure. They also assume they control a situation when it turns out the way they want. But when an unanticipated and undesirable result occurs, people assume that the situation was out of their control.

According to other researchers, however, the motivation for ego-enhancement is so strong that people even employ it on behalf of other people. Thus, observers attribute success to a person's skill and attribute failure to outside circumstances when they explain the behavior of others (Taylor & Koivumaki, 1976). Karaz and Perlman saw a similar pattern when people predicted the outcomes of videotaped horse races; winning horses, and those whose performances were consistent with their previous records, received more actor attributions (that is, the ability of the horse). Losing horses, however, were excused with circumstantial attributions (the weather, the field, bad luck), and losers whose performances in prior races had been more successful received even greater situational excuses. These researchers suggest that the self-serving bias has been overemphasized in attributions of success, and that a more general bias attributing positive outcomes to internal causes on the part of the self or of others may be the key factor (1975).

The motivational–cognitive bias debate continues. Zuckerman (1979) reviewed a body of studies of success–failure attributions. He found that although there were self-serving explanations for both success and failure in most of the studies, other factors were also identified in significant numbers. Tetlock and Levi (1982) have argued that it is impossible to distinguish between cognitive and motivational theories based on the empirical research now available.

As Miller and Ross (1975) admit, "The self-serving bias hypothesis . . . is too intuitively appealing to be summarily abandoned. (But) the challenge remains for future researchers to assess the relative explanatory values of the motivational and nonmotivational interpretations of asymmetrical causal [self-serving] attributions" (p. 224).

also, a higher percentage of those subjects who had chosen their own tickets re-fused to sell at all. Apparently, their illusion of control (choice) made them place a higher value on the ticket. As a result of this and similar experiments, Langer concluded that in the presence of such factors as competition, choice, familiarity, and involvement, which may, of course, objectively have nothing to do with the outcome of an event, people believe they have control of something even as chancy as a lottery. There is evidence, too, that people attribute control to them-selves or to others when the outcomes are unfavorable or even disastrous. Why should people want to assign blame for events that are clearly beyond their con-trol? People need to believe they can control their own destinies, thus they prefer to view even a negative event as something that could have been controlled. It may be less disturbing to believe that an accident could have been prevented and to blame ourselves for not preventing it, than to believe that we could have done nothing to affect the outcome.

This perception is related to the **just world hypothesis** (Lerner, 1965). People want to believe that they live in a "just world" where good things will happen to good people, and evildoers get what they deserve. Walster (1966) presented sub-jects with a description of an accident. Lennie B parks his car on a hill, sets the handbrake, and leaves. Later the brake cable snaps and the car rolls down the hill. Some subjects learned that the consequences of the accident were trivial (the car hit a tree stump and came to a halt), while others learned that the car was badly damaged. All of the subjects were asked to decide if Lennie had responsi-bility for the accident. Interestingly enough, the subjects assigned *more* guilt to Lennie when the consequences of the accident were great. The reasoning here appears to be in line with the just world hypothesis: I do not want an accident like this to happen to me. Therefore, I believe that accidents like this happen only to those who have done something wrong. Therefore, Lennie must be guilty of carelessness or negligence, even if there is no evidence to support this (Schneider, Hastorf, & Ellsworth, 1979).

It has similarly been observed (Janoff-Bulman, 1979) that rape victims fre-quently blame themselves for their victimization, even when they were randomly attacked by unknown assailants. This overattribution of responsibility for a nega-tive outcome is a desperate attempt on the part of the victim to assert control over life's seemingly random disasters.

Cognitive Biases

Cognitive biases are errors in perception caused by characteristics inherent in the human mental processes. A body of research shows that all of us make sim-ilar errors in attribution and judgment. Analysis of these systematic inaccuracies (that is, the same kinds of errors repeatedly made by experiment subjects) has led to the description of several specific cognitive biases.

Biases in Judgments of Covariation   Social psychologists are interested in the difficulty people have in accurately inferring relationships among events. Does effect Y always follow cause X? Nisbett and Ross (1980) found, for example, that most people were unable to understand the possible combinations of outcomes when two different factors co-varied independently. For example, suppose you are to meet someone for the first time, and are told that his or her attitudes are very similar to yours. Suppose further that you then meet this person and have a pleasant and rewarding interaction. You conclude that you like the person you just met. What caused this liking? It could have been a result of attitude similarity, the rewarding experience, or a combination of the two. Suppose you are then told about another person whose attitudes are similar to yours, but you do not interact with that person. Nevertheless, you conclude that you like him or her. Therefore the liking must be due to the attitude information itself. Different combinations of attitudes and interactions would produce different outcomes: for example, if the person's attitudes were *not* similar to yours you might not like the person. As a "naive scientist," however, you probably do not analyze your feelings in this manner. Crocker (1981) described six steps that the "naive scientist" must take in order to reach a covariation judgment:

1. decide what kinds of data to collect;
2. sample cases from the population of cases (that is, choose representative samples from all known instances);
3. interpret the cases;
4. recall data that have been collected and estimate the frequencies of conforming and disagreeing cases;
5. integrate the evidence; and
6. use the estimate as a basis for making predictions or judgments (p. 273).

As Crocker points out, errors can occur in any of these steps.

We have already examined one example of a relationship bias, inferring a cause-and-effect relationship where none exists (Heider & Simmel, 1944; see also Bassili, 1976). A similar bias is **illusory correlation,** the perception of a relationship between two variables where none in fact exists (Chapman, 1967; Chapman & Chapman, 1967; Ward & Jenkins, 1965). For example, Chapman (1967) found that subjects who were shown pairs of words overestimated the frequency of word pairs that seemed to "go together," such as bacon–eggs, lion–tiger, relative to word pairs that were not related. In fact all types of pairs were shown equally often.

Fundamental Attribution Error   A tendency to overestimate the importance of personal or dispositional factors relative to situational or environmental influences is widespread. Ross (1977) sees it as so pervasive, in fact, that it constitutes a **fundamental attribution error.** A classic demonstration was provided by an experiment in which paired subjects were arbitrarily assigned to be questioners or contestants in an oral quiz game. "Questioners" were asked to make up difficult questions on any subject based on their own specialized knowledge. When all subjects were later asked to rate their own and their partners' general knowledge, the "contestants" systematically overestimated the general knowledge of the "questioners." Thus, they made the fundamental attribution error of underestimating the natural advantage the "questioners" had over them (Ross, Amabile, & Steinmetz, 1977; see also Yandell & Insko, 1977). A recent review of fundamental attribution bias research continues to support Ross's hypothesis (see Jones, 1979). An even more recent study (Harvey, Towne, & Yarkin, 1981) seriously questions the pervasiveness of the fundamental attribution error. These

One that does ill never wants for excuses.
Portuguese proverb

authors suggest that it may be neither "fundamental," since it does not occur under all circumstances, nor an "error," since under some circumstances dispositional attributions may be appropriate. Thus the ultimate importance of the fundamental attribution error has yet to be established.

False Consensus Bias   We regard our own attitudes and behaviors as normal and customary. To the extent that the attitudes and behaviors of other people differ from our own, we regard them as unusual or abnormal. By evaluating our own behavior as the standard by which others should be judged, however, we are exhibiting a **false consensus bias**. That is, we are assuming, without evidence, that behavior in general corresponds to our own. This is, of course, relative; revolutionaries perceive more or less accurately that they are advocating a new and unusual course; burglars expect most people to be home and in bed at 3 A.M. But false consensus bias may lead a tightrope walker to assert that her career choice is no more unusual than that of a physician (Ross, 1977).

Ross, Greene, and House (1977) asked subjects to walk around a college campus wearing large sandwich board signs that read "EAT AT JOE'S." Subjects were told that they could refuse to take part, but that they would be helping the experimenter if they agreed. They were then asked to predict if other students would take part in this experiment, and to make trait inferences about those who agreed or refused to participate. Subjects who agreed to take part in the experiment estimated that 62 percent of their peers would also agree, while those who refused estimated 67 percent would refuse. Moreover, the subjects who did take part made more negative inferences about the personal characteristics of those who did not; likewise, those who did not take part had strong negative feelings about those who did. In other words, subjects believed most people would do as they did, and made strong adverse judgments about those who did otherwise.

Ross (1977) describes another related bias: considering events that do occur but ignoring the significance of what does not happen. For instance, suppose you presented a report at a committee meeting. Afterward you had a vague feeling that the committee members did not respond positively to your message. You search your memory—did you do or say something wrong? You cannot think of anything you did and thus you dismiss the feeling. But it is possible you are overlooking what you did *not* do. Perhaps you failed to ask for feedback, questions, or comments. Perhaps you failed to indicate that you were willing to continue working on the problem. Under such circumstances, you would be more likely to focus on what you did do than what you neglected. But omissions can be just as important in social interaction.

Every shut eye ain't asleep.
Black American proverb

Cognitive Heuristics   Typically, our sensory organs are receiving countless simultaneous messages at all times. Our task is to decipher and interpret this overload in order to decide which stimuli we must respond to, and how to respond. Our response depends on the judgment we make about the significance of a particular input. Our data are limited to what is at hand plus our past experience. Our experience, too, is limited. Somehow, though, we accomplish our task dozens or perhaps hundreds of times a day, and make more or less appropriate responses to the events in our lives. How do we do this?

One answer is that we appear to rely on some fairly standard mental shorthand devices, or **heuristics**. These give us an organizing system to reduce the complexities of observable (or potentially knowable) data. Heuristics constitute our personal information-processing programs. We depend on them continually to make decisions about our world. Usually they allow us to make sound judgments—but they can also cause us to err.

As naive psychologists we are, according to Tversky and Kahneman, incredibly poor statisticians. They identify (1974) three heuristics that contribute to cognitive error:

1. *Availability.* People tend to make estimates of the probability of events based on the availability of relevant information—how well they remember or imagine the event to be remembered. But this often is based on flawed information. A recent study demonstrating the effects of availability in judgments of a defendant charged with a crime was done by Reyes, Thompson, & Bower (1980). These authors manipulated availability by varying the vivid-

Application: Self-Observation on Videotape

The family therapist saw the child cower in the corner of the room, but the child's parents did not as they continued their argument. After a few minutes, however, the therapist succeeded in enforcing a truce. "Is that pretty much what happens when you argue at home?" she asked. Both parents agreed. "Now let's see what's really happening," the therapist said, and turned on the recorded videotape of the incident.

Scenes such as this are taking place daily, as portability, costs, and the easy operation of videotape equipment have made instant playback possible in clinical and other settings. Videotape is used in business, for example, in sales training sessions where new employees act out their roles and then view their own performance. After Alderfer and Lodahl reported that videotape in T-group (sensitivity training) sessions caused greater "openness" (1971), it became popular in groups and therapies.

Studies of the use of videotape in traditional psychotherapy have generally concluded that patients' increased understanding of their own behavior after viewing videotapes aided their progress (Storms, 1973, p. 173). In a number of studies examined in this book, videotape was used to manipulate the information given to subjects and to controls. What can attribution research tell us about the use of this technology in training and therapeutic situations?

Storms (1973) attempted to find out. He used videotape to manipulate the viewpoints of some actors (participants in an introduction conversation) and observers. Two actor-subjects engaged in a conversation while two observer-subjects looked on. All subjects responded afterward to a questionnaire measuring their attributions, each actor-subject answering for his or her own behavior and each observer for the individual actor he or she was observing. Actors typically attributed their behavior to the situation when they were not videotaped and also when they saw a tape showing what they had seen in the original conversation. But when they saw a videotape showing themselves instead of the other participant, actors more often attributed their behavior to internal factors. Meanwhile, observers who now saw both conversing actors instead of only one cited more situational factors.

Why did the change in viewpoint result in the changed attribution? Storms speculates that both actors and observers

ness of trial evidence while keeping its strength constant. For example, one piece of evidence implying that the defendant was drunk was that he staggered and fell against a table at a party, and the vivid version included the fact that in doing so he knocked a bowl of guacamole dip onto a white shag carpet. After a 48-hour delay, subjects were affected by the vividness of the evidence they had been given. When the evidence for the prosecution was vivid they thought the defendant was more likely to be guilty than if the evidence for the defense was vivid—even though its strength was the same in both cases!

2. *Adjustment.* This principle leads one to make estimates and predictions by inappropriately adjusting an initial estimate or value, or by some other partial computation that is insufficient. In one study, subjects were given an initial figure representing an incorrect estimate of the percentage of African countries in the United Nations. Subjects given a high figure tended to lower it somewhat; subjects given a low figure tended to increase it somewhat. But

may have received some totally new information. . . . The actor may have realized for the first time some new aspects of his own behavior; the observer may have seen new aspects of the situation or of the other participant. (1973, p. 172)

What are the implications for the use of videotape in training and therapy? The self-viewing actor, and perhaps patient, according to Storms,

is more likely to accept personal, dispositional responsibility for his behavior and is less likely to deflect responsibility to the situation. (Thus,) the husband or wife who sees himself or herself on videotape may realize for the first time his or her own behavioral contribution to the marital conflict and may be more willing to place a dispositional blame on himself or herself. (1973, p. 174)

In other words, videotape may work in some therapeutic situations because it enhances a traditional goal of therapy: to make a person aware of and accept responsibility for his or her own behavior and its consequences. By emphasizing internal factors, though, self-observation may lead people to underestimate the extent that factors beyond their control are responsible for a situation. And, as Storms points out, videotape could harm patients whose problems are related to poor self-image and low self-esteem. Alcoholics, depressed patients, and schizophrenics have responded negatively to self-observation on videotape (see, for example, Geertsma & Reivich, 1965; Parades, Ludwig, Hassenfeld, & Cornelison, 1969). Storms and Nisbett (1970) suggest that when anxiety is a major aspect of the problem (as in alcoholism, stuttering, insomnia, and many other conditions), and negative personal attributions increase an individual's anxiety, self-observation might be harmful.

As an aid to psychotherapy, then, videotape should be used with informed caution. Storms advises therapists to consider the potential consequences of self-observation for each patient, and to use videotape as an aid only if a personal attribution of behavior will aid the patient's awareness of the problem and help him or her deal with it (1973, p. 175).

all tended to "anchor" their revised estimates around the initial information, instead of trying to bring new information to the problem (Tversky & Kahneman, 1974).

3.   *Representativeness.* We also tend to make estimates of the likelihood of an event based on unrepresentative data that we assume to be representative. Thus we may overestimate the importance of prominent information while ignoring other potentially significant factors.

The errors that arise using the representative heuristic can be further broken down into three kinds: (1) We generally ignore prior probabilities and readily available baseline information. For instance, in one study Tversky and Kahneman showed subjects brief personality descriptions of people supposedly sampled from a group of 100 lawyers and engineers. The subjects were asked on the basis of the descriptions to assess the probability of whether the description fit a lawyer or an engineer. Subjects were told that the group consisted of either 70 engineers and 30 lawyers or 30 engineers and 70 lawyers. An example of one of the descriptions is:

Jack is a 45-year-old man. He is married and has four children. He is generally conservative, careful and ambitious. He shows no interest in political and social issues and spends most of his free time on his many hobbies which include home carpentry, sailing and mathematical puzzles (Kahneman & Tversky, 1973, p. 241).

What would you say Jack is, a lawyer or an engineer, based on the above description? Subjects in this study ignored the probability baseline, and relied instead on their own perceptions of what kinds of personalities were more likely to be associated with each profession. (2) We are also insensitive to sample size, and generally make decisions as though the cases we are familiar with constitute all possible cases. (3) We tend to infer strong relationships or make extreme predictions, instead of realizing that most outcomes fall into a range that clusters around the average. It should be emphasized that the heuristics or rules of thumb that we use to predict outcomes can lead us astray, but they are generally very effective devices for handling the large amounts of complex information we typically encounter in our social world.

Failure to Use Consensus Information   Just as we are imperfect statisticians, failing to use quantitative data that is available to us, it seems we are imperfect detectives as well. We typically ignore evidence that is right before our eyes. We especially overlook consensus information (how other people have behaved) and base-rate information (how many people behave in a given way). In one study, subjects who had been told the actual outcomes of previous experiments did not use that information in predicting their own responses to the experimental situation or in attributing the responses of the original subjects (Nisbett & Borgida, 1975). In another experiment, students who heard a course evaluated by other students were more influenced than those who read the evaluations, even though only a few opinions were presented in the face-to-face situation while many more were represented by the base-rate data (Borgida & Nisbett, 1977). Thus, it appears that we tend to rely more on concrete and specific encounters or cases than on such abstract or nonpersonalized sources of information as statistical tables (Hamill, Wilson, & Nisbett, 1980; Nisbett, et al., 1976). We seem also more likely to infer the general from the particular than the other way around.

Our tendency to overlook consensus information would seem to contradict Kelley's attribution theory that relies on judgments that are influenced by consensus. But it appears that both possibilities coexist. In some situations, apparently, consensus information is relied on. Subjects did, for example, rely on base-rate information in studies when other information was weak or ambiguous (Manis et al., 1980). And Zuckerman (1972) found that when subjects were given consensus information for helping or positive behavior, they tended to use it, whereas they tended to discount or ignore consensus information about cruel or negative behavior. (This is itself a rather nice and positive finding about human nature.) Similarly, Hansen and Donoghue (1977) found that consensus information was taken into greater account by subjects who believed that the information agreed with their own perceptions than when the information seemed to contradict what they themselves believed. In still another study, subjects who were informed about random representative sampling procedures used consensus information, but those who did not learn about the statistical procedure did not use it (Wells & Harvey, 1977).

Perseverance Effects   People do not easily alter their perceptions. We persevere in our social inferences and social theories even when confronted with contradictory information.

For example, subjects in one study who were asked to distinguish real suicide notes from false ones were continually given false feedback. But even after they learned that they had been deceived in the experiment process, they still believed the initial manipulated information (Ross, Lepper, & Hubbard, 1975). Another example of belief perseverance is provided by Lord, Ross, and Lepper (1979), who found that subjects were more likely to accept information that confirmed, rather than contradicted, their own viewpoints.

Such experiments show the failure of the standard postexperiment debriefing (see chapter 2). Debriefing does not always leave subjects with an accurate picture of the study they have participated in; they retain what the experimenters told them in the first place.

Why? Ross (1977) argues that we assign more weight to evidence that is consistent with our first impressions, and that we distort and negate evidence that contradicts those first impressions.

Salience Effects   One conclusion we might draw from the research on cognitive biases is that people are extremely selective in what they perceive and to what they respond. The **salience effect** is a form of attribution bias in which we respond—usually without thinking of what we are doing—to the most outstanding or *salient* stimuli in the environment. As Taylor and Fiske (1978) state,

> the causal attributions people make, the opinions people express, and the impressions they form of others in work or social situations are often shaped by seemingly trivial but highly salient information. (p. 252)

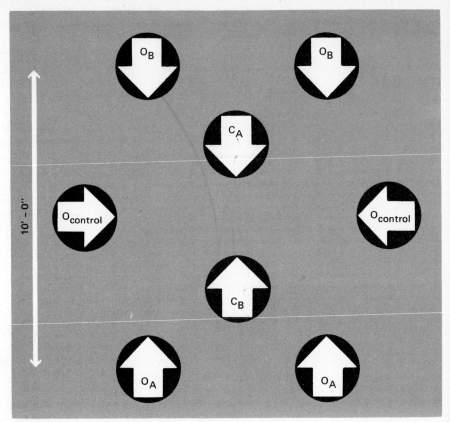

FIGURE 5-6.

Seating arrangement for confederates (C) and (O) with arrows indicating visual orientation.
A and B indicate matched actors and observers.

Source: *From "Point of View and Perceptions of Causality," by S. Taylor and S. Fiske,* Journal of
Personality and Social Psychology, *1975, 32, 439–445.*

They observed that our perceptions of causes are largely a function of what
has caught our attention; what gets our attention is salient (p. 256). If, for example, we are working on a paper with an approaching deadline, we concentrate
on that task and avoid unimportant, competing inputs: the sunny day outside our
window, the distant blare of a phonograph, or a faintly thirsty feeling. However, if
any of these peripheral stimuli become more insistent—a sudden darkening of
the bright day, a crashing noise, or a persistent thirst—we would most likely
leave our task to investigate or attend to whatever has become a more immediate
concern—or most salient.

In one experiment, Taylor and Fiske (1975) manipulated perceptual salience
through a seating arrangement. Six observers watched a staged dialogue between two confederates. The observers were seated so that for two of them, one
confederate (A) was more salient, for two the other confederate (B) was more

salient, and for two control observers both actors were equally salient. (See Figure 5–6.) All observers believed that the actor who was salient for them was the one who set the tone of the conversation and who determined what information was exchanged. The control observers, on the other hand, did not attribute causality to one or the other. This study showed that the actor who dominates an observer's visual field is perceived as the one responsible for an event; this is an example of an **engulfing** or **dominant stimulus effect.**

Motion and novelty are two other factors that affect salience. Subjects have changed their attributions when researchers manipulated lighting and dress. Observers make more dispositional, internal attributions about actors who are brightly lit, moving, or wearing different colored clothing than they do for those who are less salient (McArthur & Post, 1976). Why are salient stimuli more influential? Recently Fiske, Kenny, and Taylor (1982) have suggested that memory processes may mediate (be responsible for) the effects of salience on attributions.

Awareness of Cognitive Processes

People want to believe that they make objective decisions and that they are good judges of character, that their perceptions are not contingent on such trivial matters as novelty and bright lights. But in truth we all appear to be very susceptible to trivial influences. The purpose of much of the original research in person perception was to describe both the processes involved in reaching judgments, and the ways we try to understand what we see. But perhaps you did not recognize some of the perceptual processes we have been discussing. Perhaps you wondered, "Do I really use averaging or the covariation principle to arrive at my perceptions of others? Can I distinguish between a true consensus and a false one?"

These are important questions. As we noted in the last chapter, there is research that confirms that we are not always aware of how our thought processes work.

Taylor and Fiske, in their study of salience noted before, observed that most day-to-day responses are of the "top-of-the-head" variety (1978, pp. 252–253). We admit we have not considered the problem or situation—but we do not hesitate to give an opinion anyway. Salient factors in the immediate situation, such as novelty, motion, visual domination, and color distraction, are far more influential than controlled experiments can indicate.

It also appears that much complex social behavior is performed in a state of "mindlessness;" we often act without thinking. Such behaviors are considered *scripted*. In a series of studies, Langer and her colleagues showed that when a well-learned script (that is, pattern for behavior) does not exist, people are forced to make conscious efforts in their responses. In one experiment, students randomly divided into three groups were intercepted as they were about to use a copying machine. One group was asked to let the experimenter use the machine, but was given no reason for the interruption. A second group was asked to let the experimenter use the machine but was given an "empty" reason—one that really conveyed no information: "May I use the Xerox machine because I have to make copies?" The third group was given a reason that was considered meaningful: "May I use the Zerox machine because I'm in a rush?" Subjects were more likely to comply when they were given a reason, even one that had no meaning—an apparently automatic response. Only when responding required some effort (more work or a greater delay—20 copies as opposed to 5 copies—on the part of the subject) did the adequacy of the reason seem to be a factor (Langer, Blank, & Chanowitz, 1978).

In another study, subjects were asked to speak into a tape recorder about a subject they had obviously considered in the past. When they were asked to speak immediately, their responses were *more* articulate than when they were asked to "think about it" before answering (Langer & Weinman, 1981). Perhaps a "top-of-the-head" response isn't so bad after all!

By definition, a lack of conscious awareness in perception is difficult to demonstrate in an experimental situation. In their studies, Nisbett and Wilson (1977) found that we are often unaware of the stimulus that was influencing our response; that we may be unaware of the kind of response we make to a given stimulus; that we may be completely unaware of being influenced at all. You may remember the nightgown study discussed in the last chapter. In yet another study designed to see if people were aware of what influenced them, subjects were asked to memorize a list of word pairs. Some of the word pairs were meant to set up mental associations that would suggest specific target words later in the experiment. For example, memorizing the word pair *ocean–moon* was expected to cause subjects to say "Tide" when they were asked later to name a detergent. As predicted, subjects who memorized the word pairs consistently came up with the target words twice as frequently as controls who had not been exposed to the associative word pairings. However, when asked to explain why they chose *Tide* over some other detergent, almost none of the subjects mentioned the word association. Instead, they responded with such "top-of-the-head" remarks as, "It's the best known detergent," or, "My mother used Tide."

It appears, then, that people frequently are unable to give an accurate account of their cognitive processes. Moreover, attempts to make them more aware of these processes may even confuse them and interrupt their normal perceptions and judgments. When asked to report on stimulus influence, most people respond not by attempting to understand the process by which they have made an attribution, but instead by creating their own theories about how plausible it is for a particular stimulus to have influenced them.

Of course, we should not overemphasize the problems that arise from our motivational and cognitive biases, our reliance on cognitive heuristics, and our lack of awareness of the subtle influences on our behavior. Even though we, as naive scientists, may not perform perfectly, almost all of us perform adequately in almost all situations. And indeed, people sometimes do understand accurately what influenced their responses (Nisbett & Wilson, 1977).

In closing, it is important to note that person perception is not merely of academic interest. Such practical issues as control of bias and countering negative stereotypes depend on our understanding of our cognitive processes. In order for us to live more rationally together, it is important that we understand how our minds work. Thus, it is important that we study the various ways we judge and perceive—and sometimes misjudge and misperceive.

Answering Questions about Person Perception and Attribution

1. There are several theories describing the ways we combine information about people. According to *central trait theory*, certain key personality characteristics determine our overall impression of an individual. We also have *implicit personality theories* about traits that seem to go together. An *information integration* model holds that our overall impression of a person is a weighted average of our initial disposition and all subsequent information we receive about that individual.

2. According to Cantor and Mischel (1979), we use similar systems for organizing information about people and objects. This system consists of prototypes at three levels: superordinate (e.g., an extrovert), middle (e.g., a "PR Type"), and subordinate (e.g., a door-to-door sales representative). Similarly, an object can be classified as a vehicle, an automobile, and a Ford Falcon.

3. Several attribution biases have been identified in research, which suggests that people are often inaccurate when they attempt to assess causality. These attribution biases include fundamental attribution error, false consensus, and illusory correlation.

4. The theory of correspondent inferences says that people make attributions based on social desirability, noncommon effects, and freedom of choice. Kelley's covariation principle holds that attributions are based on the distinctiveness, consensus, and consistency of the behavior being observed. Finally, Kelley's causal schemata model predicts that attributions will depend on whether there are multiple sufficient causes or multiple necessary causes.

5. People use many shorthand devices, or heuristics, when called upon to predict events. Although these may simplify the task, they often lead to error.

6. Behavior that is well learned or "scripted" is often performed mindlessly or without much thought. When responding requires some effort, information is processed more thoughtfully.

Summary

The study of person perception is the study of how we perceive and judge the behavior and personalities of other people. **Central trait theory** holds that certain personality traits are particularly influential in determining how we see other people. **Implicit personality theories** help us determine other people's behavior. It appears, too, that there is widespread agreement about what traits are associated with each other.

To evaluate another person, we must first integrate all the information we have about that person. When we have inconsistent information we use an averaging model to help weight some characteristics more heavily than others. Other principles that govern information integration include order effects, primacy effect, and the change-of-meaning effect (by which traits can have different values in different contexts).

We rely on schemas or organizing categories to coordinate our perceptions. Schemas are small information-containing systems that help us anticipate how others will act toward us and influence what we recall about an event, scene, or person. Through stereotypes, a kind of schema, we supplement the scanty information available to us. Stereotypes are, however, often based on an illusory correlation of traits.

Attribution theory is concerned with how perceivers determine the causes of behavior. Heider observed that all people are naive psychologists when they try to interpret their observations. We tend to attribute behavior either to internal (subjective or dispositional) or external (situational or environmental) factors.

Correspondent inferences are observations about behavior that agree with other observed actions. Correspondent inferences are enhanced by *non-common effects* (unique aspects), when there is no *social desirability* involved, and when the person being observed is acting under *free choice.*

According to Kelley's covariation model, people assume that two or more associated factors have direct causative relationships. We seek covariance of three aspects of behavior: the *person*, the *stimulus*, and the *context*. The attributions we make depend on distinctiveness, consistency, and consensus.

Kelley also described a causal schemata model for attributions that were made when little information was available. We attempt to locate multiple sufficient causes, identify multiple necessary causes, and use the discounting principle to eliminate least probable causes.

We make internal or dispositional attributions for success and external or situational attributions for failure, of our own or of others' performances. Actor–observer differences are the distinctions in the ways we perceive reasons for our own behavior and that of others. We make more external attributions for other people's behavior and dispositional attributions for our own.

Attribution biases are prejudgments that may be motivational or cognitive in origin. Motivational biases, such as ego-enhancing bias and illusion of control, are in some way self-serving. Cognitive biases, which arise from characteristically human patterns of processing information, include covariation bias, illusory correlation, fundamental attribution error (overestimating the importance of dispositional factors), false consensus, and cognitive heuristics (flawed principles by which we reduce the complexities of information). Perseverance effects describe our tendency to cling to our original, perhaps false, perceptions. The salience effect is the influence of perceptions by seemingly trivial but attention-catching factors.

It seems, though, that we are often unaware of how our higher cognitive processes operate. Instead, we often make "top-of-the-head" judgments, and most of our daily actions are scripted and carried out in a state of "mindlessness." We are often unaware of the influential effect of given stimuli, or even that we have been influenced at all. Despite the problems we encounter, though, our person perception skills do seem to be adequate for most of the social situations we confront.

Suggested Additional Reading

Asch, S. Forming impressions of personality. *Journal of Abnormal and Social Psychology*, 1946, *41*, 258–290.

Harvey, J. H., & Weary, G. *Perspectives on attributional processes.* Dubuque, Iowa: Wm. C. Brown Company, 1981.

Heider, F. *The psychology of interpersonal relations.* New York: Wiley, 1958.

Higgins, E. T., Herman, P., & Zanna, M. P. (Eds.). *Social cognition: The Ontario Symposium.* Hillsdale, N.J.: Erlbaum, 1981.

Nisbett, R. E., & Ross, L. D. *Human inference: Strategies and shortcomings of social judgment.* Englewood Cliffs, N.J.: Prentice-Hall, 1980.

Schneider, D., Hastorf, A., & Ellsworth, P. *Person perception* (2nd ed.) Reading, Mass.: Addison-Wesley, 1979.

6

LONELINESS, AFFILIATION, ATTRACTION, AND SEXUALITY

Questions about Loneliness, Affiliation, Attraction, and Sexuality

1. If you were shipwrecked on a deserted island, how much would the absence of human companionship bother you?
2. Are some people destined to be lonely much of their lives?
3. What qualities do you look for in a friend? How do they differ from the qualities you look for in a lover?
4. How do we know, after one or two encounters, that we like or dislike another person? How often are we later proved wrong?
5. What clues in the behavior of two people allow an observer to assess their relationship accurately?
6. What effect do you think changing sexual attitudes and behavior will have on the structure of society? What do you think will be their effect on the structure of the family?

In the *Symposium*, Plato tells of the "hermaphrodite," a mythical being that inhabited the earth before there were men and women. This creature had human characteristics, but it contained both sexes in one body. Because it was complete in itself, it was so powerful that it rivaled the gods. Therefore, Zeus took one of his thunderbolts and split the hermaphrodite into two sexes. From that time on, according to the myth, men and women have been forced to seek one another out and to join together to overcome their sense of incompleteness.

The myth of the hermaphrodite is a poetic attempt to come to grips with the need for human contact, which we will study in various forms from a social psychological perspective in this chapter. Because "no man is an island entire of itself," as the English poet John Donne wrote, we do not find our meaning in life alone. Rather, we find life's meaning in relation to others—friends, family members, or lovers. When we are deprived of human contact, we experience loneliness. We are attracted to people in various ways, and thus the affiliations that we form differ both in kind and in degree. Finally, our sexuality, which in its origins has a biological function, is closely tied to our social needs—which is why it is appropriate to consider it in this chapter on intimate social behavior.

Loneliness

Most people have experienced loneliness at some point in their lives. Yet, if they are asked to explain the meaning of this word, they are often unable to do so, and instead describe how they *feel* when they are lonely. Loneliness, then, is a subjective phenomenon. It is, however, possible for social psychologists to formulate operational definitions of loneliness that allow them to measure it along with its causes and effects, as we shall see.

Loneliness frequently occurs during solitude or isolation, but sometimes people may feel lonely even when they are not deprived of contact with others. Moreover, loneliness is not inevitable even when individuals *are* deprived of human contact. The experience of loneliness and the intensity of this experience vary from person to person and from time to time, according to the situation.

What Is Loneliness?

Most people who experience isolation do not do so by choice. Consider, for example, the elderly person whose spouse is deceased, whose friends have either moved away or died, whose children live in distant cities, and who, on account of physical disabilities or economic condition, is unable to travel far from where he or she lives. A person in this or a similar situation— and there are unfortunately all too many in our society—is likely to experience intense loneliness.

However, in some cases social isolation is self-imposed. Withdrawal from society is practiced by many religious orders, and often by private persons who wish to expand their spiritual horizons or to fulfill some personal goal. For such people, the experience of loneliness, however painful, is an enriching one.

In April 1977, a young Australian woman, Robyn Davidson, began a trek of 1,700 miles across Australia's western desert accompanied by four camels and a dog. She arrived at Ayers Rock National Monument 21 days and 250 miles later and found a friend from her home town who had flown in to meet her. "We talked—or rather, I talked," Davidson wrote, "for four straight days. Having traveled for most of three weeks without company, I had undergone considerable change without realizing it. I babbled on to Jenny like a madwoman, and, as is often the case, one makes oneself better by making others sick. Dear Jen. She flew home feeling depressed, and I rode out of Ayers Rock feeling on top of the world!" (1978, p. 589). Of her long, often physically painful, 195-day journey, with only occasional company of aborigines or homesteaders, Davidson reported that "Some times were miserable. . . . Other times were euphoric, days of extraordinary freedom" (p. 581).

Much the same feeling was expressed by Admiral Richard E. Byrd, after his 6-month, solitary expedition to the Antarctic in 1934. Byrd found the experience of intense loneliness to be an inner confrontation with the meaning of existence. By his own account, Byrd came to recognize "man's oneness with the universe" (1938, p. 85) and to appreciate the simple pleasures of life. Confronted with the harshness of nature and the imminence of death, Byrd learned not to take the preciousness of life for granted.

But it is also possible to be lonely in a crowd, as at a party where you do not know a soul, for example, and the experience of loneliness in this situation can sometimes be more intense than when no one else is present. Perhaps this is because when people go to parties they generally hope to make intimate contact with others; if they are unable to do so, their feelings of loneliness may be heightened by their disappointed expectations.

Loneliness Defined Loneliness, according to Perlman and Peplau (1981), "is the unpleasant experience that occurs when a person's network of social relations is deficient in some important way, either quantitatively or qualitatively"

(p. 31). This definition focuses on the subjective nature of loneliness. It also stresses that loneliness arises from the interaction of a person's need for social contact with the availability of others. What one person experiences as a satisfactory "network of social relations" may be felt as deficient by another.

Forms of Loneliness   Moustakas (1961) has identified two different kinds of loneliness. **Loneliness anxiety,** a totally negative feeling, results from alienation between people. **Existential loneliness,** on the other hand, is a universal aspect of the human condition. It stems from our awareness of ourselves as separate individuals, and from our awareness of the inevitability of death. As existential loneliness broadens our understanding of reality, it stimulates self-confrontation and leads to personal and spiritual growth. Loneliness anxiety, then, is our experience of being "alone in a crowd," while existential loneliness describes the intense experiences of Davidson and Byrd.

Causes of Loneliness

When Bradburn (1969) asked a cross section of Americans the following question, "During the past few weeks, did you ever feel very lonely or remote from other people?" 26 percent answered in the affirmative. The experience of loneliness results from the interaction of situational factors and personal characteristics. Situational factors are events that reduce the quantity or quality of social interactions and thus generally cause loneliness. Personal characteristics may dispose some individuals to becoming lonely or to feeling lonely much of the time. Thus, we must examine both sets of factors.

Situational Factors   Many factors in modern life contribute to the disruption of the individual's network of relationships and hence to loneliness. Peplau and Perlman (1981) identify four kinds of events that reduce social contact and can precipitate loneliness in all of us:

1. Ending a close emotional relationship, as by divorce or death of a partner.
2. Physical separation from family and friends, as by moving to a new community.
3. Status changes, such as unemployment, promotion, or the leaving home of one's children.
4. Reduced quality of an existing relationship. (p. 103)

We live in a highly mobile society, which means that we change jobs, schools, and neighborhoods frequently. Packard (1972) noted that the average American moves 14 times during the course of his or her life. Each move generally involves a separation from friends and community and a termination of relationships. Moreover, there is much in modern life that can cause even those who remain in the same location to feel lonely. Those left behind when neighbors and family members move away may become profoundly lonely; they have lost not only their accustomed social contacts but also experience changes in their familiar environment. City and even suburban neighborhoods have changed rapidly in recent years, and close-knit communities dissolve. As populations grow and

Loneliness can be experienced at any age.

Ken Karp

life becomes more complex, institutions from schools to banks have become more impersonal. The self-service supermarket may speed up shopping chores, but it does not provide the familiar personal exchanges of daily visits to the grocer or to the fishmonger.

In America today, one out of three marriages ends in divorce; and according to the 1980 United States Census, a significantly greater proportion of the population lives alone than formerly. These demographic changes suggest that loneliness may become an increasing problem for Americans generally.

Certain life stages increase the individual's desire for social contact and thus precipitate the experience of loneliness. Rubenstein and Shaver (1979) found that young people were particularly vulnerable to feelings of loneliness, perhaps because at that stage of life there is a greater need for personal intimacy or perhaps because they are at college and away from home. Elderly people—especially those who have lost spouses and close friends—and the divorced are similarly affected. The loneliness of the young is different from the loneliness of the middle-aged or elderly; the former occurs at a time when sexual feelings are intensified, while the latter is often made more bitter by feelings of loss.

Finally, there are extraordinary circumstances when our needs for social contact and intimacy increase, such as when we are about to enter a hospital or are facing a difficult or critical period. At such times, and for some people, a previously satisfactory level of social relations may be experienced as inadequate.

Personal Characteristics Certain people are characteristically more likely to experience loneliness than others, and for these people the experience may be more intense and more enduring. A predisposition to loneliness will not necessarily cause the experience of loneliness at a particular time, but it will make the individual more vulnerable to situational factors.

People who are shy, who think poorly of themselves, or who have inadequate social skills may unwittingly discourage others from making contact with them. Shy people, for example, may be unable to overcome their feelings of self-consciousness and their fears of rejection. In spite of their desire for intimacy, they may shrink from social contact. Such shyness appears to be widespread. Zimbardo (1977) reported that 80 percent of the people in one survey indicated that they had personally experienced feelings of shyness.

Personal characteristics that are considered unattractive or undesirable within a particular social milieu—be they physical, personality, or sociocultural characteristics—hamper a person's ability to make friends, and thus lead to situations when loneliness will be experienced. Moreover, as others respond negatively to these characteristics, the person often reacts either by retreating further from social contact or by resorting to even more bizarre behavior in a futile attempt to gain attention. In this way poor social skills have an increasingly negative effect on the individual's social relationships.

Coping with Loneliness

When people feel lonely they can reduce their need for social contact, increase the quantity or quality of social contacts, or reevaluate the gap between desired and achieved levels of social relations (Perlman & Peplau, 1981). One way people change their need for others is by choosing activities that do not require others. Thus, a woman whose husband has recently died may return to the interest in painting that she had set aside while raising a family.

Increasing contact with others can be achieved by meeting new people or by deepening existing relationships. Thus, a student dissatisfied with the social relationships in his dormitory may join a club or make a special effort to become closer to his roommate.

Finally, people cope with loneliness by reducing their expectations to fit the reality of their situation. They may develop new interests and abilities, a positive adaptation, or they may turn to alcohol or drugs to compensate for unsatisfactory social relationships—a negative adaptation.

As this negative coping strategy indicates, and the rest of our discussion implies, loneliness exacts a cost from the individual and society. We know from personal experience, and from our discussion of human development in chapter 3, the importance of social contact for human beings. In the section that follows, we will examine the ways people meet their need for interaction with others.

Affiliation

Despite its importance in our lives, surprisingly few studies have explored friendship. How do we meet and make friends? What do we do with our friends when we spend time with them?

Everyday Affiliation

Deaux (1978, unpublished) asked students to record their activities at 15-minute intervals for 3 days. Subjects of both sexes spent approximately 12 percent of their time with a person of the opposite sex, 15 percent of their time with a person of the same sex, and about 25 percent of their time alone. However, there was a difference in the amount of time that men and women spent with groups of the same sex: Men spent 20 percent of their time with other men, while women spent only 14 percent of their time with other women.

Deaux found that women spent about 1 hour more each day talking than men did, and that women spent more time talking to another woman than men spent talking to another man. In a related study, Deaux found that women held more numerous longer conversations than men did, an average of 10.7 versus 7.0 in 3 days.

The findings of Deaux's self-reporting study may be compared to those found by Latané and Bidwell (1977), who observed students on two campuses. Here, both young men and women spent significantly more time in groups than they did alone, with 65 percent of the women observed in groups as against 55 percent of the men. The social instincts of these students were alive and well: Questionnaire responses from students leaving a cafeteria indicated that 66 percent ate lunch with other students whom they had either planned to meet or encountered in the cafeteria. Of students entering the cafeteria alone and not finding a friend to eat with, 40 percent decided to leave rather than to eat alone. A significantly higher percentage of women than men were in the group that decided to leave rather than to stay and eat alone.

Familiarity breeds contempt.

But we do need time alone. Rasmussen (1973) found that when people see too much of one another, they begin to behave negatively toward one another. Altman et al. (1971) conducted a laboratory study of men who were cooped up together for 8 days. They found the time spent interacting went from 50 percent of their waking hours during the first 4 days to 25 percent during the last 4 days. These findings suggest that those who are confined for long periods in prisons and other institutions may suffer as much from overexposure to fellow inmates as from the lack of significant social contact.

Conditions Promoting Affiliation

Patterns of affiliation that occur under normal circumstances tend to be fairly stable. Psychologists have found, however, that under certain conditions people feel a greater urgency to seek out others than they would ordinarily.

He is my friend who grinds at my mill.
Portuguese proverb

Patterns of affiliation that occur under normal circumstances differ from those that occur in crisis situations. Under normal, everyday circumstances, it is apparent that such factors as age, sex, race, and religion play an important role in influencing affiliation patterns. In crisis situations, ordinary influences may fade. For example, in a classic laboratory study that examined the influence of anxiety (the threat of a series of shocks) on affiliative behavior, Schachter (1959; see box) found that the threat of shocks increased the desire of the subjects to wait with others before the study began.

Research: Stress and Affiliation

The classic experiment on affiliation was conducted by Stanley Schachter (1959). Struck by the fact that emotional stress regularly occurs as a consequence of isolation, he hypothesized that "if conditions of isolation produce anxiety, conditions of anxiety would lead to the increase of affiliative tendencies" (p. 12).

In the experiment that Schachter designed to test this hypothesis, college women who were strangers to one another were divided into two experimental groups. (These students had originally signed up for the experiment to earn a course credit.) Subjects in both groups entered a room where they found the experimenter, a man who was dressed in a white laboratory coat and who introduced himself as "Dr. Gregor Zilstein of the Medical School's Departments of Neurology and Psychiatry." This "Dr. Zilstein" (the name has the ominous ring of "Frankenstein") went on to explain that the students were to participate in an experiment dealing with the effects of electric shock.

In the "high-anxiety" condition, subjects were shown ominous looking machinery and told that the shocks from it would be painful. Dr. Zilstein's script for these subjects included the following remarks:

> Now, I feel I must be completely honest with you and tell you exactly what you are in for. These shocks will hurt, they will be painful. As you can guess, if, in research of this sort, we're to learn anything at all that will really help humanity, it is necessary that our shocks be intense. (p. 13)

These subjects also saw the equipment they would be attached to while the shocks were administered.

In the "low-anxiety" condition, subjects were told that they should not be disturbed by the word "shock." Dr. Zilstein's script for these subjects included the following remarks:

> We would like to give each of you a series of very mild electric shocks. I assure you that what you feel will not in any way be painful. It will resemble more a tickle or a tingle than anything unpleasant. (pp. 13–14)

These subjects were not shown any experimental apparatus.

All subjects were told that they would have to wait outside for 10 minutes while the equipment was being set up. Subjects were given the choice of waiting alone or in the company of others. After all the subjects had indicated their preferences, Dr. Zilstein took off his white coat, told the subjects that they would not be shocked after all, and explained what the real purpose of the experiment was.

The results, as shown in the table, confirmed Schachter's hypothesis. In the high-anxiety condition, approximately 66 percent of the subjects preferred to wait with other subjects, and 6 of the 32 subjects chose not to participate. In the low-anxiety condition, only approximately 33 percent chose to wait with others, and none chose to leave. Schachter concluded that his hypothesis had been confirmed. In a stressful situation (anxiety over the prospect of painful electric shocks), people were eager to affiliate with others.

Relationship of Anxiety to the Affiliative Tendency

	Number Choosing		
	Together	Don't Care	Alone
High Anxiety	20	9	3
Low Anxiety	10	18	2

Source: From *The Psychology of Affiliation* by S. Schachter, Stanford, Calif.: Stanford University Press, 1959, 18.

Fear or Anxiety?   In his classic experiment, described in the box on page 216, Schachter assumed that he was manipulating *anxiety* as a variable. However, most psychologists would now agree that his experiment actually tested the effects of *fear* on affiliative behavior. The distinction is an important one. Fear is elicited by an objectively realistic source of danger, whereas anxiety is not. Most people do find it comforting to be with others when they are afraid. Fear would certainly have been an appropriate response to impending electric shocks. However, as we shall see, anxiety may produce different affiliative behaviors.

Sarnoff and Zimbardo (1961), in an experiment designed to clarify Schachter's findings, attempted to prove that the distinction between fear and anxiety had important implications for affiliative behavior. They were the first to replicate Schachter's experiment, but they used the label *fear* instead of anxiety. In the second part of this experiment, however, the effect of *anxiety* on affiliation was manipulated. In the high-anxiety condition, male subjects were led to believe that they would have to suck on baby bottles, oversized nipples, pacifiers, and other such objects for 2 minutes. It was expected that since these objects are associated with infantile sexuality (according to Freud's theory of development), they would arouse anxiety—particularly in men, for whom breasts retain erotic connotations. In the low-anxiety condition, subjects were told that they would have to put less provocative objects, such as whistles and kazoos, in their mouths.

The researchers found a strong positive correlation between fear and affiliative behavior (confirming Schachter's findings), but a strong negative correlation between anxiety and affiliative behavior. Other experiments have since demonstrated that the semantic distinction between fear and anxiety remains problematic. We are, then, left with the question of *which* stressful situations lead to affiliation and which do not.

Anxiety or Embarrassment?   Although Sarnoff and Zimbardo framed their experiment in terms of "anxiety," the situation they constructed might just as well have been labeled "embarrassment." It stands to reason that when people are embarrassed, they prefer to be alone; indeed, part of the meaning of embarrassment is the desire not to reveal the embarrassing situation. With this in mind, Teichman (1973) attempted to distinguish between the effects of embarrassment and "generalized anxiety" on affiliative behavior. The embarrassment portion of Teichman's experiment replicated the procedure used by Sarnoff and Zimbardo to test the effects of anxiety, and a similar negative correlation was obtained. In the generalized anxiety portion of Teichman's experiment, subjects initially filled out an anxiety inventory. Following this, subjects in the high-general anxiety condition were led to believe that, on the basis of their answers, they would have difficulty coping with certain psychological problems and that they would be required to reveal intimate secrets about themselves in further testing. Subjects in the low-general anxiety condition were told that they would be participating in an innocuous experiment dealing with physiological psychology. Teichman found that affiliative behavior increased for the high-general anxiety subjects.

These studies are somewhat confusing because labels such as "stress," "anxiety," and "embarrassment" encompass a wide variety of actual states. As

Fish, Karabenick, and Heath (1978) point out, the crucial variable in all these studies is whether or not people are ashamed to share their feelings with others. Under conditions of high stress, people are motivated to share their feelings, but if they are afraid that their integrity will be compromised by doing so, they may prefer to remain aloof.

Same State or Other State?   A basic principle of affiliation research is that people generally prefer to affiliate with people who are in "the same boat" rather than with people whose situations are different. In a modification of his original experiment on affiliation (see p. 216), Schachter (1959) demonstrated this principle by dividing his subjects into "same-state" and "different-state" conditions. For both groups, the initial procedure replicated that of the "high-anxiety" condition in the original experiment. However, some subjects were told that they could either wait alone or in the company of other students—that is, with people in the same "state" or condition as the subject. Other subjects were given the choice of waiting alone or with students who were waiting to talk to their advisers about unrelated matters—that is, with people in a different "state" or condition. As Table 6–1 indicates, the affiliative tendency was much greater in same-state subjects than in different-state subjects. Apparently, whether a person seeks out others under conditions of stress is highly dependent on whether these others share similar concerns. Or, as Schachter put it, "Misery doesn't just love any kind of company, it loves only miserable company" (p. 24).

In an experiment intended to refine Schachter's conclusions, Zimbardo and Formica (1963) divided "high-fear" subjects into same-state and other-state conditions on the basis of whether the subjects with whom they would be allowed to wait were in the same stage of the experiment or had already completed it. Again, the affiliative tendency was greater in the same-state subjects. Indeed, "high-fear, other-state" subjects showed a weaker affiliative tendency than "low-fear, same-state" subjects. Zimbardo and Formica also examined the motives for affiliation of all those who did affiliate (see Table 6–2). Whereas emotional comparison for the purpose of knowing how to act was a strong motive for "high-fear, same-state" subjects, this was not the case for "high-fear, other-state" subjects, for whom catharsis (i.e., tension reduction) was an important motive.

In an attempt to distinguish between the effects of fear and anxiety on affiliative behavior, as influenced by same-state or different-state conditions, Firestone, Kaplan, and Russell (1973) replicated the procedure used by Sarnoff and Zimbardo in the experiment discussed earlier (see p. 217). Contrary to their find-

TABLE 6–1.

Affiliating with Others "In the Same Boat"

	Number Choosing to Wait		
	Together	Don't Care	Alone
Same State	6	4	0
Different State	0	10	0

Source: Adapted from *The Psychology of Affiliation* by S. Schachter, Stanford, Calif.: Stanford University Press, 1959, 24.

TABLE 6–2.
Motives for Choosing Affiliation*

	Comfort	Emotional Comparison	Catharsis	Social Curiosity	All Others
High Fear					
Same	43	29	0	14	14
Other	38	6	31	6	19
Low Fear					
Same	25	6	19	38	12

*Percentage of subjects within each condition choosing affiliation for the reason given.

Source: From "Emotional Comparison and Self-Esteem as Determinants of Affiliation," by P. G. Zimbardo & R. Formica, *Journal of Personality*, 1963, *131*, 152.

ings, however, Firestone and his colleagues found that "anxiety" (again, "embarrassment" might be the preferred term here) is not necessarily negatively correlated with affiliation. Subjects in the "anxiety, dissimilar-state" condition (see Table 6–3) preferred affiliation to isolation. It seems that some subjects will prefer to wait with others even when embarrassed—provided the company is ignorant of the subject's embarrassing circumstances.

Theories of Affiliation

Experiments such as the one conducted by Zimbardo and Formica discussed above indicate that there are various possible motives for affiliative behavior. The theories of affiliation that have been developed tend to emphasize either **social comparison** or **stress reduction** as a primary motivational source.

TABLE 6–3.
Effects of Type of Emotion-Arousal and Similarity-of-State on Affiliation

	Number Choosing to Wait	
Experimental Condition	Together	Alone
Fear		
Similar state	20	10
Dissimilar state	14	17
Anxiety		
Similar state	11	19
Dissimilar state	21	11

Source: Adapted from "Anxiety, Fear, and Affiliation with Similar-state versus Dissimilar-state Others: Misery Sometimes Loves Miserable Company" by L. J. Firestone, K. J. Kaplan, & J. C. Russel, *Journal of Personality and Social Psychology*, 1973, *26*, 411. Copyright 1973 by the American Psychological Association. Adapted by permission of the author.

The 92-year-old man on the left was sad and solitary until the somewhat younger man on the right befriended him. Social comparison theory explains that, particularly when people are under stress, it is important to spend time with others who are understanding.

Bartlett / Action

Social Comparison Theory   Social comparison theory (see chapter 4) suggests that we seek out others in order to interpret our reactions and to find social support for these reactions (Festinger, 1954). Particularly when a person is under stress, faced with a threatening, ambiguous, or novel situation, it becomes important to be with others who can understand and clarify an emotional reaction (Schachter, 1959; Cottrell & Epley, 1977). According to social comparison theory, people form their identities and establish their sense of reality in relation to others. Consequently, the motivation to seek out others is stronger under conditions of stress than at other times (Gerard & Rabbie, 1961; Wrightsman, 1960; and Zimbardo & Formica, 1963).

How does social comparison function to provide a motive for affiliation? A person under stress must have a plausible basis for comparing his or her situation to that of another person. For example, in Schachter's second experiment (see p. 216), the fact that the subjects expected to receive electric shocks made this shared expectation the salient basis for affiliation. Whether or not they might have had other things in common was not relevant at that point.

Thus, perceived *similarity* to the person or people who serve as the comparison object is important in affiliation. However, the salience of particular personality characteristics or shared experiences depends on the immediate situation and also on how much information the subject has about the others for comparison. For example, in an experiment that manipulated fear in relation to affiliative behavior, Miller and Zimbardo (1966) gave subjects the choice of waiting with other subjects or with people whose personalities were similar but who were not involved in the experiment. In this case the subjects chose to join the people who were not involved in the experiment. Apparently, it was more important for the subjects to have common personality traits with the comparison others than for these others to be in the same situation.

The notion that *uncertainty* leads to affiliation has long been an axiom in affiliation research, although it has not been established in all cases (Cottrell & Epley, 1977). Nevertheless, new studies continue to show the importance of uncertainty. For example, Mills and Mintz (1972) told subjects in three experimental groups that they would be given a drug and then would subsequently be tested on their vision and hearing. In one group, the subjects were given 300 milligrams of caffeine (a stimulant) and were told that they were receiving an analgesic (relaxant); in the second group, the subjects were given the same 300 milligrams of caffeine and were correctly informed that they were receiving a stimulant; and in the third group, the subjects were given a placebo of milk–sugar lactose but were told that they were receiving an analgesic. After the drugs had either actually or (in the case of the placebo) supposedly been allowed to take effect, all of the subjects were given the choice of participating in 1 of 4 experiments. They were told that each would require a 10-minute adaptation period and that for 2 experiments this period would have to be spent alone.

Subjects in the "caffeine–analgesic" condition had a significantly higher tendency to choose the wait-with-others experiments than either the "caffeine–stimulant" or "placebo–analgesic" subjects. The implication is that in the caffeine–analgesic condition, subjects were confused by their physiological reactions and sought out comparisons with others for this reason. Subjects in the caffeine–stimulant condition required no confirmation of their experience because it corresponded to what they had been told. Subjects in the placebo–analgesic condition were also misinformed, but since their information was not contradicted by drug-induced physiological arousal, any uncertainty they may have experienced was probably less than that of the subjects in the caffeine–analgesic condition.

In most of the experiments that have attempted to validate social comparison theory, the comparison others have been strangers to the subjects. Psychologists have little direct information so far about how the prior existence of social relationships and the strength of those relationships affect affiliation (Cottrell & Epley, 1977). It seems reasonable to expect, however, that when people feel compromised by a particular situation, they will weigh the costs of confiding in various acquaintances. In some types of situations, an existing social relationship may discourage affiliation (Buck & Parke, 1972).

Reduction of Arousal   Social comparison theory suggests that we affiliate to interpret and receive support for our responses. Some psychologists emphasize instead a reduction of arousal as a primary motive for affiliation, particularly for people who are under great stress or anxiety (Cottrell & Epley, 1977). This view holds that under conditions of stress (fear or anxiety, for example), we seek out others for "creature comfort," to distract ourselves from our own reactions, and as models of relaxed (i.e., desirable) behavior (Epley, 1974). Thus, where social comparison theory suggests that we seek out others on the basis of *similarity*, arousal-reduction theory proposes that, under conditions of high stress, we seek out others on the basis of *difference*, so that we can change our own reactions to a more comfortable level.

Rabbie (1963) provided support for arousal-reduction theory through an experiment in which subjects monitored the emotional states of coparticipants. Arousal-reduction theory would predict that fearful subjects would avoid others who were fearful. When asked to indicate their preference for waiting with a companion who was calm, moderately fearful, or highly fearful (as shown on a false "emotionality meter") subjects—even those in a highly fearful state—showed the least preference for highly fearful companions.

Social comparison theory and arousal-reduction theory may both give us some part of the truth; they are not necessarily mutually exclusive. Social comparison theory states that we seek out others to interpret our own reactions. However, it agrees with stress-reduction theory that minimizing unpleasant stimuli is often a major purpose of affiliation. Social comparison theory is perhaps more useful for explaining affiliation in ambiguous situations, when a person has difficulty interpreting his or her reactions without some feedback from others. Under conditions of intense stress, however, when the problem facing the person is quite clear, the stress-reduction theory may be a better guide to understanding the need for affiliation.

Interpersonal Attraction

Attraction has always been considered a mysterious process. Greek mythology portrays Eros, the god of love, as blind. Those struck by his arrows were powerless to resist the charms of whomever they next encountered. Even today, we speak of "falling in love" as if it were an irresistible force over which we have no control. Is attraction really as mysterious as we like to believe in our most romantic moods? Are there identifiable factors that determine whom we choose as friends? In our discussion of affiliation we looked at the circumstances under which people choose to associate with others. In this discussion of attraction we will turn our attention to those whom we choose as close companions, friends, and lovers. Why do we like some people and not others? How do we know when we like someone? How do we find out that others like us? Why do some friendships lose their value after a short time, while others last a lifetime? How and when does "liking" turn into "love"? In this section we will examine this question from a social psychological point of view.

The Determinants of Attraction

We meet people in a variety of social situations. What happens after we say "Hello" usually depends on whether we get some degree of pleasure from being with that other person. Many factors can promote friendship, while others have a discouraging effect. Is it true that "opposites attract"? What is the role of similarity of values or interests? What is it that makes one person popular and another a "loner"? Social psychologists have identified a number of general factors that play a role in attraction, regardless of the personalities of those involved. We will examine some of these: frequency of contact, proximity, similarity, complementarity, physical attractiveness, and reciprocity.

Frequency of Contact Do we like people more if we spend more time with them? Zajonc (1968) found that the more often subjects were exposed to a particular photograph, the more favorably they responded to the person who was pictured. Zajonc therefore concluded that mere exposure enhances attraction, a conclusion subsequently supported by other studies (Moreland & Zajonc, 1979;

Saegert, Swap, & Zajonc, 1973). In general, as people get to know one another better, they respond more favorably to one another—provided that there is some basis for the attraction and that negative factors (racial bias, for instance) do not intervene. Brockner and Swap (1976) found, for example, that we rate people more favorably if we encounter them more often and if their attitudes are similar to our own. But they also found that the effects of familiarity can override a good deal of divergence in attitudes. (See also Insko & Wilson, 1977.)

Where there's honey, there will be flies.
Russian proverb

It has also been observed that the expectation of continued interaction increases liking. In a study conducted by Darley and Berscheid (1967), college women rated prospective partners more favorably than people with whom they expected to have no further contact—even though both of these groups were randomly selected and were therefore equal in attractiveness. Since it would be unpleasant to have extended contact with a person whom one disliked, the expectation of continued interaction might motivate the individual to form a favorable impression of the person in question. (This explanation coincides with dissonance theory; see chapter 8.)

While repeated contact or exposure is the best predictor of favorable impressions, mere familiarity does not necessarily make us like another person. The importance of frequent contact is demonstrated in the strong alliances—and rivalries—that can develop among co-workers over the years. Frequency of contact, though, does not function in isolation from other factors.

Proximity Related to the notion that repeated exposure increases attraction is the notion that proximity or nearness has the same effect. Most of us, indeed, have had the experience of becoming friendly with neighbors or classmates, and the effects of proximity have been supported by several studies. One classic study found that proximity was a key factor in the friendship patterns of married graduate students who had been randomly assigned apartments in a new housing community (Festinger, Schachter, & Back, 1950). The closer the couples lived together, the more likely they were to develop friendships.

An ingenious study was conducted by Segal (1974), who investigated friendship patterns among students at the Training Academy of the Maryland State Police. When the trainees were asked to identify their 3 closest friends at the Academy after 6 weeks of training, the friends they mentioned tended to have names beginning with a letter close to theirs in the alphabet. Since they had been assigned alphabetically to living quarters and to classroom seats, they had more contact with those whose names began with letters close to theirs in the alphabet.

In these studies it is difficult to separate the role of exposure from the effects of proximity; proximity implies frequent contact. How can we explain the strong role of proximity? Apparently, people take care to respond favorably to those whom they expect to see more often. There is also a predictability effect: When you see people more often or at close range, you get to know their habits and can more easily make appropriate responses; moreover, they are responding appropriately and positively to you at the same time, for the same reasons. They want to get on well with you, too. Another explanation comes from dissonance theory: You are likely to experience dissonance ("bad vibes") when you are in frequent or close contact with an unpleasant person, and you therefore try to reduce the dissonance by focusing on the better qualities of your neighbor. It seems, though, that proximity alone is a powerful determinant of liking.

Similarity The notion that people are attracted to those who are similar to them in various respects is contradicted by the proverbial notion that "opposites attract"—i.e., that people seek out those who complement their qualities and needs. Both of these factors are probably operative in most relationships. People need to share things in common with others, but they are also attracted to those who can provide experiences that would not otherwise have been accessible.

In the classic study of the effects of similarity, Newcomb (1961) arranged for 17 male college students to be given rent-free rooms on campus in exchange for participating in his study. The students were first given an attitude questionnaire and then assigned roommates. In some cases, the roommates held similar attitudes and in other cases they held dissimilar attitudes. During each week of the study, the students filled out questionnaires measuring their attitudes to their roommates. Newcomb found that the roommates chosen on the basis of similarity were more likely to develop close friendships.

Application: Proximity Reduces Prejudice

Social psychologists have found that prejudice is often the result of the lack of personal contact between different social groups (see chapter 10). When people have negative stereotypes about the members of other social groups, they tend to maintain their distance from them—this, in turn, tends to perpetuate their prejudices.

Deutsch and Collins (1958), in a landmark study, compared the racial attitudes of people living in integrated housing projects in New York City to those of people living in housing projects in Newark, New Jersey, where blacks and whites were assigned to different parts of a particular development. The surrounding neighborhoods and socioeconomic characteristics of the housing projects in both cities were roughly equivalent. Systematic interviews with homemakers and teenagers were conducted in all of the developments. The major finding of the study was that interracial attitudes were significantly more favorable in the integrated housing projects where blacks and whites were in closer contact with one another, and interracial friendships were more likely to develop among both teenagers and their mothers. Moreover, there was some evidence that the more positive racial attitudes of blacks and whites living in the integrated hous-

ing projects extended beyond the home environment to their outside activities. Deutsch and Collins concluded that "the implication of our study is that official policy, executed without equivocation, can result in large changes in behavior and attitudes despite initial resistance to that policy" (p. 622).

Were the results found by Deutsch and Collins the effects of proximity, or could other factors have been involved? Perhaps New Yorkers who were biased refused to be assigned to an integrated project, while those who were relatively free of bias to begin with chose this mode of housing. There is, then, the possibility of a self-selection factor among one, and possibly both, groups of subjects. Those who were biased to begin with might have avoided the housing situation in New York City, while the less prejudiced would not have avoided it. We cannot tell, in this case, for certain. Corroboration for the lessening of prejudice in a situation of interracial contact comes, however, from two other studies: Palmore (1955) found similar results among workers in a meat-packing plant, and Mann found similar results (1955) among university students in a classroom.

To test the hypothesis that similarity is correlated with attraction, Kandel (1978) studied the friendship patterns of nearly 2,000 high school students in New York State. The students' attitudes were measured on a variety of issues and socioeconomic and personal data were collected for each. Each subject was then asked to indicate his or her best friend in school. Since these best friends were also included in the subject pool, Kandel was able to correlate each subject's characteristics with those of the friend that he or she had named. Friendship pairs generally proved to be similar, particularly in regard to scholastic level, sex, race, and age. There was also a slighter tendency for friendship pairs to share the same religious and socioeconomic background. It was found, moreover, that the attitudes and activities of friendship pairs were similar, particularly in relation to issues such as drug use.

Kandel's study presents us with a "chicken or egg" question. Did similarity lead to attraction, or do people who are attracted to each other and develop friendships mutually influence each other and thus become similar? There is no doubt that the similarity–attraction process is a cyclical one. Kandel notes, however, that such factors as sex, age, and race are not subject to social influence. Thus, similarity along these dimensions must precede rather than follow friendship. Similarity in attitudes and behaviors, however, may well develop under social influence.

Complementarity   The notion that complementary needs is a foundation for attraction may come from folklore, but it is supported by studies of married couples. Winch (1958) noted that in happily married couples, each spouse manifested qualities that the other lacked.

Seyfried (1977) suggests that, in practice, similarity and complementarity are not opposed to each other because each is involved in the gratification of different needs. The fact is that most people have many different kinds of relationships, with each kind serving a different purpose. For example, a man who loves music may choose friends who share this interest, but as a wife he may choose a woman who possesses the emotional strength that he lacks.

Ken Karp

Secord and Backman (1964) attempted to transcend the similarity–complementarity dualism by suggesting that people are attracted to each other on the basis of *congruence*. According to this point of view, we are attracted to people who confirm our self-concept. Confirmation may be obtained from people whose characteristics are either similar or complementary to our own. For example, a woman who conceives of herself as independent might be attracted to someone with a similar self-concept; but she might just as well be attracted to someone whose feelings of dependency and need reinforce her self-image.

Beauty is a good letter of introduction.
German proverb

Physical Attractiveness   To say that physical attractiveness is an important component of sexual attraction is, of course, to employ circular reasoning. Social psychologists have, however, found that physical attractiveness, as defined by cultural stereotypes, plays an important role in our choice not only of sexual partners but of friends and role models as well. People in our society place a premium on physical attractiveness and associate it with other socially desirable characteristics. For example, Dion, Berscheid, and Walster (1972) found that people who were perceived as physically attractive were presumed to be more intelligent, happy, and successful, and to make better husbands and wives, than people who were not perceived as physically attractive. In other words, as the authors suggest, people still subscribe to the medieval doctrine that physical beauty is an expression of inner, spiritual beauty. Dion and her colleagues, however, did not conclude that this doctrine is always false.

Where the hostess is handsome, the wine is good.
French proverb

The fact that people treat attractive people more favorably than unattractive people may itself facilitate the development of other socially desirable characteristics. For example, an attractive child who receives more attention and encouragement may do better in school than a less attractive child. Indeed, unattractive children are picked on or singled out for criticism more often by their peers and by their teachers.

Attractive people are seen as having more social skills than unattractive people (Goldman & Lewis, 1977) and as being more talented than unattractive people (Landy & Sigall, 1974); they are also apparently judged to be less guilty by juries (Landy & Aronson, 1969). Dermer and Thiel (1975), however, found that attractive people are more likely to be seen as vain and as more likely to be involved in extramarital affairs than unattractive people. Moreover, people who were thought to use their attractiveness as an aid in committing crimes received stiffer sentences than usual for the same offense (Sigall & Ostrove, 1975). Attractiveness, then, may be a mixed blessing.

Walster and her colleagues (1966) randomly paired students as partners at a dance, and subsequently questioned them about their responses to their partners. In accordance with the similarity hypothesis discussed above, these researchers had predicted that the subjects would find those partners most congenial who were most similar to them in terms of physical attractiveness. The authors reasoned that the subjects would be realistic in their appraisal of the relative gains and risks involved in seeking out partners, and would therefore choose those who were not necessarily the most physically attractive. As it turned out, however, physical attractiveness rather than similarity was the major determinant of whether a particular subject wanted to date a particular partner.

Other studies, however, have confirmed the *matching hypothesis* originally formulated by Walster and her colleagues in the study cited above. According to this hypothesis, people choose mates who are close to them in terms of physical attractiveness (Berscheid et al., 1971; Walster & Walster, 1969). In a study conducted by Price and Vandenberg (1979), for example, it was found that married couples are often similar in attractiveness regardless of the length of the marriage or their ages.

Reciprocity   Although we may prefer to believe that our likes and dislikes are based on objective criteria, there is clear evidence that we tend to like people who like us. This is reciprocity. Backman and Secord (1959) tested the notion that the perception of being liked both precedes and influences liking. They experimentally manipulated subjects' perceptions of whether or not they were liked by another person, and found that subjects did indeed like those who they thought liked them. However, if their subsequent experience showed otherwise, the attraction diminished.

The stranger says he saw no one in the town; the people he met say they did not see anyone come.
Ashanti proverb

In an important study that offered a refinement of the reciprocity hypothesis, Aronson and Linder (1965) had subjects interact with a confederate who expressed attitudes toward the subjects that were either uniformly positive, uniformly negative, negative turning to positive, or positive turning to negative. Subsequently, the subjects were asked to indicate their attitudes about the confederate. Although the reciprocity hypothesis, as originally formulated, would suggest that the subjects should have responded most favorably to the confederate when he expressed uniformly positive attitudes about them, this was not the case. In actuality, the subjects responded most favorably to the confederate who initially expressed negative attitudes and then changed them to positive ones; they responded least favorably to the confederate who initially expressed positive attitudes that then became negative. In other words, a uniformly positive attitude was valued less than a gain in appreciation. Aronson and Linder suggest that the subjects attributed uniform responses to the characteristics of the confederate, but attributed an attitude reversal to their own characteristics. (Recall our discussion of attribution theory in chapter 5; see also chapter 8.) Consequently, they were more gratified by an attitude that becomes increasingly positive and more hurt by an attitude that becomes increasingly negative.

How We Communicate Liking

There is more than one way to say "I like you." We communicate our feelings to others nonverbally as well as verbally, and sometimes without being aware of it. We often rely on *eye contact* to communicate whether or not we like someone.

Have you ever had the sense that someone was observing you closely, and then looked up to find that it was so? Argyle and Kendon (1967) report that when people become aware that a person is spending more time gazing at them than at others, they infer that they are valued more highly by that person. If we see two people looking longingly—and for a long time— at each other, we assume a close and affectionate relationship exists between them (Kleinke, Meeker, & LaFong, 1974). However, as with all behavior, the meaning of eye contact depends on the context in which it occurs. When a man and a woman gaze at each other, this may indeed indicate mutual attraction; but it may also indicate a predatory attitude toward the man on the part of the woman, and his defending attempt to

Ken Karp

stare her down in return. Staring may also indicate open aggression, as when two boxers glare at each other before a bout. (These and other implications of eye contact are discussed in greater detail in chapter 7.)

The amount of space that two people maintain between themselves is indicative of their relationship. (The subject of distance, or *proxemics*, is also covered in chapter 7.) Distance between people also depends on cultural norms. For example, in American culture, touching behavior between men often connotes homosexuality; in Europe, however, men kiss or hug without sexual overtones.

Status also influences the amount of distance people maintain between each other. We sit closer to those whose status is equal to our own than we do to people of higher or lower position (Lott & Sommer, 1967). Mehrabian (1968) found that, regardless of sex, the more people like one another, the closer together they will come. In addition, Mehrabian found that disliking and lack of trust were accompanied by rigid body posture and asymmetric shoulder orientation.

Theories of Interpersonal Attraction

Now that we have looked at whom we like, and examined some of the ways we show others that we like—or dislike—them, the question remains: Why? Why do we like other people? Why are we attracted to some people and not to others? The most important social psychological theories of interpersonal interaction have been applied to the problem of attraction. These include cognitive balance theory, reinforcement theory, and gain–loss theory.

Cognitive Balance Theory   Balance theory (which will be discussed in greater detail in chapter 8) is based on the notion that people strive to maintain a consistent balance among their attitudes, beliefs, and feelings. Balance theory suggests, therefore, that people will generally like others with similar attitudes and beliefs and dislike others with dissimilar attitudes and beliefs.

Newcomb (1961) used Heider's (1958) three-part model (see chapter 8) to show how liking or disliking may develop when people first meet. According to Heider, if two people (A and B) feel the same way about another person (X, or idea, event, object, etc.), they will be attracted to each other. However, if one likes X and the other does not, they will have an *unbalanced* relationship, and be indifferent to or dislike each other, and A may well try to change B's mind. But suppose you and someone you met at a party are both avid players of Dungeons and Dragons. Or perhaps you both were glad to escape a conversation about a Dungeons and Dragons marathon and thus began talking to one another. According to Newcomb, because the two of you have developed a positive relationship on the basis of your first encounter, when you later disagree about other ideas (or people or objects) you will probably be able to iron out your differences. The model is thus a dynamic one, and it can be extended to represent the relationship between A and B over the course of time.

It is also possible to encounter an unbalanced relationship. In this case you and your new acquaintance feel very differently about Dungeons and Dragons, and on the basis of this first encounter, you would be very surprised if the two of you ever found anything to agree about, and would probably not be eager to meet again to find out.

Newcomb (1971) has noted still another possibility, *nonbalanced* relationships. Here, too, there is a difference in attitudes, but the differences are not really very important to you (you are not a game freak). While a nonbalanced relationship may be less stressful than one that is unbalanced, if there is a cumulation of minor differences over time (that guy does not play bridge, does not like Indian food, will not join the anti-nuclear protest), the two of you would probably choose not to prolong your acquaintance.

There seems to be some logic to the balance theory approach, and all of us

can certainly think of friendships in our own lives that started—or ended—on just such a basis. However, there are a number of problems with this perspective, as you have probably already found. For one thing, Newcomb's focus on one of the two participants in the relationship, A, does not take the behavior of B toward A into account. Moreover, our attitudes are seldom as simple as "like" or "dislike." Rather, we are aware of a whole range of attitudes in between, and we frequently like something (a movie) for one of its components (the music and special effects, for example) but do not care for another aspect (a basically unoriginal good-guys versus bad-guys story line). The same is true of our attitudes toward people.

Reinforcement Theory   Reinforcement theory focuses on the power of a reward (or a rewarding or positive experience) to make us want to continue the behavior that led to the reward. This approach proposes that people will like those whose company is rewarding. We have a positive feeling, or *affect*, then, to a rewarding person.

Clore and Byrne (1974) developed a *reinforcement–affect model* based on the idea that social interactions experienced as rewarding elicit positive feelings while those felt to be punishing lead to negative feelings. Thus we are attracted to people whose presence makes us feel good or who are associated with experiences that are rewarding or have been so in the past.

The reinforcement–affect model, which is based on learning theory (see chapter 3), can encompass situations in which positive or negative feelings can be evoked directly or indirectly by another person. For example, suppose that you are watching a beautiful sunset at the seashore and enjoying it very much. A few yards away, a young woman whom you do not know is also taking in the scene with obvious pleasure. You may be attracted to her directly because of her qualities, or indirectly attracted to her simply because her presence is associated with the pleasurable sunset.

Among ancient peoples, a messenger who was the "bearer of bad tidings" was sometimes severely punished or even killed. This was certainly irrational, since it was not the messenger's fault that the news he was delivering was bad; but the reinforcement–affect model could explain this phenomenon by suggesting that the messenger had become associated with his bad news. It would be nice to think that we do not behave this way today, but Veitch and Griffitt (1976) found that a stranger who had just heard good news on the radio was more liked by subjects than a stranger who was passing on bad news.

Gain–Loss Theory The gain–loss theory, actually a special case of reinforcement theory, suggests that certain changes in praise or criticism are more rewarding or punishing than if the praise or criticism had remained stable. The classic experiment conducted by Aronson and Linder (1965) to demonstrate the effects of gain–loss theory (see p. 227 above) showed that changes from criticism to praise were experienced as more rewarding than stable praise, and that changes from praise to criticism were experienced as more punishing than stable criticism.

Aronson (1969) has pointed out that since praise is expected from one's spouse, a spouse's withdrawal of praise would be experienced as more punishing than if criticism were received from a stranger. Conversely, praise from a stranger would be more rewarding than praise from one's spouse. The net result of this is what Aronson facetiously calls the "law of marital infidelity."

In an experiment designed to test gain–loss theory, Berscheid, Brothen, and Graziano (1976) wondered whether the effects would be the same if the praise or criticism came from two sources instead of one. The results of their single-evaluator versus double-evaluator study confirmed the theory only for the former. Criticism turning to praise was experienced as more rewarding only when the subject was presented with one critic at a time. When there were two critics, however, one of whom gave stable praise while the other expressed criticism that then turned into praise, the subject paid more attention to the stable-praise evaluator and expressed a preference for this person. These results indicate that the *context* in which an evaluation occurs is a significant predictor of attraction within a gain–loss model.

Human Sexuality

For most living beings, sex provides the means of perpetuating their species. For us as human beings, it is a potent emotional and physiological event as well. In our society, sex accompanies, and colors, our deepest personal relationships. Although it is clearly a form of social behavior—and in many ways one of the most important forms of social behavior—human sexuality has become an object of social psychological study only within the last decade. Sexuality has probably always been a delicate topic of inquiry, and the so-called Victorian barriers to open discussion of sexual behavior have only gradually been broken down.

It will be apparent from the materials in this section that social psychological research on sexual behavior is recent in origin. Indeed, much of the research is still at a descriptive stage. You will recall from chapter 1 that the collection of data about a phenomenon is the first step toward the development of a theory. At present there are few distinctive social psychological theories of sexuality, but as a reservoir of knowledge grows, the theories will undoubtedly follow.

What do we know about sexual attitudes and behavior? Most of us learn about sexuality in an almost clandestine manner, and it is difficult for us to assess systematically what we know. It is equally difficult for us to assess our attitudes about sexual behavior. Unfortunately, the popular press and "pop psychologists" have sometimes exploited this situation, publishing "research" on sexual behavior that places more emphasis on titillation than on science.

To take one recent example, Shere Hite in 1981 published *The Hite Report on Male Sexuality*. Although this best-selling book was reportedly based on

Controversy: Can We Really Measure Love?

What is love? Poets and lovers through the ages have asked this question. "Love rules the gods," avowed Sophocles. "Love is complete agreement," said the seventeenth century poet Lope de Vega. "Heaven is love," added Sir Walter Scott a century later. And nineteenth century humorist Josh Billings asserted that "Love iz like the meazles; we kant have it bad but onst, and the later in life we have it the tuffer it goes with us."

But what do social psychologists say? Rubin (1970, 1974) distinguished between the "moderately correlated" feelings of liking and loving (1974, p. 387). He defined liking as a favorable attitude toward another person, while loving involved attachment to and caring for the other person. This distinction is clear in the fill-in questionnaire Rubin devised to measure both emotions. (See Table A.)

It is clear from the questions in Rubin's Love Scale that they apply primarily to the love we feel for a lover, but not to the love of a parent for a child, or vice versa. Berscheid and Walster (1978) take a different approach, distinguishing between *passionate love* and *companionate love*. In passionate love, intense physiological arousal is interpreted in terms of romantic symbols that are deeply embedded in the culture. Passionate or romantic love often involves the *idealization* of the love object in addition to feelings of intense sexual longing. The image of the "knight in shining armor" or of the "gentle damsel" (romantic love, virtually unique to Western or European civilization, originated in medieval times) plays a part in the fantasies associated with this kind of intense (but fleeting) love.

Table A.
Love Scale and Liking Scale Sample Items

Love Scale
1. I feel that I can confide in _____ about virtually everything.
2. If I could never be with _____, I would feel miserable.
3. One of my primary concerns is _____'s welfare.

Liking Scale
1. I would highly recommend _____ for a responsible job.
2. Most people would react favorably to _____ after a brief acquaintance.
3. _____ is the sort of person whom I myself would like to be.

Note: Subjects are asked to fill out the questionnaire in terms of their feelings for their boyfriend or girlfriend, and in terms of their feelings for a platonic friend of the opposite sex.

Source: "Measurement of Romantic Love," by Z. Rubin, *Journal of Personality and Social Psychology*, 1970, *16*, 267. Adapted by permission.

7,239 responses to a questionnaire, the respondents in the study were not a scientifically drawn sample. Rather, nearly 120,000 copies of the questionnaire had been randomly distributed thoughout the country.

The 7,239 respondents are hardly a representative sample of American men, and the scientific value of the 1,200-page book is perhaps best indicated by the fact that vast portions of the book contain direct citations from the questionnaires collected by the author Hite. These quotations, of course, are more gossip than science (Robinson, 1981).

TABLE B.
Mean Love and Liking Scores for Dating Partners and Same-Sex Friends

	Women	Men
Love for partner	89.46	89.37
Liking for partner	88.48	84.65
Love for friend	65.27	55.07
Liking for friend	80.47	79.10

Source: Adapted from "Measurement of Romantic Love," by Z. Rubin, *Journal of Personality and Social Psychology*, 1970, *16*, 268. Reprinted by permission.

In companionate love, on the other hand, there is a greater ability to see the other person as a real individual—apart from one's fantasies. Passionate love is often "blind"; Eros and his arrows have hit the mark again. But when the flames have died down, the couple may find that there is little to hold them together. If the two people are able to discover qualities in each other that foster respect, attachment, and mutual growth, however, they will be able to sustain their relationship in a way that they could not have done if it were based only on the excitement of sexual attraction. This is not to say that companionate love is asexual or even necessarily less passionate than passionate love, but rather that it is based on reality rather than on fantasy.

What is the point of distinctions such as those made by Rubin and those of Berscheid and Walster? Can they tell us anything about social behavior? It was Berscheid and Walster's research on love and affection that drew Senator Proxmire's ire and earned the scientists his "Golden Fleece" award (see chapter 1). Although they concluded that "psychologists know very little about passionate love" (1974, p. 378), their studies supported a two-component theory to explain it: There must be both physiological arousal and the people involved must identify or label the emotion they feel as "love."

Rubin used his scales to derive scores for both loving and liking. He found that the average love scores for women and their boyfriends were virtually identical with those of men for their girlfriends. However, women had higher liking scores for their boyfriends than did men for their girlfriends (see Table B). When Rubin evaluated liking and loving for same-sex friends, he found women loved their women friends significantly more than men loved their men friends, although their liking scores for friends of the same sex were nearly the same. He suggests that male role socialization in our society may cause men to channel their capacity for loving exclusively into opposite-sex relationships.

Studying Human Sexuality

Ethical considerations limit the degree to which social psychologists can use experimental procedures in studying human sexuality. As a result, most of the research findings reported in the following sections are from questionnaires or interviews. Questionnaires can reach a large study population; interviews require a close relationship between the researcher and the subject. Both can be affected by subject-related bias; generally, more liberated and sexually active people, and younger people, would be more likely to agree to answer the most personal kinds of questions. Or people may give socially desirable answers, or not accurately recollect their behavior of last week, last month, or many years ago.

Laboratory studies in sexuality, which were pioneered by Masters and Johnson (1966), make it possible to have controlled conditions, objective observation (part of Masters and Johnson's method included observations by both male and female experimenters), and sophisticated measurements of physiological responses. Subject and researcher bias are potential hazards; and informed consent is essential. There are, moreover, real questions as to whether any laboratory setting can duplicate the privacy of one's own bedroom. The answer can only be a pragmatic one; the laboratory is as close as we can come, and indeed these studies have told us an enormous amount that we could not have learned in any other way (Byrne & Byrne, 1977).

There are many reasons for studying sexual behavior. First, all sciences seek knowledge for its own sake, and although we are starting late to gain knowledge about sexuality, we are no less eager to do so. Second, the importance of sexuality to human life and happiness—and the demonstrated unhappiness that disturbances or disruptions in this can produce—give a practical urgency to learning what we can. Another practical application is that such knowledge may help us control overpopulation of our planet and aid us in planning for the future of humanity. A final reason draws on social comparison theory: What is the range of expressions of human sexuality, and where are we, as individuals, located on that continuum?

Finally, human sexuality permeates virtually all human activities, and has many components. Our discussion in the remaining pages of this chapter will be brief, and focus on sexual attitudes, some varieties of sexual experience, and sexual relationships of cohabitation or marriage. We will not have space to discuss such other topics as childhood sexuality or sexual dysfunction and therapy, which are less directly relevant to the concerns of social psychology. (Information about these and other topics can be found in texts devoted to the subject of human sexuality; see, for example, Nass, Libby & Fisher, 1981; Victor, 1980.)

Changes in Sexual Attitudes and Behavior

It is by now a truism that the "sexual revolution" that began in the 1960s profoundly altered attitudes toward sexuality as well as the actual sexual behavior of the American public. But how much have the attitudes of Americans really changed over the past few decades? How much do these attitudes correspond to actual behavior? Indeed, has behavior truly changed, or has it merely become fashionable to adopt the attitude that "anything goes"? In an era of "permissiveness," some people may be as embarrassed to admit that they hold "old-fashioned" attitudes about sex as their grandparents would have been to talk about the subject at all. And whose behavior has changed, anyway?

It is quite obvious that television programs, movies, and magazines are much more explicit today than they were a generation ago. It is generally agreed that there has been a dramatic shift toward permissiveness in regard to many—if not all—aspects of sexuality. Although not all segments of the public reflect this shift, the expressed attitudes of Americans (if not their underlying ones) are more liberal than they were formerly.

Sources of Sexual Attitudes   We acquire our attitudes toward sex, as toward politics, primarily from parents and peers. Schools, religion, and the media also play a role. Generally, peers and the media push us toward a more liberated attitude, while parents, schools, and organized religion are restraining forces. However, some studies suggest that although people glean information about sex from their peers and the media, the attitudes inculcated by their parents are not easily lost (Nass, Libby, & Fisher, 1981).

Indeed, today the tables seem to be turning, and adult attitudes toward sex are being influenced by the attitudes and behavior of young people. Many a middle-aged couple, envious of the freedom seemingly enjoyed by the "Now Generation" as portrayed in film and television, has eagerly greeted such popular books as *Open Marriage* (O'Neill & O'Neill, 1972), *The Joy of Sex* (Comfort, 1972), and numerous magazine articles. Advocating guilt-free enjoyment of this natural function and, in many cases, providing instruction as well, the popular press and cable television have brought the sexual revolution to people of all ages. Many adults have been glad to change their attitudes (and often behavior as well) with the times. Others, however, have been made more adamantly conservative by what they perceive as a threat to traditional values and mores.

Sexual Behaviors

To see how sexual attitudes and behaviors have changed, we will briefly examine several specific expressions of human sexuality from a social psychological point of view. The topics we will discuss include masturbation, sexual orientation, premarital sex, sex in marriage, contraception, and abortion.

Masturbation   Historically, the only form of sexuality that was officially sanctioned by Western society was sexual intercourse within the institution of marriage. Masturbation was considered sinful. (The term "onanism," a synonym for masturbation, stems from the Old Testament story of Onan who was condemned for "spilling his seed" on the ground.) In medieval and puritanical times, and even in the last century, ingenious devices were used to restrain the body movements of young children in their beds. Then, and more recently, adolescents who engaged in masturbation, or thought of doing so, were burdened by feelings of guilt and even terror, since moralistic tales and folklore linked masturbation to insanity and acne.

Hunt (1974) found that people now feel less troubled about masturbation than they did formerly. While the percentage of males and females who have

Because of changing attitudes, homosexuality is more accepted today than it was in the past. One result has been that parents of homosexuals have become supportive of their children, as shown by this mother who has joined male and female homosexuals in a Gay Pride March in New York City.

ever masturbated has not increased significantly since earlier studies (90 percent of all males and 60 percent of all females), girls are more likely to begin masturbating during adolescence, and young adults of both sexes masturbate more frequently than in the past.

Masturbation is highly effective in producing orgasm—more effective, for some people, than sex with another person. Masters and Johnson (1966) found that masturbation produces more intense orgasms, on the average, than other forms of sexuality. In a study conducted among college students, however, it was found that only 33 percent of the female students and only 9 percent of the male students considered that orgasms produced by masturbation were more intense than those produced by intercourse (Arafat & Cotton, 1974). The reason, of course, is that since sexuality has a strong emotional component in addition to being a physiological response, people prefer sex with a partner to sex alone. Therefore, the subjective experience of orgasm may be more intense during intercourse.

Sexual Orientations Sexual orientation refers to one's preference for a sexual partner. Human sexual preferences can range along a continuum from exclusively male to exclusively female. This is true for both men and women. Individuals with a heterosexual orientation have an exclusive preference for opposite-sex partners. People with a homosexual orientation exclusively prefer partners of their own sex. Bisexuals have sex with both male and female partners.

Although homosexuality is more acceptable than it was formerly, it is still condemned by a majority of Americans. Levitt and Klassen (1974) found that approximately 86 percent of the public viewed homosexual behavior as being "always" or "almost always" wrong. In general, homosexuality is more strongly condemned by those who have not attended college than by college educated people, by older than by younger people, by religious than by nonreligious people, and by those who live in rural environments than by city dwellers (Nass, Libby, & Fisher, 1981; Stephan & McMullan, 1982).

These differences in attitudes toward homosexuals, combined with an increasing tolerance of homosexual behavior in recent years, suggest that people who have a greater exposure to people of different sexual orientations are likely to have a more favorable attitude. Within the past decade both male and female homosexuals have been more open about their sexual orientations, and in a few cities in the United States homosexuals form well organized and highly visible political and social entities. One index of increased public acceptance is the fact that in 1973 the American Psychiatric Association removed homosexuality from its list of mental illnesses.

Sexual Orientation vs. Experience Many people do report having had at least one homosexual experience, but the percentage of individuals who report an exclusively homosexual preference is relatively small (see Table 6-4). Moreover, the percent of those expressing an exclusively homosexual preference appears to have changed little over the years.

Contrary to the stereotype, many people who engage in homosexual activities on a regular basis also maintain heterosexual contacts. In a study conducted by the Kinsey Institute for Sex Research, a significant minority of self-described homosexuals had experienced heterosexual intercourse during the previous year and a majority of the respondents had experienced it at some time in their lives. Moreover, about half the respondents indicated that they had some sexual feelings for the opposite sex (Bell & Weinberg, 1978). Bisexuality may be situational; that is, people who are basically heterosexual may engage in homosexual activity because of a lack of access to the opposite sex—as in prisons, for example. In other cases, bisexuality is the result of choice. Among the population as a whole, however, active bisexuals are relatively rare.

TABLE 6-4.
Percent of the Population Reporting Homosexual Experiences and Homosexual Preferences

	Kinsey Studies (1948, 1953)	Hunt Study (1974)
Males		
Homosexual experiences	37%	25%
Exclusively homosexual	4%	6%
Females		
Homosexual experiences	28%	25%
Exclusively homosexual	3%	3%

Sources: Adapted from *Sexual Behavior in the Human Male*, by A.C. Kinsey, W.B. Pomeroy, and C.E. Martin, Philadelphia: W.B. Saunders, 1948; *Sexual Behavior in the Human Female*, by A.C. Kinsey, W.B. Pomeroy, C.E. Martin, and P.H. Gebhard, Philadelphia: Saunders, 1953; and *Sexual Behavior in the 1970s*, by M. Hunt, Chicago: Playboy Press, 1974.

Premarital Sex and the "Double Standard"   Hunt (1974), reporting on a nation-wide survey, points out that in surveys conducted in 1937 and 1959, only 22 percent of the sample populations found premarital sex acceptable. In 1974, however, between 60 and 84 percent of the male respondents felt that it was acceptable for men, and between 44 and 81 percent felt that it was acceptable for women. (The variance depended on the emotional commitment of the unmarried couple, which was scaled in the questionnaire.) Women, although more restrictive in their expressed attitudes than men, were far more liberated than they had been in earlier surveys. Between 37 and 73 percent felt that premarital sex was acceptable for men and between 20 and 68 percent felt that it was acceptable for women.

A number of recent studies have suggested that the *double standard*—the notion that different sexual norms should be applied to men and women—is declining in the United States (Delameter & MacCorquodale, 1979). One reason for this may be that young adults of both sexes seem to be strongly in favor of premarital sex (Nass, Libby, & Fisher, 1981), and there is evidence that male and female college students now have similar levels of sexual activity (Curran, 1977). However, as Hunt's study shows, the double standard is still with us. Not only do men and women differ in their acceptance of premarital sex in general, but both men and women are less accepting of women egaging in premarital sex. Indeed, this is true even in the most liberal age group, the 18- to 24-year-olds.

Premarital Sex and Its Effect on Marriage   Although most young Americans take a favorable attitude toward premarital sex, a majority of older people continue to disapprove of it, especially for teenagers (Glenn & Weaver, 1979). It is sometimes argued that premarital sex has an adverse effect on marriage, and that when people engage in sex before marrying each other they will become

TABLE 6–5.

Percentage of Husbands and Wives Reporting Various Effects of Premarital Sexual Experience on Their Marriages

	Individuals Who Had Premarital Intercourse with Spouse		Individuals Who Did Not Have Premarital Intercourse with Spouse	
	Husbands	Wives	Husbands	Wives
Favorable effect	22	19	27	50
No effect or mixed effect	63	70	64	45
Unfavorable effect	15	11	8	5

After 20 years of marriage, husbands and wives were asked to evaluate the effect of their premarital sexual experiences on their relationship. The vast majority of both those who had had premarital intercourse and those who had not felt that their premarital activity or lack of activity had a favorable effect or no effect on their marriages.

Source: Adapted from: "Premarital Sexual Experience: A Longitudinal Study" by B.N. Ard, Jr., *Journal of Sex Research* (a publication of the Society for the Scientific Study of Sex), 1974, *10*, 32–39.

bored with the marriage relationship. However, in a longitudinal study addressed to this issue, Ard (1974) found that both those who had and those who had not engaged in premarital sex with their future spouse did not believe their behavior had a negative effect on their marriage. In this study, couples who had been surveyed on a variety of issues, including whether they had engaged in sex with their prospective mates while they were engaged, were contacted 20 years later. The 227 couples (of the original 300) that remained together were queried as to whether they felt their experience had had a positive or negative effect on their marriages. Table 6–5 shows that people—whether or not they had engaged in premarital sex with their future spouses—felt that their experience had had "no effect."

Cohabitation occurs when a couple lives together without being legally married. In 1980, approximately 1.3 million Americans were cohabiting, despite the fact that it was illegal in many states. Although cohabitation has become a social issue, particularly where college students are concerned, it is more common among poor and minority people than among college students (Clayton & Voss, 1977). Cohabitation may be a substitute for marriage or a convenience arrangement, but it is often a prelude to marriage as well.

Bachelor, a peacock; betrothed, a lion; married, an ass.
Spanish proverb

Sexual Behavior and Marriage Although marriage has been presumed by some sociologists to be a declining institution, the fact remains that approximately 90 percent of the population will marry at least once in their lives and that although many of these marriages will end in divorce, many (perhaps most) divorced people will eventually remarry. For most people, marriage continues to be synonymous with raising a family and maintaining a long-term commitment to another person, as well as to establishing roots in a community. Indeed, marriage remains one of the basic American values.

The sexual revolution has, it seems, had a definite effect on sexual behavior within marriage. Surveys indicate that married people tend to have intercourse more frequently than in the past and that married women are more orgasmic than formerly (Masters & Johnson, 1966). However, marital sex is not free from difficulty: A study of letters received by the American Association of Marriage Counselors indicated that 40 percent of the husbands and 20 percent of the wives identified sex as the main problem in their marriages (Pietropinto & Simenauer, 1979). Among the sexual problems that continue to trouble married couples are impotence, premature ejaculation, failure to achieve orgasm, and lack of desire. Both physiological and emotional factors can be involved in sexual dysfunction. The range of effective modern therapies includes hormone treatment and prosthesis implantation as well as guided instruction and psychotherapy.

Although surveys indicate that most Americans strongly disapprove of extramarital affairs, this does not prevent people from having them. Pietropinto and Simenauer (1979) found that 25 percent of the respondents in their study (30 percent of the husbands and 17 percent of the wives) admitted to having had affairs, and some researchers speculate that for people who have been married 10 years or longer the figures are still higher (Nass, Libby, & Fisher, 1981).

What tempts people to have extramarital affairs even though they may disapprove of them? A frequently given answer is dissatisfaction with sex with their spouses. The cliché that "my wife (or husband) doesn't understand me" may, however, be closer to the mark. Certainly, a spouse may fail to meet an important need of his or her married partner. Moreover, sex with one partner can be predictable, and even boring; without question a new, especially illicit, liaison adds "spice" to one's love life. Affairs generally impose profound strains on a marriage, but some people may be so bored with their lives generally that they are willing to risk even the destruction of their marriages that may come with discovery. The underlying causes of marital infidelity are difficult to establish because they are obviously so deeply embedded in contemporary life (Pietropinto & Simenauer, 1979).

Contraception   The sexual revolution is widely believed to have begun with the mass-marketing of birth control pills in the 1960s. In the early 1970s, for example, there was a 30 percent increase in the prevalence of sexually active unmarried women. Unfortunately, the percentage of sexually active teenage girls who did not use any contraception actually increased between 1971 and 1976 (Zelnick & Kantner, 1977). More than 30 percent of sexually active teenage girls never use any form of contraception, and 60 percent use no contraception for the first experience of intercourse.

Negative attitudes toward sex can, paradoxically, lead to sexual activity without contraception (Schwartz, 1973). As Byrne and his associates point out, there are four behavioral steps involved in making contraceptive decisions:

1.   planning to engage in intercourse;
2.   publicly acknowledging the fact, as by seeing a physician for a prescription or going to a drugstore to purchase supplies;
3.   communicating about both sex and contraception to one's partner;
4.   actually using the contraceptive method chosen (1977, pp. 333–335).

Those who consciously plan to engage in sexual intercourse are more likely to plan as well to guard against the risk of pregnancy than those who simply "get carried away." Because premarital sex is still generally frowned upon, young people may be unable or unwilling to admit to themselves the reality of what they are doing and, as a result, fail to take precautions against pregnancy.

Abortion   The subject of abortion is now so controversial that few people are aware that until the 1860s there were few laws against it in the United States. Abortions were common in the early years of the nineteenth century because of the lack of effective contraception. According to reports of physicians of the time, the women seeking abortions were much more likely to be married than unmarried. For many married couples, abortion was less a moral issue than a practical form of contraception (Degler, 1980).

The anti-abortion laws that increasingly came into effect after the Civil War were promoted not by religious groups—which were much less interested in the issue than they are today—but by the medical profession. Their concern grew out of the prevalence of late abortions and fatalities or severe injury suffered by many women. The various state laws against abortion remained in effect until 1973, when the Supreme Court nullified all state laws that restricted a woman's right to choose an abortion during the first 3 months (trimester) of a pregnancy.

Proponents of legal abortion today argue that women should have control over their own bodies and that they must be allowed to choose when and under what conditions they will have children. Proponents also point out that a ban on legalized abortion would result in greater numbers of illegal abortions, which would endanger the lives of many women. Opponents, on the other hand, argue that abortion sanctions the taking of a human life (i.e., that it is "legal murder"). Some also maintain that it encourages premarital sex by eliminating the fear of pregnancy.

As many as 85 percent of the American public have supported legalized abortion in recent polls in specific circumstances: when a woman's health would be endangered by a continued pregnancy; when the fetus is defective (as indicated by prenatal testing); or when pregnancy has resulted from rape or incest. In a Harris Poll conducted in 1975, 54 percent of the public supported first-trimester abortion unconditionally (*New York Times*, 1975). In a 1982 poll of New York State residents, only 6 percent of the respondents advocated a ban on all abortions (Gannett News Service, May 30, 1982).

What about the attitudes of those who are most intimately affected by abortion, the women who undergo it and their male partners? Smith (1973) studied 125 women who had legal abortions, and found that while 22 percent had negative feelings immediately afterward, (guilt, minor depression) a year later only 3 percent expressed strong regret and another 3 percent felt ambivalent. Those most likely to experience regret or guilt were unmarried teenagers who had little emotional support from others.

In contrast, Shostak (1980) studied 100 men, aged 17 to 34, whose partners had undergone abortions and found many of them troubled about the experience as long as a year later. For more than 33 percent of the couples involved, the experience had brought them closer together; however, nearly 50 percent of the men studied felt that their relationships were weakened or destroyed by the experience. Only 10 percent had received counseling with their partners; 40 percent had talked to no one except their partners about the experience.

The Development of Sexual Relationships

A sexual relationship encompasses much more than specific sexual acts and we enter into sexual relationships for reasons that are varied and complex. Before we enter into a sexual relationship, we communicate desirability and availability. We plan (and/or fantasize) for our sexual encounters, try to reduce undesired consequences and increase their pleasurability. We encourage and stimulate our partners in a variety of ways, which in turn enhances our own enjoyment. We try to keep emotionally satisfying sexual relationships alive, and when conflict grows out of our sexuality we are devastated. We will briefly examine some of the pleasures and problems that accompany even a satisfying sexual relationship.

Sexual Communication   Lower animals have evolved specific physiological and behavioral patterns to communicate readiness to engage in copulation, patterns that are basically the same for all members of a species. But sexual communication in humans is much more complex and much less restricted to definite patterns. We use verbal and nonverbal, direct and indirect signals (see Table 6–6 on pp. 242–43). A verbal signal may be relatively direct ("You're beautiful!") or relatively indirect ("Let's get together Saturday night"). Before most people in our society (and many others) establish physical intimacy, they approach the is-

TABLE 6–6.
Men's and Women's Strategies for Influencing Sexual Encounters

Strategy	Definition	Examples	Subject's Sex	Type of Influence — Have Sex	Type of Influence — Avoid Sex
Indirect Reward	Giving gifts, providing services, and flattering the date in exchange for compliance	"I would tell my date that I really liked (———) a lot and make references to (———'s) attractiveness . . ."	Male	2	1
			Female	1	3
Coercion	Punishing or threatening to punish noncompliance by withdrawing resources or services or by sharing negative feelings	"I try to make love [and] if [my date] does not, I get mad," or "If (———) still insists [on making love], I'd remind (———) that it's my apartment and (———) can just leave."	Male	0.5	3.5
			Female	0	11
Logic	Using rational, but not moral, arguments to convince the date to have or avoid sexual intercourse	"I would tell (———) there's no harm—that we are two people with sexual needs", or "I would give reasons why I didn't want to."	Male	2	10
			Female	2	7
Information	Telling the date whether or not sex was desired in a straightforward or direct manner	"I would casually ask (———) if (———) wanted to have sex," or "I would just say that I'm not in the mood."	Male	12.5	15
			Female	8.5	16
Moralizing	Telling the date that it is the influencer's legitimate or socially sanctioned right to have or avoid sexual intercourse	No student in the present study used this strategy for the have sex situation. An example of moralizing in order to avoid coitus is: "I would state directly that that type of relationship is reserved for marriage."	Male	0	6.5
			Female	0	6.5
Relationship conceptual- izing	Influencing a date by talking about the relationship and indicating concern for the date's feelings	"I would tell my date that we have a very strong, close relationship and that it is time to express it through sexual intercourse," or "I would tell (———) very plainly . . . 'The relationship has only just begun. I don't feel we are ready for sex at this stage.'"	Male	9	20.5
			Female	9	27

Category	Description	Sex		
Seduction[a]	A definite plan for getting a date to have sexual intercourse, especially a plan focused on sexual stimulation of the date	Male	39	—
		Female	26	—
Direct				
Manipulation	Hinting at sexual intent by subtly altering one's appearance, the setting, or the topic of conversation	Male	5.5	14.5
		Female	10.5	8.5
Body language	Using facial expressions, posture, physical distance, and relatively subtle gestures to communicate one's sexual intentions	Male	6.5	6
		Female	22.5	8.5
Deception	Giving the date false information	Male	0	0.5
		Female	0	1
Non-scorable		Male	22.5	22
		Female	20	11

Seduction often included the use of body language, manipulation, and other techniques. When the use of other strategies appeared to be organized into an overall seductive plan, the entire approach was coded as seduction, e.g., "First of all I would put on some soft music and offer (——) some wine, then I would start kissing (——) gently and caressing (——'s) body, then I would give (——) a massage with oil."

"The lights would be turned down, some music put on and I'd probably offer a drink with the atmosphere right," or "I would encourage something more cerebral, a chess game etc., so as to get their mind off their intended activity."

"I would test my limits by holding hands, sitting closer to this person . . . doing more listening and minimal talking," or "I would refrain from petting and touching . . ."

Although deception could be used to seek intercourse, in actuality it was only used to avoid sex, e.g., "I would probably lie and say I had my period or didn't have any birth control [technique]."

[a] Seduction is codable only in the "Have Sex" condition

Sources: Adapted from "Come-ons and Put-offs: Unmarried Students' Strategies for Having and Avoiding Sexual Intercourse," by N.B. McCormack. *Psychology of Women Quarterly*, 1979, *4*(2), 194–211.

sue of sex tentatively; indeed, most would think it crude, and would "turn off," otherwise. Much depends on the context in which people meet, of course. In singles' bars people get to the point much faster than those who meet at work or a church picnic. When sexual intercourse is the culmination of a developing intimacy, the two people will probably have made it clear that they regard each other as "special." For some people, the transition from casual acquaintance to hand-holding may be more risky—since it first establishes an intention of intimacy—than actually going to bed will prove to be. For others, the points of risk will be different.

Cavan (1976), asking how we know when we are talking about sex, describes a ritual that begins in an appropriate environment when conversational participants perceive one another as potential sexual partners. Our culture has taught us to interpret some smiles, winks, and jokes as a "come-on," or casual sex talk, that paves the way for a prolonged encounter. Once the potential partner responds in kind, a ritual exchange of information begins, leading to a more open degree of flirtation.

It is sometimes assumed that women take a more indirect approach than men. However, a study by McCormick (1979) showed that men and women were remarkably similar in their strategies for influencing a sexual encounter. Male and female college students were asked to respond to various questions in the context of ten strategic categories for influencing sexual encounters (see Table 6–6). Interestingly, although seduction, an indirect strategy, is widely believed to be used primarily by men, it was the strategy most frequently cited by both men and women. However, men were significantly more likely than women to indicate their desire directly. Both male and female subjects used indirect strategies to indicate when sex was desired but used direct strategies to void it when it was not desired.

Sexual Arousal   For human beings, sexual arousal cannot be separated from complex psychological processes. Victor (1978) developed a social psychological model of sexual arousal in which the distinction was made between sexual arousal per se and erotic response. Sexual arousal, which involves physiological changes, is influenced by erotic response—that is, by the activation or suppression of desire. Erotic response, in turn, is influenced by the person's perceptual set, which is formed as the result of social learning processes (see Figure 6–1).

The cues that activate sexual arousal therefore depend on the person's perceptual set, on cultural norms, and on the situational context. For example, although a nude model in a *Hustler* centerfold is expected to activate sexual arousal, nudity in nudist camps generally does not because it has been defined in a nonsexual way from the outset. Similarly, although the female breast has strong erotic connotations in our society, there are many societies in which women do not cover their breasts and in which breasts play no role in sexuality. Kissing, a highly erotic stimulant for us, is unknown among the Eskimo and some other non-Western cultures.

Sexual Response   Among the factors that influence sexual responsiveness are emotional intimacy, previous sexual experience, and attitudinal predisposition. For most people, emotional intimacy intensifies sexual desire and responsiveness, but for those who associate sexuality with shame or guilt emotional in-

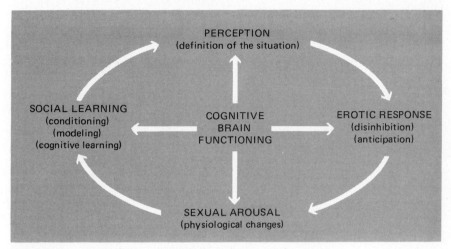

FIGURE 6-1. Factors in the Social Psychology of Sexual Arousal

Victor's model distinguishes between sexual arousal and erotic response. The social learning processes (conditioning, modeling, and cognitive learning) guide our perception of a situation. When we are sexually aroused, we respond with erotic behavior only if we define the situation as one in which that response is appropriate (that is, if the person making advances is physically and socially desirable, if the time and place are right, and so on). However, if our perception of the situation makes an erotic response inappropriate, we "turn off" instead.

Source: *Adapted from* Human Sexuality: A Social Psychological Approach, *by J.S. Victor, 1980. Reprinted by permission of Prentice-Hall, Inc., Englewood Cliffs, N.J.*

timacy may be a barrier to sexual responsiveness. There is some evidence that a greater proportion of men than women are responsive only to impersonal sex (Victor, 1980).

It has sometimes been claimed that men and women experience sexual arousal and orgasm very differently. However, Masters and Johnson (1965) identified four phases of the sexual response cycle (*excitement, plateau, orgasm,* and *resolution*) as being the same for both men and women, although the physiological mechanisms of orgasm and resolution differ. To study whether orgasm itself is experienced differently by the two sexes, Vance and Wagner (1976) obtained descriptions of what an orgasm felt like from both sexually active men and women. They then asked the subjects to identify whether each description had been written by a man or a woman. The descriptions were so similar that the respondents were unable to systematically distinguish whether they described male or female orgasms (see Table 6-7 on page 246).

The Value of Research on Intimate Behavior This chapter has focused on the development of intimate social relationships, beginning with loneliness and moving from affiliation to attraction and finally to sexual behavior. With the exception of studies and theories of affiliation, most of the research on these topics has been conducted only within the past decade. Further study is clearly necessary before we can achieve an integrated and comprehensive understanding of the social psychology of intimate relationships.

TABLE 6–7.
Excerpts from the Sexual Orgasm Questionnaire

Indicate in the space before each description whether you think it was written by a male (M) or female (F).

1. _____ A sudden feeling of lightheadedness followed by an intense feeling of relief and elation. A rush. Intense muscular spasms of the whole body. Sense of euphoria followed by deep peace and relaxation.

2. _____ To me an orgasmic experience is the most satisfying *pleasure* that I have experienced in relation to any other type of satisfaction or pleasure that I've had which were nonsexually oriented.

3. _____ Obviously, *we* can't explain what it feels "like" because it feels "like" nothing else in human experience. A poetic description may well describe the emotions that go with it, but the physical "feeling" can only be described with very weak mechanical terminology. It is a release that occurs after a period of manipulation has sufficiently enabled internal, highly involuntary spasms that are pleasurable due to your complete involuntary control (no control).

4. _____ A build-up of tension which starts to pulsate very fast, and there is a sudden release from the tension and desire to sleep.

5. _____ Begins with tensing and tingling in anticipation, rectal contractions starting series of chills up spine. Tingling and buzzing sensations grow suddenly to explosion in genital area, some sensation of dizzying and weakening—almost loss of conscious sensation, but not really. Explosion sort of flowers out to varying distance from genital area, depending on intensity.

6. _____ Orgasm gives me a feeling of unobstructed intensity of satisfaction. Accompanied with the emotional feeling and love one has for another, the reality of the sex drive, and our culturally conditioned status on sex, an orgasm is the only experience that sends my whole body and mind into a state of beautiful oblivion.

7. _____ Tension builds to an extremely high level—muscles are tense, etc. There is a sudden expanding feeling in the pelvis and muscle spasms throughout the body followed by release of tension. Muscles relax and consciousness returns.

8. _____ A release of a very high level of tension, but ordinarily tension is unpleasant whereas the tension before orgasm is far from unpleasant.

9. _____ Intense excitement of entire body. Vibrations in stomach—mind can consider only your own desires at the moment of climax. After, you feel like you're floating—a sense of joyful tiredness.

Answer key:
1-F; 2-M; 3-M; 4-F; 5-M; 6-M; 7-F; 8-M; 9-F.

Source: Adapted from "Written Descriptions of Orgasm: A Study of Sex Differences," by E.B. Vance and N.N. Wagner, *Archives of Sexual Behavior*, 1976, 5, 87–98.

Some critics have questioned the value of research on intimate behavior, some on the grounds that it is trivial, and others on the grounds that intimate behavior is too important to be tampered with. However, most social psychologists are committed to the view that better research and theories can promote healthier and happier social relationships and relieve problems such as loneliness.

Answering Questions about Loneliness, Affiliation, Attraction, and Sexuality

1. People differ, of course, in the amount of companionship they desire. But you would probably be quite distressed to be stranded on an uninhabited island. After all, you did not choose to be marooned, and humans are very social animals. Adjustment to life without human contact is not easy, but it is certainly possible.

2. Even when people are not deprived of the physical presence of others, they can be lonely, and some are particularly susceptible to such feelings. Internal factors—pathological shyness, an inability to reciprocate warmth, or other reasons—may cause some people to feel isolated much of the time.

3. The qualities we want in a friend—affection, integrity, humor, common experiences, and so on—are similar to those we want in a lover. Still, we can tolerate flaws of character in a friend far more easily than in the person we are closest to emotionally. The typical loved one was first a friend.

4. Impression formation occurs spontaneously when people meet socially for the first time. Whether you are favorably disposed to a new acquaintance depends in part on whether that person seems to like you, and in part on the rewards present in the situation in which you meet.

5. Nonverbal behavior—eye contact, interpersonal distance—is an excellent indicator of the closeness of a relationship between two people.

6. Some changes that have already begun to appear include greater tolerance of homosexuality and premarital cohabitation, and greater numbers of single-parent households. Do *you* think these trends are likely to continue?

Summary

Loneliness occurs when a person's network of social relations is deficient either qualitatively or quantitatively. It may be caused by objective conditions of isolation, but it may also be experienced in crowds. **Loneliness anxiety** results from alienation between people; **existential loneliness** stems from one's consciousness as a separate entity. Loneliness may be associated with such other feelings as depression, boredom, and anxiety, but although it shares some of the symptoms of depression it is a distinct emotional state.

The experience of loneliness is determined by a variety of situational and personal characteristics. The three basic strategies for coping with loneliness include: reducing the desire for social contact, increasing the quantity and quality of social contacts, and changing the perceived discrepancy between desired and achieved levels of social relations.

Affiliation patterns are influenced by such factors as age, sex, race, and religion. Schachter's classic study of affiliation found that a feeling of "anxiety" causes people to affiliate. Other psychologists observed that Schachter was manipulating "fear" rather than "anxiety," and that under some conditions feelings of "anxiety" or "embarrassment" may cause people to avoid affiliation.

Social comparison theory suggests that we seek out others in order to interpret our reactions and to find support for them. This seems to explain affiliation for people faced with threatening, ambiguous, or novel situations. **Stress reduction theory**, on the other hand, emphasizes the reduction of tension as the primary motivation for affiliation. This seems a valid explanation when a situation is not ambiguous.

The determinants of attraction include **frequency of contact, proximity, similarity, complementarity, physical attractiveness,** and **reciprocity.** We communicate liking through *eye contact, body gestures,* and the *amount of distance* we maintain between ourselves and another person. **Cognitive balance theory** suggests that people like other people with similar attitudes and beliefs. **Reinforcement theory** suggests that we are attracted to people whom we associate with positive feelings. **Gain–loss theory** (a special instance of reinforcement theory) suggests that a change from criticism to praise is more rewarding, or a change from praise to criticism more punishing, than praise or criticism that remains stable.

We define the quality of our attraction to another by labeling our responses. Liking involves a favorable attitude to someone; loving involves attachment and caring. Passionate or romantic love involves the idealization of the loved one in addition to sexual desire. In companionate love, there is a greater ability to see the other person as distinct from one's fantasies.

Changes in sexual attitudes and in the behavior of Americans are reflected in greater acceptances of such behaviors as premarital sex, cohabitation, marriage, extramarital sex, masturbation, homosexuality and bisexuality, contraception, and abortion. The double standard, which is apparently in decline but still operative, is the notion that different sexual norms should be applied to men and women.

Sexual communication is more complex and various in humans than in other animals, since it is not restricted to definite patterns. Sexual arousal, which involves physiological changes, is influenced by psychological factors even more than situational determinants.

Suggested Additional Reading

Berscheid, E. & Walster, E. H., *Interpersonal attraction* (2nd ed.). Reading, Mass.: Addison-Wesley, 1978.

Byrne, D. *The attraction paradigm.* New York: Academic Press, 1971.

Duck, F. W. (Ed.). *Theory and practice in interpersonal attraction.* London: Academic Press, 1976.

Huston, T. L. (Ed.). *Foundations of interpersonal attraction.* New York: Academic Press, 1974.

Peplau, L. A. & Perlman, D. (Eds.). *Loneliness: A sourcebook of current theory, research, and therapy.* New York: Wiley-Interscience, 1982.

Walster, E. & Walster, G. W. *A new look at love.* Reading, Mass.: Addison-Wesley, 1978.

COMMUNICATION, ATTITUDES, AND SOCIAL INFLUENCE

7

COMMUNICATION

Questions about Communication

1. We often hear that a foreign phrase has "lost something in translation" when an attempt is made to express the concept in English. Why should this be so? Do people who speak different languages perceive the world differently?
2. Is "body language" really a language? Can we express meaningful concepts without words?
3. Do people from all over the world smile the same way? Are facial expressions universal?
4. Can you tell when someone is lying to you? What kinds of things do you look for in that person's behavior?
5. Do people really think violent television programs are more interesting and entertaining than the same programs would be if the violent scenes were omitted?
6. How do the media influence us in the course of an election? Do we vote for the candidate whose name we have heard and face we have seen most often?
7. Can watching *The Waltons* make you a better person?

"Your electrical system is malfunctioning, prompt service is required." Hearing this warning, you pull your car onto the shoulder of the road and shut off the engine. As you step out to investigate, you hear another message: "Don't forget your keys." At Chrysler Corporation, which introduced speech synthesis devices into some 1983 luxury cars, development engineers believe that "it is very hard to ignore a car that is talking to you" (Freedman, 1982).

From modern speech synthesized messages to the old-fashioned friendly letter, communications are an important part of everyday life. When social psychologists use the term **communication**, they have in mind any way one mind affects another (Shannon & Weaver, 1949). Communication encompasses not just written or spoken words but everything from hand signals, eyebrow movements, and interpersonal distance to political slogans, popular records, and television commercials.

Communication is essentially a social process. But since human beings are not the only social animals, communication is not a uniquely human process: It occurs throughout the animal world. By their dance patterns, honey bees tell each other in what direction nectar is to be found and how far away it is. Fish communicate their territorial claims and warn off intruders. Chimpanzees have a vocabulary of gestures and calls to alert one another to danger, to indicate a food supply, and to threaten strangers.

252

Communication and Language

Communication is essential to all animals that live in organized groups and form cooperative relationships for providing food, shelter, and other necessities. While the higher primates—monkeys, apes, and humans—use several similar methods of communication, only humans have a capacity for true **language**. For our purposes, language may be defined as the system of vocal sounds used by human beings to transmit meaning to one another. By the use of signs and signals, chimpanzees can convey general messages but they cannot say exactly *what* kind of food or danger is at hand. Only human language transmits precise messages, which it does by **symbols**, arbitrary systems of sounds and images. Symbolic languages have been developed by human beings over many thousands of years. They allow us to refer to things not immediately present and to store complex information for future use.

Communication events occur not just between individuals and small groups, but also between a few senders and many millions of recipients. Such large-scale communication includes television, radio, and all printed matter—the mass media. For millions of people in this country, television has become the prime source of information about the world. As we shall see, the messages that people receive over television shape their beliefs, determine their social outlooks, and regulate their social relationships. The mass media, and especially television, have become the primary means by which human beings "explain the world to themselves and to each other" (Gerbner & Gross, 1976, p. 50). However, before we consider the functions and effects of the mass media, we will examine the uses of language, and the variety of nonverbal means of communication at our disposal. First, though, we will take a closer look at communication itself.

A Model of Communication

While other animals communicate not only by sounds and images but also by taste, touch, and smell, human beings rely primarily on sounds and images. **Sounds** include all spoken words and music; **images** include all written words, pictures, signs, and body movements.

A communication occurs when a **sender** decides to send a message to a **receiver**. (See Figure 7–1.) A message begins in the sender's brain; this is the **information source**. It will ultimately come to rest in the brain of the receiver; this is its **destination**. To get from the sender to the receiver, a message has to be transmitted in some way. When speaking to another person, for example, the sender must **encode** the message into sound symbols, and transform the symbols by means of his or her vocal cords into sound waves, which are transmitted to the receiver. The air space between sender and receiver through which the sound waves travel is the **communication channel**. When they reach the eardrums of the receiver, the sound waves are translated into nerve impulses that travel to the receiver's brain, where they are **decoded** back into the original message. The message has now reached its destination.

This description is a model of an ideal communication. However, messages

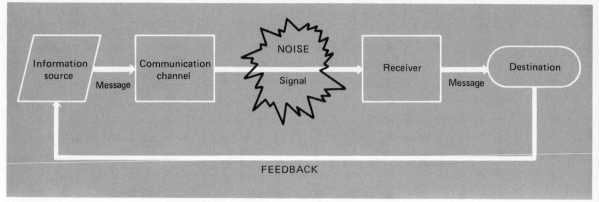

FIGURE 7–1. A Model of Communication

often become distorted in the process of transmission. There may have been loud music playing in the background, the speaker may have mispronounced a word, or the receiver may not have been paying attention. Any of these conditions during transmission can distort a message and make it difficult for the receiver to understand what the sender was trying to communicate. Distortion caused by extraneous sound is said to be due to **noise.**

A word and a stone once let go cannot be recalled.
Portuguese proverb

Communication is, of course, a two-way process. Senders are also receivers, and both can send messages to each other simultaneously. A sender usually wants to know whether the message got through to the receiver; he or she must depend on **feedback** for this information.

Meaning

Communication, then, is a social interaction that conveys information from one participant to another. Each message has meaning for both the sender and the receiver. The meaning consists not only of the factual information contained in the message, but also of the context in which it occurs. A message that states, "Rita ought to be proud of herself, she's done a fine job," has a literal meaning. The speaker has been impressed with something Rita has done. But the message could have other meanings also, and, depending upon who is sending it, Rita will feel varying degrees of pleasure. She may feel only slightly pleased if it comes from her husband, who may have other jobs for her to do. She may feel highly pleased if her boss says it; it may mean a raise and a promotion. The meaning of a message thus depends on the relationship between sender and receiver. It also depends on the social setting. Consider the following exchange:

"What's your name, boy?" the policeman asked.
"Dr. Poussaint, I'm a physician."
"What's your first name, boy?" (Ewin-Tripp, 1969, pp. 97–98)

Dr. Poussaint was a young, black physician traveling in the South. He wanted to present himself as a physician, but the receiver did not accept this message and asked him to retransmit it in a form the receiver could accept. Mes-

sages therefore have a *relational* level of meaning that indicates the amount of power and control the participants have in a relationship.

Social psychologists often look at communication in relational terms, and have devised ways of coding interactions that reveal such patterns of dominance and control. To study the exchanges between two people, researchers classify utterances according to the speaker, the grammatical form, and the direction of control. In some exchanges the speakers have the same amount of power; they feel equal to each other, and both try to minimize any differences. In other exchanges, though, speakers try to maximize their differences, with the result that one speaker gains control (or is "one-up"), and the other yields it (or is "one-down") (Rogers & Farace, 1975). A speaker who wants to gain control of a conversation may ask questions that demand an answer, give instructions or orders to the other person, disagree with what the other person says, change the subject abruptly, interrupt the other person's ongoing speech, or keep talking when the other person tries to interrupt. Speakers who yield control in an exchange accept or agree with what the other person says, ask questions that seek supportive answers, utter incomplete sentences that invite the other person to finish them, or ask questions that continue the dialogue. Much communication, therefore, is a form of interpersonal transaction with many underlying meanings.

Language

Our definition of language states that it is a characteristic of human beings. Indeed, when we think of communication we usually have spoken or written human language in mind. As we will see, though, we have other means of communication as well. This is not to say that animals do not communicate. For example, most primates have very similar call signals and body postures to indicate states of hunger, pain, and fear. But other animals, including the higher primates, do not have the highly specialized encoding and transmitting abilities that make true language possible.

There is at present some controversy over exactly how to characterize the communication abilities of other primates. Researchers have taught some chimpanzees, for example, as many as 200 words in American Sign Language. They have demonstrated that they can understand concepts such as *small–large*, *young–old*, *fruit–vegetable*, and *open–closed* (Premack & Premack, 1972). Others are apparently able to use grammatical structures such as negatives, plurals, questions, and conditionals. A chimpanzee named Washoe used signs for *water bird* when she saw a swan; another named Sarah has been able to construct sentences such as "Mary give Sarah banana" (Terrace, 1979).

What is Language?   Do primates, then, have language? To answer this question, researchers have had to look closely at what sets off human language from other forms of primate communication. They have found that chimpanzees lack several important linguistic capabilities that humans possess. Although they can learn new words and form sentences, chimpanzees display little ability to create new, original sentences. They learn by imitating their trainers over and over (Terrace, 1979). Human children, by contrast, are able to create new sentences spontaneously, and say things that have never been said before (Cairns & Cairns, 1976). They can change sentences from the active to the passive voice, and distinguish between words that are similar (Farb, 1978). Human children seem to have an inborn grasp of grammar that allows them to create new meaning by freely substituting one word for another (Chomsky, 1965).

Human children possess another ability that sets them off from primates: They can create and use **symbols**. Symbols are an abstract code by which humans assign meanings to objects, images, and vocal sounds. Thus, it has been asserted that "no chimpanzee is capable of understanding the difference be-

When psychologist H. S. Terrace began a 5-year research project with a male chimpanzee, he hoped to show that apes could not only learn to communicate with sign language but could create sentences as well. Here Terrace, aided by Ernie the Muppet, has succeeded in getting Nim Chimpsky to make the sign for *nose*. However, Terrace's research demonstrated that while apes can learn words and even learn to string them into meaningful sequences, they are not capable of creating sentences like humans.

Susan Kuklin

tween holy water and ordinary drinking water, but human beings can" (Farb, 1978, p. 68). The most frequently used symbols are *words*. Whether they write them or speak them, human beings arbitrarily assign word sounds to objects and ideas and then make the association permanent. Whereas chimpanzees' call signals express their immediate excitement at a particular moment over finding food or seeing a leopard, they do not indicate *what kind* of food has been found, or *where* the leopard is located, nor can they refer to food eaten yesterday or to leopards seen last month. Only human beings, by means of symbols that stand for distinct ideas, can do this. Symbolic language allows human beings to talk to each other about things thousands of miles away or events that transpired thousands of years ago. Human language is thus independent of any immediate stimulus from the environment: Human beings can sit in a hut in a remote rain forest and discuss computer programs or baseball batting averages.

Language makes it possible for human beings to transcend their environment. Because observations and discoveries can be written down in symbols and stored for future use, each human generation does not have to rediscover or reinvent all the devices and inventions of the past. Instead of having to learn to build airplanes from scratch every time they want to construct a new one, they consult written plans and continue from where previous airplane builders left off.

Human language also differs from animal communication in other ways. Whereas human cultural groups have developed over 3,000 separate languages, all chimpanzees, whether raised in the wild or in a laboratory, use the same vocalizations to represent the same things. Human beings, on the other hand, have created many different words to represent small distinctions among things and ideas, and invent wholly new words for new concepts or ideas whenever necessary. Consider, for example, the many words we have to describe colors, or even shades of one color: red, crimson, scarlet, fuchsia, carnation, oxblood.

Each of the literally thousands of human languages is governed by rules. In every language, the rules of **grammar** govern such areas as the forms of words, their order in a sentence, sentence structure itself, and the possible meanings phrases and sentences can have. **Syntax** is the branch of grammar that governs the order of words in a sentence and the relationship between parts of a sentence. In addition to having a literal dictionary meaning, words also have a **semantic meaning** that includes situational or expressive elements. For example, to a non-Catholic the phrase "the mystic rose" has only literal meaning. A Catholic, however, knows that it stands for the Virgin Mary (Hunter & Whitten, 1976).

Linguistic Relativity   Some linguists have thought that as children learn their native language they also acquire a way of perceiving and interpreting the world that is unique to speakers of that language. This **theory of linguistic relativity** (also known as the **Sapir-Whorf hypothesis,** named after Edward Sapir and Benjamin Lee Whorf who developed the theory) holds that language determines the way we interpret our environment and helps to perpetuate the distinctive characteristics of our culture. Slobin (1971) believes that the grammatical and semantic structure of specific languages imposes a structure on the speakers' thought processes and thus influences their behavior. Eskimo children, for example, become alert to many different types of snow because their language has many words for different kinds of snow. Other linguists have argued that the relation-

FIGURE 7–2.

The Semantic Differential

The mean ratings of three words placed on a continuum between various paired qualities that could be associated with them.

Source: *From* The Measurement of Meaning *by C. E. Osgood, G. S. Suci, P. H. Tannenbaum, Urbana, Ill.: University of Illinois Press, 1957. Reprinted by permission.*

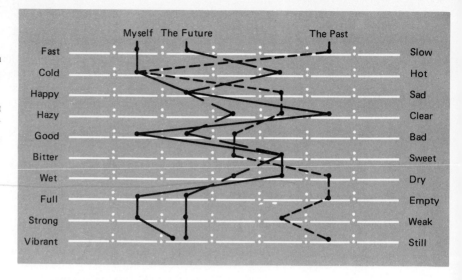

ship between culture and language is reciprocal, and that language reflects cultural differences that already exist (Cairns & Cairns, 1976). Thus, while English speakers do not discriminate among as many different kinds of snow as do Eskimos, we might if we needed to.

Even when we speak to someone of our own culture and use a shared language, we can still encounter problems of meaning. For example, abstract words such as *freedom, justice,* or *peace* tend to have many connotative meanings. Concrete words such as *triangle* or *table,* on the other hand, are more specific. We can generally communicate our meanings effectively, but this can be difficult and time-consuming—even for social psychologists who would like to be able to measure meaning with great precision.

The Semantic Differential   A technique for measuring the meanings of words has been devised by Osgood, Suci, and Tannenbaum (1957). With this method, subjects are asked to rate words such as *past, future,* and *myself* in terms of a range of possible meanings. Each word is placed on a continuum between various paired qualities that could be associated with it—*happy* to *sad, good* to *bad, strong* to *weak,* and so on. (Examples of such word pairs are shown in the left- and right-hand columns in Figure 7–2.) The mean of subjects' rating of each word for each set of qualities can be plotted on a graph (see figure). By applying a complex method of data analysis (factor analysis), Osgood and his colleagues have found that three main factors account for half the variability in meaning for a large number of words:

1.   evaluation (*good–bad, clean–dirty, valuable–worthless*)
2.   potency (*hard–soft, rough–smooth, heavy–light, strong–weak, large–small*)
3.   activity (*fast–slow, hot–cold, active–passive*)

These sets of scales are known collectively as the **semantic differential.**

The semantic differential has been used by researchers to rate presidential candidates (Osgood et al., 1957), to reveal cultural differences in attitudes (Helper & Garfield, 1965), and to examine the Sapir-Whorf hypothesis (Osgood, May, & Miron, 1975). Osgood (1971) has developed a new system for analyzing concepts derived from the semantic differential method, which he calls *semantic space*. (In chapter 8 we shall discuss in more detail how meanings are measured.)

Nonverbal Communication

The semantic differential scales were devised to provide an accurate measure of distinctions in meaning. Human languages are tools that provide us with precise meanings, but they are infinitely flexible, too. They can accommodate new concepts (digital computer), incorporate ideas from other cultures (boomerang), and describe our most intimate feelings ("How do I love you?/Let me count the ways"). Human language is constantly changing: It changes in vocabulary as new words are added (skinflicks) and old words acquire new meaning (grass) or fall by the wayside (quoth). Human language also changes its sounds (as any English speaker knows who travels to another English-speaking country, or even through one country); no one today, for example, is certain of how the ancient Greeks pronounced their tongue. And human languages are extraordinarily varied.

We should bear in mind all these characteristics of spoken language as we turn to an important means of communication that has none of these characteristics. Nonverbal communication does not have precise meanings, and does not possess an infinitely expandable vocabulary. It is, indeed, quite stable and universal, and generally understood by most people everywhere. And it does convey a great deal of information, sometimes supplementing and sometimes contradicting the spoken language that goes with it.

Nonverbal Channels of Communication

The main channels of nonverbal communication include vocal cues (paralanguage), eye contact, facial expressions, body movements (kinesics), and interpersonal distance (proxemics). We can and do use all of these at once, and at the same time as we use spoken language. Any and all of these forms of nonverbal behavior can intensify the literal meaning of our spoken words or overlay them with an entirely different meaning of their own. These nonverbal channels by themselves contribute strongly to our impressions of another person; they can also regulate the flow of a conversation, cause physical and emotional arousal, indicate the relative social status of the people involved, and determine the degree of intimacy between them.

Paralanguage   Much of the content of what we say depends on how we say it: what tone of voice we use, what words we emphasize, how loudly or softly we speak, and how fast or slowly we say it. These vocal effects, called **paralanguage,** accompany almost all speech and help convey the meanings in our conversation. How many ways can you say, "That's very kind of you"? How would you say it if you did not really mean it? If you did not like the person to whom you were speaking? By using a high-pitched tone of voice, we might convey an impression of nervousness or insincerity. By putting the emphasis on the word "YOU," we would be saying that you alone have been very kind, not the other people in the room. By putting the emphasis on "VERY," we could sarcastically suggest that it really was not—or, with a change in pitch, that it truly was.

Researchers have several techniques for investigating the uses of paralanguage. If the actual words of a statement are electronically filtered out of a tape recording, the tone of the voice alone remains. Subjects' reactions allow us to measure the effects of vocal tone by itself. Or the actual content of a message can be masked by randomly splicing words together or by using nonsense syllables or alphabet letters, which have no meaning (Davitz, 1964).

Researchers also use tape recordings to investigate the ways pitch and the rate of speech can influence the perceptions of a speaker. It has been found that a person under stress (telling a lie or attempting to deceive) tends to speak at a higher than normal pitch (Streeter et al., 1977). In another study, after listening to a number of recordings of male speakers answering interview questions, subjects were asked to evaluate the speakers on a variety of scales. The recordings had been altered by computer to raise or lower the vocal pitch and speed up or slow down the speech rate without affecting other vocal qualities such as loudness (Apple, Streeter, & Krauss, 1979). Men with high-pitched voices were thought to be smaller, weaker, less honest, and more nervous than those with lower voices. Men who talked too slowly were perceived as being colder, more passive, weaker, and less truthful than those who spoke at a normal rate. Men who spoke at a normal rate were seen as calmer and more fluent and persuasive than either fast or slow speakers. There is, of course, no evidence that fast talkers really are more active than slow talkers, or that men with high-pitched voices are weaker than deep-voiced men.

Besides influencing our perceptions of speakers, paralinguistic cues also help regulate communication. We have already seen that we can signal a speaker that we are paying attention by means of feedback such as "uh huh." We employ a number of other vocal cues to indicate that we want the floor (Duncan & Fiske, 1977). We can audibly inhale as if we were about to speak or raise the volume of our feedback. If the speaker wants to keep the floor, he or she can talk louder, talk faster, talk very softly or slowly, or fill the pauses between sentences with fillers such as "um . . .," "ah . . .," or "er . . ." (Duncan & Niederehe, 1974; Knapp, 1978). One study has found that people who are high self-monitors (see chapter 4) are more sensitive to paralinguistic cues than those who do not monitor themselves as closely (Snyder, 1979).

No sooner met, but they
    looked;
No sooner looked but they
    loved.
As You Like It, v, ii

Eye Contact and Social Interaction   What do we see when we look into another person's eyes? Perhaps the most useful nonverbal source of information is *eye contact.* The importance we place on eye contact is reflected in such phrases as, "eying someone up and down," "seeing eye to eye," "look me in the eye," or "making eyes at one another."

Although most people can tell with a high degree of accuracy (even at some distance) whether other people are looking at them, observers have difficulty in telling whether an individual is looking at someone else's eyes or at another aspect of the face (Stephenson & Rutter, 1970). For this reason, researchers have had to rely on a more general type of visual behavior—the direction of the gaze—in order to measure whether eye contact has occurred.

Eye contact discloses certain aspects of personality, becomes a way of seeking information, and influences others' behavior. For example, in our society women generally engage in more overall eye contact than do men while speaking, while listening, and during silences. Some psychologists feel that visual feedback from others has traditionally been more important to women because their physical appearance has been of paramount concern. In most social circumstances, they have been the performers and men the audience. Because some women have felt they were being constantly observed, they "adjusted their social performance" to gain the maximum amount of visual feedback (Ellsworth & Ludwig, 1972). (Such behavior may also indicate lower status, as we shall see.)

Eye contact regulates turn-taking in conversations. Before starting to speak, speakers will look away from their listeners in order to keep them from interrupting or responding prematurely. To ensure that the listeners have comprehended complicated points, speakers look toward the listener from time to time. Speakers look at their listeners to indicate that it is someone else's turn (Ellsworth & Ludwig, 1972).

Eye contact also helps two people synchronize their speech to conduct a two-way conversation. One study rated the frequency of pauses in a conversation between two people in four conditions: (1) both wearing masks so that only their eyes showed; (2) both wearing dark glasses so that only their faces showed; (3) both heads concealed behind screens so that only their bodies were visible; and (4) both in total darkness. The fewest pauses and interrruptions occurred in the first, or eyes-only, condition; the most pauses occurred in the second, or faces-only, condition. Conversation, then, is best regulated when speakers can see each other's eyes. But the study also showed that speech can be synchronized

Ken Karp

Eye contact is used by people when they talk to one another to regulate turn-taking in conversation, to indicate interest in what the other person is saying, and, of course, to indicate interest in the other person.

even when the speakers cannot see each other; the reseachers speculate that this may be due to the fact that the telephone has accustomed people to conversing without visual cues (Argyle, Lalljee, & Cook, 1968).

Prolonged Eye Contact   While mutual eye contact increases the effectiveness of a social interaction, it can be carried to extremes. During most interactions, *mutual gazing* occurs about 31 percent of the time and overall gazing occurs about 61 percent of the time. The mean duration of any kind of gazing is about 3 seconds, but mutual gazing lasts only about 1 second (Argyle & Inghan, 1972). A gaze that goes on for too long becomes an uncomfortable *stare*. Prolonged eye contact causes physiological and emotional stress (Ellsworth & Ludwig, 1972; Strom & Buck, 1979); it is a stimulus that demands some form of response to relieve the anxiety that has been aroused. Staring is often construed as hostile, and most people try to avoid the threatened confrontation by averting their own gaze as a sign of appeasement, by getting away as fast as possible, or by counterattacking (Ellsworth et al., 1972; Ellsworth & Carlsmith, 1973; Van Hoof, 1967). But staring can also signal distress; in one study passersby were more apt to help a "victim" (actually a confederate) who made prolonged eye contact with them than one who did not (Ellsworth & Langer, 1976).

In any case, staring creates tension and people will act immediately to reduce it. To see what kind of avoidance behavior staring would elicit, researchers positioned confederates at various distances away from a three-way intersection with their backs to the traffic. When a car pulled up to stop for a red light, the confederates would turn around and stare intently at the driver until the light turned green. The closer the confederate was to the curb, the more often drivers would stop well short of the intersection or well into it. It was believed that they did so in order to avoid the possibility of being in the confederate's line of sight. Almost all of those who did stop at the normal point would look away quickly when stared at and pull away abruptly when the light changed (Ellsworth & Carlsmith, 1973; Greenbaum & Rosenfeld, 1978). (See Figure 7–3.)

Our language distinguishes between *gaze*, which means to look intently and steadily, and *stare*, defined as looking fixedly with wide-open eyes. Stares cause us discomfort, but we really do not mind being gazed at. Indeed, the recipient of a gaze should be flattered: We look more at people we like, and like those people who are most frequently the objects of our gaze (Exline & Winters, 1965).

Intimate couples (married or dating) engage in more visual behavior than pairs of individuals who are not intimately involved. Since intimate couples spend more time looking at each other than a pair of strangers do, we might expect them to be more accurate at decoding each other's nonverbal behavior than strangers. Gettman and Porterfield (1980) found some support for this notion, but only for husbands who reported that they were satisfied with their marriages. Presumably, when the marriage is not satisfactory, the partners do not spend as much time looking at one another.

Married couples who love each other tell each other a thousand things without talking.
Chinese proverb

Gazing is also an indicator of social status. A low-status person generally looks more at a high-status person than vice versa (Exline, 1971; Exline et al., 1975). However, a person with high status tends to exert *visual dominance*—that is, he or she will look more at a low-status person when speaking than when listening. This is an indication that the higher status person does not have to attend closely to the low-status person.

FIGURE 7–3.
Schematic Diagram of the
Staring Experiment Setting

Source: *Adapted from "Patterns of Avoidance in Response to Interpersonal Staring and Proximity: Effects of Bystanders on Drivers at a Traffic Intersection," by P. Greenbaum and H. M. Rosenfeld,* Journal of Personality and Social Psychology, *1978, 28, 578.*

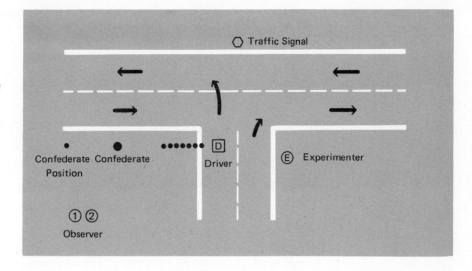

Facial Expressions   Eyes are said to be the windows on the soul. They are regarded as being the most truthful indicators of what is passing through a person's mind. In the same way, other facial features can also indicate very clearly what emotion a person is experiencing. Unless they are closely monitored—as they often are—facial expressions will occur involuntarily and automatically (Ekman & Friesen, 1975).

Charles Darwin was one of the first to observe and describe facial expressions (1872). In his travels about the world, he observed that facial expressions seem to have universal meanings: People everywhere used the same expressions to convey the same emotions. Although rules vary about when certain expressions are appropriate, people in every society convey at least six basic emotions through the same expressions: anger, happiness, sadness, disgust, fear, and surprise (and possibly others such as shame). From Norway to New Guinea, people turn the corners of their mouths up when happy and draw them down when sad. From Alaska to Africa, infants are born possessing the full adult range of facial expressions. Modern researchers show photographs of various faces to subjects in different cultures and ask them to identify the emotion expressed. They also photograph people who are asked to look as though they were angry, terrified, disgusted, and so on. (Ekman & Oster, 1979, is a review of many such studies.) As a result of such research, we can largely agree with Darwin that facial expressions are biologically determined and not culturally derived (Ekman & Friesen, 1975). It also seems to make little difference whether a person's facial expression is due to a felt emotion or is posed. That is, a person will frown in exactly the same way regardless of whether she is really angry or just pretending to be; and a person observing her will not be able to tell the difference between her spontaneous and posed frowns.

Look how we can, or sad, or merrily,
Interpretation will misquote our looks.
Henry IV, i, v, 2

People are thus capable of "managing" their facial expressions, of "putting on a face" for certain occasions. In fact, every society has conventions that determine what emotions people can display in public—especially emotions that are apparent in facial expressions. These *display rules* "specify who can show what

Members of the Fore tribe of New Guinea were asked to show on their faces the appropriate expression for each of several emotion stories. From left, the emotion stories were: "Your friend has come and you are happy"; "Your child has died"; and "You are angry and about to fight."

emotion to whom" (Ekman, 1979). For example, most middle-class American women learn at an early age not to show anger—or at least to camouflage it, while men learn not to show fear. The young woman who has just won a beauty contest may cry in public, but not the young women who have just lost (Ekman & Friesen, 1975; Ekman, 1979).

Social motivation plays a large part in determining the face we show to others. While a smile may be caused by feelings of happiness or joy, it may also be a display of friendliness and have no relationship to other aspects of the person's internal state. People often smile when they are in uncomfortable social settings, when apologizing for awkward behavior, or when violating some social norm. Firestone (1970) has observed that in our society women and some minority group members smile more than men, and in situations where men do not. She believes that this is an indicator of lower social status intended to be ingratiating to and complying with the higher status individual. Kraut and Johnston (1979) found that bowlers smiled, not when they got a strike and would have been expected to be happiest, but when they turned around to talk with their teammates. This form of social smiling is also found in nonhuman primates. Chimpanzees, for example, will often assume a smilelike grin when confronting other chimpanzees. Researchers feel such facial displays are a sign of submission or appeasement and are adopted to establish friendship and to "deflect the hostile behavior of more dominant animals" (p. 1,540).

Kinesics In addition to facial expressions, we use a host of arm, hand, and postural gestures to emphasize what we are saying or to convey messages, sometimes even without our knowing it. The study of body movements and postures is called **kinesics,** and is popularly known as *body language* (Fast, 1970). Much of the original work in this area has been done by Ray Birdwhistell (1976), who applied methods of linguistic analysis to body movements, such as facial expressions, including brow and scalp movements and body posture. Kinesicists study in minute detail how, when, and why people raise their eyebrows, flare their nostrils, purse their lips, fold their hands, and so on. The work can be tedious; 3 minutes of body language may take months to code.

Kinesics researchers distinguish between body movements and postures that can substitute for spoken communication, called **emblems,** and gestures that accompany speech, called **illustrators.** Emblems, which include head nods, shrugs, winks, and finger wags, have very precise meanings and are often used when people are unable to speak or do not want to, but still want to exchange a message. People nod or shake their heads to signal "yes" or "no" across a crowded room; they may shrug to indicate "I don't know," wave to indicate greeting or farewell, wink to indicate collusion or flirtation, or wag fingers to admonish children. Other specific emblems exist for insults, replies, giving directions, referring to physical states such as tiredness and pain, or to emotional states such as anger or surprise. People all over the world use emblems, but not necessarily the same ones. Unlike many facial expressions, emblems are not universal (Ekman, 1979). Nor is the extent to which they are used; Italians and people of other Mediterranean cultures rely more on "hand language" than people in English-speaking cultures.

Illustrators are employed to supplement speech, as when people snap their fingers when they cannot find the right word, but do not want to stop talking. By drawing shapes in the air, we may explain difficult concepts such as where to turn off a winding road, how to take something apart, or how helicopter blades move. People punctuate and add emphasis to their speech by means of a variety of finger pointings, hand wavings, and fist poundings. Unlike emblems, most of these gestures are invented on the spot and have little universal or specific meaning in other contexts (Ekman, 1979).

It has been found that people in social interactions tend to coordinate their body movements. We nod our heads or fold our arms when the person with us does, and we speak at the same rate as the other person. These coordinated actions are referred to as **nonverbal synchrony**. Risser (1979) observed subjects with confederates who were either sitting or standing with their arms folded. Subjects mimicked the arm-folding behavior only when the confederates were standing, which suggests that the meaning of folded arms may change according to whether a person is sitting or standing.

In an earlier study, Mehrabian (1968) found that women who were seated with their legs crossed and arms folded were rated as less pleasant than women who were seated with both feet on the floor and their arms resting in their laps. In this case, the uncrossed legs and arms seemed to signal accessibility and friendliness. Another study found that low-status people will stand with their feet close together, hold their arms close to their bodies, and nod and smile frequently when talking to a person of higher status. High-status people, on the other hand, hold their heads still, seldom smile, and assume casual poses, often touching a low-status person. Regardless of their individual competence or ability, women tend to use low-status gestures and men to use high-status gestures in interactions with the opposite sex. It has even been suggested that highly competent women may be consigned to lower level positions by men who perceive them as less able because they display such low-status nonverbal behaviors (McKenna & Denmark, 1978).

Interpersonal Distance (Proxemics)   How close do you get when you are talking to the college president? To your psychology professor? To your mother? To your best friend? As we noted in chapter 6, the study of interpersonal distance is called **proxemics,** and it deals with some of the subtlest forms of nonverbal behavior. Hall (1966) has identified four zones of interpersonal distance—intimate,

Proxemics is the study of interpersonal distance and its meanings. Is the distance between these two people intimate, personal, social, or public? If you know that the young man on the left is a student and the older man a professor, would your interpretation of the distance between them change? What if they were son and father? Potential voter and political candidate? Demonstrator and passer-by?

personal, social, and public—that are each appropriate for a certain kind of behavior and relationship (see Table 7-1).

Touching   Lovers and very close friends—at least in Western societies—may touch each other frequently without feeling uncomfortable, but touching between adult strangers can stir up anxiety, raise blood pressure, and cause resentment. Yet in itself, the act of touching can have very beneficial effects. In fact, tactile stimulation is of crucial importance to children's and adult's emotional, social, intellectual, and physiological development. It can have profound effects on adult psychiatric patients, making them more verbal and self-revealing, and even improves their attitude. Centuries ago, the "laying on of hands" by a ruler or religious leader was believed to have curative powers; even today charismatic "faith healers" use this principle. In other contexts, touching can have negative effects. It can communicate greater intimacy than the other person desires, as when men make "passes" at women; or it can communicate condescension, as when a superior pats a subordinate on the head (Fisher et al., 1976).

Men and women generally have quite different reactions to touch, as shown by two studies. In the first (Fisher et al., 1976), a library clerk touched individuals in the process of handing back library cards. The researchers hypothesized that such touching would arouse pleasant, positive feelings toward the toucher and the setting. They found, however, that while women had consistently positive responses to being touched, men seemed to have mixed feelings about it.

In the second study (Whitcher & Fisher, 1979), nurses would touch male and female surgery patients while introducing themselves and explaining surgical procedures. (A control group of similar patients was not touched by the nurses.) The researchers expected that all patients would react positively to being touched, feel less anxiety before and after surgery, and have lower blood pressure. Again, only those women who were touched reported feeling less anxiety than women in the control group, and the blood pressure of the touched women was also lower. Touched men, on the other hand, reported more anxiety and had

TABLE 7–1.
The Four Zones of Interpersonal Distance

Zone	Distance	Appropriate People	Characteristics
Intimate	Touching– 18 inches	Parents and children, lovers, close friends, husband and wife	Able to sense body warmth and odors, feel breath of other person. Public intimacy at this distance is generally frowned upon in the United States. People so close that vision of the other is distorted.
Personal	1½–4 feet	Lovers, husband and wife	The individual's private, inviolable space; people are close enough to touch, but able to see each other without visual distortion. Able to smell perfume but not to sense body warmth.
Social	4–12 feet 4–8 feet 7–12 feet	Co-workers, social gatherings Friends Work situations	Cannot see details of face or eyes or detect body odors, but can clearly see clothing, hair, skin, etc. Most of our social interactions occur within this zone.
Public	12–25 feet or more	Actors, total strangers, important officials (heads of state)	Cannot determine eye color, overall image less detailed, impossible to hear normal speech or see normal gestures. Voices must be louder and gestures broader for communication to take place.

Source: After *The Hidden Dimension* by E. T. Hall, Garden City, N.Y.: Doubleday, 1966.

higher blood pressures than men in the control group. In both studies, the differences between male and female responses are probably due to sex-role socialization. Perhaps girls are touched more often by parents and friends than boys and thus become more comfortable with the experience in adulthood, while boys may come to interpret a touch as a threatening, dominating gesture.

Heslin and Boss (1980), in another field study, report results consistent with this interpretation. They observed 103 pairs of travelers arriving or departing at an airport in the United States. Both men and older people were more likely to initiate touching in cross-sex pairs than were women and younger people. Presumably, men and older people have more status than women and younger people (Goffman, 1967) and, consequently, have more freedom to initiate touching. In same-sex pairs, however, women touched more intimately (i.e., hugging each other) than men (who were more likely to simply shake hands).

A woman's strength is a multitude of words.
Hausa (African) proverb

These results are consistent with the sex differences we have noted throughout our discussion of nonverbal behavior. Women gaze more than men, smile more, maintain closer personal distance, and use more nonverbal cues than men. As we have seen in chapter 6, women have more and longer conversations than men. Why should this be so? Again, the answer probably lies in sex-role socialization. In our society, the "strong, silent type" is still held up as a desirable manly image. Generally, as girls pattern their behavior after their mothers, they will adopt the speech and gesture behaviors of women. Young boys, however, will avoid patterning their behavior after their mothers, with whom they generally spend more time than with their fathers.

There is some evidence that for today's younger generations a change has been taking place. More and more young men are being encouraged, by society, their girlfriends, and one another, to "be open" and express their "real selves." It will be interesting to see, when social psychologists replicate some of these communications studies in a few years, whether the results will be different.

Multichannel Communication

Most of the time we communicate through a range of channels: We choose not only words, but also our tone of voice, facial expressions, and gestures. We can intensify a message by using more than one of these communication channels at the same time. If a father wants to demonstrate approval of something his child has done, he will not just say "That's a good boy," or just hug his son, or just kiss him; he will probably do all three at once. The question for psychologists is which channel is the strongest communicator of feeling. To find out, they have devised experiments in which strong, but *inconsistent* emotional messages are given to subjects at the same time.

The Relative Importance of Channels Some early studies have found that when an inconsistent message is delivered simultaneously over verbal and vocal (paralinguistic) channels, the person addressed will interpret the message almost totally on the basis of the vocal channel. For example, if a negative word such as *scram* is spoken in a warm, inviting tone of voice, the literal negative content will be disregarded and the message will be interpreted as positive (Mehrabian & Ferris, 1967). This led researchers to predict that a message in which vocal tones and facial expressions are inconsistent will be interpreted on the basis of facial expressions alone. Mehrabian & Ferris (1967) found that this was indeed the case; in laboratory situations, subjects gave more weight—1½ times more—to facial expressions than to the tone of voice, although they continued to base much of their evaluation on vocal tone also.

Mehrabian and Ferris' studies found that emotional messages are communicated overwhelmingly (93 percent) by means of nonverbal channels. But the influence of nonverbal channels seems to depend on the situation. Krauss and his colleagues (1981), for example, found that when subjects were shown more realistic situations, such as the heated vice-presidential television debates of 1976, they evaluated the speakers' emotional states mostly on the basis of verbal content, and much less on paralinguistic cues or facial and body gestures. Thus, the channel that reveals the most information about a person's emotional state differs according to the emotion being evaluated and the social situation in which it occurs (Ekman et al., 1980). Sometimes no explicit verbal messages are given, as when people are behaving according to social conventions and concealing their true feelings. Then of course we can only look to "nonverbal leakage" for indications of the true emotional state, as we shall see shortly.

The Equilibrium Model of Multichannel Communication Every social interaction is a product of several interacting channels. For example, we have seen that eye contact can regulate the flow of conversation by signaling turn-taking, and that prolonged eye contact can raise tension and anxiety. While no single channel of communication seems to be more effective than any other, all channels influence each other. For every social interaction there is an expected or preferred amount of *intimacy*, or interpersonal closeness. On the one hand, we want to be sure that the person we are talking with is attending to us and holds us in reasonably high regard. Thus we monitor the amount of eye contact between us, how closely we sit to the other person, the intimacy of the topic we are discussing, and how much we smile. On the other hand, we are afraid of revealing too much of ourselves and of being rejected by the other person. Thus we may decrease the amount of eye contact, move farther away, change the subject to something more impersonal, smile less, and so on. Every social interaction thus has an *equilibrium* or optimal balance among the various verbal and nonverbal behaviors (Argyle & Dean, 1965). If any of these behaviors increases above a certain point, we may feel anxious and try to compensate by shifting the other behaviors in the opposite direction.

Argyle and Dean (1965) demonstrated that people compensate for too close an interpersonal distance by reducing the amount of eye contact; but they increase eye contact when the distance becomes too great. In one experiment, male or female confederates gazed continually at subjects while holding 3-minute conversations with them at distances of 2, 6, and 10 feet. Using a room with a one-way observation window, the observers recorded only the eye behavior of the subjects. In all cases, regardless of sex, the closer the subjects sat to the confederate, the less eye contact they displayed. Eye contact increased dramatically when subjects moved from 2 to 6 feet away from the confederates. All subjects seemed tense and anxious at the closest distance, and tried to compensate by leaning backward, looking down, shading their eyes, scratching their heads, or smoking. At 10 feet, on the other hand, they tried to compensate for the increased distance by leaning forward and by increasing the amount of eye contact. Women generally engaged in more eye contact than men, but the difference between the sexes was small. The greatest differences were found at the 2-foot distance: Opposite-sex pairs maintained only half as much eye contact (30 percent of the time) as did same-sex pairs (55 percent of the time).

The equilibrium theory of intimacy has been supported by many experiments and has been shown to apply in many other situations (Patterson, 1973). For example, Carr and Dabbs (1974) found that people reduce eye contact as the conversation becomes more personal. They also found that the amount of lighting in the room affected people's perceptions of the intimacy of the interaction: A brightly lit room was seen as inappropriate for discussion of intimate topics, while a dimly lit room seemed inappropriate for formal topics.

The Arousal Model of Intimacy   However, people do not always compensate when the equilibrium in a social interaction is disturbed (Patterson, 1976). Sometimes an increase in intimacy on one side will lead to a reciprocal increase on the other side. For example, in a romantic setting, lovers will increase their intimacy and the looks between them will grow longer and more intense. Patterson suggests that changes in equilibrium generate arousal, and that small changes in arousal are not unpleasant. However, when arousal exceeds a threshold point, it must be explained and dealt with. If we consider the source of the arousal to be positive (for example, a lover), we will reciprocate; if negative (for example, a stranger), we will compensate. Thus our response to arousal depends on how we label the source.

According to the arousal model of intimacy, an increase in intimate behavior from one person will lead to a corresponding increase from the other. Increasing intimate behavior leads to increased arousal, which is experienced as pleasant if the interacting people are lovers. Increased arousal from excessive intimacy with a stranger, however, would be unpleasant and disconcerting.

Deception

We all have to conceal our emotions at some point in daily life. As we saw in the discussion of display rules, we learn at an early age not to show certain emotions at certain times. In our more public moments, as representatives of our organizations, or as actors, diplomats, politicians, physicians, teachers, and other professionals, we may have to conceal our true feelings because of the demands of our professions or to avoid antagonizing supervisors or co-workers. Circumstances dictate when others must control their facial expressions, as when guilty parties testify to their innocence. Sometimes we practice deception out of consideration for others, as when a depressed person tries to appear happy at the dinner table, or we try not to look pleased at our good fortune when others are suffering.

Nonverbal Leakage   Much of the current interest in nonverbal behavior is due to the common belief that we cannot help but communicate certain emotions despite our attempts to conceal them. As Freud noted, "He that has eyes to see and ears to hear may convince himself that no mortal can keep a secret. If his lips are silent, he chatters with his fingertips; betrayal oozes out of him at every pore" (1905, p. 94).

Does betrayal ooze out? Not through the face, as researchers have discovered. Most people are quite skilled at managing their facial expressions to conceal their true feelings. They can smile to qualify a negative emotion; they can moderate their frowns or grimaces. There are a number of ways to falsify facial expressions; by simulating a smile or frown, we can pretend to an emotion that we do not feel; or we may use a neutral expression to conceal and mask our true feelings (Ekman & Friesen, 1975). People conceal their feelings by keeping their facial expressions under steady, conscious control when they know that others are monitoring their facial expressions closely.

Nevertheless, even with the most closely monitored faces, people give off **deception cues** and **leakage cues** (Ekman & Friesen, 1969, 1974). Deception cues are nonverbal behaviors that indicate an attempt to conceal true feelings. Deception cues may appear as "smiles that last too long or frowns that are too severe" (Ekman & Friesen, 1969, p. 98), or as tensed limbs and rigid posture. Leakage cues are nonverbal behaviors that do betray the underlying emotion. For example, a faint smile may cross the face of a person who is telling a falsehood or pretending to be sad. A person listening to a boring tale may tap a pencil against the table. People do not monitor the rest of their bodies as closely as they do their faces. Leakage and deception cues occur primarily in the hands, legs, and feet. Leakage may occur as "aggressive foot kicks, flirtatious leg displays, or autoerotic or soothing leg squeezing; deception cues can be seen in tense leg positions, frequent shifts of leg posture, restless or repetitive leg and foot acts" (Ekman & Friesen, 1969, p. 99). A clenched fist is a sure sign of tension or anger.

Detecting Deception   Ekman and Friesen (1974) wanted to learn to what extent people are aware of how they attempt to deceive others. They also wanted to see whether deception actually is more easily judged by body movements than by facial expressions. They asked nursing students to watch both a pleasant film and an unpleasant film and to give their honest reactions to them in an interview afterward. The students were then asked to watch the films again and to attempt to conceal their negative reactions in the postfilm interview. Finally they were asked what means they had used to deceive the interviewer. Almost all of these subjects reported that during the interview they had used facial expressions far more often than any other part of the body. Subjects were videotaped during their interviews and these tapes were then shown to observers who were asked to judge which students were telling the truth and which were lying. The observers were able to detect deception more easily from their body movements than from their facial expressions. They were not as successful, however, in judging facial and body movements that accompanied truthful behavior.

It is important to distinguish between those who recognize when deception is occurring and those who recognize what is being concealed. Both abilities depend on the deceiver's skill at deceiving and the perceiver's skill at detecting (Zuckerman et al., 1981). People may be less accurate in detecting leakage cues than at detecting deception clues; also, those who are good at detecting leakage are not necessarily good at detecting when deception is occurring (De Paulo & Rosenthal, 1979). Perhaps different skills are involved, but it is most likely that leakage cues are much more subtle and difficult to decode.

What cues indicate that someone is trying to deceive us? Miller and Burgoon (1982) have summarized the results of several studies (see Table 7–2). Generally, deceivers smile less, fidget more, employ nervous gestures, and speak in a higher tone of voice than individuals giving honest responses. They may also hesitate and pause when speaking, or give inconsistent or contradictory messages through the various nonverbal channels. Decoders report that they more or less use these same behaviors as cues when trying to decide whether someone is telling the truth. However, these nonverbal behaviors do not necessarily reflect deception. Nervous movements, for example, may reflect the fact that an individual is anxious about being in an experiment or interview. Consequently, observers are not very accurate in detecting deception, as we mentioned earlier. Indeed, Miller and Burgoon (1982) report that the mean accuracy in detecting deception across several studies is 55 percent—or only 5 percent better than chance. Observers are, however, quite good at detecting cues they believe to indicate deception, and moreover are quite confident that they have accurately identified honest or deceptive behavior.

TABLE 7–2.

Nonverbal Correlates of Deception

Nonverbal Channel	Cues Encoded as Deceptive	Cues Decoded as Deceptive
Kinesics	Reduced eye contact (fewer, briefer glances)	Less eye contact
	Fewer head nods	
	Less smiling; less happiness; displeased mouth movements; micromomentary expressions; but more pleasant faces by highly anxious	Less seriousness; less empathy; more smiling
	Fewer gestures; fewer illustrators; more hand shrugs	Excessive gestures
	Frequent shifts in leg/body position; tense leg and foot positions; less leg and foot movement; leg crossing by males; body blocks; abortive, restless flight movements	More tension and anxiety; more postural shifts
	Physiological indicators: blushing, blinking, shaking, perspiring, dilated or unstable pupils	
Proxemics	Body less directly facing audience	
	Less forward lean	
	Greater distances	
Paralinguistics	Slower or faster speaking rate than normal	
	More nonfluencies	More nonfluencies
	Higher pitch	
	More pauses or probe openings	
	More response latency	More response latency
	Shorter word duration; shorter speaking time	
Overall	Contradictions or inconsistencies among nonverbal cues	
	More information from hands and feet than face	Greater reliance on voice than face and on face than body

Source: Adapted from G. R. Miller & J. K. Burgoon, "Factors Affecting Assessments of Witness Credibility," in *The Psychology of the Courtroom* by N. L. Kerr & R. M. Bray (Eds.), New York: Academic Press, 1982, 176–177.

Research: Detecting Deception

Two recent studies have pinpointed some of the verbal and nonverbal cues that people use to detect deception. The first study showed that under certain conditions people use the verbal content of a person's speech rather than paralinguistic or facial expressions for deception cues. The second revealed the kinds of nonverbal behavior that aroused the most suspicion, even when deception may not have been occurring.

In the first experiment, 81 subjects were shown selected segments of the television show *To Tell the Truth* (Littlepage & Pineault, 1978). In this program, three contestants try to win money by claiming to be a specific person—for example, an expert on the Middle Ages. They are asked probing questions by a panel of judges. One of the contestants actually is the expert and answers truthfully; the other two are impostors who try to convince the panelists they are the experts by lying.

There were four groups of subjects. The first group watched full, unedited portions of the program; these subjects were able to observe the contestants' full facial expressions, and hear their replies and all their vocal inflections (paralinguistic cues). The second group saw nothing, but heard the contestants' replies to the panelists' questions. The third group saw all the contestants' facial and body gestures, but heard dubbed-in versions of their voices, which canceled out any paralinguistic cues. The fourth group saw facial and body gestures only and heard nothing.

The second group, which heard only the voices, were just as accurate at guessing who was lying as the first group. The removal of visual cues had no effect on the ability to perceive deception; verbal content and paralinguistic cues sufficed. The fourth group, which saw the visual portion only, was the most inaccurate, confirming that removal of verbal content and paralinguistic cues seriously hampers the ability to detect deception. (This also supported Ekman

and Friesen's belief that people are very good at using facial expressions to conceal their feelings.) However, removal of paralinguistic cues had no effect on the third group's accuracy; this group performed better than the fourth group, which heard no verbal response. Thus, the verbal content of contestants' replies, and not facial or paralinguistic ones, was by far the most important indicator of who was telling the truth.

In the second experiment, the researchers wanted to know precisely what verbal and nonverbal cues tip off people that someone is trying to deceive them (Kraut & Poe, 1980). Here, 110 airline passengers at an airport were asked to participate in a mock inspection procedure. Some were given "contraband" to conceal, others carried nothing but their own luggage. All were to present themselves as honest persons, thereby forcing the "smugglers" to deceive inspectors. Later, real customs inspectors and uninvolved subjects watched videotape playbacks of each of the performances and were asked to decide which passengers ought to be searched. The researchers expected the professional inspectors to be more proficient than the uninvolved subjects in spotting deceptive behavior, possibly because they would look for different behavioral cues. Both sets of observers failed to identify a good many of the "smugglers," but both agreed about which passengers ought to be searched and which could pass on. The verbal and nonverbal behaviors that aroused the most suspicion were displays of nervousness, such as hesitating before answering questions, evading a question, and self-grooming. Other behaviors that would make a traveler suspicious included taking too long a time to answer a question, shifting position frequently, giving short answers, avoiding eye contact, and volunteering extra information. Judgments about deception, in this case, were heavily based on paralinguistic cues and body movements, but not on facial expressions.

Mass Communication

So far, we have discussed the communications that take place between two people or among small groups of people. However, the field of communication also encompasses television, radio, newspapers, books, magazines, recordings, films, and other **mass media** that reach an audience of millions.

Television is, without doubt, the most pervasive of the mass media. Watching television is effortless: It comes directly into our homes; for most Americans it is free; and it both displays and discusses. Each day, more people watch television than read newspapers or make use of any other mass media. As of 1981, 98 percent of all American households owned at least one TV set (*World Almanac*, 1982), and popular shows can reach millions of people on a single evening (see Table 7–3). Not surprisingly, the influence of television extends to other media as well. *TV Guide*, for example, with a circulation of nearly 18 million, is the most widely read magazine in the United States. TV commercials persuade enormous numbers of watchers to buy designer jeans, perfume, and breakfast cereal—as well as books, newspapers, magazines, and records. As we will soon see, television has the power not only to shape purchasing habits, but also to shape our perceptions of reality and to influence social behavior.

Television may be the most pervasive but it is not the only influential mass

TABLE 7–3.
All-Time Top Television Programs

Program	Date	Network	Households
Dallas	11/21/80	CBS	41,470,000
Roots	1/30/77	ABC	36,380,000
Super Bowl XIV	1/20/80	CBS	35,330,000
Super Bowl XIII	1/21/79	NBC	35,090,000
Super Bowl XII	1/15/78	CBS	34,410,000
Gone With The Wind, Pt. 1	11/7/76	NBC	33,960,000
Gone With The Wind, Pt. 2	11/8/76	NBC	33,750,000
Roots	1/28/77	ABC	32,680,000
Roots	1/27/77	ABC	32,540,000
Roots	1/25/77	ABC	31,900,000
Super Bowl XI	1/9/77	NBC	31,610,000
Roots	1/24/77	ABC	31,400,000
Roots	1/26/77	ABC	31,190,000
World Series Game 6	10/21/80	NBC	31,120,000
Dallas	11/9/80	CBS	31,120,000
Roots	1/29/77	ABC	30,120,000
Jaws	11/4/79	ABC	29,830,000

Source: Adapted from *The World Almanac & Book of Facts, 1981*, Newspaper Enterprise Associates, Inc., 1980, 430.

TABLE 7–4.
Network TV Program Ratings and Audience Composition

Program or Type	TV Households		Audience Composition (thousands)			
	Rating (%)	No.	Men (18+)	Women (18+)	Teens 12–17	Children 2–11
Today (7:30–8:00)	5.3	4,120	2,020	3,140	130	150
Morning (7:15–8:00)	3.1	2,410	1,080	1,700	70	360
Good Morning Amer. (7:30–8:00)	5.3	4,120	1,490	3,210	260	440
Daytime Drama (Soaps)	7.1	5,540	1,170	4,950	440	530
Quiz & Aud. Participation	4.6	3,560	1,160	2,890	160	450
All 10am–4:30pm	6.2	4,850	1,160	4,180	380	570
Evening Informational News Mon.–Fri.	14.1	10,970	7,100	8,260	760	1,260
General Drama	25.4	19,740	11,240	17,750	3,000	3,920
Susp. & Mystery	17.6	13,730	8,660	11,240	2,290	1,150
Sit. Comedy	21.7	16,910	9,680	14,190	3,150	4,750
Feature Film	17.2	13,350	8,890	10,550	2,440	2,200
All 7–11pm regular	19.4	15,090	9,890	11,920	2,570	3,140

Source: From *The World Almanac & Book of Facts*, 1982 edition, © 1981, Newspaper Enterprise Association, 200 Park Avenue, New York.

communicator. More than 50 percent of the nation's viewers receive fewer than 10 TV channels (*World Almanac*, 1982), but readers have a wide choice of newspapers, books, and magazines. From *Playboy* to *Children's Playmate*, from the *National Enquirer* to the *Christian Science Monitor*, the print media reach people of all ages and life-styles. Films and recordings also reach communities across the country. Individual records by such groups or artists as "Led Zeppelin," John Denver, Bette Midler, and The Muppets have sold over 2 million disks.

Users of Mass Media

Who watches all those TV shows and movies? Who buys the changing assortment of newspapers, magazines, and records? The answer is, "almost everyone." Communications experts use scientific sampling and survey techniques to determine which of the media will reach which segments of the population. Depending on your sex, socioeconomic status, and most important, your age, media analysts can predict with surprising accuracy the particular TV shows, films, newspapers, and magazines you are most likely to see. (See Table 7–4.)

Predictors of Television Use Surveys throughout the United States have shown a steady rise in the time Americans spend watching television. In 1965, the average TV-viewing time was 10.5 hours per person per week. By 1980, the figure had risen to 29.46 hours (Robinson, 1981; *World Almanac*, 1982). In the 1960s and 1970s, viewers with a lower educational level, income, and occupational status tended to watch the most TV. However, that difference between education groups may be narrowing, since statistics for 1970 to 1976 showed an increase in TV-watching time of nearly 1 hour a day in households whose head had more than 1 year of college (Bower, 1973; Comstock et al., 1978). Studies also indicate that blacks at all educational and income levels view more television than do whites. However, well-educated blacks watch *more* than do poorly educated blacks.

Age and sex also influence TV-watching habits. Children pick up the television habit at age 2 or 3, long before they know how to read. Indeed, this was the fact that led to the creation of *Sesame Street*, which was an attempt to improve the "reading readiness" of preschool children. By the time they reach grade school, children have spent more time in front of the TV set than most young adults will spend in college classrooms (Gerbner & Gross, 1976).

Differences Between Viewers and Nonviewers Before the era of television people spent more time listening to the radio, visiting with friends, reading newspapers and books, taking short trips, going to movies, and participating in organizations. Today many people look to television for almost all of their entertainment and information, and steady TV-watchers spend far less time on such "old-fashioned" activities. They also spend less time sleeping, doing housework, and caring for their children (Robinson, 1981). In contrast, nonviewers spend somewhat more time on childrearing, reading, listening to records, writing letters, and housework, and a great deal more time going to movies, museums, and restaurants, visiting friends, and participating in political and religious groups. Despite their increased activity—or perhaps because of it—nonviewers also spend more time resting and napping (Jackson-Beek & Robinson, 1981).

Studies comparing the attitudes of television viewers emphasize its influence: Regardless of age, place of residence, or exposure to other media, heavy television viewers—those who spend 4 hours a day or more in front of the "tube"—have very different ideas about the world than do nonviewers or light (2 hours a day or less) viewers. Heavy viewers may be so steeped in the dramatic realism of TV that they confuse TV fantasies with real-life events, believing Lou Grant to be a real newspaperman and Trapper John to be a real doctor. They also believe that the TV world of the predominantly white, free-wheeling, unattached, professional is an accurate reflection of the real world (Gerbner & Gross, 1976). After spending so many hours in a TV world teeming with criminals, outlaws, and other enemies of society—all of whom are invariably caught, violently punished, or killed—heavy TV-watchers tend to overestimate their own chances of being involved in a violent incident, overestimate police use of firearms, and feel that other people cannot be trusted (Gerbner et al., 1979).

One picture is worth a thousand words.
Chinese proverb

Predictors of Newspaper Use Where the most popular television shows may be seen in 20 million or more households, few magazines come close to having a circulation of 20 million copies and only 5 newspapers in the United States have a circulation of over 1 million. However, more than 60 million newspapers are read daily (see Table 7–5). Not surprisingly, the same factors that influence TV-watching also affect newspaper-reading—or nonreading, as is often the case today. According to recent studies, the proportion of adults who read a newspaper each day has declined from 73 percent in 1967, to 66 percent in 1975, to only 57

TABLE 7–5.
What Americans Read

Magazine	Circulation per Issue[a]	Newspaper	Circulation per Issue[b] Daily	Circulation per Issue[b] Sunday
TV Guide	17,981,657	Wall Street Journal	1,948,121	
Reader's Digest	17,898,681	New York News	1,491,556	1,995,702
National Geographic Magazine	10,711,886	Los Angeles Times	1,026,092	1,271,603
Better Homes & Gardens	8,052,693	New York Times	930,546	1,479,263
Woman's Day	7,748,069	Chicago Tribune	790,475	1,150,540
Family Circle	7,529,734	Total of all English-language		
McCall's	6,218,169	U.S. newspapers[c]	62,201,840	54,676,173
Ladies' Home Journal	5,601,449			
Good Housekeeping	5,290,833			
National Enquirer	5,051,496			
Playboy	5,011,099			

[a]**Source:** Audit Bureau of Circulations' FAS-FAX Report, based on total average paid circulation during the 6 months prior to Dec. 31, 1980. Adapted from *The World Almanac & Book of Facts*, 1982 edition © 1981 Newspaper Enterprise Association, 200 Park Avenue, New York, New York 10166.

[b]**Source:** Audit Bureau of Circulations' FAS-FAX Report. Average paid circulation for 6 months to March 31, 1981. Adapted from *The World Almanac & Book of Facts*, 1982 edition, © 1981 Newspaper Enterprise Association, 200 Park Avenue, New York, New York 10166.

[c]For 6 months prior to Sept. 30, 1980.

percent in 1978 (Robinson & Jeffres, 1979). Whereas we saw that higher educational and income levels were associated with *fewer* TV-viewing hours, the reverse is true for newspaper-reading. However, as more highly educated people continue their trend toward more TV-watching, each generation is more likely than its predecessor to use TV, rather than newspapers, as its major source of news (Roper Organization, 1977).

Violence and TV

Researchers warn that television violence affects more than our perceptions of reality; it may also affect our behavior. They have found, for example, that heavy TV watchers tend to feel "it is almost always all right to hit someone if you are mad at them for a good reason" (Gerbner et al., 1978, p. 196). After all, that is what the "good guys" do on television.

How Violent is TV? TV researcher George Gerbner defines violence as "the overt expression of physical force with or without a weapon, against self or other"; it may compel "action against one's will on pain of being hurt or killed, or actually hurting and killing" (1979, p. 1978). In one widely respected survey, Gerbner and his colleagues found that eight out of ten television programs contained episodes that met this definition. Six out of every ten leading characters were involved in violent actions.

The extent of violence proved even greater in children's shows. Nine out of ten weekend children's hour programs contained violent episodes. Between the

Application: Television Violence and Behavior

If television stimulated as much violence and aggression as some people fear, no one would need to do research to discover the consequences. Bruises and broken bones would afflict almost everyone (Gerbner et al., 1979). Although violence is increasingly prevalent in our society, television surely is not the only cause. Nevertheless, research studies provide firm evidence that witnessing television violence does make adults, adolescents, and children more aggressive in their behavior.

Loye (1978) provided one group of married men with a cable TV selection of only nonviolent, prosocial programs such as *The Waltons*. Another group viewed strictly violent programs such as *Hawaii Five-0*. Each man's wife was asked to monitor how often he was "helpful" or "hurtful" during the week of the experiment. According to Loye, the wives reported much more "hurtful" behavior—cutting criticism, insensitive remarks, and so on—when violent shows were the standard fare.

ages of 5 and 15, the average child witnesses over 13,400 violent deaths on television, in addition to several hundred assaults and rapes, Gerbner estimates.

As these figures suggest, the amount of TV violence varies with the hour of the day and the day of the week (Slaby et al., 1976). Slaby and his colleagues agree with Gerbner's findings that violence is most prevalent during the evening "prime time" (8 p.m. to 11 p.m.), during the afternoon, and on weekends—all the times when children are home from school. They recorded an average of 7.51 violent episodes per hour in the afterschool hours, 7.97 per hour in prime time, and 12.80 on Saturday mornings, when children comprise the majority of watchers. The rate for cartoons alone was 21.50 violent episodes per hour, "nearly three times the overall average rate of violence" (Slaby et al., 1975, p. 95). The inescapable conclusion is that heavy viewers of TV, particularly children, are exposed to large doses of violence every day.

Effects of Violence on Children and Adolescents   Harsh criticism and insensitive speech are indirect forms of aggression, and are often used by adults who have learned to inhibit their aggressive impulses, particularly around the home, where physical aggression is socially unacceptable. Unlike adults, children are considerably less inhibited in expressing hostility toward others. Many studies have addressed the problem of children imitating the violent models they see on TV (Bandura, Ross, & Ross, 1963). We will see in chapter 11 that children display aggressive behavior after watching a model who behaves aggressively. A 1977 Canadian study focused on children in a previously isolated community into which television was just being introduced. The investigators found a dramatic increase in aggressiveness among children in this town, but not among those in a comparison town that did not yet have TV reception (Joy et al., 1977).

Children do not simply imitate the violence they see on television. Studies suggest that TV violence stimulates a wide range of violent behavior that increases over time. In one study by Steuer et al. (1971), preschool children were

Exposure to violent television episodes, such as the scene from a cartoon shown here, has been shown to have behavioral consequences in children and adults. Children who watch TV violence behave more aggressively in many situations, and are more tolerant of violence in real life. When they watch television a great deal, adults overestimate the extent of violence in the real world, and even come to expect that it will occur in their lives.

carefully observed over a 10-day baseline period to establish the amount of aggressive behavior that normally occurred. One group of children spent the next 11 days watching regularly scheduled short cartoons that portrayed a variety of physical aggression; another group watched the same cartoons with the scenes of physical aggression edited out. Those who watched the violent cartoons became increasingly more aggressive toward their playmates than those who watched the nonviolent cartoons. Significantly, their violent behavior grew worse over the 11-day period. This suggests that television violence has a cumulative effect; the more children see, the more violent they become.

Exposure to TV violence also makes children more tolerant of real-life violence, researchers find. In one study (Drabman & Thomas, 1974) grade-school children who watched a violent TV western were asked to monitor the behavior of two younger children, and to call for an adult assistant if there was any trouble. After exposure to the TV violence, these children waited much longer than another group who had not seen the TV western to report the destructive confrontations of their younger charges. The investigators concluded that witnessing filmed violence encourages children to accept conflict and destructive behavior as a normal, acceptable part of life.

Similar findings were reported in studies of adolescents and young adults who watched violent scenes from full-length films (Berkowitz et al., 1963; Berkowitz & Geen, 1966). The investigators observed adolescent boys in a minimum security penal institution. When these aggressive and angry adolescents viewed violent films and were then given a socially sanctioned opportunity to subject another person to electric shocks, they were far more willing to do so than were similar adolescents who had not seen the violent films.

Some critics have attributed American adolescents' aggressive tendencies to the uniquely violent character of American society, but research does not bear this out. In a comparison of juvenile delinquents in Belgium and in the United States, Parke et al. (1977) found that boys from both countries became more physically aggressive after a week's exposure to films such as *Bonnie and Clyde*. Interestingly, boys who watched nonaggressive films sometimes showed a *decrease* in aggressive behavior.

As these examples from the substantial body of research in this area show, witnessing violence on television and on film fosters aggressive behavior in children, adolescents, and adults. Given this fact, why do the networks and movie studios continue to produce features with so much violence? Some entertainment experts claim that they are just providing what the public demands, and most people, they say, demand the excitement generated by filmed violence. But some researchers disagree. Diener and DeFour (1978), for example, found very little correlation between TV shows' violence levels and their popularity levels in national Nielsen viewer ratings. In another study, they showed college students both an uncut version of the adventure program, *Police Woman*, and the same episode with almost all the violence edited out. Although the uncut version was judged to be significantly more violent, it was *not* judged to be significantly more entertaining. In fact, some students disliked it because of the violence.

These findings are corroborated, oddly, by analysis of the ten top-rated series of the 1981–1982 television viewing year. The two favorites were *Dallas* and *Sixty Minutes*, while seven others were situation comedies. The only significantly violent series that was popular was *The Dukes of Hazzard*—which displayed more automobile crashes than interpersonal violence (Schwartz, 1982).

Politics, News, and Information

As newspaper readership declines, television has become the primary source of news information for millions of Americans. How well is television doing its job?

Actions speak louder than words.

TV News: What Do You Really Learn From It?   By its very nature, television depends primarily on images to convey information. Images capture action and show what people are doing, but they cannot reveal what people are thinking. That is where speech comes in, but studies show that on TV it does not come in often enough. According to one analysis, the script of a 30-minute newscast would not even fill one page of a newspaper (Patterson & McClure, 1976, p. 55).

What is the problem? Analyses of network news programs find that they present very little solid information. In its search for exciting visual scenes, TV often focuses on action "events" rather than on issues and policies. During an election, for example, TV watchers see crowds, motorcades, and rallies but hear only snatches of the candidates' speeches on important issues. Repeatedly, studies have shown that people who read newspapers are better informed about political issues than television watchers, and far better informed than radio listeners (Atkin et al., 1976; Atkin & Heald, 1976; Clarke & Fredin, 1978; Tan & Vaughn, 1976). As one study concluded, "People who faithfully tuned in the network news during the (1972) election learned not much more than people who spent the time doing something else" (Patterson & McClure, 1976, p. 51).

Mass Media and Politics   Although people do not learn much from watching television news programs, they do learn something, and studies have shown that that something is usually negative (Robinson, 1975). Most news accounts emphasize problems, not solutions; confrontations, not compromises. By emphasizing the negative, television encourages people to distrust elected officials in particular, and the political system in general. During the Watergate scandal, for example, people who relied solely on television for their news became hostile to our government, whereas those who regularly read newspaper accounts maintained their confidence in our political system, under the belief that Watergate was an "atypical" event (Becker et al., 1979; Becker & Whitney, 1980).

News features such as in-depth analyses or candidate debates are usually better than regular news coverage (Quarles, 1979). Before-and-after surveys of voters who watched the 1976 presidential debates between Jimmy Carter and Gerald Ford found, for example, that before the debates about 14 percent of the sampled citizens did not know Ford's positions on major issues, and 20 percent did not know Carter's positions. By the end of the debate series, the "don't knows" dropped to 6.62 percent. Since about 70 percent of all eligible voters watched the debates, political analysts concluded that most voters went to the polls relatively well informed about the issues (Chaffee, 1978).

Many voters rely on the candidates' TV advertisements to make their choices (Atkin & Heald, 1976; Patterson & McClure, 1976). This may seem surprising in view of the fact that 1 minute after a commercial fades from the TV screen, viewers generally cannot recall what was advertised (Patterson & McClure, 1976, p. 109). But presidential commercials are different. They depict the person whose decisions will affect every aspect of the viewer's life over the next 4 years, and they appear only once every 4 years, so they capture people's attention. They therefore have greater immediate impact than do commercials for denture adhesives, decaffeinated coffee, and other consumer products. Not surprisingly, more than 50 percent of the TV viewers in one poll were able to recall the content of political spot commercials aired in the 1972 election campaign and knew specific details about the candidates' issue positions (Atkin & Heald, 1976).

Public Opinion Polls and the Media   In addition to news reports and political advertisements, voters are also influenced by public opinion polls. Polls are designed to measure what people think about an issue or a candidate. However, poll results are able to alter the factors that they are supposed to measure. For example, undecided voters are more likely to vote for a candidate who is ahead in the polls, simply because that candidate looks like a winner; this is the "bandwagon effect."

Not surprisingly, when candidates fall behind in the polls they disparage the polls' influence, while those who are ahead advertise their poll standings. Pre-election polling provides both sides with a chance to respond and attempt to influence the next polls in their favor. However, sophisticated TV networks have created a new form of poll that is seemingly immune from response: election day polling. Using multimillion dollar computer technology, ABC, CBS, and NBC, the three major networks, compete with each other to see who can predict election victors first. On election night in 1972, for example, 30 minutes before even going on the air, NBC indicated that Nixon would win by a landslide. Consequently, many voters in western time zones concluded that their votes were meaningless

The fool who holds his tongue may pass as wise.
Spanish proverb

and decided not to vote (Bohn, 1980). In the 1980 election, much the same thing happened: NBC announced the presidential results at 8:15 P.M. E.S.T., and President Carter conceded the election hours before the polls closed on the West Coast. As democratic voters from Oregon to Hawaii stayed away from the polls thinking that their votes would not affect the biggest race, they unintentionally affected the results in scores of local contests (Waters & Hackett, 1980).

Mere Exposure   Although media experts criticize news reports, political advertising, and polls for "manipulating" the voters, at least these communications have direct relevance in an election. They supply identifiable information about candidates' viewpoints, personal attributes, and activities. However, several studies show that a voter's final choice often depends on seemingly irrelevant, noninformational factors, such as the candidates' position on the ballot (the name that appears first frequently gets more votes), or a familiar sounding name (Mueller, 1970).

Ballot position is determined by chance; names, of course, are determined by birth. Although there is little a candidate can do about the former, most candidates work hard to exploit the latter. Other than changing one's name to that of a famous, successful politician—and some candidates have done just that—advertising is the best way to make an unknown name into the proverbial "household word."

As we mentioned earlier, advertising provides what Zajonc (1968) called *mere exposure* (see chapter 6). And research shows there is nothing "mere" about it. Simply seeing and hearing someone's name often enough enhances voters' opinions of that individual, particularly if the individual is otherwise unknown. In a study of 51 Congressional primary elections, for example, Grush et al. (1978) found that nonincumbents who were not well known could get elected simply by frequent media exposure. In fact, media exposure alone successfully predicted 83 percent of the primary winners in these races.

What are the implications of this finding? It appears that money might enable a previously unknown candidate to "buy" an election. Limitations on the amount of money individuals can spend on their own campaigns may curtail somewhat the number of "bought" elections. It is clear, though, that candidates who are unable to raise substantial amounts of money are at a disadvantage.

Sex Roles and Sex Role Socialization

We have seen that both children and adults may model their behavior after violent characters and situations that they see on television. This modeling effect is true not only for violent models but also for sex roles, and other social stereotypes as well.

Feminists have long criticized television's tendency to portray women in passive or negative roles. Since children of both sexes are strongly influenced by television role models, this is a serious charge (Bandura, 1973). And, according to several studies, feminists' criticism is well founded.

In a content analysis of such popular children's programs as *Pebbles and Bamm Bamm, Popeye, Superman, Bewitched, I Dream of Jeannie,* and *Scooby-*

Controversy: Does Watching *The Waltons* Make You a Nicer Person?

The studies cited in the text have, for the most part, emphasized the variety of negative effects of television. Does anyone—other than the millions of apparently uncritical viewers—have a good word for this medium? In the language of social psychology, is television a "prosocial influence"? (See chapter 12.)

From the beginning, there have been television programs that encouraged caring and cooperation. The *Lassie* series, for example, typically portrayed dramatic examples of a boy helping his dog, or the dog helping the boy and his family. In one experiment, children who watched a particularly prosocial episode of *Lassie* subsequently showed considerably more willingness to help a dog in distress, even at a cost to themselves, than did nonviewers (Sprafkin et al., 1975). Another study found that second and third grade children were more cooperative in problem-solving tasks and behavioral helping measures after watching an episode of *The Waltons* (Baran et al., 1979).

Of course, experimental demonstrations may not reflect everyday situations in which children and adults face more ambiguous choices between prosocial and antisocial behaviors. We might wonder whether children who watch *The Waltons* might still increase their prosocial behaviors if an episode of *Dallas* was also on that day's TV agenda. Nevertheless, such studies do suggest that television's prosocial potential is as great, if not greater, than its antisocial potential. Whether that potential will be tapped remains to be seen.

As the *Summary Report* of the National Institute of Mental Health (1982) concluded, constructive behavior can be learned from television, especially by children who have adults available to help them understand the program material. The report questioned, however, whether the beneficial content that does exist in programs is actually viewed under circumstances that enhance the learning of prosocial behaviors, and recommended research that would study the effects of television-viewing on family beliefs and life-styles.

Doo, Sternglanz and Serbin (1974) found "striking sex differences in both the number of male and female roles portrayed and in the behaviors which were emitted by male and female characters" (p. 710). Males were portrayed more than twice as often as females, and their roles were usually more active, aggressive, or constructive (building and planning). In contrast, females were shown as passive and deferent, and those female characters who were shown as active generally got their comeuppance.

It appears that television gives American children very different messages about appropriate behaviors for males and females. Not surprisingly, those children who watch many hours of television are more likely to accept the traditional role models they have observed than those who spend less time in front of the "tube" (Fruen & McGhee, 1975). TV-viewing appears to exert a particular influence on career-related sex stereotypes, according to Beuf (1974). She studied 63 children aged 3 to 6, and found that 76 percent of the heavy TV watchers selected sex-stereotyped careers as "what they wanted to be when they grew up," whereas only 50 percent of moderate TV watchers made stereotyped choices. As well as knowing about their sex, these preschoolers already understand the social implications—and limitations—of gender for their future life.

Stereotypes continue to be reinforced throughout childhood by regular TV programs and by commercials. Tan (1979) found, for example, that teenage girls exposed to commercials for soaps, toothpastes, and other personal products rated beauty characteristics as "highly important" in a woman's ability "to be liked by men" and as "desirable" personal characteristics for a woman.

If television reinforces sex-role stereotypes, can it also reduce their influence? Some studies have indicated that this is possible. A survey of children from seven different areas of the United States, for example, found that the television program *Free Style*, which portrayed egalitarian sex roles among 9- through 12-year-olds, increased both male and female viewers' approval of nontraditional roles for girls (Johnston et al., 1980). Nontraditional sex-role acceptance was even stronger and more persistent when *Free Style* was viewed in a school setting (Johnston & Davidson, 1980), and its message was presumably enhanced by the school's authority.

McArthur and Eisen (1976) had similarly encouraging results when they exposed boys and girls in nursery school to nontraditional sex-role portrayals. Boys who saw men engaged in nurturing, domestic, and artistic behaviors later showed more of these behaviors. However, after seeing films in which men engaged in traditional behaviors, the boys engaged in more of those behaviors. Girls, too, tended to identify with and imitate same-sex role models, whether they were performing traditional (nurturing, domestic, or artistic) or nontraditional (adventuresome, leadership, or problem-solving) activities.

Sexual Innuendo Experimental efforts to show nonstereotyped behavior are rather obvious, even to children. Perhaps their clear-cut nature helps to explain the marked effects they have on children's imitative behavior. However, in most everyday situations, sex-stereotyped behavior is more subtle. This subtlety may explain why stereotypes exert such an insidious effect on our society, despite great efforts to discard them.

Research studies show that the mass media play a strong role in perpetuating sexual stereotypes, not through blatant examples but through subtle innuendo. Silverman et al. (1979) found, for example, that in 64 prime-time television programs, "suggestive" touching and flirtatious or seductive behaviors occurred more than 75 times per hour, on the average. Comparison of the 1975 and 1977 TV seasons showed a dramatic increase in the frequency of sexual behaviors, these authors reported.

Interestingly, "soap operas," which are known for their sexually suggestive material, have been found to include many explicit references to sexual behaviors widely discouraged by society—adultery, rape, incest, prostitution—and dramatized love-making scenes, but comparatively few "innuendos" (Lowry et al., 1981). Analyses of soap opera content indicate that a steady viewing diet of role models who engage in socially unacceptable sex acts may be just as damaging as a steady diet of TV violence, for both children and adults (p. 96).

Other Stereotypes Perpetuated by the Mass Media

Added to the criticism of violence and sexism in the mass media is a growing concern about racial, ethnic, and age stereotypes. Content analyses show that most characters portrayed on American TV are white, young, and middle-class

(Williams et al., 1977). However, when blacks are shown on TV, the portrayals are generally positive. Donagher et al. (1975) found, for example, that black men on *The Bill Cosby Show, Firehouse, Mannix, Maude, Mission Impossible*, and other shows were predominantly nonaggressive, persistent, altruistic, and more likely than other groups to make reparations for injuries. Black women on these shows exhibited superior abilities to explain feelings, increase understanding, resolve strife, and reassure others. Unfortunately, blacks appear so rarely—one study found that they were seen during less than 9 percent of commercial and regular program time (Weigel, Loomis, & Soja, 1980)—that such positive images may have little effect on popular attitudes and beliefs. Cross-racial interactions between blacks and whites also tend to be portrayed positively, but were even less frequent, totaling about 2 percent of the time on the shows sampled.

The lack of exposure to positive racial role models on TV is particularly damaging, since television serves as the prime source of race information for many Americans. Despite increasing integration of the races and ethnic groups across the country, most American children grow up in relatively homogeneous communities, where they seldom see, let alone interact with, people of different backgrounds. One study of 300 white elementary school children found, for example, that TV was their primary source of information about how blacks look, talk, and dress (Greenberg, 1972). Gorn et al. (1970) found that 3–5-year-old white children showed a strong preference for playing with nonwhites after being exposed to *Sesame Street* segments containing nonwhite children. In the same study, English Canadian children who viewed segments in which a French Canadian boy appeared subsequently showed a strong preference for French Canadian children as well. This is an indication that TV could make a strong contribution to positive racial relations, if producers were willing to use their opportunities.

Commercials

Although they certainly influence behavior, most television shows are designed to entertain, not to change the viewers' behavior. Commercials, on the other hand, strive specifically to affect behavior, to make a certain life-style or product seem appealing enough to purchase. The media wizards who create commercials are perhaps even more brilliant than the producers of the programs on which the commercials appear. Against their persuasive powers, children do not stand a chance. Even the most skeptical children can be swayed by repeated exposure to toy commercials during the Christmas season (Robertson & Rossiter, 1974).

According to A. C. Nielsen surveys, the average 2- to 11-year-old watches about 4 hours of television each day. Depending upon the time of day, from 9½ to 16 minutes per hour is taken by commercial messages. That comes to more than 3 hours of television advertising each week, or some 20,000 commercial messages each year—and that is without adjusting for the Christmas rush (Adler, 1977).

There is some cause for concern about whether children are able to differentiate between the informational and entertainment messages of the regular program and the persuasive messages of the commercials. A number of studies have shown that children often request products they have seen advertised (Comstock et al., 1978); just watch any kid in the supermarket! Children younger than

7 or 8 years particularly place considerable faith in commercial messages and are less able than older children to discern their persuasive, sales-oriented intentions (Robertson & Rossiter, 1977; Ward, Wackman, & Wartella, 1977). But efforts to teach young children to be more skeptical about TV advertising have been successful. Fourth-graders who viewed the Consumer's Union Film, *The Six Billion $$$ Sell*, for example, were more skeptical of advertising claims than children who viewed a control film (see Table 7–6) (Roberts et al., 1978).

However, sixth and eighth graders appeared to have been discriminating viewers even before exposure to the film. The researchers performed a similar study on younger children—"When someone famous tries to get you to buy something in a TV commercial, you can be pretty sure it is as good as he says it is" (agree or disagree). They found again that it was quite effective to teach consumer skepticism to very young children, and that the youngest children were more susceptible to both advertising messages *and* to consumer education.

Critical Viewing Skills

The results of such experiments strongly suggest that critical viewers are made, not born. Roberts and his colleagues puzzled over the mechanism that might underlie their finding that those children who watched television most were those who were most influenced by the instructional film. It is possible, they suggest, that such children are also receiving the least consumer training from their parents. But they consider it possible also that these children might have more actual examples in their minds to refer to when they received explanatory information in *The Six Billion $$$ Sell*.

This suggests that an adult audience too might be made more skeptical of

---

TABLE 7–6.
Content Analysis of *The Six Billion $$$ Sell*

Announcer comments on various "tricks" used in commercials and says we will look at some.	"The Giveaway"—promoting premium offers rather than the product itself.
"Selling the Star"—use of celebrity testimonials.	"Promises, Promises"—association of product with glamour, success, fun, and the good life.
"Now You See It, Now You Don't"—exaggerations, irrelevant claims, tricks of camera and lighting.	"Brand Loyalty"—promoting a brand rather than the product itself.
"New! New! New!"—use of the word "new" to imply superiority.	Children conduct a group discussion about commercials in general and come to the conclusion that people should make their own product choices and should be very careful about the claims made in commercials.
"Word Games"—use of scientific sounding words to imply superiority.	

Source: Adapted from the summary of two instructional films: 'The Six Billion $$$ Sell' from "Developing Discriminating Consumers" by D. F. Roberts, et al., *Journal of Communications*, 1980, *30*, 97. Reprinted by permission.

advertising claims in a like manner. In the years following the 1971 Report of the Surgeon General's Advisory Committee on Television and Social Behavior, efforts were made to counteract the negative effects of extensive television viewing through development of school curricula to increase viewer awareness. In 1982, after 10 years of efforts and research, a follow-up report summarized that

> accumulating evidence suggests that such educational programs are welcomed by teachers and pupils and that the programs do produce changes in awareness of television production, special effects, the nature of commercials, the excesses of violence and so on.

This report concluded, though, that

> longer term effects of genuine critical viewing at home or of reduced viewing or more selective viewing have yet to be demonstrated. Teaching about television is considered by many television researchers to be one of the most significant practical developments of the 1970s, one that needs to be continued, expanded, and evaluated in the 1980s. (NIMH, 1982)

The role of social psychology in this effort is sure to be as extensive as it has been in the past.

Answering Questions about Communication

1. It is believed that the grammatical and structural aspects of a language greatly influence the way people think. Eskimo children, for example, become alert to many different types of snow, probably because their language has many different words for types of snow.
2. Yes, we can express meaningful concepts without words. The fields of paralanguage (wordless sounds), kinesics (body language), and proxemics (interpersonal distance) have demonstrated those channels to be quite important in communicating messages.
3. As Darwin noted, people throughout the world use the same expressions to convey the same emotions. Although the rules for what expressions are appropriate, and when, vary according to culture, there are universal facial expressions for emotions such as anger, happiness, sadness.
4. You can tell a person is lying to you by noticing nonverbal cues. Most of these cues are not given by the face, but "leak" out through the body. A person who is lying will smile less, fidgit more, employ nervous gestures, and speak in a higher tone of voice than a person who isn't.
5. No, they do not. Researchers have shown versions of TV shows such as *Policewoman* to groups of undergraduates, either cutting violent scenes or leaving the shows intact. They have found no difference in the enjoyment levels between those who saw the edited and the complete versions.
6. There is substantial evidence that people vote for a candidate because they have been exposed to his or her name many times. The amount of media exposure is a good predictor of which candidate will win an election.

7. Yes. The National Institute of Mental Health has concluded that constructive behavior as well as destructive behavior can be learned from television programs.

Summary

Communication is any means by which one mind affects another, and can include both *verbal* and *nonverbal* communications between two or more individuals. Only humans have a capacity for true **language,** the system of vocal sounds used to convey meaning to others. Many animals can use signals or sounds to convey general information, but only human language can transmit precise messages. The use of **symbols,** arbitrary systems of **sounds** (such as spoken words and music) and **images** (written words, pictures, and body gestures), permits this precision and enables us to refer to nonmaterial concepts and store complex information. In the communication process, a **message** travels through a **communication channel** from a **sender** to a **receiver. Noise** may distort the message at any point.

Language consists of specific symbols or words. Their uses and meanings are governed by rules of **grammar. Syntax** rules determine the order of words in a sentence. **Semantic meanings** go beyond the literal meanings of words to include contextual or expressive content.

The **theory of linguistic relativity** (also known as the **Sapir-Whorf hypothesis**) holds that language determines the way we interpret our environment. The **semantic differential technique** can be used to determine the range of meanings attached to a given word.

Nonverbal communication lacks the precision and the infinitely expandable vocabulary of verbal communication. It is stable and universal: A smile or grimace is understood everywhere. Nonverbal channels of communication include vocalizations or **paralanguage** (the uh-huhs and tones we use when we speak, for example), *eye contact*, *facial expressions*, body movements or **kinesics,** and interpersonal distance or **proxemics.**

Prolonged eye contact or gazing can indicate admiration; however, an overly prolonged gaze is a discomforting stare. Kinesics researchers distinguish between **emblems,** body movements that can substitute for spoken communication, and **illustrators,** gestures that accompany speech.

Nonverbal communications can emphasize or contradict verbal content. They can also convey an impression of another person, regulate the flow of conversation, cause physical and emotional arousal, indicate the relative status of interacting persons, and the degree of intimacy between them.

In every social interaction a number of communications channels are employed. According to the **equilibrium model of multichannel communication,** for each interaction there is an optimal balance among the various verbal and nonverbal behaviors that is unique to that situation. If any one behavior increases or decreases an inappropriate amount, we feel anxiety and try to compensate by adjusting other factors: If voices become too loud, for example, we may shift our gaze away.

According to the **arousal model of intimacy,** a modest increase in intimacy (closer personal distance) generally causes a pleasant amount of arousal; too great an increase in intimacy leads to greater arousal and anxiety. Thus, we will reciprocate when arousal is positive, but find a way to compensate when arousal is negative.

Deception cues are nonverbal behaviors that indicate an attempt to conceal true feelings; tensed body posture, fixed smiles, and nervous movements are some examples. **Leakage cues** are nonverbal behaviors that betray the true emotion underneath and may contradict the content of a verbal message. Generally, people are quite good at identifying the behaviors that accompany deception, but are less adept at detecting deception itself.

Television, radio, newspapers, books, magazines, recordings, and films—the **mass media**—reach millions of receivers. Of all mass media, television is the most wide-reaching.

Factors of gender, socioeconomic status, and age influence the reading and viewing habits of Americans. Children, the elderly, and women of all ages tend to watch the most TV. Well-educated people read more newspapers and watch less TV than those who are less well-educated.

Exposure to television and other mass media has been blamed for such problems as increasing violence and sexual aggression. Studies have confirmed that TV programs, and especially children's programs, containing violent episodes can stimulate imitative violent behavior in both adults and children.

Candidates' political advertisements on television provide a substantial amount of information to the public. The most powerful effect, however, comes about simply by increasing viewers' exposure to the candidate's name and face.

TV programs have also been found to perpetuate gender, racial, age, and ethnic stereotypes. Television programs that portray prosocial behavior can do much to stimulate caring and cooperation and to break down negative stereotypes.

Television advertisements, which are designed to affect certain behaviors, are found to have a greater impact than regular programs on subsequent actions, particularly those of children. However, studies suggest that children can be taught to recognize and question the persuasive messages of commercials.

Suggested Additional Reading

Haney, W. V. *Communication and organizational behavior.* Homewood, Ill.: Irwin, 1979.

Mayo, C., & Henley, N. M. (eds.). *Gender and nonverbal behavior.* New York: Springer-Verlag, 1982.

Miller, G. R., & Burgoon, J. K. Factors affecting assessments of witness credibility. In N. L. Kerr & R. M. Bray (eds.), *The psychology of the courtroom.* New York: Academic Press, 1982.

National Institute of Mental Health. *Television and behavior: Ten years of scientific progress and implications for the eighties* (Vol. 1). Rockville,

Md.: U.S. Department of Health and Human Services, 1982.

Terrace, H. S., et al. Can an ape create a sentence? *Science, 206,* 891–902.

Whitney, D. C., Wartella, E., & Windahl, S. *Mass communication review yearbook* (Vol. 3). Beverly Hills: Sage, 1982.

Wilhoit, G. C., & DeBock, H. (eds.). *Mass communication review yearbook* (Vol. 1). Beverly Hills: Sage, 1980.

Wilhoit, G. C., & DeBock, H. (eds.). *Mass communication review yearbook* (Vol. 2). Beverly Hills: Sage, 1981.

8

ATTITUDES AND ATTITUDE CHANGE

Questions about Attitudes and Attitude Change

1. Consider your own experiences since you have been to college. Can you think of any important changes in your own attitudes and behavior that have taken place since you left home?

2. Do you smoke cigarettes? You are probably aware that cigarette smoking has been linked as a possible cause in several types of cancer. You think of yourself as a rational person, don't you? Then why don't you stop smoking?

3. You are watching a television talk show on which the host is interviewing an ex-convict who advocates more severe punishment for criminals. Would you be more persuaded by this source of communication than if you heard an ex-convict arguing for less punishment? Why?

4. In the course of watching television in prime time, you may encounter 50 commercials. Although you generally hate commercials, you can't help mentally tuning in whenever you hear the words "new and improved." Why?

5. If you want to deliver a complex message, should you write it down or present it orally? What does your psychology professor do when he or she has a particularly complex lecture to deliver? Does receiving a handout help you to get the message?

6. You are listening to the president of the United States making a televised speech defending his administration's foreign policy in a controversial Latin American nation. At the same time your roommate is talking on the phone in the next room. You find the phone conversation mildly distracting. Do you think this mild distraction will make you more or less susceptible to the president's persuasive message?

What is your attitude toward women who pursue careers outside the home? Does the term "career woman" conjure up positive or negative images? What do you believe about the personalities of career women as opposed to the personalities of homemakers? How do your beliefs and feelings affect the way you behave to women you know or meet?

Fifty years ago, most Americans, women as well as men, believed that "a woman's place was in the home," and, in fact, most women did not work unless it was economically necessary. The term "career woman" itself reflects this attitude. Did you ever hear of a "career man"?

In the last few years attitudes toward working women have changed radically, but only after their participation in the work force increased substantially. For many years, women in record numbers entered the work force despite the prevailing attitudes about women and work. This demonstrates clearly how complex the relationship between attitudes and behavior can be, and that one is not necessarily a reliable predictor of the other. For this reason, the study of attitude formation and attitude change has absorbed social psychologists since the beginnings of the discipline. In fact, there has probably been more social psychological research on attitudes and attitude change than on any other topic. In this chapter we will examine some of the classic research on these topics, and in chapter 9 we shall look at an area of attitude research that is receiving active attention from social psychologists today: How do attitudes relate to behavior?

When these women went to work during the Second World War, in what had previously been men's jobs, the nation's attitude toward them was very supportive. Attitudes toward working women, and especially women in maintenance and construction work, changed to disapproval after the war. Today relatively few women are found in such jobs, although the public's attitude is slowly becoming more favorable.

The Nature of Attitudes

Although we all have some notion about what an "attitude" is, social psychologists have struggled over the past half-century to develop a workable, scientific definition. During that time various "operational definitions" (recall our discussion in chapter 2) have been offered by social psychologists. For the purposes of the present chapter, we shall define an **attitude** as a predisposition to respond in a certain way to a particular object, event, or experience. This "predisposition to respond" is essentially a mental state, but it also has physiological implications (Detweiler & Zanna, 1976). For example, suppose that hearing a police siren late at night arouses the emotion of fear in you. The fear is a subjective mental state, which you may be able to identify by labeling it "fear"; it is also a neural state of arousal processed by your brain and nervous system; finally, it may be associated with physical symptoms, such as tenseness and sweating.

As Gordon Allport stated in a classic work on attitudes, an attitude is a "preparation or readiness for response. . . . It is not behavior but the precondition of behavior" (Allport, 1935, p. 805). Although it prepares the individual to respond, an attitude need not be conscious; a person may not even be aware of its existence. People often hold attitudes without being either able or willing to express them as definite opinions (Eagly & Himmelfarb, 1978). Allport argued that whether the attitude is consciously or unconsciously maintained, its formation in the individual is the result of prior experience, as we discussed in chapter 3 (1935). The experiences that form attitudes may be extremely subtle, and in many cases people are unaware of why they hold attitudes.

The Three Components of Attitudes

As part of a more complex operational definition, psychologists generally define attitudes in terms of three components: affective, cognitive, and behavioral. The **affective component** refers both to the subjective feeling-states or moods and the physiological responses that accompany an attitude. The **cognitive component** refers to the beliefs and opinions through which the attitude is expressed, although these are not always conscious. And finally, the **behavioral** (or **conative**) **component** refers to the physical and mental processes that prepare the individual to act in a certain manner.

These three components do not function separately; they are highly interrelated. As an example, let us suppose that your attitude toward deer hunting as a sport is extremely negative. You happen to go to a party where someone you have not previously met recounts the story of how he shot a deer and had its head mounted above his mantelpiece. You may feel revulsion for this person (the *affective* component); you may form various negative opinions about him (the *cognitive* component); and you may find yourself thinking of a nasty remark or looking for a way to make a quick exit (the *behavioral* component). Your actual responses will depend on the strength of your attitude as well as on a number of other variables.

The Measurement of Attitudes

As we have emphasized before, one of the most important components of an effective operational definition is the ability to measure the defined concept. Furthermore, although attitudes are important determinants of behavior, they are often expressed in too general or too vague a manner for researchers to be able to correlate them with specific behavioral patterns. For these reasons, social psychologists have developed a number of measurement scales to quantify attitudinal differences.

The Likert Scales   Likert (1932) devised one of the earliest and most influential methods of measuring attitudes. Likert examined five major attitude areas: international relations, race relations, economic conflict, political conflict, and religion. (Despite the passage of over 50 years, these topics are still timely!) He noted that within any of these broad categories, an individual might hold different attitudes on specific issues. For example, an individual who believes in a separation between religious and political issues might still oppose legalized abortion. Likert devised specific questionnaires for each of the five attitude areas. There were several different types of questions; some required a "yes," "?" or "no" response, some were multiple choice, and so on. Each response was given a numerical value. In this way, each individual could receive a cumulative score in each attitude category, which could then be compared against those of other subjects. Table 8–1 contains sample questions from Likert's "Internationalism Scale." The form of the questions resembles that of questions used every day in public opinion surveys. You can easily find similar questions in your newspaper or in newsmagazines such as *Time* or *Newsweek*.

The Semantic Differential Scale While the Likert scale directly elicits attitude responses from subjects, the semantic differential scale (Osgood, Suci, & Tannenbaum, 1957) employs a more indirect method for assessing attitudes. The semantic differential is a more subtle method of attitude measurement than the Likert method, and it depends on a key premise: Attitudes are composed of the meanings (semantics) people assign to key words or concepts (stimuli or signs), and these meanings can be determined through responses to word associations. Suppose, for example, we wished to measure an individual's attitude toward the concept "father"—without asking the person to respond directly with his feelings

---

TABLE 8–1.

Sample Questions from Likert's Internationalism Attitude Scale

1. Do you favor the early entrance of the United States into the League of Nations?
   YES (4)   ? (3)   NO (2)
2. Ought the United States to consult other nations in making her immigration laws?
   YES (4)   ? (3)   NO (2)
10. Is it an idle dream to expect to abolish war?
   YES (2)   ? (3)   NO (4)
13. How much military training should we have?
   (a) We need universal compulsory military training.   (1)
   (b) We need Citizens Military Training Camps and Reserve Officers Training Corps, but not universal military training.   (2)
   (c) We need some facilities for training reserve officers but not as much as at present.   (3)
   (d) We need only such military training as is required to maintain our regular army.   (4)
   (e) All military training should be abolished.   (5)
17. The United States, whether a member or not, should cooperate fully in the humanitarian and economic programs of the League of Nations.
   Strongly Approve   Approve   Undecided   Disapprove   Strongly Disapprove
        (5)   (4)   (3)   (2)   (1)
24. Moving pictures showing military drill and naval maneuvers should be exhibited to encourage patriotism.
   Strongly Approve   Approve   Undecided   Disapprove   Strongly Disapprove
        (1)   (2)   (3)   (4)   (5)

Note 1: Numerical values in parentheses did not appear in the questionnaire as presented to subjects. These values were for use in scoring.

Note 2: The actual questionnaire used by Likert was a Survey of Opinions in which questions on all five attitudes were mixed.

Note 3: A fourth type of question, the headline format, was also used. Here, from the Imperialism Scale, is a sample:

As a result of inflammatory press dispatches, mobs in a small Latin American country have repeatedly attacked United States flags and torn them to shreds. The United States citizens feel that their lives are in danger. MARINES ARE SENT TO PROTECT THE LIVES AND PROPERTY OF THESE CITIZENS.

Strongly Approve (1)   Approve (2)   Undecided (3)   Disapprove (4)   Strongly Disapprove (5)

Source: Adapted from "A Technique for the Measurement of Attitudes" by A. Likert, *Archives of Psychology*, 1932, No. 140, 15–20.

about his own father. With the semantic differential scale, this could be done by asking the subject to associate this concept with certain apparently unrelated adjectival pairs, such as *hard/soft* or *warm/cold* (recall our discussion in chapter 7 and see Figure 7–1). Once the subject has rated the particular concept on a number of dimensions, a pattern is extracted by means of statistical analysis. This pattern is then assumed to represent a coherent picture of the subject's attitude.

Bipolar Scales   A bipolar attitude scale is a scale that measures a subject's attitude on a continuum. One pole of the continuum represents the highest degree of a particular attitude and the other pole represents the highest degree of the opposing attitude. For example, if a simple bipolar scale were constructed to measure the attitudes of subjects to policemen, the two poles of the scale might be "extremely positive" and "extremely negative." Bipolar scaling, as we have seen, is also a feature of semantic differential scaling. There are many examples of bipolar scales throughout this text, and the use of bipolar scales to measure specific attitudes is frequent in social psychological research.

How Attitudes Form

In chapter 3 we talked about the socialization process, and the effects on our lives of some early experiences. Our attitudes are the product of our various life experiences. As a result, they are influenced by significant people in our lives and the ways we process information about the world. In this section we will examine some early socialization research and briefly review the effects of parents, peers, and reference groups on attitude formation. Then we will study some of the ways attitude formation occurs.

Parents, Peers, and Reference Groups   Although we would like to believe that we form our attitudes independently, research has repeatedly shown that our attitudes are influenced by the people who play significant roles in our lives. As we noted in chapter 3, in early childhood parents are the primary socializing agents; consequently, the attitudes they communicate, both verbally and indirectly, have a profound and often lasting effect on us.

Do as I say; don't do as I do.   The pervasive influence of parental attitudes has been confirmed by numerous studies (see, for example, Ashmore & Delboca, 1976; Tedin, 1974). However, it has also been found that when adolescents and young adults are removed from the immediate influence of the home environment—when they go away to college, for example—their attitudes often change profoundly as a result of new peer group and reference group pressures. Newcomb (1943) found that the attitudes of Bennington College freshmen to presidential candidates closely paralleled those of their parents, but that the attitudes of seniors diverged sharply from those of their parents (see Table 8–2). Newcomb explained his findings by pointing out that while the Bennington faculty was predominately liberal in its political outlook (and therefore tended to support the Democratic party candidate), the majority of the students came from homes where the parents were conservative in their outlook (and therefore supported the Republican party candidate). As students progressed in their college careers, they increasingly adopted the outlook of their professors.

Fellow students too are often important sources of attitude change. Consider your own experience in college. Can you think of any important changes in your own attitudes (and behaviors) that have taken place since you left home?

How are new attitudes and behaviors acquired? Social psychologists have drawn upon a variety of learning theories to explain attitude formation. In turn, these theories have produced some interesting research on attitude formation.

Classical Conditioning Theory The basic principle of **classical conditioning** is that when a neutral stimulus is paired with a stimulus that naturally elicits a particular response (the unconditioned stimulus), the neutral stimulus will elicit a similar response and thus become a conditioned stimulus. In Pavlov's famous experiment, a dog was conditioned to salivate at the sound of a bell, because the dog was always given meat after the bell rang. Thus, the bell, originally neutral, came to elicit the same response, salivation, as the natural stimulus, meat. (See Figure 8–1 on the next page.)

A similar process has been observed in attitude formation as a result of the repeated pairing of a neutral concept with one that is socially charged with positive or negative meanings (Staats & Staats, 1958). For example, the word *student* is by itself a neutral adjective that simply indicates a particular educational status; but if this word is repeatedly associated with the adjective *radical* it acquires the connotation of the latter and, as a result, creates the stereotype that "students are radical." Moreover, once the stereotype has taken hold, it does not have to be confirmed by actual experiences in order for it to have an effect on attitudes. Since the concept of *radical-ness* has now become part of the definition of *student*, those who are affected by the stereotype will respond accordingly—just as Pavlov's dog salivated at the tone of the bell. (For other studies, see Lohr & Staats, 1973; Zanna, Kiesler, & Pilkonis, 1970.)

TABLE 8–2.

Percent of Preference by Bennington Students and Their Parents for Presidential Candidates in 1936

Candidate	52 Freshmen Students	Parents	40 Sophomores Students	Parents	52 Juniors-Seniors Students	Parents
Alfred Landon (Republican)	62	66	43	69	15	60
Franklin Roosevelt (Democrat)	29	26	43	22	54	35
Norman Thomas* (Socialist)						
Earl Browder (Communist)	9	7	15	8	30	4

* The Socialist and Communist candidates were grouped together because of a low preference for both.

Source: Adapted from *Personality and Social Change* by T. M. Newcomb. Copyright © 1943 by T. M. Newcomb. Reprinted by permission of Holt, Rinehart, and Winston, CBS College Publishing.

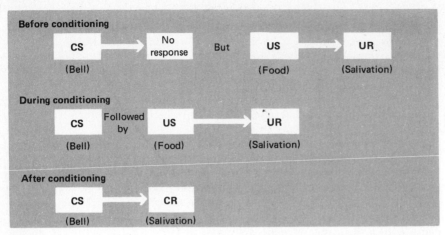

FIGURE 8–1.
Classical Conditioning Theory

Key:
CS Conditioned Stimulus
US Unconditioned Stimulus
UR Unconditioned Response
CR Conditioned Response

Reinforcement and Instrumental Learning   In contrast to the principles of classical conditioning, which view attitude formation as an automatic process in which the individual plays a passive role, the principles of **instrumental learning** (or operant conditioning) emphasize the role of reinforcement on attitude formation. When individuals receive social approval for their attitudes, these attitudes will be reinforced; conversely, if the attitudes are disapproved of, they will not be reinforced (see, for example, Insko & Nelson, 1969). It should be noted, however, that much depends on the source of the approval or disapproval. For teenagers who rebel against their parents' attitudes by smoking marijuana, reinforcement from peers may carry more weight than their parents' disapproval. (We will discuss instrumental learning in more detail as an aspect of attitude change.)

Modeling and Observational Learning   As we saw in chapter 3, Bandura (1977) has shown that we often learn new responses—and hence new attitudes—by observing and attempting to imitate the behavior of role models. Through **modeling,** children acquire various attitudes from their parents even when these attitudes have not been expressed directly through verbal instruction. In some cases, in fact, children are more strongly influenced by deeds than by words (Rushton, 1975): A child whose parents have a selfish attitude toward material possessions may internalize this attitude and refuse to share toys with playmates—even when told to do so by the parents.

Actions speak louder than words.

Self-Perception and Attitude Formation   Although we normally assume that people behave in ways that are consonant with their attitudes, that is, that their behavior is a function of their attitudes, many social psychologists have argued that this is frequently not the case. Remember that in chapter 4 we discussed Bem's (1972) self-perception theory. Bem's theory was that people do not always know how they think or feel about an issue, and that, as a result, they sometimes *infer* their attitudes from their behavior. If this hypothesis is correct, the statement, "I eat ice cream because I like it" should be changed to, "I like ice cream

Even in his posture and facial expression, this boy is modeling after his father.

because I eat it." (We will look at the relationship of attitudes to behaviors in the next chapter.)

In order for people to know what their attitudes are, they must be able to reflect upon their cognitive processes; that is, they must be capable of *introspection*. However, recall Nisbett and Wilson's (1977) suggestion (chapters 4 and 5) that when people are not able to report on their cognitive processes, they may attempt to construct plausible explanations about the causes of their behavior. Even people who are not capable of accurate introspection nevertheless provide accurate explanations of why they behaved as they did.

The Function of Attitudes   In discussing the various ways we form attitudes, we have not yet dealt with two related issues: why we *form* attitudes and why we *maintain* them. If the basic motivation of the organism is survival, then it follows that attitudes have survival value for human beings, and are adopted in response to real or perceived needs.

Katz (1960) proposed that our attitudes serve four basic functions: *adjustment*, *ego defense*, *value expression*, and *knowledge*. The adjustment and ego-defensive functions serve practical needs; they enable us to regulate or adjust our behavior so we will be rewarded rather than punished. The value-expressive and knowledge functions, on the other hand, correspond to higher level needs relating to our quest for self-fulfillment. We derive satisfaction from expressing values that agree with our views of ourselves, however idealized these self-concepts may be. Moreover, we have a need to understand the world around us and our place in that world.

Through our attitudes we attempt to endow human existence with clarity and consistency. They let us interpret our experiences in ways that are consistent with our needs, and they provide the context in which we seek out new experiences (Freedman & Sears, 1965). In structuring the ways we view ourselves in relation to the world, our attitudes determine the kinds of information we seek.

Changing Attitudes: Theoretical Perspectives

Our attitudes, then, help us to make sense of our environment and to function within it. Attitudes lead us to seek particular kinds of experiences and information. But the human environment is constantly changing; the other beings with whom we interact, the events going on around us, the information we must respond to—none of these is ever completely stable. Particularly in the modern world, change itself has become a constant. Thus, being able to change our attitudes to keep up with the changing times has survival value. The remainder of this chapter is devoted to the subject of attitude change. We will first examine the approaches of social psychologists to the theoretical issues of how and why attitudes change. We will conclude the chapter with an extensive discussion of the varied ways attitude change takes place.

In the 1940s and 1950s social psychologists gave more research attention to attitude change than to any other topic. The theorists of that era were particularly interested in figuring out what was going on "in the heads" of people whose attitudes changed. Several different types of theories were proposed.

Consistency Theories of Attitude Change

The **consistency theories** of attitude change all maintain that if a particular attitude is inconsistent either with other attitudes that the individual holds or with the individual's behavior, the person will be motivated to change either that attitude or the behavior to which it corresponds, or—in certain rare cases—an entire belief system. Consistency theory thus views attitude change as an attempt on the part of an individual to achieve cognitive equilibrium. There are three significant consistency approaches: balance theory, congruity theory, and cognitive dissonance theory.

Balance Theory Balance theory is derived from the work of Fritz Heider (1946, 1958), who argued that people maintain consistent attitudes by balancing their feelings and beliefs about one another against their feelings and beliefs about salient aspects of the environment. In Heider's model, a single individual (P) formulates or changes an attitude toward another individual (O) in relation to the similar or dissimilar attitudes that they hold to (X), which may be an object, an idea, an event, a situation, and so forth. From the standpoint of P, a "balanced" cognitive state exists if (1) P likes O and their attitudes toward X are in harmony; or (2) P dislikes O and their attitudes toward X are not in harmony. On the other hand, an "unbalanced" state will exist if (1) P likes O but their attitudes toward X are not in harmony; or (2) P dislikes O but their attitudes toward X are in harmony. Figure 8–2 illustrates the possible combinations of balanced and unbalanced cognitive states in Heider's model.

It is useful to illustrate Heider's model through a concrete example. Mr. P is a man who holds strong moral views. As he is now retired and has a certain amount of time on his hands, he serves as a volunteer for a civic organization that is devoted to helping disadvantaged teenagers. Mr. O also works for this or-

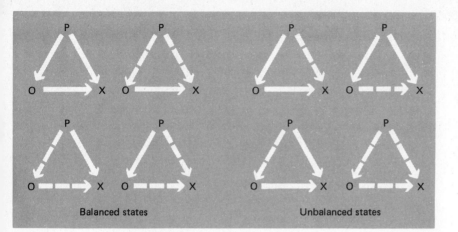

FIGURE 8–2.

Examples of balanced and unbalanced states according to Heider's definitions of balance. Solid lines represent positive, and broken lines negative relations.

Source: *From "The Concepts of Balance, Congruity, and Dissonance" by R. Zajonc,* Public Opinion Quarterly, *1960, p. 283. Copyright 1960 by The Trustees of Columbia University.*

ganization. Through their joint efforts, the two men get to know each other and Mr. P comes to admire Mr. O for his selfless devotion to others. One day, however, Mr. P discovers that Mr. O is a homosexual. Now, Mr. P has always felt that homosexuals are "sick and immoral." He thus experiences a state of cognitive unbalance that he will have to resolve in some way.

Congruity Theory   Related to balance theory but more limited in its scope, **congruity theory** is concerned with attitude change that may occur when a particular source makes a statement about a particular concept. Are such statements or messages congruent (consistent) or incongruent (inconsistent) with the individual's frame of reference (Osgood & Tannenbaum, 1955)? In congruity theory (Figure 8–3) there are three variables: (1) the individual's attitude to the source of a message; (2) the individual's attitude toward the concept or issue evaluated by the source; and (3) the nature of the assertion made by the source about the concept (Osgood & Tannenbaum, 1955). Thus, if sources we like promote ideas that we approve of, their assertions will be congruent to our frames of reference. However, if sources we like promote ideas that we disapprove of (or, conversely, if sources we dislike promote ideas we approve of), their assertions will be incongruent to our frames of reference. An individual who experiences incongruity is motivated to change attitudes to either the source or the concept evaluated by the source.

To illustrate, let us take the following situation. In a nationally televised speech, the president argues for "busing" as a solution to the problem of educational inequality. If you have a positive attitude toward that president and a positive attitude toward the concept of busing, or if you have a negative attitude toward the president and a negative attitude toward the concept, you will not experience incongruity. However, if you have a positive attitude to the president and a negative attitude toward busing (or vice versa), you will experience incongruity. If the sense of incongruity that you experience is intense enough, you will be motivated to change your attitude about either the president or the concept of busing.

FIGURE 8–3.
Congruity Theory

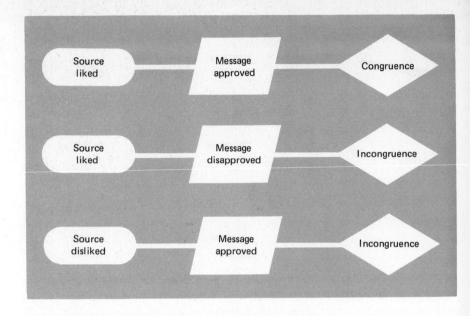

Cognitive Dissonance Theory   The theory of cognitive dissonance, which was developed by Leon Festinger (1957), is both the best known and most fully elaborated of the consistency theories of attitude change. Like balance theory and congruity theory, **cognitive dissonance theory** focuses on the ways particular beliefs or attitudes are either consistent or inconsistent with one another. However, where these earlier theories regarded consistency in terms of the external logic of a situation, dissonance theory emphasizes the psychological comfort or discomfort of the individual. As a result, it is more closely linked to motivation than these earlier theories, and it has fuller implications for the relationship between attitudes and behavior.

In Festinger's terminology, we feel **dissonance** (or psychological discomfort) whenever two related "cognitions" do not fit together harmoniously (see Figure 8–4). The term **cognition** (or *cognitive element*) refers to any belief, opinion, or perception that an individual has about the self, about his or her own behavior, or about any aspect of the environment. Since dissonance is, by definition, psychologically painful, it leads to attempts at **dissonance reduction,** much as the experience of hunger will lead to attempts to reduce hunger. Moreover, just as our attempts to reduce hunger will depend on how hungry we are, so our attempts to reduce dissonance will depend on the intensity of the dissonance we experience. However, whereas hunger reduction requires that the individual act upon the environment, this is not necessarily the case with dissonance reduction. To reduce dissonance, it is necessary for the cognitive elements that produce **consonance** (psychological comfort) to be substituted for the dissonant elements. This realignment of cognitive relations may occur in a number of different ways. It may correspond to a change in the individual's actual behavior, but it may also be restricted to the cognitive level.

FIGURE 8-4.

Cognitive Dissonance Theory

Left: Consonance—two
related cognitions fit together
harmoniously.
Right: Dissonance—two
related cognitions clash—do
not fit together.

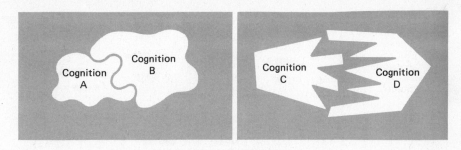

In order for cognitive dissonance to occur, there must be two cognitive elements that are *relevant* yet *opposite* to each other. Festinger formalized this principle by pointing out that "*x* and *y* are dissonant if *not-x* follows from *y*" (1957, p. 13). Thus, given the cognition that smoking is dangerous to one's health, it follows that *not* smoking is the appropriate behavior, and, therefore, if one smokes, one will experience dissonance. To reduce the dissonance, one could, of course, quit smoking, in which case the health threat that led to the dissonance would no longer be present. But if quitting smoking were the only way to remove the psychological discomfort caused by the knowledge of its dangers, many more of us would have done so. As Aronson points out: "Dissonance theory does not rest upon the assumption that man is a *rational* animal; rather, it suggests that man is a rational*izing* animal—that he attempts to appear rational, both to others and to himself" (1968 p. 6). When we say, for example, that if we stop smoking we will gain so much weight that we will be susceptible to heart attacks, what we are doing, in effect, is building up consonant cognitions about smoking in order to defuse the experience of dissonance. (See Figure 8–5.) (For studies exploring attempts to reduce cognitive dissonance, see Aronson & Mills, 1959; Walster, Berscheid, & Barclay, 1967.)

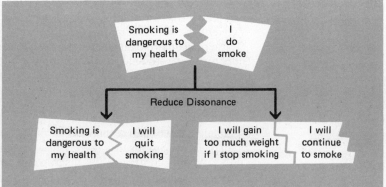

FIGURE 8–5.   Dissonance Reduction

Left: Consonance—reduction not necessary.
Right: Dissonance—one or the other cognition must be changed.

Anyone who smokes must be aware that cigarette smoking is a health hazard. These young women experience cognitive dissonance when they smoke and believe that they should not; perhaps they resolve the dissonance by thinking that they are too young to get cancer.

IS THIS WHAT YOUR KISSES TASTE LIKE?

If you smoke cigarettes, you taste like one.
Your clothes and hair can smell stale and unpleasant, too.
You don't notice it, but people close to you do.
Especially if they don't smoke.
And non-smokers are the best people to love.
They live longer.   **AMERICAN CANCER SOCIETY**

In a classic experiment designed to investigate the effects of forced compliance on cognition, Festinger and Carlsmith (1959) found that subjects changed their opinions to correspond to statements they were forced to make. You will recall from chapter 4 that in this experiment, the subjects initially spent an hour performing a couple of extremely boring, repetitive tasks. Each subject was then asked to explain these tasks to a person whom the subject was led to believe was another subject, but who was actually a confederate of the investigators. However, at this point the subjects were divided into three groups: a control group, whose members were not advised as to what, specifically, they were to say to the other person; and two experimental groups, both of whose members were told to describe the tasks as extremely interesting and enjoyable. The only difference between the two experimental groups was that the members of the first were paid $1 while those in the second received $20.

The subjects in all three groups were then interviewed about their own attitudes to the tasks they had performed. As expected, the members of the control group responded most negatively. Interestingly enough, however (although this had been predicted by the investigators), the response of the $20 group was distinctly more negative than that of the $1 group, which, indeed, was the only one of the three groups to give the tasks a positive rating.

What accounts for the discrepancy between the two experimental groups? Festinger and Carlsmith explain it by observing that the $20 condition was a sufficient inducement to the subjects in that group to present the task in a way that was contrary to their own experience of it. As a result, these subjects did not experience a high degree of cognitive dissonance and felt little pressure to bring their attitudes into line with what they had said to the confederate. The subjects in the $1 condition, on the other hand, felt underpaid; they experienced cognitive dissonance between the totally unrewarding work they had had to do, and the positive comments about it they had had to make. Thus, they felt pressured by their psychological discomfort to align their attitudes more closely with their behavior.

Dissonance theory has been criticized on a number of grounds, and several attempts have been made to revise Festinger's original formulations. For example, it has been argued that dissonance reduction is a powerful motivation only when the individual's actual behavior is linked to one of the inconsistent conditions (Brehm & Cohen, 1962; cited by Greenwald & Ronis, 1978)—as in our previous smoking example. According to this view, cognitive dissonance must be reduced only when it is important for the individual to resolve the inconsistency. Although Festinger had originally formulated his theory to encompass all situations in which *not-x* follows from *y*, these critics would narrow its scope to include only situations in which logical inconsistency translates into psychological inconsistency. Other critics believe that people are more motivated to seek novelty—that is, new or additional stimuli—than consistency (Shaw & Skolnick, 1973; see also Abelson, 1968).

Self-Perception Theory

The self-perception theory of attitude change grew out of the dissatisfaction of certain behaviorally oriented theorists with consistency theories in general and cognitive dissonance theory in particular. Bem (1967), who pioneered self-perception theory (see chapter 4), showed that the results of dissonance experiments could be explained by his own paradigm: People will generally infer attitudes from behavior. In **self-perception theory,** attitude change is a direct consequence of behavioral change. From this perspective the notion of attitudinal "consistency" is a superfluous (or metaphysical) assumption. According to this view, for example, the fact that a person smokes cigarettes *is* that person's attitude—whether he or she is aware of the dangers of smoking or is not. Consequently, for self-perception theory, the problem of consistency does not exist.

Social Judgment Theory

The **social judgment** approach to attitude change is based on the notion that the *structure* of a particular attitude determines how receptive the person who holds the attitude will be to a persuasive message that is pertinent to that attitude (Eagly & Telaak, 1972). By the "structure" of an attitude, social judgment theorists mean the range of possible positions that an individual can hold in relation to the attitude. The range of positions that the person is willing to accept is called the *latitude of acceptance*, while the range that the person rejects is called the *latitude of rejection*. The central assumption of social judgment theory is that if a particular message falls within the individual's latitude of acceptance, attitude change occurs in the direction of the message. Conversely, if a message is within the latitude of rejection, attitude change either does not occur or occurs

Research: Cognitive Dissonance at the Racetrack

Dissonance theory suggests that the more committed we are to a particular decision or behavior pattern, the more we bring our attitudes and beliefs into line with it. In order to test this hypothesis, Robert E. Knox and James A. Inkster (1968) investigated the attitudes of bettors at a Vancouver racetrack both before and after they had placed their bets.

The experimental procedure involved interviewing a random sample of subjects who were about to place a $2 bet on a particular horse and a similar sample of subjects who had just placed a $2 bet. The subjects in both the pre-bet and post-bet groups were asked to rate the chance that they thought their horse had of winning on a scale of 1 to 7 (see Figure).

The median for the pre-bet subjects was 3.48—which meant that they gave their horse a slightly better than "fair" but less than even

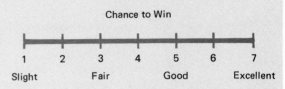

chance of winning. The median of the post-bet subjects, however, was 4.81—which meant that they gave their horse a "good" chance of winning.

Statistically, the difference between the two medians was highly significant. Moreover, the results agreed with the predictions that the investigators had made on the basis of dissonance theory. Since the actual placing of the $2 bet made the decision irrevocable, it had the effect of increasing pressures for dissonance reduction. Thus, the bettors hold more positive attitudes about the horses they had just bet on.

in the opposite direction of the message (Eagly & Telaak, 1972; Sherif, Sherif, & Nebergall, 1965).

In a pioneering study of the limits of social judgments, Sherif, Taub, and Hovland (1958) observed that an individual's prior attitude on a particular issue serves as the focal point around which latitudes of acceptance and rejection are located. Suppose, for example, a person believes that within 5 years Detroit will be able to produce an automobile that goes 100 miles on a single gallon of gas. Subsequently, he reads an article suggesting that this will not be possible for 10 years. If the latter figure falls within the person's latitude of acceptance, his position may be revised accordingly—assuming, of course, that he trusts the source of the message. This does not necessarily imply that he will accept the figure offered by the source—he may compromise by settling on 7 years, for example—but the change will occur in the direction of the message.

In general, the *wider* the individual's latitude of acceptance, the more amenable he or she will be to persuasion (Eagly & Telaak, 1972; Sherif & Hovland, 1969). Persons who hold extreme views tend to have correspondingly narrow latitudes of acceptance for messages related to those views, while persons who hold moderate views have correspondingly wide latitudes of acceptance.

We can illustrate this principle by citing an emotionally charged issue that is currently dividing many Americans: the issue of abortion. Persons A, N, and S hold different views on this issue: A believes that abortion is *always* justified; N believes that it is *never* justified; and S believes that it is *sometimes* justified. Both A and N hold extreme, although opposite, views on the issue and, as a result, their latitudes of acceptance will be narrow: Neither is likely to be convinced by anything the other has to say. Person S, on the other hand, has a wider latitude of acceptance and, although unlikely to accept either of their positions entirely, may be amenable to some of the arguments of both A and N.

Changing Attitudes Through Persuasion

In the previous sections, we examined how attitudes form and change from the perspective of the individual who undergoes these experiences. Many factors can persuade people to change their attitudes, and during the Second World War the government sponsored an active program of research to determine exactly what these factors were. The impetus for this research was practical, and there was a great deal at stake: The government desired to design propaganda to demoralize the enemy, and to promote domestic attitudes that would help the war effort. (There was, for example, research on the best way to persuade homemakers to purchase, prepare, and serve unpopular but widely available organ meats such as kidneys and liver.)

Following the war, many of these pioneering attitude researchers continued to examine persuasion and attitude change in academic settings. A notable example was Carl Hovland who, together with a number of colleagues, investigated attitudes in the Yale University Communication Research Program during the 1950s. This group was largely responsible for providing the insights into persuasive communication that we are about to consider.

We will consider five components of persuasion and their influence on attitudes. These are: 1) the *source* of the communication, 2) the *communication* itself, 3) the *target* of the communication, 4) the communication *channel*, and 5) the *environment*. You can see how these components fit together by looking at Figure 8–6. As we begin to discuss each of these components, pause and make your own predictions about the ways in which that component might affect persuasion. Even if you are a very good "budding" social psychologist, you may be in for some surprises!

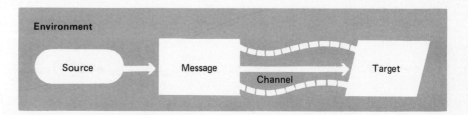

FIGURE 8–6. Factors in the Persuasion Process

The Source

What effects do the source of a communication have on the message and its influences? In this section, we examine some aspects of sources that influence the way in which their communications are received. *Think for a moment. Who is your Representative in the U.S. Congress? Suppose you were considering whether to run against him or her in the next election. Think about the problems you might encounter as a result of your status as a "source" when you discuss important campaign issues.*

Credibility *Would you be a believable source of information?* If several sources produce a message with the same content, it stands to reason that sources with higher credibility are better able to persuade people than low-credibility sources and, in fact, this has been confirmed (Hovland & Weis, 1951).

A related finding is that the impact of a high-credibility source is most pronounced immediately following a communication, but lessens with time (Kelman & Hovland, 1953). Exposure to a highly credible source may lead people to change their views, but after a time they may revert to their previous positions.

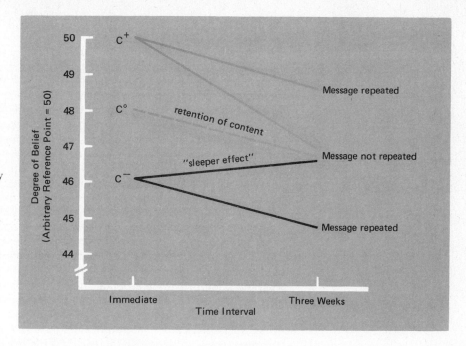

FIGURE 8–7. Effects of Credibility of Source on Acceptance of Message Content

Key:
C+ Content from high-credibility (prestige) source
C° Content from neutral source
C⁻ Content from low-credibility (non-prestige) source
Content from a low-credibility source tended to be better accepted over a period of time; this is the "sleeper effect." However, repetition or reinforcement of the message and its source appeared to counteract other effects: Reinforcement of a message from a high-credibility source increased acceptance, while reinforcement of the low-credibility source's message decreased acceptance even further, thus negating the sleeper effect.

Source: *From " 'Reinstatement' of the Communicator in Delayed Measurement of Opinion Change" by H. Kelman & C. Hovland,* Journal of Abnormal and Social Psychology, *1953, 48, 333.*

Conversely, low-credibility sources gain impact with time. At first people may not accept the statement of a source considered untrustworthy, but, surprisingly, they may eventually accept this source's viewpoint. This is known as the **sleeper effect.** However, repeated exposure to the source may counter the sleeper effect; a repeated message from a low-credibility source may even prevent the sleeper effect from occurring. Similarly, a repeated message from a high-credibility source may enhance the message to the point where it will endure over time (Kelman & Hovland, 1953). (See Figure 8–7.)

The sleeper effect may be illustrated by the following example. Suppose that *Pravda*, the official Soviet Union newspaper, reports that by the year 2000 thermonuclear fusion reactors will solve the world's energy problems. If you generally doubt the veracity of *Pravda's* pronouncements, you may be inclined to discount this one in particular. However, the message may have been implanted in your mind, and over time you may mentally separate the message from its source. At that point, you may even come to accept the message. This is the sleeper effect.

Credibility is generally defined as a function of two factors: *expertise* and *trustworthiness.* Thus, in the example given before, you would probably discount *Pravda's* story on fusion energy because you did not consider it a trustworthy source. However, if your cousin Louie, a recent high-school graduate working as a grocery clerk, makes the same point, you may think that he lacks the necessary expertise to be a credible source.

The perception of expertise depends on the *qualifications* (including experience, education, and competence) of the communicator to provide information on a particular issue (Horai, Naccari, & Fatoullah, 1974). Ex-football players are generally regarded as more credible play-by-play "color commentators" than those who have no experience with the sport because their qualifications are related directly to the issue at hand. In this respect, expertise contrasts with trustworthiness, which operates in a more subtle manner. It should be noted, however, that expertise is not always obvious and can be negated. For example, if two equally expert sources issue conflicting statements, the expertise factor may be neutralized (Ference, 1971). You might confront this problem if you wanted to purchase a product, such as a home computer, that involved advanced technology. Many companies produce them, and with an equal degree of expertise. Presidents may have similar problems, as when the Secretary of State and the Secretary of Defense give conflicting advice on foreign policy.

Trustworthiness depends on whether the communicator is perceived as basically honest or basically dishonest in attempts at persuasion. Honesty may depend on the degree the communicator is motivated by self-interest and the degree his or her self-interest will result in a loss of objectivity. In studies of the role of trustworthiness in persuasion, it has been found that sources are regarded as more credible when they argue *against* their own best interests than when arguing for them (Walster, Aronson, & Abrahams, 1966). Walster and her colleagues found that while criminals (who would normally be considered low-credibility sources) are much less effective than prosecutors (high-credibility sources) when advocating that the courts should have less power, they are *more* effective than prosecutors when advocating that the courts should have more power—that is, arguing *against* their own best interests. (See Figure 8–8.)

Liking, Attractiveness, and Similarity *As a candidate for Congress, are you likable, attractive, and not too different from your prospective constituents?* In chapter 6 we saw that attractiveness is an important determinant of social behavior. Not too surprisingly, persuasion is also influenced by how much the audience identifies with the communicator. If the communicator insults or alienates the audience, the audience may become resistant to persuasion (Abelson & Miller, 1967). But a communicator who unduly flatters the audience may arouse

FIGURE 8–8. Subjects' Reactions to High-Prestige and Low-Prestige Communicators.

Whether prosecuting attorneys argued either for more powerful courts or for less powerful courts, they were equally persuasive to their audience. But when low-prestige criminals advocated more powerful courts, they were even more effective than prosecutors in convincing their audience.

Source: *Adapted from "On Increasing the Persuasiveness of a Low Prestige Communicator" by E. Walster,* E. Aronson, & D. Abrahams, Journal of Experimental Social Psychology, *1966, 2, 333.*

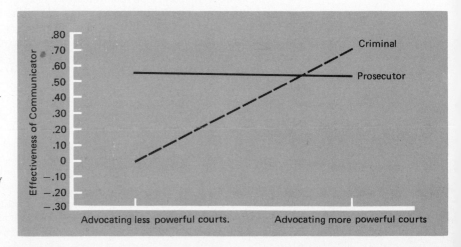

A political candidate is a source of persuasive communication. The audience's response depends on such factors as credibility, attractiveness, similarity, and style of speech-making. Here, delegates to the 1980 Democratic Party Convention in New York City, as well as passersby, listen to several speeches at a midday rally.

its suspicions. In an experiment testing the effects of approval and disapproval on audience reactions, Aronson and Linder (1965) found that although subjects generally responded more positively to speakers whose remarks indicated approval of them than to those expressing disapproval, they responded even more favorably to speakers who began critically but ended on a positive note.

The more attractive we find a particular source, the more likely we are to identify with him or her and, as a result, the more likely we are to be persuaded by his or her appeals (Kelman, 1965). Mills and Aronson (1965) found that when a communicator was presented as attractive there was a greater willingness on the part of the subjects to please her; consequently her attempts at persuasion in this condition were enhanced. However, when the communicator was not perceived as attractive, persuasion was neither enhanced nor impaired.

In general, people respond more positively to people who are similar to themselves than to people who are perceived as dissimilar. Consistency theory suggests that people evaluate their own views against those of people who are perceived as similar (Goethals & Nelson, 1973). Thus, communicators who are perceived as dissimilar may fail to be persuasive even if they hold the same views as the audience; to agree with someone who is different from ourselves would result in dissonance.

An interesting experiment on the effects of similarity in persuasion was performed in the paint department of a large retail store (Brock, 1965). In this experiment, communicators attempted to persuade customers to purchase a brand of paint at a different price from the one they had requested, either at the same or different quantity. The results showed that the persuasion attempts of the communicators were significantly more effective if they were in the *similar* condition, that is, if the quantities of paint they had mentioned using were the same as those requested by the customer. In fact, the effect of similarity significantly outweighed the effect of expertise: Nonexpert but similar communicators were more effective in persuading customers than expert but dissimilar communicators. The similarity factor apparently provided additional relevant information in support of the actual message (Simons et al., 1970).

In your congressional campaign you will no doubt want to consider the way in which you present yourself to your various audiences. Perhaps you will want to reread chapter 6 and think of ways to enhance your personal attractiveness. You will probably also want to emphasize your similarity to your audience.

Power *Do you have "clout"? Your congressional campaign may get a real boost if you do!* The power of the source to punish or reward the individual is also an important factor in opinion change. McGuire (1969) suggests that people evaluate the power of communicators in the following sequence: They evaluate the extent to which the source can administer rewards or punishments; then they estimate how much the source cares whether they conform to the communcation; and finally, they evaluate the source's ability to discover whether or not they have conformed. If the power of the source is considered to be high for all three conditions, the individual's likelihood to agree with the source—at least overtly—would be correspondingly high. (See also Rosenbaum & Rosenbaum, 1975.)

Is overt conformity to a powerful source a genuine attitude change? History shows many examples of groups who were forced to obey powerful authorities but who still maintained their own identities. During the Spanish Inquisition, for example, Jews were forced—upon pain of death if they disobeyed—to convert to Catholicism; but many continued to practice their religion in secret.

There is some evidence, however, that power-induced conformity may result in genuine opinion change. Dissonance theory suggests that responding in ways that contradict one's covert attitudes could, in certain instances, create attitude change. Under extreme conditions, such as those that prevail in totalitarian societies, covert attitudes might pose a significant threat to people's very existence, and, as a result, the motivation to change attitudes is great. In the next chapter we will consider in more depth whether changes in behavior—even when they are induced—can lead to changes in attitude. We will also consider the opposite situation, inquiring under what circumstances changed attitudes will lead to changed behavior.

The relationship between power and attitude change depends not only on the particular social situation but on the personalities of the individuals involved. Under some conditions, for example, mild threats may be more effective than severe ones in inducing long-term attitude change (Aronson, 1966b).

Speech Style How do you come across as a public speaker? Since ancient times, it has been recognized that the effectiveness of a message depends on the style in which it is delivered. Rhetoric, or the art of persuasion, depends not only on the actual words that are used, but the speaker's strategy in addressing the audience. Have you ever listened to a speech that should have been fascinating, but turned out to be dull because the speaker spoke slowly and in low, even tones? Have you ever been excited by a speaker whose style of delivery was more dramatic than the message being delivered?

In recent years, social psychologists have attempted to determine the relationship between various aspects of speech style and persuasion. Zillman (1972) found that when arguments are stated in the form of rhetorical questions, their effectiveness is increased—especially when the audience is initially opposed to the communicator's point of view. A rhetorical question is one for which the answer is already known (*e.g., We would all like to see the economy improve, wouldn't we?*). Consequently, by using rhetorical questions communicators can gain the gradual agreement of the audience to their point of view.

Other researchers have found that the rate at which a communicator speaks is taken as an indication of credibility. In general, rapid speech enhances persuasion (Apple, Streeter, & Krauss, 1979; Miller et al., 1976). People who speak rapidly, we seem to believe, must know what they're talking about. In spite of the stereotype of the fast-talking salesperson who is regarded with suspicion, MacLachlan (1979) found that audiences generally prefer communicators who speak rapidly, and apparently learn more from them in a given amount of time. Television advertisers have, unfortunately, discovered these research findings— just listen to the rate of speech on commercials and compare it to the rate of speech on the programs they accompany. Do you think that politicians are aware of these findings too?

Conclusion-Drawing   *As a candidate, would it be better for you to state conclusions explicitly, or should you let your audience form its own conclusions on the basis of your discussion?* In a pioneering study, Hovland and Mandell (1952) presented subjects with two communications that were identical in every respect except that in one the conclusion was specifically stated by the communicator while in the other the audience was left to draw its own conclusions. The results strongly indicated that persuasion was more effective when the conclusion was explicitly drawn. This was also true when the communicator was seen as acting in his or her own self-interest. (See also Thistlethwaite et al., 1955).

Cooper and Dinnerman (1951), however, suggest that the degree of explicitness of a message is a factor that must be considered. They found that while messages that are not explicitly stated may be lost on the less intelligent members of the audience, a message that is overgeneralized and lacking in specificity may be rejected by the more intelligent members of the audience, who may resent being "talked down to." This is one aspect of the **boomerang effect,** which occurs when the message produces the opposite results of those intended.

The Communication

One of the reasons you have decided to run for Congress is that you hope to contribute to the national effort to protect the natural environment. How can you most effectively inform the voters about the environmental issues that concern you? Part of the answer will lie in your communication *itself. You must consider its content, its form, and the effect it will have on the audience.*

Communication Discrepancy   Can attitudes be changed when the opinion of a listener is opposed to the position of a communication? This question is of practical concern to politicians, editorial writers, advertising managers, missionaries, teachers, and a host of other communicators in our society. Social psychologists have addressed this issue from two perspectives.

According to consistency theory, a discrepancy between the position of a communicator and that of a recipient results in pressures for attitude change. Aronson, Turner, and Carlsmith (1963) have pointed out that attitudes can be changed even when greatly discrepant positions are advocated—if the source is highly credible. If, however, discrepant positions are advocated by low-credibility sources, opinions change only up to a point; when discrepancy increases, opinion change declines (see Figure 8–9). Too much discrepancy, however, causes subjects enough conflict to resort to source-disparagement in order to reduce dissonance (Nemeth & Endicott, 1976).

Recall that from the point of view of social judgment theory, though, the relationship between attitude change and source disparagement will depend on the subject's latitudes of acceptance and rejection. The point at which discrepancy is tolerated and contributes to attitude change, in this perspective, is a function of the breadth of the subject latitude to accept discrepant positions (Sherif & Hovland, 1961; Sherif & Sherif, 1969).

Both perspectives, then, face the problem of determining the extent of discrepancy that can be tolerated and lead to attitude change, and the point at which the discrepant position begins to be rejected (Nemeth & Endicott, 1976).

Fear Content   Appeals that arouse fear are generally used either to pair an undesirable practice with a negative result or to associate a desirable practice with the avoidance of a negative result (Higbee, 1969). Some messages make use of both approaches: Advertisements for automobile seat belts typically emphasize both the positive and negative outcomes that result from the use or non-use of seat belts.

It is difficult to generalize about the relationship between fear arousal and persuasion for all situations (Higbee, 1969; Leventhal, 1970). Early studies in-

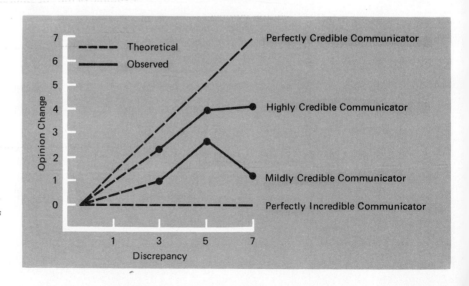

FIGURE 8–9. Opinion Change as a Function of Message Discrepancy and Source Credibility.

Source: *Adapted from "Communicator Credibility and Communication Discrepancy as Determinants of Opinion Change" by E. Aronson, J. Turner, & J. Carlsmith,* Journal of Abnormal and Social Psychology, *1966,* 67, *34.*

Application: Fear, Persuasion, and Attitude Change

Some researchers believe that the complex relationship between fear arousal and persuasion depends on the nature of the communication factors. In the model proposed by Rogers and Mewborn (1976), the fear communication is located on three dimensions: (a) the severity (or "noxiousness") of an event; (b) the probability that the event will occur in the absence of a coping response; and (c) the effectiveness of a coping response in averting the noxious event. According to this model, the relationship between fear arousal and attitude change depends on the interaction of these three factors.

In the experiment they designed to test this model, Rogers and Mewborn divided each factor into a "high" and a "low" condition. Students who were heavy smokers were shown films on smoking. The subjects in the "low noxiousness" condition viewed the first segment of a film about a man who developed lung cancer. This segment portrayed his discovery of the disease, an interview with his physician, and the surgical preparations for the operation. The "high noxiousness" subjects saw the same film plus a 5-minute segment showing the actual lung removal.

After viewing the films, the subjects in both conditions responded to a questionnaire measuring fear arousal. Then they all read separate essays that dealt with the probability of occurrence of lung cancer and the efficacy (or effectiveness) of a coping response. Both of these factors also had a high and a low condition. In the "high probability" condition, subjects learned that if one smokes cigarettes, there is a high chance of contracting lung cancer. In the "low probability" condition, subjects learned that although smoking can cause lung cancer, the chances of any given smoker contracting the disease are small. The "high efficacy" essay indicated that stopping smoking was an extremely effective way of avoiding lung cancer. The "low efficacy" essay, however, provided little reassurance that giving up smoking would be effective in avoiding the disease.

After reading the two essays, subjects were asked in a questionnaire to rate the effectiveness of the coping response and to indicate if they intended to adopt it. All subjects who saw the high noxiousness films displayed greater fear than those who viewed the low noxiousness versions. Those who read the high probability essay thought it more likely that they would get lung cancer. Those who read the high efficacy essays likewise believed them, expressed their intentions of giving up smoking, thus demonstrating attitude change. This effect was especially pronounced for those in both the "high noxiousness" and "high efficacy" conditions, or in the "high probability" and "high efficacy" conditions. However, in the "low probability" condition, "high noxiousness" had little influence, and "high probability" actually had a negative effect—subjects who were led to believe that stopping the habit would have little effect on their future health actually planned to increase the number of cigarettes they smoked daily. This was an example of the "boomerang effect."

These researchers performed similar experiments in other health related areas and found similar results. They concluded that of the three variables of noxiousness, probability of occurrence, and efficacy of a coping response, the most influential factor in altering attitudes was the strength of the belief that danger could be averted by adopting the recommended response. This has clear implications for those who are concerned with public health policy. (Other studies have explored the use of emotional appeals: Dabbs and Leventhal (1966) studied attitudes toward tetanus shots; Haefner (1965) and Leventhal and Singer (1966) looked at dental care; and Leventhal and Niles (1965) focused on attitudes toward seat-belt use.)

dicated that low-threat appeals were more persuasive than high-threat appeals (Janis & Feshbach, 1953), perhaps because the tension associated with high-threat appeals led the audience to block out the message. More recent studies, however, reach the opposite conclusion: Increased fear is more persuasive (Dembroski, Lasater, & Ramires, 1978; Griffeth & Rogers, 1976; Watts & Pagano, 1967). The relationship between fear and persuasion depends on the personal characteristics of the audience and the credibility of the source. The more credible the source, the more seriously its fear-arousing appeals will be taken.

How does fear appeal research relate to your congressional campaign and your concern for the environment? Does it suggest ways in which you can more effectively communicate the threats to the environment over which the voters in your district should be concerned?

One-Sided vs. Two-Sided Arguments   Arguments that present both sides of an issue are generally more persuasive than arguments that merely advocate the communicator's view. Hovland, Lumsdaine, and Sheffield (1949), who conducted the initial research in this area, found that two-sided arguments are especially effective with better educated people who are initially opposed to the communicator's view. These findings, however, were qualified by Chu (1967), who found that a one-sided argument was more effective with subjects who were unfamiliar with an issue. According to Chu, subjects who are familiar with an issue view a one-sided argument as biased. This led Chu to suggest that the effects of communication are related to the detection of bias. When bias-detection was held constant, Chu found that the difference in effectiveness between one-sided and two-sided arguments disappeared, just as it did when subjects were initially in agreement with the communicator's view.

Agreeing that two-sided arguments were more effective than one-sided arguments, Jones and Brehm (1970) suggested that this effect could be caused by *psychological reactance*. According to reactance theory, individuals who feel coerced into adopting a particular view react strongly against it in order to safeguard their sense of free will. Because two-sided arguments are perceived as more even-handed, people evaluate them less defensively.

Novelty vs. Repetition   Because people turn a deaf ear to timeworn arguments, novelty is often an effective strategy in communication. Of course, as dissonance theory suggests, when a message is so novel as to be opposed to the audience's views, this strategy may backfire; but the use of novelty in moderation has a positive effect on persuasion.

Sears and Freedman (1965) found that the expectation of novelty makes a communication more attractive. In the simulated courtroom situation that these experimenters designed, experimental subjects were told that they were about to hear a novel argument. Although the communication that they subsequently received was actually identical to the one received by control subjects, who had not been told that it was novel, the experimental subjects found it more persuasive. Apparently, the term "new" has the connotation of "better" or "more interesting" in many people's minds. Perhaps this explains why advertisers and politicians make such generous use of the term.

Novelty is a good strategy when people are familiar with a particular issue. If they have never been exposed to a given point of view, however, they are unlikely to be persuaded by it the first time they hear it. Remember from chapter 6 that Zajonc (1968) found that in certain instances repeated exposure to a stimulus could be sufficient in itself to enhance the evaluation of that stimulus. Various studies of subjects' reactions to such diverse stimuli as art prints, drawings, and even photos of their own faces have concluded that increased familiarity breeds favorable perceptions (Heingartner & Hall, 1974; Mita, Dermer, & Knight, 1977; Smith & Dorfman, 1975). *This suggests that your messages about protecting the environment will have a cumulative effect; are you planning enough campaign appearances?*

Familiarity breeds contempt.

It has been observed, however, that while moderate exposure to a stimulus enhances evaluation, a point is reached when repeated exposure has a negative impact (Miller, 1976). Citing psychological reactance theory, Miller noted that excessive exposure may lead individuals to react defensively against a perceived insult or threat to their intelligence and/or volition. *Have you yourself ever had this reaction to a television commercial? Can you make too many campaign appearances?*

Number of Arguments   The effectiveness of a communication depends not only on the quality but also on the *quantity* of the arguments it contains. In a simulated courtroom experiment, Calder, Insko, and Yandell (1974) found that agreement with either the prosecution or the defense depended on the amount of evidence and the number of different arguments that each side presented relative to the other. A rather alarming finding of this study was that the more arguments developed by the prosecution, the greater the tendency to evaluate the defendant as guilty. Although clearly there is no logical connection between the quantity of evidence and its quality, this study suggests that people make a connection between the two. *Since you are trying a run a clean and informative campaign, you will undoubtedly try to fill your campaign speeches with better arguments rather than simply more arguments—won't you? Just how much information about different environmental issues should you give your constituents?*

the greater # of arguments, the more convincing

The Target

In the preceding pages we have looked at factors in the source of a persuasive communication and in the communication itself that cause people to change their attitudes. But attitude change occurs *within* an individual. Therefore, the impact of a particular message depends on the particular characteristics of the individual receiving it. In this section, we examine what variables make the **target,** or recipient of the message, amenable to persuasion. *Consider the many different people you normally encounter in the course of a week. If you set out to convince all of them to contribute to your political campaign (using the improved "communication" that you planned after reading the last section), what techniques would you use with each of them? Do you think, for instance, that:*

1.   *You are more likely to get a big contribution later in the campaign if you first ask people for small contributions?*
2.   *Women will be more easily persuaded to contribute than men?*
3.   *Intelligent people will be harder to persuade?*

Commitment   People who have committed themselves to a particular position or course of action are likely to commit themselves further in the same direction. This has been dubbed the *foot-in-the-door technique* (Freedman & Fraser, 1966). Sales representatives using this approach know that the first hurdle is to get prospective customers to talk to them. Once this has been accomplished—once the foot is in the door—it becomes more difficult for the target person to withdraw from the interaction, and thus increases the likelihood of a sale.

Pliner and her associates explain the foot-in-the-door phenomenon by suggesting that people who comply with a request begin to perceive themselves as "the kind of person who does this sort of thing" (1974, p. 21). Since the person has now adopted a self-image that includes making a particular commitment, an even greater commitment in this direction in the future will be consistent with this self-image.

The relationship between an initial or tentative commitment and attitude change appears to be strengthened when the commitment is made public. Jellison and Mills (1969) found that attitude change was greater among subjects who had publicly committed themselves to a particular position than among subjects who did not make their commitment known. This has been confirmed by Kiesler et al. (1971), who found that public commitment makes subjects more resistant to counterpersuasion. *How can your campaign committee make use of these findings? Have you thought of asking supporters to invite constituents to a party or picnic so they can meet you informally?*

Personality Variables   Numerous studies have been conducted to investigate how personality characteristics are related to attitude change. Hovland and Janis (1959), in their classic study of personality and persuasion, found that subjects who are easily persuaded under one set of conditions will often be easily persuaded under another. They suggest that persuasibility (sometimes called *positive bias*) is a consistent personality trait in some individuals. Sears and Whitney (1973) assert that many people will agree with any persuasive message.

Other researchers have found that there is a relationship between self-esteem and persuasibility. McGuire (1969) attributes this to the fact that people with low self-esteem do not value their own opinions, and therefore they easily give them up under pressure.

Research conducted 10 to 20 years ago suggested that, in general, women were more susceptible to influence than men (Gergen & Marlowe, 1970). More recent research by Alice Eagly (1981) has shown that the sex difference is only a very small one. Moreover, after examining nearly 150 studies, she suggested that while there was a small difference between men and women in persuasibility experiment results, the difference may depend on the gender of the experimenter. Seventy-nine percent of the authors of influenceability studies were male, and their studies showed larger sex differences in the direction of greater persuasibility among women. In studies conducted by women no sex differences in influenceability have been found. It has also been pointed out that sex-linked susceptibility to influence should be considered in relation to specific contexts. For example, in our culture women might feel less confident about their financial opinions than men, but more confident about their ideas on childrearing. Thus, women might be more readily persuaded to change opinions on financial matters, but may resist persuasion on childrearing.

Selective Attention   In our society, people are constantly being bombarded by various messages. We are urged to buy a particular brand of bread or toothpaste, to support a local bond issue, to decide which film to view, to take a position on nuclear energy, or to contribute to volunteer police patrols. There is evidence, however, that people are selective in the attention they give to messages, and that their selectivity is biased toward their attitudes (Klapper, 1960).

Lord, Ross, and Lepper (1979) found that when people are presented with two pieces of evidence—one that confirms and one that contradicts a particular belief—they not only retain their original beliefs, but use the confirming evidence to solidify them. Apparently, the confirming evidence is accepted at face value while the contradictory evidence is closely scrutinized for flaws so that it can be rejected. We all experience this when, for example, we hear a speech by a candidate whose policies we oppose. *You can expect to have great difficulty persuading some constituents about the importance of the natural environment.*

Counter-Arguing and Inoculation   Generally, little attention has been paid to the cognitive activity of the recipient of a persuasive communication. The very term "target" conjures up the image of the recipient as passive and unresponsive. Researchers have recently begun to recognize, however, that "targets" are active processors of information. They sift through incoming messages, selectively attend to stimuli, and relate new information to preexisting knowledge (Greenwald, 1968; Petty, Ostrom, & Brock, 1981).

An analogy can be drawn between the way people are inoculated for physical diseases and the way they become resistant to persuasion. Just as weaker strains of bacteria are used to strengthen the organism against stronger strains that cause disease, so exposure to a weakened form of an argument can be used to strengthen the person against the argument in a stronger form.

In a study that confirmed the inoculation hypothesis, McGuire and Papageorgis (1961) suggested that when subjects are initially presented with a weak version of an argument, they are stimulated to develop counterarguments in support of their own beliefs. These counterarguments are later rallied against stronger forms of the opposing argument. Thus, subjects who were "inoculated" are in a better position to resist persuasion than subjects who were not. *Can you use this finding in your televised debate with your opponent for Congress?*

Role-Playing   Role-playing—situations where people espouse attitudes that they do not actually hold—is an effective way to get them to change their attitudes (Zimbardo et al., 1967). Incentive theory suggests that people who are made to argue in favor of a particular attitude in order to gain the approval of an authority figure or to receive some other kind of reward will be motivated to actually change their attitudes (Janis & Gilmore, 1965). Dissonance theory, however, predicts that as the incentive for role-playing increases, attitude change decreases. As Festinger and Carlsmith (1959) found in their classic study of cognitive dissonance, subjects who received large rewards for role-playing experienced less dissonance than subjects who received small rewards, and as a result felt less pressure to change their attitudes.

The explanations of role-playing on attitude change provided by incentive theory and dissonance theory appear to be mutually exclusive, and yet there is empirical evidence to support both. To reconcile these two approaches, one must note that attitude changes can refer to changes in behavior, beliefs, and feelings. The incentive theory explanation may be more relevant in predicting attitude behavioral change, whereas dissonance theory explanations may hold for attitude belief changes and similar cognitive–affective processes.

Ego-Involvement *How important are environmental issues in your congressional district?* Whether an individual can be persuaded to change his or her views on a particular issue depends in part on how ego-involving the issue is—that is, how significant it may be in that person's life (Apsler & Sears, 1968; Sherif, Sherif, & Nebergall, 1965). (For this reason the term "issue-involvement" is sometimes used to express the same concept.) Ego-involvement is fundamental to attitude change because it affects other factors of the persuasion process. For example, ordinarily a highly credible source will lead to attitude change, but an individual's strong commitment can negate source credibility. *If you have proved to be a knowledgeable candidate you have probably gained several votes—but how did you make out when you spoke to the management team at the chemical plant?*

Gorn (1975) measured the importance of ego-involvement in relation to the separatist political movement in the Province of Quebec, Canada. The subjects were students at McGill University (located in Montreal, Quebec) and at the University of Calgary (located in Calgary, Alberta). Both groups were strongly opposed to the separatist movement; however, the ego-involvement of the McGill students was much higher than that of the Calgary students, for obvious reasons. Groups of students were presented with communications that were either moderately against, moderately in favor, or extremely in favor of separatism. The sources of the communications were identified as either low or high in prestige.

For the moderately involved University of Calgary students, attitude change was affected by the degree of dissonance evoked by the message as well as by the prestige of the source. For the highly involved McGill students, however, neither of these factors had an effect on attitude change. (Related studies have been done by Kiesler, Collins, & Miller, 1969; Rhine & Severance, 1970; Sherif et al., 1973.)

Retention Information that is presented first is retained more easily than subsequent information. This is known as a *primacy effect*. Conversely, we also easily retain information that is presented last; this is referred to as a *recency effect*. In order for persuasion to occur, a message must be retained or remembered. Therefore, attitude researchers are interested in whether the primacy or the recency effect will occur in a given situation.

Attempts to determine the specific conditions under which primacy and recency effects occur have yielded conflicting evidence. Miller and Campbell (1959) suggest that the time that elapses between arguments and the time between the communication and the assessment of attitudes are key factors in whether a primacy or a recency effect is obtained. For example, a long delay between arguments followed by an immediate attitude assessment after the last one yields a strong recency effect. When these time conditions are not present, however, the primacy effect is dominant. (See also Rosnow, 1966.) *Can these results help you organize your campaign speeches?*

Reactance The theory of psychological reactance, which was initially formulated by Brehm (1966), is based on the idea that people are motivated to safeguard their ability to act of their own free will. When individuals feel coerced into adopting an attitude they do not hold, reactance theory suggests that they react by moving in the opposite direction. (See also Sensenig & Brehm, 1968; Worchel & Brehm, 1971.)

Recently, however, it has been suggested that people are less concerned with actual freedom than with its appearance. It has been found, for example, that subjects who are given the opportunity to affirm their freedom in the presence of someone who is curtailing it, are less likely to respond defiantly even when their freedom continues to be curtailed (Baer et al., 1980; Heilman & Toffler, 1976). In this view, then, it is the public appearance of autonomy that is important and not freedom itself.

Intelligence It is difficult to establish a consistently positive or negative relationship between intelligence and persuasibility. McGuire (1968) suggests that two factors, *reception* and *yielding*, affect persuasion. Reception, the ability to understand a message, is positively related to intelligence. Yielding, or giving in to persuasion, is negatively related to intelligence. The fact that persuasion is not effective unless the individual is both receptive and yielding accounts for the ambiguous findings in this area. Education has similar effects: It enhances the individual's ability to understand a message, and fortifies the individual to withstand it at the same time (Sears & Riley, 1969).

The Channel

By now you should have acquired some ideas on the most effective methods to employ with the different "targets" of your congressional campaign. Now the question arises: How do you best deliver your message to the voters?

The **channel,** or **medium of communication,** is the vehicle that carries a message from the source to the target or recipient. To be persuasive, a message must reach the appropriate audience in the appropriate way. If one wanted to advertise a particular brand of laundry detergent, for example, it would be more appropriate to choose as the medium an afternoon television drama (hence the term "soap opera") than an F.M. radio program devoted to late-night lovers of classical music. Of course, you probably want your campaign to reach as wide an audience as possible. How can you identify the best medium to carry it?

We can generally distinguish between a message and the medium through which it is communicated. However, it is clear that the medium is not merely the conveyor of the message but an important aspect of its impact as well. This view was popularized by Marshall McLuhan (1964), who asserted that "the medium is the message." If one thinks of the difference between watching a debate between presidential candidates on television and reading a transcript of the debate in the newspaper the following day, McLuhan's point is very clear. With a "hot" medium such as television, one evaluates not only what each candidate said, but how it was said, how the candidate looked while saying it, and so on. The communication contains nonverbal as well as verbal factors. With a "cold" medium like newsprint, on the other hand, one can evaluate only what was actually said. This medium does, however, offer the advantage that one can reread certain passages at one's leisure without losing the train of the argument.

Social psychologists have found that the media play an important role in both reinforcing and transforming attitudes. *Here's some research that applies specifically to your campaign:* Grush (1980) found that highly accurate predictions could be made about the winners of various political primaries by analyzing the amount of media exposure each had received. Since frequency of exposure is, in general, positively correlated with persuasion (as we have previously discussed), candidates who receive more exposure were evaluated more positively. Thus, the media shape voter attitudes in ways that have nothing to do with the actual communication itself.

Because it presents live images, television is widely considered the most persuasive of the media. This is especially true when a message is relatively simple and when it is directed toward a less educated audience. In a study that demonstrated the power of the image factor in persuasion, Chaiken and Eagly (1976) found that uncomplicated messages were more persuasive when videotaped than when they were either audiotaped or written down. Interestingly, however, complicated messages were more persuasive when written down. The audiotaped versions were the second most persuasive media for both complicated and uncomplicated messages. Apparently, for relatively uncomplicated messages at least, the more closely a particular medium represents face-to-face interaction, the greater its power of persuasion (Frandsen, 1963; Williams, 1975). *(Remember these findings when you mail position papers to prospective voters!)*

Media influences have been examined in a variety of contexts. The role of television programs and commercials in reinforcing sex roles and other stereotypes has been noted extensively in recent years. Peterson and Thurstone (1933), in an early study, found that the choice of medium can alter racial attitudes. Jennings and her associates (1980) found that not only do television commercials function as social cues that trigger and reinforce sex-role stereotypes, but that unstereotyped commercials could produce attitude changes in many women.

Apt media choices can also influence consumer purchases (Bauer, 1965), as advertising managers and copywriters well know. On the other hand, a choice of the wrong medium has no impact on attitudes or behavior (Berelson, Lazarsfeld, & McPhee, 1954; Campbell, Gurin, & Miller, 1954).

Environmental and Situational Factors

As you campaign for a seat in Congress, you will find yourself giving speeches in many different situations. As the campaign heats up you might be confronted by demonstrators or hecklers (at least they are taking you seriously!). What effect do you think these demonstrators (and the distraction from your message) will have on your persuasibility?

In addition to the factors that are immediately related to the persuasion process—those that pertain to the source, the communication, the target, and the channel—attitude change is also influenced by many incidental and contextual variables. **Situational factors,** such as *distraction*, *forewarning*, and *censorship*, may have a significant impact on the persuasion process.

Distraction   We do not usually devote our total concentration to the messages that we receive. We are easily distracted, so that we momentarily lose some of what is being communicated or pay only partial attention to it. The distractions may be *internal*, when other thoughts and feelings crowd into our minds, competing with the message being communicated. Or they may be *external*, when we become aware of additional stimuli that are extraneous to the message. Both kinds of distractions constitute what communication theorists call **noise** (see chapter 7).

   Distraction shortcircuits communication. If you feel hunger pangs (internal distraction) while watching a television commercial and retreat to the kitchen for a snack, you will obviously not be able to receive the advertiser's message. If your child interrupts the commercial to explain something that happened at school (external distraction), the result will be the same. In any situation, the possibilities for distraction are potentially endless.

   Paradoxically, however, social psychologists have found that distraction can sometimes enhance persuasion. In the first study in this area, Festinger and Maccoby (1964) found that when an audience is initially opposed to the communicator's viewpoint, persuasion is more effective if the audience can be distracted from the communication. The distraction apparently makes it more difficult for the audience to rehearse counterarguments while listening to the message (Keating & Brock, 1974).

   It has been shown, however, that the effects of distraction on persuasion depend on the degree to which the audience pays attention to the message and the degree to which it pays attention to the distraction (Zimbardo et al., 1970). When the audience is set to pay attention to the message, distraction increases persuasion. But when the audience is set to pay attention to the distracting stimulus, persuasion and attitude change decrease. Of course, the relationship between distraction and persuasion depends on the intensity of the distracting stimulus. If the stimulus·is strong enough to block out the message itself, then persuasion will not occur (Petty et al., 1976). *So—will your congressional opponent help or hurt you when he or she creates a distraction (such as coughing, interrupting, nose-blowing) during your speech when you debate? Should you create a distraction when your opponent is talking?*

Forewarning   Forewarning an individual that an attempt at persuasion is about to occur may weaken that person's beliefs, as he or she worries about appearing too susceptible to influence (McGuire & Papageorgis, 1962). But when a person's commitment to a particular belief is strong, forewarnings about attempts to change the belief may cause a defensive reaction that reduces the effects of persuasion. Freedman and Sears (1965), for example, forewarned teenagers before they heard an argument against licensing teenage drivers—a position that they might be expected to react negatively to—and found that their defenses against the argument increased, thus reducing the effectiveness of the persuasion.

   The findings on forewarning are mixed, but the most important factors that

Controversy: The Ethical Implications of Attitude Change

Rokeach (1971) confronted students with inconsistencies in their value systems. After rating 18 values in rank order of importance (see Table A), subjects were told that students generally rated "freedom" highly, in first or second place on an 18-value scale, while "equality" came up in eleventh or twelfth place. However, subjects were further informed that students who had participated in the civil rights movement rated both terms equally (see Table B).

On three posttests, ranging from 3 weeks to nearly 1½ years later, subjects increased the value ratings of both concepts significantly more than controls who had not been given the value inconsistency information. In fact, the value ratings for both "freedom" and "equality" increased even further with the passage of time for the subjects in the experimental condition, and decreased somewhat for the controls (see Table C).

Rokeach was troubled by the implications of his findings:

Obviously, the finding that relatively enduring changes in values, attitudes, and behavior can be brought about as a result of a rather brief experimental treatment has important implications for the fields of political science and propaganda, as well as for the

TABLE A.
Values in Rank Order of Importance to 298 Michigan State University Students

Rank	Value
13	A comfortable life
12	An exciting life
6	A sense of accomplishment
10	A world at peace
17	A world of beauty
11	Equality
9	Family security
1	Freedom
2	Happiness
8	Inner harmony
5	Mature love
16	National security
18	Pleasure
14	Salvation
15	Social recognition
4	Self-respect
7	True friendship
3	Wisdom

fields of education and therapy. But . . . if such socially important values as equality and freedom can be altered to become more important to human subjects, they can surely be altered to also become less important.

determine the effect of forewarning on persuasion seem to be, first, the strength of a person's commitment to a particular belief, and second, that person's desire to maintain agreement with the communicator. If an issue is highly relevant, or if an individual is strongly committed to a belief, forewarning creates the opportunity for developing counterarguments to withstand persuasion (Hass & Grady, 1975; Petty & Cacioppo, 1977). But if the individual is strongly motivated to maintain agreement with the communicator, forewarning lets the person modify his or her beliefs beforehand to reduce the amount of last-minute attitude change (that is, from immediately before the persuasion to immediately after) (Hass, 1975; Hass & Mann, 1976).

Who shall decide which values are to be changed and who shall decide the direction of such change? Is it ethically possible to defend experimental work that may lead to relatively enduring changes in a person's values, attitudes, and behavior without his informed consent? To what extent should our educational institutions shape values as well as impart knowledge, and, if so, which values and in which direction? If we have indeed learned how to bring about changes in values, attitudes, and behavior, as I think the experiments described here suggest, we must make certain that this kind of knowledge will be put to use for the benefit rather than the detriment of mankind. (pp. 458–459)

Source: From "Long-Range Experimental Modification of Values, Attitudes, and Behaviors," by M. Rokeach, *American Psychologist*, 1971, *26*, 458–459.

TABLE B.

Average Rankings of Freedom and Equality by Michigan State University Students for and against Civil Rights

Value	Yes, and have participated	Yes, but have not participated	No, not sympathetic to civil rights
Freedom	6	1	2
Equality	5	11	17
Difference	+1	−10	−15

TABLE C.

Mean Increases in Value for Equality and Freedom for Experimental and Control Groups

Value	Posttest 1 (3 weeks later) Experimental	Control	Posttest 2 (3–5 months later) Experimental	Control	Posttest 3 (15–17 months later) Experimental	Control
Equality	1.91	.68	2.80	.71	2.68	.32
Freedom	1.48	.20	1.16	.21	1.59	.22

Source: Tables A, B, and C adapted from "Long-Range Experimental Modification of Values, Attitudes, and Behavior," by M. Rokeach, *American Psychologist*, 1971, *26*, 454, 456.

Another important factor may be the length of the interval between the warning and the communication itself. Is there enough time for the person to strengthen or modify beliefs? Also important is information about the content of the warning. A person who is told the actual position that the communicator will espouse can be expected to react differently than if he or she only knows that a persuasive argument is about to be presented (Hass & Grady, 1975).

Censorship The issue of censorship is clearly linked to such basic political concepts as the manipulation of information by those in power, and the relationship between freedom and social responsibility. For this reason, it has been debated throughout history. Social psychologists are not in agreement over the effectiveness of censorship in changing attitudes in a desired direction. On the one hand, behaviorally oriented psychologists contend that limiting people's exposure to socially undesirable attitudes and behavior will extinguish these undesirable patterns. By this reasoning, for example, if violent pornography did not exist, there would be a lower incidence of rape and other forms of sexual violence.

Other psychologists contend, on the other hand, that censorship can intensify undesirable attitudes and behavior: Reactance theory holds that when their freedom is limited people will react by moving in the opposite direction. In an experiment designed to test the reactance hypothesis in regard to censorship, Ashmore, Ramchandra, and Jones (1971) found that subjects who were told that they would not be allowed to hear a speech they agreed with became even more favorably disposed to the communicator's position. But those who were told they would not be allowed to hear a speech they disagreed with changed their attitudes in the direction of agreement.

Attitude Change Over Time

Once a person has been persuaded to change an attitude, will the new attitude endure *(at least until election day, to ensure your campaign success)* or will the old one regain prominence? When attitudes have been built up over a long period of time and are deeply rooted in a personality, changes are often short-lived. Much depends on the specific individual and the specific situation.

Maccoby and his associates (1962) report that follow-up studies indicate that approximately 6 months after attitude change has occurred, the amount of change has diminished to about half of what it was immediately following persuasion. In some cases, however, the lapse back into former attitudes may be less extreme. In a follow-up study of smokers who had engaged in role-playing in order to give up cigarettes, Mann and Janis (1968) found that 18 months after the sessions had been conducted, the cigarette consumption of experimental subjects was still considerably less than that of an equivalent group of control subjects.

The **duration of attitude change** has been found to depend on the manner in which attitude change occurs in the first place. Kelman (1958, 1963) proposed a model of social influence that distinguished between attitude change that occurred as a result of three factors: *internalization, identification,* and *compliance*. When attitude change is a function of internalization, the individual's value system undergoes transformation to incorporate the new attitude. When it is a function of identification or compliance, however, change occurs either to receive approval from someone else or for the sake of expediency. According to Kelman, attitude changes are lasting only when they are a function of internalization. Attitude change that is a function of identification or compliance persists only as long as the identification source or the necessity for expediency persists.

Smith (1976) used Kelman's model to test the duration of attitude change for subjects who were involved in sensitivity training sessions. Subjects whose attitudes had been changed as a result of either identification or compliance were classified as *externalizers*, and subjects whose attitudes had been changed as a result of value-system transformation were classified as *internalizers*. Five months after the training sessions, it was found, as predicted, that the duration of attitude change was significantly higher for internalizers than for externalizers.

A petty consistency is the hobgoblin of little minds.
Ralph Waldo Emerson

Environmental factors are often important in determining if attitude change is permanent or transitory. Newcomb's (1943) study of the political attitudes of Bennington College students (see above, p. 296) found that the students became more liberal during the course of their college careers as a result of exposure to liberal faculty members. A follow-up study conducted by Newcomb, Koenig, Flacks, and Warwick (1967) also indicated that the women maintained their liberal views over a 25-year period. One reason for this is that they chose husbands with similar liberal views. Thus, continual contact with a person who shared similar attitudes provided a supporting environment for the retention of their views.

Long-lasting attitude change seems to require active involvement in an issue as well as a supportive environment. Hollen (1972) found that induced value change increased one month after subjects were given material relating to preservation of the natural environment. Sherrid and Beech (1976) changed attitudes of New York City police officers in a similar fashion. *That's good news for your political future; after you are elected you will want to keep your constituents actively involved with the key issue of the environment.*

Answering Questions about Attitudes and Attitude Change

1. The Bennington study conducted by Newcomb and his colleagues indicated that going to college has a profound effect on attitudes. During the college years, apparently, we change from the attitudes of our parents to those of our peers.
2. Dissonance theory suggests that people are not "rational" but "rationalizing." People will change either their behavior or their attitudes to make them psychologically consistent with one another. What rationalizations have you heard people use to explain their cigarette smoking?
3. Research findings indicate that when people argue against what appears to be their self-interest they are more persuasive. An ex-convict arguing for harsher sentences will be more effective than an ex-convict arguing for more lenient sentences.
4. Research has shown that when old arguments are recast in a new package they become more persuasive.
5. According to research results, the most effective presentation of complex messages is in writing; the most effective presentation of simple messages is face to face.
6. It has been shown that mild distractions may actually increase persuasion. The hypothesized explanation is that the listener hears the message, and is prevented by the distraction from counter-arguing.

Summary

An **attitude** is a predisposition to respond in a certain way to a particular object, event, or experience. The **affective component** of an attitude consists of the subjective moods or feeling-states and the physiological responses that accompany it. The **cognitive component** consists of the beliefs and opinions through which the attitude is expressed. The **behavioral** (or **conative**) **component** is the physical and mental process that prepares the individual for action.

The scales that measure attitudes include the Thurstone scale, the Likert scale, the semantic differential scale, and bipolar scales.

Attitudes form through learning experiences and are influenced by the significant people (or groups) in a person's life. A **membership group** is a group to which the individual belongs; a **reference group** is a group to which the individual aspires to belong.

Classical conditioning is the process that forms attitudes by the repeated pairing of a neutral concept with one that is socially charged with positive or negative meanings. **Instrumental learning** occurs when an attitude is reinforced because of the social approval the person receives. Attitudes are also learned through **modeling** and **observational learning**. **Self-perception theory** suggests that people often infer their attitudes from their behavior.

Attitudes serve four basic functions: adjustment, ego defense, value expression, and knowledge. The adjustment and ego-defensive functions are geared to rewards and punishment; the value-expressive and knowledge functions are geared to high-level needs.

Consistency theories of attitude change are based on the premise that individuals strive to achieve cognitive equilibrium. **Balance theory** suggests that people maintain consistent attitudes by balancing their feelings and beliefs about one another against their feelings and beliefs about aspects of the environment. **Congruity theory** views attitude change as a function of whether the assertions that a communicator makes about a concept are congruent with or fit the individual's frame of reference. According to **cognitive dissonance theory**, when two related cognitions are not harmonious the individual is motivated to reduce his experience of dissonance.

Social judgment theory suggests that the structure of an attitude determines one's receptivity to messages relevant to that attitude. The range of attitudinal positions that a person can hold depends on that person's latitude of acceptance; other positions fall into the latitude of rejection.

The factors that make up the persuasion process include the source, the communication, the target, the channel, and the environment or situation.

The **credibility** of the source is generally defined in terms of expertise and trustworthiness. The impact of a high-credibility source lessens following the communication. The impact of a low-credibility source is heightened with the passage of time; this is the **sleeper effect**. Other important factors that relate to the source are intentions and motives, the degree the audience likes and identifies with the communicator, the communicator's power to punish and reward, speech style, and whether the conclusions are explicitly drawn.

The factors that are related to the **communication** and that affect attitude change are the degree of discrepancy between the positions of the source and the recipient; the degree to which the message arouses fear; whether it is one-sided or two-sided; the amount of novelty and repetition it contains; and the number of arguments it includes.

Whether the **target** of the message is amenable to persuasion depends on the previous commitment to a particular belief. According to the foot-in-the-door technique, if a person can be induced to make a commitment to a particular position, further commitment is likely to follow. Another important factor is if the individual's personality is susceptible to influence. Other target-related variables include the degree to which selective awareness sifts out opposing evidence; the degree to which inoculation stimulates the individual to develop strong counter-arguments; ego involvement; retention; and intelligence.

The **channel** or **medium of communication** has an important influence on how the communication is experienced. Television, which of all the media is closest to face-to-face interaction, is for that reason the most persuasive medium.

Situational factors may also influence the outcome of persuasion attempts. The specific effects of distraction, forewarning, and censorship depend on other variables and specific situations.

The **duration of attitude change** may be short or long, depending on situational and environmental factors, including the personalities of the individuals involved. When attitude change corresponds to internalized value-system change, it is likely to be of longer duration than when it occurs as a result of identification or compliance. If the environment reinforces the change in any way, it is also likely to be longer lived. The whole subject of attitude change may pose ethical problems for researchers and for society at large.

Suggested Additional Reading

Oskamp, S. *Attitudes and opinions.* Englewood Cliffs, N.J.: Prentice-Hall, 1977.

Petty, R. E., & Cacioppo, J. T., *Attitudes and persuasion.* Dubuque: Wm. C. Brown, 1981.

Petty, R. E., Ostrom, T. M., & Brock, T. C., eds. *Cognitive responses in persuasion.* Hillsdale, N.J.: Erlbaum, 1981.

ATTITUDES AND BEHAVIORS

Questions about Attitudes and Behaviors

You are interested in whether attitudes will predict behavior. You administer a questionnaire because you want to predict the number of people who will volunteer to work in a door-to-door campaign for nuclear disarmament. Which of the following will give you the most accurate predictions? Explain your answers.

1. Measures of general attitudes about nuclear disarmament or specific intentions to volunteer for the door-to-door campaign, or both?
2. Measures of attitudes to be taken immediately before requests that respondents work on the campaign, or measures taken some time before the request for volunteers will be made?
3. Measures of whether the respondents believe other friends are in favor of or disapprove of nuclear disarmament?
4. Questions about whether the respondent has had any prior experience as a volunteer in a door-to-door campaign for a socially idealistic cause?

What is your attitude toward cheating on exams? Have you ever cheated on one? Do you plan to cheat on your social psychology final? If you were asked these questions in an actual interview, all of your answers would probably be no. But, strange to say, cheating does sometimes occur.

If you find these questions amusing (or uncomfortable), it may interest you to learn that a social psychologist has studied cheating. Corey (1937; reported by Petty & Cacioppo, 1981) tested his students' attitudes to cheating and then used these measures to predict if particular students would cheat on the tests he gave them during the semester. He did this by grading his students' true–false tests, and then telling them that they would grade themselves. The difference between the grades Corey assigned to the tests and the grades the students gave themselves served as a "cheating index." Interestingly, Corey found that the attitudes that the students expressed about cheating did *not* serve as a reliable indicator of actual cheating behavior.

It is not surprising that, with respect to an issue such as cheating, the attitudes that people express do not necessarily conform to their actual behavior. But sometimes attitudes *can* serve as reliable indicators of behavior. Thus, the problem for social psychologists is to determine the variables that lead either to consistency or to inconsistency in the attitude–behavior relationship.

Predicting Behavior from Attitudes

The question of whether attitudes can be used to predict behavior has been studied in three distinct stages. During that time social psychologists went from an optimistic view about attitude–behavior relationships to a relatively pessimistic view, and then back to a more optimistic perspective (Ajzen & Fishbein, 1980; Petty & Cacioppo, 1981). Since the term **attitude** is generally defined as a predisposition to behave in a certain way, the implicit assumption of attitude research has always been that there is a *direct* relationship between attitudes and behavior. This assumption accounts for the optimism of the earliest researchers, such as those who devised the first attitude scales (see chapter 8).

Early in the history of attitude research, however, investigators discovered—to their surprise—that a clear relationship between attitudes and behavior could not always be found. By the 1960s, researchers were discouraged to find so many obstacles to the prediction of behavior on the basis of attitudes. However, this pessimism did not last long. By the middle 1970s, researchers were again confident that attitudes could be used to predict behavior if the right variables were measured with precision. In the next few pages we will trace the history of the debates on the attitude–behavior relationship. At each stage of this story you might consider how you—as a future social psychologist—would have responded to the problems encountered by researchers.

Do Attitudes Foretell Behavior? LaPiere's Findings

LaPiere (1934) conducted one of the most famous of the early studies that showed that the attitude–behavior relationship was more of a problem than was first thought. During the early 1930s, LaPiere traveled extensively throughout the United States with a young Chinese couple. As LaPiere described them, "both were personable, charming, and quick to win the admiration and respect of those they had the opportunity to become intimate with" (p. 231). But they were traveling during a period when the attitudes of Americans to Chinese were generally negative. Therefore, LaPiere expected it to be hard to find hotel and restaurant accommodations—especially in smaller towns where few Oriental people lived.

As it turned out, however, in over 10,000 miles of travel, LaPiere and his Chinese friends met with rejection only once—in a rural California camping ground. In fact, according to LaPiere, many of the hotels and restaurants treated them with "more than ordinary consideration" (p. 232).

Between saying and doing there is a long road.
Danish proverb

Since this experience was directly contrary to what one might have expected on the basis of attitude studies of the time, LaPiere decided to investigate the matter further. Six months after the trip, he mailed questionnaires to the hotels and restaurants that he and the Chinese couple had patronized. There were two types of questionnaires (see box), but both asked the following question: "Will you accept members of the Chinese race as guests in your establishment?" (p. 233). Astonishingly, more than 90 percent of the hotel and restaurant proprietors that filled out the questionnaire said they would not. Apparently, then, the negative attitudes of these establishments' proprietors to Orientals was *not* a good predictor of how they would actually treat them.

LaPiere's findings led many researchers to conclude that behavior could not be predicted on the basis of questionnaire-assessed attitudes. But over the years the methodological procedures of his study were criticized by others (Dillehay, 1973; Triandis, 1971). It was argued, for example, that the proprietors of the establishments that LaPiere and the Chinese couple visited may not have recognized that the couple was Chinese, or that the staff of these establishments may have reacted only to LaPiere, who was white. It was also pointed out that it was the owners or managers of the establishments who had responded to the questionnaires, not the staff members whom LaPiere and the Chinese couple probably encountered. The staff members might not have been sure what the owners' policies were in this situation or might not have shared the same feelings.

Although these criticisms are relevant, they do not negate the value of LaPiere's study. The discrepancy between the behavior of the establishments' personnel and the attitudinal responses to LaPiere's questionnaires is too glaring to be considered a result of incidental methodological flaws. Moreover, subsequent studies that did not contain methodological flaws of this kind also failed to establish a high degree of correspondence between attitudes and behavior.

In addition, the conclusions of LaPiere's landmark study have often been misunderstood. LaPiere himself did *not* conclude from his study that there is *no* correspondence between attitudes and behavior, but only that the attitudes that show up on questionnaires are too general, abstract, and removed from actual experience to serve as reliable predictors of behavior. He himself recommended that "social attitudes . . . be derived from a study of humans behaving in actual social situations" (p. 237). Thus, instead of answering questions about the relationship of attitudes and behavior, LaPiere's study actually posed a new question: If we can devise more accurate measures, will we then find that attitudes correspond more closely to behavior? Research on attitudes and behavior continued for another 30 years. Then social psychologists stepped back to reassess the accumulated research—and were discouraged by the results.

Problems in Attitude–Behavior Research

In 1969, Wicker published a comprehensive review of the empirical studies of the relationship between attitudes and behavior that had been performed since the classic LaPiere study of 1934. Wicker found that "taken as a whole, these studies suggest that it is considerably more likely that attitudes will be unrelated or only slightly related to overt behaviors than that attitudes will be closely related to actions" (p. 65). According to Wicker, only rarely did these studies show a correlation coefficient of more than .30 (low significance), and often the correlation was near zero.

Abelson (1972) suggested that Wicker may have overlooked a number of studies that showed a higher correlation between attitudes and behavior, or analyzed some data inaccurately. Yet his argument does not negate Wicker's general conclusion. No matter how optimistically one regards the data, it is still apparent that the majority of studies had failed to demonstrate a high correlation between attitudes and behavior.

Research: LaPiere's Study—Design and Findings

In the study examined in the text, LaPiere mailed one of two versions of a questionnaire to each of the hotels and restaurants that he and the Chinese couple had visited. Both questionnaires contained the question: "Will you accept members of the Chinese race as guests in your establishment?" In the first questionnaire, this question was included among similar questions relating to other national groups; in the second questionnaire no other group was mentioned. LaPiere felt that respondents receiving the second questionnaire might have become suspicious about its source, and not give truthful answers. By camouflaging the question about the Chinese, the first questionnaire served to safeguard the study. As the table indicates, the two questionnaires elicited different answers.

In addition to mailing the questionnaires to the hotels and restaurants that he and the Chinese couple had patronized, LaPiere also mailed the same questionnaires to hotels and restaurants that they had not visited. Since the personnel at these hotels and restaurants were not influenced by an actual encounter with LaPiere

and the Chinese couple, they served as a control group.

LaPiere's findings are presented in the table below. As it turned out, 92 percent of the proprietors who filled out the multi-group questionnaire and 91 percent of those who filled out the questionnaire that only asked about the Chinese responded negatively to the question about accepting members of the Chinese race into their establishments. Thus, the difference in response between the two questionnaires was negligible. Similarly, there was no significant difference between the responses of proprietors of establishments that had been visited and the responses of those that had not. All subjects held about the same degree of anti-Chinese prejudice, whether or not they were queried about their other prejudices as well, and whether or not they had actually acted contrary to their expressed prejudice. Therefore, this study seems to show that attitudes—in this case a prejudice against Chinese people—are not always a good indication of actual behavior—giving the Chinese couple room and board.

Replies to the Question: "Will You Accept Members of the Chinese Race as Guests in Your Establishment?"

	Hotels, etc., Visited		Hotels, etc., Not Visited		Restaurants, etc., Visited		Restaurants, etc., Not Visited	
Total	47		32		81		96	
	1*	2*	1	2	1	2	1	2
Number replying......................	22	25	20	12	43	38	51	45
No................................	20	23	19	11	40	35	47	41
Undecided: depend upon circumstances....................................	1	2	1	1	3	3	4	3
Yes	1	0	0	0	0	0	0	1

* Column (1) indicates in each case those responses to questionnaires which concerned Chinese only. The figures in columns (2) are from the questionnaires in which the above question was inserted among questions regarding Germans, French, Japanese, etc.

Source: From "Attitudes and Actions," by R. T. LaPiere, *Social Forces*, 1934, *13*, 234.

Methodological Implications   More important than Wicker's empirical findings—which basically confirmed what many social psychologists already believed—were the methodological implications that he drew from his survey. Wicker pointed out, for one thing, that specific attitudes do not exist in isolation from other attitudes or from environmental variables. Because, in a given situation, a person's specific attitude can interact with other factors, it would be impossible to predict behavior from any one attitude considered alone.

In the LaPiere study, for example, the possible negative attitudes of the hotel and restaurant personnel to Chinese guests might have been balanced by their positive attitudes to courteous, attractive people (which is how LaPiere described his friends), or by some other set of attitudinal variables evoked by the situation. Or, environmental variables might have determined the behavior of the personnel. For example, staff members might have felt that refusing to admit the couple would have created an unpleasant scene. Theoretically, the number of variables is infinite. Nonetheless, Wicker's critique provides a useful overview of the attempts of previous investigators to categorize the factors that influence attitude–behavior relationships. For example, he cites the following *personal factors*:

1. *Other attitudes.* Other attitudes, besides the attitude in question, which are relevant to and evoked by a specific situation, may influence behavior and either strengthen or weaken the salience of the attitude in question.
2. *Competing motives.* If other motives or drives that lead to a particular behavior are stronger than those connected to a particular attitude, the importance of that attitude may be weakened.
3. *Verbal*, *intellectual*, and *social abilities.* If individuals are unable to make the connection between an attitude that they hold and the response that logically follows from it, the importance of that attitude for behavior may be weakened. Wicker (p. 68) gives the example of a voter who is unaware that the candidate he opposes holds positions that are in agreement with his own.

Wicker also mentions the following *situational factors*:

1. *Actual or considered presence of other people.* The presence of others may strengthen or weaken the importance of a particular attitude in behavior. Moreover, attitude information obtained under conditions of anonymity or secrecy (as in some studies) may not reflect how the individual will behave when others are present. The person who admits to an attitude under private conditions may be too afraid or ashamed to behave that way in public.
2. *Normative prescriptions of proper behavior.* Attitude–behavior inconsistency may result from the fact that a particular attitude is contrary to a particular behavior that the individual considers to be appropriate in a given situation. Thus, a hotel proprietor might be prejudiced against Chinese people, and might express this attitude on a questionnaire, but might also consider it inappropriate to turn them away when they are actually standing at the door.
3. *Alternative behavior not available.* In some cases, a particular course of action that would be consistent with a particular attitude is simply not avail-

Ken Karp

Civil disobedience is a situation in which normally law-abiding citizens use nonviolent confrontation to call attention to an issue they believe is unjust. In New York City in June 1982, demonstrators sat on the street in front of missions of foreign countries that have nuclear capability. When the demonstrators refused to move, police lifted them bodily to bring them to a police station for arraignment. Which of the situational factors listed by Wicker do you think caused these demonstrators to behave in ways that did not reflect their attitudes as law-abiding citizens?

able to the individual. Wicker (p. 71) gives the example of a person in a small town who dislikes the local newspaper but subscribes to it because it is the only one available.

4.   *Specificity of attitude objects.* In actual situations, the stimuli that evoke attitudes are both more specific and more concrete than the verbal stimuli that elicit attitudes in questionnaires. Thus, attitudes evoked in actual situations often do not correspond to the abstract, categorical attitudes elicited by a questionnaire. In the LaPiere study, for example, the question about members of the Chinese race may have evoked a stereotype in the respondents' minds, but their perception of the couple that actually entered the door may not have corresponded to this stereotype. It may be, then, not that attitudes fail to correspond to behavior, but rather that the attitudes elicited by a questionnaire are different from attitudes evoked by actual events.

5.   *Unforeseen extraneous events.* Unforeseen factors may intervene to cause a person to behave in ways that are inconsistent with attitudes. For example, someone who disapproves of people who receive welfare checks might suddenly become disabled and be forced to apply for public assistance.

6.   *Expected and/or actual consequences of various acts.* Attitude–behavior inconsistency may result from a person's fear of punishment or hope for reward. For example, a person who is prejudiced against blacks is not likely to voice those negative feelings while being interviewed for a job by a black

person. On the contrary, such an individual might even "lean over back-
wards" to avoid giving the interviewer the impression of prejudice.

Wicker's review of the attitude–behavior research was very influential in social psychology. First, it underscored the fact that many researchers had failed to
obtain the strong attitude–behavior relationships they expected. Next, he outlined some plausible explanations for those discouraging results. In particular,
Wicker's stress on the importance of personal and situational factors to the
attitude–behavior relationship led other researchers to reformulate their
attitude–behavior theories and devise new research methods. Within a few years,
researchers would be more optimistic about their approach to this attitude–behavior research.

Improving Attitude–Behavior Research

In 1976, Schuman and Johnson reviewed the attitude–behavior problem and attempted to establish guidelines for improving research procedures. Among
other things, they suggested that attitudinal measures that would successfully
predict behavior would have to be designed to be as *specific* as possible to the
behaviors being predicted. In addition, the *strength*, *clarity*, and *reliability* of
the attitudes being measured would also have to be precisely defined.

Schuman and Johnson also assert that behavior should be viewed not
merely in terms of single acts but in terms of overall behavioral tendencies. The
results of single acts can be misleading. For example, in the LaPiere study, the
behavior of the hotel and restaurant staffs contradicted—in this one instance—the
stated attitudes of the proprietors. But who is to say whether, over the long term,
the behavior of these staffs to Chinese people would not have been congruent to
the attitudes of their owners? It is quite possible that many of these staffs would
have refused to accommodate Chinese customers, and that only the presence of
LaPiere or the extraordinary charm of this particular couple induced them to deviate from their general rule. From this point of view, a behavioral scale basing
its predictions on overall tendencies at various times, rather than on single acts,
would provide a truer picture of the attitude–behavior relationship.

Finally, Schuman and Johnson point to the need to consider how reference
group pressures might offset attitudes in some situations, and how environmental factors may influence an outcome. The more we know about the psychological
and social pressures that influence an individual, and whether these pressures
strengthen or weaken specific attitudes in various situations, the better we can
predict behavior.

In general, Schuman and Johnson would improve research by increasing
measurement specificity and by accumulating more data. The problem, as these
investigators admit, is knowing where to stop. LaPiere might have asked the hotels and restaurants whether they would admit a "young, well-dressed, pleasant,
self-confident, well-to-do Chinese couple" (Fishbein & Ajzen, 1975; as quoted by
Schuman & Johnson, p. 171), but then the questionnaire would not have been
valid for members of the Chinese race who did not fit the description. Even if it
were possible to devise an attitude scale that corresponded perfectly to a specific
situation, the result would only be applicable to that very narrow area.

Areas of Successful Prediction

In an attitude survey or questionnaire, the questions asked must be as detailed or specific as the particular behavior one wants to predict. This may sound like a very difficult problem (and it can be!), but there are many examples of attitude–behavior research in which highly successful predictions have been achieved. We will briefly consider four of these: voting behavior, consumer behavior, race relations, and the women's movement.

Voting Behavior Attitude surveys have been used successfully to predict the outcome of elections. For example, the Gallup Poll preelection surveys have overall had an average error of only around 1 percent in recent elections, and the error rate for other polling organizations has also been extremely low (see Table 9–1).

TABLE 9–1.

Percentage Error of Forecasts by Major Polls in 1972, 1976, and 1980 Presidential Elections

1972 Polls	Sample Size	Predictions		Results		Percentage Error
		Nixon	McGovern	Nixon	McGovern	
Gallup (11/6/72)	3500	62	38	61.8	38.2	0.2
Harris (11/6/72)	—	60	37	61.8	38.2	1.8
Yankelovich (10/30/72)[a] (*New York Times* pollster)	"Approx. 1500"	65	36	61.8	38.2	3.2

1976 Polls	Sample Size	Predictions		Results		Percentage Error
		Carter	Ford	Carter	Ford	
Gallup	3500	48.0	49.0	50.0	48.3	2.0
Harris	—	49.0	48.0	50.0	48.3	1.0
Roper/PBS	2000	51.0	47.0	50.0	48.3	1.0
NBC News	—	49.0	49.0	50.0	48.3	1.0

1980 Polls	Sample Size	Predictions[b]		Results		Percentage Error
		Carter	Reagan	Carter	Reagan	
Gallup	3500	44.0	47.0	41.6	51.7	4.7
Harris	—	41.6	46.8	41.6	51.7	4.9
CBS/N.Y. Times	2264	44.7	46.8	41.6	51.7	4.9
NBC/AP	—	40.0	48.0	41.6	51.7	3.7

[a]The Yankelovich polls are not strictly comparable. They consisted of telephone interviews with potential voters in 16 states important in the electoral college.

[b]In 1980, the Anderson predictions and votes are not given, and "undecided" votes are distributed proportionately among all three candidates.

Source: Adapted from *Public Opinion*, 4th Edition, by B. Hennessy. Copyright © 1965, 1970, 1975, 1981 by Wadsworth, Inc. Reprinted by permission of the publisher, Brooks/Cole Publishing Company, Monterey, California.

TABLE 9–2.
Housing Law Survey in Detroit

Question Posed to Respondents on First Survey:[a]	Percent in Agreement (Number)	Experiment Design: Housing Petition Presented (Number)	Percent Refusing to Sign	(Number)[b]	Percent Signing
Suppose there is a community-wide vote on the general housing issue. Which of two possible laws would you vote for?					
1. A homeowner can decide for himself to whom to sell his house, even if he prefers not to sell to Negroes. (Owner's rights position)	82 (525)	Owner's rights (406)	15	(293)	85
		Open housing (119)	78	(85)	22
2. A homeowner cannot refuse to sell to some-one because of race or color. (Open housing position)	16 (101)	Open housing (101)	30	(76)	70
Neither or Not Answering	2				

[a] Respondents to the first survey were 640 white adults in Detroit. The survey was conducted in 1969.

[b] Not all of the original respondents could be reached when the follow-up petition was presented 3 months later.

Source: Adapted from "Attitude and Action: A Field Experiment Joined to a General Population Survey" by R. Brannon et al., *American Sociological Review*, 1973, *38*, 629. Reprinted by permission of H. Schuman and The American Sociological Association.

What accounts for the extraordinary success of polling organizations in predicting voting behavior? One reason may be that their predictions are based less on attitudes than on *intentions*, that is, on attitudes that have become fixed and that have taken on a behavioral direction. For this reason, as Crespi (1971) points out, surveys can pose questions that simulate the actual voting situation. Thus, if the voter expresses the intention to vote for Candidate X, this survey response should be replicated in election day behavior. Of course, many voters are undecided when the survey is taken, and some change their minds before the election actually occurs. The polling organization must take account of the intensity of the voter's attitudes and intentions, the time frame (how close the poll is to the election), and the possibility that a polled individual may fail to vote. Advanced statistical methods have made it possible for polling organizations to weigh these and other variables with a high degree of accuracy.

Consumer Behavior   Marketing researchers have found that in many instances consumer behavior can be successfully predicted from consumer attitudes toward a particular brand. For example, General Motors found that consumers' expressed liking for a specific model was a good indicator of future sales (Bogart, 1967). Of course, there are a variety of economic and other factors that can intervene to make an individual's behavior deviate from his attitude. Mr. A, a blue-collar worker, may prefer Cadillacs to Chevrolets, but this does not mean that he will actually purchase a Cadillac. Therefore, when companies conduct attitude surveys, they must ensure that the sample populations on which they are basing their predictions are representative of the intended market for the product.

Race Relations   Despite the lack of correspondence between attitudes and behaviors found by LaPiere and in subsequent studies of attitude–behavior consistency concerning race relations, a number of more recent studies have shown positive correlations. Apparently, if the general population is well-informed about a particular race-related issue, and if the specific behavior in question is the same for both the survey and the situation to which it is geared, the likelihood of a successful prediction is high.

Ego involvement

For example, Brannon et al. (1973) surveyed attitudes toward laws prohibiting racial discrimination in housing in Detroit. Respondents were asked to choose between a law in which homeowners retained the right to sell their homes to anyone they wanted, and a law that prevented them from refusing someone on the basis of race. Table 9–2 shows the questions asked in the survey and the percentage of respondents that chose each of the two options.

Three months later, the respondents were approached by confederates of the examiners who asked them to sign petitions that were either consistent or in-

TABLE 9–3.
Women's Liberation Ideology Scale*

1. There should be legislative restrictions on abortion. (Disagree)
2. Community day-care centers should be established nationally. (Agree)
3. Men and women should be paid equally for equal work. (Agree)
4. Motherhood is the most fulfilling role for women. (Disagree)
5. It is important for me to be physically attractive to the opposite sex. (Disagree)
6. Women should not be able to obtain an abortion merely on request. (Disagree)
7. I would place my children in a day-care center. (Agree)
8. There are circumstances in which women should be paid less than men for equal work. (Disagree)
9. There are some jobs for which women are emotionally unfit. (Disagree)
10. A woman's career should always be secondary to her husband's. (Disagree)
11. The wife should not always have primary responsibility for household duties. (Agree)
12. The mother should have primary responsibility for care and nurturance of children. (Disagree)

* Items in parentheses indicate the direction of the scoring.

Source: From "The Women's Liberation Movement: Attitudes and Action" by Goldschmidt et al., *Journal of Personality*, 1974, *42*, 604.

consistent with the positions they had previously taken. The behavior of the respondents in either signing or refusing to sign the petitions was very consistent with the positions they had taken earlier.

The Women's Movement   Goldschmidt et al. (1974) showed that whether women identified with and actively participated in the women's movement could be predicted on the basis of their attitudes to work, marriage, children, and other issues. In this study, college women were asked to respond to a "Women's Liberation Ideology Scale" that contained 12 questions (see Table 9–3). The researchers also found that the behavior of these women was highly consistent with their expressed attitudes: Of the 60 women who scored lowest on the scale, 50 had not participated in activities related to the women's movement. On the other hand, of the 30 highest scorers, only 4 had not participated in such activities.

Avoiding Measurement Pitfalls

As the above examples indicate, while there is a good correspondence between attitudes and behaviors in some domains, there is not a *perfect* correspondence between expressed attitudes and behavior. For this reason, investigators have attempted to identify measurement problems in attitude–behavior research in an effort to increase the correspondence. In the next section we will examine some of the more common measurement pitfalls, and discuss possible techniques for avoiding them.

Biases in Attitude Measures

Since LaPiere's classic study, many investigators have observed that attitude scales used in questionnaires may fail to reflect the authentic attitudes of respondents. If a particular item is ambiguously worded, or if the subject interprets it incorrectly, the response to that item will obviously not reflect the subject's attitudes. As we discuss later in this chapter, this is an *objective* problem of interpretation. It can be dealt with by constructing attitude scales so that several items measure the same basic attitude. These are sometimes termed **multiple indicators**. In this way, individual idiosyncrasies that affect comprehension are overcome, and we may have greater confidence that we have reliably measured the basic underlying attitudes.

A more serious measurement problem arises when, for *subjective* reasons, people's responses to questionnaire items do not reflect their real attitudes. People may offer misleading responses if, for example, they are ashamed of the attitudes they hold. Sometimes, moreover, they may be unaware of deep-seated attitudes that differ from the overt attitudes they express to others and even to themselves. In all such cases, the problem arises of the validity of the attitude scale as a measurement tool. We briefly discussed this problem in chapter 2 when we examined survey research techniques. How can such problems be offset? Several clever techniques have been suggested as safeguards against these subjective biases. We will describe a few of them as we look more closely at two kinds of reasons for subjective bias: the desire to give socially desirable responses; and the individual personality patterns that can lead to response bias.

Social Desirability In some cases, people respond in a misleading manner to attitude questionnaires because they are aware that certain attitudes are socially desirable while others are not. In order to deal with this problem, researchers have developed a technique known as the **bogus pipeline**. The experimenter claims to have access to the subject's genuine attitudes by means of a machine that provides a direct physiological measure of these attitudes (Jones & Sigall, 1971). In reality, of course, the experimenter could not possibly make such a claim because the correspondence between attitudes—which are influenced by verbal factors—and physiological states of arousal is, at best, an indirect one. Nevertheless, unless subjects become aware of the ruse, they are motivated to make authentic responses since they believe the examiner can "catch" false ones.

The bogus pipeline technique has been used effectively in a number of attitude surveys as a safeguard against distorted responses that result from social pressures. In one such experiment, Sigall and Page (1971) predicted that subjects' attitudes would correspond to socially desirable stereotypes more closely when a traditional rating method was used alone than when it was used in conjunction with the bogus pipeline technique. The basic assumption of this experiment was that as a result of social pressures, college students would tend to express less favorable attitudes toward "Americans" and more favorable attitudes toward "Negroes" than they actually felt. (This was at a time when protests against the Vietnam War and demonstrations in favor of the Civil Rights Movement were important issues on many college campuses.)

The subjects of the experiment were 60 white male undergraduates at the University of Rochester. The first group of 30 responded to a trait profile about "Americans," while the other 30 subjects responded to a similar profile about "Negroes." In each of the 2 groups, 15 subjects were hooked up to an apparatus labeled "EMG"; they believed that physiological measures of their attitudes were being taken that allowed the experimenter to know when their verbal responses were dishonest. The other 15 in each group served as controls, receiving only the trait profile, and were not attached to the bogus pipeline apparatus.

As predicted, there was a much greater tendency for the subjects to express attitudes that conformed with socially desirable stereotypes when the traditional rating method was used alone than when it was used in conjunction with the bogus pipeline technique (see Table 9-4). If the bogus pipeline did tap into attitudes that were more "real" or "authentic" than those obtained with the traditional rating method alone, we could conclude that the subjects were more favorably disposed to "Americans" and less favorably disposed to "Negroes" than they would have been willing to admit.

Methods other than the bogus pipeline have been suggested to detect socially desirable responses. Some researchers have proposed that behavioral indicators be used as a safeguard against misleading verbal responses. It has been observed, for example, that when people listen to messages with which they agree, they make more vertical and fewer horizontal head movements (Wells & Petty, 1980). Conceivably, examiners could use such movements as a warning

TABLE 9-4.
Mean Assignment of Traits*

	Condition			
	Americans		Negroes	
Trait	Bogus Pipeline	Traditional Rating	Bogus Pipeline	Traditional Rating
Talkative	1.40	1.60	.67	.47
Happy-go-lucky	.53	.53	.93	−.13
Honest	.60	−.27	−.33	.67
Musical	−.20	.53	1.53	2.00
Conventional	.87	1.33	−.60	−.73
Ostentatious	1.07	1.27	1.13	.33
Progressive	1.47	1.33	.47	.40
Ignorant	−.53	−.07	.60	.20
Practical	1.20	1.33	−.40	−.27
Superstitious	−.40	−.13	.20	.00
Intelligent	1.73	1.00	.00	.47
Pleasure loving	1.93	2.07	1.80	1.07
Imitative	.80	.33	.33	.20
Stupid	−1.07	−.20	.13	−1.00
Industrious	2.33	2.20	.07	.00
Physically dirty	−1.67	−1.53	.20	−1.33
Ambitious	2.07	2.13	−.07	.33
Aggressive	1.73	1.60	1.20	.67
Unreliable	−.73	−.40	.27	−.67
Materialistic	2.42	2.20	.60	.87
Sensitive	1.47	.07	.87	1.60
Lazy	−.80	−.40	.60	−.73

* Responses to specific traits could range from −3 (uncharacteristic) to +3 (characteristic).

Source: Adapted from "Current Stereotypes: A Little Fading, A Little Faking" by H. Sigall and R. Page, *Journal of Personality* and *Social Psychology*, 1970, *18*, 250.

of misleading or inaccurate verbal responses. In practice, however, this would probably be too cumbersome.

In addition to behavioral indicators, some researchers have experimented with physiological measures of arousal as a safeguard against misleading verbal responses. One such is the GSR (galvanic skin response), which measures how well the skin conducts electricity; another is the EMG (electromyograph), which measures muscle tension (Petty & Cacioppo, 1981). Physiological measures such as these do not have direct access to attitudes (which is the claim the bogus pipeline method pretends to have); but in their capacity to measure arousal levels, they may be able to chart dishonest responses. Thus they would operate along the same lines as polygraphs or lie detectors. Their value for attitude research, however, remains controversial.

Response Styles   In addition to the social variables that may intervene to distort an individual's responses to an attitude survey, there are also personality variables that can have the same effect. Researchers have found that some people respond in a certain pattern to questionnaires and tests regardless of their attitudes or beliefs. A patterned series of responses forms what has been called a **response style** (Cronbach, 1960). Thus, people with an *acquiescent* response style will tend to give "yes" or "agree" responses to items in a questionnaire, even if those answers do not reflect their true attitudes. Conversely, people with a *rebellious* response style will tend to give negative responses.

As we noted earlier, perhaps the best way to safeguard the validity of a test against response-style distortions is to design attitude surveys with multiple questions for the specific attitudes being tested. In such studies, the questions used to gauge a particular attitude can be phrased in various ways. Some might require "agree" answers and some "disagree" (as we saw in the Women's Liberation Ideology Scale, Table 9–3) to reflect the same attitude. By this method, an acquiescent or rebellious response style would cause internal contradictions, which the examiner could interpret. In some cases, the data might have to be thrown out and that subject's responses invalidated, but this is preferable to making predictions on the basis of misleading information. Multiple questions also minimize problems of misunderstanding and ambiguity—both for the subject and for the researcher.

Correspondence between Attitude Measures and Behavior

Let's pause for a moment. Up to now, our quest for attitudes that are related to behavior and methods for measuring those attitudes has come up against a number of theoretical and practical problems. Most of the pitfalls that researchers have encountered over the past 50 years have been methodological rather than theoretical. Indeed, most social psychologists (even during the gloomy period in which critical views such as Wicker's held sway) have consistently subscribed to theories that assumed that at least some attitudes are related to some behaviors. We have already examined several areas of attitude–behavior research (such as voting behavior) where attitudes can be used to predict behavior. Recently two social psychologists—Martin Fishbein and Icek Ajzen (1974, 1975, 1980)—have led a theoretical and methodological effort to improve behavioral prediction through effective attitude measurement. A key principle of the Fishbein and Ajzen approach is that an expressed attitude can be an appropriate basis for predicting behavior only if it corresponds to the behavior being predicted. That is, the attitude must be measured at the same level of specificity as the behavior. Correspondence also requires that the time at which the attitude measure is taken be close enough to the onset of the predicted behavior to make it unlikely that the attitude will change in the interim. If the attitude measure does not correspond in both specificity and time frame to the predicted behavior, it will not be valid. These concepts can be stated as three related principles:

1. General attitudes predict general behaviors.
2. Specific attitudes predict specific behaviors.
3. The less time elapses between attitude measurement and behavior, the more consistent the relationship between attitude and behavior will be.

We will briefly discuss each of these principles.

General Attitudes Predict General Behaviors   General attitudes are the best predictors of behaviors that may consist of several actions (as opposed to only a single act). Fishbein and Ajzen (1974), for example, showed that the religious attitudes of subjects were not necessarily consistent with any one act (giving to charity or observing a religious holiday) but corresponded closely to the performance of a number of different religious acts. Thus, general attitudes correspond to what has been called a **multiple-act criterion,** which averages the various forms of behavior that relate to a specific attitude in an attempt to arrive at a general behavioral tendency (Fishbein & Ajzen, 1975). With respect to the LaPiere study, we might speculate that if the general attitudes of the hotel and restaurant staffs toward Chinese people had been measured in terms of a multiple-act criterion, no inconsistency would have been found. (Voting is a single-act behavior that cannot be accurately predicted from a general attitude.)

Weigel and Newman (1976) conducted a study that gave subjects the opportunity to engage in behaviors that related to attitudes. First they queried the subjects about their attitudes on a broad range of environmental concerns, and later they presented the subjects with several concrete ways to express these concerns. The attitude questionnaire enabled the researchers to derive a general profile for each subject. They found only slightly significant agreement between the general attitudes of the subjects and several of the specific activities. However, when all of the suggested activities were grouped to obtain a comprehensive behavioral index, the relationship between general attitudes and general behavior was highly consistent.

Specific Attitudes Predict Specific Behaviors   Ecological issues were also at the heart of the research designed to test another attitude–behavior principle: Specific attitudes predict specific behavior. Weigel, Vernon, and Tognacci (1974) attempted to correlate the attitudes of subjects toward environmental issues with their behavior at three levels of specificity. The specific behavior under consideration was whether or not subjects would commit themselves to participating in the activities of the Sierra Club, an organization dedicated to the protection of the natural environment. "High-specificity" questions concerned attitudes about the Sierra Club itself; "moderate-specificity" questions dealt with attitudes toward conservation and pollution, two issues that are the major focus of the Sierra Club; and "low-specificity" questions covered general attitudes toward the environment (the importance of clean air and pure water, for example).

After completing the attitude questionnaires, the subjects were asked to sign a consent form allowing their names and addresses to be forwarded to the Sierra Club so that they could be included in its mailing list. Those subjects who agreed to sign were approached by members of the Sierra Club several months later. These subjects were classified as "no consent," "low commitment," "moderate commitment," or "high commitment" according to their willingness to involve themselves in Sierra Club activities.

The high-specificity measure that asked about attitudes to the Sierra Club proved to be the best predictor of whether subjects would later follow through with behavior (payment of dues, work on committees) benefitting the Sierra Club. The moderate-specificity questions were somewhat correlated with subsequent commitment, while the low-specificity scale did not yield significant correlations.

We can again consider LaPiere's study. Might he have found a better correspondence between proprietors' attitudes and their behavior (or perhaps the behavior of their employees) if the questionnaire had pointedly (and specifically) asked whether a well-dressed Chinese couple accompanied by an adult white male would be refused service if they appeared at the proprietor's establishment?

Time Lag Between Attitude Measures and Behavior   Since attitudes often shift over time, it has been found that the longer the time between the measurement and the onset of the relevant behavior, the greater the chance for inconsistent results (Oskamp, 1977). This was demonstrated by Schwartz (1978) who gave Israeli undergraduates a questionnaire in which items about specific altruistic acts (such as volunteering to tutor blind children) were included. Then, either 3 or 6 months later, or both 3 and 6 months later, the subjects received in the mail an appeal to serve as volunteer tutors for blind children. Their responses to the mailed appeal showed greater attitude–behavior consistency at the 3-month interval than at the 6-month interval. This was true not only for those who received the appeals at either 3 or 6 months, but also for those who received the appeals at both 3- and 6-month intervals.

Kelly and Mirer (1974) also observed that errors in election prediction declined when preelection interviews were made closer to election day. (Time-lag issues have also been found by Cialdini et al., 1976, and Hass & Mann, 1976.)

Were LaPiere's results similarly affected by a time lag? It is not clear whether he would have obtained a better correspondence between behavior and attitudes if he had conducted his survey within a few days of actually seeking service at the hotels and restaurants. That study's failure in measurement specificity was probably a more important source of the weak relationship between behavior and attitudes that LaPiere obtained.

Conditions Promoting and Reducing Consistency

Up to this point we have concentrated on the problem of measuring appropriate attitudes using appropriate methods. In this section we turn our attention to the attitudes themselves as we consider whether there are characteristics of attitudes that might promote stronger attitude–behavior relationships. As a brief introduction we might note that attitude–behavior correspondence depends on a number of factors: whether the attitude is formed through direct or indirect experience; how deeply it is engrained in the individual's personality; and on a variety of other situational and individual factors. In the following sections, we will examine some of these factors.

Attitudes Formed Through Experience

In the fall of 1973, more than 100 members of the incoming freshman class at Cornell University found themselves assigned to temporary living quarters be-

Both Ken Karp

Personal involvement
increases the importance of
an attitude and its
correspondence to behavior.
This wounded veteran of the
Vietnam War makes a very
strong behavioral statement
by attending a nuclear
disarmament rally.

cause of an unexpected housing shortage. This gave Regan and Fazio (1977) an
opportunity to test a key attitude–behavior hypothesis: Attitudes formed as a result of direct experience are more consistently related to behaviors than attitudes based on indirect experience. The subjects of their study included those
freshmen assigned to temporary housing and an equivalent group of freshmen
living in permanent housing. A survey of attitudes toward the housing crisis was
administered to both groups. In addition, several suggestions for actions that
students could take to help solve the crisis were included at the end of the questionnaire. Predictably, the students living in temporary quarters were more likely
to take the suggested actions: sign a petition, write a letter to the housing office,
join a committee. The attitudes they held about the situation, too, were stronger
than those of the control group. Similarly, Fazio and Zanna (1978) found that the
attitudes of students who had participated in psychology experiments were more
accurate predictors of whether they would do so again (regardless of whether
their attitude was favorable or unfavorable) than the attitudes of students who
had not participated in psychology experiments.

Clearly, attitudes formed when people are personally involved in an issue or
engaged in a particular activity will be more consistent with their behavior than
when they are not personally involved (Ray et al., 1973; Rothschild, 1978). Per-

sonal involvement increases the importance of the attitudes formed in relation to the activity in question; it makes people more aware of the implications and consequences of the behavior stemming from these attitudes (Snyder & Swann, 1976). It has also been shown that people are more likely to act in accordance with previously expressed attitudes if they are reminded of those attitudes ("Yes, but you said . . .") (Sherman et al., 1978). We will look again at the effect of experience on attitudes later in this chapter when we examine the cyclical relationship between attitudes and behavior.

Individual Differences and Personality Factors

Some people are naturally more disposed than others to maintain a close correspondence between their expressed attitudes and their behavior. Norman (1975) found that subjects with high "affective–cognitive consistency"—agreement between their feelings and their expressed attitudes—were more likely to act in accord with their attitudes than subjects whose feelings and beliefs were in conflict.

Another personality factor that may affect attitude–behavior consistency is flexibility. People who try to fit into or adapt to social situations are less likely to behave consistently with their attitudes than people who are socially inflexible. This characteristic is related to the trait of self-monitoring that we discussed in chapter 4. You may recall from that discussion that people who are defined as high self-monitors tend to fit their responses to suit specific occasions. Consequently, they are less likely to act in a way that is consistent with their internal attitudes. (Snyder & Tanke, 1976).

Zanna, Olson, and Fazio (1980) studied religious attitudes and behavior in an attempt to relate attitude–behavior consistency to both self-monitoring and behavioral variability. Behavioral variability is the degree to which past behavior was either flexible (high variability) or inflexible (low variability) in regard to an attitude object. They found that self-monitoring and past-behavior variability were independent of one another. Thus, low self-monitors were not necessarily less variable in their behavior than high self-monitors. Only those subjects who were low in both self-monitoring and past-behavior variability maintained attitude–behavior consistency. In other words, people who do not monitor and shape their behavior to fit different situations *and* who also behave consistently over time and in different situations are most likely to be behaving in a way that is consistent with their attitudes. This study implies, then, that attitude–behavior consistency depends on both of these personality variables (i.e., self-monitoring and past behavior variability).

Social Norms

The relationship between attitudes and behaviors also depends upon the ways we are expected to behave in given situations. For example, as Kiesler (1971) points out, since one is not supposed to express negative feelings about others directly, it is difficult to get subjects to admit that they have negative attitudes toward other subjects in experiments.

Both our attitudes and our behaviors are influenced by those people and groups that play significant roles in our lives. This does not, however, mean that our attitudes and behaviors will remain consistent with each other or with the attitudes and beliefs of those who are important to us. Suppose, for example, that a person is brought up to believe that smoking marijuana is bad. Now, let us suppose that in college this individual wants to impress a group of friends who smoke marijuana. Thus she is in the position where the social norms of two important reference groups are in contradiction. Depending on a variety of personal and situational factors, this student may decide to start smoking marijuana, not to smoke it, to convince her friends to give it up, to find other friends, and so on. In the process, her attitudes may change or remain as they were, and she may behave in ways that are either consistent or inconsistent with either her old or her new attitudes. In any event, she will be influenced by social norms, but the influence that they exert and the ways she deals with them will depend on numerous factors. Some of these are discussed below.

Competing Attitudes

A tree often transplanted will never be loaded with fruit.
Italian proverb

It is rare for our behavior to be influenced by only a single attitude. Most situations evoke a variety of attitudes in us, and often these attitudes conflict. In such cases, in order for us to act, some attitudes must override others. When this happens, the resulting behavior appears to be inconsistent with the less influential attitudes (Kiesler, 1971). However, if the situation were only slightly different, these less influential attitudes may have taken precedence, and as a result our behavior would have been consistent with them (Cook & Selltiz, 1964).

Suppose, for example, as you leave work every evening, you encounter the same man on the same street corner begging for money. On the spur of the moment, you may either dig into your pocket for coins or pass by; and since you en-

Which social norm—to smoke or not to smoke—will prevail with these 12-year-old boys?

Drawing by Leo Cullum; © 1981 The New Yorker Magazine, Inc.

"Let's take the next one, Stoddard. These people aren't going anywhere."

counter him every evening, you probably behave sometimes one way and sometimes another. In any event, it is likely that your behavior is influenced by a variety of attitudes, some in conflict with others. How you feel about being charitable may or may not be in conflict with how you feel about beggars. You may feel that people should be compassionate to others who are less fortunate, but you may also feel that governments should care for the poor. How you act, finally, will depend on which of these attitudes takes precedence at the time.

Situational Context

Attitudes are translated into behavior in the context of particular situations. Thus, the nature of the situation will influence the particular attitudes that will be important and lead to a particular behavior. People have attitudes toward situations as well as toward objects in a situation (Rokeach & Kliejunas, 1972). Moreover, just as attitudes toward objects are influenced by situations, so attitudes toward situations are influenced by objects. Both kinds of attitudes must be assessed to predict behavior.

Rokeach and Kliejunas (1972) hypothesized that to the extent that attitudes toward a particular object and attitudes toward a particular situation are independent, each will have some bearing on behavior. Predictions of behavior, however, will be more accurate if both sets of attitudes are considered in terms of their relative importance.

To test this hypothesis, the investigators examined the frequency of class-cutting in specified psychology courses at Michigan State University. It was assumed that class-cutting was primarily a function of each student's attitude toward the specific professor—the attitude object—and the general activity of attending class—the attitude situation. When the attitude object and the attitude situation were considered separately they were found to be moderate predictors of behavior, but higher correlations were obtained when both of these factors were considered together; and when each was weighted in terms of its relative importance, the correlations were higher still.

Attitude–Behavior Models

In previous sections, we have discussed a number of factors that influence the attitude–behavior relationship and that must be considered when predictions are made. Since there are so many factors, and since they interact in many ways, a number of theorists have attempted to integrate them into general attitude–behavior models. We shall now consider the most important of these, the behavioral intentions model developed by Ajzen and Fishbein.

Ajzen and Fishbein: The Behavioral Intentions Model

The behavioral intentions model developed by Ajzen and Fishbein (1980) is based upon the authors' **theory of reasoned action**. This theory, although simple in its basic outlines, is designed to integrate and explain many of the problematic aspects of attitude–behavior relationships that other investigators have noted.

Briefly stated, Ajzen and Fishbein's theory of reasoned action argues that people consider the implications of their actions and that most actions are consciously controlled. Therefore, the most immediate determinant of whether a person will perform a specific action is the *intention* of that person to perform that action. The authors propose that if intentions are substituted for attitudes as the key behavior causing variable, behavior is not difficult to predict in most situations:

> For example, to predict whether an individual will buy a video game, the simplest and probably most efficient approach is to ask him whether he intends to do so. This does not mean that there will always be a perfect correspondence between intention and behavior. However, barring unforeseen events, a person will usually act in accordance with his or her intention. (p. 5)

As the authors go on to explain, however, a person's intentions are a function of two variables: the person's *attitude toward the behavior* in question and the person's *subjective norms*—his or her perception of social pressures to perform or not to perform the behavior. If both of these variables are positive, the person's intentions in regard to the behavior will also probably be positive. If one is positive and the other is negative, then the person's intentions will depend

No sensible person leaves a
stream to drink from a pool.
Ashanti proverb

on the priority or weight of each of the two variables for that person in that situation.

Two people may have identical attitudes and subjective norms in regard to a particular behavior, and yet their actual intentions may be different. For example, suppose that two students, Stan and Suzanne, both would like to own motorcycles and both encounter parental opposition. As it turns out, Stan may not respond to parental pressures and may develop the intention of purchasing a motorcycle, whereas Suzanne may respond more positively to her parents' wishes, and never develop this intention, although she may desire a motorcycle as much as Stan does. Of course, whether or not Stan actually follows through on his intention by purchasing a motorcycle is another matter. The main point, however, is that even though the attitudes and subjective norms of two people in regard to a particular action may be identical, their intentions may differ because of a quantitative difference in the importance they give to different attitudes and norms.

Ajzen and Fishbein suggest that both attitudes and subjective norms are a function of beliefs about particular behaviors. Behavioral beliefs are concerned with the outcomes of behavior, whereas normative beliefs are concerned with the individual's perception of how others believe he or she should act. Thus, as Figure 9-1 shows, behavioral beliefs lead to attitudes, while normative beliefs lead

FIGURE 9-1.   The Ajzen-Fishbein Behavioral Intentions Model of Factors Determining a Person's Behavior
Note: Arrows indicate the direction of influence.
Source: *From* Understanding Attitudes and Predicting Social Behavior *by I. Ajzen & M. Fishbein,* ©
1980, p. 8. Reprinted by permission of Prentice-Hall, Inc., Englewood Cliffs, N.J.

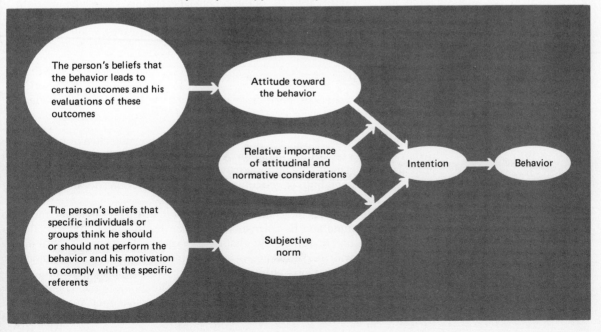

Application: Will Sally Take Birth Control Pills?

As an illustration of the Ajzen and Fishbein attitude–behavior model, we might draw on one field study of family planning behavior. Bear in mind that this example is intended only to illustrate the behavioral intentions model; it is not meant to recommend any particular family planning method for you or any other individual.

Sally M is a senior at a large midwestern state university. She and her boyfriend Ed, who plan to marry as soon as she finishes school, have become sexually intimate. Both Sally and Ed, however, are concerned that she may become pregnant if precautions are not taken. They have talked about various birth control methods and have concluded that the best method for them would be for Sally to take "the pill."

How can we know whether Sally will actually do so? In order to predict with certainty whether she actually will use the pill, we must consider some of her beliefs about the outcomes of taking the pill and her evaluations of the relative merits of those outcomes. We must also consider Sally's evaluation of what her friends and family might say about her taking the pill, and how much she values their opinions.

According to Ajzen and Fishbein, beliefs about outcomes associated with using birth control pills and evaluations of those outcomes as good or bad constitute Sally's attitudes toward the act of taking birth control pills. Her beliefs about what others think and whether or not their opinions are important to her comprise the subjective norm for using birth control pills. Both of these factors are combined to form an "intention" by Sally to use birth control pills. This intention, in turn, is then generally translated into behavior.

The diagram at right shows how the Ajzen and Fishbein model can be used to understand the ways in which Sally's attitudes might translate into behavior.

In their field study of birth control attitudes among unmarried college women in their freshman year, Jaccard and Davidson set out to test Ajzen and Fishbein's behavioral intentions model. As a first step, small samples of college women were personally interviewed in order to identify the important attitudes and beliefs for the behavior under study. The researchers then constructed questionnaires containing measures of these beliefs; evaluations of outcomes, normative beliefs, and motivations to comply with norms; intentions to use birth control pills; attitudes toward personal use of birth control pills;

to subjective norms. At this point, the attitude and the subjective norm come together to form a behavioral intention. As indicated in Figure 9-1 and by our Stan and Suzanne example, the attitude may be more or less important than the personal norm, depending on circumstances. Once the behavioral intention is formed, it leads, in turn, to the actual behavior.

The value of this model is that it accounts for the variables that can intervene between an attitude and its corresponding behavior to change the direction of the person's actual behavior. Note that the key issue is the person's attitude to a particular behavior (e.g., buying a video game), as influenced by subjective norms, and *not* the person's attitude to the object (video games) in general.

To explain why this is so, let us consider the situation of a male business executive who has never hired a female employee for any management position. Indeed, he has often remarked that women should stay home where they belong

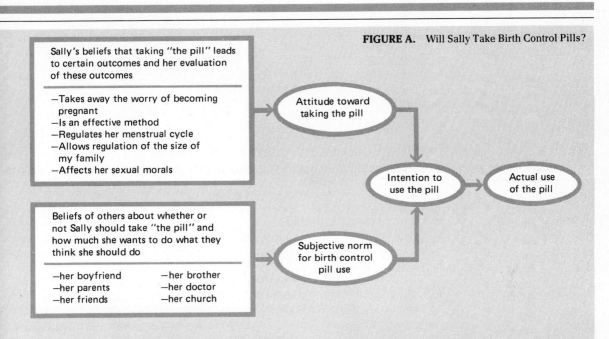

FIGURE A. Will Sally Take Birth Control Pills?

Sally's beliefs that taking "the pill" leads to certain outcomes and her evaluation of these outcomes

—Takes away the worry of becoming pregnant
—Is an effective method
—Regulates her menstrual cycle
—Allows regulation of the size of my family
—Affects her sexual morals

Beliefs of others about whether or not Sally should take "the pill" and how much she wants to do what they think she should do

—her boyfriend   —her brother
—her parents   —her doctor
—her friends   —her church

Attitude toward taking the pill

Intention to use the pill

Actual use of the pill

Subjective norm for birth control pill use

and subjective norms concerning use of the pill. These questionnaires were then administered to a larger sample of college women.

Jaccard and Davidson found a high correlation between positive beliefs about using the birth control pill and favorable attitudes toward its use. Similarly, there was a strong relationship between normative beliefs and subjective norms concerning the use of birth control pills. And both the specific attitude and the subjective norm showed an extremely high correlation with intent to use birth control.

A determined heart will not be counseled.
Spanish proverb

and not take men's jobs away from them. On the basis of his attitudes, we might predict that he will not hire a woman to be his next marketing manager. However, according to the model of behavioral intentions, his general attitudes would be irrelevant. The crucial issue would be his attitude toward the behavior—how he evaluates the consequences of hiring (or failing to hire) a woman (the most qualified candidate he has seen so far), and how he perceives the normative beliefs stemming from his social environment (he has been seeing more women at trade association conventions). In this particular case, the executive, however prejudiced, might develop positive attitudes to hiring women because of his belief that the consequences of his action would be to his advantage. He might then develop the intention to hire the female marketing manager whom he has interviewed, and actually do so.

Ajzen and Fishbein also distinguish between behavior and the outcome of behavior. Behavior, as a function of intentions, is under the control of the individual. But the outcome of the behavior is subject to factors over which the individual may have no power. One may intend to purchase a house, and one may do everything in one's power to purchase it, but at the last minute the owner may decide not to sell it, or the bank may refuse to grant a mortgage. As long as the outcome of a behavior follows as a matter of course from the behavior itself, the outcome can be predicted within the model; but if the outcome is subject to outside influences (such as the actions of the house seller), it cannot be inferred from the model.

The Reciprocal Relationship Between Attitudes and Behavior

The study of birth control intentions described in the box on pages 354–355 did not assess the later target behavior—the actual use of birth control measures. We will conclude this chapter by examining a recent field study, also concerned with a socially significant activity, in which attitudes, norms, intentions, and behavior were all measured.

In an article published in 1974 entitled "Attitudes are Alive and Well and Gainfully Employed in the Sphere of Action," Kelman emphasized a point made in the last chapter: Attitudes and behavior operate in a reciprocal relationship with one another. As we saw in chapter 8, behavior—even behavior such as forced compliance brought about in relatively artificial laboratory situations—can significantly influence attitudes. And, as Regan and Fazio's (1977) housing shortage study demonstrated, personal experiences can also strengthen the attitude–behavior relationship. In fact, it has been argued that changes in public policy that lead to changes in people's behavior also have the effect of changing people's attitudes. Examples are the legal decisions and civil rights laws of the 1960s that mandated the desegregation of schools and public facilities. These not only produced profound changes in interracial behavior, but were also followed by significant changes in white attitudes toward minorities.

It is difficult to separate the effects of changed behavior on attitudes from the effects on attitudes produced by the simple passage of such legislation (Congress and the Federal courts essentially told the American public that discriminatory behavior and attitudes were no longer as acceptable as in the past). Nevertheless, social psychological research suggests that the legally mandated changes in behavior should lead to changed attitudes.

The reason whites came to change their attitudes after mandated desegregation may be found in Bem's self-perception theory of attitude learning (chapter 8). As you recall, this theory asserts that we often use our behaviors as cues for perceiving our own attitudes, much as an outsider would. It is possible that when most white school children had less personal experience with minority children, they simply embraced the typical negative stereotypes about minorities. But once white school children came to know minority classmates and had positive experiences with them, the white children could observe themselves behaving in a friendly way. They could then begin to infer positive attitudes toward minority classmates on the basis of their actual behavior.

Change yourself, and fortune will change with you.
Portuguese proverb

Changes in behavior can lead to changes in attitude, which can lead to further changes in behavior. Changes in American race relations mirror this pattern: Civil rights laws increased interracial contacts; many people's attitudes toward members of other racial groups became more favorable; and association between members of different racial groups became more frequent as well as more social.

Influence of Previous Behavior

Any complete model or theory of the relationship between attitudes and behavior would have to take account of previous behavior in attempting to predict future behavior. Bagozzi (1981) examined the influence of both attitudes and prior behavior on actual blood donations during a campus blood drive. Bagozzi's study used a number of elements from the Ajzen and Fishbein behavioral intentions model and from Schwartz's normative model of altruism which we discuss in chapter 12. Thus, it serves as a good illustration of how that model can be applied to behavior in the real world.

One week before the first of two annual blood drives, a total of 95 students, faculty, and staff members answered questions about their attitudes regarding the act of blood donation, about their personal normative beliefs about donating, about their social normative beliefs; and about their beliefs concerning the consequences of giving blood. They were also asked whether these consequences would affect their personal decision to donate blood, what their behavioral intentions were in regard to the campus blood drive, and about their past blood donation behavior (see Table 9–5). Actual behavior was measured twice, following the blood donation drive in November, and again 4 months later after the March blood drive.

Surprisingly, Bagozzi found only a weak relationship between the measures of norms and behavioral intentions and actual behaviors: All the correlations were .03 or less. Why norms regarding so pro-social an act as donating blood

TABLE 9–5.

Sample Questions from Bagozzi's Blood Donation Study

Behavioral intentions:

Please check the box which best reflects your intentions with regard to future campus blood drives this year.

1. ☐	2. ☐	3. ☐	4. ☐	5. ☐	6. ☐	7. ☐
definitely plan to donate	plan to donate	lean toward planning to donate	not sure	lean toward planning not to donate	plan not to donate	definitely plan not to donate

Past behavior:

How many times have you donated blood in the past 5 years? _____

Personal normative beliefs:

Now we would like to get an indication of your own felt moral obligation to donate blood. Do you think that donating blood is something you *personally* ought to do or something you should not do?

1. ☐	2. ☐	3. ☐	4. ☐	5. ☐	6. ☐	7. ☐
Obligated not to donate			No obligation either way			Obligated to donate

Social normative beliefs:

We would also like to know how the people whose opinions you value most would react if you discussed with them whether you should be a blood donor. *Regardless of your personal views*, would these people think that this is something you ought to do or something you should not do?

1. ☐	2. ☐	3. ☐	4. ☐	5. ☐	6. ☐	7. ☐
Ought to donate			Neutral			Ought not to donate

Beliefs (expectancies):

1. ☐	2. ☐	3. ☐	4. ☐	5. ☐	6. ☐	7. ☐	8. ☐	9. ☐	10. ☐	11. ☐
No chance					50–50					Certain

_____ I would get a sore arm.
_____ It would hurt.
_____ I would faint.
_____ I would be dizzy and nauseated.
_____ My resistance to colds or infection would be lowered.
_____ I would be weak and have to curtail strenuous activity for a few days.
_____ I would lose time from work or study.

Source: Adapted from "Attitudes, Intentions, and Behavior: A Test of Some Key Hypotheses," by R. P. Bagozzi, *Journal of Personality and Social Psychology*, 1981, *41*, 614, 618. Copyright 1981 by the American Psychological Association, Inc. Reprinted with permission of the author.

would be so slightly related to intended and actual behavior is unclear; it appears that, although most people feel some obligation to donate, their intentions and actual behaviors are determined more by the consequences of donating (after all, it is neither convenient nor fun).

Since in this case norms were not related to intentions or behavior, Bagozzi was able to examine two simpler models, shown in Figures 9–2 and 9–3. The two models differ in several respects. Figure 9–2 (Model 1) shows the direct influence of attitudes on behavioral intentions and actual behavior after 1 week and after 4 months. The strength of these direct influences is reflected in the values alongside the causal "paths" or arrows in the figure. These values can be thought of as correlations that measure the causal impact of one variable on the variable at the end of the path or arrow.

You can see in Figure 9–2 (Model 1) that attitudes had their primary effect on behavioral intentions (.45) but had almost no effect on behavior at either 1 week (−.14) or 4 months (.02). Behavioral intentions, on the other hand, were clearly related to behavior at 1 week (.51) but not at 4 months (.01). Bagozzi found, in fact, that the best predictor of behavior after 4 months was actual behavior at 1 week. (.54).

Figure 9–3 (Model 2) incorporates the effects of previous blood donating behavior. This model uses some of the results from the test of Model 1 to simplify the analysis (in particular, all the weak values of Model 1, such as the link between attitudes and actual behaviors, are removed). The key new piece of information shown in Model 2 is the correlation between past behavior and attitude (.44). However, you will note that the path between these variables does not have a "causal" arrowhead because we cannot really be sure whether the attitude influenced past behavior or vice versa.

How does the inclusion of past behavior in the model affect our interpretation of causal relationships? First, as Bagozzi points out, the direct link of attitude to behavioral intention is weakened, since past behavior proved a somewhat better predictor of intention. Triandis (1977) predicted that prior behavior would have such an effect. He reasoned that as a behavior becomes more habitual to us, we rely less on evaluating its positive and negative consequences (recall Langer's notion of mindless behavior from chapter 5). This may explain why predictions of behaviors such as voting can be so accurate. Voting does get to be

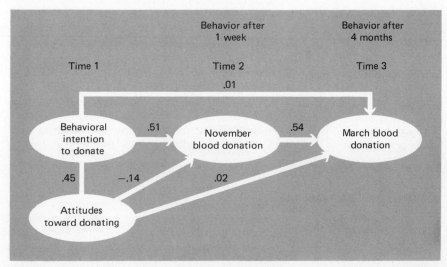

FIGURE 9–2. Bagozzi's Findings, Model 1: Attitudes, Intentions, and Subsequent Behavior.

Source: *Adapted from "Attitudes, Intentions, and Behavior: A Test of Some Key Hypotheses," by R. P. Bagozzi,* Journal of Personality and Social Psychology, *1981, 41, 609. Copyright 1981 by the American Psychological Association, Inc. Reprinted with permission of the author.*

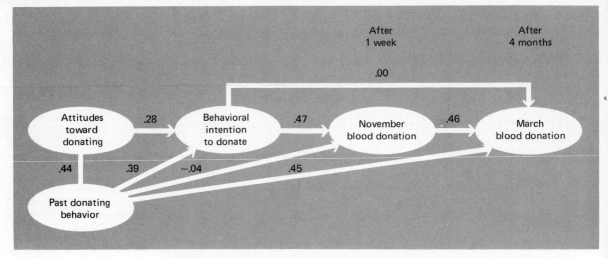

FIGURE 9–3. Bagozzi's Findings, Model 2: Attitudes, Intentions, Past Behavior, and Subsequent Behavior.

Source: *Adapted from "Attitudes, Intentions, and Behavior: A Test of Some Key Hypotheses," by R. P. Bagozzi,* Journal of Personality and Social Psychology, *1981, 41, 612. Copyright 1981 by the American Psychological Association, Inc. Reprinted with permission of the author.*

habitual for many people, and in fact a significant portion of the electorate consistently "votes the party line." Many such voters may be only dimly aware of campaign issues in a particular election, and simply follow old habits. This behavior may be mindless, but it is not irrational: The voters probably have a good notion of major party differences even though they don't rethink the party positions in every election.

A second major conclusion from Bagozzi's study confirms Ajzen and Fishbein's view that intentions are related to behavior only in the short run. As we saw in Model 1, intentions did not predict behavior 4 months later. However, both past behavior and quite recent behavior (after 1 week) appear to be reliable predictors of future behavior.

This section began by raising questions about the reciprocal relationship between attitudes and behavior. Bagozzi's results are consistent with the idea that attitudes are influenced by past behavior (the .44 correlation in Model 2), and provide a real-life confirmation of the influence of behavior on attitudes and later behavior.

Other experiments have also been conducted that illustrate the reciprocal relationship between attitudes and direct experience to those behaviors to which the attitudes refer. The results of these experiments have revealed that attitudes formed on the basis of direct experience are: held with more certainty (Fazio & Zanna, 1978); more persistent over time (Watts, 1967); and are more resistant to subsequent attitudes than those that are not based on experience (Kiesler, 1971). Fazio and Zanna (1981) have suggested that

without the benefit of prior behavior and without the opportunity to infer an attitude from that behavior, an individual is forced to, in some sense,

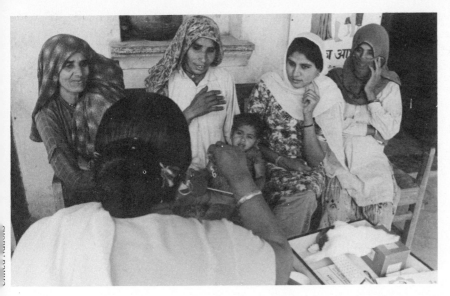

Despite the fact that India has had an official family planning policy since 1952, it continues to have one of the highest birth rates in the world. Here a family planning fieldworker from a government agency displays a contraceptive device to village women and describes its use. What factors might cause these women to form the intention to use this means of birth control? What factors might prevent them from carrying out such an intention or cause them to carry out such an intention? Consider their previous experience with unwanted births, with other birth control methods, with the opinions of relevant others.

"guess" his or her attitude from other less attitudinally reflective information. . . . The more certain an individual is of his or her attitude toward some object, the more likely it is that this attitude will guide later behavior. (p. 180)

The last word on the cyclical relationships between behaviors and attitudes is not in. Although social psychologists have been trying for more than half a century, through periods of optimism and despair, to understand these relationships, this work continues. New insights continue to be found and new methods (such as those employed by Bagozzi) enable social psychologists to ask and answer increasingly complex questions about the reciprocal relationships between attitudes and behavior. Indeed, as this chapter emphasizes, the history of research on attitudes and behavior suggests not only that Kelman was correct in arguing that "attitudes are alive and well," but also that attitudes are likely to remain a lively area of research in the future. There are, in fact, signs of a new resurgence in attitude research. It will be interesting to see whether this research fosters a new wave of optimism or despair among attitude researchers.

Answering Questions about Attitudes and Behaviors

1. The most accurate predictor of behavior will probably be the intention to perform that behavior. This intention, in turn, will probably be related to respondents' general attitudes about nuclear disarmament. Your questionnaire should measure both components.

2. The longer the time delay between the attitude measure or the intention measure and the actual behavior, the less use the attitude will be in predicting behavior. For example, if we measure a person's intention to vote for a candidate the day before the election, we will be more accurate in predicting how one respondent actually votes on election day than if we measure the intention 2 weeks earlier; we will be more accurate still if we catch the voter about to enter the polls. Thus, your questionnaire will be more accurate in predicting volunteer behavior if you administer it shortly before the door-to-door campaign is scheduled to begin.

3. Whether or not friends or other significant people also support the nuclear disarmament campaign will be important determinants of whether respondents form an intention to volunteer.

4. Experience with the behavior in question allows a person to determine more accurately exactly what his or her attitude really is toward a particular act. By measuring the respondents' experience with behavior similar to that which you are trying to predict, you will have a good idea of how people may react to your request.

Summary

The early optimism of attitude research was tempered by the classic LaPiere study, which led to a period of pessimism about the possibility of predicting behavior on the basis of attitudes. LaPiere had found that the negative attitudes of hotel and restaurant owners to receiving Chinese guests contradicted their actual behavior. By the middle of the 1970s, however, researchers were again confident, as a result of methodological improvements, that attitudes could be used to predict behavior.

For accurate predictions of behaviors, attitude measures should be as specific as possible to the behaviors being predicted. The strength, clarity, and reliability of the attitudes must also be defined. Investigators also point to the need for viewing behavior in terms of overall tendencies rather than merely in terms of specific acts. Reference group pressures must also be taken into account.

Biases in attitude measures can result from social pressures and from individual response styles. The **bogus pipeline** and other techniques have been developed to counteract various measurement biases.

General attitudes are reliable predictors of general behavior, but not of a specific act. Conversely, specific attitudes are good predictors of specific behavior. Accurate predictions are also more likely when there is only a short time lapse between attitude measurement and the start of the related behavior.

A variety of conditions may promote or reduce attitude–behavior consistency. Attitudes formed through direct experience tend to be more consistent with behavior than attitudes that are formed indirectly. Low self-monitors (less flexible individuals) show more attitude–behavior consistency than high self-monitors. Social norms may either promote or reduce consistency, depending on individual and situational variables. Consistency also depends on whether competing attitudes are present, the importance of a given attitude to the individual, and a variety of situational factors.

The most important attitude–behavior model is the Behavioral Intentions Model of Ajzen and Fishbein. This model, which is based upon the authors' **theory of reasoned action**, states that the most immediate determinant of a person's behavior is that person's intentions. Intentions, in turn, are the result of a person's attitudes toward the behavior in question, and a person's beliefs about whether or not others think he or she should perform the behavior.

Finally, in order to predict people's future behavior with accuracy, it is necessary to be attentive to *prior behavior*, and to measure attitudes and normative beliefs at appropriate levels of specificity.

Suggested Additional Reading

Fishbein, M., & Ajzen, I. *Understanding attitudes and predicting social behavior.* Englewood Cliffs, N.J.: Prentice-Hall, 1980.

Heberlein, T. A., & Black, J. S. Attitudinal specificity and the prediction of behavior in a field setting. *Journal of Personality and Social Psychology,* 1976, *33*, 474–479.

Zimbardo, P. G., Ebbesen, E. B., & Maslach, C. *Influencing attitudes and changing behavior: An introduction to method, theory, and applications of social control and personal power.* Reading, Mass.: Addison-Wesley, 1977.

10

CONFORMITY, COMPLIANCE, AND PREJUDICE

Questions about Conformity, Compliance, and Prejudice

1. Why do people conform?
2. The events that took place in Nazi Germany were extremely unusual. Do you think anything like that could ever happen in the United States?
3. It has been said that you can't legislate morality. Is this true?
4. Are some people especially susceptible to social influence?
5. Can you see any psychological principles at work in the sales techniques used by people who have waited on you?

Before the beginning of World War II, there were approximately 3.3 million Jews in Poland; by the end of the war, 3 million, or 90 percent, had been killed by the Nazis. In Europe as a whole, almost 6 million Jews fell victim to Hitler's "final solution to the Jewish question," his attempt to annihilate an entire people. Men, women, and children, the old and the young, were ruthlessly and systematically slaughtered. In concentration camps such as Auschwitz, Dachau, Bergen-Belsen, and Treblinka, they were gassed, shot, starved, or killed in the "medical experiments" conducted by Nazi "doctors." Those strong enough to work were used as slaves to fuel the Nazi war machine; as soon as they could no longer work, they were considered "useless eaters" and destroyed.

This historical event, which took place only 40 years ago, resists comprehension. As Lucy S. Dawidowicz asks in *The War Against the Jews* (1975): "How was it possible for a modern state to carry out the systematic murder of a whole people for no other reason than that they were Jews? How was it possible for the world to stand by without halting this destruction?" (p. xiii).

The Holocaust, as it has come to be known, poses profound questions about Western civilization and about the nature of the human condition generally. What are the factors that feed mass conformity and irrational prejudices such as that of anti-Semitism? How could a modern nation of 50 million people, the nation of Bach and Goethe, have allowed a criminal madman such as Hitler to come to power, and how could its people have complied with his genocidal policies? And finally, we must ask whether what happened in Germany could happen again, elsewhere—whether, indeed, it could happen here, though perhaps in a different form.

Most of us would like to believe that if we had been in the situation of the Germans at the time, we would not have gone along with the policies of the

Nazis. It must be remembered, however, that once Hitler had consolidated his power, any resistance would have led to death—and did so in the case of those few who did try to resist. But there was a time when resistance and lack of compliance might have been both possible and effective. Why did it not occur? The question haunts many Germans, and others, even now.

The issues posed by dramatic events such as the Holocaust, the mass killing and suicides at Jonestown (chapter 1), and the My Lai massacre of Vietnamese civilians by American soldiers, are central not only to theologians, philosophers, historians, and political scientists but to social psychologists as well. Indeed, it was partly because of the Holocaust that social psychologists began to focus their attention on such social processes as conformity, compliance, obedience, and prejudice—the subjects of this chapter.

Conformity

All societies, from that of the simplest hunter-gatherers to that of the most complex space explorers, are based on customs and patterns of interaction that allow life to proceed in an orderly manner. Wearing proper clothing, driving on the right side of the street, and waiting patiently in line for service are examples of the customs we habitually conform to without being aware of it. Most of us would agree that this kind of conformity is necessary because it gives order and predictability to our lives.

In countries such as the United States, however, where a high premium is placed on individuality, conformity is looked on with disfavor, particularly when it results from social pressure. Kiesler and Kiesler (1969) define **conformity** as "a change in behavior or belief toward a group as a result of real or imagined group pressure" (p. 2). This view of conformity presupposes conflict between the individual and the group, conflict that is resolved when the individual "goes along with" the group. Conformity does not, however, always involve prior conflict between an individual and the group. Fashions and fads are examples of how easy it is for many of us to conform to even trivial social pressures.

He who follows the crowd has many companions.
German proverb

A simple experiment performed by Milgram, Bickman, and Berkowitz (1969) illustrates how subtly social influence operates. The experimenters had research confederates stand on a busy New York City sidewalk and stare up at a sixth-story window. When only 1 confederate looked up at the window, 40 percent of the passersby also looked up. When 5 confederates stared at the window, over 75 percent of the passersby also looked up. Although the behavior of the passersby could have been the result of idle curiosity, it is clear the informal group of 5 confederates influenced and enhanced their normal curiosity to a significant degree.

Conformity may or may not involve the private acceptance by an individual of the group's position. If a person merely goes along with the group in public but privately does not accept the group's position, the person is acting out of **compliance**. In this section, we shall discuss various factors that relate to conformity in general, and in the next section we shall focus on compliance.

Deutsch and Gerard (1955) make a distinction between two kinds of social influence: When **informational social influence** predominates, a person accepts the group's opinions as evidence about reality. Informational social influence usually results in private acceptance. Thus, when the individual conforms, there is no discrepancy between his or her beliefs and behaviors and those of the group. But when others exert **normative social influence**, the individual is pressured to advocate positions he or she does not believe. Whether or not the individual gives in to this pressure by conforming to the group's norms, there is a felt discrepancy between his or her subjective beliefs and those of the group. We will first discuss the formation of norms and research on informational social influence, and then we will consider research on normative social influence.

Social Norms

All groups have certain rules that their members are expected to obey. These rules, which are referred to as **norms** because they define standards of behavior, may be explicit (e.g., stop at a red traffic light) or implicit (e.g., give an elderly person a seat on the bus), and they may or may not correspond to legal sanctions. Norms include all of the conventions, customs, and laws that apply to a particular group's behavior. Some norms apply to the society as a whole while others apply only to a particular group within the society. Generally, those members of a group who adhere to its norms will be rewarded for doing so, while those who violate them will be punished. New group members are expected to learn and adhere to the established norms. In this way, the group's norms are maintained and transmitted from generation to generation.

For society, then, the function of norms is to provide stability and continuity. For the individual, norms provide a *frame of reference* for interpreting and acting on information. As a result, people perceive their world in terms of their relationship to various norms.

When in Rome, do as the Romans do.

A classic study by Muzafer Sherif (1936) showed how norms develop in small groups. Sherif's study made use of an optical illusion known as the autokinetic effect: In a totally dark room, a single small light will appear to move, sometimes erratically, in various directions. This illusion occurs in part because in complete darkness there are no points of reference by which to determine the actual position of the light. Sherif placed subjects in a dark room, and asked them to judge how far a light moved (although it in fact did not move). Some subjects were in the room by themselves, and some were in groups. Individual estimates varied widely—some subjects thought the light moved as little as 1 or 2 inches, and one subject actually gave an estimate of 80 feet! What Sherif was interested in was the degree the perceptions of subjects in group situations were guided by those of other group members.

The results showed that the group had a significant effect. When individual subjects were presented with the autokinetic effect for a series of trials, their estimates of the distance the light moved raised considerably. The researchers concluded that they had formed subjective or personal estimates for their perceptions of the distance the light had moved. However, in the group situations, these subjective norms gradually converged through a process of consensus, until a group norm was established. When subjects initially viewed the autokinetic effect in isolation, and then viewed it later as part of a group, it took longer for their subjective norms to converge into a group norm than when subjects first viewed the effect in a group situation (see Figure 10–1). In both conditions, however, the group norm definitely influenced subjects' later perceptions—an indication that the conformity that had been established did involve private acceptance. At the end of the study, after the group norms had been established, each subject alone was presented with the autokinetic effect. Interestingly, subjects' estimates continued to reflect the group norm, and did not return to the perceptions they had had intitially, before the group norm was established. Moreover, most of the subjects seemed unaware of the influence of the other subjects on their perceptions.

Of course, in Sherif's studies the subjects were presented with an ambiguous situation, in which it is natural to rely on others as sources of information. That study, then, did not clarify the extent to which people depend on others when generally making judgments. Partly to answer this question, Jacobs and Campbell (1961) conducted an interesting variation of the Sherif study. Instead of groups composed entirely of naive subjects, these researchers used 4-person groups in which 3 of the "subjects" were actually experimental confederates. The 3 confederates stated that they saw the light move 15 to 16 inches. This was in sharp contrast to the perceptions of the naive subjects, who, before being influenced by the confederates, typically estimated the movement of the light to be about 4 inches. Nevertheless, after a series of trials in the group situation, the naive subjects also began to report a movement of 15 or 16 inches. In other words, under group influence, their perceptions became consistent with the group norm, even when that norm was extreme.

This study also demonstrated that group norms may continue to be transmitted even when the conditions under which they were originally established

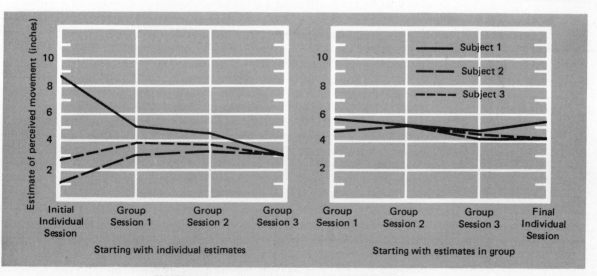

FIGURE 10–1. A Group's View of an Optical Illusion

Median estimates of individuals in three-member groups.

Source: *From* The Psychology of Social Norms *by M. Sherif, New York: Harper & Row, 1936.*

are no longer present. After the group norm of 15 to 16 inches had been estab-lished, the membership of the groups was then completely changed over a pe-riod of "generations"—as old members were gradually replaced by naive new members—and the group norms were recorded for each generation. Although the tendency of each successive generation was to return nearer to the individual norm of 3.8 inches, 4 or 5 generations were required to do so completely. In other words, the groups transmitted a norm—one that had no basis in fact—through as many as five successive changes of membership.

Social Pressure

The studies we have just described are examples of informational social in-fluence, for in them there was little or no discrepancy between the private beliefs of the subjects and the beliefs they expressed in public. We now turn to some classic investigations of normative social influence. Here the stimulus contexts are less ambiguous than those in the earlier studies; and thus when conformity occurs, it does not usually result in private acceptance.

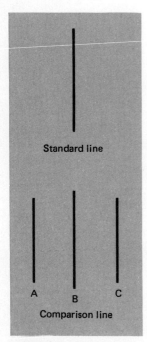

Standard line

A   B   C

Comparison line

FIGURE 10-2.
A Group Compares Lines:
Asch's Study
Source: *After "Opinions and Social Pressure" by S. Asch,* Scientific American, *1955,* 193, *31-35.*

The Asch Experiment   The classic experiment on normative social influence was conducted by Asch (1951), who suspected that when stimuli were not am-biguous there would be less conformity. In this experiment, a group consisting of 6 confederates and only 1 naive subject was asked to make a series of 18 judg-ments about which of 3 comparison lines corresponded in length to a standard line (see Figure 10-2). The correct answer was readily apparent, and thus the sit-uation was not at all ambiguous. The experimental situation had been arranged so that the naive subject was the 6th of the 7 subjects to make his or her judg-ment. On the first two "trials" everything proceeded smoothly, but on the third trial the real subject heard one confederate after another choose what was ob-viously the wrong line. Of course, the confederates had been coached to choose the wrong comparison line—and to do so unanimously—on 12 of the 18 trials. The purpose, of course, was to see whether the subjects would continue to express their own—and correct—perceptions in the face of group pressure or whether they would conform to the opinion of the majority. Only 25 percent of the subjects remained completely independent in their responses, despite group pressure. About 33 percent of the subjects altered their responses to fit the distorted opin-ions of the confederates in 50 percent or more of the trials.

On the basis of interviews conducted with the subjects, the experimenters identified different characteristics in the independent and the yielding subjects. Some independent subjects were confident of their perceptions and had little dif-ficulty in withstanding group opposition; others were less confident, quiet, and withdrawn, but still managed to respond accurately; and a third group mani-fested considerable tension and doubt, but gave accurate judgments out of a de-sire to remain honest. Of the yielding subjects, very few had experienced per-ceptual distortion and actually believed the estimates of the majority to be correct; other subjects experienced distortions of judgment, concluding that their own perceptions were inaccurate; and finally, still others agreed with the

Subjects in Asch's conformity experiment wait to hear the response of the sixth person, seated second from the right. The five previous "subjects" were confederates of the experimenter, and all gave an incorrect response. Will the naive subject conform by also giving an incorrect response, or will he "vote his conscience"? Asch found that about 33 percent of the naive subjects in this situation gave incorrect responses in 50 percent or more of the experimental trials, while only 25 percent consistently stood by their independent—and correct—views.

group not because they believed their perceptions were wrong, but out of a desire not to appear different from the others—even though the other group members were strangers who might never be encountered again. Asch's research triggered a large number of conformity studies. For instance, Deutsch and Gerard (1955) conducted a modification of the Asch study in which one group of subjects was allowed to respond anonymously. In this situation, conformity was sharply reduced. The logical inference is that an important factor in conformity is whether or not a response is made in *public*.

Hear one person before you answer; hear several before you decide.
Danish proverb

The Crutchfield Experiment   Crutchfield (1955), in a refinement of the Asch experiment, eliminated the costly need for confederates and thus provided for greater objectivity. The stimulus situation in the Crutchfield experiment also used comparison lines. However, the groups consisted of 5 subjects each seated in front of an electric console with a screen for receiving information about other "subjects'" choices and switches for transmitting their own choices. Subjects, who could not see one another's consoles, were told that their responses would be shown on the screens of the other subjects. When it was the turn of a particular subject to respond, he or she would press the appropriate switch and signal lights would supposedly flash on the other subjects' screens. However, what each subject saw did not reflect the responses of fellow subjects as they had been led to believe, but was actually transmitted by the experimenter.

What happened? Crutchfield's findings were similar to those of Asch, but the level of conformity was slightly lower. This may be because the situation of the Crutchfield experiment was less public and therefore less intimidating than the situation of the Asch experiment. On the other hand, the elimination of confederates and the use of machines might have been expected to eliminate the subjects' suspicions about the nature of the experiment, and therefore increase conformity. But this did not actually happen. Crutchfield's method was rapidly adopted by other researchers interested in factors that govern conformity.

Factors Influencing Conformity

Research has revealed a wide range of situational factors that influence the degree of conformist behavior; and since two people may respond differently to the same basic situation, personality variables have also been considered.

Situational Factors   Although the *size* of the group is an important variable in conformity, the assumption that conformity increases with the size of the majority group has not been borne out by research (Allen, 1965). Asch (1956) himself had varied the size of his groups, using 1, 2, 3, 4, 8, or 15 confederates. He found that the amount of conformity leveled off once there were 4 confederates. Rosenberg (1961) obtained similar results using Crutchfield's technique. Further support was provided by Gerard, Whilhelmy, and Connolley (1968), who presented subjects with the Asch situation, but varied the number of confederates from 0 (subject answers alone) to 7 (as in the original Asch experiment). (The results are shown in Figure 10–3.) There was a sharp increase in conformity up to a majority size of 3 or 4, but further increases in majority size did not produce corresponding increases in conformity.

Wilder (1976) attempted to explain this phenomenon by suggesting that "social influence varies with the number of social entities present rather than with the number of individuals, *per se*" (p. 254). Wilder's point, which makes use of a principle from Gestalt psychology, is that people tend to classify those who have different points of view into particular groups. If, as in the Asch experiment, the majority constitutes a single viewpoint or entity, a point will be reached at which increasing the size of this majority will not increase conformity. In an experiment devised by Wilder (1976) to test this hypothesis, 2 groups of 2 persons each influenced subjects' opinions (about a consumer lawsuit) more than 1 group of 4 persons. Wilder's results indicate that both the number of people advocating a position (up to perhaps 4 people) and the apparent independence of the advocates will influence conformity.

An individual's *status* in a particular group may influence the degree of his or her conformity to that group's positions. A low-status member is more vulnerable to rejection by the group than a high-status member because the latter has greater power in shaping group norms; therefore the low-status member is likely to experience greater pressure to conform to group norms. Moreover, people typically rise in status within a group by conforming to its norms. This conformity typically meets with favorable impressions from the group, which accumulate over time. Hollander (1958) refers to this process as the build-up of *idiosyncracy credits*—that is, the degree that an individual may depart from the norms of the group without being penalized. Early conformity typically allows for later nonconformity. It should be noted, however, that high-status members do not always have greater latitude than low-status members. Since high-status members are

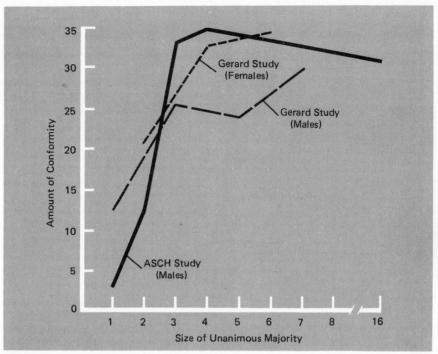

FIGURE 10–3. Three Studies of Conformity

Source: *Adapted from "Effects of Group Pressure Upon the Modification and Distortion of Judgments," by S. E. Asch. In H. Gvetzkow (Ed.),* Groups, Leadership and Men: Research in Human Relations, *Pittsburgh: Carnegie Press, 1951; and "Conformity and Group Size," by H. B. Gerard, R. A. Wilhelmy and R. S. Conolley,* Journal of Personality and Social Psychology, *1968,* 8, *79–82.*

responsible for the maintenance of the group, they must appear to set an example to low-status members (Hollander & Willis, 1967).

Another important influence on conformity is the degree to which the majority group maintains *unanimity.* Asch (1951) found that the presence of only a single confederate who agreed with the subject was enough to reduce conformity by almost 80 percent. There are various reasons why the lack of unanimity might work against conformity. First, the presence of a co-thinker might reinforce the subject's belief in his or her perceptions and thus make it easier to withstand pressure. Moreover, a lack of unanimity might make the majority appear to be weaker.

In an interesting series of studies, Allen and his colleagues (Allen, 1965; Allen & Levine, 1969, 1971; Wilder & Allen, 1973) explored the impact of dissenters or deviants in Asch-type situations. Allen and Levine (1969) used the Crutchfield procedure with 5-person "groups." The subjects, who all thought they were answering last, had to make judgments either about visual stimuli (similar to the Asch experiment) or about difficult general knowledge questions, or they had to give opinions on some mildly controversial topics. The first three "members" of the group always made the same erroneous or unusual judgments (designed to be different from the real subject's judgments). The fourth "subject" to answer either agreed with the majority, gave a judgment that was consistent with that of the real subject, or gave an incorrect or unusual response that was different from that of the majority. Allen and Levine found that when all 4 group "members" unanimously gave unusual responses, conformity with the group was high in all categories of judgments. When the dissenter gave a different but still unusual response, conformity on visual and general knowledge judgments was reduced. When the dissenter gave a response consistent with the other subjects' responses, conformity was reduced on all three categories of judgments.

Of course, the effect of a lack of unanimity depends on how the subject evaluates the person or persons who are dissenting from the majority. For example, Allen and Levine (1971) found that a dissenter who claimed he was almost blind, but still gave correct responses on a visual judgment task, did not reduce conformity nearly as much as a dissenter with apparently normal vision.

Another factor that can influence conformity is a person's goal in a particular situation. Thibaut and Strickland (1956) found that subjects who were encouraged to be concerned about their social relationships were more likely to conform as social pressures on them increased, while subjects concerned about finding the best solution to a problem grew more resistant to social pressure as the pressure increased.

Personality Factors Psychologists disagree about whether it is possible to identify personality types as either "conformist" or "nonconformist" in their basic orientation. Prior to his experiment, Crutchfield's subjects were given a series of personality tests. Crutchfield found that those subjects who remained independent in the experiment were also those who scored higher on the personality inventory in intellectual effectiveness and leadership ability, and who had fewer feelings of inferiority and less authoritarian attitudes than the subjects who conformed readily. One provocative difference was noted: The conformists described their parents in idealized terms while the independents took a more balanced view of their parents. Finally, a follow-up study found that female students tended to be more conformist than male students, and middle-aged women were less conformist than their male counterparts. This last finding may reflect the influence of the workplace, where men have traditionally been dominant and where conformity is often rewarded—despite the verbal emphasis habitually placed on "leadership." In addition, other studies have correlated conformist behavior with racial prejudice (Malof & Lott, 1962) and low self-esteem (Stang, 1972); and it has been suggested that conformists blame themselves for negative outcomes more than nonconformists (Costanza, 1970).

Findings such as these must be interpreted cautiously, however, especially since they are often difficult to replicate. Moreover, since few people conform in all situations, the notion that there is such a thing as a conformist personality is a misleading abstraction. Whether or not an individual will conform depends on a variety of factors, including the type of judgment task, the individuals comprising the majority group, and so on. Some individuals may have a greater tendency to display conformist behavior than other individuals—or at least a greater tendency in regard to particular situations—but, as Allen (1975) concludes, a "consistent personality syndrome characteristic of 'conformers' and 'nonconformers' has not been observed" (p. 3).

Is there a "conformist" personality type? This question has been raised often in recent years with the proliferation of religious cults that demand obedience, such as the Hare Krishna sect whose members are shown here. They have positioned themselves in front of the New York Public Library, and are trying to get donations and make converts. Who will be susceptible to their efforts?

Conformity versus Innovation

If the individual or the minority group always deferred to the beliefs and wishes of the majority, it is doubtful that civilization would have proceeded very far. Majority groups, once established, have a tendency to maintain the status quo. Substantive change requires innovators (who, by definition, are in the minority) who bring pressure to bear upon the majority. Innovators have often faced enormous pressures to conform—to the extent that failure to do so can result in loss of liberty or life. Galileo, for example, who demonstrated the truth of the Copernican theory that the planets revolve around the sun, was forced on pain of death to recant his beliefs. But his recantation could not suppress the growth of science for long.

The leading theorist on minority influence is Moscovici (1980). One of his early studies (Moscovici & Faucheux, 1972) suggested that a minority's *style of behavior* plays a role in determining whether it will be successful in affecting the majority. To be influential, a minority must be consistent, coherent, and forceful. The persistence of the minority raises doubts in the minds of the majority group members, who begin to question the correctness of their group's position as well as its ability to maintain itself as the majority. The minority, in short, provides an alternative view against which the majority must evaluate its own position. Gradually, some members of the majority may come over to the side of the minority; if this process accelerates, the minority may actually be transformed into a new majority.

Nemeth and Wachtler (1974) devised an experiment to explore the role of leadership in determining a minority individual's influence on the majority. Four subjects and one confederate were seated at a rectangular table and asked to discuss a case study that involved the settlement of an insurance claim. The "deviant" confederate consistently argued for a substantially smaller award than the subjects did.

There were four experimental conditions. In the "assigned side" condition, the confederate was assigned one of the side chairs; in the "assigned head" condition, the confederate was assigned the chair at the head of the table; in the "chosen side" condition, the confederate chose a side chair; in the "chosen head" condition, the confederate sat in the chair at the head of the table. The results showed that only in the "chosen head" condition did the confederate measurably influence the subjects; only in this condition did the subjects lower the awards in accordance with the confederate's arguments. Apparently, in the "chosen head" condition, the fact that the confederate assumed a position of lead-

Research: Conformity and Sex Differences

In the past, it was generally believed that women had a greater tendency to display conformist behavior than men. A number of the early studies of social influence, including the Crutchfield (1955) study described earlier, seemed to confirm this. As we saw in chapter 3, more recent studies have demonstrated that these early findings stemmed from biases in the experiments rather than from real differences between males and females (Eagly & Carli, 1981).

Sistrunk and McDavid (1971) showed that conformity is always a function of a particular set of determining variables, and therefore sex differences can never be viewed in isolation. Thus, if in a particular instance women conform more than men (or if the opposite occurs), this finding cannot be generalized to all women (or all men) in all situations.

The researchers presented male and female subjects with a 65-item "Inventory of General Information." In this inventory, 45 of the statements were classified as either "masculine" or "feminine" issues. The other 20 statements were filler items, not relevant to either masculine or feminine concerns. Within the inventory booklet that the subjects filled out, there was a column to the right of the statements labeled "Majority Response." The word "agree" or "disagree" was printed beside each item in this column, and it

was explained to the subjects that these notations corresponded to the majority responses of a group that had previously been tested. In actuality, however, these notations either contradicted the content of the factual statements or were randomly placed next to the opinion statements. By means of this falsehood the experimenters were able to manipulate pressures toward conformity. The subjects were asked to indicate whether they agreed or disagreed with the statements. They were unaware of the real purpose of the experiment.

The researchers found that males yielded to the "majority" to a greater degree than females where "feminine" issues were concerned, but females conformed more where "masculine" issues were concerned. (Interestingly, the males actually conformed more than the females on neutral issues.) This pattern seems to confirm the hypothesis of the experimenters that the relative conformist tendencies of men and women depend on specific situations. Furthermore, the pattern suggests that certain areas of concern do have masculine or feminine overtones in the minds of many people. Thus, men tend to defer to the majority more than women where "feminine" issues are concerned, while the opposite holds true where "masculine" issues are concerned.

Can a minority exert influence over a majority? These friends have joined hundreds of thousands of other people who are attempting to do just that in a demonstration against the proliferation of nuclear weapons. Of course, while they are not conforming to the attitudes and behavior of a national majority, they may be part of a sizable minority that seeks to change prevailing views.

ership of his own accord—as if to fill a power vacuum—was striking. This effect did not occur when the confederate behaved deferentially, by choosing a side chair, or when the experimenter, by assigning seating arrangements, was clearly the "higher authority." The results of this experiment have obvious implications for all who attend meetings!

As the Allen and Levine (1969) study demonstrated, the amount of social support available to a dissenter also affects conformity. Several studies indicate that a dissenter with an ally conforms less (e.g., Allen & Levine, 1971; Morris & Miller, 1975), and Nemeth, Wachtler, and Endicott (1977) demonstrated that the majority was more likely to "conform" to the minority position as the size of the minority increased.

Resistance to Conformity

When an individual or a minority group differs with the norms of the majority, the ensuing struggle can be analyzed from the standpoint of both the group and the individual. The majority exerts increasing pressure on the deviant members in an attempt to get them to conform. The amount of pressure exerted on these members depends on a variety of factors, including the prior cohesiveness of the group, the degree to which it is able or willing to accept disparate views, the status of the minority, and the importance of the issue being debated (Schachter, 1951). At first a good deal of communication may be directed at the deviants. If this does not succeed in reconciling them to the majority position, the next step is rejection and exclusion. These measures serve two interrelated purposes: to punish the deviants and to maintain the cohesiveness of the majority. But as we saw in the Thibaut and Strickland (1956) study discussed earlier, sometimes pressuring deviants can backfire.

From the standpoint of the deviant member, **reactance theory** suggests that when a person's freedom to engage in a particular behavior is threatened, he or she will be motivated to regain that freedom (Brehm, 1966, 1972). In an experiment conducted by Worchel and Brehm (1971), for example, subjects who were pressured by a confederate to choose a particular task reacted against this pressure by choosing a different task. Thus, reactance theory suggests that pressure to conform may cause a person to take an even more deviant position.

It should be noted, however, that if reactance theory held true in all situations, an increased resistance to majority group pressures would be universal—and clearly this is not the case. When individuals react against conformity pressures, they apparently evaluate the likelihood that their actions may be effective as well as any penalties they may suffer as a result. The applicability of reactance theory thus depends on situational as well as personality factors.

Compliance

Earlier in this chapter, we distinguished between conformity and compliance by noting that compliance does not involve private acceptance of the majority group's position. In actuality this distinction is not clear-cut, for it is often difficult to determine on the basis of overtly conforming behavior whether the individuals actually accept the majority group's position or are merely acting as though they do. How many of the people who collaborated with the Nazis actually accepted Nazi ideology and how many merely pretended to do so in order to save their lives? It is impossible to know.

While both conformity and compliance involve some pressure exerted by a majority, compliance involves coercion as well. We will examine some of the forms of pressure that can be brought to bear on individuals to bring them into compliance.

The Foot-in-the-Door Technique

In chapter 8 we briefly encountered the **foot-in-the-door technique** of attitude change. The foot-in-the-door technique is a term that is derived from marketing strategy, but its relevance to the issue of compliance has far broader ramifications. This technique asserts that a customer who complies with a small request (e.g., answering a few survey questions), will eventually comply with larger ones (e.g., purchasing merchandise). In other words, studies show that if the demands brought to bear on the individual increase by small increments, the individual will be more likely to comply with them.

In the most famous such study, Freedman and Fraser (1966) asked suburban homemakers to comply with a small request that had to do with driving safety—either to place a sign in their window or to sign a petition. Two weeks later, a different experimenter returned to ask the subjects to place a rather large, unattractive sign related to driving safety on their lawns. A control group of homemakers was asked only to place the sign on their lawns. Of the women who had complied with the small request, more than 55 percent later complied with the larger one as well. In contrast, fewer than 20 percent of the women in the control group complied with the larger request.

Why does the foot-in-the-door technique work? It is perfectly rational to comply with a request such as to sign a petition relating to driving safety. Most of us are in favor of safe driving (at least in the abstract), and signing a petition is not much of an inconvenience. However, as self-perception theory suggests (see chapter 4), once one has taken even so small a step, one begins to perceive oneself as a person who "does this sort of thing." It is now logical to make a slightly larger commitment to driving safety. At each step, however, the stakes get higher and thus the individual must decide whether to continue to comply or to break the logic of the progression. Doing the latter may be difficult because an entire process involving a chain of mutual expectations has been built up.

Research by Rittle (1980) suggests that after people have agreed to offer assistance, their perception of helping may change so that they see helping as more pleasant and less threatening, and therefore they will be more inclined to offer assistance at a later date.

How far into the door can the foot be pushed? Several researchers have found that this technique may not work if the second request is too large (e.g., a study by Ross & Dempsey, 1979, who tried to increase blood donations) or if the initial request is too small (Zuckerman, Lazzaro, & Waldgeir, 1979).

The Door-in-the-Face Technique

The **door-in-the-face technique** is basically the opposite of the foot-in-the-door technique. Its rationale is that if the initial request is very large, most people will refuse it, but many will comply later with a smaller request. Apparently, subjects view the second, lower request as a concession on the demander's part, and thus feel pressure to reciprocate by giving in (Cialdini et al., 1975).

Cialdini and his colleagues tested the door-in-the-face technique by asking randomly chosen college students to comply with requests to help juvenile delinquents. In the *rejection-moderation condition*, the subjects were first asked to serve as counselors to juvenile delinquents for at least 2 years; those who refused were asked if they would accompany a group of delinquent youths on a trip to the zoo some afternoon or evening. In the *smaller-request-only control condition*, the subjects were only asked to accompany the youths on an outing. Finally, in the *exposure control condition*, both requests were described and the subjects were asked if they would perform either one.

No subjects complied with the extreme request; but the subjects were more likely to accede to the smaller request when it followed the extreme demand, than in either of the other two conditions. Specifically, in the rejection-moderation condition, 50 percent complied with the smaller request; in the exposure control condition, 25 percent complied; and in the smaller-request-only control, 16.7 percent complied. A study by Pendleton and Batson (1979) lends some support to a self-perception explanation for door-in-the-face effects: Their subjects said other people would view them as unconcerned and unfriendly if they did not respond favorably to small requests.

The Low-Ball Technique

With the low-ball technique, the individual agrees to perform a particular activity, and later discovers that the terms of the agreement go beyond the original activity. In other words, the "rules of the game" are changed in midstream, and thus the individual is forced to decide whether to withdraw or to continue with the new rules. When the technique is successful, the individual goes through with the activity. The rationale behind the low-ball technique is that once a commitment has been made, it may be more difficult for a person to withdraw than to proceed, regardless of the additional cost of going ahead. The low-ball technique is thus a form of gangsterism. (The term is derived from a type of poker game.)

At one time low-balling was extremely widespread in the automobile industry (Cialdini et al., 1978), and it continues to be prevalent in many industries despite its illegality. Demonstrating the potential effectiveness of the low-ball technique, several studies have shown that it is much easier to get subjects who have previously committed themselves to favorable requests to subsequently comply with unfavorable ones than to get control subjects who have made no commitment to comply with unfavorble requests (e.g., Burger & Petty, 1981). In a study by Cialdini and others (1978), one group of students was asked by the researchers to participate in a study that would start at 7:00 A.M. Of those asked, about 25 percent agreed and showed up on time. Other students were first asked to participate in a study (and 55 percent agreed to) and were *then* told to come at 7:00 A.M. Despite the obvious inconvenience of the hour, nearly everyone who had initially agreed to participate actually showed up!

Obedience

Every social system requires of its members obedience to some form of authority. Obedience to those in power can, however, serve political ends at the expense of moral or ethical considerations. Without the willingness of large numbers of people to obey the commands of their leaders, atrocities such as those committed by the Nazis would not have occurred. The willingness of some people to follow orders is dramatically illustrated by the case of Adolf Eichmann, a Nazi official who had served under Hitler. In 1961, Eichmann was brought to trial in Jerusalem for war crimes. As part of his defense he asserted that he was merely following orders from superiors who had led him to believe that his actions were lawful and even patriotic (Arendt, 1963). A similar defense was raised by Lieutenant William L. Calley, Jr., who was tried in a court martial for the 1968 massacre by American soldiers of more than 100 Vietnamese women, children, and old men at My Lai (Hersh, 1970). (Eichmann was convicted and hanged. Calley was convicted of murdering "at least" 22 civilians; he was paroled in 1976 after serving 40 months in Federal custody, part of the time under house arrest.) The subject of obedience thus focuses on one of the most profound dilemmas of the individual in society—the point at which the individual's higher moral responsibility comes into conflict with the legal authority of the state.

Milgram's Experiments

The well-known experiments conducted by Stanley Milgram (1963, 1965) represent the most dramatic study of obedience in social psychology. The subjects in Milgram's original experiment (1963) were 40 males between the ages of 20 and 50 living in New Haven, Connecticut. Sales representatives, postal clerks, engineers, laborers, and high-school teachers were represented in a subject population that was occupationally and educationally diverse.

Subjects were told that the experiment was a scientific study of the effects of punishment on learning. They were then informed that they would be working in two-person teams, in which one subject would take the role of the teacher and the other would take the role of the learner. In actuality, however, the subject designated as the learner was a confederate of the experimenter.

In his role as the teacher, the naive subject was required to punish the learner if and when he made mistakes or failed to respond on a memory test. The punishment consisted of electric shocks of varying duration and intensity. Although no shocks would actually be delivered, the subjects were provided with a bogus shock generator. On it a panel of 30 switches was labeled from 15 to 450 volts, grouped under labels that ranged from "slight shock" through "moderate shock," past "danger: severe shock" to "XXX" (see Table 10–1). To enhance the

TABLE 10–1.
Shock Levels in Milgram's Obedience Study

Verbal Designation and Voltage Indication	Number of Subjects for Whom This Was Maximum Shock	Verbal Designation and Voltage Indication	Number of Subjects for Whom This Was Maximum Shock
Slight shock		Intense shock	
15	0	255	0
30	0	270	0
45	0	285	0
60	0	300	5
Moderate shock		Extreme-intensity shock	
75	0	315	4
90	0	330	2
105	0	345	1
120	0	360	1
Strong shock		Danger—severe shock	
135	0	375	1
150	0	390	0
165	0	405	0
180	0	420	0
Very strong shock		XXX	
195	0	435	0
210	0	450	26
225	0		
240	0		

Source: From "Behavioral Study of Obedience," by S. Milgram, *Journal of Abnormal and Social Psychology*, 1963, *67*, 376. Copyright 1963 by the American Psychological Association. Reprinted by permission.

Controversy: The Authoritarian Personality

Earlier in this chapter we examined the research on the personality characteristics of those people who conform more than others. Similar research has been conducted on the characteristics of people who are obedient to authority. The issue of whether there is such a thing as an "authoritarian personality," and whether it can be linked to particular political systems, has been an important subject of debate in the twentieth century, especially since the Second World War. In *The Authoritarian Personality*, as its title implies, Adorno and his colleagues (1950) not only proposed that a personality type of this kind could be defined, but attempted to identify the social attitudes to which this type would correspond. Since its publication, the book has been extremely influential and has generated a good deal of research.

One of the main purposes of *The Authoritarian Personality* was to investigate the psychological roots of anti-Semitism (Brown, 1965). Although anti-Semitism had assumed its most diabolical form in Nazi Germany, it had been present throughout European history, and in the twentieth century was not unknown in democratic nations such as England and the United States or in Communist countries such as the Soviet Union. By investigating the psychological roots of anti-Semitism, Adorno and his colleagues were attempting to link the authoritarian personality to ideological factors in a way that transcended national boundaries and overt political systems.

In relating ideological to psychological factors, these researchers developed four scales from which they generated questionnaire items: the *Anti-Semitism (A-S) Scale*, the *Ethnocentrism (E) Scale*, the *Political and Economic Conservatism (PEC) Scale*, and the *Implicit Antidemocratic Trends or Potentiality for Fascism (F) Scale*. The first three of these scales related to ideological factors, but the *F Scale* was directly concerned with the personality variables (such as rigidity, conventionality, and sadism) that might define an "authoritarian personality." Examples of the questions appearing on the *F Scale*—which has been widely used in research over the past 30 years—are shown in the accompanying tables.

One of the reasons that research on the authoritarian personality has been controversial is that the original studies were criticized severely by other scientists almost immediately after they were published. A volume of studies evaluating the original *F Scale* research was published in 1954 (Christie & Jahoda). Critics have noted a number of problems with the *F Scale* over the years. As an example, Hyman and Sheatsley (1954) criticized the methodology: The original studies were conducted on a homogeneous sample of white, native-born, middle-class, non-Jewish Californians; could such a sample be generalized to the American public?

By equating the "authoritarian personality"—as measured by the *F Scale*—with the "potentiality for fascism," Adorno and his colleagues had defined this personality type beforehand in right-wing political terms, probably because fascism originated as an extreme rightist movement. However, as a number of critics noted, there is no logical reason why authoritarianism could not take an extreme leftist form (Brown, 1965). Moreover, it is quite possible that people with conservative political and economic views—that is, who are opposed to government intervention and centralized planning—will also oppose authoritarianism. Others noted that the scale items were written in such a way that high authoritarians always "agreed" on the critical questions. Thus, the scale might in part be tapping an "acquiescent" response set (recall our discussion of response sets in chapter 9) (Bass, 1955; Campbell, Siegman, & Rees, 1967).

Most of the defects in the *F Scale* have been corrected and research has revealed some interesting behavioral and attitudinal differences between people who score high and low on the *F Scale*. High-*F* (or authoritarian) people have been found to be more prejudiced (Hanson, 1975; Siegman, 1961); to come from families that use harsher discipline (Martin & Westie, 1959); to prefer militaristic presidential candidates (Higgins, 1965; Milton, 1952); to support traditional authority figures (Fink, 1973; Izzett, 1971); and to be more conviction prone and punitive as jurors (Bray & Noble, 1978).

TABLE A.
Characteristics of the Authoritarian Personality

a. *Conventionalism.* Rigid adherence to conventional, middle-class values.
b. *Authoritarian submission.* Submissive, uncritical attitude toward idealized moral authorities of the ingroup.
c. *Authoritarian aggression.* Tendency to be on the lookout for, and to condemn, reject, and punish people who violate conventional values.
d. *Anti-intraception.* Opposition to the subjective, the imaginative, the tender minded.
e. *Superstition and stereotypy.* The belief in mystical determinants of the individual's fate; the disposition to think in rigid categories.
f. *Power and "toughness."* Preoccupation with the dominance-submission, strong-weak, leader-follower dimension; identification with power figures; overemphasis upon the conventionalized attributes of the ego; exaggerated assertion of strength and toughness.
g. *Destructiveness and cynicism.* Generalized hostility, vilification of the human.

These nine variables, believed by Adorno and his colleagues to characterize authoritarian individuals, formed the categories on which their F Scale was based.

Source: From "The Measurement of Implicit Antidemocratic Trends," by R.N. Sanford et al. *In The Authoritarian Personality* by T.W. Adorno and R.N. Sanford et al., New York: Harper & Row, 1950, 228.

TABLE B.
Representative Items from the *F Scale*

(Letters in parentheses indicate the characteristics from Table A of which each item is an indicator.)

Obedience and respect for authority are the most important virtues children should learn. (a, b)
A person who has bad manners, habits, and breeding can hardly expect to be liked and accepted by decent people. (a, c)
Science has carried man very far, but there are many important things that can never possibly be understood by the human mind. (b, e)
Every person should have complete faith in some supernatural power whose decisions he obeys without question. (b, e)
An insult to our honor should always be punished. (c, f)
Sex crimes, such as rape and attacks on children, deserve more than mere imprisonment; such criminals ought to be publicly whipped, or worse. (c)
There is hardly anything lower than a person who does not feel a great love, gratitude, and respect for his parents. (c)
When a person has a problem or worry, it is best for him not to think about it, but to keep busy with more cheerful things. (d)
Nowadays more and more people are prying into matters that should remain personal and private. (d, h)
People can be divided into two distinct classes: the weak and the strong. (e, f)
It is possible that wars and social troubles will be ended once and for all by an earthquake or flood that will destroy the whole world. (e)
Most people don't realize how much our lives are controlled by plots hatched in secret by politicians. (f)
Human nature being what it is, there will always be war and conflict. (g)
The American way of life is disappearing so fast that force may be necessary to preserve it. (g)

Source: Adapted from R.N. Sanford, T.W. Adorno, E. Frenkel-Brunswik, and D.J. Levinson, *The Authoritarian Personality*, New York: Harper & Row, 1950, 248–250.

realism of the experiment, each naive subject was given an actual sample shock of 45 volts, so that he could gauge the intensity of the shocks he would be administering. Needless to say, all of the subjects were convinced of the authenticity of the procedure.

The confederate-learner was led into an adjacent room, where he was strapped into an "electric chair." At this point, the subjects were told: "Although the shocks can be extremely painful, they cause no permanent tissue damage" (p. 373). They were instructed to administer a shock each time the learner gave an incorrect response and to increase the shock level by 15 volts after each mistake. The accomplice received no actual shocks, but he acted as if he did. He made mild protests when he received 75 volts, louder protests when he received 150 volts, and agonized screams when he received 285 volts.

When the subjects hesitated about administering a shock, the experimenter urged them on by saying, "Please continue." If the subject continued to hesitate, these verbal prods increased to the point where the experimenter actually said, "You have no other choice, you must go on." Under these conditions, all 40 of the subjects administered 300-volt shocks, even though at this intensity the learner was heard to pound on the wall and then ceased responding to further questions. Moreover, 65 percent of the subjects continued to the final 450-volt shock level (see Figure 10–4).

Although the majority of the subjects was willing to obey the experimenter, it was evident that obedience caused many of them considerable anxiety and conflict. Subjects were observed to sweat, tremble, stutter, or break into uncontrollable fits of nervous laughter. Apparently, however, in the majority of cases this moral anguish was not enough to stop them from obeying "authority."

In further studies, Milgram tried to encourage acts of disobedience among the subjects. The "victim" cried out, claimed he had heart trouble, pleaded to be released—but to little avail: Only 37.5 percent of the subjects disobeyed the authority. Next Milgram moved the "victim" close to the subject, and now a majority—60 percent—of the subjects disobeyed. Then Milgram placed the "victim" within touching distance of the subject, and altered the experiment so that the supposed shock would be received only when the "victim's" hand rested on a shock plate. At the 150-volt level the "victim" would no longer rest his hand on the plate voluntarily, and the experimenter commanded the subject to hold it there. To their credit, 70 percent of the subjects refused to obey at this point—but 30 percent continued to be obedient, administering the supposed shocks up to the highest level (Milgram, 1965, 1974).

Milgram and other researchers have found that obedience could be considerably reduced under several special circumstances: when instructions were given in person (Rada & Rogers, 1973), when the learner's suffering was emphasized (Milgram, 1965), and when the subject's responsibility was emphasized (Tilker, 1970). A study by Hofling and his colleagues (1966) demonstrated that Milgram's findings held up in natural as well as laboratory settings. In this study, nurses were telephoned by an unfamiliar doctor and ordered to administer an extremely large dosage of a relatively uncommon drug to patients in the hospital. Of the 22 nurses contacted, 21 complied with this order, even though their actions could have had harmful results. The researchers, of course, went to great lengths to assure that no harm could result.

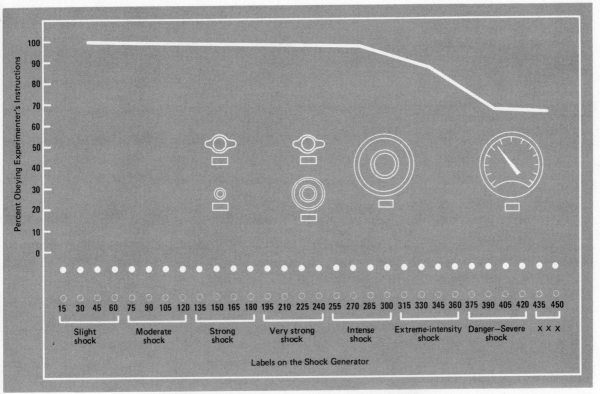

FIGURE 10–4. Results of Milgram's Obedience Experiment

The high percentage of subjects who continued to obey an experimenter's command to deliver high-voltage shocks to a suffering victim is shown against a schematic diagram of the shock generator used in Milgram's experiments.

Source: *Based on data in S. Milgram, "Behavioral Study of Obedience," Journal of Abnormal and Social Psychology, 67, 1963, 371–378.*

Conformity and Obedience in other Societies

Americans like to think of themselves as strong individualists, nonconformists, independent-minded thinkers whose very nation began as a rebellion against authority. Against this background Milgram's findings are particularly jarring. They seem to imply that in little more than 200 years Americans have gone from resisting an unjust authority to blind compliance. Is this the case? Is obedience to authority greater in the United States today than it is elsewhere?

Milgram (1971, 1977) examined conformity in Norway and France using a procedure similar to Asch's (1951; see above, page 370) and found high levels of conformity in both countries, although somewhat less in France than in Norway. Frager (1970) also used an Asch-type procedure with Japanese subjects, and found somewhat higher levels of nonconformity. Although there were variations

In Nazi occupied Holland, Jews who could not escape went into hiding in order to avoid being sent to concentration camps, or worse. Their hiding places were often attics over commercial buildings. This woman is climbing into her refuge in an unused space above a tobacco dealer's warehouse. The photographer, a non-Jew, had been an anti-Nazi activist even before the war. During the Nazi Occupation, he put his professional skills to use by creating thousands of pictures for the false identity cards needed by the Resistance. When he photographed the suffering of the citizens of Amsterdam at the height of the Occupation, he was arrested and sent to a concentration camp. After his release he returned to the city and continued to defy the authorities by photographing the agony of Jews and non-Jews alike in the extreme conditions of famine and oppression that characterized the last year of the Second World War in Holland.

among these three nations, there was still clear evidence, regardless of nationality, of a predominant tendency to conform.

Moreover, other researchers using Milgram's procedure in other countries such as Germany and Australia (Kilham & Mann, 1974; Mantell, 1971) obtained findings similar to those of Milgram's American study. It does appear, then, that obedience to authority is widespread and perhaps even a universal human phenomenon.

Controversies over Milgram's Research

From the time of its publication, Milgram's research has provoked an enormous amount of controversy. Critics have contended that the study was both unethical and unrealistic, and that the findings cannot be extended beyond the laboratory situation. Baumrind (1964), for example, maintained that obedience is specific to the artificial nature of an experimental situation. According to Baumrind, subjects perceive the experimental situation as a kind of game whose rules are, by definition, laid down by the experimenter. Indeed, prior to Milgram's experiments, Orne (1962) had argued that the compliance of subjects in experimental situations was a function of their high regard for the scientific method, and thus had no bearing on their behavior under normal conditions. Orne's thesis was corroborated by a study that showed that subjects who participate in psychological research believe that they should be cooperative during experiments and that experimenters, as a group, are decent human beings and competent professionals (Epstein, Suedfeld, & Silverstein, 1973). If this is the case, it follows that the subjects of Milgram's experiments, trusting in the good-will of the experimenter, may not have believed that they were inflicting harm. On the other hand, the fact that people could have such blind faith in scientists could be interpreted as a corroboration of Milgram's position.

Milgram's experiments provoked fierce debates about the ethics of conducting psychological research with human subjects. Baumrind (1964) argued that the well-being of the subjects taking part in an experiment should always take precedence over the possible benefits that might result from scientific discoveries. Since Milgram himself reported that his subjects experienced considerable emotional disturbance during the course of the experiments, Baumrind argues that it is impossible to know whether any subjects were permanently damaged by them. Many researchers would now agree that even the most remote possibility that an experiment will cause harm to a subject is sufficient to invalidate that experiment from an ethical point of view. Otherwise, the grotesque experiments carried out by Nazi physicians on human guinea pigs could be justified in the name of "scientific progress."

In response to these criticisms, Milgram (1977) reported that 84 percent of his subjects indicated that they did not regret participating in his experiments, and that the debriefing sessions had ensured that the subjects left in a state of well-being. Milgram also charged that those who attacked his experiments were really reacting to the disturbing implications of his findings: "If everyone had broken off at slight shock or moderate shock, this would be a very reassuring finding and who would protest?" (p. 98).

Intergroup Competition

At work or at play, at home or at school, much of our daily activities occur in groups. We learn skills and socially approved behaviors from the other members of our groups—families, classes, co-workers, friends—and sometimes we compete with them. All the groups to which we belong exist within a framework of other groups. A given family has ties to other related families and interacts with neighboring family units. The local democratic club competes against the local republican club (and perhaps others) and has ties to a network of county, state, and national democratic clubs. Thus, social psychology studies intergroup behavior to learn more about such issues as conformity and attitude formation.

Us and Them

In most cases, the groups we belong to have existed for some time and reflect actual differences between ourselves and those who are members of other groups. Such factors as gender, socioeconomic status, and ethnic background frequently form the basis for in-group and out-group identification. Within each group, norms develop that regulate the behavior of members toward other members of the group as well as toward nonmembers. As a result of these norms, people favor those in their own group. However, it is often unclear whether this positive bias is the result of actual human differences or a mere function of the ways people label themselves. Do baseball fans in Los Angeles favor the Dodgers over the Yankees because there is something intrinsically different about the Dodgers, or simply because the Dodgers are the Los Angeles team?

Some years ago in New York City, efforts to alter the administration of the public schools led to a conflict between the city's Board of Education and the union that represented most of the school system's teachers. As the conflict intensified and the United Federation of Teachers went on strike, parents throughout the city began to take sides. In many schools, Parents Associations broke down into two camps as some parents sided with the teachers' union and others with the Board of Education. More than a dozen years after the strike was settled, its legacy remains: People still pass each other on neighborhood streets and turn away from a parent or teacher who was in the opposing camp.

This intensity of feeling is not unusual following a bitter conflict. When there are differences in belief or opinion between a majority and a minority, group members feel tension and pressure one another to change positions. The conflict is often resolved when the minority conforms to the majority's position. But if the differences remain unresolved and the minority maintains its independent position, the conflict and psychological tension remain. When this happens, the boundaries separating the two groups may solidify, and group members may strengthen their identification with their own group and begin thinking in terms of "us" and "them."

In one experiment, Tasaki (1980) created majority and minority groups from a previously undifferentiated group of students. Tasaki found that tension was reduced in the minority group subjects who conformed to the majority, while those who remained independent felt increased tension over the course of the experiment. Tasaki concluded that intergroup differences can be a potent source of conflict even when group membership is informal or transitory. But these subjects were not members of conflicting groups before the experiment began.

The Minimal Group Situation

In a number of studies, Tajfel and his colleagues have demonstrated that certain aspects of intergroup behavior manifest themselves even under *minimal group situations* in which people are classified into groups on a trivial or random basis (Billig & Tajfel, 1973; Tajfel & Turner, 1979; Turner, Brown, & Tajfel, 1979). In Tajfel's original study (1970), subjects were told that they were being classified into two groups on the basis of a superficial distinction, when in fact the basis of classification was random. They were then asked to allocate money anonymously to pairs of other subjects who were either members of their own group or members of the other group. The results indicated that the subjects favored their own group members and that they were more concerned about maximizing the differences between in-group and out-group allotments of money than with maximizing the profit of the in-group. This suggests that a strong competitive motive was operating despite the fact that there was no objective basis for this competition. In-group bias has also been observed when subjects are asked to evaluate others in terms of personality traits (Rabbie & Wilkens, 1971), and when the competition is merely for symbolic points rather than for actual money.

While objective factors certainly play a critical role in real-life intergroup conflicts, studies of minimal group behavior are highly provocative. Since there is no previous conflict of interest in experimental group situations such as those described above, and since there is no objective reason for subjects to favor their own group, "social categorization *per se* is sufficient to trigger intergroup discrimination favoring the in-group" (Tajfel & Turner, 1979, p. 38). As Brewer (1979) points out in her review of research on this topic, it appears that the mere existence of an out-group is enough to produce in-group favoritism.

Social Identity and Social Competition

A number of theorists have suggested that in-group biases serve a *hedonic* function—that is, they indirectly bolster the individual's self-esteem by creating a positive social identity (Tajfel & Turner, 1979; Turner, 1975). Tajfel and Turner (1979) point out that people derive aspects of their self-image from the social categories with which they identify. To maintain a positive self-image, then, people will evaluate their own groups more favorably than other groups. In the process, they often exaggerate the differences that exist between groups. Social psychologists often refer to the attempt to differentiate the in-group from the out-group as *social competition*, and they distinguish between this and the *real competition* that results from objectively conflicting interests.

The fact that people strive to preserve a positive social identity has a bearing on conformity behavior. By conforming to the in-group, people may feel that they are achieving a positive social identity. On the other hand, those who refuse to conform and who remain independent of the majority may be identifying with a "group" that they have internalized and that they feel would support them in their convictions.

Real Competition: Intergroup Conflict

Hatred renewed is worse than at first.
Italian proverb

Intergroup conflict is not always motivated only by psychological needs, of course. Politics, whether at the local, national, or international level, are motivated by the fact that competing groups desire to maintain control of important resources; and when these resources are scarce, competition often leads to overt hostility. Thus, this kind of intergroup conflict is based on real competition. The most extreme forms of intergroup conflict—race riots, lynchings, wars, and so

Application: Competition in the Robbers Cave

In a classic study, Sherif and his colleagues examined the conditions that foster intergroup conflict in a summer camp for boys (Sherif & Sherif, 1953; Sherif, White, & Harvey, 1955). Although this study was not designed as applied research, it nonetheless addresses a very real and common social problem—intergroup competition—under highly naturalistic circumstances.

Participants in the study, which came to be known as the "Robbers Cave" experiment because the camp was located near a famous Jesse James hideout, were all white, middle-class boys between the ages of 11 and 12. The study proceeded in three stages lasting one week each. During the first week the boys were arbitrarily divided into two groups (the "Rattlers" and the "Eagles") and the groups were kept apart in order to promote the development of in-group identity. Each group organized itself and chose its own leaders. The two groups played and "worked" separately at their camp activities (hiking, canoeing, swimming, baseball, and so on).

At the end of the first week (after the boys had developed in-group solidarity and friendships within their groups), the two groups were pitted against one another in a series of athletic and camping competitions. They competed gladly. The competition was intense, and the frustrations of losing and the perceptions that the other side was unfair led to greater in-group cohesiveness. The intense rivalry sparked antagonisms and conflicts between members of the two groups. There were fights, name-calling, and even nighttime "raids" on the other group's camp areas.

In the third week of the study the researchers set out to reduce the hostility between the two groups by creating mini-crises in which the boys had to cooperate in order to achieve "superordinate" goals. For example, when the water supply "broke down" (actually, it was sabotaged by the researchers) the two groups had to work together to restore it. In order to rent a movie the

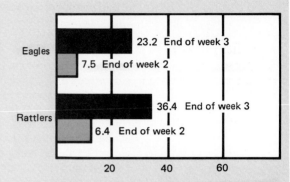

Percentage of friendship choices from out-group

Growth of Friendship between Members of Formerly Competing Groups

In the Robbers Cave experiment of Sherif et al. (1954), boys in two groups became quite hostile toward each other during a week of competing activities (week 2). However, when they spent a week working together to accomplish superordinate goals, the number of friendships between boys in different groups increased.

Source: *Adapted from* Intergroup Conflict and Cooperation: The Robbers Cave Experiments, *by M. Sherif, et al., Norman, Okla.: University of Oklahoma Intergroup Relations, 1961.*

two groups had to pool their money. At one point the camp truck got "stuck" (actually, Sherif, who was masquerading as a janitor at the camp so that he could talk to the boys in both groups in a nonthreatening way throughout the study, was sitting in the truck with his foot on the brake) and the boys had to push and pull together in order to move it. As a result of the third week's cooperative activities, the hostilities between the Eagles and the Rattlers dissolved and the boys developed friendships with their peers in the other group (see Figure).

The Robbers Cave experiment demonstrated that intergroup hostility, prejudice, and conflict are not inevitable but are the result of specific social conditions. And it also demonstrated that the need for cooperation can even override previous intergroup conflict.

on—are often related to economic factors. For example, Hovland and Sears (1940) have pointed out that the numbers of lynchings of blacks between 1880 and 1930 decreased in periods of prosperity but increased when times were hard.

Prejudice and Discrimination

In early 1982, the *New York Times* ran the following report:

> Over the last two months, the Army has acknowledged that bias against the 200,000 G.I.'s in West Germany is increasing. . . . (In one) highly publicized incident of discrimination . . . a West German newspaper, Welt am Sonntag, . . . sent a reporter out with two black soldiers trying to find something to eat and drink in Aschaffenburg, a town of 58,000 where about 4,300 Americans are stationed. The Americans were kicked out of a pizzeria, told they were not welcome at two discothèques and a bar, and were allowed into a jazz club on the condition they would leave "when the band stops playing." . . .
>
> According to the reporter's account, young people . . . shouted "Bimbo, Bimbo!" at the Americans and "give some bananas to our guests" when they tried to enter a dance club. . . .
>
> The discrimination clearly does not stop with young, black recruits. A white army captain is now involved in litigation . . . after he was refused entrance into a club in the city of Würzburg.
>
> "Owners and operators of allegedly discriminatory establishments readily admit exclusion of Americans, but deny discriminatory conduct," the Seventh Army said.
>
> Excuses for barring the Americans are found elsewhere, such as in objections to dress or accusations of rowdyism.*

Prejudices are the props of civilization.
Andre Gide, The Counterfeiters

At some time or other, and perhaps without having been aware of it, most of us have probably been victimized by prejudicial attitudes and discriminatory behavior—either because of our ethnic group, sex, socioeconomic background, or physical appearance. Similarly, there have probably been occasions when we too have responded to others on the basis of group stereotypes. Prejudice and discrimination frequently go unnoticed—especially when the people involved believe that they are responding to the characteristics of particular individuals. In the following sections, we will discuss the relationship between prejudice and discrimination and look at ways to reduce the hostility between social groups.

Attitude versus Behavior

A **prejudice** is a biased, generally negative, attitude. Social psychologists use this term to refer to bias directed against the members of a specific group. **Discrimination**, on the other hand, is a form of behavior; it may be defined as an overt action taken against one or more members of a group simply because of their group affiliation. Recall the study discussed in the last chapter, in which La Piere detected prejudice when he surveyed restaurant and hotel proprietors, but encountered virtually no discrimination when he actually visited their establishments.

It is important for us to distinguish between prejudice and discrimination because, although prejudiced attitudes are often associated with discriminatory behavior, this is not always the case. For example, a personnel manager may believe that Jews are "shrewd," that women are "frivolous," and that white Anglo-Saxon Protestants are "cold" without necessarily discriminating against members of these groups who apply for positions in her company. Moreover, just as prejudice does not always result in discrimination, discrimination does not always reflect prejudice. In some instances, people may discriminate against members of a particular group because of social pressure to do so. This would be true, for example, of the member of a golf club that does not accept blacks, who finds membership convenient and does not care about the club's discriminatory policies.

Theories of Prejudice

A number of theories have been advanced as to why people hold prejudiced attitudes. Generally these theories are of two kinds: theories that focus on the personality of prejudiced individuals and theories that emphasize the social context in which prejudice develops.

Those that are unkind to their own will not be kind to others.
Galician proverb

Psychological Reasons for Prejudice Allport (1954) proposed that while prejudiced attitudes toward members of minority groups reflect sociocultural factors and pressures to conform, they also may satisfy the needs of the prejudiced person in a variety of ways. According to Allport, when people turn minority groups into scapegoats, they feel justified in venting feelings of anger and frustration they could not otherwise express. Moreover, Allport observes that in addition to displacing their anger, prejudiced people are using the psychological mechanism of *projection:* They ascribe to members of the minority group those personality characteristics in themselves that they want to repudiate: "Suppose there are unwanted traits in oneself—perhaps greed, lust, laziness, and untidiness. What the sufferer needs is a caricature of these attributes—a simonpure incarnation of these evils. He needs something so extreme that he need not even suspect himself of being guilty. The Jew is therefore seen as wholly concupiscent; the Negro as completely lazy; the Mexican as filthy. One who holds such extreme stereotypes need not even suspect himself of having these hated tendencies" (p. 388).

We have already seen that "projection" is one of the components of the authoritarian personality, and that authoritarian people condemn anyone who is perceived to violate the conventions and rules of society. Researchers who emphasize the personality characteristics of prejudiced people have noted that childhood socialization plays an important role in fostering such beliefs. Even

Prejudice does not have to result in discrimination, but it very often does. This scene is typical of public facilities in the American South before passage of the Civil Rights Act of 1964: lunch counters, drinking fountains, and restrooms were segregated and labeled for "white" and "colored."

Library of Congress

children as young as 3 years old can show evidence of prejudice (Vaughan, 1964), and these attitudes are learned from parents. Research shows that the parents of authoritarians also tend to be authoritarian (Levinson & Huffman, 1955). In a sense, parents are among the situational factors that may promote prejudice.

Socialization and Modeling   Social psychologists who have been interested in the external conditions that promote prejudice have suggested that children develop prejudices by modeling the behavior of adults and by internalizing the values of the society. A landmark study conducted by Clark and Clark (1947) found that black children as well as white children preferred to play with white dolls and to attribute more favorable characteristics to white dolls than to black dolls. The investigators concluded that in the process of socialization, the prejudiced values, attitudes, and beliefs prevalent in the society are learned by minority children as well as majority children.

Parents, peer groups, schools, and the mass media are all sources of prejudiced attitudes. Since prejudiced attitudes are often shared by the victims of such attitudes, it follows that such attitudes are learned and do not necessarily satisfy intrapsychic needs (Brigham, 1971). In fact, a study by Griffitt and Garcia (1979) indicates that authoritarian punitiveness can be reversed later in life if the authoritarian behaviors are not reinforced by important social groups. And, more generally, research has shown that better education is associated with less prejudiced ethnic and racial attitudes (Campbell, 1971; Selznick & Steinberg, 1969).

Stereotypes

It is generally agreed that a **stereotype** is a broad generalization about the characteristics of a group of people (Brigham, 1971). Stereotypes in themselves do not necessarily result in prejudice; in fact, as we saw in chapter 5, they are essential for organizing the multiplicity of experiences we have from infancy on through adulthood (Hamilton, 1979). However, when our stereotypes are so rigidly maintained that no new information can modify them, they no longer contribute to our understanding of the world, but in fact insulate us from reality.

In chapter 5 we discussed the classic study conducted by Katz and Braly (1933) that found ethnic stereotypes prevalent among college students. We looked also at a more recent study by Karlins and his colleagues (1969), who found that while the content of a number of stereotypes had changed since the Katz and Braly study, students continued to be consistent in their descriptions of different ethnic groups. For example, stereotypes about blacks and Jews were considerably more favorable in 1969 than in 1933. One important difference, however, was noted: In 1969 many students protested when asked to make generalizations about the characteristics of ethnic groups. For some students at least, there was a greater tendency than had previously been the case to regard generalizations about ethnic groups with skepticism or distaste.

Reducing Intergroup Hostility

The reduction of prejudice and intergroup hostility is clearly a tremendously important societal goal. Based on their studies of intergroup conflict, social psychologists have formulated a number of different methods for dealing with these problems.

Establishing Superordinate Goals   As demonstrated in the Robbers Cave experiment (Sherif et al., 1961) in situations where your group's loss is the other group's gain, hostilities escalate and prejudices develop. When, however, differ-

Several social psychological studies suggest that contact between groups can improve understanding and reduce prejudice. In South Africa, where the hundreds of laws of Apartheid keep "Whites" separate from (black) Africans, as well as from "Asians" and "Coloureds" (South African terminology is used here), contact is rare and often punishable by law. The White crowd at the left is watching a sports event in a stadium at a recreation park near Johannesburg. The black African crowd has gathered at another stadium near Johannesburg to hear a black political leader plea for multiracialism.

ent groups can unite for the purpose of achieving a superordinate goal—that is, one which is of benefit to all parties—hostilities and prejudices are reduced.

Applications of this principle, whether at the local level or in the context of international politics, would require a commitment to universally beneficial goals, and that certain groups make sacrifices for the betterment of all. Unfortunately, this is easier said than done, but efforts are being made. For instance, Kelman and Cohen (1979) have reported their efforts to bring members of hostile groups (such as Egyptians and Israelis) together in problem-solving workshops.

The Contact Hypothesis   As suggested by Sherif's Robbers Cave study, contact between members of groups that previously were isolated from each other can, under certain conditions, lead to attitude change and a reduction of prejudice. When people interact personally with members of other groups that they had remained aloof from before, stereotypes are frequently disproved (Deutsch & Collins, 1951; Wilder, 1978). However, intergroup contact does not always lead to a reduction of prejudice, and under certain conditions such contact can lead to an escalation of conflict (Amir, 1969).

For example, in New York City, when members of different ethnic groups come into close physical contact with each other when riding the subway, friendships do not develop. In fact, strangers rarely even speak to one another. Thus, although inhabitants of New York and of other large cities may have a good deal of superficial contact with different ethnic groups, this kind of contact is unlikely to significantly alter any prejudiced attitudes they might have. The characteristics of the contact situation, as well as the characteristics of the individuals involved, thus determine the outcome.

The kind of contact that is most likely to have a favorable impact on reducing prejudice occurs when people are working together or otherwise interacting on an equal basis. For example, after World War II, several studies measured the attitudes of white soldiers to black soldiers (Amir, 1969). It was found that white soldiers who had actually fought alongside black soldiers had fewer prejudicial attitudes toward blacks than white soldiers who had not had that combat experience. However, other variables such as the intensity of the initial prejudice, the attitudes of relevant authority figures, and the presence or absence of superordinate goals are also factors to be considered in estimating the effects of reducing prejudice by increasing contact. Similar results have been reported following the integration of suburban areas (Hamilton & Bishop, 1976) and elementary schools (Koshin et al., 1969).

Individuation of Out-Group Members   When we respond to people in terms of their group affiliations, we lose sight of what makes them unique as individuals, and thus we deindividuate and dehumanize them. We saw some of the effects of deindividuation in chapter 4. In that discussion we concentrated on the effects of deindividuation in small groups. A similar process can occur at larger—even at societal—levels. This process of dehumanization is most clearly observed in times of war, when those who are fighting on the other side are simply seen as "the enemy." When we refer to Vietnamese as "Gooks," Japanese as "Japs," and Russians as "Reds" or "Commies," we are expressing the fact that we do not recognize their human qualities.

Reversing this process of dehumanization through emphasis on the individuality of the members of the out-groups is an important step in reducing prejudice and discrimination. We even have a sense of the importance of this notion in our everyday language: "Some of my best friends are. . . ." Individuation is part of what *can* make social contact a successful method of reducing prejudice. Individuation also helps to break down stereotypes: Any prescribed "role" like a stereotype can bear only so many "violations" before it will give way. It is easy to say that all extra-terrestrials are hideous monsters when you do not know any extra-terrestrials. But if you do make the acquaintance of a number of extra-terrestrials and none of them are hideous monsters, it is much more difficult to maintain the original belief.

Answering Questions about Conformity, Compliance, and Prejudice

1. All of us conform to a large number of social conventions in order to communicate and work cooperatively with others. Much of this conformity is based on our knowledge of social norms and some of it is based on pressure from others to conform. Situational factors such as group size, group consensus, and social status affect the extent to which people conform.
2. Forty years of research on conformity, compliance, and obedience have underscored the fact that these behaviors are part of normal and typical social activity. If Nazi Germany is viewed from this perspective, you can see that genocidal societies—although rare—are, in part, built upon social influence processes carried to their extreme.

3. Chapters 9 and 10 have both shown that efforts to change attitudes—including moral attitudes—may be facilitated when people's behaviors are consistent with the new attitudes. If the new behaviors are widely adopted, the relevant attitudes may come to agree with them. In principle, it might be possible to legislate morality. Contrast the American experience with Prohibition and desegregation.

4. Although researchers have looked for personality characteristics associated with conformity, the search has been largely unsuccessful.

5. Think about some of your recent encounters with salespeople. Have any of them used the foot-in-the-door or low-ball techniques? And how often have you declined a "big" purchase only to turn around and make a small purchase—the door-in-the-face technique?

Summary

Conformity is a change in behavior or belief toward a group as a result of group pressure. The individual resolves conflict with the group by going along with the group. Conformity may or may not involve private acceptance of the group's position. Compliance occurs when an individual goes along with the group in public but privately rejects the group's position.

The group uses social influence to gain conformity. With informational social influence, the group's positions are taken as evidence about reality, and dissenting members can more readily accept the majority position. With normative social influence the individual is pressured to accept the majority position, but a discrepancy between the individual's private beliefs and those of the group remains.

Social norms are the implicit or explicit rules and standards of the behavior of a society. Their function is to provide the individual with a frame of reference.

The situational factors that influence conformity include the size of the group, the individual's status in the group, and the degree to which the majority maintains unanimity. The existence of a conformist personality type has not been confirmed by research.

Substantive change develops from the nonconforming and innovative ideas of individuals or minorities. In order to influence a majority, a minority must be consistent, coherent, and forceful.

When individuals resist group norms, group members respond by exerting pressure on the deviant members to join the majority. The foot-in-the-door technique suggests that if demands are increased by small increments, the individual will be more likely to comply with them. The door-in-the-face technique suggests that if the initial request is very large, most people will refuse it but later comply with a smaller request. The low-ball technique suggests that if the terms of an agreement are made less favorable after the individual has made a commitment, the individual will nevertheless go through with the action. If pressure does not work, the group may resort to rejection and exclusion. Reactance theory suggests that conformity pressures may sometimes lead individuals to adopt more deviant positions than they would ordinarily have done in an effort to regain their sense of freedom.

Milgram's obedience experiments demonstrated that subjects complied with orders to deliver high levels of what they thought were electric shocks. Although obedience evoked considerable anxiety for many subjects, it was not enough to make them refuse the commands of the authority figure. The research of Milgram and his associates has been extremely controversial and has often been criticized on ethical and other grounds.

Intergroup conflict often results in the solidification of group boundaries; conversely, the mere fact that people are divided into groups may lead to intergroup competition, even when there is no objective basis for competition. Intergroup behavior patterns are found even in minimal group situations—that is, situations in which people are classified into groups on a trivial or random basis.

In social competition, the individual's attempt to differentiate the in-group from the out-group is based, not on objective factors, but rather on the fact that the individual's self-concept depends on identity derived from membership in the group. In real competition, objective factors, such as a desire to maintain control of scarce resources, are the source of intergroup conflict. A superordinate goal is one that transcends the narrow interests of competing groups and thus serves to bring them together.

A **prejudice** is a biased negative attitude directed against the members of a specific group. **Discrimination** is an overt action taken against one or more members of a group merely because of their group affiliation. Prejudice, an attitude, and discrimination, behavior, are often but not always linked. Theories of prejudice that focus on personality processes emphasize the subjective needs of the prejudiced person that are satisfied by the prejudice. Theories of prejudice that focus on the social context in which prejudice occurs emphasize the fact that children internalize prejudiced attitudes from parents, peer groups, schools, and the mass media.

A **stereotype** is a broad generalization about the characteristics of a group of people. Intergroup hostility may be reduced by establishing superordinate goals for the competing groups, by promoting contact between them, and by educating people to respond to the members of other groups as individuals rather than in terms of social stereotypes.

Suggested Additional Reading

Allen, V. L. Situational factors in conformity. In L. Berkowitz (Ed.), *Advances in experimental social psychology* (Vol. 2), 135–175. New York: Academic Press, 1965.

Allport, G. W. *The nature of prejudice*. Garden City, N.Y.: Doubleday-Anchor, 1958.

Milgram, S. *Obedience to authority*. New York: Harper & Row, 1974.

Moscovici, S. *Social influence and social change* (C. Sherrard & G. Heinz, trans.). London: Academic Press, 1976.

Sherif, M. *The psychology of social norms*. New York: Harper & Row, 1936.

Wheeler, L., Deci, E., Reis, H., & Zuckerman, M. *Interpersonal influence*. Boston: Allyn & Bacon, 1978.

ANTI- AND PROSOCIAL BEHAVIOR

11

AGGRESSION AND VIOLENCE

Questions about Aggression and Violence

1. Are humans by nature aggressive?

2. Turn on a television set at nearly any time of the day on nearly any channel, and you are likely to see one person expressing aggression against another, be it in a cartoon or a police drama. What is the effect of this exposure to so much television violence on our behavior toward others?

3. Examine a copy of a fashion magazine or a "men's magazine." You will probably find some illustrations showing very attractive women as the apparently "willing" victims of mild abuse or violence. Do such portrayals affect men's attitudes and behaviors toward women in our society?

4. It is often said that the best way to reduce violence is to find a socially acceptable release for it, such as watching a football game rather than whacking your neighbor. Do you think such releases lead to less violence?

5. After some people have a few drinks, they are quite likely to behave aggressively. What is the effect of smoking marijuana on aggressive behavior?

6. Think about the major urban riots of the 1960s and 1970s. They usually occurred in the peak of summer. Is there a relationship between heat and aggression?

Shortly after Christmas in 1981, a young mail carrier named Karen Green was going about her job in Mesa, Arizona. No one knows why, but she was assaulted by three men and two women, all drunk. Neighbors who heard her frantic cries for help telephoned the police several times, but did not directly intervene during the approximately 15 minutes Mrs. Green struggled with her attackers. Finally, the five assailants drove off with their victim. Two days later, Mrs. Green's body was found in a dump; she had been beaten and stabbed, her throat had been cut, and the attackers had tried to smother her. Three persons were later arrested and charged with the crime.

This brutal and bizarre occurrence is an example of wanton violence. There was no apparent provocation. The attackers were all drunk, but that is no reason to kill. It seemed almost as though one blow led to another. Does aggression function in this escalating fashion? How can human beings attack another human being and increase the level of violence to the point of murder? Even more appalling is the fact that observers did nothing to intervene, although they outnumbered the attackers. Why didn't the neighbors act? Were they frozen by fear? *Justified* fear?

Violence in Our Society

How many assassinations or assassination attempts have taken place in your life-time? A United States president receives an average of 100 threats upon his life every month. The number of threats increases after an actual assassination attempt, as when an aborted attempt on President Ford's life in 1975 brought the number of threats the following month to over 300, and led to a second assassination attempt.

The United States Secret Service, charged with guarding a president's life, maintains a computerized list of potentially dangerous people. Although it contains as many as 60,000 names, this list did not include those of either President Kennedy's assassin or of President Reagan's would-be assassin (Blaska, 1981).

Not only political figures are assassins' targets, of course; all popular figures share at least some of the danger as well as the limelight. Artist Andy Warhol was shot and survived; John Lennon was shot and did not. It is chilling to think that at any given time in a free society such as ours, a number of uncontrollably violent people are at large, armed, and unrestrained by social or legal codes.

As the examples above illustrate, and as your experience with television and newspaper accounts suggests, our society seems to be teeming with violence. Violence—aggression that involves the intentional use of physical force—occurs in various contexts. In this chapter we will take a look at some of them. We will examine laboratory research that has been designed to explain why we behave aggressively, and discuss some theories about the origins of human aggression. Finally, we will look at several specific aspects of aggression and violence: their relationship to pornography, women as both victims and aggressors, fear of violence, and ways to reduce aggression. First, we will look at violence in our everyday lives.

Violence in the Home

The family is generally seen as a social group committed to nonviolence between its members. Yet the empirical data and relevant theory leave no doubt that violence between family members is so common as to be almost universal (Straus, 1973, p. 105).

Familial violence is often either denied or not considered as deviant—passing, for instance, as acceptable punishment. Yet of all the murders committed in the United States in 1980, 16.1 percent were committed by members of a family upon other members of the family; over half of these were murders of one spouse by the other, and one of eight was the murder of a child by a parent (Uniform Crime Reports, 1981).

Domestic violence—child abuse and spouse abuse—has received much attention from the press and is beginning to receive attention from social psychologists. A widespread problem in need of solutions, domestic violence may also be an "attractive" research topic. A social learning theory (see chapter 3) per-

Domestic violence, long hidden from view, has begun to receive attention from social psychologists and the media as well as from the women's movement. As a result, in many communities a variety of resources are available to abused women and their children. The women shown here share an apartment that has been set up as a shelter. The woman at the right is a new arrival who left her husband immediately after the first violent episode—testimony to the success of publicity about services for abused women as well as to her strength of character.

Ann Chwatsky

Spare the rod and spoil the child.

By beating love decays.
French saying

spective would predict that what happens in the home is likely to have a major impact on subsequent behavior. As we shall see, this is indeed the case. Children spend a good deal of time in the home; parents are important and pervasive models for behavior; and home life therefore affords many children opportunities for repeated observation of aggressive or even violent behavior, as well as for "practice" on younger siblings. A number of researchers (e.g., Morris, Gould, & Matthews, 1964) have observed that an abusing parent was probably also an abused child. Most studies of abusive parents seek to identify personality disorders that lead to abuse (Spinetta & Rigler, 1977), yet these studies have not shown a great deal of consistency in their findings.

Spouse abuse is apparently more pervasive than child abuse. Straus and his associates interviewed 2,000 married couples and found that 25 percent of them reported having engaged in some form of physical violence in their married life. Comparisons of social class differences revealed that white-collar workers expressed less approval of marital violence than blue-collar workers, but the actual frequency of reported violent behavior did not differ between the two classes (Steinmetz & Straus, 1974; Straus, 1977). One study asked battered women whom they blamed for the causes of violence in their relationships; interestingly, there was no correlation between whom they blamed (themselves or their husbands) and whether or not they attempted to leave their husbands (Frieze, 1979).

Alcohol definitely has an effect on domestic violence: Gelles (1972) found that fully half of the cases of wife abuse that he investigated involved the use of alcohol. Richardson and Campbell (1980) tested what effect the use of alcohol had on attributing blame for spouse abuse. Subjects read scenarios describing a single violent incident in which one or the other spouse was drunk. Subjects assigned less blame to the husband when he was sober than when he was drunk, but more blame to the wife when she was drunk than when she was sober.

Many writers have emphasized the crucial role of the police in spouse assault. Traditionally, domestic disturbance calls have been given the lowest priority by the police; and when the police have responded to such calls, they have pursued an almost universal policy of nonarrest (Loving, 1980). Traditional police training has instructed officers to avoid arrest (Langely and Levy, 1978; Saunders, 1979). Loving (1980) noted that this policy was not only ineffective in reducing the number of spouse abuse cases, but also "may aggravate the problem by suggesting to assailants that their violent behavior can be overlooked" (p. xvi).

Gelles (1972) also found that men who abused their wives had often come from homes where violence between spouses had occurred, or were themselves victims of violence. Similarly, abused wives often came from violent families and had been beaten as children (Gelles, 1976).

Studies of violence between family members have generally depended on after-the-fact interviews and data analysis, and have concentrated on situational factors. Gelles (1972), for instance, found that violence between spouses usually takes place at night in the home, and specifically in the kitchen, and with no outsiders present. Meiselman (1978) described a cyclical relationship between wife abuse and incest: men who committed father–daughter incest were likely to abuse their wives as well, and women who had been victims of an incestuous relationship in their childhood ended up more often than other women as battered wives. Thus it appears that prior experience or learning may be related to later victimization.

Some of these forms of violence and aggression may have touched all of our lives at one time or another. Parents do not plan to abuse their children, nor do spouses plan to injure one another. But when people interact with one another daily in the confines of a home, and are pressured by different needs and external influences, irritation can escalate and self-control can wear thin.

Human aggression and violence have been addressed by social psychologists in some depth in laboratory studies. As the examples above indicate, many issues remain, and research is by no means at an end. Nevertheless, this chapter provides some tentative answers to some of the problems we have discussed, as well as to the origins and operation of aggression in other areas.

What Is Aggression?

A Supreme Court justice, referring to pornography, once quipped that even though he could not define it, he could recognize it when he saw it. Quite likely this sums up the way most of us feel about aggression—we know what it is without defining it. Many of the behaviors we have just described are generally considered aggressive. What are the characteristics of such acts that make them aggressive?

Anger is a short madness.
Dutch proverb

Aggression, according to Robert Baron (1977), is any behavior intended to harm or injure another individual who does not want to be treated in that way. This definition focuses on four factors: behavior, the intent to harm, human beings as actor and victim, and the unwillingness of the victim. Are these elements shared by the acts of family violence we have just described? Would the definition include war? Football? Boxing?

Other social psychologists have offered other definitions. Berkowitz (1969), for example, distinguishes between aggression as behavior (as in our definition above), and aggression as the feeling or emotion leading to aggressive acts. Baron's definition (which we shall use in this chapter) also differs from the way we often use the word "aggressive" in everyday speech. When we say a salesperson is "aggressive," we mean that the person is persuasive and insistent, not that he or she seeks to injure others.

Measuring Aggression

In experiments investigating aggression, social psychologists most commonly make use of a "Buss aggression machine." This device is given to subjects with an explanation that they can deliver shocks to someone else; in reality, though, no shocks are produced (see box).

The amount of aggression is easily quantified with a Buss aggression machine, making it attractive for experimentation. This approach to measuring aggression has been criticized, however, because the subjects may only be com-

Aggression—or good clean sport? The New York Rangers and the Philadelphia Flyers get into a melee when a game ends in a tie.

plying with the characteristics of the experimental situation, and not expressing their own aggression. Baron and Eggleston (1972) claim that the technique is neither very reliable nor a direct enough measure of aggression. Furthermore, the ethics of inducing people to deliver electric shocks to others have also been questioned, especially when modified versions of the Buss device are used that do deliver real, although mild, shocks.

A more direct way of measuring aggression is simply to observe aggressive behavior and record the observations. For example, Albert Bandura (1973) placed children in experimental laboratory situations and then measured aggression by counting the number of punches and kicks they inflicted on a "bobo doll."

Laboratory measurement of aggression has been criticized on methodological grounds. Some investigators, for example, have found that subjects who realize that their aggressive impulses are under study apparently refrain from giving full vent to them (Turner & Simons, 1974). This consideration may make the results less than ideally representative; but it also makes the high measures of aggression that are obtained in spite of such an awareness doubly impressive (Berkowitz & Donnerstein, 1982).

Is There a Biological Basis for Aggression?

Social psychologists are not the only behavioral scientists to study and to attempt to explain aggression. Theories past and present span a wide range between those that place responsibility for aggressiveness on human nature itself and those that place it on the environment. Indeed, an evolutionary approach holds that both nature and nurture have interacted: Environmental pressures favored the survival and procreation of people predisposed to aggressive and violent behavior. In this section we will look at some theories that deal with human nature; in the section that follows we will examine some theories that are concerned about the influence of the environment on human aggression.

Freud: Aggression as Instinct

According to Freud (1920), human beings have a natural disposition to aggression that must be controlled in socially acceptable ways. Freud's approach to aggression is similar to his approach to the sex drive or libido, which he felt must also be channeled into more acceptable activities through sublimation or displacement. Recall from chapter 3 the discussion of Freud's model of the human mind: an uneasy juxtaposition of the primal urges of the *id* existed with the parental and societal values internalized in the *superego*, leaving the *ego*—the harassed executive seeking a middle way between the two extremes—to control the resulting behavior. With aggression as with libido, the id often wins out.

Here the analogy ends, however. Because unchecked aggression can lead to the destruction of the individual, it can be more readily displaced than the sex

Research: The Buss Aggression Machine

To measure the *intensity* of aggression in an easily quantifiable way, Arnold Buss (1961) developed an electronic device and an associated methodology. (Drawings of early versions of the Buss machine are shown in Figures A and B. You can imagine what a modern version would look like!) Subjects use the Buss aggression machine to (they think) deliver electric shocks to a victim. A subject is told that he or she is to control a learning experiment. Another subject (really an accomplice of the experimenter) is to learn the correct responses to the stimuli that the real subject presents, and the real subject is instructed to administer an electric shock whenever the accomplice makes an incorrect response.

Figure A shows the subject's side of the Buss machine, and Figure B shows the accomplice's side. The two people are visually separated from each other by a barrier. A simple task that the accomplice might ostensibly be learning is to press button "A" whenever the upper left light on the panel (Figure B) is lit, and to press button "B" whenever the upper left light is not lit. The real subject is given a random sequence in which to press the buttons marked 1, 2, 3, and 4 (Figure A) that will turn on the lights at the top of the accomplice's panel (Figure B). The lights just above the stimulus buttons on the subject's panel indicate the accomplice's responses. The subject notes the response, decides whether or not it is correct, and presses either the "correct" button on the extreme left of the panel, or one of the ten shock buttons.

The shocks are, of course, the crux of the matter, and before the experiment begins, the subject is given the chance to sample the intensity of the shocks he or she will supposedly deliver. The electrodes are attached to one of the subject's fingers, and shocks are given from buttons 1, 2, 3, and 5. The shock from button 1 is barely perceptible, while that from button 5 is painful. The higher levels, untried, will presumably be more painful still.

When the accomplice is invited to the other panel and the actual experiment begins, the accomplice never receives any shocks. Instead, he or she records the number that is flashed on the panel (a "2" appears in Figure B), corresponding

drive from its actual target to a substitute, sublimated into productive channels, or otherwise reduced.

The aggressive instincts were a relatively late supplement to Freud's theory. Indeed, this addition was made only at the insistence of Alfred Adler and others that aggression must have a place in any theory of human nature. In his time, Freud's intuitive constructs to explain human behavior were revolutionary acts of genius; today, we examine them primarily because of their impact on subsequent theory and research.

Konrad Lorenz on Aggression

Although the primary concern of ethologist Konrad Lorenz is animal behavior, he also extended his theorizing to humans. Like Freud, Lorenz (1966) believed that aggression was an instinct. Unlike Freud, Lorenz did not take a basically negative view of aggression but viewed it as adaptive for the survival of a species: If

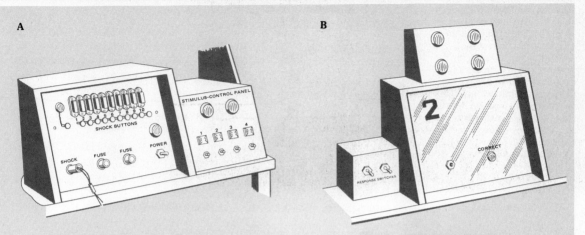

FIGURES A and B.   An early version of the Buss aggression machine, subject's panel, left, and accomplice's panel right.

Source: *From* The Psychology of Aggression, *by A. H. Buss, New York: Wiley, 1961, 47. Reprinted with permission.*

to the shock button the subject presses. The intensity of the shock that is supposedly administered, as well as its duration, give a possible measure of aggression. This device and the associated technique, often with modifications and variables, have been extensively used in social psychological experiments.

natural selection means that only the fittest of a species can survive, then the traits found in living animals, including humans, must have had survival value for the species.

Most animals, Lorenz points out, show aggression. But in most animals inhibitions act to curb their aggression against their own species, in order that the species can continue to exist. Animals that are capable of killing creatures about their own size can, in principle, also kill members of their own species. With rare exceptions, however, they do not. As Lorenz states:

> A raven can peck out the eye of another with one thrust of its beak, a wolf can rip the jugular vein of another with a single bite. There would be no more ravens and no more wolves if reliable inhibitions did not prevent such action. (1966, p. 240)

Many animals need no such inhibitions because they are not so readily capable of inflicting harm. Chimpanzees, doves, or rabbits cannot kill each other

Lions are among those animals capable of killing members of their own species. Usually, however, an instinctive inhibition prevents their intra-species conflicts from reaching that point. In this picture, taken at the Nairobi National Park game reserve, the lion on the left is responding to an attack. The lion on the right, well known for his evil disposition, won this battle by clawing out the eye of his rival. Previous fights had left him with a mangled mane.

Ian Cleghorn/Photo Researchers, Inc.

It is because of man that the blacksmith makes weapons.
Ashanti proverb

with a single thrust. Their "weapons" are poor, and their survival depends instead on escape advantages over their predators. In the face of aggression from a fellow species-member, the victim can escape before it is killed, and hence no inhibitions against intraspecies aggression develop. However, when these animals are defeated in a fight and cannot escape, they are indeed often killed by their own kind. Lorenz cites as an example the dove, the symbol of peace, which is capable of torturing another dove to death, and has no built-in inhibitions against such extreme aggression.

In the course of human evolution, argues Lorenz, the inhibiting mechanisms did not evolve. Without a weapon, a human being can rarely kill another human being with a single blow. A potential victim of unarmed aggression has plenty of chance to escape or to evoke pity from the aggressor by gestures, expressions, appeals, promises. The invention of weapons, however, upset the balance. Without inhibitions against aggression—and with the means of inflicting considerable damage—the human situation became "very nearly that of a dove which, by some unnatural trick of nature, has suddenly acquired the beak of a raven" (Lorenz, 1966, p. 241).

Lorenz believes that humanity has, at all stages of its development, been in continual danger of self-destruction. Although his approach differs radically from that of Freud, he has nevertheless come to a conclusion that is quite similar to Freud's concept of sublimation: Lorenz suggests that we should develop more ritualized and channeled forms of aggression that drain off our natural aggressive tendencies.

Critique of Instinctual Theories

In the opinion of many social psychologists, the instinct theories of Lorenz, Freud, and others do not adequately account for human aggression. The prime

Nature does nothing uselessly.
Aristotle

strength of Lorenz's theory is in his detailed observation and analysis of aggression among animals. But Rudolf Schenkel (1967) has also analyzed animal postures and believes that Lorenz's interpretation of some behaviors is wrong. For instance, when a dog or wolf is getting the worst of a fight with another dog or wolf and wants to stop, it stands stiff and offers the side of its neck without any protection. Lorenz says this a gesture of submissiveness; Schenkel, however, believes such gestures can be interpreted in other ways. Many biologists also question Lorenz's thesis; they point out that the presence of a trait in a given species does not necessarily indicate its survival value for that species. Like some organs that serve no obvious function but still are retained (the appendix, for example), a trait can be retained *because* it has no significant negative effects on the survival of the species.

Generally, social psychologists do not agree with the theories of aggression that are rooted in the instincts. Instead, learning and environmental factors are given the upper hand. Bandura (1973), for example, feels that Lorenz's analysis is too simple even for animals. Bandura's standpoint is, of course, that aggression is learned behavior. With this brief examination of instinct theories as a historical perspective, we will move on to examine more closely the social psychological theories of aggression.

Frustration and Aggression Theory

By far the most pervasive theory used by social psychologists to explain aggression, the frustration and aggression theory was developed over 40 years ago by Dollard and his associates (1939, p. 7). They asserted that frustration occurs when something interferes with the achievement of a goal at "its proper time in the behavior sequence." When frustration occurred, the theory went, the natural result was aggression.

The frustration–aggression hypothesis led to a substantial amount of research, and many social psychologists themselves became frustrated because of their repeated failures to verify the frustration–aggression hypothesis. There is no record, however, that frustration in these cases led to aggression. Our little play on words in this paragraph indicates a reason for these research failures: The definition of frustration by Dollard is quite broad.

Evidence for Association of Aggression and Frustration

The evidence to date suggests that aggression may indeed result from *some* forms of frustration. Kulik and Brown (1979) conducted an experiment that demonstrated the effects of frustration on aggression, specifically of frustration that results when progress toward a goal is interrupted. Kulik and Brown told subjects that they could earn money by soliciting pledges to donate to charity over the phone. One group of subjects was told that previous callers had been very successful at obtaining donations, while another group was told that previous callers were much less successful. Subjects then telephoned potential donors, all of whom were experimental accomplices who had been instructed not to pledge any money. Those subjects who expected a high rate of success more often slammed down the phone and made harsh comments than did those whose expectations were lower. In addition, when the frustration was seen as illegitimate (e.g., the potential donors declared that charities were a waste of money), the subjects displayed even more aggressive behavior.

Worchel (1974) devised a laboratory experiment that tested the effects of three types of frustration: random frustration, frustration resulting from expectations not being met, and frustration due to the elimination of a behavioral freedom. The subjects in this study were first asked to rate the attractiveness of three items: a bottle of perfume, cash, and course credit for participating in an experiment. They were then told that they would receive one of these items for participating in a study. One group of subjects was told that the experimenter would assign them one of these items (they were not told which one); another group was told they would receive the item they had rated as most attractive; and a third group was told they could choose the item they wanted.

After completing a task, each subject met another experimenter who arbitrarily gave the subject one of the items, regardless of the subject's preference or attractiveness rating. Worchel claimed that the subjects should have experienced three types of frustration from these manipulations: random frustration when they received an unattractive item despite not having any expectations; frustration from expectations that were not met when they did not receive the item they rated as most attractive; and frustration due to the elimination of a behavioral freedom when they were not permitted to choose the item they desired. Worchel found that when subjects were given the opportunity to act aggressively against a second experimenter by filling out a questionnaire evaluating him for a job, the subjects who had experienced the third type of frustration were significantly more aggressive than the subjects in the other conditions who exhibited little aggression.

In another laboratory experiment (Rule & Percival, 1971), aggression was measured by the level, duration, and the frequency of the shocks that were delivered by the subjects using a Buss aggression machine. Subjects were frustrated in their attempts to "teach" a list of nonsense syllables to an accomplice, and such frustration did lead to heightened aggressiveness as measured by the electrical shocks the subjects thought they were delivering. Frustration was found, however, to interact with other variables—provocation by the accomplice and sympathy for the accomplice—in such a way that called the results of the frustration–aggression experiments into question.

Buss (1963) also used his machine to try and find a link between frustration and aggression. The forms of frustration he investigated were task failure, interference with the attempt to win money, and interference with getting a better course grade. All three did lead to more aggression, as measured by the supposed shocks, compared to the level exhibited by a control group that was not frustrated. But Buss found that the effects of frustration in provoking aggression were slight. He suggested that this was because the available means of aggression had no instrumental value in overcoming the specific frustrations.

These studies, then, indicated that the frustration–aggression formula was oversimplified as an explanation. Indeed, some experiments showed no link whatsoever between the aggression shown by the subjects and their frustration (Gentry, 1970). One experiment employing actual rather than simulated shocks could not, despite a careful design, document any effects on aggression when subjects were frustrated (Taylor & Pisano, 1971).

Refining the Frustration–Aggression Hypothesis

This lack of consistent empirical support for the frustration–aggression hypothesis has led some psychologists to abandon it and others to attempt to refurbish it. Leonard Berkowitz (1965) has been the experimenter most influential in reformulating the frustration–aggression hypothesis. Berkowitz claims that two factors are prerequisites of aggression:

1.   A readiness to act aggressively, which is usually provided by frustration.
2.   External cues that trigger the expression of aggression.

In other words, Berkowitz added the need for a situational influence to the familiar hypothesis. Unless the external conditions indicate to an individual that aggression is appropriate, the potential aggressive behavior will not be expressed. One corollary of this hypothesis is generally referred to as the weapons effect (see box on next page).

UPI photo by Leslie H. Sintay

There is clear evidence of a link between aggression and some forms of frustration. This picture shows one of the many street battles between anti-war demonstrators and city police that erupted in Chicago during the Democratic National Convention in 1968. The news story accompanying it cited "youthful frustrations" at the failure of leading American politicians to heed anti-war protests. Looking at the photo one might well ask about the role of police frustration in precipitating confrontations of this kind.

Controversy: The Weapons Effect

Taking research findings out of the laboratory and trying to apply them to the world at large is a risky affair. What are the practical implications of experimental studies? How far can we make generalizations based upon them? To what extent should government officials, who understand the studies even less than behavioral scientists, base public policy upon them?

The weapons effect was demonstrated by Berkowitz and LePage in 1967, when they found that the mere availability of weapons could increase aggression. One hundred students were asked to take part in an experiment purportedly measuring their physiological reactions to stress. After being told that they would be given mild electric shocks, the students were given the chance to back out of the experiment (none did). Each student was asked to come up with some ideas to help a publicity agent boost the image and record sales of a popular singer. If a partner (really an accomplice of the experimenter who was hooked up to the student via a machine that actually delivered shocks) liked the ideas, the partner would respond with one shock. If the partner found the ideas poor, the response would be several shocks.

The shocks delivered by the partner were determined by the experimental design. Half of the subjects received one shock, and half received seven. Those that received seven shocks would presumably be rendered more aggressive due to the mild pain and the negative evaluation. Subjects then got the chance to trade places with their partners, and to deliver shocks to the person who had shocked them, based again on the quality of the ideas that were presented. One group of students sat at a table with nothing but the shock machine's telegraph key on the table; a second group also found neutral objects (badminton rackets and shuttlecocks) on the table; and the third group found a shotgun and a revolver.

The experiment found what its designers hypothesized: The mere presence of the weapons increased the number and the duration of the shocks that were given. Furthermore, the subjects who received seven shocks gave the most shocks when they saw the guns. As Berkowitz says, "I contended, and still contend, that we sometimes react mindlessly and impulsively to the presence of guns" (Berkowitz, 1981, p. 12).

Several attempts have been made by other researchers to replicate the weapons effect. Leyens and Parke (1975), using slides of guns or neutral objects, found that the subjects shown the guns gave more shocks. Ann Frodi (1975) repeated Berkowitz and LePage's original experiment on a group of Swedish high-school students and got the same results.

Some attempts to replicate the weapons effect have failed, however. One series of experiments (Buss et al., 1976), most of which involved actually firing guns in target practice before delivering the shocks, did not find any weapons effect. Page and Scheidt (1971) found that they were able to obtain the effect only on a third attempt and only with sophisticated subjects who were aware of the purpose of the guns.

How can we account for such conflicting laboratory "evidence"? Page and Scheidt concluded that subjects try to second-guess experimenters, and that "demand effects" (see chapter 2) invalidate experiments that try to study a negative behavior. Leyens and Parke suggest that inhibitions that are evoked by the presence of guns are stronger than aggressive reactions that are also evoked by the guns. This is why these researchers used pictures rather than actual guns—or indeed, rather than firing guns (as in the Buss et al. experiments).

In the face of such varied results, how valid is the weapons effect? Does the finger pull the trigger—or, as Berkowitz argues, does the trigger pull the finger?

The frustration–aggression hypothesis remains just that: a tentative hypothesis. Empirical evidence for it is not strong, and evidence against it exists; we have looked at some examples of both in this section. Berkowitz's addition to the frustration–aggression hypothesis acknowledges that more than one causal variable is at work. However, two variables may still be inadequate to account for aggressive behavior.

Situational Determinants of Aggression

Frustration is not the only condition that evokes aggressive responses in human beings. Social psychologists have examined through research aggression evoked by emotional arousal; deindividuation; verbal and physical attacks; and heat and other environmental factors.

Emotional Arousal

Let us assume that a student goes to the college pool, swims a number of lengths at a swift pace, and then climbs out of the pool. Her body is still in a state of physical arousal. On her way to the shower room someone does something deliberately to taunt her—pushes her, slides a bar of soap at her feet, or calls her an insulting name. How would the student react? Would she react differently if she had just been relaxing instead of working out?

Nonspecific arousal, when it is labeled as anger, is one source of aggressive behavior. Following Schachter's theory of emotions (see chapter 4), any arousal could facilitate aggression if it is labeled as anger. In an experiment by Zillmann and Bryant (1974), some subjects pedaled bicycles to reach a high-arousal condition, and others engaged in a sedentary task to remain at a low-arousal condition. The subjects then played a game with an opponent who was an accomplice of the experimenters, and were attacked verbally by the opponent at one of five levels of intensity. The subjects were given an opportunity to vent their aggression by delivering a harsh noise, supposedly into the opponent's headphones. Predictably, those subjects in the high-arousal condition delivered more noise; and those in this group who were attacked at the highest level of intensity delivered the most. However, high-arousal people also displayed less aggression and more benevolent behavior than their low-arousal counterparts when they were left alone and not attacked.

Not only does general arousal have a powerful effect on the human "animal," but it has an effect that lingers. Following their original study, Bryant and Zillmann (1979) found that even a full week after arousal, subjects who had been in a high-arousal condition demonstrated more aggressiveness when they were annoyed than subjects who had previously been in the low-arousal condition. After such a time lapse, endocrine and other physiological arousal factors could no longer be at work; cognitive factors, such as subject attributions or learning, had to be responsible.

Deindividuation

Individuation means the differentiation of individuals from one another in society. As we show in chapters 4 and 10, **deindividuation** is its opposite, a lack of feelings of distinctiveness and uniqueness, and it has been put forward as one situational determinant of aggression. When people are in a deindividuated state they are, according to Zimbardo (1969), more likely to act aggressively because they feel that the likelihood of being identified is less, and because their social concern is lowered. Zimbardo conducted an experiment in which anonymity was assured to some subjects by not using their names (even the experimenters did not know their names), by having them wear large robes and hoods that masked their faces, and by stressing their shared responsibility for their actions. Another group of subjects wore easy-to-read nametags, were unmasked, and were told that individual reactions were paramount to the experiment. All of the subjects were female students in an introductory psychology class.

The subjects heard a tape recording of an interview between the experimenter and a "victim" who was portrayed either as altruistic and likable, or as obnoxious and self-centered. The subjects were told that this person was being paid to go through a study on conditioning, in which she would receive shocks; the present experiment, which subjects were told was to test empathy judgments, was being combined with the conditioning experiment so that the victim only needed to receive one series of shocks.

The subjects were then seated so that they could not see each other but could see the victim through a one-way glass. They were asked to deliver the electric shocks to her whenever a lamp lit up; and she reacted with signs of extreme pain (simulated; she actually received no shocks).

Aggressiveness in this study was measured by how long the subjects held down the shock keys. As expected, the subjects in the deindividuated condition delivered the shocks for a considerably longer time—about twice as long—as did the subjects in whom individuality had been stressed. Also, the aggressive responses of the deindividuated subjects were unaffected by which of the "victims" (nice or obnoxious) they were supposedly shocking. The individualized subjects, in contrast, shocked the likable "victim" less and less as the experiment progressed, and the obnoxious "victim" more and more. It is worth noting, however, that both groups of subjects did not hesitate to administer the shocks whenever the signal light went on. It should also be noted that there was no "weapons effect" in this experiment, nor was there any incitement toward aggression or violence on the part of either the experimenter or the victim.

Watson (1973) confirmed the effects of deindividuation when he examined war records from 23 different countries. Extreme aggression (e.g., the torture and the execution of the enemy) was more common in those countries whose soldiers used some sort of disguise or otherwise changed their physical appearance when going into battle.

Who overcomes by force hath overcome but half his foe.
John Milton, Paradise Lost

It has also been asserted that modern warfare is both increasingly destructive and deindividuated. Missiles and bombs are launched against unseen enemies by unseen and untouched soldiers and pilots. Not only are combatants increasingly distant from the scene of combat, but because the victims—especially civilians—may never be seen, there is a tendency to dehumanize them as faceless, anonymous, deindividuated "enemies." It has been said that one reason opposition to the war in Vietnam was so intense was that the media—particularly television—helped to individuate both combatants and civilians. Once the war was brought home in living color, showing the faces of real people being hurt, the enemy could not remain a faceless and deindividuated mass target any longer.

Verbal and Physical Attack

Another situational determinant of aggression is direct attack. Research has shown that attacks, both verbal and physical, are very reliable instigators of ag-

For decades, deindividuation came to the aid of white-robed and masked Ku Klux Klan members as they attacked black people and their property in several states. Here a Florida "Imperial Wizard" of the Klan faces an angry, mostly black, crowd. The Klan members, who were conducting a protest demonstration, had to take refuge in a Jacksonville courthouse. A judge placed them under protective custody when the Klan leader, unaware of the irony of the situation, appealed, "Your Honor, I fear for my life!"

gression. For example, Geen (1968) provoked subjects with insults about their intelligence and motivation; these subjects demonstrated more aggression than a group of controls. Using a reciprocal shock-delivery situation, Taylor (1967) found that subjects retaliated with an escalating or decreasing delivery of shocks to an accomplice of the experimenter in direct relationship to the accomplice's increases or decreases in shocks. Further studies have found that a judgment of another person's intent to cause harm affects aggressive reactions (Rule & Ferguson, 1978). In fact, in an experiment involving noise interference with the performance of a task, Dyck and Rule (1978) showed that the provoker's intent was a more important factor than the actual inflicted harm in determining the level of aggressive response.

Heat

"The long hot summer" meant, in the late 1960s and early 1970s, urban riots. The media and popular wisdom held that hot weather encouraged violence. The annual crime reports of The Federal Bureau of Investigation supported this view (see Figure 11–1).

Baron and Ransberger (1978) reviewed archival data to determine the relationship between the weather and 102 serious riots that took place in American cities between 1967 and 1971. They found that the popular view was correct up to a point: The likelihood of a riot increased as the temperature rose, reaching a peak when the thermometer read 81° to 85°F. But at higher temperatures the probability of riots decreased. The implication was that, while heat may indeed lead to aggression, very hot weather discourages it.

Carlsmith and Anderson (1979), however, questioned these findings. After reexamining the same data, they found that there were more riots when the temperature was 81° to 85°F simply because there were more days in the year in that temperature range, and that riots were more likely to occur on any given day as temperatures became higher.

Despite the differences of opinion between them, Baron and Ransberger (1978) and Carlsmith and Anderson (1979) agree that there is a relationship between hot weather and riots. What these studies do not indicate, of course, is the possible influence of other environmental or situational factors that might be associated with hot weather, such as seasonal unemployment. The influence of the environment on aggressive behavior will be discussed in more detail in chapter 14.

Drugs and Alcohol

The image of the drunken husband terrorizing his wife and children was much used a century ago by the Temperance Movement to point out the evils of alcohol. Is violent behavior stimulated by the use of liquor and drugs? The stimuli that affect aggression are not only cognitive, as are the stimuli that affect modeling behavior or the exposure to violent pornography. Some stimuli are purely physiological, as are heat and the topics of this section, alcohol and marijuana.

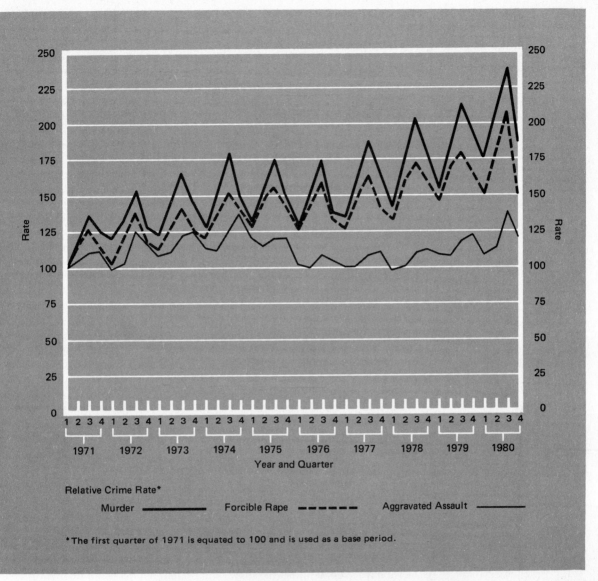

FIGURE 11-1. Seasonal trends in aggressive crimes, 1971–1980

Shown here are 10-year rates for murder, forcible rape, and aggravated assault, by quarter. For all three of these aggressive crimes, peak periods are the generally warmer months of the third quarter of the year, and rates are lowest in the cold winter months of the first quarter. The rate for murder, however, seems to rise in the third quarter and maintain its higher level longer, often until the end of the year (e.g., 1977–1979). The sharper increase in rates of rape since 1971 is accounted for, according to many observers, by improved reporting of this crime.

Source: *Adapted from* Uniform Crime Reports for the United States, *Federal Bureau of Investigation, U.S. Department of Justice, 1980, pp. 357, 359, 363.*

Taylor and his associates (1976) tested 50 male students to compare the effects of alcohol and marijuana on aggression. The subjects received one of five doses: alcohol in a high dosage, alcohol in a low dosage, marijuana in a high dosage, marijuana in a low dosage, or peppermint oil. The drugs were mixed in with a glass of ginger ale. For the marijuana, a concentrated solution of tetrahydrocannabinol—the chief chemical intoxicant of marijuana—was used. The subjects were told that the experiment involved ingesting either alcohol or marijuana (both true), or librium (not true), but they did not know which one they were given.

Once the drugs had taken effect, each student was placed in a cubicle, an electrode was attached to his wrist, and he was told that he would compete in a reaction-time study with someone else in the next room. He was asked to press one of ten buttons corresponding to the shock intensity he wanted his opponent to receive when the opponent was slower at a given task. The subject was also told that he would receive the shock his opponent set for him if the opponent were faster at a trial.

The trials then began. The "opponent" was really the experimenter, who increasingly provoked his subject by administering higher levels of the actual shocks as the trials progressed. For each trial, the subject was allowed to reset the shock intensity that he thought his opponent would receive if he lost, and these settings were taken as the measure of aggression. Subjects who received a small dose of either alcohol or marijuana were slightly less aggressive than the peppermint-oil control group. When larger doses of the drugs were consumed, however, a clear difference between alcohol and marijuana emerged. The subjects who had been given a heavy dose of alcohol used the most intense shock settings of any group, while the subjects who had received a heavy dose of marijuana delivered the lowest level of shocks.

It is interesting to note that several studies of crime statistics have emphasized the link between alcohol and crime. For instance, Wolfgang and Strohm (1956) examined homicide statistics over a 5-year period and found that in only 36 percent of the cases was alcohol "entirely absent" as a factor contributing to the homicides.

Modeling and Aggression

Train up a child in the way he should go: and when he is old, he will not part from it.
Proverbs 22:6

If, as we have seen, aggressive behavior in human beings is not instinctive, then it must be learned. Social psychologists generally agree that individuals learn this (and other) behavior by modeling. The old saying "monkey see, monkey do" certainly applies quite visibly to young children and, according to social learning theory, to the rest of us as well. Bandura's social learning theory, as we saw in chapter 3, emphasizes two processes: reinforcement and imitation. Reinforcement helps to develop aggressive behavior, since children are often rewarded for such behavior. The rewards may take the form of praise from adults for certain types of behaviors ("I like to see you stick up for your rights"). Aggressive behavior can also be rewarded directly, as when a child uses aggression to take a toy away from another child. Or the rewards may be vicarious, as when a child sees another child take a toy from somebody else. A great deal of laboratory evidence supports the contention that reinforcement helps to develop aggressive behavior (Bandura, 1973; Cowan & Walters, 1963; Geen & Stoner, 1971).

The second key process at work in social learning theory is imitation. A child who sees an admired adult or peer behaving aggressively is very likely to reproduce such behavior. Bandura has amply demonstrated this in his laboratory studies of 3 to 5-year-olds who observed an adult sitting on a 5-foot version of the Bobo doll, punching it repeatedly in the nose, striking it with a mallet, throwing it in the air, and kicking it around the room—abusing the doll verbally all the while. The children who watched that performance duplicated it when they were given a Bobo doll, while children who had viewed a nonaggressive adult were notably less aggressive (Bandura, Ross, & Ross, 1961).

In a related study, the experimenters found that children more readily imitated a person who gave them positive rewards (fascinating toys and snacks) than one who gave the rewards to someone else (Bandura, Ross, & Ross, 1963a). It has also been found that models who are rewarded for aggressive behavior are more likely to be imitated than models who are not rewarded (Bandura, 1965; Walters & Willows, 1968). Other studies strongly suggest that modeling effects occur within the family; Not only do the children of criminals tend to become criminals (McCord, McCord, & Zloa, 1959), but conventional middle-class parents who behave aggressively and reinforce such behavior in their children, also end up with aggressive children (Bandura, 1960; Bandura & Walters, 1959).

In a variation of the original Bobo doll experiments, aggressive models shown on film were found to have, like the live models, the effect of increasing both imitative and general aggression; films of violent cartoon characters had the same effect as those depicting real people. As we saw in chapter 7, violence on television does influence the behavior of adults as well as children, and leads to skewed perceptions of the extent of violence in the real world.

In a laboratory experiment, children observed an adult hitting a Bobo doll with a mallet (left). Shortly afterward, given the opportunity, they exhibited similarly aggressive behavior (center and right).

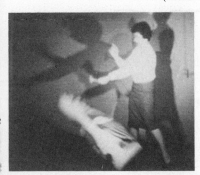

Media and Modeling

If modeling of aggressive behavior is in fact one source of such behavior, we would expect to find some evidence of this not only in the laboratory but also in real life. In fact, there are periodic news reports of aggressive acts modeled after those which people have seen on television and in the movies. In 1973 in Boston a group of youths doused a young woman with gasoline and set her on fire; the woman was fatally burned. Two days earlier a similar incident had appeared in a nationally televised film, *Fuzz*. A few years later a 15-year-old Florida youth who had killed an elderly neighbor, used as his defense the claim that he had been crazed by watching violence in television programs such as Kojak. There have been periodic reports of violence breaking out after young adults viewed the gang warfare movie *The Warriors*, and more recently there have been news stories concerning "accidental" suicides by people imitating the Russian roulette scenes in the movie *Deerhunter*. A flurry of such deaths were reported after the film was shown on cable television. And in 1981 the nation was shocked by an attempted assassination of President Reagan by a young man who admitted that his acts were inspired by television and film violence (see box).

It is perhaps not surprising that movies and television can have such prominent modeling effects, since they are graphic media that literally draw the viewer into the picture. However, a modeling effect has also been observed to follow newspaper accounts of violent episodes. In a series of studies, for example, Philips has found support for modeling after highly publicized events. In 1974 he reported that the national level of suicides increased following newspaper accounts of suicides (including, most dramatically, a 12 percent increase following the suicide of actress Marilyn Monroe). His 1978 research found an increase in airplane accident deaths following newspaper accounts of murders and suicides related to air travel. In 1979 he reported that motor vehicle deaths increased by 31 percent three days after news accounts of suicides; the greatest increase was for single-car accidents, which are often suicides in disguise; moreover, the percentage increases were related to the amount of publicity received by a given news story. In 1980 Philips reported that homicides dropped nearly 36 percent immediately following highly publicized executions, but within several weeks the number of homicides increased by an equal amount. It thus appears that the death penalty, if it does have a deterrent effect (as its supporters claim), has only a very short-lived one.

Philips's research suggests that modeling effects are stronger when the antisocial behaviors are publicized than when the punishment is publicized. Further support for the modeling effects of antisocial acts is supplied by Mazur (1982), who found that bomb threats increase following news reports of bomb threats.

Violent Pornography and Aggression

Does pornography have a modeling effect? Do men who view scenes of sex-related violence translate the screen images into aggression toward real women?

Much public concern has been expressed on this issue. The President's Commission on Obscenity and Pornography set out in 1971 to determine whether

Application: "Media Freak" Attempts Assassination

It was 7:20 P.M., network evening news time, on March 30, 1981, when the Secret Service began interrogating John W. Hinckley Jr., five hours after the shooting of President Reagan.

The young man had one question of his own: "Is it on TV?"

"It's about the only thing that is on television," replied agent Steven Colo, to Mr. Hinckley's evident satisfaction.

A significant aspect of the Hinckley case, say those acquainted with the history and the record of his examinations, is the "media factor."

He emerges from this record as a "media freak" who felt impelled to proclaim his identity by starring in a media event.

Nearly 27, he is of a generation that has lived with television since birth. The psychiatric reports indicated that the more he retreated from family and peer relationships, the more he embraced violent fantasy. In the months before the shooting, Mr. Hinckley spent thousands of hours in hotel rooms watching television alone. . . .

He [has] said that watching so much television was not a good way to pass the time because "a fantasy life" that can be "quite dangerous" tends to develop "the longer a person stays in front of the tube."

Mr. Hinckley has talked of "hypnotic movies," especially the film "Taxi Driver," which he saw several times in theaters and once on television. He speaks of Travis Bickle, the gun-slinging hero of the film, as his model. When asked why he had bought so many handguns, Mr. Hinckley replied: "I bought so many handguns because Travis bought so many handguns. Ask him, not me." . . .

Responding to the perverse incentives offered by our media culture, Mr. Hinckley, to put it objectively, accomplished his purpose. He has become a celebrity in the medium that celebrates violence. His "historic deed" has conferred identity upon him for all time.

But even as he joined the hall of fame of presidents' assailants, Mr. Hinckley appeared concerned about future emulators. While expressing pleasure on March 30, 1981, that his action was dominating television, he reflected: "That's too bad, because it's going to affect other people."

Source: © 1982 by The New York Times Company. Reprinted by permission.

a link existed between viewing pornography and aggressive behavior. Although many studies were conducted to this end, no link was demonstrated. For instance, in one study male subjects were exposed to massive quantities of pornographic movies, photographs, magazines, and books for 1½ hours a day for 15 consecutive days. No detrimental effect on attitudes—extensively surveyed both at the beginning and at the end of the experiment—could be found. Physiological measures of the subjects' sexual arousal showed that interest in and response to pornography actually decreased with exposure to it. The investigators concluded that "pornography is an innocuous stimulus which leads quickly to satiation and that public concern over it is misplaced" (Howard, Liptzin, & Reifler, 1973, p. 133). The President's Commission came to similar conclusions.

Exposure to mild erotic stimuli has even been shown, in laboratory experiments involving Buss aggression machines, to reduce aggressive behavior

(Baron & Bell, 1973; Frodi, 1977). But one experiment that confirmed this also found that highly erotic stimuli led to greater aggression (Donnerstein, Donnerstein, & Evans, 1975).

The consensus—of the President's Commission on Obscenity and Pornography in 1971, and of most behavioral scientists who have continued to investigate the matter since then—is that most pornography is harmless. Yet one area of concern remains: pornography that portrays violence against women.

The Commission did not adequately address stimuli that combine aggression and sexuality. Aggressive pornography—pornography that depicts rape and other coercive rather than voluntary sexual acts—was relatively rare in earlier years. Recent reports have suggested, however, that aggression has become increasingly prevalent in sexually oriented materials (Malamuth & Spinner, 1980). Social psychologists have begun to study the effects of this form of pornography on sexual arousal, attitudes toward rape, and aggression against women.

Does violent pornography lead to actual interpersonal violence against women? In a laboratory context, exposure to aggressive pornography increases the aggression of men against women but does not seem to influence the aggression of men against other men (Donnerstein, 1980; Donnerstein & Berkowitz, 1982; Donnerstein, in press).

Some research has indicated that depictions of aggressive sexual acts result

What effect, if any, does pornography have on violent behavior and aggression? The findings to date are mixed. Indications are, though, that violent pornography does make some men more likely to behave violently, while mild pornography seems to have little effect on normal men's attitudes or behavior.

in less arousal than depictions of nonaggressive sexual acts; only rapists are pleased by scenes of rape (Abel et al., 1977). Other studies, however, suggest that even a nonrapist population can be sexually aroused by rape depictions in some circumstances, such as when the victim is shown as enjoying the experience of being raped (Malamuth, Haber, & Feshbach, 1980; Malamuth, Heim, & Feshbach, 1980).

Such depictions can also produce a lessened sensitivity to rape, by reinforcing the "rape myth," shown to be held by convicted rapists, that women secretly enjoy being raped; it is, of course, *not* the case that women enjoy being raped. (Malamuth & Check, 1981; Malamuth & Check, in press). Evidence also exists to suggest that exposure to violent pornography causes men to have rape fantasies (Malamuth et al., in press). In one study, over half of the men who viewed violent pornography "indicated some likelihood that they themselves would rape if assured of not being punished" (Malamuth, Haber, & Feshbach, 1980, p. 122).

In an era in which "adult films" are available not only on 42nd Street in New York but to everyone who can own or rent a video-cassette player, questions about the influence of pornography on behavior remain. Findings that mild pornography has little influence on normal men's behavior or attitudes is reassuring, but to many people that is almost beside the point. Findings that men are more accepting of the "rape myth" ("they really want it") after viewing scenes of a victim "apparently" enjoying being raped indicate cause for real concern. So do findings of increased aggression toward women after viewing violent pornography.

While we may not yet know as much as we would like about all the effects of pornography on behavior, we do know that it is not socially harmless. Any depiction of abuse of one person or group of people by another implicitly dehumanizes the victims, who in these materials are usually women but may also be young boys. Clearly there is a fine line, one that can only be drawn by the courts, between First Amendment rights of freedom to publish (or produce films), and society's interest in curbing materials that may lead to antisocial behavior. The fact that the courts have been grappling with these questions for decades indicates that the answers are complex and, moreover, change with community standards over time.

Media Violence against Women

Feminists such as Susan Brownmiller (1975) have contended that mass media portrayals of violence against women lead to the acceptance of nonsexual as well as sexual violence perpetrated on women in real life. They further contend that the acceptance of violence within a culture leads to a greater incidence of violent acts, deters victims from reporting violent offenses, and decreases society's outrage at these crimes. As we have seen, Donnerstein (1980) among others found that exposure to violent pornography increased the levels of electric shocks delivered by male subjects to a female confederate of the experimenter. But nearly all of this research has been conducted in laboratory settings, using the kind of pornographic material few of us have seen. What influence do media portrayals of violence against women have on us in real life?

Malamuth and Check (1981) decided to test the feminist charge that movies portraying violence against women have adverse effects on viewers, using films many of us have probably seen. They recruited 271 introductory psychology students to participate in, as they were told, a pilot study designed to develop general measures for rating movies. The students were given tickets to two films being shown as part of a campus cinema program. Students in the experimental group received tickets to *Swept Away* (on a deserted island, a woman is "swept away" into a tender romance with a man who had previously physically abused and raped her), and *Getaway* (a woman falls in love with her assailant). Students in the control group received tickets for *Hooper* (about an aging stuntman and his compassionate woman friend) and *A Man and A Woman* (a tender romance).

One week after they viewed the second film, all subjects were contacted by a "public opinion center" and asked to complete an "attitude survey." Embedded in the survey were questions designed to measure the acceptance of interpersonal violence (i.e., "a man is never justified in hitting his wife"). Malamuth and Check found that male subjects who had viewed *Getaway* and *Swept Away* were significantly more accepting of interpersonal violence against women than those who had seen the control films.

Violence by Women

Woman [is] the female of the human species, and not a different kind of animal.
George Bernard Shaw, Preface, Saint Joan

We have already touched on the possible effects of violent pornography on violence *toward* women. Murder and rape are the most extreme forms of violence against women. But what about violence committed *by* women? Female perpetrators of crimes (except murders) are on the increase. In 1980, about one in seven identified murderers was female. Female offenders accounted for: one in eight aggravated assault offenders (aggravated assault means the attempt to inflict severe bodily harm); almost one in three larcenies (thefts without force, such as shoplifting); and about one in fourteen robberies (thefts by force or threat of force) (Uniform Crime Reports, 1981).

It is noteworthy that the biggest female criminal activity is larceny, which is nonviolent; nationally, males accounted for 90 percent of all *violent* crime arrests (for murder, rape, robbery, and aggravated assault), and 84 percent of all arrests (Uniform Crime Reports, 1981). The feminist position that aggression is essentially a male problem is partly supported by crime statistics.

But for many years now women have apparently been committing more crimes. The first significant increase in crimes committed by women was noted during the Second World War, when such crimes nearly doubled and crime patterns for women came to resemble those of men (Adler, 1975). More recently, the arrest rate for women engaged in violent crimes jumped 18.5 percent between 1971 and 1980 (Uniform Crime Reports, 1981).

Suggested Causes The increase in arrest rates for women has given rise to questions about causes. One explanation is that the increase may appear greater than it actually is. Improved reporting may account for the higher figures; in 1950 Pollak believed that women's crimes were underreported. (His reasoning would be considered sexist today. Pollak explained that crimes by women could be easily hidden, and women were deceitful by nature. He also felt that women would commit more crimes if they had more opportunity; they were, for example, less likely than men to be out at night, and thus less likely to commit crimes such as arson that are best performed under cover of darkness.)

More recently, it has been charged that the women's movement, in encouraging equality, has been encouraging equal criminality as well. Another version of this thesis states that since women are less occupied with traditional activities such as mothering and homemaking, they have more time and opportunity for negative activities (Katzeff, 1977). There seems little support for this point of view; studies have found that the majority of women sentenced to prison for their criminal activities were traditional in orientation. Most were, however, poor, held low-paying unskilled jobs, and had few economic resources. In one study of 1,600 imprisoned women, 60 percent had been married, but only 10 percent were living with a spouse at the time of sentencing (The Women's Movement and Crime, 1977). The presumption, then, is strong that property crimes committed by women have a primarily economic motivation.

If the women's movement has had an influence, we may suppose it to be in encouraging women to act in self-defense when attacked or provoked. Wolfgang (1958) found that, compared to the victims of male murderers, the victims of female murderers were twice as likely to have committed the first aggressive act. This view receives some support when the situations in which women kill are analyzed. Ward and his associates (1969) found that women generally acted alone when committing murder, although they often served as accessories during burglaries and robberies; that they were more likely to kill their husbands, lovers, or other family members than unrelated people; that most of their murders were unpremeditated; and that 19 percent of their victims were children, and 42 percent were elderly, ill, sleeping or intoxicated—in other words, more than half of the persons killed by women were unable to put up a significant struggle.

The Influence of Socialization   Despite the increase in violent crimes committed by women, the rate of violence among women is still a fraction of that of men. Many social psychologists point to the differences in socialization between boys and girls as the primary reason for this difference in aggressiveness. Bartol (1980) has summarized some of these differences in socialization. In various ways, boys learn early that aggression is a mark of masculinity. In regions where hunting is popular, for example, boys are taught early to handle firearms. Boys are also continually exposed to aggressive male models such as football players and gun-toting detectives.

The traditional social training of girls has been markedly different, and women's recent movement toward equality in many areas has not (fortunately!) been translated into equal opportunity for aggressive socialization. Parents generally discourage aggressive behavior in their daughters, who are taught to handle anger-provoking situations in a passive way. (Indeed, women generally recoil from the very word "aggressive," and even feminists speak of the need to be "assertive" in situations where men would use the more violent term.) Even the most active female models available to girls today tend to act passively, according to Bartol:

Wonder Woman, Isis, and the Bionic Woman are relatively unaggressive characters compared to Superman, Batman, and other male models. The female prototype of justice-for-all exerts just enough "passive" force [repelling bullets] to terminate attacks on herself and the others she protects, without appearing overly aggressive. (p. 282)

In reviewing the literature on women's violence, Bartol found that women express more guilt feelings about aggressive behavior than men do. Women also demonstrate more empathy with their victims than men. The relationship between empathy and lack of aggressiveness is not fully known. However, Bartol does speculate that the ability to empathize with the victim is probably one factor inhibiting female aggressiveness.

There is also evidence that aggressive situations are perceived differently by women than by men. Men, for example, are more likely to find aggressiveness in an ambiguous story, and women seem to have a higher "boiling point" than men, which makes them less likely to react violently to weak or ambiguous provocations. Bartol concludes that:

Overall, when we examine the available aggression models, the reinforcement patterns, and the conditioning attitudes of the American culture, we see that the opportunities to acquire aggressive and violent behavior are clearly in favor of males. Furthermore, this socialization process begins early. Aggressive behavioral patterns established at age eight appear to be by far the best predictor of aggressive behavior in later life. As early as age three, there appears to be a strong tendency for boys to engage in more vigorous, destructive, and aggressive play than girls. (p. 283)

The Victims of Violence

It is estimated that a forcible rape occurs every 6 minutes in the United States. In addition, 23 percent of murder victims in 1980 were female (Uniform Crime Reports, 1981).

Victims of aggression often find it difficult to gain the social support they need after being victimized. The results of one study suggest that failure to gain support from society may be due in part to the ways victims "portray" themselves (Coates et al., 1979). Over 200 male and female subjects, who believed they were evaluating materials for possible use in a community crime-awareness program, listened individually to a tape-recorded account of an attack on a rape victim. Following the description, the "victim" answered an interviewer's questions on the tape, such as, "Do you feel in any way responsible for what happened?" Some subjects heard the victim reply that the rape was largely her fault, while other subjects heard her reply that the event was due to chance. After the questions and answers were finished, the subjects were then asked various questions themselves to tap their attitudes toward the rape victim.

In general, the subjects appeared to be making "defensive" attributions—blaming the victim is one way for people to avoid confronting the possibility that they themselves could become victims. The subjects' attitudes were more favorable when the victim appeared to have regained her balance after the attack than when she still suffered the consequences, and when she accepted some respon-sibility for the attack. Subjects who were told that the incidence of rape in their neighborhood was high seemed to perceive themselves as likely to encounter a similar fate, and were also more sympathetic. In other words, the amount of sym-pathy for the victim was due to factors unrelated to the violent act itself.

Coates and his colleagues believe, moreover, that their findings point to ad-ditional hurdles for victims. For instance, rape victims tend to be wary of men and to avoid them for some time after an attack. The victims turn to other women for support; but in the experiment, while women empathized more with the vic-tim, they also blamed her more and expressed more derogatory feelings toward her. It seems that people generally react negatively to victims precisely when they are most worried, frightened, vulnerable, and most in need of company and understanding.

Although, as we have often seen, any leap from the laboratory to the real world must be made with caution, the difficulties of victims would seem to be worsened by the reactions of others. One can only welcome the increase in re-cent years of rape hotlines and victim advice services—which exist in most metro-politan areas. Through these organizations—if nowhere else—victims can en-counter people who really do grasp their need for aid and understanding.

Fear of Violence

Most of us read newspapers or at least glance at the news on television. Even if we could manage to avoid both for a period of weeks, we would still hear people around us discussing the more catastrophic events that they learned of through the media. Partly because of the competition among nations, partly because vio-lence is always dramatic and attention-grabbing, a substantial proportion of the news describes violence, including violence perpetrated on people like our-selves. Short of finding ourselves on a desert island, we are seldom unaware of the violent events portrayed in the media.

We saw in chapter 7 that people who watched television a lot overestimated the extent of violence in the real world. We often hear of people who fear to visit large cities because "crime is everywhere and you can't even walk in the streets." In the cities people are reported to seldom leave their homes for fear of being at-tacked. Are such anecdotal accounts a reflection of widespread fear? Or are they exaggerations, unrepresentative opinions held by a few unrealistic people?

One survey seems to shed light on this question. The Figgie Report (*New York Times*, September 21, 1980) used a telephone survey of 1,047 American adults to investigate their fear of crime. Of the respondents, 40 percent were "highly fearful" that they would become victims of murder, rape, robbery, or assault. (In point of fact, the actual odds of being murdered in a given year are about 1 in 11,000; of being raped, 1 in 1,700; robbed, 1 in 525; assaulted, 1 in 385.) Respondents were fearful to the point that 86 percent routinely identified visitors before letting them into their homes, 52 percent owned guns, 67 percent were in favor of the death penalty, and 45 percent thought forced sterilization should be performed on habitual criminals.

The Figgie Report concludes that, given such a high level of fear, the Ameri-can people have changed the way they live: they have become more reclusive, dress unobtrusively, and travel more cautiously. Strangely, however, the fearful respondents included not only those people who are in fact most often the victims of violence—the poor, minorities, and ghetto dwellers—but also those people who are least often the victims—the more affluent and more educated. Why? The survey suggests that one reason may be that everyone is exposed daily to reports of violence on television and in the newspapers. This could explain why the fear the survey tapped is so out of proportion with the actual crime rate, especially for the more affluent.

In another interesting study, also a telephone survey, Lewis and Maxfield (1980) investigated the fear of crime at the neighborhood level. They chose four Chicago neighborhoods of widely varying socioeconomic status and condition, studied the actual crime rates in the neighborhoods, and compared these to the residents' perceptions of the crime rates. Again, even in the more dangerous neighborhoods, people's fears were excessive compared to the actual crime levels. The researchers concluded that "citizens' perceptions of crime are shaped not so much by the neighborhood conditions reflected in the crime statistics, but rather by the level of incivility in their communities" (p. 160). By "incivility" the authors mean signs of disorder in the neighborhood, such as abandoned buildings, vandalism, drug use, and loitering teenagers. These things exacerbate neighborhood residents' fear of crime, although they may in fact have very little relationship to how much serious crime actually takes place in a neighborhood:

> Loud boisterous groups of teenagers or skid row denizens may be perceived as more dangerous than muggers and purse snatchers who take pains to be inconspicuous. Also, abandoned buildings and empty streets may generate more fear than do the private residences where violent personal crimes most often occur. (p. 179)

It would seem that the fear of crime can be influenced by exposure to media accounts of crimes and by neighborhood conditions, both of which may be inaccurate indications of how really dangerous an area is, and by the probability of being victimized. While this does not reduce the problem of a crime rate that has in fact risen steadily in recent years, it does suggest that fear of violence has so affected people's lives as to be a problem itself.

Does Violence Beget Violence?

There never was a good war or a bad peace.
Benjamin Franklin

That violence is not an innate human behavior is shown by the existence of societies such as the Yaruro of Venezuela and the Pueblo Indians of the United States, where it is not found.

Margaret Mead (1935 and 1963) described the Arapesh as a society in which

> warfare is practically unknown. . . . [although] brawls and clashes between villages do occur. . . . The beginning of hostilities they regard as an unfortunate accident [and] not unfriendly acts on the part of the next community. . . . [C]lashes between hamlets start in angry conversation, the aggrieved party coming, armed but not committed to fighting, into the village of the

offenders. An altercation follows . . . [which] may progress from reproach to insult, until the most volatile and easily angered person hurls a spear. [But] this is not a signal for a general fracas. . . . [The] carefully recorded exchange of spears in which the aim is to wound lightly, not to kill, goes on until someone is rather badly wounded, when the members of the attacking party immediately take to their heels. Later, peace is made by an interchange of rings, each man giving a ring to the man whom he has wounded. (pp. 24, 25)

Even in our own society, our moral attitude is opposed to violence. Indeed, violence and aggression would seem to be forbidden by the Judeo–Christian tradition, which tells warriors to "beat [their] swords into plowshares . . . neither shall they learn war anymore," (Isaiah 2:4) as well as to "turn the other cheek." But that same tradition has also glorified warfare for a just cause, leaving it to each generation, in its time and place, to determine what constitutes a just war. As history has shown, the causes of war are many and varied—but seldom absent from our world for long.

War is, of course, violence sanctioned by the government. What effect does this institutionalized violence have on violence in society as a whole? Archer and Gartner (1976) noted that during the Vietnam War the murder rate in the United States more than doubled; this increase followed a nearly 30-year decline. This data seem to contradict some other theories. In 1906, for example, Sumner maintained that wars produced "social solidarity" within the warring societies, and therefore internal rates of violence should decrease. Another predominant theory, the catharsis model (which we will discuss further in the next section), maintains that wars are a good substitute for individual tendencies toward violence, and consequently murder and other violent crime rates should decrease during periods of warfare.

War and Violence in other Cultures In view of these theories, Archer and Gartner examined postwar homicide rates by using a Comparative Crime Data file that contained homicide statistics for more than 100 nations. They found that most nations that had been at war experienced a dramatic increase in postwar homicide rates (see Table 11–1). These increases did not occur in nations that had not been at war. Furthermore, this increase in homicides occurred for both men and women after small-scale wars as well as large-scale wars, and in losing nations as well as those that won.

The researchers concluded that the notions that war results in increased solidarity or has a cathartic effect on domestic violence does not hold up. Instead, the data seem to support a legitimation model that maintains that government sanctioning of killing during a war spills over into civilian life immediately after the war. This theory was eloquently summarized, Archer and Gartner point out, by the Reverend Charles Parsons during World War I:

When the rules of civilized society are suspended, when killing becomes a business and a sign of valor and heroism, when the wanton destruction of peaceable women and children becomes an act of virtue, and is praised as a service to God and Country, then it seems almost useless to talk about crime in an ordinary sense (1917, p. 267).

TABLE 11–1.

Homicide Rate Changes after World Wars I and II

	Homicide Rate Change					
	Decrease	Percent	Relatively Unchanged	Percent	Increase	Percent
Combatant Nations	Australia (I)	−23	England (I)	−5	Belgium (I)	24
	Canadaª (I)	−25	France (I)	4	Bulgariaª (I)	22
	Hungary (I)	−57	S. Africaª (I)	−1	Germany (I)	98
	Finland (II)	−15	Canadaᵇ (II)	6	Italy (I)	52
	N. Ireland (II)	−83			Japan (I)	12
	U.S.ᵇ (II)	−12			Portugal (I)	47
					Scotland (I)	50
					U.S. (I)	13
					Australia (II)	32
					Denmarkᶜ (II)	169
					England (II)	13
					France (II)	51
					Italy (II)	133
					Japan (II)	20
					Netherlandsᵇ (II)	13
					New Zealand (II)	313
					Norway (II)	65
					Scotland (II)	11
					S. Africa (II)	104
Control Nations	Norway (I)	−37	Ceylon (I)	8	Finland (I)	124
	Ceylon (II)	−19	Chile (I)	−3	Thailand (I)	112
	Chile (II)	−67	Netherlands (I)	−2	Colombia (II)	34
	El Salvador (II)	−20			Sweden (II)	14
	Ireland (II)	−22			Turkey (II)	12
	Switzerlandª (II)	−42				
	Thailand (II)	−17				

ªCrimes against the person; homicide included. ᵇMurder and manslaughter.
ᶜDenmark is included because it was occupied, although it never declared war.

Note: Roman numerals I and II in parentheses following name of nation refer to World War I and World War II.
     Minus sign (−) denotes decrease.

Source: Adapted from "Violent Acts and Violent Times: A Comparative Approach to Postwar Homicide Rapes," by D. Archer & R. Gartner, *American Sociological Review*, 1976, *41*, 937–962.

Reducing Aggression

In this chapter we have considered the sources and some of the effects of violence and aggression. We have seen that aggression may have aided the evolution of the human species, and we have briefly looked at the differences made by the availability of tools for violence—specifically, Lorenz's belief that humans did not develop a prohibition against violence among themselves (intraspecies violence) because they were not naturally able to kill one another without weapons. We saw that the accessibility of weapons can encourage aggression—the "weapons effect."

History has shown clearly the paradoxical role of violence in the development of civilization. Every war has dwarfed its predecessors in violence as more advanced methods of destruction were developed. Today the tools of war—institutionalized aggression—can spell an end to human civilization.

On an individual scale, virtually every year sees an increase in the violent crime rate in our country. Only disturbed or abused people would attempt to defend murder, rape, child and spouse abuse, and assault. Clearly, it would be desirable to reverse this trend. But can aggression be reduced? And how?

Catharsis

What do you do when you get "fighting mad"? Do you go out and do battle? Run around the block three times? Count to ten? Work out in the gym? Study all night? Sit and simmer? If you run around the block, study all night, or work out in the gym you are practicing *catharsis*, the use of other activities to provide a safe emotional release. It has been proposed that there are two kinds of catharsis:

1. Arousal reduction. Doing something—anything—when one is angry expresses the aggression and thus reduces the general level of emotional arousal. In other words, shouting instead of hitting a person vents enough aggression to lower the arousal level below the boiling point.
2. Aggression reduction. Any expression of aggression may make a subsequent expression unnecessary by decreasing the level of aggression one feels.

Geen and Quantz (1977), who reviewed studies dealing with the first form of catharsis, found some support for an arousal-reduction effect in some circumstances. The second form of catharsis appears even less effective. Konečni (1975), for example, tested the proposition with a Buss machine experiment and found that one act of aggression did not reduce the likelihood of a second; instead, it usually led to further aggression.

Social Learning and Control

To find a more satisfactory method for reducing aggression, social psychologists have turned to social learning theory. Albert Bandura and his colleagues (1963a, b), for example, have shown that when children watch a film of an aggressive person who is rewarded for that behavior, they become more aggressive under conditions that are similar to those in the film than do children who viewed models who were punished for being aggressive. But seeing a model punished for aggressiveness does not decrease subsequent aggressive behavior to levels below those of control group children who saw no model at all. Children may, therefore, be best off by never seeing an aggressive model at all. By con-

Social learning theory suggests that children may develop into nonaggressive citizens if they never see aggressive behavior. That would probably not be possible in today's media-oriented society. Perhaps training in karate and similar highly structured "martial arts" is one solution. In Tae Kwon Do, for example, novices (such as the youngsters shown here) learn to use force only in self-defense, and are first taught a nonviolent but quite intimidating vocal and body movement form of attack.

trolling social learning experiences, society and parents can reduce the aggression to which children are exposed. The amount of aggressive behavior displayed by parents and other models, and the aggressive images shown on television, can all be decreased. In their place, models can demonstrate acceptable nonaggressive behaviors.

That observation of nonaggressive models leads to development of nonaggressive behaviors has been demonstrated by other studies. This is especially true of models who are respected, and when the models are seen being rewarded for their nonaggressive behavior. Baron and Kepner (1970) tested 72 students on the effects of a peer model—another student—on their aggressive behavior, as expressed with a Buss machine. Some subjects saw the model as attractive (rewarded) and some as unattractive; some saw the model behaving aggressively and some nonaggressively. Generally, those subjects who had seen a nonaggressive model delivered lower level shocks, while those subjects who had viewed an attractive and aggressive model delivered the highest level of shocks.

Comparable results have been obtained in similar experiments by Donner-stein and Donnerstein (1977) and Baron (1971). In Baron's experiment, not only did the subjects view aggressive and nonaggressive models, but some groups of subjects viewed them in combination: they viewed either the nonaggressive models first, or the aggressive models first. Both groups of subjects exposed to both models showed lower aggression than subjects who had viewed only an aggressive model. The sequence in which the models were viewed did make a significant difference; however, the subjects who viewed the nonaggressive models *before* seeing the aggressive models had the lowest level of aggression of all the groups.

Baron suggests that this effect might be applied to the prevention and control of crowd violence—that is, a nonaggressive model might be effective in averting such violence, particularly if potential rioters were exposed to the model's restrained behavior before being exposed to any violence from aggressive models. The other experimenters also suggest that their findings have practical applications in the real world, and underscore the importance of nonaggressive models in reducing aggressive behavior.

Answering Questions about Aggression and Violence

1. There does not seem to be any evidence to date that as a species humans are naturally aggressive. In fact, in some cultures aggressive acts are virtually unheard of. Rather, aggression appears to be a learned response to frustration and a socially acceptable means to some positive end.

2. There is a definite link between continued exposure to violence in television and in the movies and aggressive behavior, particularly among children.

3. Exposure to depictions of violence against women, even in mass exposure films such as *Getaway*, can cause negative changes in many men's attitudes towards women. In a laboratory setting, exposure to violent pornography in which the woman is shown being raped and apparently "enjoying" the experience, can lead to greater violence by men against women as measured by the number of shocks given in a learning task experiment.

4. There is little evidence that the catharsis effect exists. In fact, the evidence seems in favor of a violence-begets-violence interpretation. Societies engaged in a war, for example, experience more rather than less violence at home during the war period, probably because violence is temporarily legitimized in the culture.

5. Researchers have found that consumption of a moderate to large quantity of alcohol by experimental subjects increases the tendency toward aggression in laboratory tests. Similar doses of marijuana, however, result in the inhibition of aggressive behavior in a laboratory situation.

6. There seems to be a relatively straightforward relationship between heat and aggression. At least with respect to street violence, the hotter it gets the more likely it is that a riot will break out.

Summary

Aggression has been defined as "any form of behavior directed toward the goal of harming or injuring another living being who is motivated to avoid such treatment." Social psychologists most often measure aggression in the laboratory with a Buss aggression machine. This is a device that subjects operate in the belief that they are controlling a learning experiment. The subjects are instructed to administer an electric shock to the "learner" whenever a mistake is made; the aggression subjects demonstrate is measured by the number, selected intensity, and the duration of the shocks. The original Buss aggression machine did not deliver actual shocks, but some subsequent variations of the machine do. Another means of measuring aggression is to observe and categorize behavior.

Theories of aggression can be divided into two broad categories: **instinctual theories** and **environmental theories**. Sigmund Freud offered an instinctual theory in which human beings have a certain amount of aggression that must find an outlet. Konrad Lorenz believes that because human beings are not equipped by nature with weapons, they evolved without any inhibitions against intraspecies aggression.

Social psychologists prefer environmental explanations of aggression. One situational theory claims that when frustration occurs, aggression follows. However, although aggression may follow some kinds of frustration, there is not a simple causal relationship. Some theorists, notably Leonard Berkowitz, have added to the **frustration–aggression theory** a need for aggressive cues that set off the expression of aggression caused by frustration. This modification is often called the **weapons effect**, since subjects have sometimes been shown to deliver more shocks with Buss-like devices when weapons are nearby than when weapons are absent.

Other situations or stimuli besides frustration can evoke or contribute to aggressive responses. These include a heightened general level of arousal; deindividuation; verbal and physical attack; heat, and alcohol.

Social learning theory stresses the importance of reinforcement and modeling as factors that contribute to aggression. Reinforcement of aggressive behavior helps to develop it; those who view the aggressive behavior of models generally imitate them. Experiments by Albert Bandura and his associates have used "Bobo dolls" to demonstrate these effects on small children.

In view of the importance of models, the media would seem to play a strong role in fostering aggression. Bandura found that aggressive models on film produced as much aggression in observers as live models did. Pornography, apparently not a cause of aggressive behavior, may nevertheless become one when violence toward women, such as rape, is portrayed.

Only one in five murder victims is female, and even fewer violent criminals are female; the latter proportion is on the rise, however. Victims of violence face—because of other people's attitudes toward them—more hurdles than simply recovering from the effects of an attack. Media accounts of violent crimes also seem to foster a fear of violence that is out of proportion with the actual danger people face.

Laboratory experiments have shown that an absence of aggression displayed on the part of models results in the development of nonaggressive behavior. This is especially true if the models are respected, and if the observer sees them being rewarded for their nonaggressive acts. Such control of social learning experiences would seem to offer one means of reducing the amount of aggression in society.

Suggested Additional Reading

Bandura, A. *Aggression: A social learning analysis.* Englewood Cliffs, N.J.; Prentice-Hall, 1972.

Baron, R. A. *Human aggression.* New York: Plenum, 1977.

Berkowitz, L. (Ed.). *Roots of aggression.* Chicago: Aldine, 1969.

Zillmann, D. *Hostility and aggression.* Hillsdale, N.J.: Erlbaum, 1979.

12

PROSOCIAL BEHAVIOR

Two repairers were working on a power line when one of them received a
severe shock. The other quickly climbed the pole to his dangling co-worker and
began mouth-to-mouth resuscitation. The heroic effort, which threatened the
life of the rescuer, was successful. A photographer for the *Jacksonville*
(Florida) *Journal*, passing by, earned a Pulitzer Prize for this photo.

Questions about Prosocial Behavior

1. "You scratch my back and I'll scratch yours." Everyone has heard this expression; to what extent do people follow this norm in our society?
2. When asked, most of us would probably say we feel an obligation to help the blind and the sick. Yet when it comes to translating these feelings into behavior some people act and others don't. What is the difference between those who act altruistically in a given situation and those who don't?
3. You can be assured that if you fell on the steps in a crowded stairwell and broke your leg, someone would intervene immediately to help, and that the more people present the better chance you'd have of getting help—right?
4. Whom are we most likely to help? Do we help everyone who needs help, or do we select people with certain characteristics to be helped?
5. What are the characteristics of people who help others? Are they more nurturing? Do they have higher self-esteem?

I n the summer of 1944, Raoul Wallenberg, a young business executive and a member of one of Sweden's wealthiest families, was sent to Hungary by Allied authorities and Swedish officials on a special mission to save as many Jews as possible from being captured by the Nazis. Within a few months, Wallenberg had given Swedish passports to at least 20,000 Budapest Jews, keeping another 13,000 of them in "safe" houses which he had rented and over which flew the Swedish flag, thus bringing them under the protection of his government. But 90,000 other Jews of Budapest, whom he did not reach, were killed.

In carrying out his rescue operation, Wallenberg cared little for his own safety and yet seemed immune to harm by the Germans. He stood on top of a deportation train handing out Swedish papers to all the hands that could reach them, then insisted that the people holding them be allowed off the train. With his own hands, he pulled people out of "death marches" to the Austrian border or brought them bread, soup, and medical supplies in the middle of the night when he had no more passports to give out. (Lester & Werbell, 1980)

Finally, in January of 1945, Wallenberg's work came to an end when he was apparently arrested by the Soviet security service, the NKVD, while attempting to get Russian aid in locating the thousands of people who were missing and unaccounted for as the war neared its end. He was presumably imprisoned in the Soviet Union, and former Russian prisoners have mentioned knowing or hearing about him at various locations there. But despite efforts by Swedish and American diplomats, there has been no news of Wallenberg in years (Marton, 1980).

Selfless behavior takes many forms:

> The Jerry Lewis 21-hour "Labor Day of Love" Muscular Dystrophy telethon
> . . . [is] the single most successful annual fund-raising event in charity his-
> tory. . . . By the final two hours, Jerry has gone through 21 changes of
> clothes and at least two cartons of cigarettes. His mouth is dry, and his facial
> lines have turned into pasty folds. Only his hair refuses to wilt. As the tote
> board hits $30,075,227, it is all over. . . . He ends with a brave, "I hope I
> never have to see you again," to the television audience. . . . And why does
> he do it? Jerry won't tell until a cure is found. Till then, let's say he does it
> because he does it. (Sabol, 1979)

Unlike the tyrants, muggers, and bigots whose exploits are splashed across
the front pages of daily newspapers, the Wallenbergs and Jerry Lewises of the
world represent a far more appealing side of modern society. Human beings are
not all bad or all good. Although some people's actions clearly demonstrate their
concern for others, no one is completely selfless. What intrigues social psychologists is the underlying tension between forces within an individual and the influences on a person that determine whether and how help will be given.

As part of this analysis, researchers have identified specific attributes of
prosocial behavior that characterize certain actions. For instance, Raoul Wallenberg's heroic actions in Budapest involved considerable personal risk, with little
or no gain. This regard for the interest of others, without concern for one's self-
interest, is termed **altruism**. Giving a charitable gift or monetary contribution, as
Jerry Lewis does with his donation of time and energy to aid research on muscular dystrophy, meets the definition of **helping**: giving assistance to another with a
definite object or goal in mind. Social psychologists would classify both altruism
and helping under the broader heading of **prosocial behavior,** a term that refers
to any actions that benefit another, regardless of the benefits to or self-sacrifices
of the actor (Wispé, 1972). If you have helped someone by carrying packages,
come to the aid of a stranded driver, or donated blood, you have engaged in
prosocial behavior.

*Those who have not suffered
do not know how to pity.*
Mohandas K. Gandhi

The term *prosocial* was originally used to mean *culturally desirable*, and
such activities as initiation rites or parental punishment were the initial focus of
researchers in this field. Sears and his co-workers, for example, referred to *prosocial aggression*, which they defined as potentially harmful aggressive behavior used "for purposes that the culture defines as desirable" (1965, p. 113). Or,
as Bandura and Walters (1963) explained, "prosocial aggression" was "positive"
in the sense that it aimed more to shape behavior than to injure. Other researchers later extended the term to include all positive, socially responsible behaviors, in contrast to antisocial behavior. As Wispé observes, it is one of the ironies
of psychology that a term originally introduced to characterize aggressive behavior rapidly evolved to encompass behavior that was the opposite of aggression,
namely, altruism, helping, charity, and self-sacrifice (1972).

This seeming paradox actually pinpoints the opposing forces that control
prosocial behavior. As you will read in the following section, human instincts favor self-preservation and aggression toward others who might endanger one's
personal welfare. Opposing these *internal*, instinctual motives is a vast collection of *external*, environmental influences, such as models who teach us socially

appropriate behavior, or people in need who directly request our help. Whereas these external factors are observable and quantifiable, our internal motives are not. Therefore, social psychologists have had to create experimental situations in which internal motives for altruism and other prosocial behaviors are translated into observable actions—helping someone change a tire or putting money into a Salvation Army kettle.

In this chapter we will be looking at the sociobiological approach to altruism, aspects of bystander intervention, and the characteristics of those who help and those who are helped. For each of these topics, we will follow the shifting balance between internal and external variables, and attempt to weigh the proportional influence of each. We will describe some of the different research approaches used to explore the different prosocial behaviors. Finally we will briefly look at examples of helping behavior (or its absence) among other cultures.

Origins of Prosocial Behavior

Why should people behave altruistically toward one another? Some psychologists believe that altruism is *inborn*—that is, a genetically determined, internal mechanism common to all human beings. Others see evidence that altruism is *learned* through the socialization process. Learning theorists, for example, point to modeling and imitation as the mechanism by which we acquire altruistic behavior. Which theory is correct? Let us examine the evidence.

Instincts and Helping

Many species of termites and ants live in colonies in which certain subgroups assume responsibility for reproduction, the provision of food, and the defense of the colony. When predators attack a termite nest, for example, nymphs and workers rush to conceal themselves, while "soldiers" aggressively stand to meet the intruder. Honeybees, another species of "social" insects, are protected by worker bees whose barbed stingers remain embedded in their victims. When the worker pulls away after attacking a victim, its viscera tear, leaving the bee fatally injured. As E. O. Wilson points out, the fearsome reputation of social bees and other social insects is due to their instinctive readiness to throw their own lives away to protect the colony (1975).

Risking one's own life for the welfare of the group is literally the ultimate act of altruism—for animals as well as for humans. This type of altruism is sometimes interpreted in Darwinian terms as an instinctual mechanism that insured the survival of the species, albeit at the expense of certain individuals. Some sociobiologists refer to this protection of the group-as-a-whole as *kin selection*. Wilson, for example, believes that kin, or blood relatives, bestow altruistic favors on one another for the benefit of future offspring (1975).

Others disagree on the grounds that if self-sacrificial altruism were a genetic trait, it would gradually disappear over many generations. The more altruistic the individual, the greater the chance that she or he would be killed protecting the more cowardly members of the population, who would survive to pass on their nonaltruistic genes to future generations (Campbell, 1965, 1972, 1978, 1979). (Of course, as Wilson points out, there is always the possibility that altruistic genes could be carried through brothers and sisters for whom the altruistic individual gave his life.) Campbell points out that among social insects, the altruistic members are generally sterile and so can have no genetic influence on the species as a whole. Social mammals, on the other hand, have no specialized, sterile, altruistic groups. Those who are altruistic are in direct genetic competition for mates, and indeed appear to be extremely desirable mates. Humans prefer to associate with predictable, dependable, unselfish people, as opposed to unpredictable opportunists. And, in fact, the most heroic, self-sacrificing altruists who survive are considered sexually attractive (Campbell, 1979; Ghiselin, 1976).

This nature–nurture controversy is not yet resolved. In the meantime, however, social psychologists have been most interested in searching for sociocultural and modeling processes to explain the origins of altruistic behavior.

The Development of Altruism in Childhood

In support of the idea that altruism is learned and not innate, Rubin and Schneider (1973) found that children's willingness to help and share with others increases with age, and is directly related to their level of moral reasoning. (Refer back to chapter 3 to refresh your memory about Piaget's and Kohlberg's theories of moral development in children.) In their study, children whose communication skills demonstrated a high level of moral development and a lack of egocentrism were significantly more willing to donate candy to poor children, and to help younger children at their own expense.

Green and Schneider (1974) confirmed that helping behavior increases with

For Better or For Worse   by Lynn Johnston

Even children are known by their doings, whether their work is pure, and whether it be right.
Proverbs 20:11

age in their studies of four age groups: 5 and 6 years, 7 and 8, 9 and 10, and 13 and 14 years. They found that a willingness to share candy and to help in a clean-up task increased progressively, until by ages 9 and 10 virtually all children help and share with others. What children learn during their first decade, these authors say, is the capacity to recognize and appreciate the needs of others and the understanding of "societal prescriptions" that encourage altruism (p. 250). It is not the children's age that determines altruism, but their developing ability to take the point of view of other people, which Underwood and Moore (1982) term **moral perspective-taking.**

Modeling Altruistic Behavior: Social Rewards for Helping

Just as some children learn to spell better than others, so do some children learn to be more altruistic. Since our society would greatly benefit from an increase in helping behavior, social psychologists have attempted to identify ways in which prosocial acts can be encouraged. The two most powerful prosocial techniques yet discovered are modeling and reinforcement (Midlarsky et al., 1973).

Studies have shown that the best way to teach altruism is to model the desired behavior in front of the child (or adult), and then to reinforce the desired behavior when the subject reproduces it. Midlarsky, Bryan, and Brickman (1973) demonstrated this paradigm with a group of sixth-grade girls who were given the opportunity to win prizes by playing pinball. Each time a win was scored, prize tokens were awarded. The girls were instructed to place their tokens in a jar labeled "My Money," or to donate some of the tokens to another jar labeled "Money for the Poor Children." Their attention was drawn to a nearby poster for the Denver Children's Fund, described as an organization that provided for the ill and needy children of their city "some of the silly things, like toys and candy, that make children feel remembered." When the pinball game was demonstrated by a model who donated many chips to the "Poor Children" jar, the sixth-graders also donated to the jar. If the model smiled broadly and said things like, "Boy, you're really nice to do that!" when the subjects donated to the jar, donations increased even more.

Interestingly, the experiment also demonstrated the truth of the common advice, "Do as I say, not as I do." Although all of the subjects were instructed to think about the poor children as they played and to "Let us let them know that we remember them," only those subjects who saw a model donating to the "Poor Children" jar made significant donations themselves. When the model put all her winnings in the "My Money" jar, subjects tended to do so, too.

These findings were expected. However, not all modeling effects coincide with commonsense expectations. Rushton, for example, found a difference between the short-term and long-term effects of modeling. In a playing-for-tokens game similar to that used by Midlarsky, subjects who were exposed to a model who preached generosity but behaved selfishly donated a larger number of tokens during a follow-up session than they had during an initial session eight weeks earlier. As Rushton explains, words are apparently better remembered than deeds (1975).

Whereas these studies focus on the contradictions between actions and words, other studies find that actions speak louder than words when no con-

Ken Karp

Among the many things children learn in the first years of life is to help and share with others. Research indicates that the development of altruistic behavior is learned, and not innate, and that it is facilitated by modeling and reinforcement.

tradictory messages are thrown in for confusion. Grusec and Skubiski (1970) found, for example, that children who watched an adult model donate half his winnings to charity after playing a game, later showed far more charitable behavior themselves than another group who had merely heard the adults advocate donations. Similarly, Bryan and Test (1967) found that people were much more likely to stop and help someone change a flat tire if they had just driven past a "model demonstration" in which a woman was watching a man change a flat tire.

These studies show that it is not necessary to receive direct reinforcement to learn that prosocial behavior is desirable. Aronfreed (1968) believes, for example, that after receiving praise and approval for the performance of prosocial behavior, children internalize the reward mechanism. When they engage in helping, they recognize that they are "being good," and this self-reward perpetuates the altruistic response. Of course, additional reinforcement never hurts. Moss and Page (1972) demonstrated this with an attractive 18-year-old female who approached passersby asking for directions to a local department store. When the directions were given, the woman said something positive ("Thank you"), something neutral ("O.K."), or something negative ("I can't understand what you're saying; never mind, I'll ask someone else"). When the same passersby later encountered a woman who accidentally dropped a package without realizing it, those who had been positively reinforced were more likely to help by calling out to the woman or actually picking up the dropped package.

Forget injuries, never forget kindnesses.
Confucius

This study showed, too, that just as a positive experience like a reward increases helping behavior, a negative experience can decrease it. Passersby who were rebuffed hesitated to risk helping someone else. Similarly, Rushton and Teachman (1978) found that children who were criticized for sharing tokens with others ("That's kind of silly for you to give it to Bobby—now you will have less tokens for yourself") were less likely to share later.

Decreases in helping may also occur after we have observed a very helpful model. For example, Thomas et al. (1981) found that people exposed to excessively helpful models may respond negatively to what they think is an obvious pressure to induce them to be helpful. But those who consciously resisted the influence of such exemplary models were readily persuaded by "moderately" helpful models. The difference, according to the researchers, was that subjects attribute their helping behavior to their own intrinsic feelings of sympathy, concern, and compassion after viewing a moderately helpful model; after viewing the highly helpful model, they realize that their altruistic acts were motivated from the outside rather than from within.

The vast collection of studies on modeling and altruism demonstrates that prosocial behavior is extremely malleable. Depending on the situation and the individual's perception of it, helping may be encouraged or suppressed. A model serves to remind the observer of what is appropriate in that situation (the social norm), what behaviors will lead to a successful helping response and, finally, to reduce inhibition toward actually performing the altruistic gesture.

Social Norms and Personal Ideals

Learn to do well; seek judgment, relieve the oppressed, judge the fatherless, plead for the widow.
Isaiah 1:17

All societies follow a collection of unwritten rules that stipulate how people should behave in various situations. These unwritten guidelines, or **social norms,** represent a consensus about which behaviors are acceptable and encouraged, and which are unacceptable or discouraged. By definition, prosocial behavior, which benefits society as a whole, is behavior that is rewarded, accepted, and encouraged.

Social norms are at first an *external* mechanism, existing outside of the individual. However, after growing up in a society and receiving rewards for following those norms, as well as receiving punishments for not following them, most people *internalize* the values and beliefs the norms represent. Now altruism and helping behavior occur not because society dictates these behaviors, but because the individual feels a personal, moral obligation to "do the right thing." People who do not follow these internalized, personal ideals are punished not by society, but by self-generated feelings of guilt.

Social Norms

How do we know that social norms exist? Anthropologists identify the social norms of other cultures by observing the behavior of children, adults, husbands, wives, relatives, and strangers. Someone observing our own culture would do the same thing. If, under certain conditions, almost all people in a culture behaved in the same way, that behavior would qualify as a social norm.

Think of the many behaviors that are social norms in our culture: shaking hands and introducing yourself to a stranger; wearing shoes and clothing out of doors; forming a line at the bus stop or cash register; saying "Have a good day" to a neighbor. The examples are endless, and so are the exceptions. If you met a stranger on a dark, lonely road, you would probably hurry by with your eyes averted instead of introducing yourself. In the heat of summer, you might venture out naked for a sunbath if you thought no one would see you. Or, if the line were very long and the arriving bus were almost full, you might push forward toward the door to be sure of getting in.

Reciprocity Prosocial behaviors, like the behaviors we just mentioned, also follow rules and exceptions. As George Homans (1961) explains, people almost always weigh the personal costs and rewards associated with performing an act of altruism. If the costs are low, then the rewards need not be great. For example, the cost of helping a blind person cross the street is just a few seconds out of a long day; a simple "thank you" and the internal feeling of having done the right thing is more than enough thanks. However, diving into a swiftly moving river to retrieve a child's dropped lollipop would be another matter entirely. No matter how great the child's gratitude, it could not outweigh the enormous personal risks. If it were the child, and not the lollipop, that fell into the river, of course the decision might be quite different.

Most examples of altruism reflect an equal balance of gains and/or losses to the people involved, in other words, an *equitable* social interaction (Berkowitz & Walster, 1976). For instance, Jerry Lewis donates 21 hours toward helping people with muscular dystrophy, but he receives the enormous gratitude of millions of viewers and, very likely, sufficient public exposure to receive top billing in movies and nightclub appearances.

Whatsoever ye would that men should do to you, do ye even so to them.
Matthew 7:12

But what about the people who actually donate their money through Lewis's telethon? What do they get out of it, apart from a form letter of thanks and a tax deduction? According to Homans (1961), people help where there is no apparent gain in the expectation that they can expect help in return. Just as one student may help another with an assignment in the hope that he may ask for help in return if the need ever arises, so altruistic people assume that others in society would show altruism toward them if they were ever in need. The idea of *reciprocity*—if you do it for me, I will do it for you—is a predominant social norm in our culture. In fact, Gouldner (1960) and other sociologists believe that it is a *universal* norm, "no less universal and important an element of culture than the incest taboo," in *all* societies.

What you do not want done to yourself, do not do to others.
Confucius

Several empirical studies have confirmed that intuitive notion of reciprocity. Staub and Sherk (1970) found, for example, that a child who received a large number of candies from another youngster while listening to a story, later showed a significantly greater willingness to share crayons than did youngsters who had not received shared candies. Similarly, Pruitt (1968) found that college students gave more to a partner in an experimental game when they had previously received a gift from the partner than when they had not.

Social Responsibility The studies cited above were designed to demonstrate reciprocity. However, they also showed that prosocial behavior often occurs in the absence of reciprocity. Although Staub and Sherk's (1970) subjects shared more if others had shared with them, subjects who had not received any shared candies still shared their crayons. Why? Because our social norms also dictate that people should help others, regardless of whether or not they can reciprocate. Berkowitz and his colleagues call this the norm of *social responsibility*. People follow this norm not for reciprocity, but for "the symbolic pat on the back they will give themselves for having behaved in a socially desirable manner" (Berkowitz et al., 1964, 1966, 1972).

Berkowitz and Daniels (1963) examined this norm in an experiment that required subjects to assemble paper envelopes under the direction of a helpful supervisor. The subjects were told that their construction work was actually a test of supervisory skill; the more boxes they constructed correctly, the more likely their supervisor was to win a $5 prize. Some subjects were led to believe that their supervisor's rating was greatly dependent upon their own productivity, whereas other subjects believed that the rating depended only a little on their own performance. The study showed that, even with no possible gain for themselves, the subjects helped those supervisors who seemed most dependent on them. According to the experimenters, the only motivation the subjects could have had was a feeling of social responsibility.

Personal Norms, Personal Responsibility Just because society encourages certain helping behaviors does not mean that all people will follow society's dictates. For example, some people always seem willing to help others, to donate to charity, or to take part in community activities, whereas others demonstrate less of a "social conscience." According to Schwartz (1977), some people act on their own **personal norms** or obligations (internalized social norms) and others do not. Schwartz has developed a **theory of norm activation** to try to predict when people will act on their personal norms.

According to Schwartz, a person's decision to help or not to help can be described by a four-step model (see Table 12–1). In the *activation step* a person becomes aware of another's need and perceives that there are actions he or she

TABLE 12–1.
Schwartz's Model of Altruistic Behavior

I. Activation steps: perception of need and responsibility
  1. Awareness of a person in a state of need
  2. Perception that there are actions which could relieve the need
  3. Recognition of own ability to provide relief
  4. Apprehension of some responsibility to become involved
II. Obligation step: norm construction and generation of feelings of moral obligation
  5. Activation of preexisting or situationally constructed personal norms
III. Defense steps: assessment, evaluation, and reassessment of potential responses
  6. Assessment of costs and evaluation of probable outcomes
    (The next two steps may be skipped if a particular response clearly optimizes the balance of costs evaluated in step 6. If not, there will be one or more iterations through steps 7 and 8.)
  7. Reassessment and redefinition of the situation by denial of:
    a. state of need (its reality, seriousness)
    b. responsibility to respond
    c. suitability of norms activated thus far and/or others
  8. Iterations of earlier steps in light of reassessments
IV. Response step
  9. Action or inaction response

In this model, a moral obligation must be activated in order for altruistic behavior to take place.
Source: From "Normative Influences on Altruism," by S.H. Schwartz, in L. Berkowitz (Ed.), *Advances in Experimental Social Psychology*, Vol. 10. New York: Academic Press, 1977, 241.

could take to relieve the need. In the *obligation step* an already held personal obligation to help is evoked or a new obligation is constructed. The third step in Schwartz's model is, in a way, a step backward. The person contemplating helping begins to assess the costs involved and may attempt to deny responsibility in the situation. Schwartz calls this the *defense step*. Finally, there is the *response step* in which the person either acts or does not act to help.

This model does not assume that the potential helper is consciously aware of going through all four steps. Indeed, it is quite possible that all of these steps are cognitively processed almost instantaneously and that the person is acting to help before she or he realizes exactly why.

In the model, steps I and III imply that there are two very important factors that determine whether or not a person will help: an awareness of a person in need and actions that can help; and a tendency not to deny personal responsibility in the situation. According to Schwartz,

> The hypothesis implicit in this analysis is that there will be an association between a person's moral [personal] norms and his behavior only when these conditions of awareness of consequences and ascription of responsibility are fulfilled. (1968, p. 356)

In a series of experiments, Schwartz (1977) has shown the effects of awareness of the consequences of helping. These studies typically measure awareness by having the subjects write endings to short stories about a person in need. The ending is scored on three factors: an awareness of the other person's needs, adopting the perspective of others, and reflecting on the consequences of taking actions. Some time after the subjects have completed the short stories, they are telephoned and asked to donate time to tutor the blind or to help at a bake sale that benefits needy preschoolers. In such studies Schwartz has generally found that those whose story endings demonstrated a high awareness of the consequences of their actions are more likely to act on their personal norm for helping than those whose story endings showed that they were low on this factor. The tendency to deny responsibility in a situation has also proven to be a good indicator of who will help. Those people who are low in responsibility denial (more likely to accept responsibility to help) are much more likely to act on their personal norms for helping than people who are high in responsibility denial.

Negative Personal Norms

The bread of strangers can be very hard.
Russian proverb

When do we feel morally justified in not helping? A recent report from the Housing and Urban Development Department (HUD) maintains that federal aid to urban areas in the United States has done more damage than good. The report charges that federal programs have forced big city mayors and managers to become scavengers for federal funds instead of being creative problem solvers. It seems to imply that cities would be helped more if the federal government did *not* help.

According to Schwartz (1982), there are occasions when we as individuals may feel some degree of moral obligation not to aid particular causes or other individuals (e.g., communists, ex-convicts). These moral obligations not to help have been labeled **negative personal norms**. Schwartz conducted a study to test the idea that having a negative personal norm will result in less helping behavior than having no norm at all. First he asked a sample of married women drawn randomly from the telephone directory to complete a public opinion survey for the "National Institute for Social Policy Studies." Embedded in the survey were questions asking the respondents whether they thought they *ought* or *ought not* to give free time to help welfare recipients in need, or donate money to welfare families who do not have enough food to eat. Also in the questionnnaire were items designed to measure the respondents' general level of responsibility denial.

Ten weeks later the women who had completed these questionnaires were called by a volunteer from "Food for the Elderly" (a fictitious organization). The caller requested that the subject donate some time to address envelopes for a statewide mailing describing the plight of "poor elderly people whose welfare payments are so small that they have difficulty buying food." Those women whose earlier questionnaires had shown them to have negative personal norms volunteered less often than women who had either positive norms or no norms at all for this behavior. But surprisingly, even those people who were very low on responsibility denial (or conversely, very likely to accept responsibility to act in a situation of need) refused to help. These findings led Schwartz to conclude that "for some people at least, expressions of opposition are not merely a way to show resentment at being asked to suffer costs inherent in a self-sacrificing act. Rather they represent real feelings of obligation not to act" (p. 85).

Criticism of Normative Theories   It is important to recognize that social situations rarely present obvious choices. For example, someone with a strong feeling of personal responsibility for others may decide *not* to help a criminal or an unknown charitable institution.

Give with a glad heart.

Just as ambiguity is a problem for a person trying to decide how to behave in a particular situation, so it is a problem for the social psychologist trying to explain *why* the individual behaved that way. If a person acts altruistically in a situation that calls for prosocial behavior, the psychologist might say that person had internalized the norm for social responsibility. However, if the person failed to act altruistically, that failure might be explained equally well by concluding that the person held the social norm of minding one's own business.

Charity begins at home.

Latané and Darley (1970), along with other researchers, believe that this ambiguity seriously diminishes the usefulness of norms as a scientific construct to explain helping behavior. "Since norms are so many and so vague, they can be used to explain almost any pattern of behavior," they note. If people give money to a charity, it is attributed to a norm to "help thy neighbor." If they fail to contribute, it is due to a norm to "look out for yourself" (p. 21). Such explanations really explain very little.

If norms do not determine behavior, what does? Latané and Darley believe that *situational* factors are the true determinants of behavior. Their studies on "unresponsive bystanders" provide strong support for the predominance of *external* rather than *internal* factors in increasing the likelihood of prosocial behavior.

Bystander Intervention

To Detective Sgt. Garry Meeker of the Santa Clara Sheriff's Department, it was not the killing of 14-year-old Marcy Renée Conrad that was so unusual, at least not these days.

"Not the crime itself," said the 42-year-old sergeant, who has been a police officer all his working life, like his father before him. "The unusual aspect was what followed, the kids going up there. That was the unusual aspect. . . ."

The scant official facts are that . . . a 16-year-old [high school] junior . . . is charged with strangling Marcy Conrad, possibly after raping her, and leaving her body about four miles from town in the hills where some [people] dump leaves and trash.

But what has shocked this fast-growing community of 38,000 are reports by police investigators, acknowledged by students and school administrators, that the defendant boasted of the crime, then loaded other young people into his white pickup truck and drove them into the hills to view the body. Others, hearing of "the body in the hills," went on their own to look.

Only one of the students who saw the body has been charged as an accessory. The police say he went to view the body with the defendant and dumped a garbage bag of leaves on it as an apparent attempt to hide it. As for the others, Sergeant Meeker said, "Failure to report a body is not a crime." (King, 1981)*

In this case, the nonintervention of bystanders delayed reporting a crime for two days. The murders of Karen Beth Green in Arizona (see chapter 11) and of Kitty Genovese in New York (see chapter 2) actually took place while several bystanders watched and did nothing. It is just this type of circumstance that served as the impetus for Latané and Darley's (1970) studies on "unresponsive bystanders"—those who fail to intervene in emergencies.

In their studies on nonemergency situations—such as someone needing directions on a bus or subway—they had found people quite willing to help when they were asked. If people are so willing to help in nonemergencies, it would seem that they should be even more willing to help in emergencies in which the need for help is so much greater. However, according to Latané and Darley, the very *nature* of emergencies puts people on their guard. Emergencies involve a threat of harm or actual harm; typically, life, well-being, or property are in danger. As Latané and Darley explain:

At worst, an emergency can claim the lives not only of the victims, but of anyone who intervenes. At best, the major result of any intervention is a restoration of the status quo before the emergency, or more normally, a prevention of further damage to an already damaged person or property. Even if an emergency is successfully dealt with, rarely is anybody better off afterwards than before. Consequently, there are few positive rewards for successful action in an emergency. (pp. 29–30)

* © 1981 by The New York Times Company. Reprinted by permission.

Latané and Darley found that, while people are quite willing to help in nonemergency situations, an emergency activates different concerns. People are generally not prepared to provide appropriate assistance. Police officers, shown here assisting an elderly woman who was pushed to the ground by a crowd of parade-watchers, are trained and well prepared to deal with emergencies of all sorts. Here bystanders show their concern on their faces, and one bystander does appear to have gone to the victim's aid.

These high costs and low rewards put pressure on individuals during an emergency, causing them to have distorted perceptions and to underestimate their responsibility for helping. Adding to this pressure is the fact that emergencies are so unusual that most people—aside from trained police, fire, and medical personnel—have little personal experience in handling them. In addition, because emergencies are sudden, people do not have an opportunity to prepare for the best course of action. Since our culture provides little advice in advance about what to do in an emergency—other than the laughable stereotypes of "Charge!", "Women and children first!", "Quick, get lots of hot water and towels!"—each person is left to his or her own resources. And, for many people, those resources may be sorely lacking. "The picture is a grim one," Latané and Darley conclude:

> Faced with a situation in which he can gain no benefit, unable to rely on past experience, on the experience of others, or on forethought and planning, denied the opportunity to consider carefully his course of action, the bystander to an emergency is in an unenviable position. It is perhaps surprising that anyone should intervene at all. (p. 31)

Latané and Darley's Model of Intervention

Deciding whether or not to intervene in an emergency requires several cognitive steps. First, the individual bystander must *notice* that something is happening. Next, he or she must *interpret* the event as an emergency, and then *decide* on his or her *personal responsibility* to take action. Once that is decided, the bystander must *choose the form of assistance* she or he will give, and then *implement* that assistance. (See Figure 12–1.)

At each of these decision points, numerous *social determinants* affect the bystander's decisions. For example, in deciding whether she or he is personally responsible for helping, a bystander might consider whether the victim "deserves" help, and how likely it is that other bystanders may provide that help. Not surprisingly, many more people will stop to help a frail, elderly woman sprawled on the sidewalk than will stop for a young, healthy looking, but poorly dressed teenager (Latané & Darley, 1970, p. 34). However, it is not so obvious whether the presence of other bystanders will make helping more or less likely. At first glance, we might think that the more people that are present, the more likely at least one of them will take action. But, according to Latané and Darley's research, which we examine below, the presence of others actually serves to *inhibit* the impulse to help.

The Smoke-Filled Room Experiment   Male college students who were supposedly to take part in a survey of life in large metropolitan areas, came alone to a room furnished with several tables and chairs. They were instructed by a large sign on the wall to fill out a preliminary form and then wait for the interviewer. Some subjects were alone in the room while others were with two confederates of the experimenter. After a few minutes the room started to fill with white smoke. This continued either until the subject took action or for 4 minutes. By then there was so much smoke in the room that it affected both vision and breathing.

Of course, everyone immediately reported the potential fire, right? Wrong! About 75 percent of the 24 subjects who were working alone walked out of the room and calmly reported the problem. (Interestingly, 6 subjects failed to report the smoke and kept working as the room filled with smoke.) However, in the

FIGURE 12–1.
The Intervention Model of
Latané and Darley

If the bystander answers "no"
at any decision point,
intervention will not take
place.

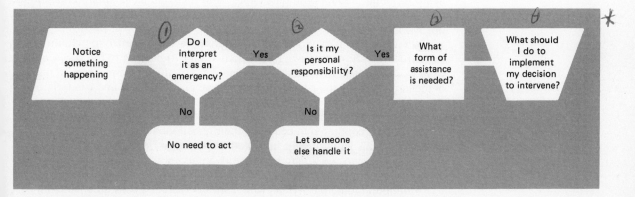

room where the confederates were present, only 1 subject took immediate action. The rest waited in the room for a full 6 minutes, "doggedly working on their questionnaires and waving the fumes away from their faces. They coughed, rubbed their eyes, and opened the window—but they did not report the smoke," the investigators found. Apparently, the presence of others had inhibited their actions. Yet, in postexperimental interviews, the subjects did not even mention the presence—or the reactions—of other people in the room. "Although the presence of other people actually had a strong and pervasive effect on the subjects' reactions, they were either unaware of this or unwilling to admit it," Latané and Darley concluded.

The smoke-filled room presented a somewhat ambiguous situation. No clear danger existed. Even the subjects who reported the problem admitted, "I thought it might be steam, but it seemed like a good idea to check it out." Nevertheless, it was surprising that without exception the subjects who failed to report the smoke hit upon astonishing alternative explanations that interpreted it as a non-dangerous event. Several thought it was smog "purposely introduced to simulate an urban environment," and two subjects actually suggested that the smoke was a "truth gas" filtered into the room to induce them to answer the questionnaire accurately. As the study notes, "surprisingly, they were not disturbed by this conviction" (p. 52). In the following experiment, similar, surprising behavior was seen in a less ambiguous situation where the danger was clear.

A Lady in Distress   The subjects were male college students who were supposedly taking a market survey test of the appeal of a number of adult games and puzzles. They were tested alone, with a friend, or with a stranger. When they arrived, an attractive young woman greeted them, introducing herself as a representative of the market research organization. While they answered a questionnaire, they could hear a woman in the open office next door, apparently putting away papers in desk drawers. After a few minutes, the subjects who listened carefully could hear her climb up on a chair. Even those who were not listening carefully could then hear a crashing noise, a scream, and a chair falling down. "Oh, my God, my foot . . ." the woman cried. "I . . . I can't move . . . it. Oh, my ankle. I . . . can't . . . can't . . . get . . . this thing off . . . me." The moans and cries continued about a minute longer, then got gradually quieter. Finally, she was heard to mutter about going outside, to bang the chair as she pulled herself up, and to limp out, closing the door behind her (Latané & Darley, 1970, pp. 57–58).

What would you expect? Did the young male subjects rush to help the "lady in distress"? As in the smoke-filled room study, 70 percent of the subjects who were working alone responded with some kind of aid, but fewer than 10 percent of those working in the presence of others stopped working and tried to help in some way. Although the subjects seemed upset and confused during the emergency and frequently glanced at the others (confederates, of course) working in the room, they continued to complete their questionnaires. Clearly, the presence of an unresponsive bystander inhibited the subjects from offering assistance to the injured woman. Yet again, in poststudy interviews, they were either unwilling or unable to admit that they had been affected by this factor.

Attempting to help a woman with a sprained ankle poses little personal cost

Is help needed here? What would be the potential costs, if any, to an intervening bystander? Would the presence of other bystanders encourage or inhibit your offer of assistance to this man?

Marc Anderson

or risk to the bystander. However, many emergencies present clear and present danger. In a dangerous situation, would you expect that the presence of others might make helping more likely, since any danger might be lessened by working together? Consider the following situation.

Witness to a Crime   Male undergraduates who had agreed to a 1 hour interview for a $2 fee arrived alone or with two other subjects (confederates) to be interviewed. They were met by a receptionist who explained that because the interviews were running a few minutes behind schedule, she would pay them beforehand to save time. She took several large bills and some smaller ones from an envelope on her desk, gave the subjects their $2, and asked if anyone in the room had change for $20. Then she put from $30 to $50 back in the envelope. She left the room shortly thereafter, ostensibly to answer a buzzer. Seconds later a "thief" (one of the confederates) got up and went to the desk. He fumbled with a magazine that was lying there and "then, clumsily but blatantly, seemingly trying to hide his actions but performing in full view of the other subject(s), he reached into the envelope, took out the cash, stuffed it into his jacket pocket, picked up the magazine, and returned to his seat. At no time did he say a word. If anyone spoke to him he either ignored them and continued reading the magazine, or answered with an innocent 'I don't know what you're talking about.' About one minute after the theft, the receptionist returned" (Latané & Darley, 1970, p. 71).

What do you think happened this time? As you might expect from the previous studies, the subjects who were alone in the room with the thief reported the theft more often than those who were in the presence of another bystander. But the most surprising finding was that under both experimental conditions—alone and in the presence of others—not only did few subjects report the theft, but few even admitted *noticing* it. More subjects admitted to "seeing" the theft in the "together" situation, but even there subjects proffered implausible interpretations such as, "It looked like he was only making change." Or even if they admitted that a theft had occurred, each subject in the group condition, looking at the in-

Research: Are Trick-or-Treaters Deindividualized?

As you will recall from chapters 4, 10, and 11, much research has been conducted on the effects of deindividuation on aggressive behavior. Most of these studies deindividuated subjects by giving them reduced concern for self-evaluation and/or making them believe that the personal consequences of a negative evaluation by others would be minimized. Lately researchers such as Maruyama, Fraser, and Miller (1982) have been asking whether deindividuation is a form of diffusion of responsibility that inhibits helping. These researchers reasoned that Halloween provides a good natural setting for testing the application of the deindividuation model to prosocial behavior. Children trick-or-treating in Halloween costumes are fairly anonymous, excited, and generally have the social support necessary to diffuse responsibility for their pranks (antisocial behavior).

Female experimenters who were assigned to six houses in a neighborhood near the University of Southern California met children trick-or-treating on Halloween night. In the front room of each house, hospital posters and pictures of hospitalized children were displayed. The experimenter told the trick-or-treaters that she was out of candies but pointed to the posters and said she was trying to collect candies for hospitalized children. She asked the trick-or-treaters to donate some of their candies in three different ways: In the first condition they were simply asked to contribute as many candies as they could; in the second condition one child in the group was arbitrarily selected by the experimenter as a leader, given a badge, and informed that his or her name would appear on the bag of candy given at the hospital; in the third condition each child was told he or she was individually responsible, each received a badge, and each was informed that his or her name would appear on the bag of candy donated to the hospital. The experimenter then left the room, and a hidden experimenter counted the number of candies donated and the size of each group of children.

It was found that as responsibility was increased from the first to the second and third conditions, the contributions increased from the children who were in small groups. In large groups of trick-or-treaters, however, the manipulation of responsibility had no effect. The researchers concluded that in the small groups the effects of diffusion of responsibility can be overcome, but that in the large groups this is more difficult.

activity of the other bystander, seemed to decide that the theft was not too serious and that "squealing" would be more inappropriate.

An Epileptic Seizure Recognizing that their experimental theft might indeed appear unimportant, Latané and Davis extended their testing to an event of unarguable seriousness. As they explained:

Even though an event clearly is an emergency, any individual in a group who sees an emergency may feel less responsible simply because any other bystander is equally responsible for helping. To test this line of thought, an emergency was simulated in a setting designed to resemble Kitty Genovese's murder. Subjects overheard a victim calling for help. Some [subjects] knew that they were the only one to hear the victim's cries; others believed that other people besides themselves were aware of the victim's distress. As with the Genovese witnesses, subjects could not see each other or know what the others were doing. (1970, pp. 93–94)

The victim, heard via tape recorder, simulated the onset of an epileptic attack. Again, the number of bystanders that the subject perceived to be present had a major effect on the subject's likelihood of reporting the emergency. *All* subjects who thought they were alone with the victim reported the problem, many responding even before the victim stopped speaking. (See Table 12–2.) In contrast, only 62 percent of the subjects who thought 4 other bystanders were nearby acted to help the victim.

Were these people uncaring and irresponsible? Not really. When they recognized the victim's distress, many were overheard to say, "My God, he's having a fit," or "Oh God, what should I do?" When the experimenter entered the room to explain the situation, the subjects often asked if the victim was "all right." "Is he being taken care of?" "He's all right, isn't he?" Many were visibly nervous and upset.

Diffusion of Responsibility and Pluralistic Ignorance

As the previous example indicates, nonhelping subjects frequently have not decided *not* to help. Rather, their inaction generally reflects a state of indecision and conflict about *whether* to respond and *how* to help most effectively. If only one bystander is present in an emergency situation, she or he carries all of the responsibility for dealing with the emergency. The point of Latané and Darley's extensive research is, first, that when other bystanders are present, the onus of responsibility is diffused, and each individual feels less personal responsibility to help. Second, Latané and Darley suggest that there is a form of shared ignorance at work: Each bystander tends to rely upon the behavior of others as a guide to his or her own behavior. If other bystanders are not taking action, an individual may be misled into believing that no action is necessary. This combination of diffusion of responsibility and pluralistic ignorance operates to reduce the likelihood that any one individual will step forward to help. Imagine

TABLE 12–2.
Intervention and Group Size in Epileptic Seizure Experiment

Group Size	Total Number of Subjects	Percent Responding by End of Fit	Percent Ever Responding	Time in Seconds
2 (Subject and victim)	13	85	100	52
3 (Subject, victim, and one other)	26	62	85	93
6 (Subject, victim, and 4 others)	13	31	62	166

Source: From *The Unresponsive Bystander*, by B. Latané and J. M. Darley, © 1970, 97. Reprinted by permission of Prentice-Hall, Inc., Englewood Cliffs, N.J.

yourself in the same place. If others were nearby, would *you* be the one to make the first move?

Interestingly, many field (as opposed to laboratory) studies of helping behavior find that the large crowds of people typically present in the "real world" make it *more* likely, rather than *less* likely that help will be offered. Contrary to Latané and Darley's explanation of diffused responsibility, other investigators (Clark & Ward, 1971; Piliavin, Rodin, & Piliavin, 1969; Schwartz & Clausen, 1970; Staub & Clawson, 1972) have found that the presence of others reassures potentially helpful bystanders that they will be assisted, and perhaps protected, in their efforts to aid a victim or prevent a crime.

Piliavin, Rodin, and Piliavin also noted that the costs and benefits associated with intervention must be considered. Morgan and Peck (Morgan, 1978) have extended and formalized this idea in a cost-reward model of helping. In an empirical test of the model, Morgan (1978) found that as the cost of intervening increased (i.e., the more valuable time the intervener must take from an important task), and as the benefits of *not* intervening increased (i.e., the important task could be completed), the diffusion of responsibility effect found by Latané and Darley held true. The more people present, the more time elapsed before anyone took action. But when the individual costs were low and the rewards associated with not intervening were also low, group size did not have any effect on action. Individuals in large groups are just as likely to help as people who are alone.

The data are not all in, but it seems reasonable to conclude that whether or not we will act in an emergency depends on two situational factors: how personally responsible we feel in the situation, and the costs and benefits for ourselves associated with helping.

Characteristics of Those Who Help

As you read about the various experimental situations designed to test prosocial behavior, you have probably been asking yourself how you might react. Probably, too, you have been reminded of past situations in which you did, or did not, help others. Were you alone, or with someone else?

Aside from examining the effects of the presence of others on an individual's willingness to help, social psychologists have also looked at the characteristics of the individual helper. What is it about a person that predisposes him or her to help? Is there such a thing as an altruistic personality? In an emergency who makes the first move to help?

Personality and Helping

The question still remains: Who will make the first move to help? As with other topics in social psychology, the field of prosocial behavior has been the focus of extensive research. Many researchers have hoped to identify personality variables that might explain why some people offer help and others do not. However, numerous studies have been unable to identify any personal characteristics or traits that reliably correlate with altruism (Bryan, 1975; Krebs, 1970; Staub & Feinberg, 1979).

Staub (1979) found, for example, that people with strong prosocial motivation and who believe that they can influence events, and who have specific competencies—appropriate to a situation—are more likely to be helpful than people with weak prosocial motivation. Children who express sympathy toward others and show an understanding of others generally rank high in social responsibility and altruism. Nevertheless, even these children may fail to exhibit altruistic behavior in specific circumstances.

Similar findings have been reported for adults. Gergen, Gergen, and Meter (1972) explored altruism in a study of 80 college students. After taking a battery of personality inventories, the subjects were asked whether they would volunteer for one or more projects (counseling male or female high-school students on personal problems; helping with a faculty research project on deductive thinking; aid in research on unusual states of consciousness; or assist in collating materials for use by the student's class). Different personality traits were, in fact, associated with each choice of assistance; however, no one trait emerged as a consistent predictor of a general willingness to help (see Table 12-3). In their studies of 176 black and white males and females 20 to 60 years old, Wispé and Freshley (1971) were also unable to correlate any variables of age, race, or sex with a willingness to help in bystander situations.

TABLE 12–3.
Relationship between Trait Dispositions and Prosocial Behavior in Males and Females

	Type of Prosocial Behavior Chosen									
	Counsel H.S. Males		Counsel H.S. Females		Help with Deductive Thinking Experiment		Aid Research in Unusual States of Consciousness		Collating Class Materials	
	M	F	M	F	M	F	M	F	M	F
Abasement	−	−	−		−					
Autonomy				−				+	+	+
Change							+	+		
Deference				+						−
Nurturance	+			+						
Order			+	+					−	
Self-Consistency	−					+	−			
Self-Esteem								+		+
Sensation Seeking		+				−	+	+		+
Succorance	+							−		

+ Indicates positive correlation between a trait disposition and a particular choice of prosocial activity.
− Indicates negative correlation between a trait disposition and a particular choice of prosocial activity.

Source: Adapted from K. J. Gergen, M. M. Gergen, and K. Meter, "Individual Orientations to Prosocial Behavior," *Journal of Social Issues*, 1972, *28*, 115.

Characteristics Associated with Helping

What characteristics do seem useful in predicting who will help? Some clues are provided in a study by Huston et al. (1981). These investigators interviewed 32 people who had actually intervened in dangerous criminal episodes such as street muggings, armed robberies, and bank hold-ups. In comparison with a matched group of people who had not intervened in either a crime or an emergency, the helpful bystanders were found to be taller, heavier, and better trained to cope with emergencies. Many had had medical, lifesaving, or police training. Despite an extensive search for shared personality traits, none were found. However, the investigators did find something else: A significant number of the helpful bystanders had previously witnessed the victimization of others or had themselves been victims of a crime.

So the answer to the question of who will intervene in an emergency appears to depend on both previous experience and the situation, factors that are somewhat external rather than internal personality dispositions. Those who have been victims themselves or who have training in ways to help victims are more likely to help. In other words, those who know how to help *will* help. However, even these people probably will not help in the absence of what Schwartz (1977) calls "a situationally specific moral norm" for helping. The circumstances must be right or people will not feel compelled to translate their experience into direct action.

Moods and Feelings

As we have shown, the likelihood of performing prosocial acts depends most greatly on *external*, situational factors. Yet, in many instances, the crucial, decisive impetus comes from an *internal* state of mind—feelings of responsibility, empathy, and a willingness to take personal risks.

Several experiments have shown that manipulating a person's feelings or moods changes his or her tendency to be altruistic. Aderman (1971) found, for example, that subjects who read a set of "elation" mood statements were more helpful to an experimenter than subjects who had read "depression" statements. Similarly, Isen and Levin (1972) reported that college students who had unexpectedly received cookies while studying in the library or who had found a dime in a public telephone were significantly more likely than those subjects who had not received any unexpected rewards to volunteer help in a research project. But, according to a later study by Isen, Clark, and Schwartz (1976), such "good mood" effects are not especially long-lasting. Their study began with a door-to-door distribution of free stationery to homeowners. The resulting good mood extended only for about 20 minutes. Within that time period, more of those who had received stationery than control, nonrewarded subjects were willing to help a stranger by looking up a telephone number and making a phone call for her. However, when the stranger's request was made more than 20 minutes later, members of the experimental group showed no difference from members of the control group in their willingness to help her.

Controversy: Can Altruism Be Selfish?

Why do people help others? Because it is the right thing to do. What makes helping "right" is the socialization process, which teaches us what behaviors are appropriate and inappropriate in almost every social situation. During childhood, when we did the "right" thing, rewards surely followed—a cookie, a pat on the head, or a parent's smile. Later on, as the socialization messages were internalized, we learned to provide our own pat on the head, even if no one else provided it for us. Because of this conditioning, our socially approved behavior became self-gratifying: *Doing* good meant *feeling* good.

Extending this analysis a bit further, Baumann and his colleagues at Arizona State University (1981) have suggested that when we do something good for someone else we are actually doing something good for ourselves as well. When we help someone else feel better, we feel better, too. And if we can save someone else from unhappiness, but do not, we feel unhappy about not helping.

Is "selfless" altruism then really selfish self-reinforcement? Is it possible that altruism can be hedonism? To find out, Baumann and his colleagues recruited 80 college students and purposely manipulated their moods. Some of them were asked to recall experiences that had made them feel sad (negative mood); others were asked to recall happy experiences (positive mood); and a third group was asked to think about their route to school that day (neutral mood). Some subjects from each condition then were assigned a task "imbued with altruistic character." They were told they were to test a technique that would "help individuals who are losing their eyesight to observe the world about them more efficiently so they can function better with their visual handicap." The subjects in the control condition were told they would test a technique to "better understand how individuals learn to observe the world around them" (p. 104).

All subjects were shown the same sets of figures and asked to decide which one in each pair of drawings was more complex. After the test, the subjects were allowed to reward themselves by taking tokens that would later be redeemed for a prize. "The more tokens you take, the more valuable the prize," they were told. "You can take up to seven tokens; you can take all, none, or some."

Mood was measured by the number of tokens that each subject took. "Negative mood" subjects who participated in the altruistic task took fewer tokens than all the other subjects, while negative mood subjects who did not perform a helping task took more tokens than the other subjects (see Table). According to the authors' interpretation, helping made the negative mood subjects happier, and was indeed so self-gratifying that those who could be helpful needed less external gratification in the form of tokens. These results, the authors concluded, "provide good support for our contention that adult altruism is the functional equivalent of self-gratification" (p. 1,044). Or, to put it more directly, doing good is its own best reward. Haven't you heard that somewhere before?

Mean Number of Tokens Taken, by Type of Task and Mood Conditions

Type of Task	Positive Mood		Neutral Mood		Negative Mood	
	M	n	M	n	M	n
Nonaltruistic	5.00	16	3.69	13	6.10	10
Altruistic	5.07	14	4.30	10	3.63	11

Note: M = mean number of tokens taken
       n = number of subjects

Source: From "Altruism as Hedonism: Helping and Self-Gratification as Equivalent Responses," by D. J. Baumann, R. B. Cialdini, and D. T. Kenrick. *Journal of Personality and Social Psychology*, 1981 *40*, 1039–1046. Copyright 1981 by the American Psychological Association, Inc. Reprinted by permission.

Whom Do We Help?

We have seen that a potential helper who feels good is more likely to help than someone who is not in a particularly good mood. Is the helper influenced by the feelings, behavior, or other characteristics of the person who needs help? Definitely, yes. Research suggests that people are most likely to help "innocent" victims—good, bright, decent people who have done nothing foolish, stupid, or spiteful to bring about their own suffering (Lerner, 1970). We prefer to help people like ourselves, people we find attractive, and those whom we do not blame for their misfortunes.

Those Like Ourselves

Several researchers have found that people are more likely to help those who are like themselves—from the same socioeconomic group, the same race, religion, and nationality, and who wear the same kind of clothing and have the same lifestyle. For example, Emswiller, Deaux, and Willits (1971) found that "hippie-style"

Would you help either of these men? Both of them? Research indicates we help those who are like ourselves, those who are attractive, and those who we do not blame for their predicament. Are we least likely to help those who need help most?

men and women—those with long hair, jeans, a worn shirt or blouse, beat-up shoes or sandals and a "typical hippie" accessory such as beads or a headband— were more likely to lend a dime (for a phone call) to other men and women dressed like hippies than to clean-cut, "straight" dressers. Similarly, "straights" were more likely to assist other "straights" than to assist "hippies." In a similar study, Feldman (1965) found that in both Paris and Boston people were more helpful to their compatriots than to foreigners.

The effects of race similarity are not so clear-cut. Gaertner and Bickman (1971) found, for example, that when a caller reached the wrong number and required assistance from the person who answered, whites were more likely to help whites than to help blacks. However, black subjects gave about the same amount of assistance to both blacks and whites. In contrast, Dutton (1973) found that black and American Indian solicitors for a charity received significantly higher donations from whites than did white solicitors. As Dutton explains, these results support part of a theory of "reverse discrimination": "when middle-class whites are involved in 'trivial' interactions with minority group members whom they perceive as belonging to groups that have been targets of discrimination, they will treat those minority group members better than they treat another white in identical circumstances" (p. 34).

Yet another investigation, by Piliavin, Rodin, and Piliavin (1969), found that race did not effect the helping behavior of either blacks or whites who were confronted by either a black or white victim who collapsed in a New York subway. Based on these varied findings, the only conclusion one can reach about the effects of a racial similarity of a victim and a helper on altruistic behavior is that there is *no* conclusion we can reach at this time.

Those We Find Attractive

As we saw in chapter 6, physically attractive people are liked better and rated as more intelligent, more friendly, more . . . well, attractive, than nonattractive people. It should come as no surprise then that attractive people are more likely to be helped by others.

One study (Benson et al., 1976) lends empirical support to this commonsense hypothesis. The researchers purposely "lost" multiple copies of eight completed graduate school application forms, each of which included a photograph and a stamped, self-addressed envelope. The picture was used to convey information about the applicant's physical attractiveness (attractive vs. unattractive), race (black vs. white), and sex. The lost envelopes were found by 442 male and 162 female white adults passing through a large metropolitan airport. As predicted, the attractive subjects were helped significantly more often (by having their lost application returned), regardless of their race or sex. Thus, being attractive appears to be a more effective stimulus to altruism than either of the other major characteristics. (We can only hope it is not a more effective stimulus to being admitted to graduate school, but we are not so sure!)

A similar field study of an emergency situation by West and Brown (1975) showed similar results. Male college students passing by a campus health center were stopped by either an attractive or an unattractive female who made the following request: "Excuse me, I was working with a rat for a laboratory class and it bit me. Rats carry so many germs—I need to get a tetanus shot right away but I don't have any money with me. So I'm trying to collect $1.75 to pay for the shot." In a "low severity" situation, in which the young woman held her hand as if she had received a bite but showed no other signs of injury, attractiveness made no difference in the subjects' willingness to help. However, in a "high severity" situation—the victim wore a gauze bandage soaked with artificial blood—the attractive female received significantly larger donations than did an unattractive victim.

An even more startling demonstration of the power of attractiveness was reported by Pomazal and Close (1973). They studied the reactions of 400 male and female motorists who passed by a hitchhiker on the highway. Passing motorists saw either a male or a female who was either wearing or not wearing a white, 24-inch knee brace and arm sling. As might be expected, females were helped ("picked up") more often than males, but notably less help was given to women and slightly less to men who wore the brace and sling. Clearly, the "handicapped" subjects were perceived as less attractive than the "uninjured" controls.

Although people are more likely to help attractive people, the converse does not appear to be true. Female subjects were more reluctant to seek help from a physically attractive woman than from a physically unattractive woman (Nadler, 1980). The researcher believes that people are reluctant to expose their inadequacy (need for help) to a person whose attractiveness makes her seem "better" than they are. Similarly, Gergen and his colleagues (1975) found that people who are able to improve their standing in a helper's eyes, for example, by repaying a debt, find the donor more attractive than a donor for whom nothing can be done in return.

Those We Do Not Blame

Nadler's finding of a reluctance to seek help in people who perceive themselves as less attractive than their potential helper works the other way as well. The more attractive potential helper is often reluctant to give help to unattractive victims. Lerner (1970) observed that medical students often resented having to treat indigent patients. Their tendency to "blame the victim" and to attribute the victim's illness to his or her self-neglect inhibited their ability to empathize and help those patients who needed help the most.

Since physicians are responsible for treating *all* patients—whether indigent or wealthy—we might expect their sense of responsibility to override the negative effects of unattractiveness. However, studies show that just the opposite may be true. Lerner and Matthews (1967) found, for example, that students who received strong electric shocks were perceived as more attractive if the subject–observer believed the subject to be shocked had chosen a "shock" slip from a bowl than those who were believed not to be responsible for their fate. Those who were themselves responsible for another person's suffering tended to devalue their victims. Since physicians are often in the position of inflicting pain, Lerner (1970) notes, it is not surprising that they often devalue and look down upon those they treat.

Why do people blame those who are victimized? According to Lerner (1970) and others (Rubin & Peplau, 1973) most people want to believe that the world is a just place where good is rewarded and bad is punished. If someone becomes a victim, these researchers suggest, people assume that he or she must have done something to deserve it despite the fact that we hear news of unjust suffering every day.

When Helping Does Not Help

Recent research has demonstrated that we may actually hurt those who are recipients of our good intentions when we think we are helping them. Research on recipients' reactions to aid (reviewed in Coates, Renzaglia, & Embree, in press) has revealed that recipients of help may later feel more out of control, incompetent, and incapable of overcoming both present and future problems. Patients confined to total care institutions, for example, often experience a feeling of helplessness that renders them incapable of making contributions to their own recovery. Similarly disabled patients, on the other hand, provided with less than total care and expected to assume control over certain aspects of their lives, showed dramatic improvement in both physical and emotional health (Langer & Rodin, 1976; Rodin & Langer, 1977; Rodin, 1980). (See chapter 16.)

Researchers have also found that people are less likely to maintain improvements that are attributed to another's help than improvements that they believe to be self-generated (Brickman et al., 1982). These findings have led social psy-

Application: If You Want Help—Ask For It!

Before intervening to assist a victim, a bystander must notice the victim's plight, interpret it as an emergency, decide that he or she has a personal responsibility to act, and believe that he or she can render the necessary assistance, according to the Latané and Darley model of intervention described earlier in this chapter (see p. 453). In most bystander situations, the crucial factor is whether the bystander assumes personal responsibility. If more people could be made to feel more responsible for more other people, a significant amount of suffering and tragedy might be averted. How can responsibility be generated?

According to Shaffer, Rogel, and Hendrick (1975), the answer is simple: *just ask!* They observed male and female students studying in isolated areas of the Kent State University Library. A confederate seated himself at the table occupied by a lone subject. After several minutes of apparent studying, the confederate got up and walked away from the table, leaving behind an assortment of personal belongings. With some subjects, the victim looked back and asked the student to watch his belongings (request condition). With the remaining subjects, no request was made.

Soon, a "thief" appeared, rummaged through the confederate's belongings, discovered his wallet, and hurriedly walked off with it. As you might expect, 64 percent of the subjects in the "request" condition tried to stop the theft, as opposed to only 14 percent in the "no-request" condition. The moral of our story is: If you want help—ask for it!

chologists to design ways to help recipients regain control over their lives. One way this has been accomplished has been by turning recipients into donors. Allen (1976), for example, found that the best way to improve the competence of slower students was to have them instruct younger children in the subjects they themselves had difficulty with. It has been suggested (Brickman et al., 1982) that one of the reasons for the success of Alcoholics Anonymous is that members not only receive help but also give it (by setting a continuing good example to others, and by round-the-clock availability to discuss problems).

Altruism in a Cultural Context

How universal are the social norms we have been talking about? Is altruism prized everywhere? Are people in all cultures socialized to help one another? Is helping behavior a truly human characteristic?

Specific research on prosocial behavior in other cultures has been rare, and therefore the few glimpses we can get are the more fascinating. Gergen and his

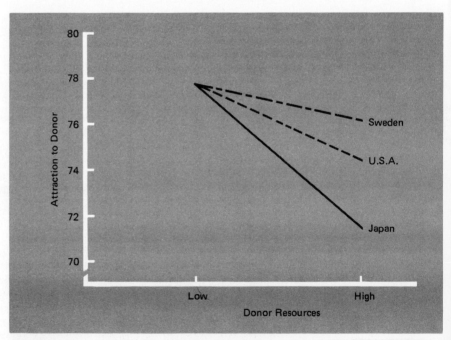

FIGURE 12-2. Attraction to the Donor in Three Nations as a Function of Donor Resources

Source: *From "Obligation, Donor Resources, and Reactions to Aid in Three Cultures," by K. J. Gergen, C. Maslach, P. Ellsworth, and M. Seipel,* Journal of Personality and Social Psychology, *1968, 10, 395.*

associates (1975) studied the sense of obligation felt when one receives aid from another person, and the aspects of giving aid that make a donor attractive to a recipient. The subjects were male college students in the United States, Japan, and Sweden. The researchers found "substantial similarities" in the "relationship between obligation and attraction" in all three cultures (p. 398). Donors with low resources, who subjects felt could ill afford to give, were perceived as more attractive than donors with high resources in all three countries (see Figure 12–2). In all three countries, too, donors who asked for an equal exchange were evaluated more highly than donors who gave with no obligation. Only one cultural difference appeared: In Japan and the United States, but not in Sweden, donors who asked for interest were evaluated less favorably than those who asked for an equal exchange (see Figure 12–3). The researchers point out, however, that despite the similar results for these very dissimilar cultures, the fact that all three countries "share in a material prosperity . . . might well have colored their reactions to economic aid" (p. 400). Moreover, we cannot "be certain that these patterns would be found in more primitive or less technologically advanced cultures" (p. 400).

In the absence of studies, we must look to field research, usually by anthropologists, to demonstrate the range of prosocial behaviors in human societies. And quite a range it is! Consider, first, Turnbull's (1972) account of the African

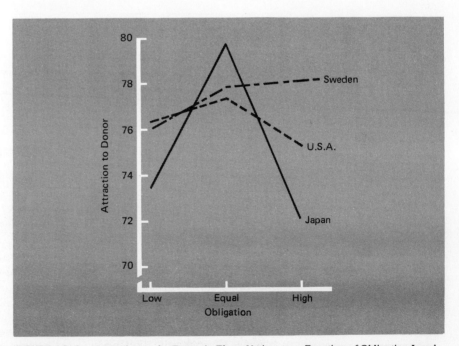

FIGURE 12–3. Attraction to the Donor in Three Nations as a Function of Obligation Level
Source: *From "Obligation, Donor Resources, and Reactions to Aid in Three Cultures," by K. J. Gergen, C. Maslach, P. Ellsworth, and M. Seipel,* Journal of Personality and Social Psychology, *1968, 10, 396.*

To ensure specific kinds of helping behavior among their people, cultures have a variety of social institutions at their disposal. Among Indians living on the Northwest Coast of North America, the potlatch serves this function and others as well. A tribal leader may prepare for years before giving a feast for people from the surrounding area. The guests are not only fed and entertained lavishly with ritual singing and dancing, but they are also the recipients of valued gifts. Those who receive gifts and hospitality are under various obligations to their host. Here, women of the Kwakiutl tribe survey some of the goods assembled for a potlatch.

mountain tribespeople known as the Ik. The Ik were farmers, struggling for existence in hostile and infertile terrain:

> The food was uneatable because there was not any, and the people were as unfriendly, uncharitable, inhospitable and generally mean as any people can be. Given the situation in which the Ik found themselves as I headed toward them, man has no time for such luxuries, and a much more basic man appears, using much more basic survival tactics. (p. 32)

> If when out walking I stumbled during a difficult descent . . . the Ik shrieked with laughter. . . . Men would watch a child with eager anticipation as it crawled toward the fire, then burst into gay and happy laughter as it plunged a skinny hand into the coals. (p. 112)

> Anyone falling down was good for a laugh too, particularly if he was old or weak, or blind. . . . The best game of all, at this time, was teasing poor little Adupa . . . [who] was a little mad. . . . Adupa did not go and jump on other people's play houses, and she lavished enormous care on hers and would curl up inside it. . . . That of course made it all the more jump-on-able, and Atum's nephew and granddaughter, Lokwam and Nialectcha, used to fight to be the first to jump. . . . Then when Adupa pulled herself from the ruins of her house, crying, Lokwam became genial and let others join in as he beat her over the head and danced around her. (pp. 113–114)*

If the Ik represent a society in which the total absence of prosocial behaviors has survival value, most American Indian cultures are at the opposite pole. Indian communities across the continent, from the northeastern Iroquois to the southwestern Pueblos, traditionally offer hospitality to every stranger. In those tribes, a child can go into any home and be sure of receiving food and shelter. Even under duress similar to the struggle for survival of the Ik, a group of American Indians, the last of the Yahi tribe, remained tender and caring toward one another (Kroeber, 1961).

We know of the Yahi's struggle because their last survivor, Ishi, appeared in a northern California town late in the summer of 1911. Befriended by anthropologists at the University of California, Ishi lived out the remainder of his life in comfort, teaching his new friends his skills, and telling them his story. By the early years of the twentieth century, only four Yahi were left:

> A man and woman became frail and old; and a second man [Ishi] and woman, able-bodied, strong, and well, but no longer young. . . . Ishi's group was master of the difficult art of communal and peaceful co-existence under permanent threat of alarm, and in a tragic and deteriorating prospect. We know from Ishi that men took on "women's work" and *vice versa* according to need. The sick, the dying, and the bedridden were cared for; the dead were sent on their way with ritual formality, nor did the living neglect to mourn for them. . . . [After their pitiful settlement was raided] Ishi somehow managed to carry his mother out of reach [of Californians looking for them. They] were together until her death. . . . That Ishi was wearing his hair burned short in sign of mourning in August, 1911, was evidence of a death or deaths in his family. (Kroeber, 1961, pp. 97, 108, 114)†

The dark side of human nature need not prevail.

---

*From *The Mountain People* by C. M. Turnbull. Copyright © 1972 by Colin M. Turnbull. Reprinted by permission of Simon & Schuster, a Division of Gulf & Western Corporation.

†From *Ishi in Two Worlds* by Theodora Kroeber. Berkeley: University of California Press, 1961.

Answering Questions about Prosocial Behavior

1. George Homans first formalized a social psychological idea that's been around for centuries: Most people will weigh the personal costs and rewards associated before they perform a given act. Acting altruistically is no exception to this "rule of reciprocity." Several empirical studies have confirmed this notion of reciprocity. Researchers have found, for example, that children who received a gift of candy from another youngster were more likely to share with that child in the future.

2. While many people feel obligated to act altruistically in certain situations, those who have a general awareness of the consequences of their actions in interpersonal situations, *and* who don't deny responsibility for taking action, are the ones who will translate their feelings of obligation into behavior. These two variables—awareness of consequences and responsibility denial—*interact* to help translate prosocial feelings into prosocial behaviors.

3. Researchers have found that increasing the number of people present in a laboratory emergency situation *decreases* the chance that any one individual will intervene and help. This phenomenon has been termed "diffusion of responsibility." It should be noted that diffusion of responsibility effects have been hard to find in the field, and that the costs and rewards associated with intervening also interact with the number of people present in the situation. In situations where the costs of not intervening are high, and the rewards for intervening are also high, people will probably help no matter how many others are present.

4. Research in the field and in the laboratory has demonstrated that people are more likely to help those who are similar to themselves than those who are dissimilar. People are also more likely to help those who they find attractive and victims whom they do not blame for their plight.

5. Researchers have not found many consistent relationships between personality type and helping behavior. People who are nurturant or high in self-esteem, for example, may help in one situation but not in others. There are, however, some characteristics that may distinguish those who will or will not intervene in a dangerous crime emergency situation: At least one investigator has found that helpful bystanders tend to be taller, heavier, better trained or prepared to help in emergencies, and that they had previously witnessed or been victims of a crime themselves.

Summary

Regard for the interest of others, without concern for one's self-interest, is termed **altruism**. Giving assistance to another with a definite goal in mind is known as **helping**. Both of these, as well as actions that benefit another, regardless of the benefits to or self-sacrifices of the actor, fall under the broad heading of **prosocial behavior**.

The term *prosocial* was originally used to mean *culturally desirable*. For ex-

ample, *prosocial aggression* was defined as potentially harmful aggressive behavior used for purposes that the culture defines as desirable.

Some psychologists believe that altruism is inborn, that it is a genetically determined, internal mechanism that insures the survival of the species, even at the
expense of altruistic (self-sacrificing) individuals. Critics of this theory point out
that since altruists are more likely than cowards to meet death at an early age,
they would not have much opportunity to reproduce and transmit "prosocial
genes" to offspring.

Learning theorists hold that altruism is an acquired behavior. They point to
studies showing that helping behavior increases with age, as children gain exposure to models and earn rewards for altruism.

Prosocial behavior follows a collection of unwritten rules—**social norms**—that
stipulate which behaviors are acceptable and encouraged, and which are unacceptable or discouraged in various situations. Although these norms are external mechanisms, most individuals internalize the values and beliefs that norms
represent. Among the altruistic social norms that have been identified are *reciprocity* (doing for others in the expectation they would do the same for you), *equity*
(creating a balance of gains and/or losses to the individuals involved), and *social responsibility* (feeling that one should help others, regardless of whether or
not they can reciprocate).

Personal norms are internalized social norms. Researchers who attempt to
predict whether a person will behave altruistically in a given situation depend on
that individual's personal norms, *awareness of the consequences* of any action,
and the human tendency to *deny responsibility* for taking action.

Studies of emergency situations indicate that, in the presence of other
people, bystanders may fail to provide help and may underestimate their responsibility for helping. Latané and Darley's diffusion of responsibility model sees
helping as a series of decisions, often made without the person's conscious
awareness. The person must first notice that something is happening, then interpret it as an emergency, and then make a decision about whether it is his or her
personal responsibility to act. If action is called for, the person must next decide
on the form of assistance required, and then how to implement that decision to
act. The reason people do not act in emergency situations, according to Latané
and Darley, is that they are led to believe that no intervention is necessary because no one else is taking action and also because they feel little personal responsibility to intervene when others are also present. Other researchers have
noted that relevant competencies and experience with helping determine
whether someone will help in an emergency, rather than personal characteristics
of the potential helper.

It has also been found that people who are in a good mood are more likely to
help. However, the characteristics of the person who needs help may be more important in determining whether help will be given than any characteristics in the
helper. People tend to help those who are most like themselves, those who are attractive, and those who are not to blame. There is a widespread tendency to
"blame the victim" and thus devalue a person in need, and therefore to provide
less assistance. In the most difficult circumstances, when altruism is most
needed and appreciated, it may often be withheld. Some researchers have also
shown that helping a person may actually do more harm than good; the person
who is helped may suffer a loss of self-competence and feel a sense of a loss of
self-control.

Suggested Additional Reading

Latané, B. & Darley, J. M. *The unresponsive bystander: Why doesn't he help?* New York: Appleton-Century-Crofts, 1970.

Rushton, J. P. *Altruism, socialization and society.* Englewood Cliffs; N.J.: Prentice-Hall, 1980.

Schwartz, S. H. Normative influences on altruism. In L. Berkowitz (Ed.), *Advances in experimental social psychology* (Vol. 10). New York: Academic Press, 1977.

Staub, E., ed. *Positive social behavior and morality* (Vols. 1 & 2). New York: Academic Press, 1978, 1979.

Wispé, L. G., ed. *Altruism, sympathy, and helping: Psychological and sociological principles.* New York: Academic Press, 1978.

APPLYING
SOCIAL PSYCHOLOGY

13

GROUPS, LEADERSHIP, AND ORGANIZATIONS

Questions about Groups, Leadership, and Organizations

1. What is a group?
2. Can an individual be more productive than a group?
3. Why do people join groups and want to remain in them? What makes people want to leave a group?
4. Does a group take more risks than its individual members would alone?
5. Is there such a thing as a "group mind" or crowd mentality?
6. Are leaders born or made? That is, are there people who are "natural leaders," or do leaders emerge as a result of being in the right place at the right time?
7. Does job satisfaction cause good performance, or does good job performance cause job satisfaction?

Several people are talking together in the middle of a hallway. You have to pass them on the way to your classroom. Would you take the straightest route, which leads you directly in their midst? Or would you walk around them?

Stated another way, would you consider these interacting people blocking the hall as so many individuals, each constituting a separate obstacle to be negotiated on your way to class? Or would you treat this collection of people as something more, having perhaps a certain life of its own, which you recognize by walking around the entire collection—around the entire **group**?

What Is a Group?

Although groups have been studied by social psychologists for more than 50 years, researchers are still actively exploring the mutual influences of groups and the individuals who form them on each other. It is easier to describe the characteristics of groups than to define what they are. Floyd Allport (1924), in his classic social psychology textbook (see chapter 2), said that "nobody ever stumbled over a group," implying that groups are illusory, existing only in people's minds. However, others have discovered that groups have quite tangible boundaries. Knowles (1973) found that in the hallway situation just described, more people walked around the group than through it. However, more

476

people walked through two-person groups than through four-person groups; and more people walked through groups of people of lower status (in this case, college students) than through groups of people of higher status (college professors). Knowles interpreted these differing behaviors to indicate that not only do groups have boundaries, but that group boundaries vary in permeability depending on the size and status of the group.

The nature of groups has interested writers for many years. Le Bon (1903) not only recognized that large groups (crowds) were distinct entities, but went so far as to say that a crowd has a "collective mind" that amounts to more than the minds of the individuals in it. As we shall see later, Le Bon believed this collective mind was destructive in nature.

Groups are sometimes defined by the factors that make a collection of individuals come together, such as the interaction and communication among its members, and shared goals and norms. For the moment, however, it might be more useful to consider "groupness" as a matter of degree. We can then distinguish three levels:

1. *Aggregate group*—a collection of individuals with no social connection whatsoever, such as people waiting at a bus stop.
2. *Minimal group*—a collection of individuals that has at least some social connection, although it may be weak, such as an audience at a concert.
3. *Identity group*—the strongest form of a group, important for the sense of identity of those who belong to it, such as the family, colleagues at work, or a church's members.

Another basic distinction is the length of time a group exists. *Ad hoc groups* are temporary, created to meet a particular need, and are disbanded when they are no longer required. Impromptu groups of rescue workers following a disaster, a jury, or the groups created for study in the laboratory by social psychologists are some examples. *Ongoing groups* interact repeatedly over a longer period of time, which may be for the duration of a semester for a university seminar, or for several years for a board of trustees.

Finally, groups can be differentiated according to their purpose. *Task groups* function to get a particular job done, and all of their activities are oriented to this end. *Social groups*, on the other hand, exist for the purpose of the social interaction and enjoyment of their members.

Individuals and Groups

If you are a jogger out on the road for your daily half-hour workout, what happens if another runner pulls up beside you? If you do not know the other person, conversation is unlikely. Instead, your interaction becomes a matter of who is going to pass whom, or whether you will keep up a common pace until one of you tires. As a result of this competition, will your performance improve? (In all likelihood it will.)

But suppose you are a new jogger, out on a day when the road is thick with

At right, an aggregate group has gathered to purchase lunch from a sidewalk vendor.

Marc Anderson

runners who are obviously old pros, moving fast with relaxed looking strides. Will being in such a group make you more enthusiastic about running, or are you more likely to go home, bury your new running gear deep in a drawer, and leave it there?

These real-life situations—you will be able to think of others—involve the relationship between individuals and groups. The group in these examples is at the aggregate level—a mere collection of individuals—or at the minimal group level. Contemporary social psychology looks at the relationship between groups and individuals from a variety of perspectives. Two of the most important are Zajonc's **social facilitation theory** which deals with the effect of the presence of others on an individual's performance, and Latané's **social impact theory,** which deals with the effect of the individual on the group as well as with the effect of the group on the individual.

Social Facilitation

The earliest social psychology experiment was in fact an experiment in social facilitation by Triplett (1898). Using a copy of the official bicycle race records of 1897, Triplett charted the times of cyclists racing alone; of cyclists racing with no competing cyclists but preceded by a swift cycle that set the pace; and of cyclists racing in competition and preceded by a pacemaker. Triplett found that the times for cyclists competing together were the fastest, and that the times for cyclists pedaling alone were the slowest. Triplett then devised a "competition machine" to use in an experiment, a device made of fishing reels that allowed two persons to turn side by side. Forty children were asked to turn the fishing reels as fast as they could. Half of the trials were performed by children "reeling" by themselves, and half by children competing together. The results showed that many children acting with others (co-action) were able to exceed the maximum they attained when working alone.

The term **social facilitation** was coined in 1924 by Floyd Allport, who theo-

Left: Ken Karp; right: Vetter/RSVP

Left: These enthusiastic participants in an outdoor rally are a minimal group, connected only for this particular event. Right: The members of this identity group meet regularly to produce quilts that are either sold to raise money for senior citizens or given to children in an orphanage. This is also an ongoing, task, and social group.

rized that "the sight and sound of others doing the same thing" are stimuli that not only trigger a reaction that a person is prepared to give, but also intensify that reaction. In 1930 Dashiell conducted a series of studies on the effects of audience and co-action. The results showed that in general the performance of individuals was improved whether they were working under observation or in co-action with others. Other studies, however, have shown that the presence of an audience can sometimes impair an individual's performance. The experimental design of such studies typically requires subjects to learn new responses in the presence of others.

A large body of conflicting research results accumulated over the next 30 years. In 1965 Zajonc explained these seemingly conflicting results with his theory of social facilitation. Zajonc hypothesized that the mere presence of others as spectators or as co-actors causes arousal, and hence increases the likelihood of people's most common responses (or so-called **dominant response tendencies**) occurring. If dominant responses are correct, either because the task is well learned or instinctive, then co-action or the presence of an audience can improve individual performance; but if the dominant responses are mostly incorrect, as when a skill is being learned (as in our second running example) or when tasks are complex, then the presence of others hampers individual performance.

Although Zajonc's explanation was quite compelling, Cottrell (1972) questioned whether the *mere* presence of others was responsible for these effects. In an experiment (Cottrell et al., 1968), subjects were placed in three different situations: alone; in an audience situation with two observers nearby; and in a "mere presence" situation, with two observers who were wearing blindfolds so they could not really "observe." Social facilitation took place only in the condition in which observers were not blindfolded. Cottrell concluded that it is not the "mere presence" of others that causes arousal, but the *anticipated evaluation* by others.

However, new evidence contradicted this interpretation. In an amusing social facilitation experiment, Zajonc, Heingartner, and Herman (1969) attempted to offset any questions of evaluation apprehension that arise in studies with human subjects by recording the maze and runway performances of cockroaches. The results: The mere presence of other cockroaches seemed to be a source of arousal that facilitated the dominant response performance!

Although concern for social facilitation has waned in recent years, a new series of articles suggests that it still holds interest for researchers and theorists. Bond (1982) has proposed an updated "self-presentational" version of the theory, which is similar to Cottrell's (1972) earlier evaluation apprehension explanation. Sanders (1981) has recently offered a distraction/conflict hypothesis to explain social facilitation results. He suggests that the presence of others is distracting, and causes a conflict in subjects' attention between the other people present and the task at hand. This may improve performances of easy tasks, which do not require full attention; but it has a negative effect on difficult tasks, which do. Other writers, such as Markus (1981) and Geen (1981), have criticized this idea, maintaining that Zajonc's original theory, with some modification, remains the best explanation of the social facilitation phenomenon.

Social Impact Theory

Over 50 years ago, the German researcher Ringlemann performed an interesting experiment. He asked workers to pull as hard as they could on a rope by themselves, or with one, two, or seven other people. Ringlemann used a gauge to measure how hard the subjects pulled (Moede, 1927). He found that the more people were in the group, the less hard each individual pulled. In other words, the collective group performance was less than the sum of the individual efforts.

Like social facilitation theory, social impact theory also deals with the effect the presence of others has on an individual's performance. According to social impact theory, when more people work together, even though the group as a whole may outperform any single individual, individuals within the group are likely to exert less effort.

In his social impact theory, Latané (1981) extended the ideas originally offered by Ringlemann. Social impact theory is a comprehensive attempt to account for a broad range of phenomena. There are two main points to the theory. The first is that the impact of a group on an individual increases as the size of the group increases. (See Figure 13-1.) The second point is that the larger the group, the smaller the impact of any individual on each member of the group. We saw some evidence of this effect in the conformity studies (particularly Asch, 1951; and Rosenberg, 1961) discussed in chapter 10.

Once in the pack, you may not have to bark, but you must at least wag your tail.
Russian proverb

Latané, Williams, and Harkins (1981) replicated Ringlemann's finding conceptually by conducting two experiments in which people were asked to shout or clap as loud as they could. As the number of co-performers increased, the output of each member decreased. Latané termed these reduced efforts *social loafing*.

Increasing the number of participants diminishes the pressure on an individual to perform because the effort is divided among the group members, and because it is less likely that individual output can be identified. This can also reduce the individual's apprehension about performance. In both a laboratory and a field study of stage fright, Jackson and Latané (1981) found that subjects were

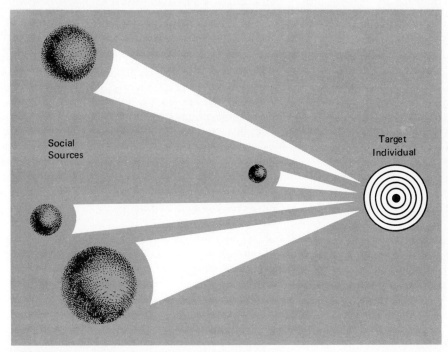

FIGURE 13–1.   Effect of the Group on the Individual

According to Latané's social impact theory, the forces exerted by a group on an individual have a "multiplicative" effect.

Source: *From "The Psychology of Social Impact," by B. Latané,* American Psychologist, *1981, 36, 344.*

less nervous when they performed in acts involving a large number of performers than when they were in acts with a few performers.

Support for the general principles of social impact comes from a wide range of research. As we saw in chapter 12, many studies have found that people in groups are less likely to help or intervene than are people alone—in groups there is a "diffusion of responsibility." If others are present, the responsibility for helping is divided among the members, diminishing individual initiative. Examples of other applications of social impact theory described by Latané (1981) are: research on chivalry in elevators (as the number of people increased, the probability that an individual will respond chivalrously decreased); tipping in restaurants (tips were proportionately less as the responsibility was divided among more people); and "declaring for Christ" (Billy Graham's impact was reduced proportionately as the size of the crowd increased).

The important point about both social facilitation and social impact theories is that they capture, in different ways, aspects of group influences on the individual. Of course, a group's influence varies depending on the type of group being considered. In the sections that follow we will consider research on a number of group characteristics.

Group Structure

Think of all the groups you have belonged to in your life. Which ones are you no longer a member of? What are the reasons why you no longer belong to those groups? What is keeping you "in" the others? Why are you a more active participant in some groups than in others?

In this section we will examine the structure of groups. First we will take a look at what holds groups together—their cohesiveness. Then we will consider the effects of differentiation in roles and status among members.

Cohesiveness

For a group to function as a group, people must be attracted to it in the first place and have a desire to join it. Cartwright and Zander (1968) have suggested three factors that affect group attractiveness:

1. *Attractiveness of members.* A person evaluates other members of a group before deciding to join.
2. *Similarity among members.* As indicated by Festinger (1954) in his social comparison theory (see chapter 4), people want to compare themselves with others who are similar.
3. *Instrumental needs.* A group is attractive to those who identify with its goals. This attraction holds even for a group that fails to reach its goals, if members view the failure as due to arbitrary, external forces that the group could not control.

Why Do People Stay in Groups?   Cohesiveness may be defined as the result of all the forces that cause members to remain in a group (Festinger, 1951). Several methods have been devised to measure group cohesiveness, each emphasizing one or another of the component forces of cohesiveness as we have just defined it (Cartwright & Zander, 1968). Friendship indexes, for example, measure the interpersonal attraction among members. There are also ways to measure group members' evaluation of their group as a whole, with a more positive evaluation presumably reflecting greater cohesiveness. For instance, Mann and Baumgartel (1952) asked a sample of employees to agree or disagree with the statement: "Our crew is better than others at sticking together." Of those employees with a low rate of absence (which is assumed to reflect high group cohesiveness), 62 percent endorsed the statement. Only 21 percent of those employees with a high rate of absence (reflecting low cohesiveness) agreed with the statement.

Other researchers have measured members' feelings of personal involvement with a group, the degree of individual identification with a group, and the strength of an individual's sense of belonging to the group. All of these factors seem related to group cohesiveness, as is the expressed desire of individuals to remain in their group.

Members of a senior center make music together. Which of Cartwright and Zander's factors that affect group attractiveness is operative here?

Ken Karp/Sirovich Senior Center

Factors That Increase Cohesiveness   Researchers have isolated several factors that can contribute to a group's cohesiveness. One of these is competition with other groups. Recall from chapter 10 the classic study by Sherif et al. (1954) in a boys' camp in Robbers Cave State Park in Oklahoma. The cohesiveness within the two groups, the Eagles and the Rattlers, increased when the groups were brought into open competition with one another. However, when the groups were given superordinate goals that could not be attained by either group alone, they learned to cooperate and even began to make friends with members of the formerly hostile opposite group.

Fear can also increase cohesiveness. Mulder and Stemerding (1963) conducted an experiment in the Netherlands in which merchants in several small towns were led to believe that a supermarket chain would soon open a branch nearby, which would substantially lower the profit of each merchant. As a result, the merchants in each of the towns demonstrated increased group cohesiveness.

In the study of the effects of initiation by Aronson and Mills (1959) mentioned in chapter 4, subjects who underwent a severe initiation in order to join a group expressed greater liking for the group than control subjects who did not undergo harsh initiations. Rewards are another factor that can increase cohesiveness, and they need not be material. Lott and Lott (1965) demonstrated that groups in which people had pleasant experiences were highly cohesive.

Effects of Cohesiveness   Beyond holding groups together, we might wonder what other effects cohesiveness has on a group. Here we will consider two: the influence on productivity, and the impaired decision-making phenomenon known as "groupthink."

A high degree of cohesiveness has several effects that should be conducive to high productivity. One of these is greater participation in the group's endeavors by each group member. Studies generally indicate that the rate of absenteeism is lower, and the work effort is greater in a cohesive group (Cartwright & Zander, 1968). In addition, communication between group members is more frequent in a cohesive group (Lott & Lott, 1961), cooperation is greater (Haythorn, 1953), and the satisfaction of group members is greater (Exline, 1957). All of these positive results of cohesiveness can be expected to lead to higher productivity.

I do not like work even when another person does it.
Mark Twain

They do not always, however. Homans (1950) found that workers in cohesive groups established norms for performance, and discouraged any group member who exceeded the group's predetermined performance level. This tendency of groups to establish and maintain a kind of "lowest common denominator" seems especially true for highly cohesive groups.

A bad compromise is better than a good battle.
Russian proverb

The word *groupthink*, or conformity to the values and ethics of a group, was coined by George Orwell in the novel *1984* (1949), and has entered our everyday language. The concept was explored by Irving Janis (1972), who found that decision-making in highly cohesive groups can be impaired. Such groups do not necessarily come up with cautious plans of action moderated by compromises, as one might expect. Instead, very cohesive groups can make radical and even foolhardy decisions. Group members may develop a strong *esprit de corps*, including an unconscious set of shared illusions. These nonrational factors interfere with factually based decision-making. Overconfidence abounds in such groups, and each member has great respect for the opinions of the other members. When an action is proposed, assent by all members is often assured by the very spirit of cooperation, rather than by any rational deliberation. Group members, often without realizing it, are reluctant to introduce any doubts they may have, lest they disturb the pleasant, consensual atmosphere of the group. A dissenting member risks being jumped upon by the others.

As an example of the destructive potential of groupthink, Janis analyzed the 1961 Bay of Pigs fiasco, in which a group of high level American policymakers, including President John F. Kennedy, devised a foolhardy plan to overthrow the government of Fidel Castro by secretly landing a brigade of Cuban exiles on a beach in Cuba. The group that came up with this plan included some very intelligent and experienced people; yet they based their decision on assumptions bordering on the absurd. The plan that resulted from this exercise in groupthink failed in its earliest stages.

Differentiation Among Members

Within a group, there is often a division of labor among the members. Some members perform one type of task, and other members perform different types of tasks. In some groups tasks are assigned. In others, though, the division of labor and the role differentiation associated with it may evolve from the interaction of the group members. Once roles have been established, the kind of behavior associated with them tends to be expected in the future by other group members.

Roles Probably the most commonly drawn role distinction is that between a group's task specialist and its social–emotional specialist. The task specialist has a high degree of competence for the task at hand, and tends to guide the group's task activities. This is an important group function, but not necessarily a popular one. The task specialist talks a fair amount of the time, and he or she has more prestige relative to other group members because of managing the group's work. However, these factors, plus any readjustments (with their attendant frustrations) that members must make in order to carry out the task, can arouse a certain amount of hostility toward the task specialist.

The social–emotional specialist represents those values that may be disturbed by the task specialist. Tending to the emotional needs of the members and to the relationships among them, the social–emotional specialist fills a prominent group role. Assent of the social–emotional specialist to the proposals of the task specialist may be necessary in order to get the group members to carry out a task effectively (Parsons & Bales, 1955). Traditionally, in mixed-sex groups, women have filled the role of social–emotional specialist, and men that of task specialist. There is no innate tie to gender, however; the roles are interchangeable, and indeed, one person can hold both. Moreover, both roles exist, and are filled, in single-sex groups.

These roles are informal roles. Institutionalized roles also exist. Institutionalized roles are more clear-cut than informal roles, spelling out the behavior expected of people as the result of their position. Such common group roles as coordinator or chairperson, recording secretary, or treasurer, for example, define generally accepted acts and behaviors. Other institutionalized roles—vice-president or co-coordinator, for example—may have to be identified and defined by the group members. The expected behavior associated with a given institutionalized role is well known, and thus it affects the attitudes and behavior of the others, and also of the person performing the role. The study by Zimbardo (1973) of subjects asked to temporarily assume the roles of prisoners and prison guards, discussed in chapters 2 and 15, strikingly confirmed how readily people can become caught up in the behavior appropriate to their roles.

Status Status is a position of social rank within a group. Each group member has a status, and every status has certain characteristics. Sometimes status is inherent in the person (as a result of socioeconomic class or professional achievement, for example) and sometimes it derives from the person's role or performance in the group. Whatever the source of their status, higher status people talk more in a group, and more communications are directed toward them (Berger, Cohen, & Zeldnick, 1973). One study found that high-status jury members tended to choose the seat at the head of the table and tried to perform the role of discussion leader during jury deliberations (Strokbeck & Hook, 1961). Torrence (1954) found that B-26 bomber crews more readily accepted the solution to a problem when it came from the person of highest status, the pilot. Decisions originating from the second highest status person, the navigator, were more readily accepted than those of the next level down, the gunner. Crew members readily accepted solutions that originated with higher-status people, even when those solutions were, objectively, wrong or ineffective. Status is also an important factor in determining which member will lead a group. (Leadership will be discussed later in this chapter.)

Group Processes

Think again of the groups you belong to. What are the purposes of these groups? (They might be work groups, athletic groups, hobby groups, drinking groups, church groups, and so on.) We have just been talking about the structure of groups in terms of the relationships between its members. How do the structures of your groups vary?

Are your groups as productive as they should be? How could their productivity be improved? How is decision-making handled in these groups? Are there splits or factions? How do group members communicate with one another? One way to see how important these group characteristics can be is to conduct a little "thought experiment." What would happen if the decision-making in your drinking group was conducted in the same way as the decision-making on your job? Or vice versa? What would happen if the communication patterns of some of your groups were exchanged?

We are now going to examine group processes—productivity, decision-making, polarization, and communication—each of which is affected by variations in group structure.

Group Productivity

Productivity is a concern of task groups (social groups are not expected to be productive in this sense). A task group is a set of people assigned to perform a task. According to Steiner (1972), productivity is determined by the interaction of three factors:

1. *Task demands* include all the requirements for performing the task: the resources needed, how the resources must be combined, and the constraints imposed by any external rules or conditions.
2. *Resources* are the knowledge, abilities, skills, tools, and materials that a group possesses.
3. *Process* consists of the means used by the group to perform its task.

The maximum performance that can be achieved, given the demands of a particular task and the available resources, is **potential productivity**. However, **actual productivity** is often lower than the potential, due to process problems in which resources are not used as effectively as possible. This can be expressed as a formula: actual productivity = potential productivity − loss due to faulty processes (Steiner 1972, p. 9).

Could Hamlet *have been written by a committee, or the* Mona Lisa *painted by a club? . . . Creative ideas do not spring from groups.*
Whitney Griswold

Productivity often depends on the type of task facing a group. Steiner distinguishes between *unitary tasks*, all aspects of which must be performed by a single individual, and *divisible tasks*, which can be accomplished through division of labor. Tasks can also be categorized according to the ways in which members' efforts can be utilized to accomplish them (see Table 13–1).

In a recent review of research on group performance, Gayle Hill (1982) ob-

Application: Brainstorming

Developed in the 1950s as a group process for creating innovative ideas for advertising campaigns, brainstorming has since been widely used in business and other settings to generate potential solutions to problems. The technique is deceptively simple: A problem is posed to a group and members are asked to come up with as many different ideas for solving it as quickly as possible. Typically, there is a brainstorming session monitor who introduces the problem and then, standing at a flip-chart supplied with blank paper, writes down the solutions of the seated "brainstormers," which come in rapid-fire order. Alex Osborn (1957), the originator, established these rules for brainstorming:

1. All criticism or analysis of suggestions is withheld until the end of a session.
2. "The wilder the idea the better."
3. A great number of suggestions is desired.
4. Building on previous suggestions, in the form of combinations or improvements, is welcome.

Brainstorming is used best to solve two kinds of problems. The first is to suggest the steps that might be followed to achieve a certain goal. For example, a brainstorming session might seek ways to dispose of all future nuclear waste safely or to package an aerosol deodorant more attractively. The second type of brainstorming problem is to think of as many consequences as possible of a particular action. For example, a brainstorming session might pose the question: "What would happen if all television programming, production, and broadcasting were directed by senior citizens?" Or, for a commercial example, "If we eliminated our natural-grain breads tomorrow, what would be the consequences on purchase patterns for the rest of our baked goods line?"

For either type of problem, once a group has generated its quota of suggestions, an evaluation process culls out usable suggestions. For instance, the nuclear waste disposal problem would include suggestions such as "fly it to the moon" and "make it into glow-in-the-dark breakfast cereal" (remember, suggestions are to be free and uninhibited). The breakfast cereal suggestion would be eliminated; "fly it to the moon," however, might be examined further.

Although brainstorming was devised as a group process, it can be done alone. In order to brainstorm alone, a person follows the same four principles enumerated above, withholding any evaluation of ideas until the end of the session.

Osborn intended brainstorming as a group method, and claimed great success with it. "The average person can think up twice as many ideas when working with a group than when working alone" (Osborn, 1957). Taylor, Berry, and Block (1958), however, found that although the number of suggestions made by a group exceeded that made by a single individual, subjects brainstorming in groups produced fewer ideas than the same number of subjects brainstorming alone. Taylor and his associates also found that the ideas generated by individuals were superior to those of the groups. Their studies combined the scores of individuals to form nominal groups for comparison purposes; much subsequent research in this area has used this nominal group process. A review of the literature produced by nominal group brainstorming studies confirms that individuals brainstorming alone do produce more ideas than individuals brainstorming in groups (Lamm & Trommsdorf, 1973).

TABLE 13-1.
Task Types and Associated Productivity

Task Type	Productivity By	Example
Disjunctive tasks	Most competent member	Solving a maze puzzle
Conjunctive tasks	Least competent member	Mountain-climbing with whole team attached to same rope
Additive tasks	Sum of individual efforts	Pushing a car stuck in the snow
Discretionary tasks	Group effort, combined as group decides (e.g., averaging, adding)	Estimating the number of beans in a jar

Source: After *Group Process and Productivity* by I. D. Steiner, New York: Academic Press, 1972, chapter 2.

A committee is a group that keeps minutes and loses hours.
Milton Berle

serves that most of Steiner's conclusions about group productivity and process loss (as shown in Table 13-1) have been confirmed by research over the past decade. She concludes that "group performance [is] generally qualitatively and quantitatively superior to the performance of the average individual. Group performance, however, [is] often inferior to that of the best individual. . . . This research confirms the belief that the performance of one exceptional individual can be superior to that of a committee. . . , especially if the committee is trying to solve a complex problem and if the committee contains a number of low ability members" (p. 535).

Decision-Making

Do you have strong opinions about politics? About religion? About environmental pollution? If so, how were your opinions formed? The odds are that they were formed in a group. Reaching a decision through group discussion—even though your opinion may have been the same before the discussion—seems to strengthen it.

During World War II when there were food shortages and rationing, Lewin (1943) was asked by a government agency to find ways to get homemakers to serve organ meats (kidneys, brains, and sweetbreads) more often. (These foods were nutritious and inexpensive, and more widely available than more popular cuts.) Lewin tried two different methods: In one, groups heard a persuasive message about serving these food items; in the other, the groups discussed the matter, and reached a decision about using the items. In a follow-up interview one week later, 10 percent of the women from the lecture groups had used the products, as opposed to 52 percent of the women from groups that had held discussions. The group decision had changed these people's previous attitudes and behaviors.

In another study, workers at a pajama factory had to adjust to changes in their work procedure. For instance, pajama examiners were told to no longer clip threads from all areas of the garment, but only from certain areas, while continuing to examine every seam. Some groups were given the opportunity to discuss the changes with management, and some were not. Those groups that participated in the discussions proved to be more productive under the changed procedures than those that did not. Apparently the discussion process helped overcome any resistance to change (Coch & French, 1948).

Models of Small Group Decision-Making   Much research on group processes has concentrated on the *product* or outcome of the group activity rather than on the processes themselves. However, studies of the processes themselves do exist, and some researchers attempted to construct models of how a group functions. Decision-making by juries is one area that has been particularly well researched in recent years. The size of a jury (generally either 6 or 12 members) and decision rules (generally everyone must agree) are fixed by law, and this makes the jury an ideal group for studying decision-making processes.

Models of jury decision-making (Penrod, 1982) have the common aim of predicting final jury verdicts based on the initial tendencies of the jurors to vote for guilt or innocence. All of them are based upon assumptions about the influence processes, such as those discussed in chapter 10. One of the most successful models—social decision schemes (Davis, 1980)—concentrates on implicit decision-making rules, which may differ from the explicit rules. (An explicit rule, for instance, is that verdicts must be unanimous.) After testing various models against data, Davis concluded that a "two-thirds majority, otherwise hung" decision scheme is generally in operation. This means that if two-thirds or more of the jurors agree when the jury takes its first ballot, that majority opinion will eventually become the unanimous verdict. But if two-thirds of the jurors do not agree on the first ballot (if there is, for example, a 50–50 split), the jury is unlikely to be able to reach a verdict (a jury that cannot reach a verdict is said to be "hung").

Other models—social transition schemes (Kerr, 1981; and related work by Klevorik and Rothschild, 1979)—focus on how jurors change their opinions during deliberation. Some models of social influences on the jury take the form of computer models that simulate the jury decision-making process. It is possible to simulate the deliberations of several hundred juries in a matter of seconds. The models refined in this manner can then be tested to see if their output matches the actual results from real jury studies. Computer models developed by Penrod and Hastie (1979, 1980) and Stasser and Davis (1981) have proven to be highly successful at predicting jury outcomes. All of the jury models capture with great precision the influence of jury members on one another. The models demonstrate that even in a complex group task such as jury decision-making (which involves reconciling differences through argument and persuasion) group influences are systematic.

Group Polarization

"Brian is an interesting person, but he's so conceited." This comment has just been addressed to you. You know Brian, and have some positive and some negative feelings about him. "What do you mean?" you ask.

"Ever hear him talk about his grades?" a third person says.

"Or his family!" says a fourth. "My God, you'd think they'd been made of gold plate for at least ten generations back."

"And then there's his hair . . ." says another.

How do you think that Brian, mercifully absent, is going to emerge from this discussion? Not well. The chances are that the group's collective opinion about Brian will drop because of each individual's eagerness to "top" other group members in describing his negative points, and as a result an overwhelmingly derogatory group consensus is likely to emerge.

Such shifts in groups to an extreme opinion also occurs in decision-making. One of the most extensively studied areas of group processes has been the phenomenon of decision shifts. In an unpublished thesis, Stoner (1961) originated this area of study by showing that groups do not make more conservative decisions than individuals, as is commonly supposed. Instead, groups make more daring decisions. Stoner termed the move from the more individual cautious solutions to the more daring group solutions the **risky shift.**

Madness is the exception in
individuals, the rule in groups.
Nietzsche

Early research on the topic confirmed the risky shift. One study posed such dilemmas as the following:

> A man with a severe heart ailment must seriously curtail his customary way of life if he does not undergo a delicate medical operation which might cure him completely or might prove fatal. (Wallach, Kogan, & Bem, 1962)

Groups that arrived at a joint decision through group discussions more often chose the riskier option (in this case, of operating) than the same individuals alone had chosen prior to group discussion. Moreover, subjects who had experienced a risky shift in the course of group discussion retained the same views when tested individually weeks later.

The term *risky shift* was changed to **group polarization** by Moscovici and Zavalloni (1969), when they discovered that the shift could be either in a more risky or a more cautious direction, depending on the initially dominant tendency in the group. In other words, a cautious shift will occur in groups initially favoring caution, and a risky shift in groups initially favoring risk.

Why do these shifts take place? Various explanations have been offered to explain the group polarization phenomenon. (One of the best discussions of these theories is by Lamm & Myers, 1978.) *Group decision rules*, for instance, have been suggested as a reason. A familiar example is majority rule, and several others have been proposed (Davis, 1973). **Informational influence** is a more strongly supported explanation, which states that group polarization results from the arguments that are made during discussion that are found important by the group members. It may be that more arguments are offered in the initially preferred direction, thus persuading people to shift further in that direction (Burnstein & Vinokur, 1977). According to **social comparison theory** (recall from chapter 9 that people use relevant others as standards for comparison), group polarization may result when people find that others share their view more than they thought. In addition, research has demonstrated that most people believe themselves superior to the "average" person; and stating the dominant position in the group somewhat more strongly may be a way to display themselves more

The Declaration Committee, drawn by Currier and Ives, consisted of, from left, Thomas Jefferson, Roger Sherman, Benjamin Franklin, Robert R. Livingston, and John Adams. Do you think informational influence during committee discussions led to the radical decision made by this group—or were the members' minds made up before they began their work? Was their decision a "risky shift"?

prominently. Recent research suggests that the best explanation of group polarization is probably a combination of all the above factors (e.g., Laughlin & Earley, 1982).

Whatever the actual explanations, the group polarization effect has been found in a wide variety of laboratory and field settings. It has been shown to influence general risk-taking (Wallach, Kogan, & Bem, 1962); attitudes (Moscovici & Zavalloni, 1969); bargaining and negotiations (Lamm & Sauer, 1974); gambling behavior (Blaskovich, Ginsburg, & Howe, 1975; Lamm & Ochsmann, 1972); and jury decisions (Myers & Kaplan, 1976).

Communication In Groups

Like decision-making, communication in groups is an area where group processes have been studied in their own right. One of the most notable characteristics of group communication is its structure: Who speaks to whom?

Communication networks of various forms exist within groups. In some groups, every member communicates freely with every other member. In other groups, the leader communicates to the members, and the members may communicate directly back to the leader. Formal groups that exist within organizations generally have an explicitly specified communication network structure, although in practice the group may depart from it. The networks in informal groups are determined by social processes within the group. The effects of the different network structures on the communications that are necessary for

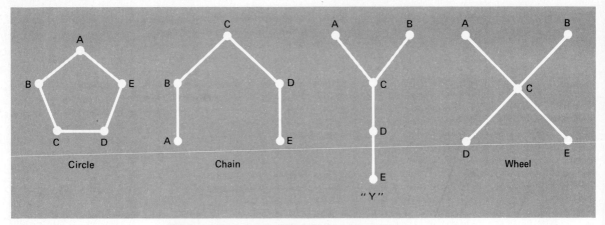

FIGURE 13-2.   Types of Communication Networks

Source: *From* Management, *2nd ed., by J. A. F. Stoner,* © *1982, p. 508. Reprinted by permission of Prentice-Hall, Inc., Englewood Cliffs, N.J.*

solving a simple problem were studied by Bavelas (1950) and Leavitt (1951). Figure 13-2 shows some of the network structures they tested. One of the testing methods was, for each pattern, to seat five people separated by partitions and to control with whom they could communicate. For example, in the chain pattern, subject C could communicate with subjects B and D; to get a message to subject E, subject C would have to go through subject D. In the "Y" pattern, subject C could communicate directly with A, B, or D; and subject E could communicate directly only with subject D.

Why are these communication patterns important? Bavelas and Leavitt found that the efficiency of groups increased but morale decreased, as the network structure became more centralized. In descending order of centrality, the patterns are the wheel, "Y," the chain, and the circle. Both Bavelas and Leavitt stressed the tentative nature of these findings.

The network structure also influenced which people emerged as the leaders of the experimental groups. In the circle, no one emerged as a leader; in the more centralized structures (the chain, the "Y", and the wheel), subject C did, since other group members necessarily came into contact more often with subject C in order to communicate with one another.

In a different kind of study, Bavelas et al. (1965) attempted to manipulate group behavior by changing the amount that the selected group member talked. Designated group members were encouraged to increase the amount that they talked, and simultaneously other group members were discouraged from talking as much. The result was that the subjects who were made to talk more were ranked high on leadership characteristics. The amount of communication apparently is one factor involved in leadership, which is discussed in the next section.

The structure of its communications may aid or hinder a group, but *what* is said—the content of the communications—is equally as important. How could you study—in a scientific manner—the content of communications in the groups of which you are a member? One person who has given this problem considerable attention over the years is Robert Bales (1950), who developed a system known as **interaction process analysis**, or IPA. IPA consists of twelve categories for coding the content of communications, or interactions (see Figure 13–3). When Bales first devised this system, the interactions were scored by an observer who coded them as they took place. Recently, analysis of interactions has become much eas-

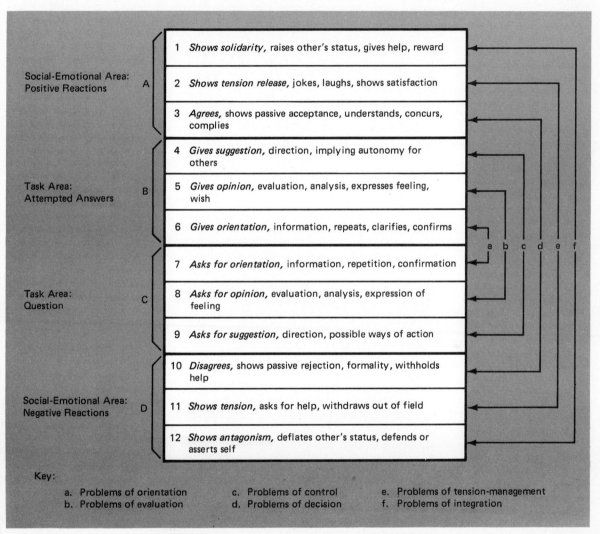

FIGURE 13–3. The System of Categories Used in Observation and Their Relation to Major Frames of Reference

Source: *From "A Set of Categories for the Analysis of Small Group Interaction," by R. F. Bales, American Sociological Review, 1950, 15, 258. Reprinted by permission of the American Sociological Association.*

ier through the use of videotape and the development of advanced computer technology. One new technique has been developed by Bales after more than two decades of research on the topic. SYMLOG (SYstematic Multiple Observation of Groups) is a highly complex system of scoring and analyzing group interactions. The mathematical analysis of the interaction data is not possible without the use of a computer (Bales & Cohen, 1979).

Note that Bales's IPA analysis is designed for general use in many types of groups and focuses on task and social-emotional aspects of group communication. You can imagine the difficulty of designing research methods that would actually measure the substantive content of group communications—e.g., that would keep track of the arguments presented during jury deliberations, or the content of a group therapy session.

Leadership

Again, think about the groups you belong to. Who are the leaders? Why are these particular individuals the leaders? This is the question that we will focus on in this section. You may be surprised by some of the answers that result from an exploration of leadership.

As in the case of "group," there is no exact and generally accepted definition of "leadership." Most popular definitions define leaders as those who intentionally influence the activities of a group, often directing the activities toward a goal. Beyond these general areas of near agreement, researchers seem to define leadership, and investigate it, according to their area of specialization (Yukl, 1981).

A distinction should be made between leaders who are appointed and those who are chosen by the group through election or some other means. An appointed leader may have less power than an emergent or a leader chosen by the group, because group support seems to increase the mandate or legitimacy with which an individual occupies the role of leader (Raven & French, 1958).

Wielding power is an important aspect of leading. French and Raven (1959) have identified five potential sources of power:

1. *Reward power*, the ability to reward a subordinate for work well done.
2. *Coercive power*, the ability to punish a subordinate for work not well done.
3. *Legitimate power*, the power that derives from the leader's position of recognized authority.
4. *Expert power*, the possession of particular skills or expertise.
5. *Referent power*, the ability to influence others because of likability or because of being admired.

To these can be added a final source of power (Raven & Kruglanski, 1970):

6. *Informational power*, the possession of important information.

How many sources of power does Zubin Mehta draw on as music director of the New York Philharmonic, shown here in rehearsal?

The Contingency Model

Fred Fiedler has developed a theory of leadership that explicitly takes into account the interaction between the leader and the situation (1978, 1981). Fiedler assumes that every leader has a personal style of leadership that cannot easily be changed. To secure the most effective performance from a group, the leader's style should be suited to the needs of the group and its task. For instance, an authoritarian supervisor might be replaced by a more democratic and socially oriented leader during a company crisis that is taking a heavy toll on employee morale. Trying to change the leadership styles of leaders, Fiedler believes, is useless; it is better to change the situation to fit the existing leader, or even to change the actual leaders to fit the needs of the group. For Fiedler, leadership is dependent, or contingent, upon situational factors; for this reason his theory is known as the **contingency model of leadership**.

Fiedler's model is concerned, then, with two key variables: leadership style and the characteristics of the situation. He measures leadership style by using a "Least-Preferred Co-worker" (LPC) index (see Figure 13–4). According to Fiedler, a leader who rates his or her least-preferred co-worker favorably—gives him or her a high LPC rating—is considerate of subordinates, human relations oriented, and permissive. A leader who rates his or her least-preferred co-worker unfavorably—gives him or her a low LPC rating—is primarily concerned with accom-

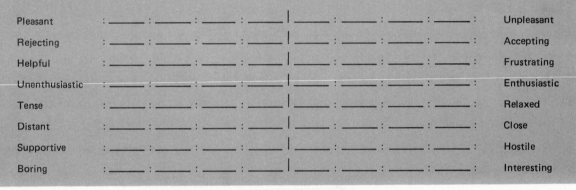

Instructions:
    People differ in the ways they think about those with whom they work. On the scale below are pairs of words which are opposite in meaning. You are asked to describe someone with whom you have worked by placing an "X" in one of the eight spaces on the line between the two words. Each space represents how well the adjective fits the person you are describing, as in the following example:

Very neat: _____ : _____ : _____ : _____ : _____ : _____ : _____ : _____ : Not neat

                1   2   3   4   5   6   7   8

            Very   Quite   Some-   Slightly Slightly   Some-   Quite   Very
            neat   neat   what   neat   untidy   what   untidy   untidy
                                neat   untidy

Now, think of the person with whom you can work least well. He may be someone you work with now, or he may be someone you knew in the past. He does not have to be the person you like least well, but should be the person with whom you had the most difficulty in getting a job done. Describe this person as he appears to you.

Pleasant   : ____ : ____ : ____ : ____ | ____ : ____ : ____ : ____ :   Unpleasant

Rejecting   : ____ : ____ : ____ : ____ | ____ : ____ : ____ : ____ :   Accepting

Helpful   : ____ : ____ : ____ : ____ | ____ : ____ : ____ : ____ :   Frustrating

Unenthusiastic : ____ : ____ : ____ : ____ | ____ : ____ : ____ : ____ :   Enthusiastic

Tense   : ____ : ____ : ____ : ____ | ____ : ____ : ____ : ____ :   Relaxed

Distant   : ____ : ____ : ____ : ____ | ____ : ____ : ____ : ____ :   Close

Supportive   : ____ : ____ : ____ : ____ | ____ : ____ : ____ : ____ :   Hostile

Boring   : ____ : ____ : ____ : ____ | ____ : ____ : ____ : ____ :   Interesting

FIGURE 13–4. Example of the LPC Scale

Fiedler used the semantic differential technique (see chapters 2 and 7) to determine how leaders viewed their least-preferred co-workers. Shown here is a portion of the LPC Scale showing some of the descriptive terms used.

Source: *Adapted from* A Theory of Leadership Effectiveness, *by F. E. Fiedler, New York: McGraw-Hill, 1967. Used with the permission of McGraw-Hill Book Company.*

plishment of the task at hand, has little interest in the feelings of subordinates, and is more rigid in style.

The second variable in the contingency model is situational control, or the extent to which the leader is able to control and influence the situation. Fiedler subdivides situational control into three aspects, or subscales:

1. *Leader–member relations*, the most important of the three subscales, specifies whether leader–subordinate relationships are good or bad. A leader who has a good working relationship with subordinates can be sure they will do what they are asked; this makes leadership more effective.

2. *Task structure*, second in importance, measures the degree to which the task to be performed is spelled out in step-by-step instructions. This gives

group members a clear idea of what they have to do; in this situation leaders gain authority.

3. *Leader position power* measures whether the intrinsic authority that is attached to a given position is strong or weak. If leaders are able to reward, punish, and otherwise enforce compliance to their directions, their authority is strengthened.

Now that we understand the basis of Fiedler's model, we can state his theory: Task-motivated leaders (those with a low LPC) perform best in situations of either high or low control; relationship-motivated leaders (those with a high LPC) perform best in situations of moderate control. Figure 13–5 expresses the theory graphically.

Fiedler has tested his theory in hundreds of laboratory and field situations. Most of the studies were done using ongoing groups, such as West Point cadets

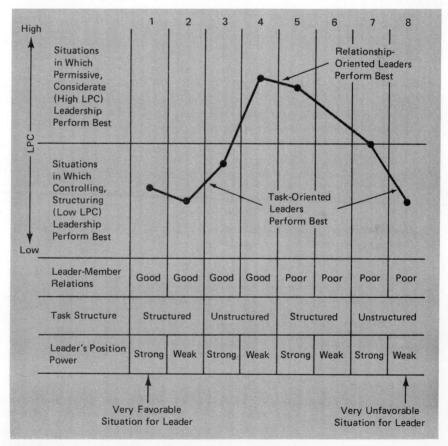

FIGURE 13–5. How Effective Leadership Varies with the Situation

Source: *Adapted from* A Theory of Leadership Effectiveness *by F. E. Fiedler, New York: McGraw-Hill, 1967, 146. Used with the permission of McGraw-Hill Book Company.*

Controversy: Are Leaders Born or Made?

People often wonder what makes a great leader—out of a curiosity that is not necessarily disinterested, since we ourselves may aspire to become important leaders. Researchers have taken two different approaches to what makes a leader, and they are diametrically opposed to one another.

THE TRAIT APPROACH

Dubbed the "great person" theory, this approach in effect says that some people are born leaders. To discover *which* people are born leaders, we can examine past and present leaders to see what personality traits they have in common (and whether we might, or might not, share them ourselves).

A review by Yukl (1981) of the vast literature on leadership traits concludes that few such traits have been consistently identified. Much of the research reports weak relationships between personality traits and leadership. Yukl concludes that some traits and abilities are frequently associated with leadership, but, while

> certain traits increase the likelihood that a leader will be effective, . . . they do not guarantee effectiveness, and the relative importance of different traits is dependent on the nature of the leadership situation (1981, p. 70)(See table).

A few characteristics of leaders stand out. One is height. Leaders are often taller than the average, as if people quite literally expected to look up to them. Keyes (1980) found that people tended to overestimate the height of people in important positions. He also found a correlation between height and salaries: Taller people earned more money.

Intelligence also seems to correlate with leadership. In a review of 60 years of research, Richard Mann (1959) concluded that of all the traits examined, the most evidence exists for a connection between intelligence and leadership. He also found that leaders demonstrated better psychological adjustment.

THE SITUATIONAL APPROACH

In opposition to the trait approach is the "Zeitgeist" approach. *Zeitgeist* means "spirit of the times" in German, and this theory says that leadership is a function of a particular situation. At any given historical time and in any particular place, people have certain needs, and require the help of appropriate individuals to lead them in meeting those needs. *Who* leads is mostly a matter of chance: It's a matter of being the right person in the right situation at the right time. Given a choice of people in the right place at the right time, this theory does concede to the "great person" theory that the individual whose traits are most suited to the particular circumstances will be chosen. But in a different place at a different time, this person would not be chosen (Cooper & McGaugh, 1963).

The Zeitgeist theory, like the great person theory, has had its share of supporters. Count Leo Tolstoy said that Napoleon's defeat occurred

and high-school basketball teams. Thus the evidence does seem to say something about how leadership works in the real world, and it supports his contention that matching leadership style to the situation leads to effective leadership. Fiedler has gone further and used his model as the basis for a training program for leaders that shows them how to alter variables of the situation to fit their leadership styles, rather than vice versa. Leaders are first tested to deter-

because of the time and place: Napoleon was no longer, in that situation, the right person to be leader; hence he ceased to be.

Simonton (1979) examined historical archives concerning nearly 600 multiple scientific discoveries. It has often happened that the same discovery or invention was made simultaneously and independently by more than one person, as with calculus (Newton and Leibniz), the planet Neptune (Adams and Leverrier), and even evolution (Darwin and Wallace). Is this due to Zeitgeist? To some extent, yes. Simonton's analysis showed that situational influences were of key—but secondary—importance in making such discoveries. Pure chance came first, and the previous technological background of the person ranked third.

WHICH APPROACH IS RIGHT?

Social scientists today generally agree that elements of both the trait approach or the situational approach are valid, although neither by itself adequately accounts for the phenomenon of leadership. However, an archival study by Suedfeld and Rank (1976) hints that some possibilities may be overlooked by both theories. Suedfeld and Rank examined the variable of cognitive complexity for leaders of historical revolutions. In the beginnings of a revolution, things are simple. Once the protesting minority achieves power, however, the situation becomes more complex. A leader who can change and become more complex along with the situation is most likely to be successful. Their review of 19 leaders

in 5 revolutions concluded that 11 of the leaders were able to adapt their personal characteristics to the demands of their new situations. And indeed, those leaders were the ones who remained in power until voluntary retirement or natural death.

As with most nature vs. nurture controversies, so it is with the question of whether leaders are born or made—the answer turns out to be both, and in permutations that are not fully understood.

Traits and Skills Most Frequently Characteristic of Successful Leaders

Traits	Skills
Adaptable to situations	Clever (intelligent)
Alert to social environment	Conceptually skilled
Ambitious and achievement-oriented	Creative
Assertive	Diplomatic and tactful
Cooperative	Fluent in speaking
Decisive	Knowledgeable about group task
Dependable	Organized (administrative ability)
Dominant (desire to influence others)	Persuasive
Energetic (high activity level)	Socially skilled
Persistent	
Self-confident	
Tolerant of stress	
Willing to assume responsibility	

Source: From *Leadership in Organizations*, by G. Yukl, © 1981, p. 70. Reprinted by permission of Prentice-Hall, Inc., Englewood Cliffs, N.J.

mine their LPC ratings, and then given training to achieve the amount of situational control best suited to their leadership styles.

Beyond question, Fiedler's approach to leadership in a situational context is a substantial contribution to our understanding of leadership. His theory, however, has some limitations: Are one characteristic of the leader and three characteristics of the situation a sufficient basis for understanding all aspects of a

complex phenomenon? Also, what influence do other members have on what happens in a group? Are leaders and followers very different from one another? A study by Hollander and Webb (1955) suggests that leaders and followers may not be so very different; people rated as good followers were also rated as good leaders. In other words, the differences between leaders and followers are probably very small to begin with. Effective leadership may depend largely on situational factors—just as Fiedler suggests.

Large Group Processes

So far we have discussed the dynamics of small functional groups. But human beings come together in large masses as well as small ones for various purposes: to attend sporting events, to worship, to watch parades, to picket. Small group experiences do provide stimulation and can be strong influences on our behavior, as we have seen. Large groups can cause us to experience an exhilaration of a different nature. Who has not at some time felt a stir of excitement from being part of a large group doing something interesting—whether it is marching in a band, competing in a race, advancing with an army, cheering our team from the stands, attending a large rock concert, or taking our political feelings to the streets? Some of the oldest social psychological theorizing concerns large groups; however, not as much research has been done on large-group behavior as on small-group behavior. Nonetheless, some of the large-group studies are quite provocative, have implications for real-world events, and are often "classic" studies within our discipline.

Contagion

"Little adapted to reasoning, crowds, on the contrary, are quick to act." So wrote Gustave Le Bon (1903, p. 17) almost a century ago. He felt that the crowd represented a more primitive species than the individual—that people were transformed by being in a crowd into a "collective mind" (p. 26). Le Bon did not define collective mind in any precise manner, but he felt it could unite even geographically isolated individuals into a kind of crowd. Not all assemblies of people would qualify as a crowd in these terms, but only those that achieved the psychological unity of the collective mind. As should be apparent, Le Bon did not like crowds:

> In consequence of the purely destructive nature of their power, crowds act like those microbes which hasten the dissolution of enfeebled or dead bodies. When the structure of a civilization is rotten, it is always the masses that bring about its downfall. It is at such a juncture that their chief mission is plainly visible, and that for a while the philosophy of number seems the only philosophy of history. (p. 19)

Le Bon believed that individuals were transformed into crowd members by three things. First, the sheer force of numbers made people experience a sensation of power and invincibility, which led them to loosen some of the restraints that normally act on behavior. Second, *contagion* occurred, a kind of hypnotic phenomenon in which the crowd's interest quickly took priority over the individual's personal interest. Contagion was a function of the third factor, the suggestibility of people in crowds. As Le Bon said, "The individualities in the crowd who might possess a personality sufficiently strong to resist the suggestion are too few in number to struggle against the current. . . . An individual in a crowd is a grain of sand amid other grains of sand, which the wind stirs up at will" (pp. 35–36).

Le Bon's strong beliefs about crowds are credited today primarily with ini-

Is a collective mind at work when a major political party holds its presidential nominating convention?

tiating interest in the subject, and little more. He held the prejudices of his era—he was afraid of the masses, and believed that they should have no part in governing a society. Nevertheless, his writings prompted other writers to develop theories of contagion. McDougall (1920) thought that contagion worked through "the sympathetic induction of emotion" that one person experiences when witnessing the facial expression and manner of another. Allport (1924) suggested that contagion was a circular reaction: A person stimulates another, sees the stronger response he or she has evoked in the other, is in turn led to a new pitch of stimulation, which the other intensifies further—and so on, as greater and greater excitement is produced.

Unlike Le Bon, Brown (1954) found that people in different kinds of crowds differed to the extent to which they would deviate from conventional behavior. Contagion does exist, but within what limits? For instance, if contagion accounts for the spread of looting in portions of a city during a riot or a power blackout, why doesn't contagion cause looting to spread to a city's entire population? Many questions remain unanswered about contagion (Milgram & Toch, 1968).

Panic

Another type of large group situation, made possible by the phenomenon of contagion, is panic. Smoke and the sound of an alarm can turn almost any audience into bedlam through the quick spread of panic. LaPiere (1938) traced the development of panic through three stages:

1. *Shock.* The stimulus that will cause panic does not do so immediately. The first effect is that all behavior is suspended as people, in a state of shock, try to grasp what is going on.
2. *Sense of panic.* The period of shock ends when some group members grasp the situation. At this point they respond to the crisis with panic, a pervasive feeling like fear or terror.
3. *State of action.* The feeling of panic leads to action. This action is not necessarily the wild and uncoordinated behavior we generally associate with panic, such as trampling others in a rush to get to the door. Soldiers may experience panic but they react as they were trained to. People caught up in a disaster also often act calmly. External factors seem largely responsible for determining whether the state of action is adapted toward problem-solving, or remains at the panic level.

Panicked action is nonadaptive. If everyone jams at the theater door at the same time, no one will get out; if people exit in a rapid but orderly fashion, everyone will, since theaters can be emptied in a few minutes. An analog to the panic situation was created in the laboratory by Alexander Mintz (1951). He placed paper cones attached to strings inside a narrow-necked bottle and asked groups of subjects to get the cones out—one cone and string per subject. The cones could only be removed singly; an attempt to get even two out concurrently would block the bottle neck, as Figure 13–6 illustrates.

Mintz told some groups that this was an experiment in group cooperation. Other groups were told that this was a game in which individuals could win

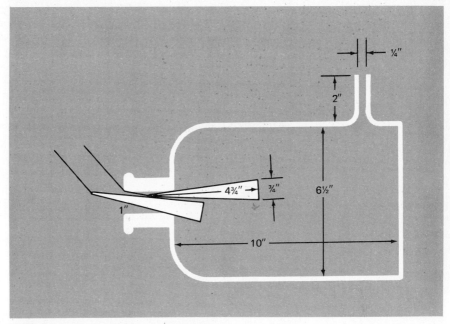

FIGURE 13–6. Getting Through a Bottleneck

Diagram showing a cross-section of the glass bottle in Mintz's experiment. Note that two cones are shown blocking the neck of the bottle, as competing subjects attempt to pull them both out at the same time.

Source: *From "Non-Adaptive Group Behavior,"* by A. Mintz, *Journal of Abnormal and Social Psychology,* 1951, *46,* 155.

money if they got their cone out. "Traffic jams" did not occur in the "cooperation" groups, but they did in the "win money" groups—which provided the same sort of "each man for himself" motivation that panicked action does. In some of the groups not even a single cone was removed from the bottle.

The designers of another laboratory experiment reasoned that *urgency* was a key factor in panic. In this study, subjects were seated in separate booths where they could not see each other. They were told they would receive punishment if they were unable to escape from a simulated danger situation within a limited time, and electrodes were attached to one hand for the purpose of administering electric shocks (which in fact were never administered). Signal lights showed each subject the position of all the subjects. At the start of the experiment, each subject's light indicated he or she was in danger. By pressing a button, a subject could escape from danger, but only if there was enough time (3 seconds) before interference was caused by another subject trying to escape. The expected bottlenecks occurred, blocking escape; and the bottlenecks were worse the higher the threatened penalty was for not escaping. Also, the larger the group, the lower the percentage of subjects that escaped. Interestingly, it was found that when one subject indicated a willingness to wait by pressing the appropriate button, the panic was lessened (Kelley et al., 1965).

This discussion has stressed some of the negative aspects of large group

processes. There is, however, a more positive view of large groups that emphasizes coordinated large groups or organizations. Organizational behavior can be
studied from a variety of perspectives and at a variety of levels. Most of the research we have examined earlier in this chapter is directly relevant to behavior
in organizations. For example, organizations frequently confront problems in
fostering group cohesiveness, avoiding the pitfalls of groupthink, and locating
and promoting effective leaders. In a sense, then, this entire chapter concerns
"'organizational" behavior. In the section that follows we will take a closer look
at research specifically focused on coordinated group behavior.

Behavior in Organizations

The investigation of behavior in organizations—known as organizational psychology, industrial psychology, or organizational behavior—began in the United
States in the early 1900s, but it was not until the 1960s that the field burgeoned,
resulting in a vast amount of research on the subject. Once again, think of the
groups you belong to. How many of them would you consider to be organizations? Are some of them part of larger organizations? How are these organizations put together, or structured? Consider these organizations, or others with
which you are involved (school, church, athletic league, place of work). What has
caused you to be happy or unhappy in an organization you are or were a member
of? The questions raised in this paragraph are some of the questions that researchers in the area of organizational psychology have tried to answer.

Studying Behavior in Organizations

What is an organization? **Organization** is a term that has been defined with more
precision and general agreement than *group* or *leadership*. An organization is:

> the planned coordination of the activities of a number of people for the
> achievement of some common, explicit purpose or goal, through division of
> labor and function, and through a hierarchy of authority and responsibility.
> (Schein, 1980, p. 15)

This definition, along with variants offered by other writers, emphasizes that an
organization has three key characteristics: a deliberate design; specific purposes
or goals; and greater reliance on formal prescriptions of acceptable versus unacceptable behavior than do less structured social systems (Katz & Kahn, 1978).

Organizations come in a bewildering variety of shapes and sizes, and with
purposes that run the gamut of possibilities: religious bodies, hospitals, industrial concerns, colleges, political parties, social clubs, the Mafia all are organizations. (You may be surprised to discover that you belong to a lot more organizations than you thought!) We can make some basic distinctions among them in

order for us to reach a better understanding of human behavior in our organizations. Schein (1980) described three types of organizations:

1. *Formal organizations.* Schein's definition at the start of this section actually described a formal organization. Businesses, governments, and universities are all formal organizations.
2. *Social organizations.* These do not involve the deliberate coordination of activities for the achievement of specific goals. Social organizations arise spontaneously out of social interactions. "Having a good time" may be a common goal. Clubs, families, communities, and gangs are examples of social organizations.
3. *Informal organizations.* Within a formal organization, patterns of coordination or relationships between people inevitably arise that have nothing to do with the formal requirements of the organization. A group of co-workers eat lunch together, share common grievances, and even become good friends outside of working hours. Informal organizations, similar to our concept of group discussed at the start of this chapter, arise within virtually all formal organizations.

As already mentioned, the study of behavior in organizations has become an interdisciplinary area of concern to many persons within and outside of the social sciences. Interest in the area continues to grow, largely due to its relevance to the business world and to some successful applications it has found there. Organizational psychologists or their equivalents are found in many formal organizations, either as staff members or outside consultants specializing in the field, and they deal with a wide range of problems concerning people in organizations. Although organizational psychology is sometimes considered a separate field from social psychology, we will look at a few examples of research that reflect a social psychological perspective on organizational behavior. We will encounter many familiar social psychological concepts such as attitudes, cooperation and competition, and group structure.

Behavior in organizations occurs, of course, at multiple levels that interact with one another. The levels are that of individuals, that of groups within an organization, and that of an organization as a whole. The remainder of this chapter will be devoted to a discussion of these three levels in turn, together with some research examples for each. Our concern will be, for the most part, with formal organizations and how they function.

Individuals in Organizations

There is hardly a time in our lives when we are not members of an organization. Our first experience as an organization member occurs in earliest childhood, when we become aware that we belong to a structured group called a family whose task is to bring us up and to nourish and support all of its members. We learn that each family member is unique, that some have more power than others, and that some are more dependent than others. When we translate the organizational skills we learned in the family to the school, we find that we are not quite so unique, but share characteristics with many other members. Here we learn to interact with peers as well as with superiors. Over the years, in after-school programs and summer camps, we learn a growing repertoire of organizational skills as we participate in special events, cooperate with others to plan projects and carry them out, and perhaps assume leadership roles ourselves. In summer or after-school jobs we get a chance to test some of the skills in the workplace, where we are exposed to multiple levels of authority. Most of us will be members of such organizations, whether they be businesses, nonprofit institutions, or government or community agencies, for most of our adult lives.

You might have heard the phrase that someone is "perfect for the job." Is there a right person for the right job, or can some organizational roles be filled by just about anybody? What affects an individual's attitude and performance on the job?

Employee Attitudes and Job Satisfaction   Employee attitudes are obviously important to the individuals holding them. But they are equally important to an organization, because the match (or lack of it) between an individual's needs and expectations and the job's actual satisfaction can influence an employee's behavior. Attitudes are not dissociated from behavior, but affect it, as we saw in chapter 9. This is generally recognized, and employee attitudes are an important topic in organizational psychology. Work-related attitudes, usually referred to under the general term of *job satisfaction*, have been the subject of numerous studies.

Three differing relationships between job satisfaction and job performance have been hypothesized by different researchers at various times and under various conditions. These are:

1.   Job satisfaction causes good performance.
2.   Good performance causes job satisfaction.
3.   There is no invariable causal relationship between job satisfaction and job performance.

Early social psychological research in industry showed a pronounced relationship between happy workers and good performance (Homans, 1969). Recently a new look has been taken at the early research upon which the "happy workers are productive workers" view is based. Those studies were not controlled experiments, and thus cannot claim to have documented a causal relationship between satisfaction and performance. The studies relied on measures of correlation, instead of experimentally manipulating satisfaction to find out its effect on performance.

In recent research, some investigators (for instance, Cherrington, Reitz, & Scott, 1971) have found satisfaction and performance to be unrelated. In fact, that is very near to the current viewpoint, which is that job satisfaction *may* influence performance, but this depends on complex circumstances.

A corollary of the current viewpoint is that job satisfaction *does* influence employee turnover and absenteeism. In a review of 13 studies of satisfaction and turnover, Porter and Steers (1973) found that dissatisfied workers were more likely to leave their jobs than satisfied workers. If alternatives to resignation exist, however—such as transfers within the organization—the connection between

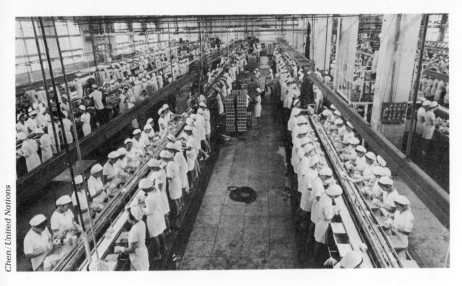

Chen/ United Nations

The relationship between job satisfaction and job performance has tantalized researchers for many years. Most recently, social psychologists have been looking at the interaction of an industry's technology and social system. Clearly, the factors that make for satisfied and high performing workers in this setting, the production line of a pineapple cannery in Taiwan, will be quite different from those we would find at General Motors in Detroit.

dissatisfaction and termination was less evident. Victor Vroom (1964) showed that voluntary absenteeism was also related to job satisfaction, with satisfied workers being absent less often.

There appears at this point to be no clear relationship between job satisfaction and performance. Think back to the last job you had. Did you like it? Why or why not? Were you good at it? Why? You probably cannot easily give simple answers to these questions.

Perhaps the most useful way to think about motivation in organizations is from a "systems view"—that is, by looking at aspects of the work situation as interrelated components. Using a systems perspective, Porter and Miles (1974) list three types of variables that affect worker motivation:

1. The characteristics of the individual, including each person's attitudes, interests, and needs.
2. The characteristics of the job, including the amount of responsibility, amount of variety, and degree of autonomy provided.
3. The characteristics of the work situation, particularly the general atmosphere of the work environment created by supervisors and peers.

In view of the complex variables involved, it is not surprising that no simple relationship between job satisfaction and performance exists. They are both probably joint functions of all of the characteristics of a given organizational system.

Groups in Organizations

All of the topics we have discussed in this chapter—group structure and processes, communication, leadership, and organizational behavior—are relevant to an understanding of groups within organizations. As a college or university student, you are a member of a large organization. You are also a member of a social psychology class within that organization. And within your class, you may be a member of a smaller group of good friends. We will see in this section that groups within organizations—groups within groups—have unique interactions. The first research to show the importance of groups in an organization was the series of investigations known collectively as the Hawthorne studies (see box).

Those who work much do not work hard.
Henry David Thoreau

Importance of Informal Groups The importance of informal groups such as those at Hawthorne was also underscored by the Tavistock Institute studies in Great Britain, performed by Eric Trist and his associates (Trist & Banforth, 1951). A change in coal-mining technology spelled the demise of the old work teams that had ranged in size from two to eight men. These were small, tightly knit social groups, with long-term relationships that extended to providing for a team member's family if he was injured or killed. When mechanical coal-cutting equipment was introduced, the old teams were dissolved and replaced by units of 40 to 50 men each. The social groups were disrupted to such an extent that, in the end, the new system could not function efficiently. The disruption of informal group relationships resulted in emotional strain, in addition to lessening the quantity and quality of the output itself.

Types of Informal Groups Informal groups are natural combinations of people in the work situation. In large organizations, several types of informal groups may exist (Dalton, 1959):

1. *Horizontal cliques.* These are informal associations of organizational members of more or less the same rank, who generally work in the same area. This is the most prevalent type of informal group.
2. *Vertical cliques.* Members from different levels within a given department can compose vertical cliques. They may be in superior–subordinate relationships to one another. Such groups serve a key function in the vertical communication process, and may form because members were acquainted earlier (for instance, before some were promoted to supervisory positions) or because they need each other to accomplish their work or personal goals.
3. *Mixed or random cliques.* These are comprised of members of different ranks, from different departments, and even from different physical locations. Such cliques may arise to serve common interests, or because of relationships outside the organization (such as living in the same community, working out at the same gym, or car-pooling). Random cliques also facilitate communication within the organization (see Figure 13–7).

The Total Organization

Have you ever wondered how a large organization operates? How do individuals within groups and groups within organizations fit together to form the "total organization" and to get things done? Issues that have been investigated at this level include the structure and design of organizations, the relationship between organizations and their environments, organizational effectiveness, and organizational change.

The classic approach to organizations as a totality was that of Max Weber in 1925 (1968). He believed that effective organizations, which he called bureaucracies, were typified by a formal, hierarchical structure. Tasks were specialized, ac-

Research: The Hawthorne Effect

In the late 1920s, Elton Mayo and his colleagues studied the effects of fatigue and monotonous operations on assembly-line workers at Western Electric's Hawthorne plant in Cicero, Illinois. They studied a group of female workers who were assembling telephone relay switches. When Mayo and his colleagues installed new lighting, the output of the work group increased. However, output also increased when the lighting conditions in the room where the women worked were deliberately worsened. Productivity increased also when the workers were given coffee breaks, and when the workday was shortened by an hour. Indeed, productivity increased even when the workday was extended. Moreover, the control group, which experienced no changes in lighting or anything else, also stepped up its output! Mayo concluded that just being studied had caused the workers to increase productivity, independently of any of the factors he had been investigating. This became known as the **Hawthorne effect** (Mayo, 1933; Roethlisberger & Dickson, 1939).

The researchers then wanted to find out why the special attention of being studied had improved group performance. The results of an ambitious interview program indicated that the informal groups that exist within formal organizations had affected workers' output. Informal groups are social, and such non-job related factors turned out to be most important to workers. Mayo had earlier discovered that job satisfaction led to good performance, a discovery that contradicted the prevailing beliefs of the times, which assumed that good pay and good working conditions were the key factors in motivating workers. These studies also marked the beginning of organizational psychology.

Later researchers followed Mayo's footsteps in using experimental methods to explore ways to improve working conditions, productivity, and employer–employee relations. A classic study by French and Coch (1948) demonstrated, for example, that in situations where new working methods have to be introduced, workers may resent simply being told to change. In that study, productivity fell and never recovered after the method change, and there was a large turnover in workers. In contrast, workers who had representatives participating in the decisions involving the change experienced a temporary drop in productivity but no turnover, while workers in a third condition—in which all workers participated in the decision-making—very quickly increased their productivity with no turnover.

Interestingly, a recent reanalysis of the original data from the Hawthorne experiments by Parsons (1974) has revealed several methodological flaws that make many of the conclusions drawn earlier invalid. Under some conditions, it now appears, worker output did not increase, and in other situations there were contaminating factors (such as absence of a true control group) that precluded any firm conclusions. Therefore the "Hawthorne effect," as it has been described in most social psychology textbooks (and in organizational behavior) probably did not exist (Rice, 1982). Nonetheless, Mayo's research was an important impetus to the social psychological study of the workplace.

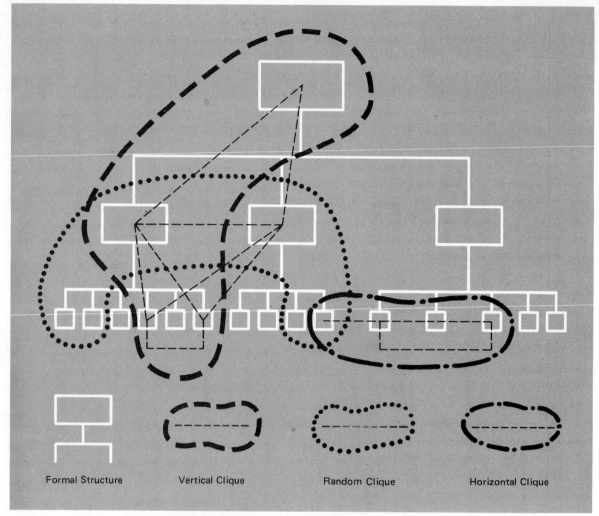

Formal Structure   Vertical Clique   Random Clique   Horizontal Clique

FIGURE 13-7.   Informal Groups within an Organization

Source: *Adapted from* Management, *2nd ed., by J. A. F. Stoner,* © *1982, 329. Reprinted by permission of Prentice-Hall, Inc., Englewood Cliffs, N.J.*

tivities routinized, career opportunities assured, and in sum, all of the characteristics of full-blown bureaucracies were exhibited. Weber viewed these characteristics as positive, but we have since come to view them as negative, perhaps because today's large organizations are much larger than those Weber knew.

Today's approach to organizations sees them as more complex than Weber did. Current theories view organizations as dynamic, open systems in constant interaction with their environment. No one structure can suit all environments and situations. The first statement of this systems approach was Katz and Kahn's 1966 edition of *The Social Psychology of Organizations*.

One attempt to view organizations as more complex systems is the **socio-technical model**, which implies that any organization is an interacting combination of a certain technology and a certain social system. This model was developed by Joan Woodward and her colleagues at the Tavistock Institute in London, who investigated the organization of nearly 100 manufacturing firms (1965). She concluded that the type of technology used by a business organization (e.g., mass production vs. custom preparation) determined the optimal size of the working groups and the number of levels in the organizational hierarchy.

As Schein (1980) has pointed out, it would be a mistake to conclude that the organizational structure is determined by technology, or that the way tasks are performed is determined by the sociocultural characteristics of the workers. Mayo's, Trist's, and Woodward's studies all indicate that all of these factors interact, with each affecting the other to some extent. For example, in Trist's study of the devastating effects of introducing new equipment to British coal mines, the researchers assumed that people had three major needs in the work situation: a sense of completion of a meaningful unit of work; control over their activities; satisfactory relations with co-workers. They also found that a homogeneity of skill levels in a group, homogeneity of prestige and status, and the individual choice about being in the group were important factors in work group stability.

All of these factors had been present in the traditional small mining teams. When technological change was introduced, and new, larger groups were formed, workers were given specialized assignments at different rates of pay (and prestige), and had to work at some distance from one another. New mechanisms for the communication and coordination among co-workers, and for forming supportive relationships, were needed. Because these requirements were ignored in the new system, however, absences increased and productivity fell.

Later, the researchers persuaded managers to modify some factors in the direction of job enlargement—such as permitting job trading and using a group-based pay system. As a result, absences declined dramatically, productivity became higher and more consistent, and the costs of supervision were lowered (Trist & Banforth, 1951).

As in so much of the research on organizational behavior, our current view of the total organization is much more complex than the early theorists supposed. The organization, as we know it today, has turned out to be a dynamic system encompassing technological, social, and structural characteristics. The nature of any particular total organization will depend upon the interaction, unique to that organization, among all of these factors.

Answering Questions about Groups, Leadership, and Organizations

1. There is no one "best" definition of a group. Groups can be classified by degree of association, length of duration, or the purpose they serve.
2. Latané's social impact theory shows that individuals will sometimes exert

less effort in a group than when they are alone. The presence of others places less responsibility on each individual member.

3. Attraction to the group, or group cohesiveness, can be due to several factors: attractiveness of the group's members, similarity of members, and whether the group meets the person's own instrumental needs. When these factors are not present, people will not join, or may decide to leave, a group.

4. Group decisions, instead of reaching a moderate compromise, often shift toward the initially dominant tendency following group discussion. This is known as group polarization. Research in this area began with studies of the "risky shift," which found that groups often make riskier decisions than individuals.

5. Le Bon, in 1903, felt that a crowd was transformed into a "collective mind," which was more primitive than the mind of the individual. Although Le Bon was probably not correct, it is true that people in a crowd act differently than they would if they were alone. Crowd behavior can be positive, as at a football game, or negative, as in a riot.

6. The "great person" theory of leadership says that certain personality traits are characteristic of leaders, whereas the "Zeitgeist" approach says that leaders are a product of the situation. In fact, leadership is probably due to both personal and situational factors.

7. Due to a lack of controlled experimental research, the direction of causality between job satisfaction and job performance is still not clear. It is true, however, that satisfied workers generally perform well at their jobs.

Summary

Groups can be distinguished at three different levels: the *aggregate group*, which is an unconnected collection of individuals, such as people waiting at a bus stop; the *minimal group*, which is a collection of individuals with a slight social connection, such as a concert audience; and the *identity group*, which is vital to the sense of identity of those who belong to it, such as a family. Groups can also be temporary (ad hoc groups), or ongoing. Another basic distinction is between *task groups*, which function to get a particular job done, and *social groups*, which are formed for the enjoyment of their members.

Two main theories exist on the relationship between groups and individuals. Zajonc's **social facilitation theory** deals with the effect of the presence of others on an individual's performance. Latané's **social impact theory** describes the effect of the group on the individual, and the effect of the individual on the group.

Cohesiveness is the result of all the forces that act on members to remain in a group. Certain factors have been found to increase cohesiveness, such as competition between groups, fear, and severe initiation to the group. Cohesiveness itself has effects beyond holding the group together. One may be an increase in productivity. Another can be *groupthink*, or conformity to the values and ethics of a group even when such conformity may result in a disastrous decision.

Within groups there is usually a division of labor. Individuals may assume such informal roles as task specialist or social–emotional specialist; there are also institutionalized roles based on the work to be done.

A number of factors determine the productivity of a group, including task demands, resources, potential productivity, and process loss. *Brainstorming*, a technique originally developed to tap group productivity by generating creative ideas, can be employed by individuals as well. Decision-making and communication within groups have been studied. Individual opinions and group decisions tend to become more extreme in groups, a phenomenon known as **group polarization.**

There are two distinct theories to explain the phenomenon of **leadership,** which has long fascinated people. The trait approach tries to identify characteristics common to leaders, and the situational approach maintains that leadership is a function of time and place. Although both may be partly correct, neither one is the sole explanation. Fiedler's **contingency model** considers both leader characteristics and their situations.

Large groups such as crowds have not been as well studied as small groups partly because of the inherent difficulties in them. Among their unique characteristics are *contagion* and *panic.*

Behavior in **organizations** has been extensively studied in recent years, and from many viewpoints. There are three basic types of organizations: *formal, social,* and *informal.* Each has been studied at the level of the individual in the organization, and at the level of groups within organizations. Organizations can also be studied as a totality of individuals and groups. Current approaches to the complete organization, such as Woodward's **sociotechnical model,** view organizations as dynamic, open systems in constant interaction with their environment.

Suggested Additional Reading

Cummings, L. L. Organizational behavior. *Annual Review of Psychology,* 1982, *33,* 541–579.

Fiedler, F. E. A contingency model of leadership effectiveness. In L. Berkowitz (Ed.), *Advances in experimental social psychology* (Vol. II). New York: Academic Press, 1978.

Lamm, H., & Myers, D. G. Group-induced polarization of attitudes and behavior. In L. Berkowitz (Ed.), *Advances in experimental social psychology* (Vol. II). New York: Academic Press, 1978.

Shaw, M. E. *Group dynamics* (2nd ed.) New York: McGraw-Hill, 1976.

Steiner, I. D. *Group process and productivity.* New York: Academic Press, 1972.

Zander, A. The psychology of group processes. *Annual Review of Psychology,* 1979, *30,* 417–451.

14

ENVIRONMENTAL INFLUENCES ON SOCIAL BEHAVIOR

Questions about Environmental Influences on Social Behavior

1. Is highrise housing necessarily "bad" for people?
2. The word "territoriality" is used to refer to an individual's staking out of an area and willingness to defend it from intruders. Is this a learned or an innate behavior?
3. Look around your apartment or dorm room. Does the arrangement of furniture and space invite people to socialize there? What factors facilitate or inhibit the social interaction of people in your living space?
4. Some years ago, one of the bloodiest, most vicious prison riots took place in a New Mexico state prison. The overconcentration of inmates in a restricted environment was one of the factors leading to the carnage. What sorts of pressures are people under crowded conditions exposed to? Why is the stress particularly acute in a prison setting?
5. What causes us to have a vague feeling of claustrophobia when our environment gets too crowded?
6. Do you think today's environment induces more stress than the environment of 100 years ago?

Think about the environment you are in right now—your room, a library, a campus lawn. What features of this environment best characterize it? Which features distinguish it from other environments you live or work in? Which features caused you to select it as *the* place in which to read this chapter? Which features make it a good (or poor) place to study?

We like to believe that our perceptions—what we see, hear, taste, smell, and feel—reflect objective reality. In actuality, however, what we perceive depends on the world around us. Consequently, environmental factors are not merely reflected in our perceptions but actually determine the way we perceive. For example, you may already see that some environments are more conducive to study than others. In fact, we are often influenced by environmental factors in ways that are so subtle that we are not aware of them.

The notion that human beings, like all other species, are influenced—indeed, partially determined—by their environment has become something of a cliché. It may surprise you to learn, however, that before the nineteenth century few philosophers or scientists paid much attention to the effects of the environment. It was not until Charles Darwin propounded his theory of evolution in *On the Origin of Species* (1859) and *The Descent of Man* (1871) that science became concerned with environmental issues. Darwin's theory had a profound impact not only on the biological sciences, but also on the developing social sciences as well.

Even before Darwin, of course, many people had observed that human beings in different parts of the world differed in both physical makeup and customs. However, the general philosophical and religious orientation of the times prevented people from examining these data systematically. Christian doctrine held that God first created all lower animal species at about the same time and in a manner that was unrelated to any interaction with the environment, and afterward created humans in His own image and endowed with a soul. From this point of view, human beings stood above and apart from the rest of creation; thus environmental factors could influence the course of human destiny, but they had nothing to do with the essence of being human.

Darwin's theories were based on his observations that related animals in different areas developed varied characteristics that helped them meet the demands of their environments. For example, finches on one group of islands had somewhat longer beaks than those on another group of islands, and this coincided with their different food sources. On the basis of such observations, Darwin proposed that variations within and between species are due to **natural selection**. According to this theory, individuals possessing characteristics that aid their survival in a particular environment have the best chance of living long enough to mate and thus passing those characteristics on to their offspring. If this were so, Darwin argued, then all species (including *homo sapiens*) were descended from a common ancestor (ultimately, a single-celled organism), and that the tendency in nature was for development to occur in the direction of increasing complexity. Since the theory of evolution seemed to challenge the very core of nineteenth century Christian thought, it is not surprising that it provoked an outcry at the time.

I have called this principle, by which each slight variation, if useful, is preserved, by the term Natural Selection.
Charles Darwin

Scientists today largely accept Darwin's theory of evolution, although natural selection and the biological mechanisms that accomplish it are still being investigated. Likewise, it is widely accepted that human beings, together with all other forms of life, are partially determined by the environment. Most scientists would agree, however, that human beings interact with the environment in a much more complex manner than other living creatures do. This is because humans are the only animals that can alter and progressively change the environment in which they live. Other animals interact with their environment in ways that are determined by instinct and that are essentially the same for all individuals of the species in every generation, but humans build on the accomplishments of their peers and predecessors. A beaver's dam may change the course of a stream one year, but it erodes into the stream after a season or two; the shape and location of a blackbird's nest have not changed in centuries. But the life of a twentieth century American is significantly different from that of an ancient Egyptian or that of a neolithic cave dweller—and they and other earlier humans have left their artifacts for us to decipher. Through intellectual and technological advances, human beings exert profound changes on their environments; these changes, in turn, alter human behavior—and even transform human nature itself.

When Aristotle said that "man is, by nature, a political animal," he meant that it is "natural" for human beings to live in cities, since the Greek word *polis* means *city.* As in Aristotle's day, cities are places where people crowded into relatively small spaces, where a great deal is happening all the time, and where change is rapid and continual. All of these effects are, of course, intensified in the modern metropolis. Today's city, and tomorrow's, is an environment that affects us all. It is an amalgam of people and structures so vast, and so economically and politically powerful, that it influences the lives and behavior even of those who do not live in it. For this reason, the urban environment has become a concern of social psychologists.

In this chapter, we shall be concerned primarily with today's complex urban environments and their impact on our behavior and psychological functioning. We will start by looking at those environments we make for ourselves—our homes and offices, the buildings and and rooms we live in. Before we discuss urban crowding, and its effects on our lives, we will examine human behaviors in relation to territory. We will then look at some specific aspects of the environment—heat, noise, and air quality—to see how they affect our behavior and performance. Finally, we will examine the effects of urban existence and our perceptions of our place within it.

Environmental Psychology

I have discovered that all human evil comes from this, man's being unable to sit still in a room.
Blaise Pascal

Environmental psychology is a branch of psychology that seeks to understand the relationship between the physical world and human behavior. Although it is a subdiscipline in itself, and sometimes taught as a separate course, environmental psychology (sometimes called **human ecology**) forms part of the curriculum of social psychology as well. This is natural, since social psychology is concerned with how people function in the context of social groups, and hence with the effects of the human environment, as well as other variables, on behavior. Environmental psychology specifically focuses on the physical and spatial aspects of the external environment.

Although environmental psychology is a fairly recent area of study, many of its concepts have been around since the beginnings of social psychology as a discipline. Early in the history of social psychology, for example, Kurt Lewin (1935) espoused the role of environment in determining behavior. Although Lewin's primary concern was with aspects of the social environment, such as the family, his work stimulated researchers to investigate other aspects of the physical environment that influence behavior.

Today environmental psychology takes a multidisciplinary approach that includes ecology, architecture, and engineering, as well as all of the social sciences (Sommer, 1980). Many researchers now attempt to integrate these separate fields. They take a **systems approach** to environmental factors, because they believe that none of the factors that play a role in the system as a whole can be understood in isolation (Altman, 1976). Like all living things, human beings are part of an ecosystem—the intertwined network of natural environmental factors and social and cultural constructs that provide for human needs. Environmental psychology sees people as factors in their own ecosystem, drawing from it and contributing to it in an organized and cumulative fashion.

Because of its scope, and despite its relative youth as a science, environmental psychology is taking on increasing practical importance for social planning. Its findings can be applied to a variety of problems—from local ones as to how to control littering in city parks to such national ones as how to reduce energy consumption.

The Impact of Our Surroundings

Our discussion in this chapter begins with aspects of our most immediate environment—the rooms and buildings we live in—and how they influence our perceptions and hence our behavior. Human beings are creatures who can tolerate a broad range of stimulation, depending on the meaning we attach to a situation or place. Our perceptions do not only reflect objective reality. Rather, what we think we see and feel reflects our mood, our past experiences, and a whole host of situational factors. To understand, then, how a person behaves in a given environment, we need to know how that environment appears to that person.

Effects of Interior Design

We are most intimately affected by the environmental influences of the interior spaces where we spend most of our time—the homes, schools, and offices where we live and work. These interior spaces offer shelter and make it possible to carry out the complicated functions of an advanced society.

Some rooms are sanctuaries—peaceful havens where we can escape from the cares and confusions of the outside world. Other rooms have an aura of excitement, and seem to invite people to come inside. There are rooms that are designed for one specific purpose—studying, listening to music, eating, sleeping. And there are rooms designed to serve multiple purposes, where a swift rearrangement of furniture, color, and texture transforms a work space to an entertainment area, a sleeping alcove to a dining space.

A man's home is his castle.

What gives a room its "personality"? Think about your own room at home. What sort of "personality" does it have? How does the impression given by your room relate to the ways you use it? Are there rooms in your house with a markedly different "personality"? Have you ever noticed the effect the rooms in your life have on your mood?

Room Characteristics The characteristics of a room—its lighting, color scheme, furnishings, accessories—have wide-ranging effects on our emotions and perceptions. Seghers (1948) demonstrated that the color of a room's walls can influence perceptions of warmth and cold, and thus whether we feel comfortable. In this study, women working in a room whose walls were a "cool" blue felt cold when the thermostat was set at 75 degrees. At the same temperature, women in "warm" yellow or "restful" green rooms were too warm.

Sherrod and his colleagues (1977) found that the qualities associated with an interior environment can have a definite influence on a person's mood, which in turn can influence that person's behavior. Subjects in the positive condition of their experiment were asked simply to list and describe some of the things they liked about their college residences; subjects in the negative condition were asked to describe some things they disliked about their residences. After completing this task, all subjects were dismissed; but upon leaving the room they encountered a confederate who mentioned that he was also an experimenter conducting research for which he needed help. The subjects who agreed to help

Our surroundings can affect our moods and behaviors. How would you feel living in the house shown at the left? Would living in the house shown at right make a difference? (This is the children's playroom of the home in which Mark Twain lived in Hartford, Connecticut. His children could play and do their homework here while he worked at the large table-desk.)

were given a series of arithmetic problems and were told to spend as much time on them as they needed. From a hiding place, the confederate then observed how long each subject worked on the problems. Since this was being done as a favor to the confederate, the length of time that was spent on the problems was considered a measure of altruism.

The subjects who had listed likable aspects of their residences spent an average of 12.6 minutes working on the problems, as against only 6.5 minutes spent by subjects who had listed negative aspects of their residences. Apparently just thinking of the positive or negative aspects of the environment had a subsequent influence on altruistic behavior. Of course, the relationship between environmental factors and behavior is not direct but is also influenced by emotional factors. Presumably, thinking of the pleasant or unpleasant aspects of their residences induced certain moods in the subjects, and these moods determined the degree to which they were willing to help the researcher.

This principle seems applicable to the findings of related experiments as well. For example, Russel & Mehrabian (1978) found that subjects were more willing to affiliate with others when they were in rooms they found attractive than when they were in rooms they found unattractive. Our perceptions of interior environments can also lead us to draw conclusions about the qualities of the people who occupy them, and thus influence how we interact with those people. Campbell (1979) demonstrated this effect by showing male and female students different slides of a faculty office. Some of the slides showed offices with plants, fish aquariums, and art objects; some did not. They also differed in seating arrangements and neatness. After viewing a particular slide, the subjects were asked to indicate whether they would feel comfortable being seated in the office, and what they thought the professor occupying it would be like. The results indicated that neatness, in particular, had a significant influence on the subjects' ratings of whether they would feel comfortable in a particular office and whether they would be compatible with the professor they imagined occupying it. The presence of plants, fish, and art works was also positively correlated with feelings of comfort and compatibility with the imaginary professor. (The only one of the four factors that did not turn out to be salient was seating arrangements.) Interestingly, female subjects were more responsive to environmental variations than males.

Room Arrangement   Some early environmental psychology research explored the effects of interior arrangements on the people who used these spaces. Osmond (1957), examining the effects of room arrangement on patients in geriatric wards, described two distinct types of arrangements: In **sociofugal spaces** furniture is arranged in rows, reducing social interaction and fostering isolation. In **sociopetal spaces** furniture is placed in groupings, fostering social interaction. Sociofugal arrangements are appropriate in public settings where intimacy is not desired, such as bus station waiting rooms, while sociopetal arrangements are desirable for private interiors, such as living rooms—and geriatric wards.

Problems arise when the interior arrangement of a room and its function are in contradiction. This problem is often the case in institutional settings, where increased social interaction would be desirable. In a classic study of this problem, Sommer and Ross (1958) visited a new hospital whose designers had hoped to foster interaction among the patients. The atmosphere of the hospital was pleasant, but the patients were nevertheless apathetic and social interaction was minimal. The reason for this, apparently, was that the furniture arrangement in the wards was sociofugal: Chairs were lined up in long straight rows so that the patients sat side by side and back to back. When the investigators rearranged the furniture, placing groups of four chairs around small tables, patients' interaction doubled within a few weeks. These findings were confirmed by Mehrabian and Diamond (1971), who had groups of four strangers choose their own seating arrangements. The more directly people faced each other, the more time they spent conversing.

Eye contact and verbal interaction seem to go hand in hand (as we saw in chapter 7) and furniture arrangement can encourage or inhibit eye contact. Silverstein and Stang (1976) conducted a field experiment in which observers joined 201 groups of 3 people (triads) seated at rectangular tables in campus areas, usually cafeterias. Figure 14–1 is a schematic representation of the position of the observer and the other persons at the table. It was found that the person facing two others spoke most often; this corresponds with the fact that only this person could maintain visual contact with the others in the triad without shifting his or her own body. The person who spoke least often was the one who had to shift to make eye contact with the others.

Although the spatial factors stemming from furniture arrangement can play an important role in shaping social interactions, people are usually unaware that this is happening. Consequently, they may incorrectly interpret their own behavior as well as the behavior of others. For example, in an experiment conducted by Aiello and Thompson (1978), subjects were made to carry on conversations while seated at an uncomfortably far distance from one another. Although the subjects felt uneasy about the situation, they failed to recognize that their dis-

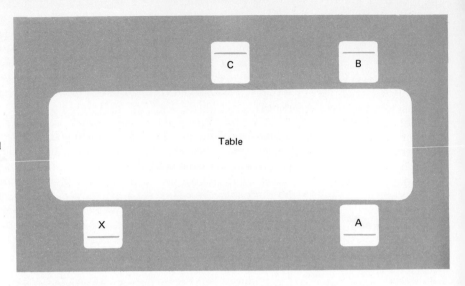

FIGURE 14-1. Seating Arrangement, Eye Contact, and Conversation

Observer X has taken a chair at a table previously occupied by persons A, B, and C. It was found that A spoke most, and C least often.

Source: *Adapted from "Seating Position and Interaction in Triads: A Field Study," by C. H. Silverstein & D. J. Stang, Sociometry, 39(2), 1976, 166.* Reprinted with permission from the author and *The American Sociological Association.*

comfort was due to situational factors. Instead, they held their partners accountable for the discomfort they felt.

Effects of Architectural Design

The effects of architectural design on behavior are generally parallel to the effects of interior design, but there are some important differences between the two. In the first place, when we speak of interior design we refer to factors contained in an enclosed and relatively small space. These small-scale factors are usually amenable to change: It is fairly easy to rearrange furniture or to paint the walls a new color. With architectural design, however, we are concerned with large-scale factors that affect a community as a whole. The location, structure, appearance, and layout of a building affect not only the people who live or work inside it, but it also affects the people who come into contact with it from the outside and temporary visitors. The planning, construction, and use of a building is thus a matter that concerns society as a whole at a great many levels and that involves the expenditure of a good deal of its resources. One can rearrange furniture but one cannot rearrange the walls of an entire building; if it fails to fulfill its function, the only recourse is demolition.

High-Rise versus Low-Rise Housing   In recent years, city planners, architects, social psychologists, and community members have all offered opinions about the relative advantages and disadvantages of high-rise and low-rise housing—especially where low-income projects are concerned (see box). To study this controversial issue, McCarthy and Saegert (1978) compared the experiences of tenants in both high-rise and low-rise buildings within the same low-income housing project. The investigators hypothesized that the high-rise tenants would be more burdened by crowding, would have more fears for their safety and privacy, and would have more problematic social interactions with their neighbors than

Application: When a Housing Project Fails

When the Pruitt-Igoe housing project was built in St. Louis in the 1950s, it was considered a showcase for what public housing should be (*Time*, Dec. 27, 1971). Its 33 high-rise buildings contained 2,800 apartments with the most up-to-date fixtures. Between the buildings ample space was provided for automobile parking. The project design even included galleries for strolling and recreation within the buildings themselves, as well as green areas and playgrounds outside. Urban planners were convinced that the project would be an enormous success and that it would be a model for low-income housing projects in cities across the country.

Only a decade later, Pruitt-Igoe was a high-rise ghost town, and the enthusiasm of planners, architects, and government officials was shattered. Instead of serving as a model for other communities, the project stood as a dire warning. By 1971 it was recognized as a complete failure, and wrecking balls were sent in to attack some of the buildings. What had gone wrong?

Part of the problem with Pruitt-Igoe was its location. Constructed in one of the worst slums in St. Louis, the complex was gradually overrun by the problems of the surrounding area. Although city planners had initially hoped that the project would help to revitalize the area, the disintegration of the surrounding inner-city community proved too great for the residents of Pruitt-Igoe to combat. Instead of providing a needed facelift for the neighborhood, Pruitt-Igoe became a monument to urban blight.

The other failing of Pruitt-Igoe was due to the people who came to live there. The original intention had been for some tenants to be working-class families and some to be welfare families, all drawn from people already living in the area. It was assumed that working-class people would be attracted to the modern facilities that the project offered, and that the rents paid by these families would supplement the lower rents paid by the welfare tenants and contribute to the project's upkeep.

Unfortunately, fewer working-class families than anticipated chose to live in the project, partly because of the area it was located in, and partly because of the exodus to suburbia that was then at its height in American cities. As a result, many apartments remained vacant, leading to financial problems and also to pressures to fill them with more welfare families from the area.

Eventually this caused an accelerating deterioration. As the money available for building and grounds maintenance was reduced, the physical condition of the project worsened. The problems of the neighboring community increasingly penetrated the project, whose high-rise buildings, long corridors, and galleries offered a haven for drug addicts and criminals of all kinds. Gangs of unemployed youths began to terrorize tenants; vandalism and theft became common occurrences; elevators and halls were used as "shooting galleries" and lavatories. Confronted with this state of affairs, the remaining tenants who could afford to go elsewhere left in droves, and their apartments were taken over by the city's destitute. The continued loss of revenue made it increasingly difficult to manage the project properly. Within a few years, the Pruitt-Igoe project, begun with high hopes, was a disaster.

As a result of Pruitt-Igoe and other similar fiascoes, city planners and government officials have learned a few lessons. They now know that high-rise buildings become vertical concentrations of the social problems prevalent in blighted urban areas. Such structures provide fewer opportunities for social interaction and offer more concealed spaces where antisocial activities can be carried on. Therefore, the tendency now in low-income housing is to construct lower buildings and disperse them throughout urban areas rather than centralizing them in a single deteriorating neighborhood.

low-rise tenants. All of these predictions were supported by interview data. It should be noted, however, that the apparent disadvantages of high-rise buildings in low-income neighborhoods probably do not apply to middle-class or affluent neighborhoods. People living in poor neighborhoods generally are more exposed to vandalism, overcrowding, and crime than are people in middle-class neighborhoods—but high-rise dwelling seems to add to their vulnerability.

Residential Proximity   In chapters 6 and 7, we discussed the role that proximity plays in interpersonal attraction and communication. Since architecture determines proximity in living and working patterns, it will also have an indirect impact on friendship patterns.

The classic study of the relationship between spatial and functional proximity and friendship patterns was conducted by Festinger, Schachter, and Back in 1950. The subjects of this study were a homogeneous group of graduate students living in housing for married students at the Massachusetts Institute of Technology shortly after World War II. Festinger and his colleagues interviewed the women of the households to determine the relationship of physical distance to their friendships with neighbors. Basically it was found that couples were most likely to become friends with their next-door neighbors and least likely to become friends with the people who lived farthest from them in the building.

If the couples surveyed had been separated by large distances, or if they had lived in high-rise apartment buildings, the findings obtained by Festinger and his colleagues would not have been very remarkable. But this, in fact, was not the case. Figure 14–2 is a schematic representation of one of the buildings surveyed. As the figure shows, this barracks-style building contained only 2 floors, with 10 dwelling units in all. The people living on the first floor entered their apartments by way of individual porches. The people living on the second floor, however, reached their apartments by way of staircases located at both ends of the first floor hall. Festinger and his colleagues found that the effect of physical distance on friendship patterns was influenced by **functional distance**—that is, by the architectural features that either increased or decreased the likelihood of contact. Few friendships developed between people living on different floors; but when they did occur, the lower-level couple almost always lived next to a stairway. Thus, whether friendship developed between two couples depended, at least to some extent, on the likelihood of their "bumping into" each other—either because of physical proximity *per se* or because the architecture affected pathways.

Festinger and his colleagues were cautious about making generalizations based on these results because of the homogeneity of their subject population, but subsequent research has supported the importance of the architectural configuration of space and the distribution of people within it to friendship patterns. Nahemow and Lawton (1975) found that, although shared attitudes, interests, and background are more important determinants of friendship than physical proximity among people of similar age and race, proximity is the determining factor in friendships among dissimilar people. Proximity, it seems, can facilitate friendships that would not otherwise occur.

Proximity can also cause hostility, however, and one recent study conducted in a housing project found hostility to be even more strongly correlated with proximity than friendship (Ebbeson, Kjos, & Konečni, 1976). Interestingly, al-

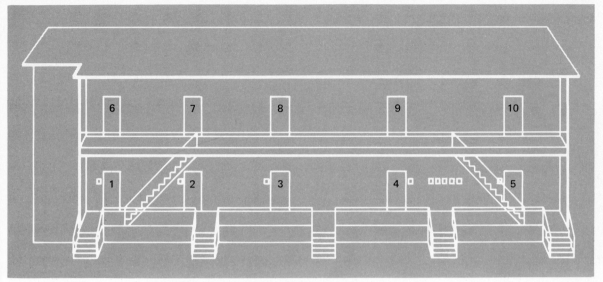

FIGURE 14–2.   Barracks-Type Housing

This is a schematic diagram of the barracks-type housing whose residents' friendship patterns were studied by Festinger et al. The ground floor porch area is the only means of entering or leaving the building. Each story has five adjacent apartments, and the two stories are connected by stairways at each end of the porch. Residents were more likely to choose as friends those living on the same floor, and those whose apartments were closer to their own.

Source: *From "The Spatial Ecology of Group Formation," by L. Festinger, S. Schachter, & K. Back,* Social Pressures in Informal Groups, *New York: Harper, 1950, 36.*

Good fences make good neighbors.
Robert Frost, Mending Wall

though the subjects tended to mention personal qualities to explain why they liked a particular neighbor, they tended to mention behavioral factors—such as whether an individual had noisy parties or failed to clean up after his dog—to explain why they disliked someone. (If you have ever had a noisy or messy next-door neighbor, you will not be surprised at these findings!)

College Dormitory Design   During our waking hours, and to a lesser extent while we are asleep, our sensory organs are continually receiving stimuli from the environment. Because our brains process information in a way that allows us to focus on important stimulus patterns, however, we are usually able to shut out extraneous stimuli. Thus, while you are reading this book, you may be hearing a variety of sounds, smelling a variety of odors, and so on; but if you are concentrating on what you read, you will probably be unaware, or only dimly aware, of these extraneous stimuli. On the other hand, if you are trying to study and your roommate is playing rock music at a high decibel level, you may be unable to concentrate. In this case, your inability to shut out extraneous stimuli will result in what psychologists term **stimulus overload.**

Unfortunately, many college dormitories seem to have been designed to maximize stimulus overload and to make it impossible for students to study. Another common complaint of students who live in dormitories is that they have little privacy and are constantly bumping into one another. This experience of social overload—too much social interaction—can be very disconcerting. Although we are social animals, when we encounter an excess of interaction we apparently crave privacy to regain our balance.

In a series of important studies, Baum and Valins (1976, 1977, 1979) examined the relationship between college dormitory design and social overload. These researchers compared the effects of corridor-design and suite-design dormitories. In a typical corridor-design dormitory, two-person bedrooms are situated on both sides of a long hall, a central bathroom is located toward the middle of the floor, and a lounge is located at one end of the hall. In a typical suite-design dormitory, on the other hand, each floor contains a number of four- to six-person suites, each with its own bathroom and lounge facilities (see Figure 14–3). The hallway is thus the only area of a suite-design dormitory that is shared by all of its residents; but, since the occupants of a suite have their own bathroom and lounge, their use of the hallway is reduced. As a result, occupants of a suite-design dormitory have less incidental contact with people who do not share their immediate living quarters than do occupants of a corridor-design dormitory. On the other hand, the members of a suite have more people with whom they must establish habitual modes of interaction than do the roommates of a corridor-design dormitory.

Baum and Valins found that subjects who lived in corridor-design dormitories felt the effects of crowding much more intensely than subjects living in suites (see Table 14–1). They found also that within corridor-design dormitories, subjects whose rooms were near bathrooms or lounges—areas that naturally have a good deal of traffic—felt more crowded than the other residents. The researchers concluded that "the dynamics of the corridor environments posed threats to residents' ability to regulate social contact" (1979, p. 156).

If those who live in corridor-design dormitories feel more intensely crowded than those who live in suites, do their different experiences lead them to behave differently in social interactions outside of the dormitory environment? To investigate this question, Baum and Valins (1977) set up a laboratory experiment in which male and female subjects from both groups were placed in a waiting room either alone or with a confederate of the same sex posing as another subject. Students from the corridor-design dormitory avoided interacting with the con-

TABLE 14–1.

Perceptions of Crowding in Dormitories of Different Design

Dormitory Design	Crowded	Not Crowded	Have Privacy	Do Not Have Privacy	Desire to Avoid Others Often	Desire to Avoid Others Seldom
Corridor	61	39	41	59	84	16
Suite	16	84	72	38	38	62

Note: Numbers are in percentages.

Source: Adapted from "Architectural Mediation of Residential Density and Control: Crowding and the Regulation of Social Contact," by A. Baum and S. Valins. In L. Berkowitz, *Advances in Experimental Social Psychology, Vol. 12.* New York: Academic Press, 1979, 156.

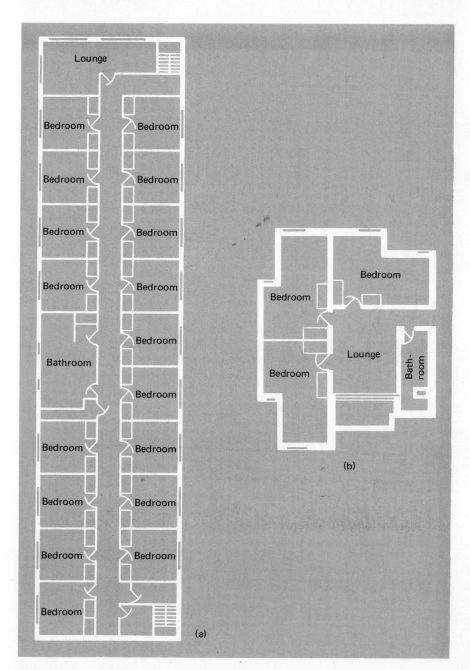

FIGURE 14-3.   Floor Plans of Corridor-Design Dormitory (a) and Suite-Design
              Dormitory (b)

Source: *From* "Architecture Social Behavior: Psychological Studies of Social Density," by A. Baum, & S.
Valins, *Hillsdale, N.J.: Erlbaum, 1977.*

federate and seemed to experience considerably more stress while waiting with another person than those from the suite-design dormitory. However, stress levels and behavior for both groups were similar when they were waiting alone. The researchers concluded that frequent contact with dormitory neighbors may result in reactions of stress and avoidance of social contact outside of the dormitory situation. Think of this the next time a fellow student rebuffs your attempt to be friendly; perhaps he or she is in a state of withdrawal after being socially overloaded from dwelling in a corridor-design dormitory.

Territoriality

The tendency of many animals to seek, mark, maintain, and defend a particular area from members of their own and other species is referred to as **territoriality**. This has long been a controversial subject, not only among psychologists but also among philosophers and other scientists as well. While it is generally agreed that many (if not most) animals display territorial behavior, some scientists claim that territoriality is a learned behavior resulting from an organism's relationship to its environment, while others maintain that it is an innate drive that corresponds to a basic instinct.

Most psychologists and other social scientists, however, are unwilling to accept the instinctivist position, at least in its entirety, and particularly in regard to human territorial behavior. Their position is that human behavior is extremely complex and that the human territorial instinct, if there is one, cannot be empirically isolated and distinguished from learned components of behavior.

Human Territorial Behavior

Despite their disagreement about the extent to which human territorial behavior is learned or instinctive, few psychologists today dispute its existence. Territorial signs are embedded in our everyday spoken and written language—in phrases such as "my turf," "members and guests only," and "no trespassing" (Altman, 1975). Indeed, territoriality is at the basis of our social, political, and legal codes and institutions. When we distinguish between public and private, and between "my property" and "yours," we are using territorial concepts that became habitual early in our childhood.

Attitudes toward personal property vary from person to person and also from society to society. Among the nomadic !Kung Bushmen of Africa, for example, there is little that belongs exclusively to any one person.

> A Bushman will go to any lengths to avoid making other Bushmen jealous of him, and for this reason the few possessions that Bushmen have are constantly circling among the members of their groups. No one cares to keep a particularly good knife too long, even though he may want it desperately, because he will become the object of envy. (Thomas, 1959, p. 22)

And the Hadza of Tanzania do not even protect property rights to the land on which they hunt and forage for food. Indeed, not only can any person from their own group use whatever resources exist in their territory, but the Hadza do not even protest encroachment on their territory by outsiders.

In its own forest the clockbird is supreme.
Ashanti proverb

But people such as the !Kung and the Hadza are exceptions. Among more complex societies, property, whether land or more portable possessions, is generally owned, identified, and jealously guarded, if not by individuals then by a collective entity such as a commune, business organization, or government.

Animals relate to territories only within the framework of the immediate group. The territory of a pride of lions, for example, includes only the actual terrain that the animals cover while they search for food. But human beings in even the simplest societies are aware that they live in communities, and that these communities exist within an area that contains other human communities. Indeed, for humans territoriality helps to identify group membership. Americans in New York know that there are Americans in California and that both states are part of the territory of the United States. If a part of this territory is attacked (as it was at Pearl Harbor on December 7, 1941), Americans living very far away respond defensively. Moreover, territorial behavior in humans even manifests itself in terms of ideas and belief systems. In most parts of the world, majority groups maintain themselves in power by strictly limiting access to the material wealth of the group as a whole to those who adhere to the group's beliefs.

This village belongs to the Castle, and whoever lives here or passes the night here does so in a manner of speaking in the Castle itself.
Franz Kafka, The Castle

Types of Territories

In everyday speech we tend to distinguish only between what is public and what is private. However, the kinds of territorial relationships that actually exist in a given society are much more complex than this simple distinction indicates. For example, suppose that you are studying in the smoking section of your university library and someone takes the ashtray next to you without asking your permission. Even though the ashtray is not your private property, you would probably be annoyed—and justifiably so—because you had been using it first. In this case, then, one might say that you had a territorial claim to the ashtray, even though it was intended for "public" use.

Altman (1975) points out that territorial distinctions are based on two factors: (1) the degree of control and the use by occupants and (2) the relative duration of users' claims to the space. On the basis of these factors, Altman distinguishes among *primary*, *secondary*, and *public territories*. These distinctions are useful because they eliminate some of the ambiguity between public and private territorial events.

Primary Territories   Primary territories are "owned and used exclusively by individuals or groups, are clearly identified as theirs by others, are controlled on a relatively permanent basis, and are central to the day-to-day lives of the occupants" (Altman, 1975, p. 112). This category includes our ordinary notion of "private property," along with territories, such as business offices, that may not be the legal property of their users. A person's relationship to a primary territory contains both real and symbolic boundaries that set the individual off from the rest of society and define the individual in terms of society. Thus, Professor

When a hurricane forced thousands from the coast of North Carolina to flee to higher ground they were taken to Red Cross shelters such as this one, hastily set up in a school building. It is public territory, open to those in need; for those taken in, it is secondary territory; and the two cots and the floor area between them have become primary territory for this family. When the building returns to its customary use, it will still represent public, secondary, and primary territories to the general public, its students, and its faculty and administrative staff respectively.

American Red Cross photo by Ted Carland

Mendez of the psychology department will have a key to her office and the office itself will be designated as belonging to Professor Mendez by a nameplate of some kind. If an outsider were to enter her office without permission, it would be considered at least a breach of manners and, in certain cases, perhaps even a crime.

Secondary Territories Whereas primary territories are exclusively controlled by those who use them, secondary territories are only partially controlled by their users, and sometimes in symbolic or even illegal ways. Thus, secondary territories form a somewhat shadowy bridge between primary territories and public ones. Private clubs, neighborhood bars, and even stretches of beach may be considered secondary territories by particular groups. In the case of private clubs, there may be a legal basis for excluding nonmembers, but in the case of neighborhood bars and beach areas, such a basis does not exist. Nevertheless, outsiders who "intrude" on these areas could be made to feel unwanted by the "regulars." Secondary territories figure prominently in the "turf mentality" of street gangs and underworld groups.

Public Territories Public territories are those that everyone, at least theoretically, has free access to, although the right of access may be controlled by certain rules. For example, a municipal zoo is a public territory, but in order to enter it one might have to pay a fee. In contrast to primary territories, which are maintained on a more or less permanent basis by their users and occupants, individual use of public territories is occasional or intermittent. Playgrounds, beaches, buses, libraries, and streets are all public territories—although they may be secondary territories for particular groups, and even primary territories for people employed in or on them.

Territorial Marking

Anyone who has ever had a male dog knows that animals mark off territories by means of the physiological mechanisms at their disposal. Human beings do not generally resort to the same procedures, but essentially the same principle applies to them as well: The purpose of territorial marking is to distinguish between "insiders" and "outsiders," between those who are privileged to occupy or use a particular space and those who are not.

People make use of both physical markers, such as fences and hedges, and symbolic ones, such as words, to indicate particular territories. The kinds of markers used as well as the ways they are used depend on the type of territory being marked. Primary territories are typically marked by obvious indicators such as doors, fences, and signs—a nameplate on a door, a number for a reserved parking place. Secondary territorial markers, on the other hand, may be more subtle or ambiguous. For instance, a bright green shamrock and a sign reading "O'Leary's Saloon" would clearly indicate that the bar was Irish, and thus in some cases discourage non-Irish patrons from entering. The markers that people leave in public spaces typically have a less formal quality. For example, people who intended to return to a particular desk in the library after making a telephone call often leave a coat or some books to indicate that the seat is "taken."

Sommer and Becker (1969) found that people can sometimes serve as territorial markers themselves, in the sense that their presence can cause others to keep their distance. For example, these researchers found that a smaller percentage of passersby used a campus water fountain when a confederate was sitting close to it and reading a book than when nobody was present. Similarly, it has been found that in public settings people often resort to touching or other

Ken Karp

Among humans, territorial marking takes many forms. Three are shown here: the two young men sprawled on a rock in an urban park are using their personal space to define their temporary use of a public territory. The man seated on the park bench has extended his arms to define the space he occupies and ward off intruders. And an unseen claimant has left his mark in white paint in the foreground.

forms of physical contact to indicate territorial claims. For example, in a study of territorial behavior in a pinball arcade, it was found that when people approached a machine (but were not yet playing) and were observed at a close distance by strangers, they were more likely to maintain physical contact with the pinball machine than were people who were not being observed at a close distance (Werner, Brown, & Damron, 1981).

The kinds of markers used to designate primary territories depend on how the occupants relate to them. For example, Edney (1972) found that homeowners who used markers such as fences, hedges, and "private property" signs tended to have lived in their residences for a longer period of time than the homeowners who did not use such indicators. Presumably, territorial markers such as fences and signs indicate both the commitment of homeowners to their residences and also their fear of intrusion from outsiders.

A marker's effectiveness in regulating access to a territory ultimately depends on the user's power to defend the territory. The means of defense used by animals are consistent within a given species. In general, though, the strongest members of the group dominate the others, first by use of threatening gestures and then, if acquiescence does not follow, by more aggressive acts. Humans, on the other hand, have a wider range of territorial defense options available. The use of more varied means instead of stereotyped ones, indirect behavior instead of direct behavior, and generally more sophisticated behavior distinguish human means of regulating claims to territory from that of other animals.

In a study of territorial behavior in a boys' rehabilitation center, Sundstrom and Altman (1974) found that the most dominant boys maintained control of preferred areas, such as the TV room, while the less dominant boys distributed themselves throughout the cottage. The investigators noted that a "pecking order" or social hierarchy was established in regard to preferred areas or activities, and that this hierarchy maintained the equilibrium of the group as a whole.

When primary territories are invaded, their inhabitants will, of course, attempt to defend them, but confrontation is rarely used in defending secondary or public territories (Becker & Mayon, 1971). You may wish to be alone while studying in the library, but if someone sits down at your table you can hardly shoo him away, since he has as much right to be there as you do. However, if a stranger were to walk in your front door, you would have every right to shoo him away— and to call on the police to enforce your right to defend your primary territory. Nevertheless, there are situations in which people do actively defend public territories: "Hey, why don't you wait your turn in line like everyone else?"

Territoriality and Behavior

For animals and human beings alike, territoriality regulates behavior by eliminating potential conflicts. In an interesting series of studies on the relationship between territorial boundaries and conflict, United States navy volunteers who were strangers were paired in socially isolated situations for periods between 8 and 10 days (Altman & Haythorn, 1967; Altman, Taylor, & Wheeler, 1971). Those pairs that made firm territorial decisions at the outset of the period they spent together were found to be more compatible than those that did not define the ground rules from the start.

The relationship between territoriality and social regulation is dramatized when territorial mechanisms fail to function. This happened in 1979, as you may recall, when "The Who" gave a concert in Cincinnati at which 11 young people were trampled to death and many more were seriously injured. As a result of a security breakdown, close to 7,000 fans with unreserved, general admission tickets, who had been waiting outside Riverfront Coliseum for hours, were allowed to rush through two sets of doors in an attempt to get as close to the stage as they could. The result was chaos—and tragedy. Reserved seating would in all likelihood have prevented these deaths.

A number of studies have shown that territorial behavior gives people a sense of control. Paterson (1978) found that elderly people who provided their homes with territorial markers were less fearful of personal assault and property loss than those who did not. There is some indication, moreover, that territorial markers actually do help to prevent crime and to ward off intruders (Sommer & Becker, 1969).

The psychological advantage of being in "home territory" is a well-known phenomenon in competitive sports. Most teams, whether amateur or professional, do better "at home" than "away." Part of the reason is that athletes are more familiar with the idiosyncracies of the fields or courts that belong to their teams, and thus can compensate for these flaws or take advantage of other factors. Visiting teams, on unfamiliar ground, are unable to do either. A baseball team that has a number of very fast "singles hitters" may want to take advantage of this by having the grounds crew water the infield in a certain way, for example. But in addition to the tangible benefits of the home-court advantage, there are also psychological benefits. Players who know that the fans are rooting for rather than against them may feel more secure.

The home-court advantage is not restricted to sports. Edney (1975) conducted an experiment in which pairs of undergraduates were asked to perform activities such as rearranging furniture and clearing floor space. The tasks were to be done in the dormitory room of one of the two students. In half of the trials, the resident was designated as being in charge, and in the other half the "outsider" was so designated. Regardless of who was nominally in charge, however, the person who lived there reported being more comfortable in the situation and also took a more active, take-charge role.

In a related study, male college students role-playing prosecuting and defense attorneys had to negotiate a jail sentence for a fictitious criminal. The debate took place in the room of one of the students, and the room's occupant tended to exert more influence on the negotiations than the outsider. He spent more time speaking than the outsider did and also argued more persuasively (Martindale, 1971).

This study suggests that in a conversation between people with dissimilar orientations, the owner or occupant of a territory tends to maintain dominance. Other studies have suggested, however, that in conversations between people with similar orientations, a so-called **hospitality effect** comes into play. When the subjects of one study met to discuss whether the university should recognize the campus Gay Liberation group, the occupant of the room dominated the conversation when the pairs disagreed. However, when they agreed on the issue, the occupant tended to defer to the visitor, who spoke more and seemed to control the conversation (Conroy & Sundstrom, 1977).

Crowding

The perpetual struggle for room and food.
Malthus

The subject of crowding has been of particular interest to social psychologists as a result of what has come to be known as the "population explosion" of the twentieth century. Actually, issues associated with the problem of crowding have been important in social science since at least 1798, when the English economist and demographer Thomas Malthus published his *Essay on the Principle of Population*. Malthus's basic thesis was that population will always increase faster than the food supply, and that therefore social progress can occur only if population growth is restricted, preferably through strict limits on reproduction. In the absence of such limits, Malthus argued, wars and periodic outbreaks of epidemics would continue to be inevitable. Although the Malthusian perspective has often been attacked—for example, by those who argue that "natural" resources should not be regarded as fixed, since what nature yields depends on human technological development—it continues to be influential.

Ehrlich (1968) pointed out that from the year 6000 B.C. to 1650 A.D. the world's population grew from around 5 million to 500 million, doubling only about every 1,000 years. There are now about 4 billion people in the world. If expansion continues at current rates, demographers estimate, it will only take another 35 years for the population of the world to double! The problem of crowding is particularly severe in the nations of the Third World, which often lack the resources to accommodate the basic needs of their people. In their attempts to limit the population growth, the governments of some nations have occasionally resorted to dictatorial measures; thus, the problem of crowding is linked to social control at many different levels.

There are more than three and a half billion people unevenly distributed over the habitable areas of the earth. When population density becomes too great, governments in underdeveloped nations and modern metropolises alike try to find means of alleviating the problems. On Tokyo's main shopping thoroughfare, the Ginza, traffic is banned for several hours a day so that pedestrians can use every foot of street space.

Animal Studies

Studies of crowding in animal populations must be interpreted with caution because the results cannot always be generalized to human beings. The coping mechanisms of humans differ from those of animals because humans are able to change their environments and their responses to them more easily than animals. Nevertheless, animal studies do provide important information on the behavioral and physiological effects of crowding.

Perhaps the best known of all animal studies of crowding was conducted by Calhoun (1962), who created an experimental situation in which groups of 80 rats were confined in a 10 by 14 foot room that was divided into 4 interconnected pens (see Figure 14-4). The pens numbered 1 and 4 could be reached only by a single ramp each, and in these pens a dominant male was able to protect his territory from incursions by other males. Two ramps entered pens numbered 2 and 3, and as a result population density was highest in these pens, and pathological behavior stemming from crowding developed.

Ample food was provided to the animals by means of food hoppers that were constructed so as to make feeding a prolonged activity. As a result, the rats became conditioned to associate feeding with the presence of others. This fostered what Calhoun termed a **behavioral sink,** in which the normal function of the feeding situation—survival—was subordinated to the desire of the animals for togetherness. Eventually, one of the hoppers came to be preferred by the majority of the animals, with the result that 75 percent of them crowded into the pen containing this hopper, making conditions even more crowded than they would have been if the animals had distributed themselves evenly in all of the pens.

In the pens numbered 1 and 4, infant mortality was only about 50 percent. The females in the harems of the dominant males were protected by them from unwanted attention by males in the other pens, and took good care of their young. In the middle pens, however, infant mortality rose as high as 96 percent. Unable to protect themselves while in heat, the females in these pens gradually stopped building proper nests for their young.

Also in the middle pens, the males developed pathological behavior patterns. A number became unable to distinguish between appropriate and inappropriate sexual partners, attempting to mount other males, females who were not in heat, and even juveniles. Other males became totally passive, remaining aloof from rats of both sexes and ignored by them as well. Finally, a third group, which Calhoun termed the "probers," displayed frenetic activity. These animals would continually wait for females in heat at the tops of the middle ramps; and even when chased away by the dominant males, with whom they never attempted to fight, they would soon return to their stations. They were hypersexual, homosexual, and also cannibalistic.

Calhoun's study stimulated a good deal of research, but his results should be interpreted cautiously. For one thing, it is probable that the pathological behavior manifested by the rats in his experiment stemmed less from crowding *per se* than from the behavioral sink produced by the abnormal feeding situation and the arrangement of the cages. With other cage and feeding arrangements, groups of healthy mice have been bred under "standing room only" conditions. Nevertheless, since crowding often occurs with other factors that may lead to behavior aberrations, Calhoun's results remain extremely provocative.

FIGURE 14–4. A Study of Crowding Using Rats

Eighty rats were confined in a 10-by-14-foot room divided into four pens. Conical objects (center) are food hoppers; trays with 3 bottles are drinking troughs. Elevated burrows of five nest boxes each (shown exposed in pen 1) could be reached by winding staircases. Ramps connected all adjoining pens but 1 and 4. Rats therefore tended to concentrate in pens 2 and 3. A "behavioral sink" of increased population developed in pen 2, where 3 rats are eating simultaneously. A female rat in heat is approaching the ramp in pen 3, pursued by a pack of males. In pens 1 and 4 a dominant male could usually expel all other males and possess a harem, but in pens 2 and 3 males outnumbered females. Dominant males, shown sleeping near the ramps in pens 1 and 4, wake to prevent other males from entering their territories. The 3 rats peering down from the ramp at right are probers, a deviant behavioral type produced by pressure of high population density. Deviant maternal behavior was also observed in female rats in pens 2 and 3.

Source: Adapted from "Population Density and Social Psychology", by J. B. Calhoun, Scientific American, 206, (2) 1962, 140–141. Copyright © 1962 by Scientific American, Inc. All rights reserved.

Density versus Crowding

We tend to treat the phrases *high population density* and *crowding* as if they were synonymous, but this can be misleading (Stokols, 1972). **Density** is a relative category that refers to an objective ratio of population to spatial area; **crowding,** on the other hand, is a psychological phenomenon that may or may not be provoked in a particular individual or group by a given level of density. Later in this chapter, we will examine a study (Mitchell, 1971) that indicates that under certain conditions even a very high density level may not provoke the subjective stressful phenomenon of crowding (see p. 539). Other studies have shown that the notion that high density always has adverse effects on people is false (Freedman, 1975).

As a psychological phenomenon, crowding has a *personal* component as well as a *situational* component. Some people, depending on their experiences and personalities, tend to be more vulnerable to the stressful feelings of crowding than other people. Moreover, certain situations may be more stressful to some people than to others. Some people, for example, may experience the stress of crowding particularly intensely on public buses, while others may feel unpleasantly crowded in a department store or at a cocktail party.

A distinction can also be made between **spatial density** and **social density** (see Figure 14–5). Spatial density is relative to the amount of space allotted to each person in a given area. Thus, if both the number of people and the spatial area are doubled, the spatial density remains the same. Social density, on the other hand, depends only on the number of people in a given area. If the number of people increases, social density increases—even if the amount of space they are allotted also increases. Interacting with many people calls for different per-

Drawing by Stevenson; © 1978 The New Yorker Magazine, Inc.

"The social fabric is extremely fragile around here."

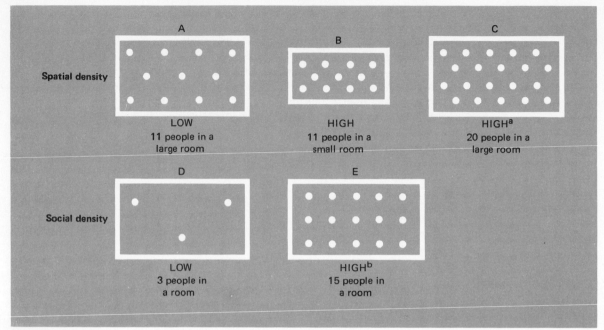

FIGURE 14–5. The Differences Between Spatial and Social Density

[a]In (C), we have a higher social density but an equivalent spatial density relative to (B).
[b]In (E), by increasing the number of people in the same size room as (D), we've reduced spatial density.

sonal resources than interacting with 2 or 3. The psychological experience of crowding may be associated with either spatial or social density, or with both at once.

Demographic Studies of Human Crowding

Early demographic studies on humans generally supported the conclusion that crowding was related to various social, physical, and behavioral problems. However, they often failed to consider other variables, such as economic and educational factors, that might also be related to such problems (Stockdale, 1979). Typically, these studies took a particular measure of crowding, such as the number of people per square mile or the amount of space per person in a household, and then correlated the figures with data on a problem such as robbery, murder, or the admissions to mental hospitals in a given city or neighborhood. This methodological approach made it impossible to know whether (and to what extent) crowding *caused* social psychological problems, or whether it was merely *associated* with them because it occurred in conjunction with poverty and/or other factors. More recent studies have attempted to control for such possibly confounding factors as socioeconomic status and ethnic background. The results of these studies indicate that crowding is not the only and direct cause of social ills such as juvenile delinquency (Freedman et al., 1975).

One study of the effects of crowding on various social pathologies usefully distinguished between **population density**—the number of people contained in a given area—and **interpersonal press**—which the authors define as a function of the number of persons per room and the number of rooms per housing unit (Galle, Gove, & McPherson, 1972). There are different problems, for example, in being one of 8 people sharing an 8-room home, or sharing the same dwelling with only 2 people. Galle and his colleagues found that interpersonal press was more highly correlated with such factors as mortality and juvenile delinquency rates than population density. These findings suggest that the effects of crowding may be mitigated if the home environment provides a haven from the stresses of the outside world, as it generally does in middle-class neighborhoods. Indeed, Booth and Welch (1974) suggest that the relationship between household density and violent crime is weaker in smaller cities and rural areas, where it is easier to escape from a crowded home environment, than in larger metropolitan areas.

The Cultural Context of Crowding: An Interview Study

City life: millions of people being lonesome together.
Henry David Thoreau

Demographic studies that merely correlate the number of persons per household with various social problems tell us nothing about whether crowding affects certain kinds of people more than others. Individual interviews, on the other hand, can tell us whether people in certain cultural contexts are more affected by crowding than people in other cultural contexts.

Mitchell (1971) interviewed a large number of people in Hong Kong, which has one of the highest ratios of population to available land in the world. Of the respondents, 39 percent shared their dwelling units with people who were not members of their families, and 28 percent slept 3 or more to a bed, with 13 percent sleeping 4 or more to a bed. In Hong Kong as elsewhere, density ratios and poverty are positively correlated.

One of the major findings of Mitchell's study was that crowding was correlated to emotional stress only when people who were not related were forced to occupy the same dwelling unit. Apparently, people's ability to function effectively within the family unit was unaffected by crowding. This suggests that the relationship between crowding and various social effects depends on the cultural conditions in which crowding occurs. In Hong Kong, where the tradition of the extended family remains extremely strong, intra-family crowding does not appear to be correlated with stress. In the United States, on the other hand, where the extended family is less prevalent than it once was, it is possible that intra-family crowding might be more strongly associated with emotional stress.

Crowding in Laboratory Settings

Laboratory studies of crowding have been concerned mainly with physiological reactions to crowding and its effects on task performance, social behavior, and sex differences. Such studies typically attempt to measure the amount of stress that subjects experience when they are crowded into a room.

Physiological Reactions and Task Performance Stress reactions associated with crowding are demonstrated by increases in skin conductance levels or cardiac function, and these reactions also correlate with subjective factors such as low frustration tolerance and negative mood swings (Epstein, 1981). Research findings on the psychological effects of crowding on task performance have been ambivalent. Some studies have found that density has little effect on task performance (Freedman, Klevansky, & Ehrlich, 1971; Nogami, 1976), but this may be because the tasks involved were relatively simple. Evans (1979) found that although crowding had little effect on subjects performing simple tasks, it had a definite effect on subjects who attempted to perform more complex tasks.

Social Behavior   The effects of crowding on social behavior depend on numerous factors, such as the personalities, interests, and backgrounds of the people involved. Individualistic people seem to suffer more intensely from crowding than people with cooperative goals. In a study conducted at Rutgers University, first year students were put three in a room that was originally intended for double occupancy (Karlin, Epstein, & Rosen, 1978). As a group, these students (who were presumably individualistic in their orientation, since they did not know one another before meeting at college and did not expect to be together long) experienced a good deal of stress. During the time they roomed together, their grade-point averages were significantly lower. The men coped with the situation by spending as little time in their rooms as possible; the women, on the other hand, invested a good deal of effort in making their rooms homelike, but were frustrated in this effort. Although the students showed few long-term adverse effects from the year of rooming together, retrospective reports were as negative as they had been in their first year (Karlin, Rosen, & Epstein, 1979).

The experience of a group of young married couples training for service in the Peace Corps, as reported by MacDonald and Oden (1973), is in direct contrast to the experience of the Rutgers University students. In this study, 5 couples were assigned to a single 30 by 30 foot room and shared a single toilet for a period of 12 weeks. These couples were a close-knit, cooperatively oriented group because of their common goals and their future expectations of their service in the Peace Corps. Not only did these trainees not show adverse effects as a result of the experience, but they apparently all enjoyed it immensely. Many from this group were selected for their leadership abilities by other trainees, many reported enhanced marital satisfaction, and as a group they regretted having to leave this dorm situation more than a control group regretted leaving their hotel accommodations.

Other studies have shown that whether crowding has positive or negative effects depends on whether the people crowded together are compatible or incompatible. Smith and Haythorn (1972) observed navy personnel in a simulated undersea laboratory. Crowding led those subjects who were incompatible with the others to withdraw from interactions; but those who were compatible sought group recreational activities such as card-playing more often than a control group that did not experience crowding.

Sex Differences   Most, but not all, of the research on how sex differences influence the effects of crowding suggests that men are more disturbed by conditions of high density than women (Aiello, Nicosia, & Thompson, 1979; Epstein & Karlin, 1975; Paulus, 1976). This may be due to differences in the ways men and women have traditionally been socialized to handle stress. Women in our society are generally more comfortable than men about sharing their feelings of distress; women tend to respond to stressful experiences by bonding with other women, whereas men often attempt to maintain a facade of self-assurance. Schettino and Borden (1976) report that when the number of students packed into a classroom increases, women react by becoming nervous whereas men become aggressive.

In another experiment, Freedman and his colleagues (1972) placed all male and all female groups in large or small rooms in simulated courtroom situations. Measures were taken of the competitiveness of the subjects and of their harshness in sentencing a mock defendant. Under high density conditions, men tended to respond competitively to others in their group and to hand out stiffer sentences. Women, on the other hand, cooperated more with one another and were more lenient in their sentencing under the same conditions. In addition, the women liked each other more than the men liked each other under these conditions.

It seems clear that the differences in men's and women's responses to crowding are not innate but are rather due to social learning. A study conducted by Karlin and his colleagues (1976) demonstrated that special training can alter the effect of sex differences. After informing crowded women that successful, intelligent people cope by keeping to themselves, and by providing female models of this coping strategy, they observed that the crowded women had adopted the "male" response to crowding that had been modeled for them.

Explanations of Crowding Effects

A number of theories have been offered to explain why crowding has psychological effects on us. The three most influential ones focus on how we interpret crowding, the social overload that crowding causes, and our sense of losing control of a crowd situation.

The Attributional Model   The attributional model of crowding is based on the Schachter–Singer theory of emotion (see p. 537). According to this theory, the feelings we report to ourselves or to others are based on our cognitive interpretations of the physiological arousal we feel. This explanation holds that, if we feel aroused under conditions of high density and *attribute* the stress we feel to the presence of many others, then we will feel crowded. We can be in a group of people, be aroused, and yet not feel crowded if we interpret the source of our feelings as something other than those around us—as we are and do at a football game, for example. The attributional model, then, distinguishes between high density as an objective phenomenon and crowding as a subjective interpretation of the situation.

Proponents of the attributional model separate the experience of crowding into two distinct stages (Worchel & Teddlie, 1976). The initial stage usually occurs in the context of a violation of personal space norms. A high density situation, as we saw above, will not necessarily be viewed as a violation of personal space; for example, people do not generally feel crowded at concerts or athletic events. But when a person does experience the violation of personal space due to the unwanted presence of others, he or she may, in the second stage, interpret this feeling as crowding.

A study conducted by Worchel and Yohai (1979) supports the role of attribution to the feeling of crowding. The authors predicted that subjects who were misinformed about the cause of their arousal under high density conditions would not feel crowded. The subjects were placed in a room and some of them

Controversy: Is Crowding In Prisons "Cruel and Unusual Punishment"?

Most of the prisons in the United States are crowded—that is, they contain more inmates than they were originally intended to house. There is no question that this is an unfortunate state of affairs. However, is the crowding that occurs in American prisons a kind of "cruel and unusual punishment," and thus a violation of the Eighth Amendment to the Constitution?

On June 15, 1981, in the case of *Rhodes vs. Chapman*, the Supreme Court, in a 8 to 1 vote, held that it was not unconstitutional for 1,400 inmates at the Southern Ohio Correctional Facility to be doubled up in 63-square-foot cells. Writing for the majority, Judge Lewis F. Powell, Jr., asserted that although crowding may result in conditions that are harsh, these conditions are "part of the penalty that criminal offenders pay for their offenses against society. . . . The Constitution does not mandate comfortable prisons."

This decision, however, did not entirely close the door on advocates of prison reform because the Southern Ohio Correctional Facility is generally regarded as a first class prison. Thus, although the court decided that "double-celling" was not unconstitutional in the relatively benign conditions at the southern Ohio prison, the practice might, under other conditions, be ruled unconstitutional.

Before the Supreme Court arrived at its decision, social psychologists and prison reform advocates had argued for years that crowding can have extremely adverse effects on prison inmates. In a study conducted by McCain, Cox, and Paulus (1976), for example, it was found that crowding is positively related to illness rates in prisons and jails. These researchers maintained that the social density aspect of crowding in prisons was more salient than the spatial density aspect—that is, prisoners housed in dormitory cells containing many inmates were more likely to suffer from the effects of crowding than prisoners doubled up in cells meant for only one inmate. (The Supreme Court decision of 1981 addressed only the issue of spatial density but not that of social density, which, if McCain and his colleagues are correct, is a more serious cause for concern.)

As the Supreme Court implicitly recognized, it is quite difficult to isolate the negative effects of crowding from those due to other factors (Bukstel & Kilmann, 1980). In the court's judgment, double-celling—an issue that relates to spatial density—at the Southern Ohio Correctional Facility was not "cruel and unusual punishment" because the overall environment at this prison was relatively good. The court ruled, in effect, that spatial density levels should not be considered in isolation from other variables.

Those who disagree with the court's decision argue that even if crowding cannot be isolated from other variables in determining the general atmosphere of an institution such as a prison, there is no point in setting limits on the number of inmates to be housed in a prison if these limits are going to be ignored. Advocates of prison reform contend that the court's decision gives comfort to those states that wish to avoid spending money on providing adequate prison facilities.

had their personal space violated while others did not. They all were told that they would hear either a stress-inducing or a relaxing subliminal noise in the background while they performed a task. There was no noise in actuality, but the aroused subjects who could blame the "subliminal noise" for their discomfort did not feel crowded. Those who expected the noise to soothe them could only attribute their arousal to the other subjects, and thus felt crowded.

Excessive Social Stimulation   Another theoretical model of crowding emphasizes the role of social overload (see p. 549). According to this model, crowding occurs when the amount of privacy desired by a person is greater than the actual amount of privacy (Altman, 1975). The social overload model does not, in principle, distinguish high density crowding from other situations in which people feel a lack of privacy. However, it recognizes that social overload is likely to be most intense under the conditions of high density.

Lack of Control   Other theorists believe that a person's perception of having no control over the environment is the key factor in feeling crowded (Epstein, 1981). (Recall our discussion of perceived control in chapter 4.) The lack-of-control hypothesis emphasizes that people often develop stress reactions under conditions of high density because of a perceived inability to cope in that environment. As Sherrod (1974) found, the simple option of being able to leave a crowded room reduced stress reactions even in subjects who did not avail themselves of this option.

Rodin, Solomon, and Metcalf (1977) conducted an experiment in which four confederates piled into a Yale University elevator with a single naive subject. Sometimes the confederates nudged their way in so that the subject did not have access to the control panel. The rest of the time the subject was allowed to stand right next to the panel. When the subject reached his floor, another confederate, posing as a student of architecture, asked him to complete a short questionnaire about the elevator design. The subjects who had been shoved away from the access panel felt that the elevators were considerably more crowded than the subjects who had access to the panel; they also estimated the size of the elevator as being smaller. Apparently, then, access to the control panel affected perceptions of crowding—a finding that supports the lack-of-control hypothesis.

It should be noted that these theories are by no means mutually exclusive and that, depending on the individual and the situation, one or more of the factors they emphasize may be salient. You can demonstrate this to yourself by thinking of some situations in which you have personally felt crowded. Which theory best accounts for your reactions? You probably see that different theories better explain some situations than others.

Environmental Quality and Interpersonal Behavior

Although there has been a substantial amount of research on crowding, it is not the only factor that can make an environment uncomfortable or unpleasant. Imagine you are driving on an expressway during rush hour in a large city. The temperature is 96° and with every window in your car rolled down you are receiving the full effects of exhaust fumes and traffic noise. What impact do you think these conditions have on you and your fellow drivers? Are these necessary consequences of modern urban life?

We know we feel "under par" on hot muggy days. We know that noise makes it difficult to concentrate or to carry on a conversation. We detest noxious odors, not only because they are unpleasant but also because we suspect that "something's in the air" that may be dangerous to breathe. More and more psychological research on the effects of heat, air quality, and noise on behavior is directly linked to a growing concern about such issues as crime, energy costs and pollution. The more we learn as a society about how the quality of the environment affects behavior, the better we will be able to make responsible decisions in shaping it.

Heat and Aggression

As we saw in chapter 11, the rate of violent crimes such as murder, rape, and assault rises in the summer months with the rising temperatures. Experimental studies provide evidence for a causal relationship between heat and both interpersonal attraction and aggression. Griffitt (1970) placed students either in comfortably heated or in overheated rooms and then asked them to evaluate strangers with similar or dissimilar attitudes. Although people generally prefer those with similar beliefs (see chapter 6), the evaluations of Griffitt's subjects varied more in response to the environmental conditions, with the subjects in the overheated rooms making less favorable evaluations.

Bell and Baron (1976) identified a relationship between heat and aggression that can be represented as an inverted U-shaped curve. Aggression levels increase as heat increases up to a certain point, after which further rises in temperature lead to lethargy rather than aggression. Presumably an increase in heat produces a negative mood that increases the likelihood of aggression. When subjects are exposed to conditions they find miserable, however, their more likely response is escape rather than aggression. This finding is suggested in another of their studies. Baron and Bell (1976) placed subjects in cool, warm, and stiflingly hot conditions and allowed them to behave aggressively against an insulting confederate. Subjects in the cool condition (whose mood was probably not affected by the temperature) were most aggressive because they became angry as a result of the insult. Subjects in the warm condition were less aggressive, and very hot subjects only wanted to escape from the experiment. Apparently, under particularly miserable conditions (i.e., when insult is added to the injury of heat), escape is the preferred response.

Baron (1976), studying the responses of motorists in naturalistic settings, observed that on a hot summer day, drivers in cars without air conditioning honked their horns more quickly at cars that failed to move when the light turned green than did drivers in airconditioned cars. However, when a competing response was aroused—such as empathy for a crippled pedestrian crossing the street—the effect caused by the heat disappeared, and drivers in nonairconditioned cars were just as patient as those who drove in cool comfort.

Air Quality

While the adverse effect of air pollution on physical health has been a source of concern for some time, few studies so far have been devoted to its psychological consequences. Two recent studies (Rotton et al., 1978, 1979), suggest that under certain conditions, air pollution may be associated with negative moods and aggressive interpersonal behavior. For example, experimental subjects who were exposed to moderately unpleasant odors displayed more aggressive behavior than did control subjects (Rotton et al., 1979). However, subjects who were exposed to extremely offensive odors were no more aggressive than control subjects.

Most unpleasant odors are perceived as unpleasant by virtually everyone, but the odor of tobacco smoke affects smokers and most nonsmokers differently. Some nonsmokers are so sensitive to the fumes from a cigarette or cigar that they can detect them at a distance of several feet, while habitual smokers seem to flourish in their smoke-filled rooms. Because of the evidence that even breathing cigarette smoke can have adverse physiological effects, some communities have recently begun to enact laws restricting smoking in public places, and many restaurants and libraries have created "nonsmoking" and "smoking" sections in response to their patrons' pressures, if not to the law. Some smokers protest against this segregation, asserting that they have a right to smoke in public places. Do you think nonsmokers have a more compelling right to clean air?

Noise

From a psychological standpoint, noise consists of unpleasant or unwanted sounds. Sounds, which are detected by our ears as a result of changes in air pressure, vary in both pitch and intensity. Extreme intensities of sound—screeching high tones, rumbling low tones, rasping, or very loud sounds—cause discomfort and even physiological damage. But the experience of noise, which varies from person to person, rarely coincides with an actual physiological disability. What one person considers music may be noise to someone else, and when you are trying to concentrate, a mere whisper can be a painful distraction.

The physiological arousal associated with intense noise has been shown to interfere with task performance (Broadbent, 1979). However, there is evidence that an adaptation to noise occurs rapidly, and when people have become used to the noise it no longer interferes with their performance of at least simple tasks (Cohen & Weinstein, 1981).

As we saw in chapter 4, when subjects believe they can control the occurrence of a noise it has a less destructive impact on their work; and when they know when a noise is going to occur, they make fewer errors in a task performance than when the noise occurred at random intervals (Glass & Singer, 1972). These findings are consistent with the effects of control on perceptions of crowding that we discussed in the previous section (see p. 543).

A simple field study dramatically demonstrated the effects of noise—and the relief from it—on grade-school children (Bronzaft, 1981). Fifteen times every day some classes in Public School 98 in New York City would have to stop work while a subway train screeched over the elevated tracks nearby. Noise levels measured 89 decibels when a train passed, and the teachers had to scream to be heard. Students in the lower grades whose classrooms faced the train tracks had reading levels several months behind those of students in the same grade on the quieter side of the building. The fifth and sixth graders fell behind by as much as a year. Finally complaints were heeded, and one summer the city's Transit Authority installed inch-thick rubber cushioning on the subway rails, while the Board of Education added sound insulation to the ceilings of classrooms on the subway side of the school building. When school began again in the fall, the noise level on the subway side had been reduced to 81 decibels, and 10 of 11 teachers reported that their rooms were significantly quieter and that the interruptions were less frequent. On reading achievement tests later that year and the next, the scores of the children in the classrooms on the side of the building by the subway were, for the first time, the same as those for their grade mates on the quiet side of the building.

That people may become habituated to noisy working conditions does not mean that noise has no effect on them. In fact, there is evidence that noise may have serious negative consequences for cognitive functioning long after the noise has abated. After the subjects of the study conducted by Glass and Singer were exposed to outbursts of noise, they were removed to quiet rooms and asked to piece together four puzzles and to proofread a manuscript. Two of the four puzzles were actually unsolvable, and the amount of time that the subjects persisted at the task served as a measure of their tolerance for frustration. Those subjects who had earlier heard unpredictable and uncontrollable noise became frustrated more readily than the other subjects. The experience of unpredictable noise apparently induced feelings of helplessness that persisted long after the noise had ceased. These feelings, in turn, made the subjects less tolerant of frustration than they might otherwise have been.

Public School 98 as seen from beneath the elevated subway tracks nearby.

The New York Times/Dith Pran

There has been little research on the long-term aftereffects of noise on human behavior. This is because in everyday life exposure to noise is confounded by other variables, such as socioeconomic status, occupation, location of residence, and ethnic background. Cohen, Glass, and Singler (1973) did observe a relationship between the auditory and verbal skills of children and the noisiness of their homes, even when they controlled for the effects of social class and physiological damage. The researchers suggest that in adapting to their noisy environments, the children lost some of their capacity to discriminate sounds, and this, in turn, had an adverse impact on their reading skills.

Matthews and Cannon (1975) have shown that in attempting to adapt to noisy environments, people may narrow the focus of their attention in a way that leads them to be less sensitive to the needs of others. Under both laboratory and naturalistic settings, the subjects of their study were less helpful to a person in need under noisy conditions than under quiet conditions.

Urban Life

In the United States there is more space where nobody is than where anybody is.
Gertrude Stein

At least 50 percent of the inhabitants of the United States live on only 1 percent of its land. The experience of urban life, however, varies enormously. Some people characterize it as vibrant, expansive, and enriching, while others find it cold, impersonal, and life-threatening. Which view do you think is more accurate?

City lovers point out that cities come in all sizes, from small to megalopolitan. They observe too that each city has its own personality and character. Philadelphia is very different from San Francisco, and Madison varies greatly from New York. The characteristics of the individual, as well as of the urban area in which he or she lives, determine the extent of that person's satisfaction with an urban way of life.

Positive and Negative Aspects of Urban Life

There's safety in numbers.

Whyte (1976) interviewed managers and other employees of large corporations in New York City who had chosen either to remain in the city or to move to the suburbs. Those who chose to remain in the city emphasized the opportunities for stimulation that the city provided, while those who chose to leave cited a desire for relaxation and a haven away from the stresses of the work place. Apparently, some aspects of urban life that are viewed as positive by some people are viewed as negative by others.

One might assume that the city's slum dwellers would invariably be discontented with their environment, but this may not always be the case. Fried and Gleicher (1961) interviewed residents of West Boston and found that those who had a strong network of social relations with neighbors and relatives expressed a sense of wellbeing and a resistance to relocation. More than half of the respondents in this interview had lived in the neighborhood for more than 10 years, and 9 out of 10 liked their neighborhood. Their attachment to the community was knit together by a collection of local meeting places—parks, the street in front of their buildings, and bars. But perhaps environments today are less cohesive and stable than they were when Fried and Gleicher conducted their study.

Perhaps those residents most supported by networks were also the most up-
wardly and physically mobile, and they took their strengths to "better" neighborhoods. And perhaps those left in today's inner city are those with the fewest
sources of satisfaction within their community. This was, for example, among the
explanations given for urban riots, looting, and vandalism.

Information Overload

There is, in any event, little doubt that life in the city is less personal than it is in
a small town. In his comprehensive study of the psychology of urban life,
Milgram (1970) suggests that the apparent aloofness of city dwellers is an adaptation to what would otherwise be an unmanageably complex environment.
Milgram estimates, for example, that a pedestrian in midtown Manhattan may
meet as many as 220,000 people during a 10-minute walk to work. Compare this
to the 11,000 others that a person would encounter in a suburban county outside
of New York City.

City dwellers employ a variety of strategies to cope with what Milgram calls
the **information overload** to which they are habitually exposed. They may give

Research: Night as a New Frontier

Melbin (1978) has proposed that with the exhaus-
tion of space in the American subcontinent,
people are expanding their activities in time,
with the result that night has become a new frontier. Over the last half-century, nighttime activities have increased dramatically. Fortunately, the
technology that makes it all possible—from electric lighting to telecommunications, has increased also. Twenty-four-hour radio and television broadcasting, all-night restaurants and
supermarkets, and continuous-process refining
plants and factories are some examples of our
expanded occupation of time.

Melbin draws a number of parallels between
the expansion of nighttime activity in urban
environments and the settlement of the western
frontier. For example, the population in both
frontiers is relatively sparse and fairly homogeneous; males predominate over females; there
are fewer social constraints and more solitude;
and there is apt to be more lawlessness and violence. Moreover, Melbin contends that, as on the
western frontier, interpersonal behavior during

the nighttime is characterized by more friendliness and helpfulness than under nonfrontier
(daytime) conditions.

Melbin tested his hypothesis by conducting
a series of field experiments in the Boston area.
He found that between the hours of 12 A.M. and
7:30 A.M., people were more likely to comply with
requests for interviews, to respond helpfully
when asked for directions, and to behave so-
ciably in a 24-hour supermarket than during
other periods. Melbin argues that, like the pio-
neers of the old West, people who inhabit the
night perceive themselves as set off from the
larger population and feel a sense of com-
radeship with those in the same situation. The
night, says Melbin, is still a relatively unpopu-
lated frontier and the night dweller may be less
afflicted by the stresses of information overload
than are others. But Melbin warns that, like the
continental United States, time is unstretchable
and that it is a resource for which there is no
substitute. "What will happen," he asks, "when
saturation occurs?" (p. 21).

less time and attention to each item of information or person they come into contact with; they may altogether ignore inputs that they consider unimportant; they may make themselves less accessible to incoming stimuli; or they may become emotionally disengaged.

Now my soul hath elbow-room.
Shakespeare, King John, *V, vii*

Field research confirms the effects of information overload on social behavior. For example, Milgram (1970) found that city dwellers are less likely to respond to the handshakes of strangers than people living in small towns. Similarly, Newman and McCauley (1977) found that the farther one travels from the center of a large city, the more one will observe eye contact between strangers. By avoiding eye contact, city dwellers can block off incoming stimuli and maintain their sense of personal space.

Another way in which people respond to information overload is to find simpler ways of organizing information. The idea that people construct **cognitive maps** of a city in their attempts to organize their experience of it was first put forth in 1960 by the architect Kevin Lynch. Lynch asked residents of Boston, Los Angeles, and Jersey City to walk mentally through their city and then to sketch a map of what they had seen. After scrutinizing these maps, Lynch found that the subjects had organized their perceptions in terms of defining features. For example, people included the city paths along which they "customarily, occasionally, or potentially moved" (p. 47). Strategic spots or "nodes" are also characteristically included in cognitive maps, as are landmarks, which may serve as practical points of reference. Also included were edges or boundaries, and districts distinguished by their function or other identifying characteristic.

Milgram (1976) suggests that our ability to represent a city as a cognitive map makes it a more manageable and pleasant place in which to live. What does your cognitive map of your community look like? What does it indicate about the environmental factors that most concern you?

Answering Questions about Environmental Influences on Social Behavior

1. While highrise apartment houses have often become vertical concentrations of problems that exist in the surrounding community, these buildings do not automatically spell trouble for their inhabitants. Highrise dwellers may be more susceptible to crime and social overload than people living in smaller housing units. Much depends on the economic standing of the residents and the socioeconomic conditions in the immediate neighborhood. Factors making for safe and successful highrise dwelling include: a population mix containing working-class and middle-class residents; closeness with neighbors; and a sense of trust and community. As the chapter points out, there are architectural means to encourage or inhibit these factors. If the residents take responsibility for the semi-public areas beyond their front doors, vandalism and noise problems are less likely. Residents can also use territorial marking to help regulate their contact with others.

2. Ethologists and certain other scientists like to point out the apparent similarities in territorial behavior between lower animals and humans. Psychologists, however, are generally reluctant to call the behavior exhibited by hu-

mans "instinctive." The question has no clearcut answer—but the evidence to date weighs in on the side of territoriality, in the complex forms characteristic of humans, as being primarily learned behavior.

3. The characteristics of a room will affect the way people interact within it. Thus, if your walls are a warm yellow rather than a cool blue, a feeling of warmth and cordiality toward visitors is promoted. Similarly, if the furniture is arranged to create sociofugal forces (so that people can face one another in an intimate way), friendly interactions among visitors are promoted.

4. Socially dense situations may—or may not—cause an individual to feel crowded. Prison inmates, however, cannot control the people they come in contact with, are subject to violations of personal space, and have little motivation to resolve difficulties with other inmates. In addition, they obviously are not in the institution by choice. Much of the stress of prison life can be interpreted by inmates as due to the close-packed conditions. Pressures build, and sometimes erupt in disturbances as serious as riots.

5. A crowded room restricts the amount of personal space alotted to each of us, and the violation of personal space becomes difficult to avoid. The "press" of many people is arousing, but not always experienced as aversive. Until the individual cognitively links this arousal to the presence of others (and thus feels "crowded"), he or she may just feel slightly claustrophobic.

6. Certain aspects of today's environment can pose problems that were nonexistent or found only in the largest cities 100 years ago: noise, air pollution, and overpopulation. But to say "the world was a better place back then" is to oversimplify. Many of the factors that cause stress have remained stable over the years: the effects of heat on social behavior, for example. Also, the problems of earlier times are not necessarily the same as today's. Years ago people often had to conquer and tame the natural environment; securing food and shelter were constant challenges; survival was the goal. Today's problems involve *accommodating* humans to their surroundings rather than *conquering* the surroundings themselves. The problems of an earlier age were probably more straightforward, but not necessarily any easier to deal with.

Summary

Environmental psychology deals with the relationship between the physical world and human behavior. Environmental factors are reflected in our perceptions and also determine the ways we perceive. The characteristics, use, and arrangement of a room can influence perceptions and behavior. Colors can cause us to feel cooler or warmer in a room than the actual temperature warrants. **Sociofugal spaces** reduce social interaction, whereas **sociopetal spaces** foster it. The structure and layout of buildings affect not only those who live and work in them but those who come into contact with them on a transient basis. **Residential proximity** has been shown to influence friendship patterns, and people who live nearer to one another are more likely to become friends.

Territoriality refers to the tendency of many animals to seek out, maintain, or defend areas from members of their own or other species. Sociobiologists generally ascribe territorial behavior to instinct, while social psychologists (and others) prefer to consider it as learned.

Three categories of territory have been identified: **Primary territories** are central to the lives of their inhabitants and users and are controlled by them on a long-term basis. **Secondary territories** are only partially controlled by their users, and often in symbolic or illegal ways. **Public territories** are those to which everyone, theoretically, has access.

Territorial markers are used to distinguish "insiders" from "outsiders." Markers may be physical and/or symbolic, and depend on the types of territories they are intended to mark. Whether a marker serves its purpose depends on the power of the individual or group to defend the territory in question. Territoriality serves to regulate behavior in a variety of ways.

Animal studies of crowding indicate that it causes considerable stress to the organism. A distinction can be made between **density,** or the ratio of population to area, and *crowding*, which is a psychological phenomenon that may or may not be provoked by a particular density level. The psychological experience of crowding has both a personal and a situational component. **Spatial density** is relative to the amount of space allotted to each person in a given area; **social density** depends on the number of people in an area.

The effects of crowding on social behavior depend on the personalities, interests, and backgrounds of the people involved, and on the situation. Men and women respond differently to the stress of crowding, probably because of differences in male and female socialization. Various crowding theories focus on attribution, excessive social stimulation, and a lack of control over the environment as explanations of the psychological effects of crowding.

Environmental factors such as heat, air pollution, and noise are broadly linked to interpersonal behavior. Both heat and air pollution have been linked to aggression; but a point may be reached at which increases in these factors lead to lethargy rather than further aggression. Physiological arousal due to intense noise has been shown to interfere with task performance, and the negative effects of excessive noise may persist long after the sound has died away.

The way the characteristics of urban life are perceived depend on the characteristics of the individual and of the particular urban environment. If there is a strong network of social relations, even slum dwellers may be favorably disposed to their environment. City people have a variety of strategies to cope with information overload. People orient themselves to the cities in which they live by means of **cognitive maps.**

Suggested Additional Reading

Altman, I. *Environment and social behavior: Privacy, personal space, territory, and crowding.* Monterey, Calif.: Brooks-Cole, 1975

Baum, A. & Epstein, Y. M. *Human response to crowding.* Hillsdale, N.J.: Erlbaum, 1978.

Freedman, J. L. *Crowding and behavior.* New York: Viking, 1975.

Proshansky, H. M., Ittleson, W. H., & Riulin, L. G. (Eds.). *Environmental psychology: People and their physical settings.* New York: Holt, Rinehart & Winston, 1976.

Sommer, R. *Personal space.* Englewood Cliffs, N.J.: Prentice-Hall, 1969.

Stokols, D. *Perspectives on environment and behavior.* New York: Plenum, 1977.

15

SOCIAL PSYCHOLOGY
AND THE LAW

In their paintings and drawings, schizophrenics often express a feeling of being caged or confined. This drawing is the work of a schizophrenic who had actually been imprisoned.
UPI

Questions about Social Psychology and the Law

1. If you had to decide whether an indicted person should be released on bail, what factors would you take into consideration?
2. How can jurors become biased during the course of a trial?
3. Do you think the sentencing policies used by judges are fair? Why or why not?

he figure of Justice, holding the balance scales of Law in her hand, adorns courthouses across the land. We take pride in being governed by law. John Adams expressed our faith when, in 1770, he defended the British soldiers on trial for the Boston Massacre:

> The law, in all vicissitudes of governments, fluctuations of the passions, or flights of enthusiasm, will preserve a steady undeviating course; it will not bend to the uncertain wishes, imaginations and wanton tempers of men. . . . It does not enjoin that which pleases a weak, frail man, but without any regard to persons, commands that which is good and punishes evil in all, whether rich or poor, high or low—'tis inflexible.

Adams won his case in a decision that was highly unpopular in pre-Revolutionary Boston. Public opinion then, as now, had no place in court. And yet today, when an unpopular verdict is reached, we protest vigorously, and legislators rush to propose new laws that will plug the apparent loopholes.

From the point of view of social psychology, how well does the law, and especially its trial proceedings, work? Social psychologists have lately found this to be an applied research area of great interest. How lawyers select jurors; how witnesses, lawyers, and judges affect the opinions of jurors; how jurors, judges, and the rest of us perceive victims; why juries decide to acquit or convict; how judges set sentences—these are but some of the topics social psychologists address when they study the law.

Although research in this area has burgeoned since 1970, it did not begin then, as Linz (1982) observes. In the nineteenth century sociologist Max Weber pondered the ways people interacted with the legal system; however, he did not conduct empirical research. In 1895 James McKeen Cattell, an early experimental psychologist, studied the accuracy of subjects asked to recall various types of information, and suggested a scheme (never employed) of assigning numerical weights to the testimony given by witnesses in the courtrooms. In 1908 Hugo Munsterberg published *On the Witness Stand: Essays on Psychology and Crime*, the first major work on psychology and the law. This work touched on many areas that remain of interest today, such as what effects a victim's "attractiveness" has on the verdict he or she receives.

The late 1950s saw the next major round of research, a study of 3,576 criminal trials at the University of Chicago. The Chicago jury project made some striking findings: For instance, judges disagreed 30 percent of the time with verdicts that juries had reached.

Most of the work on psychology and the law has been done since 1970, however, and the explosion of research literature shows no signs of subsiding. In 1981 the American Psychological Association, recognizing that psychology and the law was a unique area, formed a separate division to research it.

The present chapter summarizes some of the main findings of recent research in the area. The larger part of the research examined in this chapter has been guided by social psychological theory and conducted by social psychologists, and you will see that psychology and the law—as an applied area of investigation—makes use of a variety of the research methods that we discussed in chapter 2. Space limitations prevent us from covering some of the topics that are related to psychology and the law: the causes of criminal behavior, clinical psychological issues such as predicting dangerousness, the insanity defense, and a wide variety of topics outside the criminal law. These are equally important as the topics we do discuss, as you already know from the news events of this and any recent week.

In this chapter we will follow the actual sequence of events in the criminal trial process. We will first discuss the victims of crime; then we will look at the defendants and the factors that affect them before the trial begins, such as setting bail, plea bargaining, and publicity. Then we move on to the actual trial, examining jury selection and eyewitness and other testimony. Finally, we deal with posttrial events: how juries come to their decisions; and the sentencing, imprisonment, and parole of criminals. Although our focus is on criminal trials, most of the research we report is equally applicable to the less highly publicized civil trials.

The law is the true embodiment
Of everything that's excellent.
It has no kind of fault or flaw.
W. S. Gilbert, Iolanthe

Who Are the Victims?

"Get this, Perry," Drake said. "Get it fast. We're sitting on a keg of dynamite. My man found Ethel Garvin . . . sitting in her automobile . . . dead as a mackerel, a bullet hole in her left temple. From the angle, there's not much chance the wound could have been self-inflicted. She's slumped over the steering wheel and it's rather messy. . . . The gun . . . is lying on the ground directly beneath the window. . . ."

"What about the police?" Mason asked.

Although victimization rates for the elderly are actually lower than for other age groups, fear of being a victim of violent crime is great among older Americans. As a result, many people have begun learning self-defense measures. Here, a karate instructor (center, rear) demonstrates and members of a senior center practice resistance to an attack. Even if they never need to use their new skills, senior citizens will feel more confident after participating in such programs.

Ken Karp, Sirovich Senior Center

"My man's on the job. He discovered the body. No one else knows it's there—yet. . . . I'm working my head off trying to trace that gun before the police get all of the information. We *may* be just one jump ahead of them."

"Okay," Mason said. "I'm on my way. Get one jump ahead of them and stay one jump ahead of them."*

What was the likelihood that the victim in Perry Mason's *Case of the Dubious Bridegroom* would be a woman? In fact, the odds are 4 to 1 that a murder victim will be a man. The odds of being a murder victim in the United States in a given year are about 1 in 11,000.

Criminal Victimization of Minorities and the Elderly

In chapter 11 we saw that blacks and Hispanics formed a disproportionate share both of the victims and of the perpetrators of murder. Rapes and property crimes also fall disproportionately on different segments of the population. The causes of the greater victimization of minorities have not been fully identified, but they probably include such factors as a disproportionately greater likelihood of living in high-density, impoverished neighborhoods, a greater presence "on the street"

*Excerpts from pp. 85–87, 175–176, 187–189, 216, and 222 in *The Case of the Dubious Bridegroom* by Erle Stanley Gardner. Copyright 1949 by Erle Stanley Gardner. By permission of William Morrow & Company.

(where a large share of crimes occur) due to overcrowded or unacceptable living conditions at home, and often inadequate police protection (Wiltz, 1978).

Contrary to popular belief, older people are not victimized as much as other members of society. For instance, in 1979 the victimization rate of all people over age 65 for assault, robbery, and rape was about 8 per 1,000 people, compared to an average of 36 per 1,000 for people under age 65. The only crimes where the elderly matched the general population in victimization rates was purse snatching and pocket picking (U.S. Department of Justice, 1981).

Despite these data and according to attitude surveys, the aged fear crime more than younger people. One possible explanation is that older people feel vulnerable and unable to defend themselves. Another explanation is that the consequences of victimization are more severe for them—a fall during a mugging, for instance, could result in a fracture and a lengthy hospitalization. Fear of crime may, in fact, cause older people to restrict their activities, and thus result in their low rate of victimization (U.S. Department of Justice, 1981).

However, even within an elderly community there is a tremendous variation in victimization rates. One study of victimization among the aged found that black males living in inner city areas had the highest victimization rates among the aged (Liange & Sengstock, 1981).

Criminal Victimization of Women

As with the elderly, women as a group show a discrepancy between their fairly high fear of crime and their fairly low victimization rates. In 1978 women were the victims of violent crimes half as often as men. (Recall the discussion of violence in the home in chapter 11.) Stephanie Riger (1981) suggests that crime has an impact on women that far exceeds its frequency. Traditional explanations for this have been that women overrespond to the danger because they have been socialized for timidity; that they run the risk of an especially heinous crime, rape; and that they are physically unable to overcome male attackers. Riger finds that these explanations miss the mark:

> Since men constitute the vast bulk of criminal offenders . . . most women are victimized by men, linking criminal encounters to more general patterns of interaction between the sexes. Women are more likely to know their attacker than men, and are more often subject to crimes which affect not only their bodily safety but also their social identity and emotional well-being, such as rape and wife abuse. (Riger, 1981, p. 48)

Other factors Riger believes may affect women's fear of crime are their perceptions of their own physical incompetence and the strength of their ties to the community. Also, media reports of crime tend to emphasize the victimization of women—as well as the elderly—leading to their exaggerated fears of the chance of being victimized. It is even possible, as with the elderly, that fear of being victimized leads this population group to limit its exposure to victimization possibilities, therefore accounting for the low rate of actual victimization (Skogan & Maxfield, 1981).

Research: Rape Victims on Trial

How do we treat victims of crime—particularly victims of violent crime—in our society? As we have indicated in chapter 11, we may end up blaming the victim. This tendency takes on a doubly unfortunate significance when the "we" is a jury that is responsible for delivering an objective verdict in a rape case.

Borgida and White (1978) studied the reaction of rape victims in an experimental situation. (A group of adult subjects were gathered together and asked to reach a decision "as if" they were jurors in an actual case.) Two factors that frequently influence real rape trials were manipulated: the likelihood that the supposed victim consented, and the introduction of information on the victim's prior sexual history. The jurors showed less willingness to convict an accused rapist when *any* testimony about the victim's prior history was introduced, regardless of whether the information showed the victim in a more positive or a more negative light. Only when absolutely no evidence about prior sexual history was introduced, and when the probability was low that the victim had consented, was the victim viewed as credible by the jurors and the rapist convicted. As the experimenters concluded, the results "lend credence to the reformist contention that a rape victim is 'on trial' along with the accused" (p. 339).

Holstrom and Burgess (1978) interviewed 140 actual rape victims and found that the primary reason that the victims often did not press charges at all against their attacker was the victim's belief that she would be traumatized in the courtroom. This belief supports the contention that in a courtroom during a rape trial the victim is also on trial. Other studies also support this. Feldman-Summers and Lindner (1976), in an experiment involving 300 undergraduates of both sexes, found that "irrelevant characteristics of the victim (her marital status, her sexual experience, and her profession) influence judgments

about her responsibility for the rape and how much she was psychologically affected by either sexual or nonsexual assault" (p. 145). Numerous studies have found that the evidence of a "good" versus a "bad" character influences juror decisions in hypothetical rape cases (Catton, 1975; Jones & Aronson, 1973; Smith et al., 1976).

Calhoun, Cann, Selby, and Magee (1981) have found that the emotional characteristics of rape victims affect whether they are liked. Subjects who viewed a videotape of an emotionally contained victim perceived her as less traumatized and liked her less than an emotionally expressive victim. Calhoun, Selby, and King (1976) suggest that people expect rape victims to be visibly upset and to have psychological problems as a result of the rape. Thus, those victims who do not express sadness or distress—whose appearance is incongruent with people's expectations—may be seen as less believable.

Expressing concern about the intimidation of rape victims, the American Bar Association (1980) proposed a community-based program to provide victims of violent crimes—particularly rape victims—with a friend in court. This person, trained in social work or psychology, would support the victim by attending preliminary hearings as well as the trial. Victims may have quite a bit to cope with. Seeing the rapist in a hallway of the courthouse, the Association found, can be highly traumatic to rape victims; sometimes they are even threatened by their attackers. The Association also recommended that the victims be provided with ready information on whether a suspect has been arrested, the dates when courtroom appearances will have to be made, when they will have to take time off from work, and with a hotline for support and for protection in case of threats of reprisal. An effective support hotline would be offered both during the trial and after its completion.

Before the Trial

Let us return to *The Case of the Dubious Bridegroom.* Ed Garvin, husband of Ethel Garvin, has been charged with first degree murder as well as bigamy! It seems that Ed thought he was divorced from Ethel so he remarried. Ethel, however, had other plans. She wanted control of Ed's mining company. She had the police charge him with bigamy and tried to gain control of the company's stock. When Ethel turns up "dead as a mackerel" the police naturally suspect Ed, and he is duly apprehended.

The real world is not as exciting as the world of Perry Mason, in which all the cases he handles end up with dramatic courtroom battles. Few cases actually come to trial in real life—most are settled before an actual trial, in a process known as plea bargaining. We will cover that topic, as well as bail setting and pretrial publicity in this section.

Bail Setting

When a suspect is arrested, a police officer takes the suspect to court for a pretrial arraignment (in some instances the defendant's attorney attends the arraignment for the defendant). At the arraignment, the defendant is informed of his or her rights, especially regarding the right to a lawyer, who will be furnished free-of-charge by the court if necessary. The arraignment then moves on to a preliminary hearing on the evidence of the case—to determine that it does seem likely a crime has been committed and that there is evidence to tie the defendant to it. Finally, the court will consider setting bail.

What Is Bail?   Bail is a deposit of money with the court to help insure that the defendant will actually appear at the trial. A defendant who "skips" will lose the money on deposit. In a bail hearing the judge listens to the recommendations from the defense and prosecuting attorneys, and considers the prior record of the accused, his or her ties to the community, and the severity of the crime. In some instances, the judge accepts the defendants' statements that they will show up at their trial, and instead of requiring bail releases the defendants "on their own recognizance." In other instances, judges demand bail.

There are two kinds of bail: a cash bond, where the defendants pay an amount of money that will be refunded upon their appearance in court; or a bonding agent's release, where defendants pay a percentage of the amount of bail that is set (usually 10 to 30 percent) to a professional bonding agent, who is then responsible for paying the full amount of the bail if the defendants fail to appear in court.

Finally, some defendants, especially those who are accused of murder, are not released on their own recognizance or on bail, but are kept in jail up to the trial and in between trial sessions. Recent changes in the law have increased the likelihood that people charged with crimes of violence will not be released on bail.

Artist's rendering of a bail hearing. From left, prosecutor, judge, defense attorney, his client, a second defense attorney, and his client.

Criteria For Bail Decisions The factors that influence a judge in setting bail mark the point where social psychologists enter the picture. The amount and type of bail set obviously depends on the judge's assessment of whether the defendant will appear in court. Social psychological studies have examined both

1. factors that actually predict whether a defendant will appear in court, and
2. factors that judges employ in making bail decisions.

These two types of considerations do not always coincide.

For the first—factors that actually predict appearance in court—Ares, Rankin, and Sturz (1963) found that those defendants with strong community ties would most likely show up. Their study convinced the New York State legislature to pass the Bail Reform Act of 1964, which wrote a consideration of community ties clause into the rules for setting bail.

What criteria do judges actually use for setting bail? Goldkamp and Gottfredson (1979) examined some 8,300 bail decisions of the Philadelphia courts. The investigators found that the decision to release defendants on their own recognizance was influenced primarily by the severity of the charged crime, and that the amount of cash bail was affected primarily by whether weapons were involved in the crime. Neither community ties nor demographic variables significantly affected these bail decisions.

In an interesting experiment, real judges in their own courts were asked to set bail for defendants in fictitious cases. The variable that correlated most strongly with the amount of bail was the strength of local ties. The judges also considered the defendant's prior criminal record and the recommendations of the prosecuting and defense attorneys (Ebbesen & Konečni, 1975). But when these experimenters observed the judges making actual bail decisions rather than making recommendations based on fictitious case summaries, they found that the recommendations of the prosecuting and defense attorneys played the major role.

Some tentative conclusions can be offered on bail setting based on the studies we have cited. First, the factors used by judges in setting bail are not always those that best predict whether the defendant will show up in court. Second, the factors that judges actually use (e.g., the recommendations of the attorneys) are not necessarily the ones they report using (such as local ties and prior criminal record). It is possible, however, that attorneys take such factors as local ties and prior criminal record into account in making *their* bail recommendations to the judge, and that judges know and rely on this (Ebbesen & Konečni, 1975).

Plea Bargaining

In most areas of the country, from 80 to 90 percent of all criminal cases never reach the trial stage; instead, they are resolved by plea bargaining. A plea bargain is a sort of legal "deal" struck at the preliminary hearing, in which the defendant pleads guilty in exchange for having the severity of the charge reduced, such as from a felony (a serious crime) to a misdemeanor (a minor crime). As with any deal, there are gains and concessions on both sides. The prosecution gains because the defendant admits guilt even though the evidence that the defendant committed the more severe crime might not be strong enough to convince a jury; however, the prosecution also loses because the defendant is not found guilty for the actual crime. The defendant gains since he or she does not face a trial and therefore cannot be convicted of the greater offense for which the punishment would also be greater; however, the defendant loses because a conviction must be accepted, even though it is for the lesser offense.

An innocent heart suspects no guile.
Portuguese proverb

Gregory, Mowen, and Linder (1978) conducted two experiments concerning plea bargaining. In the first, students played the role of defendants, some of whom were guilty and some of whom were innocent. Those subjects playing guilty defendants accepted plea bargains much more readily than the innocent defendants, almost all of whom rejected plea bargaining. In the second study, some psychology students facing a difficult test as part of an experiment were given prior information about the exam by an associate of the experimenter. All the students were then told that they had done very well on the test, and that the experimenter suggested that they had cheated. The subjects were given a choice of appearing before a departmental ethics committee—which would inflict punishments such as lowering the student's final grade if the student was found guilty—or of admitting guilt and simply losing credit for having taken part in the experiment. Of eight guilty students, six accepted the plea bargain. Of eight innocent students, none did.

Houlden (1981) was concerned with how different methods of resolving disputes affected the satisfaction of the defendant, "for if defendants are dissatisfied with the methods employed, they are unlikely to perceive their sentences as justified and less likely when released to abide by the rules of a society which has

Controversy: Do Lie Detectors Really Work?

Many people believe lie detectors to be nearly infallible and to provide a direct pipeline into the soul of the person being tested. But how reliable are they?

The polygraph, or lie detector, is used in private industry and in security screenings with some frequency—for example, to verify or disprove an employee's statement about money that is missing. In the courts, the results of lie detector tests are occasionally accepted as evidence. Most often, polygraph testing is among the procedures that precede indictment.

How does a lie detector work? After a brief interview with the subject—mainly to obtain material to develop questions from, but also to determine the subject's attitude toward lying and lie detectors—the subject is hooked up to the polygraph (see Photo A). The device monitors several physical reactions simultaneously—such as galvanic skin response, blood pressure, abdominal respiration, and thoracic respiration—through external connections to the subject's hand, fingers, arms, and chest (see Photo B).

Once the device is attached the examiner asks a dozen or more questions that require yes or no answers, and the physiological and verbal responses are recorded. Three kinds of questions are asked: biographical questions or questions that are irrelevant to the case (Is your name John Doe?); crime related questions (Did you murder Suzanne Smith?); and control questions (Did you ever take anything that did not belong to you?). These control questions will usually elicit mild arousal in nonguilty subjects, since virtually everyone has at one time or another taken something. They thus establish a baseline response level for the physiological readings. The same set of questions may be repeated several times, perhaps in a different order or with variations. Any questions that evoke stronger reactions than the baseline are judged as indications of lying. No one answer is considered the critical item; rather, it is the pattern of a subject's physiological responses that is considered. Examiners evaluate the data subjectively, based

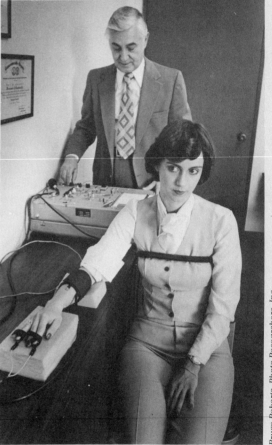

Photo A. A lie detector test being administered. The bands around the fingers monitor galvanic skin response; the cuff around the arm measures blood pressure; and the band around the chest detects changes in respiration.

Bruce Roberts, Photo Researchers, Inc.

on their experience and intuition, rather than following any codified system of objective measurement (Szucko & Kleinmuntz, 1981).

Do lie detectors really work? A psychiatrist, David Lykken (1979), reviewed the evidence and concluded that polygraphs were accurate about 64 to 71 percent of the time—not substantially better than chance (50 percent). Especially problematic, Lykken found, were subjects who can deliberately control their responses and deceive the polygraph; and a high rate of "false positives"—that is, instances of "identifying" lying in people who are actually telling the truth. This might readily occur, for example, in many people who easily get nervous or are accused unjustly. While some investigators dispute

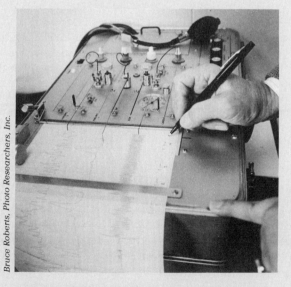

Bruce Roberts, Photo Researchers, Inc.

Photo B. Lie detector tests are known as polygraphs because the readings taken by the various measuring devices all appear together in graphic form. Here, the investigator notes at the bottom of the print-out the number of the question to which the readings refer.

Lykken's findings (Raskin & Podlesny, 1979), others have conducted experiments in which polygraphs proved no better than simply observing the subject (Ginton et al., 1982).

Because the examiner in a polygraph test relies on subjective scoring of the physiological readings, Szucko and Kleinmuntz (1981) set up an experiment to test the accuracy of seasoned examiners. Fifteen students were instructed to steal something from a desk; fifteen others did not steal. All were then tested individually by examiners within an hour of committing the theft or, for the controls, after a brief walk. These examiners did not know an experiment was involved, and followed the standard polygraph questioning and testing procedures we have described. The polygraph data were then evaluated by experts (who were informed that this was an experiment and that half of the subjects were guilty), and also fed into a computerized statistical model by the experimenters. The results? The expert polygraph interpreters proved quite unreliable, in part because they did not follow the procedures contained in their polygraph protocols consistently. The computer model—which followed its rules consistently—outperformed the examiners.

In a more recent study, Kleinmuntz and Szucko (reported in Boffey, 1982) took polygraph charts from 100 actual cases in which the guilt or innocence of the defendant had been verified by confessions. Six polygraphists judged the charts; the average accuracy was 70 percent. What was most alarming was that 37 percent of the "innocent" charts were misclassified as guilty.

Several states ban the use of polygraphs by private industry; and while a few courts prohibit the introduction of polygraph evidence, in most courts such evidence is generally allowed only when the prosecution, defense, and the judge all agree (that is, rarely).

shown so little concern for them" (p. 268). She conducted an experiment involving inmates at a Florida jail and undergraduates at the University of Florida. The subjects in both groups were asked to play the role of a defendant in a plea bargaining situation. Each subject heard a description of six different plea bargaining procedures, which varied in whether or not the defendant was allowed to participate in the plea bargaining, and in whether or not a mediator was present. The subjects were then asked which procedure they preferred. Both the inmates and the undergraduates preferred to participate in the conflict resolution procedures themselves. The inmates, however, preferred to have no mediator present in the plea-bargaining procedure, while undergraduates preferred to have one. If a mediator was to be present, inmates preferred a community volunteer, while undergraduates preferred a paid state official. The results of the study suggest that it might be a good idea for defendants to be present and active during their plea bargaining. In addition, Houlden points to the differences between the two groups as evidence of the pitfalls in formulating policy based entirely on studies that use undergraduates as subjects. Houlden's study has implications for legal policy decisions, suggesting that one way to increase the satisfaction of inmates is to encourage defendants to participate in the plea bargaining process. This may even deter inmates from committing more crimes when they are released.

Pretrial Publicity

Our law requires that a defendant be tried by an impartial jury. We will see later in this chapter that many of the events that occur during a trial may produce biases in the jurors. Potential jurors may also become biased *before* a trial takes place, through the effects of pretrial publicity.

A defendant's right to a fair trial clashes with another constitutional guarantee, the freedom of the press, on the issue of pretrial publicity. Cases are sometimes held in a different location, or even dismissed on the grounds that a fair trial is impossible due to the sensational publicity. More frequently, appeals succeed when they charge that pretrial publicity led to bias during the trial. The examination of potential witnesses and potential jurors takes longer when there is a lot of pretrial publicity, since efforts must be made to find individuals who have not been affected by it; and this lengthy process increases the amount of time before a trial and the quantity of pretrial publicity that can be generated (Padawer-Singer & Barton, 1975).

One experiment used prospective jurors to study the effects of pretrial publicity. Prospective jurors are questioned by prosecution and defense lawyers, who will reject some and select or impanel others. These jurors were given news accounts to read, some of which were prejudicial to a supposed defendant and some of which were not. The subjects then were assembled into a "jury" in an actual courtroom, where they listened to a tape recording of a trial. Following the recording, the jurors retired to a room to deliberate in the usual way, delivered their verdict, and filled out an experimental questionnaire. This procedure was followed with 33 juries. The researchers found that those jurors who had read the pretrial publicity were much more likely to find the defendant guilty. Of the juries in the experiment 80 percent delivered a guilty verdict, compared to 39 percent of the control juries (Padawer-Singer & Barton, 1975). The legal implications of this experiment are clear: Safeguards must be provided to protect defendants from the potentially damaging effects of pretrial publicity. But the public's right to know, via the press, must also be protected. Judicial and journalistic restraints both are called for.

The Trial

So far in this chapter we have discussed the events leading up to the trial. Now it is time to focus on the trial itself. We will take a look at the methodology of studying trials, and then examine the research concerning jury selection and the testimony during the trial.

Let us go back to *The Case of the Dubious Bridegroom*. The defendant, Ethel Garvin's husband, is on trial. We are in the courtroom.

> Hamlin L. Covington, the District Attorney of San Diego County, sized up Perry Mason as the defense lawyer entered the courtroom, then turned to his chief deputy, Samuel Jarvis.
> "A good-looking fellow," Covington whispered, "but I can't see that he's any wizard."
> "He's dangerous," Jarvis warned. . . .
> Abruptly the door from the judge's chambers opened and Judge Minden entered the courtroom.
> Lawyers, spectators and courtroom attachés stood in a body as the judge walked over to the bench, hesitated a moment, then nodded gracious permission to the crowd to be seated.
> The bailiff, who had pounded the court to order with his gavel, intoned, "The Superior Court of the State of California, in and for the County of San Diego, Honorable Judge Harrison E. Minden, presiding, is now in session." (Gardner, 1949, pp. 187–188)

Social Psychology in the Courtroom—How Is It Studied?

While some social psychologists may get ideas for research from reading Perry Mason, they obtain verification of those ideas from a different source. Social scientists generally study the psychological processes that may be at work during a criminal trial by means of **jury simulation studies**. These are mock trials in which subjects serve as jurors. Most such studies take place in an experimental laboratory. The subjects are often students who receive summaries of the trial facts to which they are to respond. Usually the summaries are written; sometimes they are on videotape; on rare occasions, they are live reenactments.

If you recollect our discussion of research methods in chapter 2, it will be apparent that such jury simulation studies are highly artificial situations. Most of these studies are weak in external validity. That is, what we find in the laboratory may not generalize to the real world of a juror participating in an actual trial.

More realistic simulations employ videotaped or live reenactments of an actual trial, and include all the major aspects of the procedures found at a real trial: opening statements, witnesses called to the stand, closing statements, judges' instructions, and jury deliberation. We should be aware then, when looking at studies that lack these features, that they also lack external validity.

There are two sides to the coin, however. The most realistic studies are difficult, costly, and time-consuming to conduct. Methodologically, studies lacking external validity may have greater internal validity; the experimenter is able to isolate the variable he or she wants to study—for instance, the effects of the defendant's race on jury decision making—and make that characteristic very salient to the mock juror. Written or videotaped descriptions also have an advantage over the more realistic simulations, in that the latter can never be repeated exactly. In the less realistic situations it is far easier to manipulate and control variables and conditions, and to utilize measurements that lend themselves to statistical analysis.

The disadvantages of unrealistic simulation studies are that the results may be less readily applied to a population of actual jurors outside of the laboratory. Linz and Penrod (1982) have shown that simulation studies that are low in external validity may vastly overstate the impact of experimental variables on actual jury decisions. In fact, studies with the most external validity are not found in a laboratory at all; they are field experiments in real courtrooms (such as the Padawer-Singer and Barton experiment described in the preceding section on pretrial publicity), or field observations of actual trials. There, in return for a sacrifice of control, we do in fact come to grips with the real world.

Jury Selection

"People of the State of California versus Edward Charles Garvin," Judge Minden said.

"Ready for the prosecution," Covington announced.

"And for the defendant, Your Honor," Mason said, smiling urbanely.

"Proceed with the impanelment of the jury," Judge Minden told the clerk.

Covington whispered to Samuel Jarvis, "You go ahead and impanel a jury, Sam. I'm going to keep myself in reserve. . . ."

Judge Minden made a brief statement to the jury impanelment concerning their duties, called on the district attorney to advise the jurors of the nature of the case, asked the prospective jurors a few routine questions, then turned them over to the attorneys for questioning.

Mason varied his usual courtroom technique by asking only the most vague and general questions.

District Attorney Covington, suddenly suspicious, whispered a warning to Jarvis, forced Jarvis to continue with a long line of searching questions until gradually it dawned on Covington that the district attorney's office was apparently being manueuvered into the position of trying to get a hand-picked jury, while the defense seemed casually willing to accept any twelve men who were fair. [But] . . . late that afternoon [Covington] realized that Mason . . . had somehow acquired a thorough knowledge of the characters and background of the prospective jurymen. (Gardner, 1949, pp. 188–189)

Who had the best jury selection strategy, Jarvis with his "long line of searching questions," or Perry Mason who had "somehow" learned about the jurors? Would a strategy that accepts "any twelve men who were fair" be as good? You may be surprised to learn what the relationship is between the individual characteristics of jurors and how they vote.

The first phase of a trial is what is known as *voir dire* (French for "to see, to speak") or jury selection. Social psychologists have been quite involved in studying as well as affecting the process of jury selection. In fact, an increasingly common image of the psychologist in the legal domain is an an expert assisting in jury selection. In one widely used technique, the trial lawyer consults with a psychologist at the counsel table as both scrutinize each juror. Such consultation is based on the assumption that individual characteristics will affect the decision that an individual will reach as a juror; it is also based on the assumption that the consulting psychologist can assess such characteristics reliably during the selection process.

As the preceding chapters have indicated, these are big assumptions. For instance, in chapter 5 we saw that behavior is affected by personal and situational factors. Thus, any assessment of a prospective juror should consider the particular circumstances of jury service in general and a given case in particular. Again, the Fishbein and Ajzen model described in chapter 9 would suggest that the best predictor of juror behavior in a particular trial would not be the general attitudes or traits of the jurors, but their very specific attitudes about the defendant, the charges, the evidence, and the witnesses, in this specific trial under these specific circumstances.

Attorneys' Commonsense Theories Like everyone else, attorneys have their private opinions of human nature and follow their commonsense theories about who will make a good juror for their case. Hans and Vidmar (1982) examined the handbooks used to train lawyers in trial tactics and easily identified a number of stereotypes. For instance, one manual recommends that defense lawyers choose female jurors if the main witness for the prosecution is a woman, because women are "somewhat distrustful" of other women. The same manual holds that people in unconventional occupations, such as actors, writers, and artists, are to be preferred as jurors since they have been exposed more to varied aspects of life and will not be as shocked by crimes as people in more conventional occupations will be. The manuals also recommend matching jurors to the specific case—male jurors for a rape case, or female jurors if the defendant is an attractive man.

The Research Perspective Psychological research does not provide much substantiation for attorneys' commonsense theories. Little relationship has been found between personality factors and jurors' votes (Davis, Bray, & Holt, 1977; Gerbasi, Zuckerman, & Reis, 1977; Nemeth, 1981; Saks & Hastie, 1978). Feild (1978), Penrod (1980), and Hepburn (1980) have undertaken studies that have examined literally hundreds of juror characteristics in attempts to predict trial verdicts. In the Penrod* study, demographic and attitudinal data on a sample of 367 real jurors were matched against their verdicts in four simulated cases: murder, rape, robbery, and a civil damages case. It was found that little of the variability in juror decision making could be explained by attitudes or personal characteristics. None of these or any other studies has examined juror attitudes specific to the particular case the jurors are sitting on. If it were possible to measure attitudes at a more specific level, we would probably be able to make more accurate predictions of a specific juror's vote in a particular case (Hans & Vidmar, 1982).

In addition to investigating juror selection on the basis of juror characteristics, social psychologists have been involved in other aspects of jury selection. These include helping attorneys find a jury that represents the makeup of the local community (which will be better aware of the context for the defendant's behavior), and providing survey evidence to support a "change of venue" motion. Change of venue means "change of place," moving a trial to an area where jurors are less likely to be prejudiced about the case. For instance, in 1974 Joanne Little, a black woman, was charged with murdering her jailer with an icepick; she claimed she acted in self-defense after the jailer had raped her. The trial was to take place in Beaufort County, North Carolina. The defense wanted the trial moved because of massive pretrial publicity and because of the alleged conservative, racist, and sexist attitudes of the inhabitants of Beaufort County. Social psychologists conducted an attitude survey of Beaufort and 24 other counties in North Carolina. They found that exposure to pretrial publicity did not vary from county to county, but that racist and sexist attitudes were more pronounced in Beaufort. The psychologists' evidence helped convince the judge to move the trial (Hans & Vidmar, 1982).

Eyewitness Testimony

Mason said, with feeling, "It's been demonstrated dozens of times that if you have a crime committed in front of a whole room full of witnesses and then call on those witnesses to make a written statement of what took place, the statements will contain all sorts of variations and contradictions. People simply can't see things and then tell what they've seen with any degree of accuracy."

"I suppose so," Drake said.

"Hell, it's been demonstrated time and again," Mason said. "It's a favorite stunt in classes in psychology in college. But what happens when you have witnesses in the trial of a case? They get on the stand one after another and tell a story that might have been written on a mimeograph. A witness sees something, he tells it to the police. The police point out little discrepancies between his story and that of the other witnesses. They point out what must have happened. Then they let the fellow think it over. Then they talk with him again. Then they let him talk it over with other witnesses. Then they take him to the scene of the crime. Then they get the witnesses to re-enact what happened. By the time a witness gets on the stand he's testifying to a composite of what he saw, what he thinks he saw, what the other fellow tells him *he* saw, and what he concludes he must have seen, judging from the physical evidence. Look at what's happening in this case right under our noses." (Gardner, 1949, pp. 175–176)

* Steven Penrod, the author of this book and an active researcher in the area of social psychology and law, appears in the photos on pages 173 and 176.

When Perry Mason cross-examines the main eyewitness to the crime and asks what he remembers about the "perpetrator," he quickly determines that the witness cannot remember the man's features, the colors of his clothing or shoes, whether he wore a tie or a hat. "So," Mason said, "you are identifying a man whom you saw with one eye through a crack in the door in a dark lobby, a man whose face you had never seen in your life until the police pointed him out to you in the jail . . ." (Gardner, 1949, p. 216).

Actually, this Perry Mason excerpt is closer to fact than you might imagine. It is not unusual for eyewitnesses to make questionable identifications. In fact, what is unusual about this eyewitness is how little he is actually certain about. Perry is also correct about psychological research: As we will see, eyewitnesses are often subject to subtle processes of suggestion that greatly influence the accuracy of their reports.

Eyewitnesses are much sought after in criminal trials, and their testimony often forms the heart of a lawyer's case. In this section we will consider some of the factors affecting the accuracy of eyewitness testimony, and its impact upon the jury.

Most of us would probably agree that if we have an honest eyewitness, we will know what happened, within certain obvious constraints: witnessing only part of a crime, confusion, darkness, and so on. The Rev. Bernard Pagano would heartily disagree. He was apprehended as the "gentleman bandit" wanted for six robberies in the Wilmington, Delaware, area. An eyewitness identified him from a book of photographs. After his picture appeared in the local press, several other eyewitnesses identified him in a police lineup. He was indicted, and the trial against him was proceeding smoothly until the real "gentleman bandit" turned himself in. Rev. Pagano was set free (Ellison & Buckhout, 1981).

A single witness is no witness.
Legal truism

The Lineup The legal profession is aware of the problem of mistaken eyewitness identification. Police lineups take place days, weeks, or even months after a crime. The lineup is a relatively recent addition to the methods used to identify wrongdoers, having been developed in the 1920s by the British police. It was a clear improvement over the show-up, the face-to-face confrontation between the suspect and the witness that was previously relied on (Levine & Tapp, 1982). In the lineup is one person the police believe to be the criminal, and several other individuals. Police may inadvertently or deliberately present that person in a way so as to make him or her *appear* to be the criminal. Lineups occur before formal legal proceedings against a suspect have begun.

The United States Supreme Court addressed this problem in several 1967 decisions, ruling that suspects in a lineup had the right to have attorneys present; that protection was, however, eroded by subsequent decisions (Levine & Tapp, 1982). The issue remains a lively one. In 1982 New York's highest court ruled that suspects appearing in lineups were not entitled to lawyers to protect their rights. Heated dissent accompanied the opinion, however, and in practice suspects in New York do often have a chance to contact a lawyer before appearing in a lineup (Margolick, 1982).

Factors That Affect Eyewitness Memory With or without counsel, the suspects in a lineup are at the mercy—perhaps more than they realize—of the eyewitnesses who try to identify them. Social psychologists concerned with eyewitness performance have identified factors that affect eyewitness memory. From a theoretical perspective, memory involves three steps or stages: encoding, storage, and retrieval (Penrod, Loftus & Winkler, 1982).

Several factors about an event affect how it is encoded or entered into the memory of a witness. One obvious factor is the length of time the event is seen; the longer a person can observe something, the more details he or she will notice and the better it can be recalled. Complex stimuli (such as faces and landscapes) seem to be more readily encoded than simpler stimuli (objects and words) when they are meaningful to an observer. Stress is also related to remembering an event (Clifford & Scott, 1978; Johnson & Scott, 1976; Yerkes & Dodson, 1908). Both low levels and very high levels of stress in a witness detract from encoding, whereas intermediate levels of stress contribute to it (Krafka & Penrod, 1981).

Accurately encoded information about an event must be stored or retained in the memory to contribute to eyewitness accuracy. Numerous studies have demonstrated that memory declines over time. For instance, when Shepard (1967) showed subjects pictures of various objects, waited two hours, and then showed the same subjects the same pictures mixed in with new ones, recognition was 100 percent. But when the pictures were shown to the same subjects after 4 months, recognition dropped to 57 percent, little better than chance (50 percent).

Although we may think of memory as being similar to a videotape or recording, studies indicate that it can be altered by new information and social influence. For instance, Loftus showed students a film of an automobile accident and then asked some subjects how fast the white sports car was traveling when it passed the barn, and asked other subjects how fast the car was traveling without mentioning a barn. The film had in fact shown no barn. All of the subjects were then subsequently asked if they had seen a barn: Of those asked the first question, 17 percent said they had; of those asked the second question, 3 percent said they had. New information can supplement and even replace existing information in memory (Loftus, 1975).

The recall or retrieval of stored information can be affected by the way the information is evoked. In one experiment, after viewing a film of an automobile accident, subjects were asked how fast the cars were going at the time of the accident. Speed estimates varied depending on the verb used in the question: "smashed" elicited a speed of 40.8 miles per hour; "collided," 39.3; "bumped," 38.1; "hit," 34 mph; and "contacted," 31.8 (Loftus & Palmer, 1974). Malpass and Devine (1980) found similar effects in an experiment involving a police lineup. Subjects reporting for a supposed biofeedback demonstration witnessed a staged act of vandalism, and were later asked to attend what they thought was a real police lineup. Some subjects were led to believe that the perpetrator probably was in the lineup (biased instructions); other subjects were told that the perpetrator might be present (unbiased instructions). Lineups were then presented, with and without the perpetrator, to both groups. Subjects given the unbiased instructions did far better in identifying the perpetrator. When the perpetrator was in fact not present, many subjects in both groups identified somebody else as the guilty party—but far more of the subjects who heard the biased instructions did so (see Table 15–1).

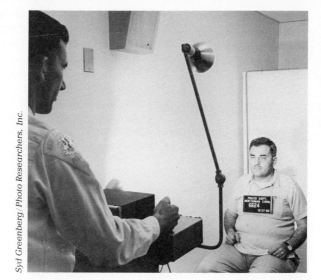

A Connecticut police officer photographs a newspaper photographer posing as a mugging suspect for a "mugshot." The black eye and mustache are makeup. Research has shown that identifications made on the basis of photographs are more often wrong than right.

Eyewitness Identification From Photographs As this discussion has already indicated, identifying people from lineups is not always reliable. The same applies to viewing photographs ("mugshots") in a police station, or in helping police artists compose a facial composite of the perpetrator. In one experiment, clerks in small stores were asked to identify—from photographs—customers who had been in their store 2 hours earlier; about 33 percent of the identifications were correct (Brigham et al., 1982). In an imaginative experiment, Buckhout (1980) went so far as to have a staged mugging presented on a television news program, followed by a televised lineup and a request that viewers phone in their identification. Of over 2,100 calls, only 14.1 percent identified the right person. The callers would have performed better by guessing!

TABLE 15–1.
Percentage of False Identifications in a Lineup Experiment

	Unbiased Instructions	Biased Instructions
Perpetrator present	0	25
Perpetrator absent	33	78

Source: Based on data from "Eyewitness identification: Line-up instructions and the absence of the offender," by R. S. Malpass & P. G. Devine, unpublished manuscript, State University of New York at Plattsburgh, 1980.

The Impact of Eyewitness Testimony   Research indicates that eyewitness testimony can have an impact on jury decision making. For instance, of subjects in a laboratory study who heard a description based on circumstantial evidence of an armed robbery involving murder, only 18 percent voted to convict. When eyewitness identification of the defendant was included, however, 72 percent of the subjects voted to convict (Loftus, 1974).

In a study of how eyewitness testimony is perceived, subject "jurors" were presented with eyewitnesses who had correctly identified the culprit following a staged theft, and with eyewitnesses who had made incorrect identifications. All of the eyewitnesses were cross-examined, some with "leading" questions (Was the jacket she had on tan or brown?) and some with "nonleading" questions (Describe what the person was wearing). The subjects then had to assess how accurate and how confident they thought the witnesses were. Although only 58 percent of the eyewitnesses had made correct observations, the jurors believed 80 percent of them. Accurate witnesses were no more likely to be believed than inaccurate witnesses, except when the leading-question style of cross-examination was used (see Table 15-2). Most interesting of all, 50 percent of the jurors' decisions to believe or disbelieve eyewitnesses were based upon how confident they thought the eyewitnesses were (Wells, Lindsay, & Ferguson, 1979).

A similar study also found that jurors were unable to distinguish between accurate and inaccurate eyewitnesses (Lindsay, Wells, & Rumpel, 1981). Some evidence was found that jurors were sensitive to the conditions under which the eyewitnesses viewed the event, and could adjust their rates of belief accordingly—but they still believed far too many witnesses. Although jurors seem to rely on eyewitness confidence as an indicator of reliability, when Deffenbacher (1908) reviewed 43 studies of the relationship between eyewitness confidence and accuracy, he found that on average the relationship was very weak. The relationship was stronger, he found, when eyewitnesses had viewed the event under optimal conditions, but of course many identifications are made under less than optimal circumstances. The legal profession itself is well aware that witness testimony delivered in a confident and positive manner is more readily believed.

TABLE 15-2.
Jurors' Decisions and Belief in Witnesses—Percent of Jurors Making Correct Decisions and Believing the Witnesses as Functions of Witness Accuracy and Type of Cross-Examination

Witnesses' Identification Accuracy	Percent of Jurors Believing the Witnesses		Percent of Jurors Making Correct Decision	
	Leading Questions	Nonleading Questions	Leading Questions	Nonleading Questions
Inaccurate	73	86	27	14
Accurate	84	76	84	76

Source: Adapted from G. L. Wells, R. D. L. Lindsay, and T. J. Ferguson, "Accuracy, Confidence, and Juror Perceptions in Eyewitness Identification," *Journal of Applied Psychology*, 1979, *64*, 444.

TABLE 15-3.

Percentage of Jurors' Guilty Votes as Functions of Witness Accuracy and Briefing

	Briefed Witness	Not Briefed Witness
Accurate Witness	40	33
Inaccurate Witness	61	28

Source: Adapted from "The Tractability of Eyewitness Confidence and Its Implications for Triers of Fact," by G. L. Wells, T. J. Ferguson, and R. C. L. Lindsay, *Journal of Applied Psychology*, 1981, *66*, 688–696.

Why are some eyewitnesses confident even when they are not accurate? A revealing experiment investigated the effects of "briefing" witnesses (recall Perry Mason's speculations!) upon the confidence that they showed and upon the jury conviction rate. A theft was staged for 80 unsuspecting students, who were later shown photographs that did, or did not, include the thief. The experimenters then randomly selected half of the witnesses who made correct identifications, and half who made incorrect identifications, and briefed them on the questions they might be asked during the trial. As expected, student "jurors" were far more attentive to testimony from the briefed eyewitnesses than from unbriefed eyewitnesses. Conviction decisions were more related to this impression than to whether or not eyewitnesses were accurate. In fact, as Table 15–3 shows, testimony by inaccurate eyewitnesses who had been briefed led to the most convictions (Wells, Ferguson, & Lindsay, 1981).

As we have often noted in this book, it is a large leap from the laboratory to the real world. Nevertheless, as members of society, it should give us pause that these experimental studies show that the truth—what actually happened—is not always related to how people subsequently judge events.

Other Aspects of Testimony

Many other witnesses aside from eyewitnesses can appear in court to testify for or against a defendant. Even defendants themselves are sometimes called upon to testify in their own behalf. There may be "character witnesses" who testify (for the defense) for the good character of the defendant, or even (for the prosecution) for the bad character of the defendant; and police officers and other expert witnesses (e.g., forensic psychologists, toxologists, and medical examiners).

Which witnesses do jurors find most believable? A large-scale field study (Linz et al., 1982; see Table 15–4) investigated 50 trials in Madison and Milwaukee, Wisconsin. Jurors were surveyed after their participation in a trial, and asked to rate witnesses, including police officers, scientific experts, eyewitnesses, victims, and defendants in terms of credibility, confidence, understandability, honesty, and likeableness. Police and expert witnesses appeared less coached, more understandable, most confident, less discredited, less dishonest, more likeable, and more believable than any other type of witness. No wonder, then, that attorneys call police and expert witnesses to the stand as

TABLE 15–4.

Comparison of Juror Ratings of Expert and Other Witnesses

Witness Characteristic*	Police and Expert Witness (N = 64)	Eye Witness (N = 22)	Victim Witness (N = 29)	Defendant Witness (N = 40)
Appeared coached	2.92	4.02	4.14	6.11
Was understandable	7.83	7.26	7.16	6.94
Appeared confident	7.52	6.7	6.09	5.69
Was discredited	3.1	3.47	3.3	4.87
Was dishonest	2.42	3.44	3.22	5.4
Was likeable	6.04	5.51	5.67	4.84
Was believable	7.5	6.68	7.01	5.0

*Rated on a scale of 1 (not at all) to 9 (extremely).

Source: Linz, D., & Penrod, S., et al., *The use of experts in the courtroom: Attorney judgments of expert witness credibility.* Paper presented at the Annual Meeting Academy of Criminal Justice Sciences, March, 1982.

much as possible, and that defense attorneys are sometimes reluctant to call the defendant to the stand. Of all witnesses, the defendant appears least credible. How are judgments about credibility made?

Consider this situation: You are a juror in a courtroom. A defendant is being questioned by the prosecutor. The defendant's testimony seems confused and hesitant. Is the defendant testifying accurately but displaying genuine uncertainty? Or is the defendant trying to deceive you?

Research has indicated (as we saw in chapter 8) that a speaker's credibility depends on such factors as his or her competence, trustworthiness, and forcefulness. Ekman and Friesen (1969) showed, for example, a witness who "lacks dynamism and composure, as reflected by a barely audible voice, high incidence of vocal disruptions such as nonfluency, and numerous nonverbal adaptors such as self-touching and fidgeting with clothing," is likely to be perceived as relatively incompetent and/or untrustworthy. In one study subjects viewed strangers on videotape without hearing them speak, and expressed their confidence that the strangers were truthful. The average rating of confidence was 58 percent—obviously based on nonverbal cues; when subjects heard an audio component in addition, the confidence judgments rose to only 64 percent (Hocking, Miller, & Fontes, 1978). As our discussion in chapter 7 made clear, people rely very heavily on nonverbal cues as a means of detecting deception.

The use of hypnosis to elicit truth from witnesses is controversial. Hypnosis has sometimes been used with spectacular success; in 1967 the "Boston strangler" detailed his crimes under hypnosis, convincing police that he was the culprit; when 26 children were kidnapped at gunpoint from a schoolbus in California, the bus driver, when hypnotized, could recall enough of the getaway van's license plate number so that the police could rescue the children (Brody, 1980).

However, an hypnosis expert, Martin Orne (1979), questions the use of investigative hypnosis because memories are not static but change over time, and people under hypnosis may give inaccurate accounts. In fact, "pseudo-memories" introduced during hypnosis are remembered with a great deal of subjective certainty. This may cause a witness to seem confident and convincing when in fact the confidence is based on a false memory developed during hypnosis. Hypnosis may be useful in some investigations, but Orne feels it cannot verify statements made in court, since memories of actual events cannot be distinguished from subsequent material. Orne recommends that hypnosis be conducted only by psychiatrists and psychologists trained to use it, that the hypnosis session and all the other interactions between the subject and the hypnotizer be videotaped, and that no third parties (with their inadvertent communications) be present. Tape recordings of any prior questioning of the subject should be made available to identify cues that may already have been planted in a subject's mind.

The Role of Defendant Characteristics

Let us return to our defendant in *The Case of the Dubious Bridegroom*, Ed Garvin. The first morning of trial testimony has been concluded, and Perry Mason is concerned with the impression that his client is making on the jury:

> "Court will take a recess until two o'clock."
> Edward Garvin reached out and caught Mason's arm. His fingers pressed into the flesh of the lawyer's arm. "Mason," he said, "for God's sake I . . ."
> Mason turned to smile reassuringly at his client, but the smile was only on the lawyer's lips. His eyes were cold and hard.

Marilyn Church

How does a jury interpret a defendant's courtroom testimony? Is hesitant speech perceived as deception? In this drawing, a defendant in a murder trial is questioned by the prosecutor, while three members of the defense counsel team (left foreground) look on. In this case, the defendant, Jean Harris, was found guilty.

"Smile," Mason said.

"I . . ."

"Smile, damn it," Mason said in a low half-whisper, "smile."

A travesty of a grin twisted Garvin's features.

"Do better than that," Mason said, "smile and keep that smile on your face until the jury have filed out."

Mason watched expression struggling on Garvin's face, laughed good-naturedly, patted Garvin on the shoulder, said "Well, let's get some eats," and turned casually away.

"Mason, I've *got* to see you," Garvin whispered.

Mason said over his shoulder in a low voice, "Try to see me now and with the jury looking at you, and with that expression on your face, and you'll be buying a one-way ticket to the death cell in San Quentin." [Gardner, 1949, p. 222]

Perry Mason obviously feels that certain characteristics of the defendant will have an effect on the jury. Is this concern justified? In fact, research shows that jurors do not, unfortunately, consider only the facts of the case when making decisions during deliberations. In a criminal trial many additional factors such as characteristics of the defendant (age, race, etc.) may enter into jury decision making. In a review of the experimental literature, Dane and Wrightsman (1982) grouped such defendant characteristics into six groups:

1. *Gender*—effects seem to differ depending on the crime, but more research is still needed.
2. *Socioeconomic status*—no consistent influence has been found.
3. *Moral character*—prior offenses (information not ordinarily allowed in a trial, but often deduced by jurors) seem to increase the likelihood of a conviction; the more repentant a defendant appears, the less likely is a conviction.
4. *Attractiveness* (both physical and interpersonal)—attractive defendants are more leniently treated, except when the attractiveness was used to facilitate the crime.
5. *Race*—defendants of the same race as the jurors are less likely to be convicted.
6. *Attitude similarity*—jurors seem to be more lenient toward defendants with attitudes similar to their own.

Although such extraneous defendant characteristics do have an effect on the decision of a jury, that effect is probably minimal. The facts of a case are supposed to, and usually do, exert the greatest influence.

The Influence of Trial Procedures

Jurors are generally unfamiliar with courtroom procedures. Court atmospheres are imposing, and the pretrial and trial rituals are time-consuming, sometimes tedious, and frequently difficult to understand. How are jurors affected by what goes on in the courtroom before they begin their deliberations? In this section we will describe the studies of several procedural or trial factors: the order in which testimony is given, the availability of alternative verdicts, the presumption of a defendant's innocence, the format of the judge's instructions, and prejudicial evidence that may not relate to the specific trial.

Order of Presentation   Numerous factors can influence persuasion, as we saw in chapter 8, including the sequence in which the information is acquired. In a trial, the standard order is for the prosecution to present its side first. The prosecution witnesses are questioned by the prosecuting attorney, cross-examined by the defense counsel, and perhaps questioned again by the prosecuting counsel. Then it is the turn of the defense; the defense witnesses are questioned by defense counsel, cross-examined by the opposing counsel, and then requestioned by the defense counselor. Some researchers, in mock trials, have manipulated this sequence and concluded that the existing system is fair to both the prosecution and the defense (Thibaut, Walker, & Lind, 1972; Walker, Thibaut, & Adreoli, 1972).

Verdict Alternatives   In criminal cases, a charge may contain "lesser included offenses"—for example, a charge of first-degree murder might contain the lesser included offenses of second-degree murder, manslaughter, and self-defense. Where such alternatives are included, instead of rendering a "guilty" or "not guilty" verdict on the greater charge, jurors may find the defendant "guilty" or "not guilty" of any one of the offenses charged.

Vidmar (1972) conducted a simulated jury experiment, presenting some jurors with the verdict alternatives of first-degree murder, second-degree murder, and manslaughter, and presenting other jurors with a simple guilty or not guilty choice on one of the charges. When alternative verdicts were offered, jurors seldom chose the "not guilty" option (6 percent), but when their choice was limited more than half (54 percent) chose "not guilty."

Presumption of Innocence and Burden of Proof   We have all heard the phrase "innocent until proven guilty." It is an assumption of United States law that jurors must presume the defendant's innocence at the start of the trial. (A trial is by definition an adversary proceeeding, in which the task of the prosecution is to show *beyond a reasonable doubt* that the defendant is guilty as charged.) This, too, has been the subject of empirical study, and the results have been mixed, primarily because of the difficulty of obtaining accurate estimates of a presumption of innocence. However, the available evidence suggests that jurors' presumptions are not always the same as those prescribed by law (Nagel, 1979; Simon & Mahan, 1971).

In fact, surveys of actual jurors have borne this out. Some surveys have found that many of them presume *guilt* rather than innocence (Buckhout & Baker, 1977). This was true, for example, of the juror overheard to say of the defendant, "He's on trial, so he must have done something." This seems consistent with the conviction rate: The majority of defendants brought to trial are found guilty. A survey of over 3,500 criminal cases in the 1960s found an 83 percent conviction rate (Kalven & Zeisel, 1966). Dramatizations of trials on television and in movies often give the false impression that the defendant is "guilty until proven innocent," and may be a factor in people's misunderstanding. In any case, "innocent until proven guilty" would not seem to describe the impression held by most jurors.

Kerr et al. (1976) were interested in whether variations in the requirements of proof actually affected verdicts. They presented mock jurors with three definitions of reasonable doubt: a lax criterion ("you need not be absolutely sure that the defendant is guilty to find him guilty"), a stringent criterion ("if you are not sure and certain of his guilt you must find him not guilty"), and a condition where reasonable doubt was not defined. More guilty verdicts were obtained with the lax criterion than with either the undefined or the stringent criterion.

Judges' Instructions   In a real trial, the judge's instructions to the jury before they begin deliberating explain the concepts of presumption of innocence and burden of proof. These instructions also explain the meaning of "beyond a reasonable doubt" and other matters of the law, such as the need to disregard prejudicial evidence. The judge also reads and explains the charges in detail.

Do jurors understand judges' instructions? A 1977 study by Sales, Elwork, and Alfini found that the instructions that were incomprehensibly legalistic should be improved, and suggested psycholinguistic and other methods for doing so. As an example of this need they cite a 1975 case in which the defendant was charged with second-degree murder and the "lesser included offense" of manslaughter. After listening to 30 minutes of incomprehensible instructions from the judge, the jurors found the defendant guilty of manslaughter; what they had meant to do, however (they later explained in a letter to the judge), was to acquit. From the judge's instructions, they thought that delivering a guilty verdict for manslaughter was the way to declare the defendant "not guilty" of second-degree murder.

Timing also seems to have a significant impact on how effective a judge's instructions are. Kassin and Wrightsman (1979) found that instructions about the presumption of innocence, the beyond-a-reasonable-doubt standard of proof, and burden of proof (which side must prove the case) were effective only if they are given *before* the trial rather than after it. This would suggest a change in procedures. Judges also typically instruct jurors to disregard prejudicial evidence; we will see in the next section that these instructions are sometimes effective, and sometimes not. Research suggests that the courts should critically evaluate the effectiveness of judges' instructions instead of simply assuming that they work.

Prejudicial Evidence   Various types of evidence may be prejudicial, causing jurors to be biased against a defendant for reasons that do not specifically relate to the case they are deciding. We will examine research about inadmissible evidence, evidence of previous convictions, joined offenses, and character evidence.

Evidence is often introduced in a courtroom but subsequently ruled inadmissible by the judge. The judge then instructs the jurors to disregard this evidence. Whether they are in fact able to do so has been the subject of empirical study, but the results are mixed. Sue, Smith, and Caldwell (1973) found that inadmissible evidence against the defendant nevertheless resulted in a higher conviction rate, especially when the case was initially weak. Wolf and Montgomery (1977) focused on the effectiveness of judicial instructions to ignore the in-admissible evidence. They found that simply ruling the evidence inadmissible was in fact successful in removing its effect, but strong judicial admonishment backfired so that subjects were influenced by the inadmissible evidence. These two studies used written trial transcripts. In a study using a realistic videotape of a simulated trial, Thompson, Fong, and Rosenhan (1981) found that inadmissible evidence favoring acquittal caused jurors to acquit more often, and that the judge's instructions had no effect. Inadmissible evidence favoring conviction, however, did not affect jurors' verdicts. Clearly, additional research on this topic is needed.

Evidence of previous convictions is normally inadmissible in the courtroom, although in certain specific conditions it is permitted. One experiment found that the knowledge of a criminal record resulted in more guilty verdicts, and that instructions to disregard the information were ineffective (Doob & Kirschen-baum, 1973). Another study found that the knowledge of a prior record had no effect on individual verdicts, but had a strong effect on the verdicts obtained by groups during deliberation (Hans & Doob, 1976).

Under federal and state laws, a defendant who is charged with more than one offense can be tried for all the offenses in a single, or "joined," trial. Convictions arising from such trials are often appealed on the grounds that prejudice resulted from the joined offenses. Several experiments have shown that a defendant tried for joined offenses is indeed more likely to be convicted, and that instructions to consider the charges separately are not very effective in removing the bias toward conviction (Greene & Loftus, 1982; Horowitz, Bordens, & Feldman, 1980; Tanford & Penrod, 1982).

Drawing by Lorenz. © 1977 The New Yorker Magazine, Inc.

"The jury will disregard the witness's last remarks."

Character evidence may also be prejudicial, and whether it is inadmissible or admissible depends on the type of evidence and its relevance to the case. In a study involving a simulated automobile negligence trial, Borgida (1979) examined the effects of evidence about a plaintiff's cautiousness. A single character witness resulted in more positive verdicts for the plaintiff, although a larger number of character witnesses did not.

Deliberation Procedures

As usual, the jury sitting on one of Perry Mason's trials has little to do. Perry has sewn up the case long before the jury deliberation begins. In *The Case of the Dubious Bridegroom*, the murderer was not Ed Garvin but a sneaky accountant for Ed's company who feared that once Ed's wife gained control she would expose his many years of fraudulent bookkeeping. Most real cases are not as clear-cut. Jurors at an actual trial are often left with the task of putting together the facts of the case in order to determine whether the defendant is guilty or not. In this section we will discuss how juries go about reaching their decisions. Are there patterns in the way jurors influence each other?

From movies, television, and plays such as *Twelve Angry Men* we are familiar with the situation in which a lone juror holds out until the rest of the jurors are, one by one, persuaded. As we will see, this is seldom true in an actual case. Most often the majority exerts sufficient pressure on a minority to win. After the jury has been instructed by the judge, it retires to deliberate. Typically, the jurors sit at a table in a closed room, with a guard outside the door to see that no unauthorized persons enter—and that no juror leaves. Twelve people are face to face with each other—and with the absent defendant as well. Now the real drama begins, right? Wrong.

A major contribution to the study of juries has been a large-scale research project begun at the University of Chicago in the 1950s and still under way. The

Artist's rendering of jury deliberations. During deliberations jurors weigh not only the evidence, but their impressions of defendant characteristics and their attitudes toward one another. Social psychological research has shown that jury decisions usually follow the initial tendency of a majority of jurors to convict or acquit. However, minority opinion has been found to have surprising influence when it is both strong and consistently held.

Marilyn Church

Chicago jury project (described at the start of this chapter) resulted in the publication of *The American Jury* by Kalven and Zeisel (1966). *The American Jury* cites evidence from 225 actual juries that suggests that "the real decision is often made before the deliberation begins." The researchers, excluded from the actual decision-making process, examined the initial vote distribution and the final verdict, but not the deliberation process in between. To study the process of jury deliberation, researchers must resort to a mock jury situation or mathematical and computer models.

Various models have been developed to simulate jury decision making. These attempts to predict final verdicts are based on the initial tendencies to consider a defendant guilty or not guilty and by means of equations that simulate the decision-making process. Divided into social decision schemes, social transition schemes, and computer models, these tools were described in chapter 13 under "Models of Small Group Decision Making."

According to the theory of group polarization (also discussed in chapter 13), groups shift their opinion in the direction of their initially preferred tendency. Myers and Kaplan (1976) studied group polarization in simulated student juries, and found that during deliberation subjects shifted toward guilty verdicts in "high guilt" cases (a preponderance of evidence indicated the defendant's guilt) and toward acquittal in "low guilt" cases.

Strong majority influences were found in all of the models of jury decision making, as well as in the actual Chicago jury project data of Kalven and Zeisel. This suggests that conformity pressures (described in chapter 10) could be at work. Wilder (1978) found that the pressure to conform was greatest when the majority members were of diverse social or personality types. To a dissenter, the majority view will seem more credible and he or she will more likely yield to it if the other jurors are perceived as heterogeneous—belonging to different social groups.

Some dissenters do hold out, however, and can—just as in the movies—bring the majority around to their view. Social scientists investigating the influence of the minority in mock jury deliberations have found that dissenters can be influential when the minority holds its opinion consistently throughout the deliberation (Wolf, 1979), or even if a lone dissenter simply takes the seat at the head of the table (Nemeth & Wachtler, 1974). However, one study has suggested that the influence of a minority may be limited to smaller 6-member juries, and are unlikely to operate in 12-member juries, where the influence of the majority will be very strong (Tanford & Penrod, 1982).

Jury Size and Decision Rules

Not to be overlooked in the jury decision-making process is the size of the jury involved and whether or not the jury must make a unanimous decision. In a series of decisions in the 1970s, the United States Supreme Court made the following rulings (Sperlich, 1979):

1. The minimum jury size is 6 members (*Ballew v. Georgia*, 1978; interestingly, this decision was based largely on social scientific, group interaction evidence).

2.   Juries of 6 members and 12 members are functionally equivalent (*Williams v. Florida*, 1970).
3.   Jury decisions may not have to be unanimous in 12-member juries (*Apodaca v. Oregon*, 1972; *Johnson v. Louisiana*, 1972), but must be unanimous in 6-member juries (*Burch v. Louisiana*, 1979).

Social scientists have gone beyond the current legal status of actual jury size and decision rules and manipulated both factors in several experiments. One study (Davis et al,. 1975) found virtually no difference in verdicts between either 6- or 12-member juries, and no differences between them in handing down unanimous or two-thirds majority decisions. Valenti and Downing (1975) found a large difference for jury size when defendant guilt was high, with 6-member juries more likely to convict than 12-member juries; but there was no difference when defendant guilt was low.

In a realistic experiment using an audiovisual trial presentation to subjects from an actual jury pool in a courtroom, Roper (1980) concluded that:

1.   Juries of 12 members were more likely to be "hung" (unable to agree on a verdict) than 6-member juries.
2.   Juries of 6 members were more easily influenced by minority dissenting members than 12-member juries.

Roper suggested that the courts need to examine more carefully the effects of jury size "on such things as the accuracy of evidence recall and the quality of deliberations." His findings were supported by two computer simulations of jury decision making (Penrod & Hastie, 1980; Tanford & Penrod, 1982).

Who Leads the Jury?

After listening to the testimony, a jury's first task is to select a foreperson. (This is true in some jurisdictions; elsewhere, the first person seated automatically becomes the foreperson.) To see if there was a pattern in who is selected, Strodtbeck, James, and Hawkins (1958) drew jurors at random from jury pools in Chicago and St. Louis courts, and asked them to participate in a mock trial. After the jurors listened to the recorded trial testimony, they were told to choose a foreperson and to begin their deliberations. In over 50 percent of the 49 deliberations that the experimenters analyzed, the foreperson was nominated by one person and quickly elected by the group. In 33 percent of the cases the person elected was the one who first spoke, or who focused the jury's attention on the task of selecting a foreperson. Although forepersons from all socioeconomic strata were selected, proprietors were 3½ times more likely to be selected than laborers, and women were chosen only 20 percent as frequently as chance would have suggested. If you recall our discussion of leadership in chapter 13 (see box, "Are Leaders Born or Made?") the processes that are involved in foreperson selection seem to follow both the situational approach and the trait approach.

Status considerations proved particularly significant during the deliberations: The researchers found that the higher-status jurors participated more in the discussion than the lower-status jurors. When the jurors were asked who they would like on a jury if they themselves were on trial, people of lower status showed a strong tendency to prefer, not a jury of their peers, but a jury composed of higher-status individuals.

Do Judge and Jury Always Agree?

In *The American Jury*, Kalven and Zeisel (1966) reported the results of questioning the judges in 3,576 jury trials held from 1954 to 1958. In 30 percent of the trials the judges disagreed with the jurors' verdicts. In a very small percentage of the cases the disagreement was due to facts known only by the judge. The primary reasons for that disagreement were the discrepancies between the weight the judge and the jurors assigned to the characteristics of the defendant—with the jurors weighing these more heavily than the judges—the interpretation of the law, and issues of evidence.

Jurors are not expected to be experts on the law; in fact, legal experts are barred from serving on juries. It would seem that jurors decide cases more according to the spirit than to the letter of the law, and that this accounts for the substantial disagreement between jurors and judges. Proponents of the American jury system cite this bias toward the spirit of the law as a strong point in its favor.

After the Trial

In a Perry Mason story, the real murderer, once exposed, usually buys "a one way ticket to the death cell in San Quentin" (p. 222). The conclusion of an actual trial may be a bit less dramatic. If the sneaky accountant in *The Case of the Dubious Bridegroom* had been convicted of first degree murder, the judge would sentence him to a term of imprisonment and, in all likelihood, the accountant would be eligible for parole after a certain period of time. In this section we will discuss the consequences of a guilty verdict: sentencing, imprisonment, and parole.

Sentencing

Of all the steps in the legal process that we have discussed so far, sentencing has the fewest legal guidelines. Upper and lower limits for sentences for a given crime are set by law. But within these limits, judges have discretion to set sentences as they see fit, allowing for wide variations in the sentences imposed for the same crime (see box).

The amount and type of sentence imposed will depend on the goal the judge has in mind. McFatter (1978) describes three sentencing strategies:

1.   Retribution—the punishment should be in proportion to the severity of the crime.

2. Rehabilitation—the punishment should be such that the offender will be reformed and not commit another crime in the future.
3. Deterrence—the punishment should be sufficiently severe so that others will be dissuaded from committing the crime.

McFatter asked some students to follow each of these strategies in an experiment. The most severe sentences were obtained using a deterrence strategy, and the least severe sentences were obtained using a rehabilitation strategy. In re-

Application: Setting Sentences

Disparity exists among judges in sentencing for the same offense. There is no general consensus on why this is the case, but a majority of federal judges believe that this is to some extent a problem (Yankelovich, Skelly, & White, 1980).

Clancy and his associates (1981) investigated both this disparity and the reasons for it. When 264 federal district court judges were each given several hypothetical case summaries for sentencing, widespread disagreement was the result. The differences among the sentences were not random, but systematically related to the characteristics of the case and the offender—as well as to the general value orientation of the judge and, to some extent, to the regional environment of the judge. The experimenters concluded that the sentences given "represent specific applications, or projections, of a judge's political philosophy and his or her core values about the desired functions of criminal sanctions. . . . Particular sentences also serve as remedies for the perceived failures in the system at large" (p. 553). The experimenters recommended that guidelines be set so that each judge need not hammer out an individual philosophy for each case.

A number of cities have introduced sentencing guidelines and five of these cities have been evaluated in an extensive research project on the effects of the guidelines (Rich et al., 1981). The five cities are Chicago, Denver, Newark, Philadelphia, and Phoenix. These guidelines generally provide a narrower range within which to sentence, and include a table containing the ranges for different offenses and offender characteristics. Judges can choose sentences from outside the range, but if they do they must provide a written explanation of their reasons.

How were the guidelines developed? First, past decisions that resulted in convictions were analyzed. Data was tabulated on:

1. offense characteristics (such as whether or not a weapon was involved);
2. offender characteristics (such as educational background);
3. victim characteristics (such as whether the victim was a person or a business);
4. the sentencing decision (such as whether it involved jail or probation, and for how long).

Analysts then determined how these variables correlated, and presented this information on the unwritten guidelines of the past to the judges. Over a number of meetings, the judges amended the preliminary guidelines until the new guidelines were accepted.

This seems a logical and desirable procedure, but unfortunately the guidelines as adopted proved ineffective in reducing sentencing disparity in those five cities (Saks, 1982). Further study of these guidelines, and of their more successful applications, can help pave the way to finding future guidelines that *are* effective.

Irene Springer

The grimness and isolation of imprisonment are conveyed by the walls and watchtower outside this state prison (Sing Sing, in Ossining, New York).

A foolish judge passes a brief sentence.
French proverb

lated research with real judges in Canada, Hogarth (1971) found that the judges regarded rehabilitation as the most important sentencing consideration, followed by deterrence, incapacitation, and "just deserts."

Imprisonment

What happens in prison? To find out, Haney, Banks and Zimbardo designed and carried out a dramatic—and controversial—simulation experiment (1973). We examined their methods briefly in chapter 2. You will recall that the subjects—a group of 24 middle-class, normal, mature, intelligent men between the ages of 17 and 30—were fully informed of the purposes of the study, and were randomly assigned to be "prisoners" or "guards." The mock prison, constructed in the basement of the Stanford University psychology building, had small, barren cells, steel-barred doors, and a solitary confinement closet. Guards were given more spacious quarters and a recreation area. All of the subjects were paid $15 a day, and were expected to remain in the experiment for at least 2 weeks.

Psychological Effects of Imprisonment   The researchers tried to duplicate the activities and experiences of an actual prison in order to produce similar psychological reactions in the subjects. In the guards and in the prisoners, respectively, they tried to create "feelings of power and powerlessness, control and oppression, satisfactions and frustration, arbitrary rule and resistance to authority, status and anonymity, machismo and emasculation" (p. 72). In order to increase the realism of the experiment, "prisoners" were "arrested" unexpectedly at their homes by members of the Palo Alto police department, and taken to the mock prison. There they were kept under constant surveillance, and most of their basic civil rights were suspended.

To promote anonymity and group identity and to reduce feelings of individuality, both guards and prisoners wore uniforms. Guards wore khaki shirts and trousers, and were given whistles, night sticks, and one-way reflecting sunglasses to prohibit eye contact. Prisoners wore "loosely fitting muslin smocks, with an identification number on front and back." They wore no underwear. "On their feet they wore rubber sandals, and their hair was covered with a nylon stocking made into a cap" in order to reduce any sense of individuality conveyed by hair length or color (p. 75). These uniforms were designed "not only to deindividuate the prisoners but to be humiliating and serve as symbols of dependence and subservience" (p. 76). Prisoners were referred to only by their identification numbers; they were given "three bland meals" and "were allowed three supervised toilet visits" a day (p. 76). Three times a day they were also lined up for a "count," which lasted ten minutes at first but became increasingly longer on successive days "until some lasted several hours" (p. 77).

The guards were told that they had to keep a "reasonable degree of order" but were not instructed specifically how to go about it. They were to be prepared for unexpected situations and were required to write reports. Physical punishment of any kind was prohibited. Both prisoners and guards were free at any time to engage in positive, supportive interactions; nothing in their instructions prevented this.

But they did not. Instead, interactions became progressively more "negative, hostile, affrontive, and dehumanizing" (p. 81) with the prisoners assuming a predominantly passive role and the guards an active one. Verbal aggression took the place of physical violence, usually in the form of commands, threats, and insults, and usually from the guards to the prisoners. Almost no helping behavior occurred either between the guards and the prisoners or among the prisoners themselves. Any sense of cohesion among the prisoners soon broke down. Subjected to the random abuse of the guards, the prisoners became passive, dependent, depressed, and helpless. After a time some even came to believe that they deserved to be insulated and harassed. Five prisoners had to be released after three days because of "extreme emotional depression, crying, rage, and

The deindividuated dress and apathy of the "prisoners" in Zimbardo's experiment are seen in the posture of the men waiting for a "parole board" hearing.

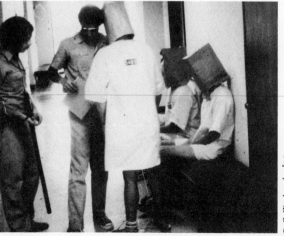

Library of Congress

Is sitting in the stocks any more "cruel and unusual" than imprisonment? Perhaps, in exposing the wrongdoer to the open censure of a close-knit community, this relatively mild punishment was a more effective form of retribution, rehabilitation, and deterrence than most sentences that are meted out today. Here, two miscreants serve their seventeenth century sentences under guard in the Boston Town House Square.

acute anxiety" (p. 81). Another was released a day later after developing an extensive body rash.

The experiment itself was brought to a halt after only six days, to the delight of the prisoners and to the dismay of the guards. The guards had become exhilarated by their sense of power and were quite reluctant to relinquish it. They enjoyed their status and the control it gave them over the lives of others. No guard was ever late for duty, and many had volunteered to work overtime for no pay. "Some went far beyond their roles to engage in creative cruelty and harassment," escalating such actions whenever they noticed a prisoner's emotional condition beginning to deteriorate (p. 81).

The Functions of Imprisonment   What, then, is the purpose of prison? The purposes of imprisonment have traditionally been threefold:

1. punishment of the criminal;
2. protection of society from the criminal by incapacitating the criminal;
3. deterrence of others from committing crimes.

The vilest deeds like poison weeds
Bloom well in prison air:
It is only what is good in man
That wastes and withers there.
Oscar Wilde

Some people (including some judges) believe that prisons should also serve a reform function, transforming prisoners into useful members of society. Most prisons do not seem to serve this function; as we saw in chapter 14 they are overcrowded and unpleasant. They also often function as a breeding ground for crime and for perfecting criminal techniques. They seldom have job training and rehabilitation programs. In many prisons inmates are subjected to violent behavior from other prisoners and guards, an absence of privacy, and general demoralizing abuse:

Convicts are subject to having their persons and their cells searched at the whim of prison officials for contraband which may range from weapons or drugs to innocuous items that the prison officials have arbitrarily decided that prisoners may not have. These searches may include rectal and vaginal searches. Having been convicted of a crime, the inmate has no Fourth

Amendment protection against such warrantless searches. There, they need not be based on probable cause. They may result merely from the prison administration's constant concern about custodial security or even from the whim of a guard. (Cohn & Udolf, 1979)

Under degrading conditions of which this quotation gives but a hint, prisons can hardly be said to win criminals over to a superior, law-abiding way of life.

A review of the available data by Blumstein (1978) suggests that imprisonment does serve the purpose of incapacitating convicted criminals and protecting society while they are confined. As for deterrence, the severity of punishment does seem to have a dampening effect on the commission of crime, which may or may not be due to the deterrent function of prisons. Blumstein stresses the need for more controlled experiments on the effects of punishment.

Carroll (1979) set up an experiment to study the effects of deterrence on the commission of a "crime." He used subjects drawn from a state prison and a juvenile detention and diagnostic center, as well as high school and community college students. Interviewers asked the subjects to evaluate the opportunities to commit a crime based on a "pie picture" such as that shown in Figure 15–1. The

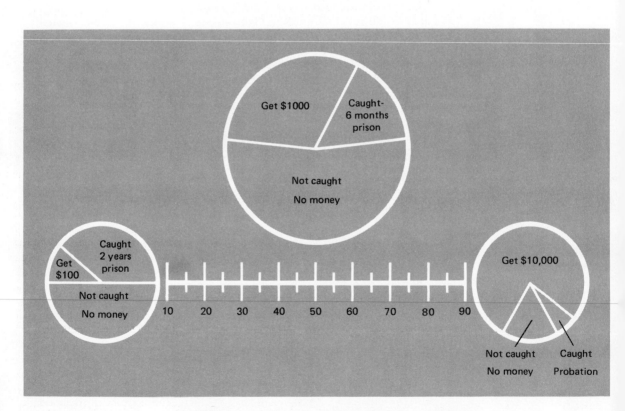

FIGURE 15–1. Crime Opportunity "Pie" with Response Scale

Source: From "A Psychological Approach to Deterrence: The Evaluation of Crime Opportunities," by J. S. Carroll, *Journal of Personality and Social Psychology*, 1978, *36*, 1515.

interviewers explained that the different segments of the "pie" were possible outcomes of the crime, and placed a spinner on the pie to demonstrate that over a series of spins the larger segments come up more often.

The crime opportunities varied along the dimensions of probability of success, the amount of money resulting from a successful crime, the probability of getting caught, and the penalty if caught. Most subjects made their judgments primarily along a single one of these dimensions. Money was the most important dimension, and probability of capture was the least important. This suggests that punishment may not have the deterrent effect that the system assumes it does.

Parole

In most decisions involving imprisonment, the judge sets minimum and maximum limits on the sentence to be served, such as from 5 to 10 years. Once the defendant is imprisoned, his or her case is turned over to a parole board. The parole board follows the case and determines when the offender should be released. Once the prisoner is released, the parole board assumes responsibility for the parolee's conduct in society until such a time as the full length of the sentence has expired. Parole decisions have been the subject of a fair amount of psychological research, most of it by Carroll and his associates.

One of the main factors in deciding whether to release someone on parole is the likelihood of recidivism, the return of a released offender to criminal behavior. Carroll and Payne (1977) examined the ways the risk of recidivism and the seriousness of the crime that the inmate had committed affected the decisions of actual parole board members and students. Both groups inferred the risk of future criminal behavior as much or more from background information about the person than from any descriptions of the crime the person had committed. These results can be explained by attribution theory (remember our discussion in chapter 5). Apparently, background information reflects more internal and stable characteristics of the person.

Carroll (1978) went on to apply attribution theory to the parole decision itself. After each of 272 actual decisions to release an offender on parole, every member of the Pennsylvania Board of Probation and Parole answered a questionnaire. They were asked to rate the importance of various factors in their decision, and to give their opinions on why that decision had been reached. Carroll found that the more stable the attributions that were made about the offense and about the convict's prior record, the higher were the predictions of future criminal behavior and the more reluctant board members were to grant parole. In addition to the risk of future crime, the board also gave high weight to the need for special (e.g., psychiatric) deterrence services and to the likelihood of rehabilitation in making their parole decisions.

Trends in Social Psychology and Law Studies

As we noted at the beginning of this chapter, social psychological research on the law started over 80 years ago, but it was only a decade or so ago that the volume of research began to expand rapidly. We are now at the point where social psychology and the law merits recognition as a major area of applied research. Moreover, it seems likely that the recent period of rapid growth in research will continue as more social psychologists become familiar with legal settings and legal problems.

This chapter has been designed to provide an overview of the many different topics investigated by social psychologists. In fact, a disproportionate amount of research has—perhaps naïvely—been devoted to juries and to issues in the criminal law. However, most of what happens in "the law" takes place outside the criminal courtroom and it is likely that social psychology will expand its interest into those areas, too. Future research will not only help us to understand how our legal system operates, but it will also enrich and extend the theoretical foundations on which social psychology is built.

Answering Questions about Social Psychology and the Law

1. Research on bail setting shows that community ties are the best predictor of whether a defendant will show up in court. However, this is not necessarily the factor judges actually use in their bail decisions. Moreover, there are discrepancies between factors actually used by judges and those they claim to use.
2. Jurors can be affected by such procedural factors as the sequence of the trial presentation and the complexity of the judge's instructions. They can also be affected by prejudicial evidence such as inadmissible testimony, a prior criminal record, and character evidence.
3. The length of prison sentence is to a large extent left to the discretion of the trial judge. Research on sentencing shows that there are wide discrepancies among sentences meted out for similar crimes.

Summary

Social psychologists study many aspects of the law as it surrounds events before, during, and after trials. Research on victims shows that people sometimes blame the victims for having been the object of a crime, although the reasons for this are unclear. Minority group members are disproportionately victimized, perhaps due to residence patterns and other aspects of poverty. The aged have a low victimization rate, contrary to popular belief, although rates greatly vary between different segments of the aged community. Women also have a low victimization rate, although (and perhaps because) women tend to have a fairly high fear of crime.

Psychologists have found that the criteria judges actually use in setting bail are not always the best predictors of whether defendants will show up in court. Plea bargaining—a type of "deal" in which the defendant pleads guilty without trial to an offense less severe than the one that the defendnt may actually have committed—takes place in 80 to 90 percent of all criminal cases. Social psychologists have studied negotiation strategies and plea-bargaining preferences, and suggest that defendants should play a role in the negotiations. Pretrial publicity has, in studies, been shown to have negative effects on jurors' objectivity.

Trial procedures are generally studied in the form of laboratory simulations. Jury selection has been extensively investigated. Little relationship has been found between personality factors and whether a juror will vote to convict or acquit. Eyewitness testimony is highly influential in trial proceedings, and is subject to a number of factors that limit its accuracy. Identification from photographs and live lineups is not reliable. Jurors are most impressed with eyewitnesses and other types of witnesses when they seem confident about their testimony, which may be increased by pretrial briefing, and may also have little to do with whether they are telling the truth. Psychologists are called as expert witnesses to caution jurors on the pitfalls of eyewitness testimony.

Jury decision making has been researched in terms of who leads the jury, how extralegal defendant characteristics such as gender and attitude affect jurors' decisions, and how judges' instructions and rules of evidence are reflected in verdicts. "Innocent until proven guilty," a cornerstone of our legal system, is seldom understood or believed by the average juror. Judges and juries often disagree about a verdict.

When a trial is completed, sentencing, imprisonment, and perhaps parole, follow. Social psychologists have researched sentencing in terms of the factors that judges employ in setting sentences. Imprisonment is meant to serve the functions of punishment of the criminal, protecting society from the criminal, rehabilitation, and deterring others from committing crimes. In reality, rehabilitation rarely occurs, and findings are inconclusive on the deterrent effects of imprisonment. The decisions of parole board members to release offenders have also interested and been studied by social psychologists.

Suggested Additional Reading

Cohn, A., & Udolf, R. *The criminal justice system and its psychology.* New York: Van Nostrand Reinhold, 1979.

Ellison, K. W., & Buckhout, R. *Psychology and criminal justice.* New York: Harper & Row, 1981.

Greenberg, M., & Ruback, B. *Social psychology and the criminal justice system.* Belmont, California: Wadsworth, 1982.

Kalven, H., & Zeisel, H. *The American jury.* Boston: Little, Brown, 1966.

Kerr, N. L., & Bray, R. M. *The psychology of the courtroom.* New York: Academic Press, 1982.

Saks, M., & Hastie, R. *Social psychology in court.* New York: Van Nostrand Reinhold, 1978.

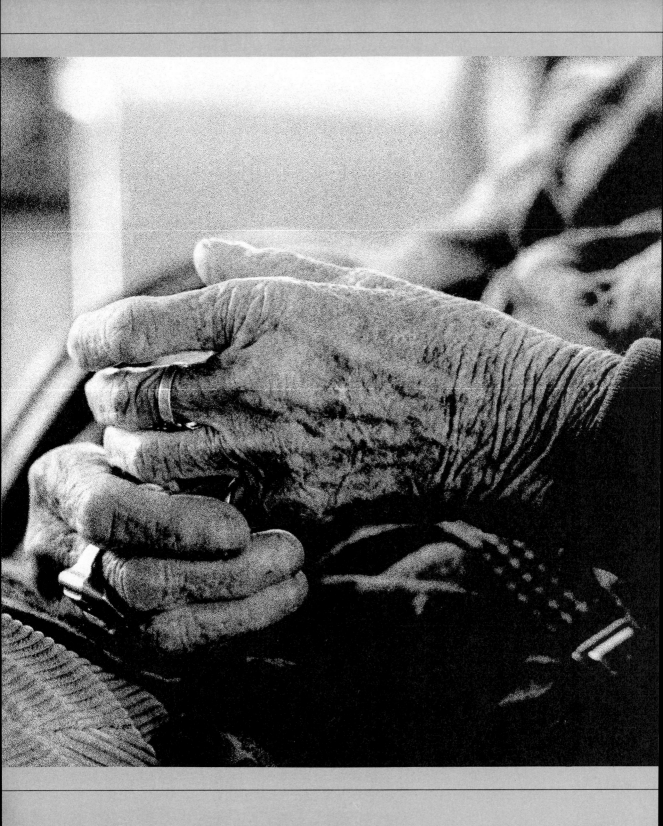

16

SOCIAL PSYCHOLOGY AND THE QUALITY OF LIFE

Questions about Social Psychology and the Quality of Life

1. What contributes most to satisfaction with life—health, wealth, love, children, friends, political freedom—or something else?
2. If you were a social psychologist, how would you measure someone's satisfaction with life?
3. In recent years, increasing numbers of married women have been entering the workforce. How has this affected them and the other members of their families?
4. Can you think of ways in which advertisers appear to make use of attitude research and theories?
5. Which social psychological theories might be applied to resolving social problems such as smoking or excessive energy consumption?
6. How true are the conventional stereotypes of old people?

Imagine the best possible life you could have. Would you choose fame, fortune, good health, a happy marriage, children, an interesting job, religious freedom, wealth? Or would you like them all—and more?

In 1932 Herbert Hoover campaigned for the presidency promising "a car in every garage and a chicken in every pot." How innocent this statement of national aspiration seems in the [present decade] and how inappropriate it would seem to any aspirant to high office today. A nation which has been known, and criticized, for its materialistic values is now asking itself whether in fact the good life can be measured in terms of consumer goods, and those who presume to define the national goals increasingly speak of quality of life rather than of further material possessions. Quality of life is seldom precisely defined in these statements, but the implication is typically given that the nation must change from its fixation on goals which are basically economic to goals which are essentially psychological, from a concentration on being well-off to a concern with a sense of well-being. (Campbell, Converse, & Rodgers, 1976, p. 1)

Well-being is a relative term. For some people, it may mean a sense of achievement at work, or a feeling of closeness to family, friends, and community. For others it means material wealth and the goods it can purchase. And for many others, well-being might be a simple but nourishing meal or a day free of pain.

As with beauty, well-being is in the eye of the beholder. Well-being, happiness, satisfaction—the **quality of life**—depends on each person's expectations and standards of comparison. But from a scientific point of view, we might question how accurate the beholder's eye really is. Many people spend their lives struggling for what they *think* will make them happy—money, prestige, a house

594

in the country, marriage, the proverbial "pot of gold" at the end of the rainbow—but when they finally attain it, find that they are still not happy.

Social psychologists, as objective researchers, attempt to look through the eyes of the beholder and to report what is really there, as opposed to reporting what the beholder thinks may be there. Guided by traditional *psychological theories* (as discussed throughout this text), and using scientific *research methods* (as described in chapter 2), social psychologists have challenged the common-sense beliefs about life satisfaction, and have addressed themselves in a practical way to improving the quality of human existence.

Obviously, this task is enormous. To make it more manageable, social researchers first isolated the individual components of everyday life that might add to—or detract from—happiness and satisfaction: economic factors, jobs and the workplace, marriage and family life, consumer behavior, health, to name but a few. These are the subjects of the current chapter. Enough research exists on each of these subjects to fill entire separate chapters and even books. Many colleges and universities now offer courses devoted solely to topics in applied social psychology. This chapter may serve as an introduction to such a course.

Because of space limitations, it is possible to discuss only a few studies for each of the "applied" topics covered in this chapter. These studies have been chosen to provide some sense of the range of research approaches employed by applied social psychologists. Although the topics are diverse, there are two major unifying themes running through the chapter: First, the topics covered in the chapter all address some aspect of the quality of our lives. Indeed, improvement in the quality of human life is an implicit goal of all applied research. Second, almost all of the studies selected for discussion are good examples of how social psychological theories and research methods can be applied to practical problems. As you read the sections that follow, you will come across numerous reminders of theoretical discussions and research covered in the preceding chapters of this text.

Quality of Life

Think again about the questions raised in the first paragraph of this chapter. People have thought about their aspirations from the beginning of time, but it was not until 1965 that the psychologist Hadley Cantril tried to analyze these aspirations. Cantril developed a list of "Subjective Quality of Life Measures" to help people identify their own personal definitions of the "best possible life," without suggesting that such a life was actually possible. "Here is a picture of a ladder," the subjects were told. "At the top of the ladder is the best life you can imagine—the ideal life. At the bottom of the ladder is the worst life you can imagine—a life that is terrible. Using a number on this card, where on the ladder would you place your life at this time?" The rungs were numbered from 1 (the bottom) to 10 (the top). The subjects also were asked about their life satisfaction: Were they completely dissatisfied (1), neutral (6 or 7), or completely satisfied (10); about their general happiness (very happy, fairly happy, or not too happy);

and about their feelings about life as a whole, taking into account what had happened in the last year and what was expected in the near future—whether they felt delighted (7 on the scale), about equally satisfied and dissatisfied (4 on the scale), or terrible (a low of 1).

Man's happiness in life is the result of man's own effort and is neither the gift of God nor a spontaneous natural product.
Ch'en Tu-hsiu

Cantril used what could be called a cognitive approach to evaluate these conceptions of the ideal life. Such cognitive measures are easy to quantify, but they may not get at the full meaning of quality of life. For Campbell (1976), however, the quality of life is to be found *not* in objective circumstances but in *affective*, subjective experiences. Campbell and other researchers tried to explore the subjects' individual experiences of pleasantness or unpleasantness, rather than satisfaction or dissatisfaction. For example, people were asked to position "their lives in general" at a point between interesting and boring, enjoyable and miserable, lonely and friendly, rewarding and disappointing.

How would you determine the quality of your life? Can you really be objective about it? Would your response depend on what was happening in your life at a given time, or would you be able to take a more global view? Every life has its ups and downs, as these captured moments of everyday experience vividly remind us.

Susan Rosenberg / Photo Researchers, Inc.

Ed Lettau / Photo Researchers, Inc.

TABLE 16-1.
Average Importance of Life Experience
Domains

Domain of Life Experience	Mean Importance Rating
Health	1.37
Marriage	1.44
Family life	1.46
National government	1.54
Friendships	2.08
Housing	2.10
Job	2.19
Community	2.21
Religious faith	2.35
Nonwork activities	2.79
Financial situation	2.94
Organizations	4.01

Note: Respondents were asked to rate the importance of each domain on a scale ranging from 1 (extremely important) to 5 (not at all important). Thus, lower mean ratings indicate greater importance.

Source: Adapted from *The Quality of American Life: Perceptions, Evaluations, and Satisfactions,* by A. Campbell, P. E. Converse, and W. L. Rodgers, Copyright © 1976 by Russell Sage Foundation. Reprinted by permission.

Measuring the Quality of Life

The cognitive and the affective aspects of life satisfaction interact in ever-changing, complex combinations. To study how people feel about their lives, researchers have designed objective scales and questions that can be scored, tabulated, and reported.

One of the most interesting and comprehensive studies of life satisfaction was conducted by Campbell, Converse, and Rodgers at the Institute for Social Research of the University of Michigan (1976). Following the model of Kurt Lewin, who theorized that experience and behavior stem from an interaction between the person's subjective perceptions and the objective environment, these researchers asked over 2,000 American adults to evaluate their lives. They wanted to know *everything:* To measure cognitive aspects, they administered Bradburn's Scale of Affective Balance, which ranks life experiences on a scale of pleasant to unpleasant. They collected objective data on age, race, occupation, family income, level of education, religion, and other factors. They identified 12 "domains of life experience" and asked the subjects to rate the importance of each domain in their lives (see Table 16-1). Then they tried to identify the attributes of each domain that directly affected satisfaction. For example, in the work domain, the challenge of a job, the physical environment where it is performed, the social relationships in the work community, even the convenience of the trip to work—all interact to produce general satisfaction or dissatisfaction. In the marriage domain, relevant factors included the number of children in the family, the family income, the ages of the respondent and his or her spouse, the amount of companionship with the spouse, and similar qualities.

The researchers ended up with a mountain of subjective estimates of life quality, and orderly, objective tallies of life achievements such as education and income. At last they were ready to answer the big question: "How well do subjective feelings of life satisfaction correlate with actual life circumstances?"

Surprisingly, the correlations were quite weak. A very few objective variables accounted for the greatest variability in subjective satisfaction. The major indicator of well-being was not income, as one might have thought, but health, marriage, family life, confidence in the nation's government, adequate housing, and job satisfaction. The most important of these were health and marriage; the least important were financial circumstances and an involvement in community or professional organizations.

This research definitely contradicts the idea that happiness can be bought. Although American society has been dominated by the belief that economic satisfactions directly determine human welfare, psychological research suggests that life is more than a bank balance. Rather, life satisfaction is a rich mixture of many components.

Domains of Life Satisfaction

Another approach to identifying quality-of-life factors was taken by Flanagan (1978). He interviewed nearly 3,000 people from all ages, races, backgrounds, and regions of the country. Flanagan collected more than 6,500 "critical incidents" by asking the subjects when was "the last time you did something very important to you," or about "a time when you saw something happen to another person that really was harmful" (pp. 138–139). "Tell me about a continuing source of pleasure to you," "a continuing source of trouble to you," "a strong positive emotional impact," and "a strong negative emotional impact," Flanagan asked (p. 139). Flanagan sorted the responses into 5 major categories containing 15 subcategories (see Table 16–2).

Consider these five major headings: Physical and material well-being; relations with other people; social, community, and civic activities; personal development and fulfillment; and recreation. If you are like most people—and like the people Flanagan interviewed—all of these categories are important in your life. But in which of these are your needs and desires being met at this time? In a follow-up study, Flanagan asked this question of both men and women, at ages 30, 50, and 70 years. More than 80 percent said their needs and wants in the area of health and personal safety were "well met," and about 75 percent of all subjects were also satisfied with their material well-being. But all age groups were dissatisfied in four sub-areas: participation in local or national government, learning, participation in active recreation, and opportunity for creative expression. In each of these domains, about 33 percent of all the subjects rated their needs as only moderately or "less well" met, and they cited these areas as significantly detracting from the quality of their lives.

TABLE 16-2.

Importance of Various Components in Quality of Life at Various Life Stages

Component	Male 30 yrs	Male 50 yrs	Male 70 yrs	Female 30 yrs	Female 50 yrs	Female 70 yrs
Physical and material well-being						
A. Material comforts—things like a desirable home, good food, possessions, conveniences, an increasing income, and security for the future.	80	85	87	75	86	87
B. Health and personal safety—to be physically fit and vigorous, to be free from anxiety and distress, and to avoid bodily harm.	98	96	95	98	98	96
Relations with other people						
C. With relatives—communicating, visiting doing things, and helping and being helped by them.	68	63	60	83	76	78
D. Having and raising children—this involves being a parent and helping, teaching, and caring for your children.	84	85	83	93	92	88
E. With a husband/wife/a person of the opposite sex.	90	88	85	94	83	46
F. Close friends—sharing activities, interests, and views; being accepted, visiting, giving and receiving help, love, trust, support, guidance.	71	76	70	79	80	87
Social, community, and civic activities						
G. Helping and encouraging others—this includes adults or children other than relatives or close friends. These can be your own efforts or efforts as a member of some church, club, or volunteer group.	60	71	64	71	74	78
H. Participation in activities relating to local and national government and public affairs.	47	62	64	42	58	58
Personal development and fulfillment						
I. Learning, attending school, improving your understanding, or getting additional knowledge.	87	68	50	81	67	60
J. Understanding yourself and knowing your assets and limitations, knowing what life is all about and making decisions on major life activities. For some people, this includes religious or spiritual experiences. For others, it is an attitude toward life or a philosophy.	84	84	80	92	90	88
K. Work in a job or at home that is interesting, rewarding, worthwhile.	91	90	55	89	85	59
L. Expressing yourself in a creative manner in music, art, writing, photography, practical activities, or in leisure-time activities.	48	39	36	53	54	58
Recreation						
M. Socializing—meeting other people, doing things with them, and giving or attending parties.	48	47	49	53	49	60
N. Reading, listening to music, or observing sporting events or entertainment.	56	45	52	53	56	63
O. Participation in active recreation—such as sports, traveling and sightseeing, playing games or cards, singing, dancing, playing an instrument, acting, and other such activities.	59	48	47	50	52	52

Percentages of a sample of 1,000 30-year-olds, 600 50-year-olds, and 600 70-year-olds reporting each of the 15 components as important or very important to their quality of life

Source: Adapted from "A Research Approach to Improving Our Quality of Life," by J. C. Flanagan, *American Psychologist*, 1978, *33* 141.

As the quality of life research we have been discussing demonstrates, our sense of well-being is affected by our experiences in various areas. In the remainder of this chapter we will examine social psychological research in several of these: economic well-being, work, the family, consumer behavior, health, energy conservation, and aging. The potential of applied social psychology to help us understand—and improve—our experiences in these areas is suggested by the variety of research projects described in the remaining pages of this chapter.

Economic Well-Being

Although income, in and of itself, does not appear to be the dominant part of life satisfaction, it is clear that gainful employment and the economic security it provides do affect the quality of life. A lack of income, by any measure, is a major part of life *diss*atisfaction.

Have you ever lost a job abruptly, or had a sudden financial burden placed on you that you were unable to meet? One graduate student who was just managing to make ends meet with a scholarship and a part-time job, abruptly found himself in urgent need of $1,500 for dental work. The student had neither the money nor the time to work still more hours to earn the money. Even finding time to consult different dentists for second and third opinions (and financial estimates) placed a strain on his schedule. Would you, in this student's shoes, still sleep soundly at night? What if the student, in addition, lost his part-time job?

It seems reasonable to suppose that economic stress affects the mental health of those experiencing the stress. Social scientists have conducted some studies in this area, especially on the effects of unemployment on the psychological condition of the unemployed, and even on his or her life itself. For example, although the exact causal relationships are not understood, it has been found that when the unemployment rate rises 1 percent,

1. First admissions to state mental hospitals increase by 4.3 percent for men, and by 2.3 percent for women.
2. Suicides increase by 4.1 percent.
3. Murders increase by 5.7 percent.
4. Imprisonments in state institutions increase by 4 percent.
5. Deaths over the subsequent 6 years from stress related causes, such as heart disease, increase 1.9 percent. (Pines, 1982)

In an interview, Louis A. Ferman, research director of the Institute of Labor and Industrial Relations at the University of Michigan, remarked: "We now feel the relationship between unemployment and physiological or psychological stress is so strong that every pink slip should carry a Surgeon General's warning that it may be hazardous to your health" (Pines, 1982).

Coping with Economic Pressures

Of course, people can experience economic hardship even without losing their jobs. Caplovitz (1981) surveyed nearly 2,000 families in 1976 to determine their inflation and recession coping strategies. Those most affected by inflation and recession were low-income families, retired persons, semiskilled and unskilled workers, and members of minority groups. These people operated on a marginal financial basis in healthy economic times, and an economic slump caused such hardships as reducing the number of meals from three a day to two or even one and a half per day, deciding which child to buy clothes for, or deciding which child to allow to remain in school and which to send to work. People of greater economic means faced less severe cutbacks: eating less steak and lobster, buying medium priced rather than expensive cars, and saving less for the future.

My life is one demd horrid grind.
Charles Dickens, Nicholas Nickleby

The coping techniques used by the families surveyed included taking second jobs, sending additional family members out to work, putting in more overtime, bargain hunting when shopping, and sharing resources (as in car pools). For the most part, however, no matter what their walk of life, people simply lowered their rate of consumption, cutting back on the money they spent for food, clothing, entertainment, and in the case of the poor, even on medical care. Moreover, about 33 percent of the families surveyed indicated that the pressures resulting from inflation and recession were damaging to their marriages. Of the respondents in Caplovitz's survey, 25 percent believed their mental health had been damaged.

When social psychologists talk about measuring economic satisfaction or economic well-being, what do they mean? In one experimental study it was found that a person's actual financial well-being was not paramount in contributing to a sense of personal satisfaction; instead, raises and cost-of-living increases were prime contributors (Levin, Faraone, & Herring, 1980). It would seem that getting a raise and keeping up with inflation have an intrinsic value to people as measures of job success.

In a second study, Levin, Faraone, and McGraw (1981) investigated how a group of 60 undergraduates perceived the effects of changes in major economic variables. One experimental group rated economic well-being, and another group rated personal satisfaction, for various "scenarios"—financial descriptions of hypothetical people contained in a booklet and also read aloud to the subjects. The scenarios contained a salary level, annual inflation rate, and annual raise rate.

The study showed that salary, raises, and inflation combined to influence ratings of financial well-being and personal satisfaction, and that actual income level and financial well-being were not as important as the perception that one was receiving raises and keeping up with inflation. The subjects evidently compared the size of the raise with the inflation rate in figuring their personal satisfaction level, and even a small change for the better or worse was able to bring about a fairly large change in personal satisfaction. Effectively coping with inflation seems to be an important aspect of people's sense of well-being, and this has been confirmed by both field and experimental research.

Recall from chapter 4 that much of what we know about ourselves is based on comparisons with other people. Similarly, our perceptions of our material well-being are based upon at least two different types of social comparisons. First, social psychologists have known since the Second World War that we compare our own status to that of people similar to ourselves. Stouffer et al. (1949) found that military police (MPs) were not more discontented than men in the Army Air Corps even though Air Corps personnel were promoted more rapidly. The MPs compared themselves to other MPs (their reference group), and therefore did not feel deprived. The researchers argued that discontent arose from relative deprivation—that is, deprivation relative to others in a similar situation. Pettigrew (1967) has used the **relative deprivation theory** to explain violent black protests during the 1960s.

A second relevant comparison we all make is with ourselves at other times. In assessing our current economic well-being, we compare our present income to how well we were doing in the past—and also to how well we hoped we would be doing now. Are we better off today than last year at this time? Than five years ago? Have we met our own financial goals? Where will we be one year from now? In five years? The resulting judgments will be tempered by our appraisal of relevant reference groups. How are our peers doing?

Let us be thankful for the fools.
But for them the rest of us
could not succeed.
Mark Twain

Work and the Quality of Life: The Working Woman

In all of the studies of life satisfaction, productive work has ranked high as a major determinant of well-being, both for those who work for pay and for those who work, unpaid, in their own homes. Not surprisingly, those in the first category—paid workers—are predominantly male, those in the second category—nonpaid, home workers—are predominantly female. Judging from the job attributes that are identified with work satisfaction—challenge, stimulation, financial rewards, co-worker relationships, among others—it is also not surprising that working males tend to get more satisfaction from their work than females working at home (Campbell et al., 1976).

Numerous studies have focused on job satisfaction for both men and women. Because of space limitations, and because of its growing importance today, we have chosen to direct our coverage to women's issues. What are women's issues? In their 1981 book *Women and Work: A Psychological Perspective*, Nieva and Gutek identify the following as women's issues: the decision to work, career choices, performance on the job, leadership ability, achievement motivation, pay, promotions, intrinsic rewards, role conflict, and sexual harassment. Except for the first and last items, it is clear that most women's work issues are really the same as men's work issues. And such factors as the decision to work, role conflict, and even sexual harassment are now beginning to affect men as well. It is certain that women are making progress if they now face the same problems as men do! However, studies show that they face many added problems that seriously impede their ability to perform as equals in the workplace. And when they are able to perform as equals, women too often find that the rewards—in pay, promotions, and "perks"—are far from equal.

Job Discrimination

In 1974, there were 21,800 women attending accredited law schools in the United States. In 1982, the number had more than doubled, to nearly 45,000—a sign of progress (American Bar Association Annual Survey, 1982). In 1981, women held 68.5 percent of the technical health jobs in hospitals and clinics. They earned an average weekly wage of $273. Men doing the same work earned $324. Female elementary-school teachers comprised 82 percent of that workforce, and earned an average $68 a week less than male teachers. Women held 76.2 percent of the sales counter jobs that were not related to food sales. They earned an average $195 per week; men in the same jobs earned an average of $240 per week—a sign of discrimination (Bureau of Labor Statistics, 1982).

Why are women treated differently than men in the workplace? Our culture stereotypes women in motherly housewife roles that are incompatible with the ambitious leadership roles of paid employment. As you will recall from chapters 5 and 7, some stereotypes are supported by factual evidence, but many are based on false notions and perpetuated by socialization processes and mass media images. Which stereotypes—the factually based or the unfounded—account for the workplace differences between men and women?

England, Chassie, and McCormack (1982) focused on skill-related differences between the sexes as a possible explanation for women's generally lower earnings potential. The researchers measured the skill demands and training requirements for various jobs. They found that traditionally male and female occupations differ in the kinds of skills they require. For example, many traditionally male occupations require manipulation of physical objects or the exercise of power over people. In contrast, traditionally female jobs are predominantly clerical (secretarial, bookkeeping) or nurturing (nursing, teaching). However, skill differences alone did not explain women's lower earnings. In occupations that were traditionally female, salaries were low. In occupations that were traditionally male, salaries were higher. Indeed, women seeking to enter some traditionally male occupations have been offered somewhat higher salaries than male job candidates: For example, in 1975–1976, female college graduates were offered $1,021 a month in accounting jobs, $1,045 in computer science, and $1,052 in chemistry—offers that topped offers to males by $4, $10, and $41 a month, respectively (National Science Foundation, 1977).

This might lead us to expect that, as more women enter previously male jobs, their salaries will increase. Unfortunately, history suggests that when women enter an occupation in significant numbers, that occupation takes a nosedive in perceived prestige—and level of compensation. Educators, librarians, telephone operators, stenographers, and typists were virtually all men a century ago.

Although the workplace is perceived by women as a source of discrimination, the workplace is a key area in which attitude change has occurred on a broad scale. According to a 1982 Harris Poll conducted for *Business Week* magazine, women are still struggling to reach the top executive levels at major corporations, but their proven expertise—and salary demands—are commanding growing respect among male business executives. The poll showed, for example, that 86 percent of those queried found women executives to perform "as well as or

Half a century separates the women stitching automobile upholstery (left) and the worker assembling carburetor parts in the early 1980s. In that period women's participation in the workforce has increased dramatically, as has women's access to a wider variety of jobs. However, discrimination in pay and promotions, and sexual harassment, are continuing problems.

Left: National Archives; Right: Will McIntyre / Photo Researchers, Inc.

better than expected." However, of the 602 top level executives polled, only 8 were women (*Business Week*, June 28, 1982, p. 10).

Stresses on Working Women

In comparison to the few women enjoying high salaries, prestige, and respect in the executive suite, most women continue to work at low paying, repetitive, low prestige jobs with little opportunity for advancement. And when they come home, these women still face the nonpaying, repetitive, low prestige, nonadvancement job of chief cook, bottle washer, face wiper, and cleaner upper. You might think that their level of stress would be almost debilitating, but surprisingly, just the opposite is true: Employment outside the home actually is associated with *improved* mental health in women.

In a review of 38 published studies, Warr and Parry (1982) found that working women were significantly less likely to commit suicide, to experience lasting depression, or to suffer low self-esteem. Women whose jobs provided rewarding prestige and social interactions that were missing in their home environments benefitted most, but no one category of women—single or married, mothers or nonmothers—emerged as having significantly lower psychological well-being than those without jobs.

In a reexamination of data from a 1976 survey of 2,440 American adults aged

Application: Bias at the Bindery

The Government Printing Office, which prints such things as the Congressional Record and the Federal Register, had 604 workers binding publications in 1973.

All 279 members of the bookbinder craft were men. All but one of the 325 bindery workers were women.

Some bindery workers did bookbinders' jobs and vice versa.

The male bookbinders made considerably more money than the female bindery workers, ranging from $3 to $10 more per hour over the years.

Skilled women were not, and have not been, promoted into the bookbinder ranks.

Was this a case of sexual discrimination?

Yes, the United States Court of Appeals for the District of Columbia ruled recently. It upheld a 1979 District Court decision under which 28 female machinists were promoted and bindery workers were given easier access to and training for bookbinder positions. The frosting on the cake is about $8 million in back pay, plus "front pay"—a kind of continuing discrimination penalty—to be imposed until half the bookbinder jobs are held by women.

The printing office's "only defense is that the bookbinder's job involves a four-year apprenticeship that has traditionally excluded women," according to the appellate court brief. The "cold numbers," it added, were brought "convincingly to life" by tales of individual bias and discouragement.

Nora A. Bailey, who represented the plaintiffs, identified as "Dorothy M. Thomson, et al.," is a Washington tax lawyer who donated her work for the cause. "It was such a clear-cut case, I thought it would be quickly settled out-of-court by the agency," she said. "That was 9½ years ago."

Drew Spaulding, an attorney for the Government Printing Office, said he could make no official comment. "It's water under the bridge," he said.

21 and older, Kessler and McRae (1982) came to a similar conclusion. They found that women with few family responsibilities or those whose husbands helped with child care reaped the greatest psychological benefits from outside employment. In addition, as a group, all employed wives had significantly lower scores than did unemployed wives on a 20-item scale of depression and anxiety, and also on additional measures of ill health and low self-esteem.

While married women benefit from working outside of the home, their husbands have a different experience. Kessler and McRae (1982) also found that husbands of working wives had significantly higher rates of nervousness, headaches, loss of appetite, upset stomach, hand-trembling, sweating, nightmares, dizziness, and weight loss than husbands whose wives stayed home. Were these men distressed by having to assume an increased burden of housework or child care? Apparently not, the authors found. Nor did they seem to be affected by the stress of being the sole provider for a family. Although evidence was not conclusive, Kessler and McRae theorize that many men—particularly older men—experience social conflict about the fact that their wives work because it is contrary to their socialization. If this explanation is valid, we might expect less male

Will the bond between them
be just as close if she goes to
work?

Suzanne Szasz/Photo Researchers, Inc.

distress in the years ahead, because the male children of today's working
mothers have had a different socialization experience.

If some husbands suffer when their wives work, what happens to the children of working mothers? One study of 28 4-year-old boys found them to be as
compliant, affectionate, and independent as those of nonworking mothers. The
researchers also found that, regardless of employment status, mothers who were
satisfied with their roles maintained the best interactions with their children
(Henggeler & Borduin, 1981). Since numerous variables are involved in any assessment of children's adjustment, much more research will be needed before
we can learn the implications of employment for mothers and children.

Marriage

In our discussion about the areas of life satisfaction, we saw that relationships
with other people were high on all of the category lists. We looked at several aspects of interpersonal relationships in chapter 6. Here we focus on what is perhaps the most important, the most demanding, and the most "institutionalized"
relationship in people's lives: the marital relationship.

Marital Satisfaction

Rhyne (1981) studied the differences in marital satisfaction between men and women. It may surprise you to learn that men are slightly more satisfied with their marriages than women. This has in fact been one of the most consistent findings of research on this topic (Atkinson, 1980; Bernard, 1972; Campbell et al., 1976). Both men and women in the sample of 2,190 married Canadians used by Rhyne evaluated their marriages using the same criteria: friendship, sexual fulfillment, spouse's help, time spent with children, and so on. One area in which women reported more satisfaction was sexual fulfillment; men were more satisfied with friendship, spouse's help, and time with children (see Table 16-3). It should be emphasized that the differences are small; and that "such findings do not, however, in themselves give evidence for differential bases of marital satisfaction or quality" (p. 945).

Lifelong Relationships   What about marital satisfaction through the life cycle? Do partners become less satisfied as their marriage and time go by? Many researchers have found that there is a curvilinear relationship between marital satisfaction and the stage in the life cycle (Rollins & Cannon, 1974; Rollins & Feldman, 1970). Marital satisfaction seems to decline during a couple's childbearing years and increases again after the children leave home.

Lupri and Frideres (1981), in a survey of 464 Canadian couples, found this to be true. The couples were asked: Different stages of family life may be seen as more satisfying than others. How satisfying do you think each of the following stages are?: I. before children arrive; II. first year with infant; III. preschool children at home; IV. all children at school; V. having teenagers; VI. children gone from home; VII. being grandparents; VIII. at retirement stage (p. 287).

The researchers found that marital satisfaction declines steadily from the beginning of the marriage until the children are gone from home (stage VI) (see

TABLE 16-3.
Satisfaction with Marriage by Gender*

Aspect of Marriage	Men	Women
Love shown by spouse	3.14	3.09
Interest shown by spouse	3.00	2.86
Help given by spouse at home	3.30	2.70
Treatment by in-laws	3.08	2.92
Time spent by spouse at home	3.32	3.11
Spouse's friends	3.07	2.98
Spouse's time with children	3.33	2.98
Friendship	3.28	3.13
Sexual gratification	3.39	3.51

*Note: Mean values on a scale of 1, "not very satisfied," to 4, "extremely satisfied."

Source: Adapted from "Bases of Marital Satisfaction among Men and Women," by D. Rhyne, *Journal of Marriage and the Family*, November 1981, 948.

Figure 16–1). An increase in satisfaction occurs, however, as couples move from postparental years toward retirement (stage VIII itself does not appear in the figure).

Love comes after the wedding.
Lapp proverb

Popular belief has it that children tend to solidify a marriage and increase marital satisfaction. A growing body of research, however, suggests that the presence of children has the opposite effect. Glenn and McLanahan (1982) examined data on married people categorized by their level of education, religion, race, sex, employment status, and age, and found that the negative impact of child-rearing on marital enjoyment held for all subgroups. The only subgroup on which children had a neutral but not a negative effect upon marital happiness was white parents who believed that an ideal family should have four or more children. Why are children associated with less marital happiness? Glenn and McLanahan suggest that one explanation for their findings is that the presence of children in the family may deter unhappily married people from divorcing.

In a second study, the same authors used a sample of older adults (age 50 and above) whose children were grown. Even here, with no children at home, there were virtually no discernible positive effects of having children on the happiness of their parents. The popular idea that children provide psychological rewards that parents can experience at their leisure in later life would seem to merit reexamination (Glenn & McLanahan, 1981).

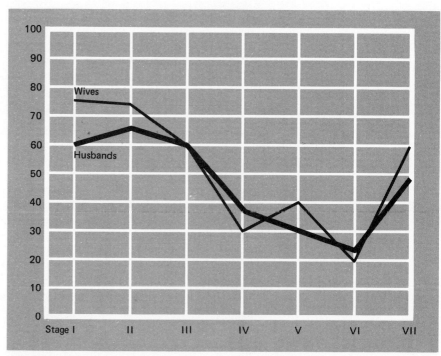

FIGURE 16–1.   Percentages of Husbands and Wives in Different Stages of the Marital Cycle Reporting "Very Satisfying" Marriages
Source: *From "The Quality of Marriage and the Passage of Time: Marital Satisfaction Over the Family Life Cycle," by E. Lupri and J. Frideres,* Canadian Journal of Sociology, *1981, 6, 289.*

In Rhyne's study (see page 607), wives expressed less satisfaction than their husbands with most aspects of their marriages. Lupri and Frideres, however, found that wives' satisfaction was greater than that of their husbands except when their children are young or are leaving home. Will her outlook improve a few years from now?

Suzanne Szasz/ Photo Researchers, Inc.

Marital Dissatisfaction

The other side of marital satisfaction, already obvious enough from our discussion, is that couples do encounter marital dissatisfaction, often to the point of divorce. Here we will look at some divorce statistics, briefly examine social psychological research on divorce, and discuss postseparation adjustment. Our discussion of divorce will not be extensive: Divorce is a topic more intensively studied in courses in clinical and counseling psychology.

America's divorce rate is the highest in the world. Between the mid 1960s and mid 1970s the divorce rate in the United States doubled; since then it has continued to increase, but not as rapidly. In some areas of the United States, 50 percent of all new marriages are likely to fail. Marriages of teenagers are particularly vulnerable: Women married at ages 14 to 17 are twice as likely to divorce as women married at ages 18 or 19, and three times more likely to divorce than women married at ages 20 to 24. Similar statistics hold for men. In terms of education, people with high incomes and/or college degrees are less likely to divorce than people with low incomes or those who did not finish high school.

A growing number of couples live together without marrying—approximately one million couples in 1977, an 80 percent increase from 1970 and representing about 2 percent of America's couple households. Although those couples do not divorce, their relationships dissolve at a similar rate, and they apparently experience similar problems in postseparation adjustment.

Reasons for Divorce   Determining the causes of divorce is difficult, and the problem has been approached from a variety of perspectives. To give an idea of the diversity, divorce has been studied as a necessary part of the contemporary family system in providing an "out" for unworkable marriages (Reiss, 1976); as a

Momma
By Mell Lazarus

Panel 1: MARRIAGE IS A BEAUTIFUL, LOVELY THING, MARYLOU.

Panel 2: I DON'T KNOW, MOMMA... LOOK AT EILEEN AND GEORGE, WHO CONSTANTLY SCREAM AND YELL AND FIGHT AND ARGUE AND THREATEN AND KICK EACH OTHER OUT, DAY AFTER MISERABLY ROTTEN DAY!!

Panel 3: BIG DEAL. IT'S WHAT THEY CALL "TROUBLE IN PARADISE."

© Field Enterprises, Inc., 1981   MELL LAZARUS.   12-18

measure of social disorgaization (Scanzoni, 1966); as a conflict resolution strategy (Sprey, 1969); and as a kind of deviance (Reiss, 1976).

All happy families resemble one another; each unhappy family is unhappy in its own way.
Leo Tolstoy, Anna Karenina

The most popular current perspective on divorce is provided by **exchange theory** (Levinger, 1976; Nye, 1979, 1982; Scanzoni, 1979). According to exchange theory, divorce becomes more likely when the benefits to a person for keeping a relationship going are lower, and the costs higher, than if that person had another relationship or was living alone. Few experiments have been devised to test exchange theory itself. Instead, most studies have examined the specific variables affecting divorce, such as the presence of children, whether or not the wife works, and the age at marriage (Kitson & Raschke, 1981). Among the factors that have been linked to higher divorce rates are the increased American emphasis on self-realization (Weiss, 1975); economic stress and unemployment (Coombs & Zumeta, 1970); different social backgrounds of spouses (e.g., Bumpass & Sweet, 1972; Levinger, 1965); premarital pregnancy (e.g., Furstenberg, 1976; Hampton, 1979); and divorced parents of either spouse (Kulka & Weingarten, 1979; Mueller & Pope, 1977). Although women who are not employed outside of the home are less likely to be divorced than women who are (Glick & Norton, 1979), the relationship of divorce to the employment status of wives is unclear. The financial stress that necessitated a two paycheck household may have contributed to the divorce, or the financial need following a divorce may have propelled former wives into the workplace in disproportionate numbers.

Advertising and Consumer Behavior

Single, married, divorced, young, old—whatever our marital status or life stage, we are all consumers. Most of us, in this era of relative abundance, in a society free from the survival pressures of food and shelter, measure the quality of our lives not in terms of what we need, but in terms of what we want. Our consumer society has a whole occupational class of specialists—the "Madison Avenue" advertisers—whose task is to convince their fellow citizens that they want the most extraordinary things! The founders of our nation could not have imagined that people, in their "pursuit of happiness," would devote their energies and means of exchange to obtain not just any clothes, but particularly those adorned with embroidered alligators and illegible signatures of someone else's name; not just any efficient means of transportation, but those that make jungle cats snarl and alluring women purr; not just any nourishing and tasty food, but only those that crackle, pop, gurgle and are eaten by smiling stars of the stage, screen, and athletic fields.

Theoretical Approaches

In surveying the quality of life, social psychologists include the area of consumer behavior and the influence of advertising on consumer behavior. These areas are of interest because advertisers have paid close attention to psychological research, particularly as it bears on attitude change and persuasion. Indeed, many marketing researchers are social psychologists and some of their research has contributed significantly to our understanding of attitudes and behavior (see chapters 8 and 9). One important area or current research draws upon cognitive response theory (Wilson & Muderrisoglu, 1980).

Cognitive response theory, which we mentioned in our discussion of attitude change in chapter 8, asserts that what most strongly facilitates attitude change is the thoughts people have after they are exposed to persuasive communications, but before they take action. Whereas some of these intervening thoughts may be positive—"You know, they're right about Crackle Flakes. They *do* make my mouth tingle. I really should buy another box"—research shows that most of them are critical (negative). These critical thoughts include **counterarguments,** disagreements with the intent of the communication—"Boy, are they wrong about Flake-Off Shampoo. Ever since I started using it, my dandruff problems have disappeared, but so have my boyfriends. I wonder if that oil-of-elephant-leaf odor could have something to do with it"—and **source derogation,** lack of confidence in the communicator, or in the source of his or her information—"What in the world does Rocky Rhodes know about toothpaste? He lost all his front teeth in the last title bout" (Kassarjian, 1982).

You have probably noticed that most advertisements do not mention competing brands. It is not lawsuits that advertisers are worried about, but the stimulation of counterarguments. A study by Wilson and Muderrisoglu (1980) found that comparative advertising elicits more counterarguments and fewer supportive arguments or positive thoughts than noncomparative advertisements.

Similarly, Sternthal and his colleagues (1978) focused on **source credibility** as an influence on counterarguments and support arguments. They gave 56 subjects copies of a booklet presenting arguments in favor of a consumer protection bill. Some subjects read that the source of the message was a highly credible source (a Harvard-trained expert in the field of consumer issues), while others read that the booklet was from a less credible source (an "unknown" consumer lobbyist). For 50 percent of the subjects in each condition, the source was identi-

fied before the message was read; for the remainder of the subjects the source was identified afterward. As expected, the "credible source" proved more persuasive than the unknown lobbyist, but only when he was identified before the subjects read the pamphlet. When the source was identified following the message, the researchers found that "credibility cues are made available too late to affect" the thoughts generated in the mind of the message recipient (p. 253).

In addition to focusing on the content and source of messages, marketing psychologists have also focused on the target of advertising messages. Several research studies have found, for example, that messages about some purchases are best directed to the woman of the house and some to the man of the house: Purchases of furniture and household goods are typically joint husband–wife decisions, but in more than 50 percent of all families surveyed husbands alone decided whether and when to purchase major items such as automobiles and housing. However, it was the wife who determined what was bought as far as the details were concerned, such as house style or neighborhood (Jenkins, 1980).

What Consumers Think about Advertising

People do not passively allow themselves to be manipulated by advertising. Consumers are skeptical of advertising precisely because they are aware that its goal is to affect their behavior. In a survey of over 300 California residents, Schutz and Casey found that over 50 percent of them viewed "most" or "all" mail and tele-

*You can tell the ideals of a
nation by its advertisements.*
Norman Douglas

phone advertising as misleading, and 38 percent regarded "most" or "all" television advertising as misleading. Certain types of advertising came in for particularly harsh criticism. Of the respondents, 66 percent found "most" or "all" advertising directed at children to be seriously misleading, and almost 50 percent found advertising directed at senior citizens to be seriously misleading. Advertising directed at young and middle-aged adults fared only slightly better. On the positive side, newspaper advertising was considered the most "credible" by a majority of respondents; only 19 percent felt that "most" or "all" newspaper ads were seriously misleading.

These consumers were, moreover, activists. Nearly 50 percent complained directly to a retail or individual advertiser and nearly 33 percent had taken their criticism directly to a manufacturer. As these collected findings show, there is often a significant difference between the business community's and the public's perceptions of advertising. But even if consumers are not getting the advertiser's message, they are certainly making sure that the advertisers get theirs!

Controversy: Who Needs Nutrition Labeling?

Scientific studies have demonstrated that the excessive intake of sugars, salt, nitrate preservatives, artificial sweeteners, caffeine, and many other food ingredients can be harmful to the health of many individuals. Consumer studies also show that most Americans are familiar with this research and are concerned about the negative effects of food ingredients. Furthermore, for many foods nutrition labels are required by the Food and Drug Administration. So now everyone reads food labels and avoids the products that contain harmful ingredients— right? Wrong!

Studies have found that very few people actually read the nutrition labels, let alone use them as a guide to purchasing. Why? Data from a 1978 *Woman's Day* magazine survey, and from other reports, indicate that only 50 percent of all consumers are able to understand what the labels say. Studies indicate that the ability to understand food labels is significantly affected by a consumer's mathematical skills. Our nationwide "fear of math" apparently causes many people to avoid reading anything that looks like a list of numbers.

Another survey, this one conducted by the Food and Drug Administration, found that 82 percent of all food shoppers rated their health as at least "good," and 79 percent thought everyone in their household had a well-balanced diet. In other words, they considered themselves too healthy to need nutrition advice or to have to be careful about what they ate. However, other studies suggest that they are wrong; most consumers generally have little knowledge about nutrition (Bauman, 1973).

In an effort to help consumers use labels better, two researchers at the University of Wisconsin Consumer Science Program surveyed over 400 shoppers at major food store chains. Asked to read a Kellogg's Corn Flakes nutrition label, those who were least successful in interpreting it turned out to be the ones who customarily do not read labels; who rated themselves low on nutrition knowledge; who were less likely to plan meals in advance; and who were less well educated (Klopp & MacDonald, 1981). In short, this study indicates that the consumers who most need the information contained on labels are those least likely to make use of it.

Public Health

Although many consumers think all advertising is profit oriented, in some cases the potential profit is all on the consumer's side. Certainly health advertising is a good example of the positive use of social psychological principles of persuasion and attitude change for the public good.

As medical psychologist Matarazzo (1982) explains, a consensus has emerged among social psychologists that "the behavior of the individual (e.g., use or abuse of tobacco, alcohol, and salt; poor practice of dental hygiene; failure to use automobile seat belts, and so on) is today's unexplored frontier in the study and understanding of health" (p. 1). He notes that the amount of money spent on health care in this country has risen from $12.7 billion in 1950 to $212.9 billion in 1979, and is the fastest growing component of the gross national product. Because "psychology is a discipline with 100 years of experience in the study of individual behavior, including behavior change," Matarazzo thinks this experience could help reduce the sums we spend on health services (p. 2). Taylor (1978) suggests five areas in which such changes are possible:

1. *Etiology*—that is, identifying the major psychological causes or possible contributants to physical illness. Among those already known are stress, depression, feelings of hopelessness and helplessness, excessive noise, crowding, and the even more relevant factors of diet, smoking, and life-style that are influenced by psychological variables.
2. *Prevention*—analysis of the ways people can be persuaded to change their behaviors—their diet, smoking, and alcohol practices, for example—to lessen their risks of disease. Social psychologists' knowledge of decision making, attitude change, fear arousal, denial and avoidance could, for example, be used in designing mass media health advertising targeted toward prevention.
3. *Management*—treatment of health problems. Psychologists can help educate patients to engage in proper "self-management"—detection and self-care—and to seek out health professionals when their help is warranted. Studies on doctor–patient communications also help to teach physicians how to improve the education of their patients.
4. *Treatment*—using psychological principles to design better therapies. For example, the psychological research on pain has shown that patients are better able to withstand both pain and uncomfortable medical procedures if they are told what to expect, and if they are given an active role in trying to control their pain.
5. *Delivery*—getting the health care services to the people who need them. In hospitals and busy doctors' offices, delivery systems are arranged more for the convenience and comfort of the staff than for the patients. Psychological studies suggest that some aspects of the delivery of health services contribute to patient dissatisfaction, noncompliance with suggested treatments, and even malpractice suits.

This is an enormous agenda, but psychologists have already made substantial progress in carrying it out. Consider their efforts in two major areas: smoking and heart disease.

Smoking

More public health advisories have been issued about smoking than about any other health related behavior. Starting with the publicity about smoking's contribution to the risks of lung cancer, heart disease, and pregnancy problems, to name but a few, followed by an official antismoking warning from the prestigious United States Surgeon General, and then capped by laws mandating a health warning on every cigarette package produced in this country, the efforts of medical scientists, public health officials, legislators, and educators have focused directly on this major potential killer. Nevertheless, lobbying efforts by industry, and addiction to nicotine, continue to put the burden of prevention and control directly on the individual. And that is where psychology comes in.

What has been done? On the negative side, advertisers, with the help of psychologists, have crafted persuasive messages to convince current and potential smokers of all ages that this habit is fun, sexually attractive, relaxing, and even pleasant tasting. On the positive side, a number of psychologists have drawn from psychological theory to examine the influences of habit, motivation, reinforcement, associative learning, resistance to extinction, personality, and addictive behavior on cigarette smoking.

Intervention   Aside from identifying problems and collecting statistics, psychological research has been the major impetus for new strategies of intervention—helping people to quit smoking, and preventing nonsmokers, particularly young adults, from taking up the habit (Leventhal & Cleary, 1980).

Therapies   Intervention studies approach the smoking problem from two perspectives: therapies to help people stop smoking, and public opinion to motivate people not to smoke. Many therapies use operant conditioning or behavior modification procedures. For example, in one study, smokers who were asked to "light up" only when a timer buzzed were able to separate their smoking from its usual situational cues, and also were able to cut down considerably when the buzzer was removed (Shapiro et al., 1971). In sensitization and desensitization techniques—the most commonly used behavior therapies—an obnoxious stimulus, such as an electric shock or excessive cigarette smoke, is paired with the act or thought of smoking. Desensitization therapies teach alternative methods of relaxation. Psychotherapy, hypnosis, sensory deprivation, and many combinations of these have also been tested.

The results of these therapies, unfortunately, have not been particularly encouraging. Whether the criterion is quitting or significant reduction, there is an impressive initial decrease in smoking during treatment with almost all of these therapies, but the dropout rate is generally high, often reaching 50 percent of those who start a therapy program. And the longer term results are even poorer. Of those who improve during treatment, the majority gradually return to smoking within 6 months. By 1 year, the people who have quit smoking or smoke less only make up from 10 to 25 percent of all those who were in a therapy program. No one therapy has a significantly better track record than the others—despite some claims to the contrary (Leventhal & Cleary, 1980).

Public Opinion   Research suggests that social psychological interventions designed to change smoking attitudes and behavior have fared little better. Among those that have been tried, the most notable is the Surgeon General's "WARNING" now mandated to appear on all cigarette packages and advertisements. Like nutrition labels, cigarette warnings are avoided by the very people they are designed to help. On a smaller but still large population scale, almost every school district in the nation has an antismoking education program, often beginning in the earliest grades. Postintervention studies at many schools suggest that these programs have been quite successful in teaching students about the hazards of smoking. Students who participate in the programs know significantly more than nonparticipants. Unfortunately, their knowledge does not translate into behavior. Most studies report only a 5 to 10 percent reduction in smoking rates among program participants (Leventhal & Cleary, 1981). Even among adults, community education programs were no more effective (see box).

Successes   Can we conclude that psychological interventions just do not work? According to Leventhal and Cleary, the answer is that the interventions psychologists have tried so far do not work. "As a whole," they explain, "the studies make clear the incorrectness of the commonsense view of communication as a process in which a message is repeated by an authoritative source (TV star, famous athlete, Nobel laureate, doctor) a sufficient number of times (a) to capture attention, (b) to produce learning of the content, (c) to change attitudes, and (d) to change behavior (p. 380)." What is needed, they believe, is greater attention paid to the people who are intended to receive the message, rather than to the message itself.

One study that did direct its major attention to message receivers, impressively reduced the smoking behavior among junior high-school students. The public opinion messages, designed by Evans and his associates (1981) as part of a National Heart and Blood Vessel Research and Demonstration Center program, did not just preach against smoking, but explained techniques viewers could use to cope with the social influences of peers, parents, and the media. The keystone of the program was a film, *Resisting Pressures to Smoke*, which recreated the actual situations in which students are exposed to pressures to smoke, and included modeling behavior demonstrating some ways to resist such pressures. This approach, based on social learning and persuasive communication theories, produced a significant decrease in both the number of subjects who intended to smoke, and in the number that had actually taken up smoking.

Of course, many of the public opinion strategies that have been attempted have also been, cumulatively, effective: Millions of Americans have dropped the smoking habit. Among your own circle of acquaintances there are probably many people who have quit smoking, or at least cut down. According to Schachter (1982), these people are most sensitive to information about the negative consequences of smoking; once they decide to quit, they are the ones who actually succeed. In contrast, the "hard core" smokers who are unable to quit on their own and then finally seek therapy are those we might expect to have problems sticking to their resolve. Schachter argues that based on the results with this group of self-selected, hard core smokers, we should not view smoking as "intractably" addictive. Many people have made positive changes in their health practices without the help of therapists. And, Schachter implies, with the indirect help of psychological theory applied to the problem, many more can be helped in the future.

Heart Disease

The American Heart Association recently issued new dietary recommendations that, according to a large body of scientific research, may significantly reduce Americans' risks of crippling heart attacks and strokes. According to the Association's Nutrition Committee, foods high in cholesterol and other fats—including egg yolks, organ meats, red meats, shrimp, butter, ice cream, and other dairy products—are implicated in coronary disease. It recommends that no more than

Research: The Mass Media and Your Health

Heart disease is the single greatest killer in the United States. Numerous medical studies have found that the control of risk factors—smoking, high blood pressure, consumption of saturated fats, excess body weight, lack of exercise, and stress—can significantly reduce the incidence of heart attacks and strokes.

To determine whether the mass media can effectively provide information about the avoidance of these risk factors, researchers in Stanford, California, designed a multidisciplinary quasi-experimental field study. They used a variety of media in a multimillion dollar, 3-year information blitz directed at two California towns, Gilroy and Watsonville; there were 50 television spots, 3 hours of television programming, weekly newspaper columns, newspaper advertisements and stories, printed material sent via direct mail, bus card advertisements, calendars, and other materials. In addition, those Watsonville residents found to be at a particularly high risk of heart disease also received "intensive instruction" in reducing their risk through individual home counseling and group sessions over a 10-week period (Maccoby & Alexander, 1980; Meyer et al., 1980).

After 3 years, residents of both towns showed dramatic increases in their knowledge of heart disease risk factors, and significant decreases in their blood pressure levels, consumption of saturated fats, and cigarette use. On the other hand, the greatest reduction in risk factors was found in the high risk Watsonville residents who received personal and group counseling. Some critics say, however, that much of the positive effects in both communities may have been due to a desire to please the investigators or to "look good" during the testing sessions (Leventhal et al., 1980).

Both supporters and critics alike agree that the Stanford program was "a bold and Herculean undertaking . . . (and) a considerable accomplishment" (p. 158). Analysis is continuing to identify which factors and procedures could improve the "media mix" that might be tried in later experiments, and put to wider use.

30 percent of a person's daily calorie intake should come from fat. That means a big shift for most people—away from hamburgers and french fries, which have become dietary staples, and toward greater consumption of currently unpopular "complex carbohydrates" (vegetables, beans, whole grains, cereals, fruits), poultry, and nonoily fishes.

As with smoking, just telling people to change their diets is not going to do the job—but sending out the word is a good start. In the past decade, significant mass media attention has focused on the health risks of a poor diet, smoking, and insufficient exercise, and the result can be seen on the roads of almost every town in the country, where joggers and bicyclists beat a path to better health. Interestingly, the effects of mass media efforts on the general population have been much stronger than those reported for the limited groups that have been studied and scientifically measured. This is consistent with Schachter's analysis of smoking studies. Health benefits do not show up dramatically in brief periods of time or for a few thousand people in the general population. It may take hundreds of thousands of subjects, studied over many years, to demonstrate that 5 or 10 people out of every 1,000 are living longer and healthier lives than they would have without taking precautions about their health.

Medicine, the only profession that labors incessantly to destroy the reason for its own existence.
James Bryce

Stress Similar positive results have been reported in studies aimed at people who have what is known as "Type A" personalities. Type A individuals are highly competitive, pressured for time, prone to hostility when frustrated, ambitious, hard driving—and have a significantly increased risk of dying from heart disease (Glass, 1976). Such individuals represent an obvious and unique target for the combined efforts of medicine and psychology. By identifying all the people who show any of the components of type A behavior, we should be able to develop programs to help those people reduce the stresses in their lives, or at least to help them to handle those stresses better. Programs like the Stanford Heart Disease Prevention Program (see box) are attempts to do just that.

Attitudes, Behavior, and Energy Conservation

In our consumer society, much of the quality of our lives depends on energy. Appliances ease our home lives, entertainment equipment enlivens our leisure lives, sophisticated machines add productivity to our work lives. We fly or drive to play, to work, to visit relatives and friends. Without our hatchbacks and data terminals, DC-7s and VCRs, stereos and food processors, life for most Americans at the end of the twentieth century would be—well, like the nineteenth century.

In the two decades following the Second World War, American energy consumption expanded dramatically, fueling a population boom and the growth of an affluent society. The expansion of the gross national product (GNP) seemed limitless, and consumers were indeed urged by energy producing utilities as well as manufacturers to buy more and bigger appliances and automobiles. The United States uses more energy than any other nation in the world. From 1920 to 1970 its annual energy consumption rate tripled (see Figure 16-2).

Electric blackouts, cutbacks in oil production, and higher prices at the gas pump signalled the end of infinite expansion. Since 1970 there has been a moderate decline in American energy use (Seligman, Becker, & Darley, 1981). Energy efficiency are now the key words in advertisements for refrigerators, air-conditioners, and automobiles. New industries have sprung up to provide alternatives to fossil fuels, and utilities are urging us to conserve.

Can the habits of a generation brought up on "bigger is better" be changed? Will we become a nation of subcompacts instead of gas guzzlers? Social psycho-

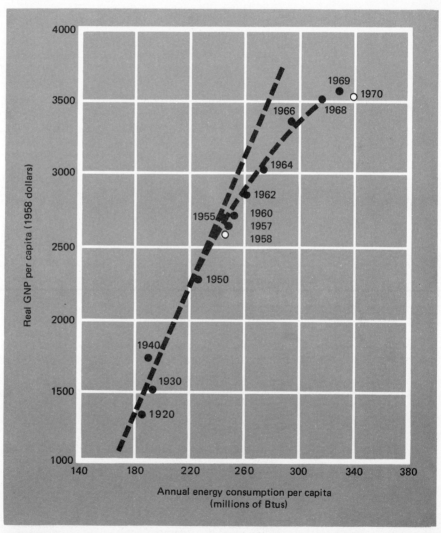

FIGURE 16–2. Energy Consumption versus Real GNP for the Period 1920 to 1970 in the United States
Source: *From* Energy, Resources and Policy, *by R. C. Dorf,* © 1978. Reading, Mass.: Addison-Wesley, *Figure 1.7. Reprinted with permission.*

logical research is being done in the area of energy conservation behavior to help us cope with this problem. Researchers have examined energy conservation from a variety of perspectives (Cook & Behrenberg, 1981), but most fall into two categories: behavioral approaches to modifying conservation behavior, and persuasive or attitude change approaches. The behavioral approach is based on learning principles much like those of social learning theory (discussed in chapters 3 and 4), while the persuasive or attitude change approach makes use of the attitude theories discussed in chapters 8 and 9.

Behavioral Approaches to Modifying Energy Consumption

Behavioral approaches to promoting energy conservation have focused on providing consumers with systematic information on how to conserve energy, promptings to encourage energy saving, monetary incentives, and feedback. In this section we will discuss one of these approaches—feedback—which has been shown to be an effective tool for lowering energy use.

In contrast to most of our behaviors, our use of energy does not really provide us with substantial feedback. The monthly utility bill is hard to understand and does not come immediately after we have turned off the lights or bought a new refrigerator. It reflects total consumption for a period of one or two months, and does not tell us whether an evening of television costs more than an evening of stereo listening. Most of the information we get from our utility companies fails to provide us with the specific, prompt, and accurate feedback that might help us conserve energy.

Social psychologists have designed programs that include specific and timely feedback components, and these programs have been quite successful in modifying energy behavior. Becker (1978), for example, provided a group of owners of identical tract homes with information on the amount of electricity typical home appliances consume, as well as some information on tradeoffs—for instance, that they would have to use no electric lights for a day and a half in order to save the amount of electricity that their airconditioners consumed in one hour (all of the houses in the sample had central airconditioning). Becker then divided the homeowners into 5 groups of 40 families. One group of 40 families was asked to cut back their electricity consumption for several summer weeks by 2 percent, and another group of 40 families was asked to cut back by 20 percent. Half of the homeowners in the 2 percent and 20 percent groups were selected to receive frequent feedback. Finally, a control group of families was studied for comparison.

Feedback was in the form of a chart taped to a window in the subjects' homes that was updated three times a week. The chart plotted the percent of electricity conserved or wasted. The 20 percent group that was given feedback cut back electricity consumption by about 15 percent. The no-feedback group and the 2 percent group did not differ significantly from the control group.

In another feedback study, Becker and Seligman (1978) also divided households into groups, this time of ten houses each. One group was given a small blue light that flashed when the outside temperature dropped below 68°F and the airconditioner was on; a situation in which energy could be saved by opening windows and turning off the airconditioner. A second group received no signalling device but was given feedback on the energy saved or wasted, plotted on a chart taped to a window and updated three times a week, as in the preceding study. The third group received both the signalling device and the feedback, while the fourth, control group received neither. This time the two groups with the signalling device decreased their energy consumption by 15.7 percent, while the feedback-only and control groups showed no significant change.

It would seem, then, that one of the best ways to induce energy conservation is to provide consumers with very specific feedback about their actual consumption and encourage them to establish conservation goals. The importance of goal-setting has been demonstrated in studies of other conservation measures such as metal recycling (McCaul & Kopp, 1982).

The Persuasive Approach

What are America's attitudes toward conservation? Olsen (1981) investigated consumers' attitudes toward energy conservation by examining a number of surveys of attitudes toward the energy crisis. He concluded that most Americans believe that an energy crisis exists and that it is acute. He found that Americans of a higher educational level took this view more often than people of lower educational levels, and younger people held this view more often than older people. No differences were found between men's and women's attitudes toward the energy problem. The problem, of course, is to translate these perceptions of an energy crisis into concrete energy saving behaviors.

The persuasive approach seeks to change and reinforce attitudes in ways that will bring about energy conserving behaviors. As we saw in chapter 9, the link between attitudes and actual behavior can be rather tenuous. Similarly, a link between attitudes toward the need for effective conservation practices, and actually taking actions to conserve, has not been proven. However, positive attitudes probably make a positive difference in bringing about conservation behavior, if only by increasing the effectiveness of persuasive campaigns to reduce energy consumption (Stern & Gardner, 1981).

One persuasive technique is to direct attention to conservation actions. People with proconservation attitudes are alerted to the fact that an opportunity for such behavior exists. Media campaigns are an example. Consistent with the findings on the attitude–behavior relationship discussed in chapter 9, those media campaigns that make very general appeals—such as "conserve energy"—have been shown in studies to be ineffective. However, those campaigns that display the message at the point where action can be taken (e.g., "turn off the lights" signs above electric switches) and at the right time for action, work better. If the message also indicates who is responsible for taking the conservation action, and when it should be taken, it is even more effective.

Advertising reminders like those just mentioned can work on people who hold proconservation attitudes and in whom these attitudes are important or salient in the appropriate situation. But if salience is low in the situation, no conservation behavior is likely to occur despite a positive attitude toward such behavior. Hence, some persuasive techniques attempt to make proconservation attitudes more salient or important to energy consumers. Although studies in this area have not examined conservation attitudes, they have examined other attitudes, such as those on religion and racial integration. Enhancing salience has been shown to make it less likely that people will forget or deny a desired attitude and its implications.

While general attitudes toward energy consumption do not necessarily result in changes in behavior, people are much more likely to conserve if they experience or anticipate experiencing direct personal consequences from an energy problem. Seligman et al. (1979) investigated homeowners' attitudes toward energy conservation in terms of personal comfort and convenience, family health, an optimistic belief in science, the legitimacy of the energy crisis, anticipated financial savings from conservation, the individual's role in saving energy, and the state of the family's finances.

Which of these factors do you think predicted energy saving behavior? Only the first two, personal comfort and convenience and family health were found to be significant. The other factors had negligible or slight influences.

A study conducted by Heberlein, Linz, and Ortiz (1981) strikes an optimistic note. This study examined people's satisfaction with shifting the time of day that they used electricity. This represents a very complicated energy related behavior: changing one's electricity use from peak hours (when energy is most expensive) to off peak hours (when it is least expensive). People were willing to adjust their household schedules to make such a shift if the economic benefit of the shift seemed worthwhile. Subjects reported little dissatisfaction with doing so, suggesting that life satisfaction need not be diminished by consuming less energy. Such findings make the energy future look somewhat brighter. (This conservation method will, of course, be possible only where public utilities install clocks on meters and actually are able to determine the time of day during which electricity is used.)

The studies noted here have focused on home energy consumption, but energy conservation in manufacturing, agriculture, and transportation are equally important, if not more important, targets for social psychological research. The role of social psychology in energy conservation is likely to expand as these areas receive greater attention.

Aging: Life Satisfaction Through the Life Cycle

In many parts of the world older people are honored, looked to for advice and approval, and generally cared for tenderly by their younger relatives, as well as by society at large. In youth-oriented America, however, the elderly are often seen as an embarrassment and a burden. We call them "old fogies," disparaging the wisdom of their years and the validity of their life's experience. We rush on past them, designing homes, fashions, films, and automobiles without thought to their inconvenience and inappropriateness for mature adults. As the number of older people grows (see Figure 16–3), we find more ways to sideline them—in mandatory retirement, senior centers, leisure villages, and "golden age residences."

Today, most people look forward to retirement with mixed feelings. The leisure that should be anticipated as the reward for years of labor and the opportunity to do things that had to be overlooked earlier has become a bittersweet time of economic retrenchment and, ultimately, physical disability. For many people, inflation has made it necessary to use savings for subsistence and emer-

Anyone can get old. All you have to do is live long enough.
Groucho Marx, Groucho and Me

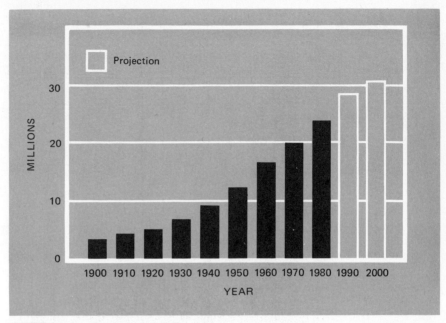

FIGURE 16–3. Population Age 65 and Over
Source: *Adapted from* Growing Old: A Social Perspective, *by R. Baum and M. Baum, 1980, Englewood Cliffs, N.J.: Prentice-Hall.*

gencies, leaving little or nothing for travel, theater-going, and other long desired recreations.

Some demographic and economic facts about older Americans are shown in Tables 16–4 and 16–5 and in Figure 16–4. While we cannot explore the implications of these statistics here, they form the background against which we will discuss several key issues that relate to the psychological quality of life for older people. You will note that these tables subdivide the elderly into narrower age

TABLE 16–4.

Income of Older Americans
(Median Total Money Income)

Age	All Units	Couples	Nonmarried Units
55–61	$12,100	$16,490	$5,260
62–64	8,830	12,750	4,450
65–67	6,250	9,710	3,770
68–69	5,630	8,620	3,740
70–72	5,110	8,140	3,550
73 and over	3,920	6,780	3,130

Source: From Income & Resources of the Aged, U.S. Department of Health, Education, and Welfare, Social Security Administration, SSA Publication No. 13-11727, January, 1980, p. 6.

TABLE 16–5.

Marital and Poverty Status of Older Americans

Age	Married couples		Nonmarried Men		Nonmarried Women	
	Number in Millions	Percent Below Poverty Line	Number in Millions	Percent Below Poverty Line	Number in Millions	Percent Below Poverty Line
55–61	6.2	5	1.2	24	2.3	34
62–64	2.1	7	.4	24	1.1	37
65 and over	6.8	9	2.3	27	8.2	38

Source: Adapted from Income & Resources of the Aged, U.S. Department of Health, Education, and Welfare, Social Security Administration, SSA Publication No. 13-11727, January, 1980, pp. 2 and 33.

groupings. Such groupings reflect the fact that the growing elderly population is not a monolith. It consists of people whose lives are very different depending on their income sources, whether they are married or not, and whether they are physically healthy or not. People today are living longer despite chronic ailments that restrict their activity.

Older people suffer more from chronic illnesses than younger people, require more frequent hospitalization and remain in the hospital longer. Health expenses become considerable, increasing the chance that the older person will have to subsist at a poverty level. Thus, not only does income fall substantially in later years, but health problems increase. None of this can be expected to contribute to a sense of well-being on the part of those older people that are affected.

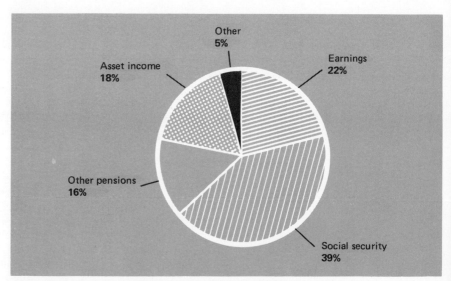

FIGURE 16–4.   Average Sources of Income of People 65 Years and Older
Source: Income and Resources of the Aged, *U.S. Department of Health, Education, and Welfare, January 1980, p. 13.*

One consequence of inadequate income and poor health is that older people may feel that they lack control over their lives. We have already noted several social psychological studies of the effects of a loss of control (see, for example, chapters 4 and 14). Later in this section we will look at some studies that examine what happens when people regain control. First, though, it will be informative to examine some social perceptions of older Americans and (since we all hope eventually to join the legions of older Americans), to ask what contributions social psychologists have made toward providing understanding of some of the problems confronted by this growing population group.

Ageism Stereotype

Like racism and sexism, ageism is a discriminatory attitude based on a stereotype. This stereotype, according to Butler (1980), has three characteristics:

1. Prejudicial attitudes toward older people and toward the aging process—including such attitudes held by the elderly themselves.
2. Discrimination against older people in employment and other areas.
3. Institutional practices that, often unwittingly, help maintain stereotypes about older people, reduce their life opportunities, and undermine their dignity. (p. 8)

As well as the negative forms of ageism that would be expected—Butler reports that many physicians refer to their older patients as "crones," "trolls," and "turkeys"—ageism also takes a benign or patronizing form. Butler, for example, tells of

> an opthamologist who was ushering an older patient with a number of physical disabilities, including severe arthritis and parkinsonism, into an examination room. As the patient entered slowly, he said apologetically, "I'm sorry to take so long—I'm just getting old, Doctor," The doctor replied, "Oh, come on, don't say that, you're not getting older." The doctor's response was certainly meant to be comforting and benevolent, but it failed to take up the older man's concerns about his slowness of movement and his disabilities. The doctor was anxious, and this anxiety interfered with the ability to be effective in helping the patient deal with his own anxiety about getting older. (1980, p. 9)

Advertising, television shows, movies, and books frequently portray older people as physically impaired and undynamic (perhaps sitting in a rocking chair). Rarely are they seen in active, coping roles. (The 1981 film *On Golden Pond* showing an elderly couple grappling with family relationships and coming to grips with diminished physical abilities, was a notable exception.) As we noted in chapter 7, the media exert a powerful influence on attitude formation, especially stereotyped attitude formation. The images portrayed of older people are no exception. Many younger people are surprised to learn—if they should stumble on this information—that a vigorous and healthy sex life for both men and women can and often does persist into the 1980s and beyond. The first reac-

Top left: Hayman / RSVP; top right: Ken Karp / Sirovich Senior Center; bottom left: Ken Karp; bottom right: Ken Karp / Sirovich Senior Center

Older people can continue to be active and contribute to the quality of their own life and that of others. Here, clockwise from upper left, a retired man serves as a volunteer for the blind (this man also recruits other retirees for this purpose); women share a meal provided by a government feeding program at a senior center (nearly all older men still live with their wives, while a majority of older women are divorced or widowed); a woman takes advantage of an art program at a senior center to develop a talent that lay dormant during her working and child-rearing years; and a group of Gray Panthers joins a demonstration (the Gray Panthers are a politically active pressure group concerned with quality-of-life issues for society in general and the elderly in particular).

of many people to the sexuality of older people has too often been crude humor and incredulity.

Rodin and Langer (1980) reviewed the literature to see how labeling or negative stigmatizing affects the perceptions and behavior of older people themselves. Labels in general have been shown to affect how one is perceived by others and, indeed, by oneself. (Recall our discussion of labeling theory in chapter 4.) Negative stereotypes of older people can be believed by older people themselves and influence their behavior. For instance, an older person who forgets something or makes a simple mistake may often say "I'm old and forgetful" and believe that his or her mental capacities are becoming impaired.

In one study, the attitudes toward the elderly of young, middle-aged, and older adults were assessed (Langer & Mulvey, n.d.). Young and middle-aged respondents believed older people to be nonsocial, passive, sickly, and to possess negative personality characteristics. Older adults, in contrast, emphasized social interactions and positive characteristics. All, however, shared a stereotype of the elderly that included senility (Rodin & Langer, 1980).

Fear of senility is very real for older people: one questionnaire study found that only 10 percent of the subjects over 70 years of age felt sure that they would not become senile, as compared to 65 percent of the people between the ages of 25 and 40. In actuality, both views exaggerated the incidence of senility, which in severe form affects only 4 percent of all people over 65, and in mild form affects another 10 percent. The fear of senility reflected by these findings is an indication of the importance we attach to having full control of our mental functions.

Loss of Control

From early infancy, human beings strive to control their environment. Older people are deprived, however, of many means of control—by loss of their work role through retirement, lowered income, physical problems, the departure of children and, sometimes, institutionalization. Schulz (1976) performed an experiment to study the effects of *increased* control on people in a retirement home. The increase in control was touchingly small, but the results were telling.

Schulz predicted that the psychological and physical health of institutionalized older people would be improved if they could predict or control the regular occurrence of some positive event in their lives. Accordingly, he randomly divided 40 subjects into 4 groups: one group could decide when and for how long they would receive visits from a college student (visitor control condition). A second group was told that they would receive such visitors, but could not control when or for how long (predict condition). The third group received visits on a random basis without being told in advance (random condition). A fourth group received no visits (no treatment condition).

That it will never come again
Is what makes life so sweet.
Emily Dickinson

Over the two months' duration of the experiment, the subjects in the visitor control and predict groups changed medication about half as often, used significantly less medication overall, and generally had better physical health than the subjects in the other groups. The visitor control group also showed significantly higher ratings on measures of psychological status. The other two groups that received visits did not perform as well on such measures, but were better off than the group that received no visitors (the no treatment group). On the psychological variable of "hopefulness," the visitor control subjects showed marked increases; they were also less often bored and lonely than the other subjects.

Other field studies have also arrived at encouraging findings. Langer and Rodin (1976), for example, conducted an experiment in a Connecticut nursing home in which the staff on one floor emphasized the residents' own responsibility for themselves. On another floor, the staff emphasized *its* own responsibility for the residents. The subjects in both groups were then given plants to care for. The "staff responsibility" group was told that the staff would water and care for the plant, while the "own responsibility" group was told that they were solely responsible for its care. Various measures of the well-being and activity levels of the groups were taken one week before and three weeks after the start of the experimental situation. The staff filled out questionnaires, the residents filled out a questionnaire. The activity level was more directly measured by unobtrusively placing white adhesive tape on the wheels of the wheelchairs one night, removing the tape the following night, and gauging the amount of activity during the day in between by the extent of the tape discoloration. (Some findings are shown in Table 16–6.) These measures showed that the "own responsibility" group improved significantly in alertness, active participation, and a general feeling of well-being, compared to the "staff responsibility" group.

These experiments show that increased control leads to healthier, happier individuals. A society that deprives its older members of such control through stereotypic labeling and unimaginative institutionalization may be depriving these people of their happiness and health as well.

TABLE 16–6.

Giving Control to the Elderly: Changes in Scores on Self-Report, Interviewer and Nurses' Ratings on 9-Point Scales and Time in Percent

Questionnaire Responses	Own Responsibility	Staff Responsibility
Self-report		
Happy	.28	−.12
Active	.20	−1.28
Perceived Control		
Have	.16	.41
Want	−.05	.17
Interviewer rating		
Alertness	.29	−.37
Nurses' ratings		
General improvement	.40	−.24
Time spent		
Visiting patients	6.78	−3.30
Visiting others	2.14	−4.16
Talking to staff	8.21	1.61
Watching staff	−2.14	4.64

Source: Adapted from "The Effects of Choice and Enhanced Personal Responsibility for the Aged: A Field Experiment in an Institutional Setting," by E. J. Langer & J. Rodin, *Journal of Personality and Social Psychology*, 1976, *34*, 191–198.

Left: Action; Right: Hella Hammid / Photo Researchers, Inc.

Not all people experience a loss of control as they grow older. In fact, as far as one important facet of life goes—the relationship of parents and their children—studies have indicated that many older Americans and their adult children live interdependent lives that are mutually satisfying to both. Older parents want to live close to their children, but they also want to maintain control over the essential aspects of their own lives. This has been called "intimacy at a distance." An informal agreement often exists between older parents and their adult children that each pursue their own interests, goals, and responsibilities, with the children providing minimal services but more substantial levels of affectionate social contact (Baum & Baum, 1980). As the older population grows, we are likely to see many changes in the life-styles of the elderly—for example, more and more older people are likely to continue working past the traditional retirement age, more older people may respond to calls for "Gray Power," and we may even see many older adults relating to—and caring for—their even older parents.

Using Social Psychology to Improve the Quality of Life

Although it has been impossible to consider any of this chapter's topics in great detail, the chapter has provided an overview of a few real-world problems that have been and can be usefully approached from a social psychological perspective. Although knowledge can be valued for its own sake, most social psy-

We should all be concerned about the future because we will have to spend the rest of our lives there.
Charles F. Kettering

chologists do believe that their research can and ultimately will improve the quality of life for people everywhere. The more we learn about our social lives—through refined research methods and refined theories of social behavior—the easier it will be for us as a society to alleviate the social problems we encounter in our personal, community, national, and international lives. As scientific social psychology matures, it is likely to play an increasing role in helping us to design and to achieve a social world in which everyone can have and enjoy—not merely a chicken in every pot—but a fully satisfying life.

Answering Questions about Social Psychology and the Quality of Life

1. It appears that life satisfaction consists of a number of components. Surprisingly, research indicates that the most important of these is not wealth. When people are asked to rank major life domains in order of importance, the list is headed by health, marriage, family life, faith in national government, and friendship, in that order.

2. Social psychologists have used a variety of approaches to measure life satisfaction. Some have asked people to think of a ladder of which the top rung is "the best life you can imagine" and the bottom is "a life that is terrible," and to rate their own lives. Others have divided life experiences into a number of domains such as health, family life, and housing, and asked people to rate the pleasantness or unpleasantness of their own experiences in each domain.

3. Increasingly, women are devoting their lives to careers outside the home. Research has shown that this has led to greater psychological health for working women and most members of their families. They are significantly less likely to commit suicide, experience lasting depression, or suffer low self-esteem than women who are not employed. Children of working mothers can be as compliant, affectionate, and independent as those of nonworking mothers. Some husbands of working women, however, report higher rates of nervousness, headaches, and weight loss, among other distresses, than men whose wives are not employed.

4. Advertisers and marketing experts have made extensive use of the findings of social psychologists who study persuasion and attitude change. Cognitive response theory and research on source credibility, for example, have guided the construction of persuasive advertising messages. Advertisers often call on prestigious or highly credible sources, such as a famous athlete or film star, to present their messages. Also, most advertisers do not give information about competing brands for fear of producing counterarguments (a central component of cognitive response theory) against their products.

5. Social psychologists have given their attention to many social problems. Helping people to stop smoking and to reduce energy consumption are two examples. One study, for example, taught teenagers specific techniques they could use to resist the pressure to smoke that was exerted by peers, parents, and the media. Social psychologists investigating energy use have found that when subjects are given goals for energy savings and receive fre-

quent and detailed feedback about their energy use, there is a significant saving in homeowners' energy consumption.

6. It is widely believed that old people are an embarrassment, a burden, passive, and forgetful or senile. In actuality, severe senility afflicts only 4 percent of all persons over 65. Social psychologists suspect, and experiments seem to confirm, that passivity in the elderly results from being deprived of control of life events, often through institutionalization.

Summary

Life satisfaction—the quality of life—is dependent on each individual's expectations and standards of comparison. The psychological components that determine life satisfaction are both **cognitive** (conscious, objective perceptions) and **affective** (subjective feelings).

Using large scale survey methods, psychologists have identified the specific areas or **domains** of life satisfaction that have the greatest impact on the quality of life, such as health, marriage, family relationships, confidence in the nation's government, adequate housing, and job satisfaction.

Although income and financial circumstances ranked low on the scale, an absence of economic well-being seems to have a statistical relationship to an absence of personal well-being. Suicides, murders, imprisonments, and deaths all increase in times of economic hardship. Social psychologists have sought measures of economic well-being. Receiving raises and salary adjustments for inflation seems to have intrinsic value to people as a measure of job success, quite apart from their actual impact on personal finances. In times of hardship people cope in a variety of ways, primarily by cutting back on expenses, even for needed items.

One domain important to both men and women was occupation. Studies of the large population of married women with and without children who have returned to the workplace indicate that they are as affected by the same job attributes as men, including challenge, stimulation, financial rewards, co-worker relationships, and tedium. However, women face the additional problems of discrimination and lower salary levels.

One consistent finding in the area of marital satisfaction is that men are slightly more satisfied with their marriages than women. Satisfaction with marriage declines from the time of marriage through the childbearing years, and increases after children leave home. The most popular current explanation of divorce is **exchange theory**, according to which marriages are dissolved when the rewards for keeping them going are lower, and the costs higher, than for living alone.

Because basic needs for food and shelter are generally met in modern American society, the quality of life today is generally measured in terms of what people *want*, not what they need. Advertising, designed according to principles of social psychological theory, helps people determine what they want.

Psychological principles have also been used to design programs aimed at better public health. Researchers have identified five areas in which behavior change could be beneficial: etiology of illness, prevention, management, treatment, and the delivery of health care. Some intervention techniques that have been tried to get people to stop smoking and to take measures against heart disease include **therapies** (operant procedures, sensitization/desensitization techniques) and **public opinion messages** (film, radio and TV advertisements, books, pamphlets). Although many studies have failed to demonstrate any benefits from either of these approaches, newer research suggests that manipulations directed more toward the message receiver, and less toward the message itself, will have greater success.

Two social science approaches have been taken to encourage energy conservation. The behavioral approach seeks to modify conservation behavior through providing information, promptings, incentives, and feedback. Studies have demonstrated the effectiveness of the behavioral approach. The persuasive approach seeks to change attitudes to favor conservation and to make the attitudes salient enough to cause conservation behavior; feedback providing information about short-term, personal consequences is particularly effective.

The increasing population of older Americans includes many who live in poverty and experience health problems. Like racism and sexism, **ageism** is a discriminatory attitude based on a stereotype. The media help to perpetuate ageism, and negative labels and stigmatization affect not only the perception of older people by others but the perception of older people by themselves. The loss of control over their lives causes depression and debilitation for many of the aged; this process has been experimentally reversed in institutional settings with impressive physical and psychological gains by the subjects who participated in the studies.

Suggested Additional Reading

Baum, A., & Singer, J. E. (eds.). *Energy conservation: Psychological perspectives.* Advances in environmental psychology series (Vol. 3). Hillsdale, N.J.: Erlbaum, 1981.

Baum, A., & Singer, J. E. (eds.). *Environment and health.* Advances in environmental psychology series (Vol. 4). Hillsdale, N.J.: Erlbaum, 1982.

Bickman, L. (ed.). *Applied social psychology annual* (Vol. 3). Beverly Hills, Calif.: Sage Publications, 1982.

Duck, S., & Gilmour, R. (eds.). *Developing personal relationships* (Vol. 2). New York: Academic Press, 1981.

Duck, S., & Gilmour, R. (eds.). *Personal relationships in disorder* (Vol. 3). New York: Academic Press, 1981.

Duck, S., & Gilmour, R. (eds.), *Dissolving personal relationships* (Vol. 4). New York: Academic Press, 1982.

Geis, M. L. *The language of television advertising.* New York: Academic Press, 1982.

Seligman, C., & Becker, L. J. (eds.). Energy conservation. *Journal of Social Issues,* 1981 *37,* (2).

Stewart, A. J., & Platt, M. B. (eds.). Studying women in a changing world. *Journal of Social Issues,* *38*(1), 1982.

Stringer, P. (ed.). *Confronting social issues: Some applications of social psychology* (Vol. 1). New York: Academic Press, 1982.

Stone, G. C., Cohen, F., & Adler, N. E. *Health psychology—a handbook.* San Francisco: Jossey-Bass, 1979.

Stroebe, W., & Meyer, W. (eds.). *Social psychology and economics.* Letchworth, U.K.: The British Psychological Society, 1982.

GLOSSARY

Actor-observer differences A pattern of perception in which a participant arrives at an attribution unlike that of an onlooker.

Affective component Subjective feeling-states or moods and the physiological responses that accompany an attitude.

Ageism A discriminatory attitude based on stereotypes about older people.

Aggression Any behavior intended to harm or injure another individual who does not want to be so treated.

Altruism Concern for the interests of others without regard for one's self-interest.

Androgyny Having both traditionally male and female characteristics simultaneously.

Archival studies The examination of documents to determine naturally occurring phenomena.

Attachment The physical and emotional closeness of an infant to a parent.

Attention decrement People's tendency to lose interest and pay less heed to recent information than to information presented earlier.

Attitude A predisposition to respond in a certain way to a particular object, event, or experience.

Attribution A person's perception of the reasons for other people's behavior.

Attribution biases Erroneous judgments that occur because of distortions in information processing.

Attribution model of crowding The theory holding that if we feel aroused under conditions of high density, we are likely to attribute the stress we feel to the presence of others and thus feel crowded.

Attribution theory The area of social psychology concerned with how perceivers determine the causes of behavior.

Averaging model Anderson's model of information integration, holding that we evaluate positively or negatively, and average all items to form an overall impression.

Balance theory Heider's thesis that people are motivated to maintain consistency and balance in their relationships with other people.

Behavioral (or **conative**) **component** The physical and mental processes that prepare the individual to act in a certain manner.

Behavioral sciences Disciplines dealing with observations about the activities, including mental operations and motor responses, of animals and humans.

Behavioral sink Calhoun's term for the subordination of a normal function to another desire.

Bias Systematic errors in an experimental situation that can distort results.

Bogus pipeline An attitude research technique in which the experimenter claims to know the subject's genuine attitudes from a (phony) machine that provides direct physiological measures.

Boomerang effect An attitude change in the opposite direction of that intended by a message.

Case study Intensive examination of an individual, group, or event.

Causality Change in one variable that directly produces change in another.

Causal schemata model Kelley's model for how we explain an event using consistency, distinctiveness, and consensus information.

Central trait theory The view that certain characteristics are of primary importance in determining how we perceive other individuals.

Chance Random occurrence.

Change-of-meaning effect The tendency for information to alter the meaning we give to other information.

Channel The medium of communication through which a message travels.

Classical conditioning theory The principle that when a neutral stimulus is paired with a stimulus that naturally elicits a particular response (the unconditioned stimulus), the neutral stimulus will elicit a similar response and thus become a conditioned stimulus.

Cognitive biases Distortions in perception or judgment due to the ways in which people process information.

Cognitive component The beliefs and opinions through which an attitude is expressed.

Cognitive dissonance An uncomfortable state that occurs when actions conflict with beliefs. *Cognitive dissonance theory* focuses on ways in which we make our beliefs and attitudes consistent.

Cognitive heuristics Standard mental shorthand devices that serve as an organizing system to reduce the complexities of observable data.

Cognitive maps Mental representations of people's environment that reflect their experience of it.

Cognitive theory A theory of behavior stating that humans actively perceive and interpret stimuli in their environment to create meaning in their social interactions.

Cohesiveness The result of all forces that cause members to remain in a group.

Communication Any way one mind affects another, including not only written or spoken words but also body gestures, nonverbal sounds, and television commercials.

Communication channel Any means by which a message travels between sender and receiver.

Complementarity The tendency for people to seek out those who have qualities they lack.

Conformity The tendency to adopt the attitudes and behaviors of others.

Congruity theory Theory of attitude change focusing on our approval of a message and its source; if sources we like promote ideas we approve (or vice versa), the message will be congruent to our frame of reference.

Consistency theories Theories of attitude change holding that people strive to achieve cognitive equilibrium.

Consensus In Kelley's theory, the degree to which people act the same way toward the same entity.

Consistency In Kelley's theory, the degree to which people act in the same way whenever a particular cause is present.

Constructs Qualities identified by the names and definitions we give them.

Content analyses The systematic study of existing material in order to identify its components.

Contextual effect Changed or enhanced meanings of words due to their association with other words.

Continuous process theories Theories that human development is primarily influenced by environment and occurs independently of any timetable or maturational sequence.

Control group A group of subjects that does not experience an experimental treatment or manipulation.

Correlation An association or relationship between variables. Changes in one variable do not necessarily *cause* changes in a correlated variable.

Correlational studies Systematic but nonexperimental studies of the relationships between specific variables.

Correlation coefficient An index of how strongly two variables are related to one another.

Correspondent inference Attribution of intentions derived from observed behavior.

Covariation bias Inferring a causal relationship between two variables where none exists.

Covariation principle The attribution of an effect to one of several possible causes.

Credibility The believability of a source of information based on expertise and trustworthiness.

Data Observations and/or factual information gathered to support a hypothesis.

Deception cues Nonverbal behaviors that indicate an attempt to conceal the truth.

Decode To translate a message from the (symbolic) form in which it was transmitted.

Deindividuation Temporarily losing self-awareness and becoming a kind of group-being.

Density The ratio of population to spatial area.

Dependent variable The variable that experimenters measure, having manipulated another (independent) variable.

Destination The place a message eventually comes to rest, e.g., the receiver's brain.

Determinism The belief that events are systematically and causally related.

Discounting hypothesis The disregard of subsequent information that contradicts previous data.

Discounting principle The dismissal of less plausible explanations in attributing the cause of an event.

Discrimination An overt action taken against one or more members of a group because of their group affiliation.

Dissonance In Festinger's theory, the psychological discomfort that occurs when two related conditions are in conflict. *Dissonance reduction* is the effort to reduce dissonance by altering one of two conflicting cognitions.

Distinctiveness In Kelley's theory, the degree to which a behavior occurs only when a particular cause is present.

Dominant response tendencies Zajonc's term for patterns of well-learned behavior.

Door-in-the-face technique A method of persuasion based on the tendency to comply with a small request after refusing a larger one.

Ego In Freud's theory, the "executive branch" of the mind, which includes reality and mediates between the id and the superego.

Egoism Behavior determined completely by the desire to serve self-interest.

Emblems Body movements and postures that can substitute for spoken language.

Empiricism Reliance on systematic data collection and observation to test theoretical predictions.

Encode To transform a message into sound or other symbols.

Engulfing or **dominant stimulus effect** The view that the object or person who dominates the visual field is responsible for an event.

Environmental psychology The branch of psychology concerned with the effects of the physical world on human behavior.

Equilibrium model of multichannel communication The view that verbal and nonverbal behaviors are kept in balance appropriate to the degree of intimacy between two communicators.

Evaluation research Systematic assessment of the effectiveness of social intervention programs.

Exchange theory The theory that the benefits of a relationship are weighed against its costs.

Experimental studies Systematic testing of a hypothesis by manipulating one or more variables.

External attribution The ascription of events to sources over which we have no control.

External validity The ability to generalize to the larger population from research results that are based on a sample.

Factor analysis Simplification of complex data by considering together variables that co-vary or are otherwise related.

False consensus bias Using one's own behavior as the standard by which others are judged.

Feedback Information from the receiver to the sender to confirm receipt of a message.

Field studies or **Field experiments** Observation of social behavior in a natural setting.

Foot-in-the-door technique A method of persuasion based on the tendency for people who comply with small requests eventually to comply with larger ones.

Free response data Subjects' responses to a questionnaire which allows them to use descriptive terminology of their own choosing.

Frustration Interference with the achievement of a goal at a particular time in the behavior sequence. The belief, unsubstantiated by experimental evidence, that this causes aggression, is known as the *frustration-aggression hypothesis*.

Functional distance The space between interacting people that affects friendship development; determined by architectural features as well as physical distance.

Fundamental attribution error The belief that personal or dispositional factors are more important than situational or environmental influences.

Grammar Rules governing the structure of language in such areas as word forms and order, and sentence structure.

Group polarization The tendency for a group decision to be either more cautious or more risky than an individual decision, depending on the dominant tendency of the group.

Halo effect The inference of other positive (or negative) traits from observation of a single but major positive (or negative) trait.

Hawthorne effect A change in subjects' behavior due to being observed and unrelated to experimental variables.

Hedonism Acting solely to gain pleasure and avoid pain.

Helping Giving assistance to another with a definite object or goal in mind.

Hospitality effect The tendency for the owner or occupant of a territory to maintain dominance in a conversation.

Human ecology Sometimes used instead of "environmental psychology."

Hypotheses Testable predictions derived from theory.

Id In Freud's theory, the part of the personality containing inherited elements such as instincts.

Identification Acceptance and internalization of another person's values and needs into one's own personality.

Illusory correlation Erroneous inferences based on apparent associations between traits.

Illustrators Gestures that accompany speech.

Images Visually interpreted means of communication, such as written words, pictures, signs, and body movements.

Implicit personality theories People's ideas about which personality traits are associated with one another.

Impression management Our efforts to make ourselves agreeable to others.

Independent variable The factor manipulated in an experiment in order to measure its effect on the other (dependent) variable.

Individuation The differentiation of individuals from one another.

Information overload An excessive amount of stimuli to which people may be exposed.

Information source The origin of a message.

Informational (social) influence Social influence produced by providing others with information.

Informed consent Subjects' permission to participate in an experiment, granted with the knowledge that they may experience psychological discomfort.

Instinctual theories of aggression The view that humans have a natural disposition to aggression that must be controlled in socially acceptable ways.

Interaction effect The tendency to view the combination of a negative trait with a positively evaluated role (such as irresponsible father), and vice versa, more negatively than it would be if perceived alone. Also, the result of two or more combined independent variables producing greater influence than any one of those variables alone.

Interaction process analysis A system for coding the content of communications by observing the behavior of the communicating individuals.

Internal attribution The ascription of events to our own actions, rather than to sources beyond our control.

Internal validity A measure of an experimenter's success in producing intended experimental manipulations; this assures that experimental results are not influenced by outside factors or by a flaw in the research design.

Interpersonal press A function of the number of persons per room per housing unit.

Interview The collection of data directly from a respondent by the experimenter.

Invariance Belief that causal relationships between events do not change over time or over location.

Jury simulation studies Mock trials in which carefully prepared "evidence" is presented as the experimental manipulation to subjects who serve as jurors, thus allowing the study of psychological processes that may take place during real trials.

Just world hypothesis The belief that good things happen to good people and vice versa.

Kinesics The study of the body movements and postures consciously or unconsciously used to convey messages.

Labeling theory The thesis that the terms or "labels" we use to describe people are incorporated into their self-images.

Language The symbol system of vocal sounds used by human beings to convey meaning to one another.

Leadership The intentional influence of a group's activities and the direction of activities toward a goal.

Leakage cues Nonverbal behaviors that communicate true emotion or information and contradict the content of a verbal message.

Learned helplessness The belief, a result of repeated failure, that no action can change one's situation.

Learning theory The belief that behaviors are acquired through a stimulus-response relationship between the environment and an individual.

Loneliness The sense of loss that occurs when a person has too few or inadequate social interactions.

Loneliness anxiety A totally negative feeling that results from alienation between people.

Low-ball technique A method of gaining compliance in which a person who agrees to a particular activity later discovers that more is being required.

Mass media Modes of communication such as television, radio, books, and recordings that reach very large audiences.

Medium of communication The vehicle that carries a message from the source to the target or recipient; channel.

Modeling The process through which new responses are learned by observation and imitation of the behavior of others.

Motivational bias A non-objective perspective that fulfills a need of the perceiver; for example, taking a positive view of our own behavior to raise self-esteem.

Multiple-act criterion A research tool that averages the various behaviors relating to a specific attitude in order to deduce a general behavior tendency.

Multidimensional scaling A method of reducing the number of individual personality traits by grouping them according to the relationships among them.

Multiple indicators Several items on a scale or questionnaire that measure the same attitude; used to overcome individual idiosyncrasies and to insure reliability.

Multiple necessary causes Preconditions to a particular outcome.

Multiple sufficient causes Several alternative factors that might produce or result in a particular outcome.

Naive psychology People's tendency to make commonsense attributions, or find logical reasons for behavior.

Negative correlation Variables change together, but in opposite directions (one increases while the other decreases).

Negative personal norms A sense of moral obligation not to help particular causes or aid particular individuals.

Negativity effect The tendency for subjects in impression integration studies to give extra weight to negative items.

Noise Extraneous sound that causes distortion of a message.

Nonexperimental observations Collection of data about some aspect of naturally occurring behavior.

Nonverbal synchrony The tendency for interacting people to coordinate their body movements and speech patterns.

Normative social influence Group pressure based on threats to reject group members who do not accept the positions of the group.

Null hypothesis A statement that the groups in an experiment are the same and that any differences between them are due to chance. By manipulation of variables, the experimenter attempts to disprove this hypothesis.

Objective self-awareness The sense of being an object of other people's observations.

Objectivity Non-biased research procedures that make possible replication by other investigators.

One-group preexperimental design A research method in which the same subjects are tested both before and after an experimental treatment.

Operational definitions The translation of complex variables into readily measured items such as test scores or survey questions.

Operationalism Agreement that theoretical terms must be objective and measurable.

Organization A structured group of people whose activities are planned and coordinated to achieve a specific purpose or goal.

Paralanguage Vocal effects that accompany speech and help to convey meaning, including tone of voice, word emphasis, volume, and speed of speech.

Peer group Individuals who are similar to the self serve as an important source of beliefs about the self and may introduce or reinforce values and attitudes.

Perseverance effect The tendency to maintain social inferences and theories even when confronted with contradictory information.

Personal construct Our own individual organizing system, the result of our unique background, experience, and values, which helps us make sense of our world.

Personal norms Internalized social norms, values, or obligations.

Physiological theory Belief that much of human behavior is determined by biological or physical make up.

Pleasure principle In Freud's theory, the id's need to discharge the excess energy of external stimuli or internal impulses to reduce tension.

Population density The number of people contained in a given area.

Positive correlation When variables change together in the same direction (both increasing and both decreasing).

Potential productivity The maximum performance that can be achieved, given the demands of a particular task and the available resources.

Prejudice A biased, generally negative attitude directed toward some people because they are members of a specific group.

Primacy effect The tendency for the first information received to be the most influential.

Primary territories Areas owned and used exclusively and permanently by individuals or groups, clearly identified as theirs, and used by them on a regular basis.

Prosocial behavior Any actions that benefit another, regardless of the costs or benefits to the actor.

Prototypes A type of schema that represents the "typical" instance of a person or object.

Proxemics The study of interpersonal distance, among the subtlest forms of nonverbal communication.

Proximity Physical closeness, a factor that influences attraction; greater proximity generally leads to increased attraction.

Psychoanalytic theory Freud's theory of human behavior and personality, holding that the key internal drives must be expressed.

Psychology The study of human and animal behavior, including mental and emotional processes.

Psychosexual stages In Freud's model, each period of human development is characterized by the focus of sexual energy on a particular area of the body; frustrations encountered at any stage can arrest development.

Public territories Areas to which everyone has free access.

Quality of life Well-being, happiness, satisfaction; a variable that depends on each person's expectations and standards of comparison.

Quasi-experimental designs Simple research which observes the effects of a manipulation (generally in a real-life situation) where random assignment of subjects is impossible.

Questionnaire A series of questions designed to elicit data from respondents.

Random assignment In an experiment, a method of ensuring that any given subject has an equal chance of being placed in the test or in the control group.

Random sampling A method of insuring that groups of individuals being studied is representative of the population as a whole.

Reactance theory The view that when people's freedom to engage in a particular behavior is threatened, they will be motivated to regain that freedom.

Reality principle In Freud's theory, the ego's function of preventing the id from discharging energy until an appropriate object is found.

Receiver The person to whom a communication is directed.

Recency effects The tendency for later information to have a greater impact on overall judgments.

Reference group A group to which an individual aspires to belong.

Relative deprivation theory The argument that one's sense of material well-being may suffer by comparison with others in similar situations, leading to discontent.

Reliability Consistency of results. The ability of experimental or test results to be reproduced.

Research hypothesis In an experiment, the prediction that a manipulated variable will have an effect and that research results will not be due to chance differences between groups.

Response styles A patterned series of responses to questionnaire items; may be acquiescent style (the tendency to give "yes" answers) or rebellious (the tendency to give negative answers).

Risky shift The tendency for groups to make more daring decisions than an individual might make.

Role-playing An experimental method that asks subjects to behave as they would in a given situation.

Salience effect A form of attribution bias in which we respond to the most outstanding or important of the stimuli in the environment at a given time.

Sapir-Whorf hypothesis The view that our language influences our interpretation of our environment; the theory of linguistic relativity.

Schemas Cognitive structures containing our knowledge about some specific domain and its attribution, allowing us to categorize and interpret new information related to that domain.

Scientific method Systematic description, explanation, prediction, and control; specifications for making observations so that a discipline can be considered a science.

Scripts A type of schema that describes the series of steps in a particular event.

Secondary territories Spaces that are only partly controlled by their users, sometimes in symbolic or even illegal ways, such as neighborhood bars or stretches of beach customarily used by certain individuals.

Self-concept Our understanding of who and what we are, based on life experience, containing certain assumptions, and enabling us to make predictions about ourselves.

Self-disclosures Revelation of information about ourselves; those who disclose too much or too little may have social adjustment problems.

Self-esteem Our appraisal of ourselves, an evaluation of what we are, including both positive and negative aspects.

Self-monitoring Our control of how we appear to others.

Self-perception The ways in which we come to understand who we are. *Self-perception theory* holds that people learn about their own attitudes, emotions, and other inner states by inferring them from their own behavior, using the same external cues that an outsider would infer from our own internal state.

Self-schemas Our understanding of the kind of person we are, based on observation of our past social interactions.

Semantic meaning The underlying content of words that adds to their dictionary or literal meanings.

Sender The transmitter of a communication.

Sex roles The socially-effected behaviors for a person of a given sex. Sex role stereotypes are commonly-held expectations about male and female behaviors and traits; like other stereotypes, these are often inaccurate, restricting, and lead to discrimination.

Sexual identification A process, beginning early in life, in which children label themselves as boys or girls, realize that this label gives them group membership, and that it is permanent.

Similarity Having something in common with another person; a factor in attraction.

Simulation An experimental method in which subjects are asked to behave as they believe they would if the situation were real.

Situational factors Incidental and contextual variables that may influence attitude change, persuasion, and other aspects of human behavior.

Sleeper effect The tendency for low-credibility sources to gain impact over time.

Social comparison theory The view that we seek out others in order to interpret and find social support for our reactions.

Social density The number of people in an area, regardless of the size of the area.

Social facilitation theory The idea that observing others engaging in the same behavior will not only trigger a reaction that a person is prepared to give but also intensify that reaction.

Social impact theory The idea that the presence of others has an effect on an individual's performance.

Socialization; socialization process The process by which individuals learn what their community considers socially important and acceptable behavior.

Social judgment theory The idea that if a message falls within an individual's range of acceptable positions in relation to an attitude, attitude change occurs in the direction of the message.

Social norms The implicit or explicit rules and standards of behavior held by a society.

Social overload An excess of social interaction; situations with little privacy.

Social psychology A discipline that attempts to understand how the thoughts, feelings, and behaviors of individuals are influenced by the actual, imagined, or implied presence of others. Begins with commonsense observations and subjects them to the rigors of scientific method.

Sociobiological theory The view that social behaviors have evolved through the process of natural selection.

Sociofugal spaces Areas in which furniture is arranged so as to reduce social interaction.

Sociopetal spaces Places where furniture is arranged to encourage social interaction.

Sociotechnical model Woodward's view that any organization is an interacting combination of a certain technology and a certain social system.

Sounds In communication, all spoken words, paralanguage, and music.

Source derogation Lack of confidence in the communicator or in the source of his or her information.

Stage theories The idea that human development occurs in successive but distinct steps.

Statistical significance Experimental group differences which are so great that there is very low probability that they are due to chance.

Status A position of social rank within a group.

Stereotype A broad generalization about a person's characteristics based on group membership. *Stereotyping* or acting on such generalizations is a potentially negative aspect of schemas.

Stimulus overload An unpleasant state that results from an inability to shut out extraneous stimuli.

Stress reduction theory The view that we affiliate with others primarily to reduce tension.

Superego In Freud's theory, one of the three parts of the personality, the enforcer of the moral code or internalization of parental authority.

Survey The collection of information about naturally occurring behavior such as voting preference, typically using interviews and/or questionnaires.

Symbolic interactionism The theory that human behavior is primarily determined by social relationships and communication with others.

Symbols Arbitrary systems of sounds and images that allow us to refer to things not immediately present and to store complex information for future use.

Syntax The rules that govern sentence word order and the relationship between parts of a sentence.

Systems approach The view that any aspect or factor must be seen in the context of related components; in environmental psychology, for example, the idea that factors can be understood in isolation.

Target The intended recipient of a communication.

Territoriality The tendency of many animals to mark, maintain, or defend areas as their own. *Territorial markers* are the physical or symbolic means used to indicate an individual's own area.

Theories Explanations of observed data that attempt to predict phenomena.

Theory of norm activation Schwartz's model that attempts to predict when people will act on their personal norms or social obligations.

Theory of reasoned action The view that people consider the implications of their actions and that most actions are consciously controlled.

Therapies Techniques used to get people to change destructive or counter-productive behaviors.

Variables Concrete and measurable representations of constructs; social status, for example, can be represented by income.

Violence Aggression that involves the intentional use of physical force.

Weapons effect Berkowitz and LePage's addition to frustration-aggression theory, that frustrated individuals will respond more aggressively when a weapon is present.

BIBLIOGRAPHY

Abel, G. G., Barlow, D. H., Blanchard, E., & Guild, D. The components of rapists' sexual arousal. *Archives of General Psychiatry*, 1977, *34*, 395–403.

Abelson, J. R. P. Are attitudes necessary? In B. T. King & E. McGinnies (Eds.), *Attitudes, conflict, and social change*. New York: Academic Press, 1972.

Abelson R. Computers, polls and public opinion: Some puzzles and paradoxes. *Trans-Action*, 1968, *5*, 20–27.

Abelson, R., & Miller, J. Negative persuasion via personal insult. *Journal of Experimental Social Psychology*, 1967, *3*, 321–333.

Abramson, L. Y., Seligman, M. E. P., & Teasdale, J. D. Learned helplessness in humans: Critique and reformulation. *Journal of Abnormal Psychology*, 1978, *87*, 49–74.

Adair, J. G., & Spinner, B. Subject access to cognitive-processes-demand characteristics and verbal report. *Journal for the Theory of Social Behavior*, 1981 (1), 31–52.

Aderman, D. Elation, depression, and helping behavior. *Journal of Personality and Social Psychology*, 1972, *24*, 91–101.

Adler, F. *Sisters in crime: The rise of the new female criminal*. New York: McGraw-Hill, 1975.

Adler, R. (Ed.). *Research on the effects of television advertising on children*. Washington, D.C.: Government Printing Office, 1977.

Adorno, T. W., Frenkel-Brunswick, E., Levinson, D. J., & Sanford, R. N. *The authoritarian personality*. New York: Harper & Row, 1950.

Aiello, J. R., Nicosia, G., & Thompson, D. E. Physiological, social, and behavioral consequences of crowding on children and adolescents. *Child Development*, 1979, *50*, 195–202.

Aiello, J. R., & Thompson, D. E. When conversation fails: Mediating effects of sex and locus of control at extended interaction distances. Paper presented at the annual convention of the American Psychological Association, Toronto, Canada, 1978.

Ajzen, I., & Fishbein, M. *Understanding attitudes and predicting social behavior*. Englewood Cliffs, N.J.: Prentice-Hall, 1980.

Ajzen, I., Timko, C., & White, J. B. Self-monitoring and the attitude-behavior relation. *Journal of Personality and Social Psychology*, 1982, *42*, 426–435.

Alderfer, C. P., & Lodahl, T. M. A quasi experiment on the use of experiential methods in the classroom. *Journal of Applied Behavioral Science*, 1971, *7*, 43–69.

Allen, T. J. *Managing the flow of technology*. Cambridge, Mass.: MIT Press, 1977.

Allen, V. L. Situational factors in conformity. In L. Berkowitz (Ed.), *Advances in Experimental Social Psychology* (Vol. 2). New York: Academic Press, 1965, 133–170.

Allen, V. L. Social support for non-conformity. In L. Berkowitz (Ed.), *Advances in experimental social psychology* (Vol. 8). New York: Academic Press, 1975.

Allen, V. L., & Atkinson, M. L. Identification of spontaneous and deliberate behavior. *Journal of Nonverbal Behavior*, 1981, *5*, 224–237.

Allen, V. L., & Levine, J. M. Consensus & conformity. *Journal of Experimental Social Psychology*, 1969, *5*, 389–399.

Allen, V., & Levine, J. Social support and conformity: The role of independent assessment of reality. *Journal of Experimental Social Psychology*, 1971, *7*, 48–58.

Allport, F. H. *Social Psychology*. Cambridge, Mass.: Riverside Press, 1924.

Allport, G. W. Attitudes. In C. Murchison (Ed.), *A handbook of social psychology*. Worcester, Mass.: Clark University Press, 1935.

Allport, G. The historical background of modern social psychology. In G. Lindzey & E. Aronson (Eds.), *The handbook of social psychology* (Vol. 1). Reading, Mass.: Addison-Wesley, 1968.

Allport, G. W. *The nature of prejudice*. Garden City, N.Y.: Doubleday-Anchor, 1954.

Allport, G., & Ross, J. Personal religious orientation and prejudice. *Journal of Personality and Social Psychology*, 1967, *5*, 432–443.

Almond, G. A., & Verba, S. *The civic culture*. Princeton, N.J.: Princeton University Press, 1963.

Alper, T. P., & Karchin, S. S. Memory for socially relevant material. *Journal of Abnormal and Social Psychology*, 1952, *47*, 25–38.

Altman, I. *The environment and social behavior: Privacy, personal space, territory, crowding*. Monterey, Calif.: Brooks/Cole, 1975.

Altman, I. Environmental psychology and social psychology. *Personality and Social Psychology Bulletin*, 1976, *2*, 96–113.

Altman, I., & Haythorn, W. The ecology of isolated groups. *Behavioral Science*, 1967, *12*, 169–182.

Altman, I., Taylor, D. A., & Wheeler, L. Ecological aspects of group behavior in social isolation. *Journal of Applied Social Psychology*, 1971, *1*, 76–100.

American Bar Association. *Reducing victim/witness intimidation: A package*. Washington, D.C., 1980.

American Bar Association. Legal education and bar admission statistics, 1963–1981. *A review of legal education in the United States—1981–1982: Law schools and bar admission requirements.* Chicago: American Bar Association, 1982.

Amir, Y. Contact hypothesis in ethnic relations. *Psychological Bulletin,* 1969, *71,* 319–342.

Andersen, S. M., & Bem, S. L. Sex typing and androgyny in dyadic interaction: Individual differences in responsiveness to physical attractiveness. *Journal of Personality and Social Psychology,* 1981, *41,* 74–86.

Anderson, N. H. Application of a linear-serial model to a personality-impression task using serial presentation. *Journal of Personality and Social Psychology,* 1968, *10,* 354–362.

Anderson, N. H. Averaging versus adding as a stimulus-combination rule in impression formation. *Journal of Experimental Psychology,* 1965, *70,* 394–400.

Apodaca, Cooper, and Madden v. Oregon, *United States Reports,* 1972, *406,* 404–415.

Apple, W., Streeter, L. A., & Krauss, R. B. Effects of pitch and speech rate on personal attributions. *Journal of Personality and Social Psychology,* 1979, *37,* 715–727.

Apsler, P., & Sears, D. O. Warning, personal involvement, and attitude change. *Journal of Personality and Social Psychology,* 1968, *9,* 162–166.

Arafat, I. S., & Cotton, W. L. Masturbation practices of males and females. *Journal of Sex Research,* 1974, *10,* 293–307.

Archer, D., & Gartner, R. Violent acts and violent times: A comparative approach to postwar homicide rates. *American Sociological Review,* 1976, *41,* 937–963.

Ard, B. N. Premarital sexual experience: A longitudinal study. *Journal of Sex Research,* 1974, *10,* 32–39.

Arendt, H. *Eichmann in Jerusalem: A report of the banality of evil.* New York: Viking, 1963.

Ares, C., Rankin, A., & Sturz, H. The Manhattan bail project: And interim report on the use of pretrial parole. *New York University Law Reivew,* 1963, *38,* 67–95.

Argyle, M., & Dean, J. Eye-contact, distance, and affiliation. *Sociometry,* 1965, *28,* 289–304.

Argyle, M., & Ingham, R. Gaze, mutual gaze, and proximity. *Semiotica,* 1972, *6*(2), 32–50.

Argyle, M., & Kendon, A. The experimental analysis of social performance. In L. Berkowitz (Ed.), *Advances in experimental social psychology* (Vol. 3). New York: Academic Press, 1967, 55–98.

Arkin, R. M., Appelman, A. J., & Burger, J. M. Social anxiety, self-presentation, and the self-serving bias in causal attribution. *Journal of Personality and Social Psychology,* 1980, *38,* 25–35.

Arkin, R. M., Gleason, J. M., & Johnston, S. Effect of perceived choice, expected outcome, and observed outcome of an action of the causal attributions of actors. *Journal of Experimental Social Psychology,* 1976, *12,* 151–158.

Aronfreed, J. *Conduct and conscience: The socialization of internalized control over behavior.* New York: Academic Press, 1968.

Aronson, E. Threat and obedience. *TransAction,* 1966, *3,* 25–27.

Aronson, E. The psychology of insufficient justification: An analysis of some conflicting data. In S. Feldman (Ed.), *Cognitive Consistency.* New York: Academic Press, 1966, pp. 115–133.

Aronson, E. Dissonance theory: Progress and problems. In R. P. Abelson, E. Aronson, W. J. McGuire, T. M. Newcomb, M. J. Rosenberg, & P. H. Tannenbaum (Eds.), *Theories of cognitive consistency: A sourcebook.* Chicago: Rand McNally, 1968.

Aronson, E. Some antecedents of interpersonal attraction. In W. Arnold and D. Levine (Eds.), *Nebraska Symposium on Motivation* (Vol. 17). Lincoln: University of Nebraska Press, 1969.

Aronson, E. The theory of cognitive dissonance: A current perspective. In L. Berkowitz (Ed.), *Advances in experimental social psychology* (Vol. 4). New York: Academic Press, 1969.

Aronson, E., & Golden, B. The effect of relevant and irrelevant aspects of communicator credibility on opinion change. *Journal of Personality,* 1962, *30,* 135–146.

Aronson, E., & Linder, D. Gain and loss of esteem as determinants of interpersonal attractiveness. *Journal of Experimental Social Psychology,* 1965, *1,* 156–171.

Aronson, E., & Mills, T. Effects of severity of initiation on liking for a group. *Journal of Abnormal and Social Psychology,* 1959, *59,* 177–181.

Aronson, E., Turner, J. A., & Carlsmith, J. M. Communicator credibility and communication discrepancy as determinants of opinion change. *Journal of Abnormal and Social Psychology,* 1963, *67,* 31–36.

Asch, S. E. Effects of group pressure upon the modification and distortion of judgments. In H. Guetzkow (Ed.), *Groups, leadership, and men.* Pittsburgh: Carnegie Press, 1951.

Asch, S. Forming impressions of personality. *Journal of Abnormal and Social Psychology,* 1946, *41,* 258–290.

Asch, S. E. Studies of independence and conformity: A minority of one against a unanimous majority. *Psychological Monographs,* 1956, *70*(9, Whole No. 416).

Ashmore, R. D., & Delboca, F. K. Psychological approaches to understanding intergroup conflicts. In P. A. Katz (Ed.), *Towards the elimination of racism.* Elmsford, N.Y.: Pergamon Press, 1976.

Ashmore, R. D., Ramchandra, V., & Jones, R. A. *Censorship as an attitude change induction.* Paper presented at the meeting of the Eastern Psychological Association, New York, April 1971.

Atkin, C. K., Galloway, S., & Nayman, D. B. News media exposure, political knowledge, and campaign interest. *Journalism Quarterly,* 1970, *53,* 231–237.

Atkin, C. K., & Heald, G. Effects of political advertising. *Public Opinion Quarterly,* 1976, *40,* 216–228.

Atkinson, J. W. Motivational determinants of risk taking behavior. *Psychological Review,* 1957, *64,* 359–372.

Atkinson, T. Public perceptions of the quality of life. In H. J. Adler & D. A. Brusegard (Eds.), *Perspectives Canada III.* Ottawa: Statistics Canada.

Babbie, E. R. *The practice of social science research* (2nd ed.). Belmont, Calif.: Wadsworth, 1979.

Backman, C. W., & Secord, P. F. The effect of perceived liking on interpersonal attraction. *Human Relations,* 1959, *12,* 379–384.

Baer, R., Hinkle, S., Smith, K., & Fenton, M. Reactance as a function of actual versus projected autonomy. *Journal of Personality and Social Psychology,* 1980, *38,* 416–422.

Bagozzi, R. P. Attitudes, intentions, and behavior: A test of some key hypotheses. *Journal of Personality and Social Psychology,* 1981, *41,* 607–627.

Bales, R. F. A set of categories for the analysis of small group interaction. *American Sociological Review,* 1950, *15,* 257–263.

Bales, R. F., & Cohen, S. P. *SYMLOG: A system for the multiple level observation of groups.* New York: The Free Press, 1979.

Ballew v. Georgia. *United States Reports,* 1978, *435,* 223–246.

Bandura, A. *Aggression: A social learning analysis.* Englewood Cliffs, N.J.: Prentice-Hall, 1973.

Bandura, A. Influence of model's reinforcement contingencies on the acquisition of imitative responses. *Journal of Personality and Social Psychology,* 1965, *1,* 589–595.

Bandura, A. *Relationship of family patterns to child behavior disorders.* Progress Report, Project #M-1734, Stanford University, Stanford, Calif.: U.S. Public Health Service, 1960.

Bandura, A. Self-efficacy: Toward a unifying theory of behavioral change. *Psychological Review,* 1977, *84,* 191–215.

Bandura, A. *Social learning theory.* Englewood Cliffs, N.J.: Prentice-Hall, 1977.

Bandura, A., & McDonald, E. J. The influence of social reinforcement and the behavior of models in shaping children's moral judgments. *Journal of Abnormal and Social Psychology*, 1963, *67*, 274–281.

Bandura, A., Ross, D., & Ross, S. A. A comparative test of the status envy, social power and secondary reinforcement theories of identificatory learning. *Journal of Abnormal and Social Psychology*, 1963, *66*, 527–534. (b)

Bandura, A., Ross, D., & Ross, S. A. Imitation of film-mediated aggressive models. *Journal of Abnormal and Social Psychology*, 1963, *66*, 3–11. (a)

Bandura, A., Ross, D., & Ross, S. A. Transmission of aggression through imitation of aggressive models. *Journal of Abnormal and Social Psychology*, 1961, *63*, 575–582.

Bandura, A., & Walters, R. H. *Adolescent aggression*. New York: Ronald, 1959.

Bandura, A., & Walters, R. H. *Social learning and personality development*. New York: Holt, Rinehart & Winston, 1963.

Baran, S. J., et al. Television drama as a facilitator of prosocial behavior: "The Waltons." *Journal of Broadcast*, 1979, *23*, 277–285.

Baron, R. A. Reducing the influence of an aggressive model: The restraining effects of discrepant modeling cues. *Journal of Personality and Social Psychology*, 1971, *20*, 240–245.

Baron, R. A. The reduction of human aggression: A field study of the influence of incompatible responses. *Journal of Applied Social Psychology*, 1976, *6*, 260–274.

Baron, R. A., & Bell, P. A. Aggression and heat: The influence of ambient temperature, negative affect, and a cooling drink on physical aggression. *Journal of Personality and Social Psychology*, 1976, *33*, 245–255.

Baron, R. A., & Bell, P. A. Effects of heightened sexual arousal on physical aggression. In *Proceedings of the 81st Annual Convention of the American Psychological Association*, 1973, *8*, 171–172.

Baron, R. A., & Eggleston, R. J. Performance on the "aggression machine": Motivation to help or harm? *Psychonomic Science*, 1972, *26*, 321–322.

Baron, R. A., & Kepner, C. R. Model's behavior and attraction toward the model as determinants of adult aggressive behavior. *Journal of Personality and Social Psychology*, 1970, *14*, 335–344.

Baron, R., & Ransberger, V. Ambient temperature and the occurrence of collective violence. The "long, hot summer" revisited. *Journal of Personality and Social Psychology*, 1978, *36*, 351–360.

Barron, F., & Harrington, D. M. Creativity, intelligence, and personality. *Annual Review of Psychology*, 1981, *32*, 439–476.

Bartol, C. R. *Criminal behavior: A psychological approach*. Englewood Cliffs, N.J.: Prentice-Hall, 1980.

Bass, B. M. Authoritarianism or acquiescence? *Journal of Abnormal and Social Psychology*, 1955, *51*, 616–623.

Bassili, J. N. Temporal and spatial contingencies in the perception of social events. *Journal of Personality and Social Psychology*, 1976, *33*, 680–685.

Bauer, R. A. A revised model of source effect. *Presidential Address of the Division of Consumer Psychology. American Psychological Association Annual Meeting*, 1965.

Baum, A., & Valins, S. Architectural mediation of residential density and control: Crowding and the regulation of social contact. In L. Berkowitz (Ed.), *Advances in experimental social psychology* (Vol. 12). New York: Academic Press, 1979.

Baum, A., & Valins, S. *Architecture and social behavior: Psychological studies of social density*. Hillsdale, N.J.: Erlbaum, 1977.

Baum, M., & Baum, R. C. *Growing old: A societal perspective*. Englewood Cliffs, N.J.: Prentice-Hall, 1980.

Baumann, D. J., Cialdini, R. B., & Kenrick, D. T. Altruism as hedonism: Helping and self-gratification as equivalent responses. *Journal of Personality and Social Psychology*, 1981, *40*, 1039–1046.

Bauman, H. E. What does the consumer know about nutrition? *Journal of the American Medical Association*, 1973, *225*, 61–72.

Baumrind, D. Child care practices anteceding three patterns of preschool behavior. *Genetic Psychology Monographs*, 1967, *75*, 43–88.

Baumrind, D. Some thoughts on ethics of research: After reading Milgram's "Behavioral study of obedience." *American Psychologist*, 1964, *19*, 421–423.

Bavelas, A. Communication patterns in task-oriented groups. *Journal of the Acoustical Society of America*, 1950, *22*, 725–730.

Bavelas, A., Hastorf, A. H., Gross, A. E., & Kite, W. R. Experiments on the alteration of group structures. *Journal of Experimental Social Psychology*, 1965, *1*, 55–70.

Becker, H. S. *Outsiders: Studies in the sociology of deviance*. New York: Free Press, 1963.

Becker, L. B., & Whitney, D. C. Effects of media dependencies: Audience assessment of government. *Communication Research*, 1980, *7*, 95–120.

Becker, L. B. et al. Newspaper and television dependencies: Effects on evaluation of public officials. *Journal of Broadcasting*, 1979, *23*, 465–475.

Becker, L. J. Joint effect of feedback and goal setting on performance: A field study of residential energy conservation. *Journal of Applied Psychology*, 1978, *63*, 428–433.

Becker, L. J., & Seligman, C. Reducing air conditioning waste by signalling it is cool outside. *Personality and Social Psychology Bulletin*, 1978, *4*, 412–415.

Becker, T. D., & Mayo, C. Delineating personal distance and territoriality. *Environment and Behavior*, 1971, *3*, 375–381.

Beckwith, H. Relationships between infants' social behavior and their mothers' behavior. *Child Development*, 1972, *43*, 397–411.

Bedell, J., & Sistrunk, F. Power opportunity costs, and sex in a mixed motive game. *Journal of Personality and Social Psychology*, 1973, *25*, 219–226.

Bell, P. A., & Baron, R. A. Aggression and heat: The mediating role of negative affect. *Journal of Applied Social Psychology*, 1976, *6*, 18–30.

Bell, A. P., & Weinberg, M. S. *Homosexualities: A study of diversity among men and women*. New York: Simon & Schuster, 1978.

Belmont, L., & Marolla, F. A. Birth order, family size, and intelligence. *Science*, 1973, *182*, 1096–1101.

Bem, D. J. An experimental analysis of self-persuasion. *Journal of Experimental Social Psychology*, 1965, *1*, 199–218.

Bem, D. J. Self-perception: An alternative interpretation of cognitive dissonance phenomena. *Psychological Review*, 1967, *74*, 183–200.

Bem, D. J. Self-perception theory. In L. Berkowitz (Ed.), *Advances in experimental social psychology* (Vol. 6). New York: Academic Press, 1972.

Bem, S. L. The measurement of psychological androgyny. *Journal of Consulting and Clinical Psychology*, 1974, *42*, 155–162.

Benson, P. L., Karabenick, S. A., & Lerner, R. M. Pretty pleases: The effects of physical attractiveness, race, and sex on receiving help. *Journal of Experimental Social Psychology*, 1976, *12*, 409–415.

Berelson, B., Lazerfield, P. F., & McPhee, W. N. *Voting*. Chicago: University of Chicago Press, 1954.

Berger, J., Cohen, B. P., & Zelditch, M., Jr. Status characteristics and social interaction. *American Sociological Review*, 1972, *37*, 241–255.

Berger, S. M. Observer perseverance as related to a model's success. *Journal of Personality and Social Psychology*, 1971, *19*, 341–350.

Berkowitz, L. The frustration-aggression hypothesis revisited. In L. Berkowitz (Ed.), *Roots of aggression: A reexamination of the frustration-aggression hypothesis*. New York: Atherton, 1969.

Berkowitz, L. Social norms, feelings and other factors affecting helping and altruism. In L. Berkowitz (Ed.), *Advances in Experimental Social Psychology* (Vol. 6). New York: Academic Press, 1972.

Berkowitz, L. Decreased helpfulness with increased group sizes through lessening the effects of the needy individual's dependency. *Journal of Personality*, 1978, *46*, 299–310.

Berkowitz, L. How guns control us. *Psychology Today*, June 1981, pp. 11–12.

Berkowitz, L. Some aspects of observed aggression. *Journal of Personality and Social Psychology*, 1965, *2*, 359–369.

Berkowitz, L., Corwin, R., & Hieronimus, M. Film violence and subsequent aggressive tendencies. *Public Opinion Quarterly*, 1963, *27*, 217–229.

Berkowitz, L., & Daniels, L. Affecting the salience of the social responsibility norm: Effects of past help on the response to dependency relationship. *Journal of Abnormal and Social Psychology*, 1964, *68*, 275–281.

Berkowitz, L., & Daniels, L. R. Responsibility and dependency. *Journal of Abnormal and Social Psychology*, 1963, *66*, 429–437.

Berkowitz, L., & Donnerstein, E. External validity is more than skin deep: Some answers to criticisms of laboratory experiments. *American Psychologist*, 1982, 37, *3*, 245–257.

Berkowitz, L., & Geen, R. Film violence and the cue properties of available targets. *Journal of Personality and Social Psychology*, 1966, *3*, 525–530.

Berkowitz, L., & Walster, E. H. (Eds.). Equity theory: Toward a general theory of social interaction. *Advances in experimental social psychology* (Vol. 9). New York: Academic Press, 1976.

Berkowitz, L., & LePage, A. Weapons as aggression—eliciting stimulu. *Journal of Personality and Social Psychology*, 1967, *2*, 202–207.

Bernard, J. *The future of marriage*. New York: Bantam, 1972.

Bernstein, A. M., Stephan, W. G., & Davis, M. H. Explaining attribution for achievement: A path analytic approach. *Journal of Personality and Social Psychology*, 1979, *37*, 1810–1821.

Berscheid, E., Brothen, T., & Graziano, W. Gain-loss theory and the "Law of Infidelity": Mr. Doting versus the admiring stranger. *Journal of Personality and Social Psychology*, 1976, *33*, 709–718.

Berscheid, E., Dion, K., Walster, E., & Walster, G. W. Physical attractiveness and dating choice: A test of the matching hypothesis. *Journal of Experimental Social Psychology*, 1971, 7, 173–189.

Berscheid, E., & Walster, E. H. *Interpersonal attraction* (2nd ed.). Reading, Mass: Addison-Wesley, 1978.

Berscheid, E., & Walster, E. A little bit about love. In T. L. Huston (Ed.), *Foundations of interpersonal attraction*. New York: Academic Press, 1974.

Best, D. L., Williams, J. E., & Briggs, S. R. A further analysis of the affective meanings associated with male and female sex trait stereotypes. *Sex Roles*, 1980, *6*, 735–746.

Beuf, A. Doctor, lawyer, household drudge. *Journal of Communication*, 1974, *24*(2), 142–145.

Bigelow, B. J., & LaGaipa, J. J. Children's written descriptions of friendship: A multi-dimensional analysis. *Developmental Psychology*, 1975, *11*, 857–858.

Billig, M., & Tajfel, H. Social categorization and similarity in intergroup behavior. *European Journal of Social Psychology*, 1973, *3*, 27–52.

Birnbaum, M. H., & Stegner, S. E. Source credibility in social judgment: Bias, expertise and the judge's point of view. *Journal of*

Personality and Social Psychology*, 1979, *37*, 48–74.

Blascovich, J., Ginsburg, G. P., & Howe, R. C. Blackjack and the risky shift, II: Monetary stakes. *Journal of Experimental Social Psychology*, 1975, *11*, 224–232.

Blaska, D. Over 100 threats made each month at the president. *The Capital Times*, April 1, 1981, p. 2.

Blumstein, A. Comment: Research on deterrent and incapacitive effects of criminal sanctions. *Journal of Criminal Justice*, 1978, *6*, 1–10.

Bogart, L. *Strategy in advertising*. New York: Harcourt, 1967.

Bohn, T. W. Broadcasting national election returns, 1952–1976. *Journal of Communication*, 1980, *30*(4), 140–153.

Bond, C. F. Social facilitation: A self-presentational view. *Journal of Personality and Social Psychology*, 1982, *42*, 1042–1050.

Booth, A., & Welch, S. The effects of crowding: A cross-national study. Unpublished manuscript, Ministry of State for Urban Affairs, Ottawa, Canada, 1973.

Bootzin, R. R., Herman, C. P., & Nicassio, P. The power of suggestion: Another examination of misattribution and insomnia. *Journal of Personality and Social Psychology*, 1976, *34*, 673–679.

Borgida, E. Character proof and the fireside induction. *Law and Human Behavior*, 1979, *3*(3), 189–202.

Borgida, E., & Nisbett, R. E. The differential impact of abstract vs. concrete information on decisions. *Journal of Applied Social Psychology*, 1977, *7*, 258–271.

Borgida, E., & White, P. Social perception of rape victims: The impact of legal reforms. *Law and Human Behavior*, 1978, *2*, 339–351.

Bower, G., Black, J., & Turner, T. Scripts in text comprehension and memory. *Cognitive Psychology*, 1979, *11*, 177–220.

Bower, K. S. Situationism in psychology: An analysis and a critique. *Psychological Review*, 1973, *80*, 307–336.

Bowlby, J. *Attachment* (Vol. 1). New York: Basic Books, 1969.

Bradburn, N. *The structure of psychological well-being*. Chicago: Aldine, 1969.

Bradley, G. W. Self-serving biases in the attribution process: A reexamination of the fact or fiction question. *Journal of Personality and Social Psychology*, 1978, *36*, 56–71.

Brannon, R., Cyphers, G., Hesse, S., Hesselbart, S., Keene, R., Shuman, H., Vicarro, T., & Wright, D. Attitude and action: A field experiment joined to a general population survey. *American Sociological Review*, 1973, *38*, 625–636.

Bray, R. M., & Noble, A. M. Authoritarianism and decisions of mock juries: Evidence of jury bias and group polarization. *Journal of Personality and Social Psychology*, 1978, *36*, 1424–1430; 120.

Brehm, J. W. Post-decision changes in desirability of alternatives. *Journal of Abnormal and Social Psychology*, 1956, *52*, 348–389.

Brehm, J. W. *Responses to loss of freedom: A theory of psychological reactance*. Morristown, N.J.: General Learning Press, 1972, 185.

Brehm, J. W. *A theory of psychological reactance*. New York: Academic Press, 1966.

Brehm, J. W., & Cohen, A. R. *Explorations in cognitive dissonance*. New York: Wiley, 1962.

Brewer, M. B. In-group bias in the minimal intergroup situation: A cognitive motivational analysis. *Psychological Bulletin*, 1979, *86*, 307–324.

Brickman, P., Rabinowitz, V. C., Karuza, J., Coates, D., Cohn, M., & Kidder, L. Models of helping and coping. *American Psychologist*, 1982, *37*(4), 368–384.

Brigham, J. Ethnic stereotypes. *Psychological Bulletin*, 1971, *76*, 15–38.

Brigham, J. C., Maass, A., Snyder, L. D., & Spaulding, K. Accuracy of eyewitness identification in a field setting. *Journal of Personality and Social Psychology*, 1982, *42*(4), 673–681.

Broadbent, D. E. Human performance and noise. In C. M. Harris

(Ed.), *Handbook of noise control*. New York: McGraw-Hill, 1979.

Brock, T. Communicator-recipient similarity and decision-change. *Journal of Personality and Social Psychology*, 1965, *1*, 650–654.

Brockner, J., & Swap, W. C. Effects of repeated exposure and attitudinal similarity on self-disclosure and interpersonal attraction. *Journal of Personality and Social Psychology*, 1976, *33*, 531–540.

Brody, J. E. Hypnotism is a powerful but vulnerable weapon in fight against crime. *The New York Times*, October 14, 1980, pp. 15, 17.

Bronfenbrenner, U. Freudian theories of identification and their derivatives. *Child Development*, 1960, *31*, 15–40.

Bronzaft, A. The effect of a noise abatement program on reading ability. *Journal of Environmental Psychology*, 1981, *1*(3), 215–222.

Brophy, J. E. *Child development and socialization*. Chicago: Science Research Associates, Inc., 1977.

Broverman, I. K., Vogel, S. R., Broverman, D. M., Clarkson, F. E., & Rosenkrantz, P. S. Sex-role stereotypes: A current appraisal. *Journal of Social Issues*, 1972, *28*, 59–78.

Brown, B. R. Face-saving following experimentally induced embarrassment. *Journal of Experimental Social Psychology*, 1970, *6*, 255–271.

Brown, R. W. Mass phenomena. In G. Lindzey (Ed.), *The handbook of social psychology*. Cambridge, Mass.: Addison-Wesley, 1954.

Brown, R. W. *Social psychology*, Boston: Little, Brown, 1965.

Brown, R., & Herrnstein, R. J. *Psychology*. Boston: Little, Brown, 1975.

Brownmiller, S. *Against our will: Men, women, and rape*. New York: Simon & Schuster, 1975.

Bruner, J. S., & Tagiuri, R. Person perception. In G. Lindzey (Ed.), *Handbook of social psychology* (Vol. 2). Reading, Mass.: Addison-Wesley, 1954.

Bryan, J. H. You will be advised to watch what we do, instead of what we say. In D. DePalma & J. Folley (Eds.), *Moral development*. Hillsdale, N.J.: Lawrence Erlbaum Associates, 1975.

Bryan, J. H., and Test, M. A. Models & helping: Naturalistic studies in aiding behavior. *Journal of Personality and Social Psychology*, 1967, *6*, 400–407.

Bryan, J. H., & Walbek, N. H. The impact of words and deeds concerning altruism upon children. *Child Development*, 1970, *41*, 747–757.

Bryant, J., & Zillman, D. Effect of intensification of annoyance through unrelated residual excitation on substantially delayed hostile behavior. *Journal of Experimental Social Psychology*, 1979, *15*, 470–480.

Buck, R. W., & Parke, R. D. Behavioral and physiological response to the presence of a friendly or neutral person in two types of stressful situations. *Journal of Personality and Social Psychology*, 1972, *24*, 143–153.

Buckhout, R. Nearly 2000 witnesses can be wrong. *Bulletin of the Psychonomic Society*, 1980, *16*(4), 307–310.

Buckhout, R., & Baker, E. Surveying the attitudes of seated jurors. *Social Action and the Law*, 1977, *4*(6), 98–101.

Buffery, A. W. H., & Gray, J. A. Sex differences in the development of spatial and linguistic skills. In C. Ormsted & D. C. Taylor (Eds.), *Gender differences: Their ontogeny and significance*. Baltimore: Williams & Wilkins, 1972.

Bukstel, L. H., & Kilmann, P. R. Psychological effects of imprisonment on confined individuals. *Psychological Bulletin*, 1980, *88*, 469–493.

Bumpass, L. L., & Sweet, J. L. Differentials in marital instability. *American Sociological Review*, 1972, *37*, 754–756.

Burch v. Louisiana, *United States Reports*, 1979, *441*, 130–139.

Burger, J. M., & Petty, R. E. The low-ball compliance technique:

Task or person commitment? *Journal of Personality and Social Psychology*, 1981, *40*, 492–500.

Burnstein, E., & Vinokur, A. Persuasive arguments and social comparison as determinants of attitude polarization. *Journal of Experimental Social Psychology*, 1977, *13*, 315–332.

Burton, R. V. Generality of honesty reconsidered. *Psychological Review*, 1963, *70*, 481–499.

Buss, A. Physical aggression in relation to different frustrations. *Journal of Abnormal and Social Psychology*, 1963, *67*, 1–7.

Buss, A. *The psychology of aggression*. New York: Wiley, 1961.

Buss, A., Booker, A., & Buss, E. Firing a weapon and aggression. *Journal of Personality and Social Psychology*, 1972, *22*, 196–302.

Butler, R. N. Ageism: A foreword. *Journal of Social Issues*, 1980, *36*, 8–29.

Byrd, R. E. *Alone*. New York: Putnam, 1938.

Byrne, D., & Byrne, L. *Exploring human sexuality*. New York: Thomas Y. Crowell Company, 1977.

Cairns, H. S., & Cairns, C. E. *Psycholinguistics: A cognitive view of language*. New York: Holt, Rinehart & Winston, 1976.

Calder, B. J., Insko, C. A., & Yandell, B. The relation of cognitive and memorial processes to persuasion in simulated jury trial. *Journal of Applied Social Psychology*, 1974, *4*, 62–93.

Calhoun, J. B. Population density and social pathology. *Scientific American*, 1962, *206*(3), 139–148.

Calhoun, L. G., Cann, A., Selby, J. W., & Magee, D. L. Victim emotional response: Effects of social reactions to victims of rape. *British Journal of Social Psychology*, 1981, *20*, 12–21.

Calhoun, L. G., Selby, J. W., & King, H. E. *Dealing with crisis*. Englewood Cliffs, N.J.: Prentice-Hall, 1976.

Campbell, A. Subjective measures of well-being. *American Psychologist*, 1976, *31*, 117–124.

Campbell, A. *White attitudes toward black people*. Ann Arbor: Institute for Social Research, 1971.

Campbell, A., Converse, P. E., & Rodgers, W. L. *The quality of American life: Perceptions, evaluations, satisfactions*. New York: Russell Sage Foundation, 1976.

Campbell, A. A., Gurin, G., & Miller, W. *The voter decides*. Evanston, Ill.: Row, Peterson, 1954.

Campbell, D. E. Interior office design and visitor response. *Journal of Applied Psychology*, 1979, *64*, 648–653.

Campbell, D. T. Comments on the sociology of ethics and moralizing. *Behavioral Science*, 1979, *24*, 37–45.

Campbell, D. T. Ethnocentric and other altruistic motives. In D. Levine (Ed.), *Nebraska Symposium on Motivation* (Vol. 13), Lincoln, Neb.: University of Nebraska Press, 1965.

Campbell, D. T. On the genetics of altruism and the counterhedonic components in human culture. *Journal of Social Issues*, 1972, *28*(2), 21–37.

Campbell, D. T. Reforms as experiments. *American Psychologist*, 1969, *24*, 409–429.

Campbell, D. T., Seligman, C., & Rees, M. B. Direction-of-wording effects in the relationships between scales. *Psychological Bulletin*, 1967, *68*, 293–303.

Campbell, D. T., & Stanley, J. C. *Experimental and quasi-experimental designs for social research*. Chicago: Rand McNally, 1966.

Cantor, N., & Mischel, W. Prototypes in person perception. In L. Berkowitz (Ed.), *Advances in experimental social psychology* (Vol. 12). New York: Academic Press, 1979.

Cantor, N., & Mischel, W. Traits as prototypes: Effects on recognition memory. *Journal of Personality and Social Psychology*, 1977, *35*, 38–48.

Cantril, H. *The pattern of human concerns*. New Brunswick, N.J.: Rutgers University Press, 1965.

Caplovitz, D. Making ends meet: How families cope with inflation and recession. *Annals, American Academy of Political and Social Science*, 1981, *456*, 88–98.

Carlsmith, J. M., & Anderson, C. A. Ambient temperature and the occurrence of collective violence: A new analysis. *Journal of Personality and Social Psychology*, 1979, *37*, 337–344.

Carlsmith, J., Ellsworth, P., & Aronson, E. *Methods of research in social psychology*. Reading, Mass.: Addison-Wesley, 1976.

Carr, S. J., & Dabbs, J. M. The effects of lighting, distance, and intimacy of topic on verbal and visual behavior. *Sociometry*, 1974, *37*, 592–600.

Carroll, J. S. Causal attributions in expert parole decisions. *Journal of Personality and Social Psychology*, 1978, *36*, 1501–1511.

Carroll, J. S. A psychological approach to deterrence: The evaluation of crime opportunities. *Journal of Personality and Social Psychology*, 1979, *36*, 1512–1520.

Carroll, J. S., & Payne, J. W. Crime seriousness, recidivism risk, and causal attributions in judgments of prison term by students and experts. *Journal of Applied Psychology*, 1977, *62*, 595–602.

Cartwright, D., & Zander, A. (Eds.). *Group dynamics: Research and theory* (3rd ed.). New York: Harper & Row, 1968.

Cavan, S. Talking about sex by not talking about sex. In J. P. Wiseman (Ed.), *The social psychology of sex*. New York: Harper & Row, 1976.

Carver, C. S., Blaney, P. H., & Scheier, M. F. Reassertion and giving up: The interactive role of self-directed attention and outcome expectancy. *Journal of Personality and Social Psychology*, 1979, *37*, 1859–1870.

Carver, C. S., DeGregorio, E., & Gillis, R. Ego-defensive bias in attribution among two categories of observers. *Personality & Social Psychology Bulletin*, 1980, *6*, 44–50.

Choffee, S. H. Presidential debates: Are they helpful to voters? *Communication Monograph*, 1978, *45*, 330–353.

Chaiken, A. L., & Darley, J. M. Victim or perpetrator?: Defensive attribution of responsibility and the need for order and justice. *Journal of Personality and Social Psychology*, 1973, *25*, 268–275.

Chaiken, S., & Eagly, A. H. Communication modality as a determinant of message persuasiveness and message comprehensibility. *Journal of Personality and Social Psychology*, 1976, *34*, 605–614.

Chapman, L. J. Illusory correlation in observational report. *Journal of Verbal Learning and Verbal Behavior*, 1967, *6*, 151–155.

Chapman, L. J., & Chapman, J. P. Genesis of popular but erroneous psychodiagnostic observations. *Journal of Abnormal Psychology*, 1967, *72*, 193–204.

Cherlin, A., & Walters, P. B. Trends in United States men's and women's sex-role attitudes: 1972 to 1978. *American Sociological Review*, 1981, *46*, 453–460.

Cherrington, D. J., Reitz, H. J., & Scott, W. E., Jr. Effects of contingent and non-contingent reward on the relationship between satisfaction and task performance. *Journal of Applied Psychology*, 1971, *55*, 531–536.

Cherry, L., & Lewis, M. Mothers and two-year-olds: A study of sex differentiated aspects of verbal interaction. *Developmental Psychology*, 1972, *12*, 278–282.

Cheyne, J. A., & Walters, R. H. Punishment and prohibition: Some origins of self-control. In T. W. Newcomb (Ed.), *New directions in psychology* (Vol. 4). New York: Holt, Rinehart & Winston, 1970.

Chomsky, N. *Aspects of the theory of syntax*. Cambridge, Mass.: M.I.T. Press, 1965.

Christian, J. J., Flyger, V., & Davis, D. C. Factors in the mass mortality of a herd of sika deer, *Cervus nippon*. *Chesapeake Science*, 1960, *1*, 79–95.

Christie, R., & Jahoda, M. (Eds.). *Studies in the scope and method of "The authoritarian personality."* New York: Free Press, 1954.

Chu, G. C. Prior familiarity, perceived bias, and one-sided versus two-sided communications. *Journal of Experimental Social Psychology*, 1967, *3*, 243–254.

Cialdini, R. B., Levy, A., Herman, C. P., Kozkowski, L. T., & Petty, R. E. Elastic shifts of opinion: Determinants of direction and durability. *Journal of Personality and Social Psychology*, 1976, *34*, 663–672.

Cialdini, R. B. et al. Low-ball procedure for producing compliance: Commitment then cost. *Journal of Personality and Social Psychology*, 1978, *36*, 463–578.

Cialdini, R. B., Vincent, J. E., Lewis, S. K., Catalan, J., Wheeler, D., & Darby, B. L. Reciprocal concessions procedure for inducing compliance: The door-in-the-face technique. *Journal of Personality and Social Psychology*, 1975, *31*, 206–215.

Clancy, K., Bartolomeo, J., Richardson, D., & Wellford, C. Sentence decisionmaking: The logic of sentence decisions and the extent and sources of sentence disparity. *The Journal of Criminal Law & Criminology*, 1981, *72*(2), 524–554.

Clark, K. B., & Clark, M. P. Racial identification and preference in Negro children. In T. M. Newcomb & E. L. Hartley (Eds.), *Readings in social psychology*. New York: Holt, 1947.

Clark, R. D., & Word, L. E. Why don't bystanders help? Because of ambiguity? *Journal of Personality and Social Psychology*, 1972, *28*, 39–57.

Clarke, P., & Fredin, E. Newspapers, television, and political reasoning. *Public Opinion Quarterly*, 1978, *42*, 143–160.

Clayton, R. R., & Harwin, L. V. Shacking up: Cohabitation in the 1970s. *Journal of Marriage and the Family*, 1977, *39*, 273–283.

Clifford, B. R., & Scott, J. Individual and situational factors in eyewitness testimony. *Journal of Applied Psychology*, 1978, *63*, 352–359.

Clifton, A., McGrath, D., & Wick, B. Stereotypes of woman: A single category? *Sex Roles*, 1976, *2*, 135–148.

Clore, G. L., & Byrne, D. A reinforcement-affect model of attraction. In T. L. Huston (Ed.), *Foundations of interpersonal attraction*. New York: Academic Press, 1974.

Coates, D., Renzaglia, G. J., & Embree, M. C. When helping backfires: Help and helplessness. In J. D. Fisher, A. Nadler, & B. De Paulo (Eds.), *New directions in helping* (Vol. 1). New York: Academic Press, in press.

Coates, D., Wortman, C. B., & Abbey, A. Reactions to victims. In I. H. Frieze, D. BarTal, & J. S. Carroll (Eds.), *New approaches to social problems*. San Francisco: Jossey-Bass, 1979.

Coch, L., & French, J. R. P., Jr. Overcoming resistance to change. *Human Relations*, 1948, *1*, 512–532.

Cohen, S., Glass, D., & Singer, J. Apartment noise, auditory discrimination, and reading ability in children. *Journal of Experimental Social Psychology*, 1973, *9*, 407–422.

Cohn, A., & Udolf, R. *The criminal justice system and its psychology*. New York: Van Nostrand Reinhold, 1979.

Coleman, J. *The adolescent society*. New York: Free Press, 1961.

Coleman, J., Hoffer, & Kilgore. *Public and private schools: A report to the National Center for Education Statistics*. Chicago: The National Opinion Research Center, March 1981.

Comfort, A. *The joy of sex*. New York: Crown, 1972.

Comstock, G. et al. *Television and human behavior*. New York: Columbia University Press, 1978.

Condry, J., & Condry, S. Sex differences: A study of the eye of the beholder. *Child Development*, 1976, *47*, 812–819.

Condry, J., & Dyer, S. Fear of success: Attribution of cause to the victim. *Journal of Social Issues*, 1976, *32*(3), 63–83.

Conroy, J., & Sundstrom, E. Territorial dominance in a dyadic conversation as a function of similarity of opinion. *Journal of Personality and Social Psychology*, 1977, *35*, 570–576.

Cook, H., & Stingle, S. Cooperative behavior in children. *Psycho-

logical Bulletin, 1974, *81*, 918–933.

Cook, S. W. Ethical issues in the conduct of research in social relations. In C. Selltiz, L. C. Wrightsman, & S. W. Cook (Eds.), *Research methods in social relations* (3rd ed.). New York: Holt, Rinehart & Winston, 1976.

Cook, S. W., & Berrenberg, J. L. Approaches to encouraging conservation behavior: A review and conceptual framework. *Journal of Social Issues*, 1981, *37*, 73–107.

Cook, S. W., & Selltiz, C. A. A multiple-indicator approach to attitude measurement. *Psychological Bulletin*, 1964, *62*, 36–55.

Cook, T. D., & Campbell, D. T. *Quasi-experimentation: Design and analysis for field settings.* Chicago: Rand McNally, 1979.

Cooley, C. H. *Human nature and the social order.* Glencoe, Ill.: The Free Press, 1922.

Coombs, L. C., & Zumeta, Z. Correlates of marital dissolution in a prospective fertility study: A research note. *Social Problems*, 1970, *18*, 92–102.

Cooper, E., & Dinnerman, H. Analysis of the film "Don't Be A Sucker": A study of communication. *Public Opinion Quarterly*, 1951, *15*, 243–264.

Cooper, J. Deception and role playing: On telling the good guys from the bad guys. *American Psychologist*, August 1976, 605–610.

Cooper, J., & McGaugh, J. C. Leadership: Integrating principles of social psychology. In C. A. Gibb (Ed.), *Leadership.* Baltimore: Penguin Books, 1969.

Cooper, J., Zanna, M. P., & Taves, T. A. Arousal as a necessary condition for attitude change following induced compliance. *Journal of Personality and Social Psychology*, 1978, *36*, 1101–1106.

Coopersmith, S. Studies in self-esteem. *Scientific American*, 1968, *218*, 96–106.

Costanzo, P. R. Conformity development as a function of self-blame. *Journal of Personality and Social Psychology*, 1978, *36*, 1101–1106.

Costanzo, P. R., Coie, J. D., Grumet, J. F., & Farnell, D. A reexamination of the effects of intent and consequence on children's moral judgments. *Child Development*, 1973, *44*, 154–161.

Cottrell, N. B. Social facilitation. In C. G. McClintock (Ed.), *Experimental social psychology.* New York: Holt, 1972.

Cottrell, N. B., & Epley, S. W. Affiliation, social comparison, and socially mediated stress reduction. In J. Suls & R. L. Miller (Eds.), *Social comparison processes.* Washington, D.C.: Hemisphere/Halsted, 1977.

Cottrell, N. B., Wach, D. C., Sekerak, G. J., & Rittle, R. H. Social facilitation of dominant responses by the presence of an audience and the mere presence of others. *Journal of Personality and Social Psychology*, 1968, *9*, 245–250.

Cowan, P. A., & Walters, R. H. Studies of reinforcement of aggression: Effects of scheduling. *Child Development*, 1963, *34*, 543–551.

Cozby, P. C. Self-disclosure and liking. *Sociometry*, 1972, *35*, 151–160.

Cozby, P. C. *Methods in behavioral research* (2nd ed.). Palo Alto, Calif.: Mayfield, 1981.

Crespi, J. What kinds of attitude measures are predictive of behavior? *Public Opinion Quarterly*, 1971, *35*, 327–334.

Crocker, J. Judgment of covariation by social perceivers. *Psychological Bulletin*, 1981, *90*, 272–292.

Cronbach, L. J. *Essentials of Psychological Testing* (2nd ed.). New York: Harper & Row, 1960.

Crutchfield, R. Conforming and character. *American Psychologist*, 1955, *10*, 191–198.

Curran, J. Convergence toward a single sexual standard? In D. Byrne & L. Byrne (Eds.), *Exploring human sexuality.* New York: Thomas Y. Crowell Company, 1977.

Curtiss, S. *Genie: A linguistic study of a modern-day "wild child."* New York: Academic Press, 1977.

Dabbs, J. M., & Janis, I. L. Why does eating while reading facilitate opinion change? An experimental inquiry. *Journal of Experimental Social Psychology*, 1965, *1*, 133–144.

Dabbs, J. M., & Leventhal, H. Effects of varying the recommendations in a fear-arousing communication. *Journal of Personality and Social Psychology*, 1966, *4*, 525–531.

Dalton, M. Formal and informal organization. *Men who manage.* New York: Wiley, 1959.

Dane, F. C., & Wrightsman, L. S. Effects of defendant's and victim's characteristics on juror's verdicts. In N. Kerr & R. M. Bray (Eds.), *The psychology of the courtroom.* New York: Academic Press, 1982.

Darley, J. M., & Berscheid, E. Increased liking as a result of the anticipation of personal contact. *Human Relations*, 1967, *20*, 29–40.

Darley, J., & Goethals, G. Peoples' analyses of the causes of ability-linked performances. In L. Berkowitz (Ed.), *Advances in experimental social psychology* (Vol. 13), Academic Press, 1980.

Darwin, C. *The expression of emotions in man and animals.* London: Murray, 1872.

Dashiell, J. F. An experimental analysis of some group effects. *Journal of Abnormal Social Psychology*, 1930, *25*, 190–199.

Davidson, R. Alone across the outback. *National Geographic Magazine*, 1978, *153*, 581–611.

Davis, G. J., & Meyer, R. K. FSH and LH in the snowshoe hare during the increasing phase of the 10 year cycle. *General Comparative Endocrinology*, 1973, *20*, 53–60.

Davis, J. H. Group decision and procedural justice. In M. Fishbein (Ed.), *Progress in social psychology.* Hillsdale, N.J.: Erlbaum, 1980.

Davis, J. H. Group decision and social interaction: A theory of social decision schemes. *Psychological Review*, 1973, *80*, 97–125.

Davis, J. H., Bray, R. M., & Holt, R. W. The empirical study of social decision processes in juries. In J. Tapp and F. Levine (Eds.), *Law, justice and the individual in society: Psychological and legal issues.* New York: Holt, Rinehart & Winston, 1977.

Davis, J. H., Kerr, N. L., Atkin, R. S., Holt, R., & Meek, D. The decision process of 6- and 12-person mock juries assigned unanimous and 2/3 majority rules. *Journal of Personality and Social Psychology*, 1975, *32*, 1–14.

Davis, K. Extreme social isolation of a child. *American Journal of Sociology*, 1940, *45*, 554–565.

Davitz, J. R. (Ed.). *The communication of emotional meaning.* New York: McGraw-Hill, 1964.

Dawidowicz, L. *The war against the Jews.* New York: Holt, Rinehart & Winston, 1975.

Deaux, K. Sex related patterns of social interaction. Paper presented at the meeting of the Midwestern Psychological Association, Chicago, May 1978.

Deaux, K., & Emswiller, T. Explanations of successful performance on sex-linked tasks: What's skill for the male is luck for the female. *Journal of Personality and Social Psychology*, 1974, *29*, 80–85.

Deci, E. Effects of externally mediated rewards on intrinsic motivation. *Journal of Personality and Social Psychology*, 1971, *18*, 105–115.

Deffenbacher, K. Eyewitness accuracy and confidence: Can we infer anything about their relationship? *Law and Human Behavior*, 1980, *4*, 243–260.

Deiner, E. Deindividuation, self-awareness, and disinhibition. *Journal of Personality and Social Psychology*, 1979, *37*, 1160–1171.

DeLamater, J., & MacCorquodale, P. *Premarital sexuality.* Madison: University of Wisconsin Press, 1979.

Dembroski, T. M., Lasater, T. M., & Ramirez, A. Communicator similarity, fear-arousing communications, and compliance with health care recommendations. *Journal of Applied Social Psychology*, 1978, *8*, 254–269.

Dengler, C. N. *At odds: Women and the family in America from the revolution to the present.* Oxford: Oxford University Press, 1980.

DePaulo, B. M., & Rosenthal, R. Telling lies. *Journal of Personality and Social Psychology*, 1979, *37*, 1713–1722.

Der-Karabetian, A., & Smith, A. Sex-role stereotyping in the United States: Is it changing? *Sex Roles*, 1977, *3*, 193–198.

Dermer, M., & Thiel, D. L. When beauty may fail. *Journal of Personality and Social Psychology*, 1975, *31*, 1168–1196.

Department of Justice, Federal Bureau of Investigation. Uniform Crime Reports, 1978. Cited in *Information Please Almanac*, 1981. New York: Simon & Schuster, 1980.

Detweiler, R. A., & Zanna, M. P. Physiological mediation of attitudinal responses. *Journal of Personality and Social Psychology*, 1976, *33*, 107–116.

Deutsch, M., & Collins, M. E. The effect of public policy in housing projects upon interracial attitudes. In E. Maccoby, T. M. Newcomb, & E. L. Hartley (Eds.), *Readings in social psychology* (3rd ed.). New York: Holt, 1958.

Deutsch, M., & Collins, M. E. *Interracial housing: A psychological evaluation of a social experiment.* Minneapolis: University of Minnesota Press, 1951.

Deutsch, M., & Gerard, H. B. A study of normative and informational influence upon individual judgment. *Journal of Abnormal and Social Psychology*, 1955, *51*, 629–636.

Devereux, E. C. The role of peer-group experience in moral development. In J. P. Hill (Ed.), *Minnesota symposia on child psychology* (Vol. 4). Minneapolis: University of Minnesota Press, 1970.

Diener, E., & DeFour, D. Does television violence enhance program popularity? *Journal of Personality and Social Psychology*, 1978, *36*, 333–341.

Dillehay, R. C. On the irrelevance of the classical negative evidence concerning the effect of attitudes on behavior. *American Psychologist*, 1973, *28*, 887–891.

Dion, K., Berscheid, E., & Walster, E. What is beautiful is good. *Journal of Personality and Social Psychology*, 1972, *34*, 285–290.

Dipboye, R. L., Fromkin, H. L., & Wiback, K. Relative importance of applicant sex, attractiveness, and scholastic standing in evaluation of job applicant resumés. *Journal of Applied Psychology*, 1975, *60*, 39–45.

Dodson, J. A., Tybout, A. M., & Steinthal, E. Impact of deals and deal retraction on brand switching. *Journal of Marketing Research*, 1978, *15*(1), 72–81.

Dollard, J., Doob, L., Miller, N., Mowrer, O., & Sears, R. *Frustration and aggression.* New Haven, Conn.: Yale University Press, 1939.

Donagher, P. C., Poulos, R. W., Liebart, R. M., & Davidson, E. S. Race, sex, and social example: An analysis of character portrayals on interracial television entertainment. *Psychological Reports*, 1975, *37*, 1023–1034.

Donnerstein, E. Aggressive-erotica and violence against women. *Journal of Personality and Social Psychology*, 1980, *39*, 269–277.

Donnerstein, E. Erotica and human aggression. In R. Green and E. Donnerstein (Eds.), *Aggression: Theoretical and empirical reviews.* New York: Academic Press, in press.

Donnerstein, E., & Berkowitz, L., Victim reactions in aggressive-erotic film as a factor in violence against women. *Journal of Personality and Social Psychology*, 1981, *41*, 710–724.

Donnerstein, M., & Donnerstein, E. Modeling in the control of interracial aggression: The problem of generality. *Journal of Personality*, 1977, *45*, 100–116.

Donnerstein, E., Donnerstein, M., & Evans, R. Erotic stimuli and aggression: Facilitation or inhibition. *Journal of Personality and*

Social Psychology, 1975, *32*, 237–244.

Doob, A., & Kirshenbaum, H. The effects on arousal of frustration and aggressive films. *Journal of Experimental Social Psychology*, 1973, *9*, 57–64.

Drabman, R. S., & Thomas, M. H. Does media violence increase children's toleration of real life aggression? *Developmental Psychology*, 1974, *10*, 418–421.

Dugger, W. M. Do genes hold culture on a leash? *Social Science Quarterly*, June 1981, pp. 243–246. (b)

Dugger, W. M. Sociobiology for social scientists: A critical introduction to E. O. Wilson's evolutionary paradigm. *Social Science Quarterly*, June 1981, pp. 221–223. (a)

Duncan, B. L. Differential social perception and attribution of intergroup violence: Testing the lower limits of stereotyping of blacks. *Journal of Personality and Social Psychology*, 1976, *34*, 590–598.

Duncan, S. D., Jr., & Fiske, D. W. *Face-to-face interaction.* Hillsdale, N.J.: Lawrence Erlbaum & Associates, 1977.

Duncan, S. D., Jr., & Mederche, G. On signalling that it's your turn to speak. *Journal of Experimental Social Psychology*, 1974, *10*, 234–247.

Dutton, D. G. Reverse discrimination: The relationship of amount of perceived discrimination toward a minority group on the behaviour of majority group members. *Canadian Journal of Behavioural Science*, 1973, *5*, 34–45.

Dutton, D. G., & Lake, R. A. Threat of own prejudice and reverse discrimination in interracial situations. *Journal of Personality and Social Psychology*, 1973, *28*, 94–100.

Duval, S., & Wicklund, R. A. *A theory of objective self awareness.* New York: Academic Press, 1972.

Dyck, R. J., & Rule, B. G. Effect of retaliation on causal attributions concerning attack. *Journal of Personality and Social Psychology*, 1978, *36*, 521–529.

Eagly, A. H. Sex differences in influenceability. *Psychological Bulletin*, 1978, 85, 86–116.

Eagly, A. H., & Carli, L. Sex of researchers and sex-typed communications as determinants of sex differences in influenceability: A meta-analysis of social influence studies. Unpublished manuscript, Purdue University, 1981.

Eagly, A. H., & Himmelfarb, S. Attitudes and opinions. In M. R. Rosenzweig and L. W. Porter (Eds.), *Annual review of psychology* (Vol. 29). Palo Alto, Calif.: Annual Reviews, 1978.

Eagly, A. H., & Telaak, K. Width of the latitude of acceptance as a determinant of attitude change. *Journal of Personality and Social Psychology*, 1972, *23*, 388–397.

Eagly, A. H., Wood, W., & Chaiken, S. Causal inferences about communicators and their effect on opinion change: The case of communicator attractiveness. *Journal of Personality and Social Psychology*, 1975, *32*, 136–144.

Ebbesen, E., Kjos, G., & Konecni, V. Spatial ecology: Its effects on the choice of friends and enemies. *Journal of Experimental Social Psychology*, 1976, *12*, 505–528.

Ebbesen, E., & Konecni, V. Decision making and information integration in the courts: The setting of bail. *Journal of Personality and Social Psychology*, 1975, *32*, 805–821.

Edney, J. J. Property, possession and permanence. A field study in human territoriality. *Journal of Applied Social Psychology*, 1972, *3*, 275–282.

Edney, J. J. Territoriality and control: A field experiment. *Journal of Personality and Social Psychology*, 1975, *31*, 1108–1115.

Ehrlich, P. *The population bomb.* New York: Ballantine, 1968.

Eisen, S. V. Actor-observer differences in information inferences and causal attribution. *Journal of Personality and Social Psychology*, 1979, *37*, 261–272.

Ekman, P. Biological and cultural contributions to body and facial movement. In J. Blacking (Ed.), ASA Monograph 15, *The anthropology of the body.* London: Academic Press, 1979, 39–84.

Ekman, P., & Friesen, W. V. Detecting deception from the body or face. *Journal of Personality and Social Psychology*, 1974, *29*, 288–298.

Ekman, P., & Friesen, W. V. Nonverbal leakage and clues to deception. *Psychiatry*, 1969, *32*, 88–106.

Ekman, P., Friesen, W. V., O'Sullivan, M. & Scherer, K. Relative importance of face, body, and speech in judgments of personality and affect. *Journal of Personality and Social Psychology*, 1980, *38*, 270–277.

Ekman, P., & Friesen, W. V. *Unmasking the face* Englewood Cliffs, N.J.: Prentice-Hall, 1975.

Ekman, P., & Oster, H. Facial expressions of emotion. In M. R. Rosenzweig & L. W. Porter (Eds.), *Annual review of psychology* (Vol. 30). Palo Alto, Calif.: Annual Reviews, 1979.

Ellison, K. W., & Buckhout, R. *Psychology and criminal justice.* New York: Harper & Row, 1981.

Ellsworth, P. C. From abstract ideas to concrete instances: Some guidelines for choosing natural research settings. *American Psychologist*, 1977, *32*, 604–615.

Ellsworth, P. C., & Carlsmith, J. M. Eye contact and gaze aversion in an aggressive encounter. *Journal of Personality and Social Psychology*, 1973, *28*, 280–292.

Ellsworth, P. C., Carlsmith, J. M., & Henson, A. The stare as a stimulus to flight in human subjects: A series of field experiments. *Journal of Personality and Social Psychology*, 1972, *21*, 302–311.

Ellsworth, P., & Langer, E. J. Staring and approach: An interpretation of the state as a nonspecific activator. *Journal of Personality and Social Psychology*, 1976, *33*, 117–122.

Ellsworth, P. C., & Ludwig, L. M. Visual behavior in social interaction. *Journal of Communication*, 1972, *22*, 375–403.

Elms, A. C., & Janis, I. L. Counter-norm attitudes induced by consonant versus dissonant conditions of role-playing. *Journal of Experimental Research in Personality*, 1965, *1*, 50–60.

Emswiller, R., Deaux, K., & Willits, J. Similarity, sex, and requests for small favors. *Journal of Applied Social Psychology*, 1971, *1*, 284–291.

England, P., Chassie, M., & McCormack, L. Skill demands and earnings in female and male occupations. *Sociology and Social Research*, 1982, 66, 147–168.

Epley, S. W. Reduction of the behavioral effects of aversive stimulation by the presence of companions. *Psychological Bulletin*, 1974, *81*, 271–283.

Epstein, S. The self-concept revisited: Or a theory of a theory. *American Psychologist*, 1973, *28*, 404–416.

Epstein, Suedfield, & Silverstein. The experimental contract: Subjects' expectations of and reactions to some behaviors of experimenters. *American Psychologist*, 1973, *28*, 212–221.

Epstein, Y. M. Crowding stress and human behavior. *Journal of Social Issues*, 1981, *37*, 126–144.

Epstein, Y. M., & Karlin, R. A. Effects of acute experimental crowding. *Journal of Applied Social Psychology*, 1975, *5*, 34–53.

Erikson, E. H. *Childhood and society.* New York: Norton, 1963.

Ervin-Tripp, S. M. Sociolinguistics. In L. Berkowitz (Ed.), *Advances in social psychology* (Vol. 4). New York: Academic Press, 1969.

Evans, G. Behavioral and physiological consequences of crowding in humans. *Journal of Applied Social Psychology*, 1979, *9*, 27–46.

Evans, R. I. et al. Social modeling films to deter smoking in adolescents: Results of a three-year field investigation. *Journal of Applied Psychology*, 1981, *66*, 399–414.

Exline, R. V. Group climate as a factor in the relevance and accuracy of social perception. *Journal of Abnormal and Social Psychology*, 1957, *55*, 382–388.

Exline, R. V. et al. Visual behavior as an aspect of power role relationships. In P. Pliner, L. Krames, & T. Alloway (Eds.), *Nonverbal communication of aggression* (Vol. 2). New York: Plenum Press, 1975.

Exline, R. V. Visual interaction: The glances of power and preference. In J. K. Cole (Ed.), *Nebraska Symposium on Motivation* (Vol. 19). Lincoln: University of Nebraska Press, 1971, 163–206.

Exline, R. V., & Winters, L. Affective relations and mutual glances. In S. S. Tompkins and C. E. Izard (Eds.), *Affect, cognition and personality.* New York: Springer Publishing, 1965.

Farb, P. *Humankind.* New York: Houghton Mifflin, 1978.

Farran, D. C., & Ramey, C. T. Infant day care and attachment behaviors toward mothers and teachers. *Child Development*, 1977, *43*, 1112–1116.

Fast, J. *Body language.* New York: Penguin, 1970.

Fazio, R. H. On the self-perception explanation of the overjustification effect: The role of salience of initial attitude. *Journal of Experimental Social Psychology*, 1981, *17*, 417–426.

Fazio, R. H., & Zanna, M. P. Attitudinal qualities relating to the strength of the attitude-behavior relationship. *Journal of Experimental Social Psychology*, 1978, *14*, 398–408.

Fazio, R. H., & Zanna, M. P. Direct experience and attitude-behavior consistency. In L. Berkowitz (Ed.), *Advances in Experimental Social Psychology* (Vol. 14). New York: Academic Press, 1981.

Feather, N. Positive and negative reactions to male and female success and failure in relation to the perceived status and sex-typed appropriateness of occupations. *Journal of Personality and Social Psychology*, 1975, *31*(3), 536–548.

Federal Bureau of Investigation. *Uniform Crime Reports for the United States*, 1981.

Feild, H. S. Juror background characteristics and attitudes toward rape: Correlates of jurors' decisions in rape trials. *Law and Human Behavior*, 1978, *2*, 73–93.

Feldman, R. E. Response to compatriots and foreigners who seek assistance. *Journal of Personality and Social Psychology*, 1968, *10*, 202–214.

Feldman-Summers, S., & Keisler, S. Those who are number two try harder: The effects of sex on attributions of causality. *Journal of Personality and Social Psychology*, 1974, *30*, 846–855.

Feldman-Summers, S., & Linder, K. Perceptions of victims and defendants in criminal assault cases. *Criminal Justice Behavior*, 1976, *3*, 135–149.

Ference, T. P. Feedback and conflict as determinants of influence. *Journal of Experimental and Social Psychology*, 1971, *7*, 1–16.

Ferguson, T. J., & Wells, G. L. Priming of mediators in causal attribution. *Journal of Personality and Social Psychology*, 1980, *38*, 461–470.

Ferris, C. B., & Wicklund, R. A. An experiment on importance of freedom and prior demonstration. In R. A. Wicklund, *Freedom and reactance.* Hillsdale, N.J.: Erlbaum, 1974.

Festinger, L. Informal social communication. *Psychological Review*, 1950, *57*, 271–282.

Festinger, L. A. *A theory of cognitive dissonance.* Stanford, Calif.: Stanford University Press, 1957.

Festinger, L. A theory of social comparison processes. *Human Relations*, 1954, *1*, 117–140.

Festinger, L., & Carlsmith, J. Cognitive consequences of forced compliance. *Journal of Abnormal and Social Psychology*, 1959, *58*, 203–210.

Festinger, L., & Maccoby, N. On resistance to persuasive communications. *Journal of Abnormal and Social Psychology*, 1964, *68*, 359–366.

Festinger, L., Schachter, S., & Back, K. *Social pressures in informal groups: A study of a housing community.* New York: Harper, 1950.

Fidell, L. S. Empirical verification of sex discrimination in hiring practices in psychology. *American Psychologist*, 1970, *25*, 1094–1098.

Fiedler, F. E. The contingency model and the dynamics of the leadership process. In L. Berkowitz (Ed.), *Advances in experimental social psychology* (Vol. 11). New York: Academic Press, 1978.

Fiedler, F. E. Leadership effectiveness. *American Behavioral Scientist*, 1981, *24*, 619–632.

Fink, H. C. Attitudes toward the Calley-My Lai case, authoritarianism and political beliefs. Paper presented at the meeting of the Eastern Psychological Association, Washington, D.C., May 1973.

Firestone, L. J., Kaplan, K. J., & Russel, J. C. Anxiety, fear, and affiliation with similar-state versus dissimilar-state others: Misery sometimes loves miserable company. *Journal of Personality and Social Psychology*, 1973, *26*, 409–414.

Firestone, S. *The dialectic of sex: The case for feminist revolution.* New York: Morrow, 1970.

Fish, B., Karabenick, S., & Heath, M. The effects of observation on emotional arousal and affiliation. *Journal of Experimental Social Psychology*, 1978, *14*, 250–268.

Fishbein, M., & Ajzen, I. Attitudes toward objects as predictors of single and multiple behavioral criteria. *Psychological Review*, 1974, *81*, 59–74.

Fishbein, M., & Ajzen, I. *Belief, attitude, intention and behavior: An introduction to theory and research.* Reading, Mass.: Addison-Wesley, 1975.

Fisher, J. D., Rytting, M., & Henslin. Hands touching hands: Affective and evaluative effects of an interpersonal touch. *Sociometry*, 1976, *33*, 178–183.

Flanagan, J. C. A research approach to improving our quality of life. *American Psychologist*, 1978, *33*, 138–147.

Foss, R. D., & Dempsey, C. B. Blood donation and the foot-in-the-door technique: A limiting case. *Journal of Personality and Social Psychology*, 1979, *37*, 580–590.

Frager, R. Conformity and anticonformity in Japan. *Journal of Personality and Social Psychology*, 1970, *15*, 203–210.

Frandsen, K. D. Effects of threat appeals and media of transmission. *Speech Monographs*, 1963, *30*, 101–104.

Freedman, J. *Crowding and behavior.* San Francisco: Freeman, 1975.

Freedman, J. L., & Fraser, S. Compliance without pressure: The foot-in-the-door technique. *Journal of Personality and Social Psychology*, 1966, *4*, 195–202.

Freedman, J. L., Heshka, S., & Levy, A. Population density and pathology: Is there a relationship? *Journal of Experimental Social Psychology*, 1975, *11*, 539–552.

Freedman, J. L., Klevansky, S., & Ehrlich, P. The effect of crowding on human task performance. *Journal of Applied Social Psychology*, 1971, *1*, 7–25.

Freedman, J. L., Levy, A. S., Buchanan, R. W., & Price, J. Crowding and human aggressiveness. *Journal of Experimental Social Psychology*, 1972, *8*, 528–548.

Freedman, J., & Sears, D. Selective exposure. In L. Berkowitz (Ed.), *Advances in experimental social psychology* (Vol. 1). New York: Academic Press, 1965, 58–98.

Freedman, J. L., & Sears, D. O. Warning, distraction, and resistance to influence. *Journal of Personality and Social Psychology*, 1965, *1*, 262–265.

French, J. R. P., & Raven, B. H. The bases of social power. In D. Cartwright (Ed.), *Studies in social power.* Ann Arbor: University of Michigan Press, 1959.

Freud, S. *Beyond the pleasure principle.* New York: Bantam, 1970. (Originally published, 1920.)

Fried, M., & Gleicher, P. Some sources of residential satisfaction in an urban slum. *Journal of the American Institute of Planners*, 1961, *27*, 305–315.

Frieze, I. H. Perceptions of battered wives. In I. H. Frieze, Bar-Tel & Carroll (Eds.), *New approaches to social problems.* San Francisco: Jossey-Bass Publisher, 1979.

Frieze, I., Parsons, J., Johnson, P., Ruble, D., & Zellman, G. *Women

and sex roles: A social-psychological perspective.* New York: W. W. Norton, 1978.

Frieze, I., & Weiner, B. Cue utilization and attributional judgments for success and failure. *Journal of Personality*, 1971, *39*, 591–605.

Frodi, A. The effect of exposure to weapons on aggressive behavior from a cross-cultural perspective. *International Journal of Psychology*, 1975, *10*, 283–292.

Frodi, A. Sexual arousal, situational restrictiveness, and aggressive behavior. *Journal of Research in Personality*, 1977, *11*, 48–58.

Frodi, A., Macaulay, J., & Thome, P. R. Are women always less aggressive than men? A review of the experimental literature. *Psychological Bulletin*, 1977, *84*, 634–660.

Froming, W. J. The relationship of moral judgment, self-awareness, and sex to compliance behavior. *Journal of Research in Personality*, 1978, *12*(4), 396–409.

Fruen, J., & McGhee, P. E. Traditional sex role development and amount of time spent watching television. *Developmental Psychology*, 1975, *11*, 109.

Furstenberg, F. F., Jr. Premarital pregnancy and marital instability. *Journal of Social Issues*, 1976, *32*, 67–86.

Gaertner, S., & Bickman, L. Effects of race on elicitation of helping behavior: The wrong number technique. *Journal of Personality and Social Psychology*, 1971, *20*, 218–222.

Gailey, P. Four rescuers praised: Courage of the fourth is known, but not the name. *The New York Times*, January 15, 1982, p. D15.

Galle, D. R., Gove, W. R., & MacPherson, J. M. Population density and pathology: What are the relations for man. *Science*, 1972, *176*, 23–30.

Gannett News Service. Poll: Death penalty OK. May 30, 1982, pp. A1; A9.

Gardner, E. S. *Perry Mason solves the case of the dubious bridegroom.* New York: William Morrow, 1949.

Garrett, C. S., Ein, P. L., & Tremaine, L. The development of gender stereotyping of adult occupations in elementary school children. *Child Development*, 1977, *48*, 507–512.

Geen, R. Effects of frustration, attack, and prior training in aggressiveness upon aggressive behavior. *Journal of Personality and Social Psychology*, 1968, *9*, 316–321.

Geen, R. G. Evaluation, apprehension and social facilitation: A reply to Sanders. *Journal of Experimental Social Psychology*, 1981, *17*, 252–256.

Geen, R. G., & Wuanty, M. B. The catharsis of aggression: An evaluation of a hypothesis. In L. Berkowitz (Ed.), *Advances in experimental social psychology* (Vol. 10). New York: Academic Press, 1977.

Geen, R. G., & Stoner, D. Effects of aggressiveness habit strength on behavior in the presence of aggression-related stimuli. *Journal of Personality and Social Psychology*, 1971, *17*, 149–153.

Geertsma, R. H., & Reivich, R. S. Repetitive self-observation by videotape playback. *Journal of Nervous and Mental Disease*, 1965, *141*, 29–41.

Geizer, R. S. Rarick, D. L., & Soldow, G. F. Deception and judgment accuracy: A study in person perception. *Personality and Social Psychology Bulletin*, 1977, *3*, 446–449.

Gelles, R. J. Abused wives: Why do they stay? *Journal of Marriage and the Family*, 1976, *38*, 659–668.

Gelles, R. J. *The violent home.* Beverly Hills, Calif.: Sage, 1972.

Gentry, W. D. Effects of frustration, attack, and prior aggressiveness training on overt aggression and vascular processes. *Journal of Personality and Social Psychology*, 1970, *16*, 718–725.

Gerard, H. B., & Rabbie, J. M. Fear and social comparison. *Journal of Abnormal and Social Psychology*, 1961, *62*, 586–592.

Gerard, H. B., Wilhelmy, R. A., & Connolley, R. S. Conformity and group size. *Journal of Personality and Social Psychology*, 1968, *8*, 79–82.

Gerbasi, K. C., Zuckerman, M., & Reis, H. T. Justice needs a new blindfold: A review of mock jury research. *Psychological Bulletin*, 1977, *84*, 323–345.

Gerbner, G., & Gross, L. Living with television: The violence profile. *Journal of Communications*, 1976, *26*(2), 173–199.

Gerbner, G., Gross, L. Jackson-Beeck, M., Jefferies-Fox, S., & Signorielli, N. Cultural indicators: Violence profile No. 9. *Journal of Communication*, 1978, *28*, 176–207.

Gerbner, G., Gross, L., Signorielli, N., Morgan, M., & Jackson-Beeck, M. The demonstration of power: Violence profile No. 10. *Journal of Communication*, 1979, *29*, 177–196.

Gergen, K. J., & Marlowe, D. (Eds.), *Personality and social behavior*. Reading, Mass.: Addison-Wesley, 1970.

Gergen, K., Green, M., & Metzer, K. Individual orientations to prosocial behavior. *Journal of Social Issues*, 1972, *28*, 105–130.

Gergen, K. J., Ellsworth, P., Maslach, C., & Seipel, M. Obligation, donor resources, and reactions to aid in three cultures. *Journal of Personality and Social Psychology*, 1975, *31*, 390–400.

Gergen, K. J., & Wishnov, B. Others' self evaluations and interaction anticipation in determinants of self presentation. *Journal of Personality and Social Psychology*, 1965, *2*, 348–358.

Ghiselin, M. T. *American Psychologist*, 1976, *31*, 358–359. (comment)

Gilbert, G. M. Stereotype persistence and change among college students. *Journal of Abnormal and Social Psychology*, 1951, *46*, 245–254.

Gillig, P. M., & Greenwald, A. G. Is it time to lay the sleeper effect to rest? *Journal of Personality and Social Psychology*, 1974, *29*, 132–139.

Ginton, A., Daie, N., Elaad, E., & Ben-Shakhar, G. A method for evaluating the use of the polygraph in a real-life situation. *Journal of Applied Psychology*, 1982, *67*, 131–137.

Glass, D. C. Stress, competition and heart attacks. *Psychology Today*, December 1976, pp. 54–57; 134.

Glass, D. C., & Singer, J. E. *Urban stress*. New York: Academic Press, 1972.

Glenn, N. D., & McLanahan, S. Children and marital happiness: A further specification of the relationship. *Journal of Marriage and the Family*, February 1982, 63–71.

Glenn, N. D., & McLanahan, S. The effects of offspring on the psychological well-being of other adults. *Journal of Marriage and the Family*, May 1981, 409–421.

Glenn, N. D., & Weaver, C. N. Attitudes toward premarital, extramarital and homosexual relations in the U.S. and the 1970s. *Journal of Sex Research*, 1979, *15*(2), 108–119.

Glick, P. C., & Norton, A. J. Marrying, divorcing, and living together in the United States today. *Population Bulletin*, 1979, *32*, Washington, D.C.: Population Reference Bureau.

Glueck, S., & Glueck, E. *Unraveling juvenile delinquency*. New York: Commonwealth Fund, 1950.

Goethals, G. R., & Darley, J. M., Jr. Social comparison theory: An attributional approach. In J. M. Suls & R. L. Miller (Eds.), *Social Comparison Processes: Theoretical and Empirical Perspectives*. Washington, D.C.: Hemisphere, 1977.

Goethals, G. R., & Nelson, R. E. Similarity in the influence process: The belief-value distinction. *Journal of Personality and Social Psychology*, 1973, *25*, 117–122.

Goffman, E. *Interaction ritual*. Garden City, N.Y.: Doubleday, 1967.

Goffman, E. *The presentation of self in everyday life*. New York: Doubleday, 1959.

Goldberg, A. S., & Cain, G. G. The causal analysis of cognitive outcomes in the Coleman, Hoffer, and Kilgore report. *Sociology of Education*, 1982, *55*, 103–122.

Goldberg, A. S., & Shiflett, S. Goals of male and female college students—Do traditional sex differences still exist? *Sex Roles*, 1981, *7*, 1213–1222.

Goldberg, L. W. Differential attribution of trait-descriptive terms to oneself as compared to well-liked, neutral, and disliked others: A psychometric analysis. *Journal of Personality and Social Psychology*, 1978, *36*, 1012–1028.

Goldkamp, J. S., & Gottfredson, M. R. Bail decision making and pretrial detention: Surfacing judicial policy. *Law and Human Behavior*, 1979, *3*, 227–249.

Goldman, W., & Lewis, P. Beautiful is good: Evidence that the physically attractive are more socially skillful. *Journal of Experimental Social Psychology*, 1977, *13*, 125–130.

Goldschmidt, J., Gergen, M. M., Quigley, K., & Gergen, K. J. The women's liberation movement: Attitudes and action. *Journal of Personality*, 1974, *42*, 601–617.

Gordon, C. Self-conceptions: Configurations of content. In C. P. Gordon & K. P. Gergen (Eds.), *The Self in Social Interaction*. New York: Wiley, 1968.

Gorn, G. The effects of personal involvement, communication discrepancy, and source prestige on reactions to communications on separatism. *Canadian Journal of Behavioral Science*, 1975, *7*, 369–386.

Gorn, G. J., Goldberg, M. E., & Kamingo, R. N. The role of educational television in changing the intergroup attitudes of children. *Child Development*, 1976, *47*, 277–280.

Gottman, J. M., & Porterfield, A. L. Communicative competence in the nonverbal behavior of married couples. *Journal of Marriage and the Family*, 1980.

Gouldner, A. W. The notion of reciprocity: A preliminary statement. *American Sociological Review*, 1960, *25*, 161–178.

Gove, W. R. (Ed.). *The labeling of deviance*. New York: Sage-Halsted Press, 1975.

Green, F. P., & Schneider, F. W. Age differences in the behavior of boys on three measures of altruism. *Child Development*, 1974, *45*, 248–251.

Greenbaum, P., & Rosenfeld, H. M. Patterns of avoidance in response to interpersonal staring and proximity: Effects of bystanders on drivers at a traffic intersection. *Journal of Personality and Social Psychology*, 1978, *36*, 575–587.

Greenberg, B. Children's reactions to TV blacks. *Journalism Quarterly*, 1972, *49*, 5–14.

Greene, E. and Loftus, E. F. When crimes are joined at trial: Institutionalized prejudice? Paper presented at the convention of the American Psychology-Law Society, Boston, 1981.

Greenwald, A. G. Cognitive learning, cognitive responses to persuasion and attitude change. In A. G. Greenwald, T. C. Brock, and T. M. Ostrom (Eds.), *Psychological foundations of attitudes*. New York: Academic Press, 1968.

Greenwald, A. G., & Ronis, D. C. Twenty years of cognitive dissonance: Case study of the evolution of a theory. *Psychological Review*, 1978, *85*, 53–57.

Gregory, W. L., Mowen, J. C., & Linder, D. E. Social psychology and plea bargaining: Applications, methodology, and theory. *Journal of Personality and Social Psychology*, 1978, *36*, 1521–1530.

Griffith, R., & Rogers, R. Effects of fear-arousing components of driver education on students' safety attitudes and simulator performance. *Journal of Educational Psychology*, 1976, *68*, 501–506.

Griffitt, W. Environmental effects on interpersonal affective behavior. Ambient effective temperature and attraction. *Journal of Personality and Social Psychology*, 1970, *15*, 240–244.

Griffitt, W., & Garcia, L. Reversing authoritarian primitiveness. The impact of verbal conditioning. *Social Psychological Quarterly*, 1979, *42*, 55–61.

Gruder, C. L., Cook, T. D., Hennigan, K. M., Flay, B. R., Alessis, C., & Halamaj, J. Empirical tests of the absolute sleeper effect predicted from the discounting cue hypothesis. *Journal of Personal and Social Psychology*, 1978, *36*, 1061–1074.

Grusec, J. E., & Skubiski, S. L. Model nurturance, demand characteristics of the modeling experiment, and altruism. *Journal of Personality and Social Psychology*, 1970, *14*, 352–359.

Grush, J. E. Impact of candidate expenditures, regionality, and prior outcomes on the 1976 Democratic presidential primaries. *Journal of Personality and Social Psychology*, 1980, *38*, 337–347.

Grush, J. E., McKeough, K. L., & Ahlering, R. F. Extrapolating laboratory exposure and research to actual political elections. *Journal of Personality and Social Psychology*, 1978, *36*, 257–270.

Haan, N., Smith, M., & Block, J. Moral reasoning of young adults: Political-social behavior, family background and personality correlates. *Journal of Personality and Social Psychology*, 1968, *10*, 183–201.

Haefner, D. P. Arousing fear in dental health education. *Journal of Personality and Social Psychology*, 1967, *7*, 387–397.

Hall, C. S. *A primer of Freudian psychology*. New York: World Publishing Company, 1954.

Hall, C. S., & Lindzey, G. *Theories of personality* (2nd ed.). New York: Wiley, 1970.

Hall, E. T. *The hidden dimension*. Garden City, N.Y.: Doubleday, 1966.

Hall, J. A. Voice tone and persuasion. *Journal of Personality and Social Psychology*, 1980, *38*, 924–940.

Hamilton, D. L. A cognitive-attributional analysis of stereotyping. In L. Berkowitz (Ed.), *Advances in experimental social psychology* (Vol. 12). New York: Academic Press, 1979.

Hamilton, D., & Bishop, G. Attitudinal and behavioral effects of initial integration of white suburban neighborhoods. *Journal of Social Issues*, 1976, *32*, 47–67.

Hamilton, D. L., & Gifford, R. K. Illusory correlation in interpersonal perception: A cognitive basis of stereotypic judgments. *Journal of Experimental Social Psychology*, 1976, *12*, 392–407.

Hamilton, D. L., & Huffman, L. J. Generality of impression-formation processes for evaluative and non-evaluative judgments. *Journal of Personality and Social Psychology*, 1971, *20*, 200–207.

Hamilton, D. L., & Zanna, M. P. Differential weighting of favorable and unfavorable attributes in impressions of personality. *Journal of Experimental Research in Personality*, 1972, *6*, 204–212.

Hampton, R. L. Husband's characteristics and marital disruption in black families. *The Sociological Quarterly*, 1979, *20*, 255–266.

Haney, C., Banks, C., & Zimbardo, P. Interpersonal dynamics in a simulated prison. *International Journal of Criminology and Penology*, 1973, *1*, 69–97.

Hans, V. P., & Doob, A. N. Section 12 of the Canada Evidence Act and the deliberations of simulated juries. *Criminal Law Quarterly*, 1976, *18*, 235–253.

Hans, V. P., & Vidmar, N. Jury selection. In N. Kerr & R. M. Bray (eds.), *The psychology of the courtroom*. New York: Academic Press, 1982.

Hansen, R. D., & Donoghue, J. M. The power of consensus: Information derived from one's own and other's behavior. *Journal of Personality and Social Psychology*, 1977, *35*(5), 294–302.

Hanson, D. J. The influence of authoritarianism upon prejudice: A review. *Resources in Education*, 1975, *14*, 31.

Harlow, H. F. The nature of love. *American Psychologist*, 1958, *13*, 673–685.

Harlow, H. F., & Harlow, M. K. The young monkeys. In P. Cramer (Ed.), *Readings in developmental psychology today*. Del Mar, Calif.: CRM Books, 1970.

Harrington, D. M., & Anderson, S. M. Creativity, masculinity, femininity, and three models of psychological androgyny. *Journal of Personality and Social Psychology*, 1981, *41*, 744–757.

Hartshorne, H., & May, M. S. *Studies in the nature of character* (Vol. 1: *Studies in deceit*; Vol. 2: *Studies in self-control*; Vol. 3: *Studies in the organization of character*). New York: Macmillan, 1928–1930.

Hass, R. Persuasion or moderation? Two experiments on anticipatory belief change. *Journal of Personality and Social Psychology*, 1975, *31*, 1155–1162.

Hass, R. G., & Grady, K. Temporal delay, type of forewarning, and resistance to influence. *Journal of Experimental Social Psychology*, 1975, *11*, 459–469.

Hass, R. G., & Linder, D. E. Counterargument availability and the effects of message structure on persuasion. *Journal of Personality and Social Psychology*, 1972, *23*, 219–233.

Hass, R., & Mann, R. Anticipatory belief change: Persuasion or impression management. *Journal of Personality and Social Psychology*, 1976, *34*, 105–111.

Heberlein, T. A., Linz, D., & Ortiz, B. P. Time-of-day electricity pricing. In J. D. Claxton, C. D. Anderson, J. R. Brent Ritchie, & G. H. G. McDougall (Eds.), *Consumers and energy conservation: International perspectives on research and policy options*. New York: Harper, 1981.

Heider, F. Attitudes and cognitive organization. *Journal of Psychology*, 1946, *21*, 107–112.

Heider, F. *The psychology of interpersonal relations*. New York: Wiley, 1958.

Heider, F. Social perception and phenomenal causality. *Psychological Review*, 1944, *51*, 358–374.

Heider, F., & Simmel, M. An experimental study of apparent behavior. *American Journal of Psychology*, 1944, *57*, 243–259.

Heilman, M. E., & Toffler, B. L. Reacting to reactance: An interpersonal interpretation of the need for freedom. *Journal of Experimental Social Psychology*, 1976, *12*, 519–529.

Heingartner, A., & Hall, J. M. Affective consequences in adults and children of repeated exposure to auditory stimuli. *Journal of Personality and Social Psychology*, 1974, *29*, 719–723.

Helmreich, R. L., Spence, J. T., & Holahan, C. K. Psychological androgyny and sex role flexibility: A test of two hypotheses. *Journal of Personality and Social Psychology*, 1979, *37*, 1631–1644.

Helper, M. M., & Garfield, S. L. Use of the semantic differential to study acculturation in American Indian adolescents. *Journal of Personality and Social Psychology*, 1965, *2*, 817–822; 380.

Hendrick, C. Social psychology as history and as traditional science: An appraisal. *Personality and Social Psychology Bulletin*, 1976, *2*, 392–403.

Hendrick, C., & Constantini, A. F. Effects of varying trait inconsistency and response requirements on primacy effect on impression formation. *Journal of Personality and Social Psychology*, 1970, *15*, 158–164.

Henggeler, S. W., & Borduin, C. M. Satisfied working mothers and their preschool sons: Interaction and psychosocial adjustment. *Journal of Family Issues*, 1981, *2*, 322–335.

Henslin, J. L. Craps and magic. *American Journal of Sociology*, 1967, *73*, 316–330.

Hepburn, J. R. The objective reality of evidence and the utility of systematic jury selection. *Law and Human Behavior*, 1980, *4*, 89–102.

Hersh, S. *My Lai 4: A report on the massacre and its aftermath*. New York: Vintage Books, 1970.

Heslin, R., & Boss, D. Nonverbal intimacy in airport arrival and departure. *Personality and Social Psychology Bulletin*, 1980, *6*, 248–252.

Hess, R. D., & Torney, J. V. *The development of basic attitudes and values toward government and citizenship during the elementary school years, Part I* (Cooperative Research Project No. 1078). Washington, D.C.: U.S. Office of Education, 1965.

Hetherington, M. E. Effects of father absence on personality development in adolescent daughters. *Developmental Psychology*, 1972, *7*, 313–326.

Hetherington, M. E., & Deur, J. The effects of father absence on child development. *Young Children*, 1971, *26*, 233–248.

Higbee, K. L. Fifteen years of fear arousal: Research on threat appeals, 1953, 1968. *Psychological Bulletin*, 1969, *72*, 426–444.

Higgins, J. Authoritarianism and candidate preference. *Psychological Reports*, 1965, *16*, 603–604.

Hill, G. W. Group versus individual performance: Are N + 1 heads better than one? *Psychological Bulletin*, 1982, *91*, 517–539.

Himmelfarb, S., & Eagly, A. H. *Readings in attitude change*. New York: Wiley, 1974.

Hocking, J. E., Miller, G. R., & Fontes, N. E. Videotape in the courtroom: Witness deception. *Trial*, 1978, *14*, 52–55.

Hoffman, L. W. Changes in family roles, socialization and sex differences. *American Psychologist*, 1977, *32*, 644–657.

Hoffman, L. W. Maternal employment: 1979. *American Psychologist*, 1979, *34*, 859–865.

Hoffman, M. L. Development of moral thought, feeling, and behavior. *American Psychologist*, 1979, *34*, 958–966.

Hofling, C. K., Brotzman, E., Dalrymple, S., Graves, N., & Pierce, C. M. An experimental study in nurse-physician relationships. *Journal of Nervous and Mental Disease*, 1966, *143*, 171–180.

Hogan, R. Moral conduct and moral character: A psychological perspective. *Psychological Bulletin*, 1973, *79*, 217, 232.

Hogarth, J. *Sentencing as a human process*. Toronto: University of Toronto Press, 1971.

Hollander, E. P. Conformity, status and idiosyncrasy credit. *Psychological Review*, 1958, *65*, 117–127.

Hollander, E. P., & Webb, W. B. Leadership, followership and friendship. *Journal of Abnormal and Social Psychology*, 1955, *50*, 163–167.

Hollander, E., & Willis, R. Some current issues in the psychology of conformity and nonconformity. *Psychological Bulletin*, 1967, *68*, 62–76.

Hollen, C. C. Value change, perceived instrumentality, and attitude change. *Dissertation Abstracts International*, 1972, *33*. (University Microfilms No. 72–22, 229.)

Holsti, O. R. *Content analysis for the social sciences and humanities*. Reading, Mass.: Addison-Wesley, 1969.

Holstrom, L., & Burgess, A. *The victim of rape: Institutional reactions*. New York: Wiley, 1978.

Homans, G. C. *The human group*. New York: Harcourt, Brace, 1950.

Homans, G. C. *Social behavior: Its elementary forms*. New York: Harcourt, Brace, 1961.

Horai, J., Naccari, N., & Fatoullah, E. The effects of expertise and physical attractiveness upon opinion agreement and liking. *Sociometry*, 1974, *37*, 601–606.

Horner, M. S. Toward an understanding of achievement-related conflicts in women. *Journal of Social Issues*, 1972, *28*, 157–175.

Horowitz, I. A., Bordens, K. S., & Feldman, M. S. A comparison of verdicts obtained in severed and joined criminal trials. *Journal of Applied Social Psychology*, 1980, *10*, 444–456.

Houlden, P. Impact of procedural modifications on evaluations of plea bargaining. *Law and Society Review*, 1980–81, *15*, 267–291.

Hovland, C. I., & Janis, I. L. (Eds.). *Personality and persuasibility*. New Haven, Conn.: Yale University Press, 1959.

Hovland, C. I., & Weiss, W. The influence of source credibility on communication effectiveness. *Public Opinion Quarterly*, 1951, *15*, 635–650.

Hovland, C., Janis, I., & Kelly, H. H. *Communication and persuasion*. New Haven, Conn.: Yale University Press, 1953.

Hovland, C., Lumsdaine, A., & Sheffield, F. *Experiments on mass communication*. Princeton: Princeton University Press, 1949.

Hovland, C., & Mandell, W. An experimental comparison of conclusion-drawing by the communicator and the audience. *Journal of Abnormal and Social Psychology*, 1952, *47*, 581–588.

Hovland, C., & Sears, Minor studies in aggression: VI. Correlation of lynchings with economic indices. *Journal of Personality*, 1940, *9*, 301–310.

Howard, J. L., Lipzain, M. B., & Reifler, C. B. Is pornography a problem? *Journal of Social Issues*, 1973, *29*(3), 133–145.

How executives see women in management. *Business Week*, June 28, 1982, p. 10.

Hunt, M. *Sexual behavior in the 1970s*. Chicago: Playboy Press, 1974.

Hunter, D. E., & Whitten, P. *Encyclopedia of anthropology*. New York: Harper & Row, 1976.

Huston, T. L., Ruggiero, M., Conner, R., & Geis, G. Bystander intervention into crime: A study based on naturally occurring episodes. *Social Psychology Quarterly*, 1981, *44*(1), 14–23.

Hyde, J. S. How large are cognitive gender differences? *American Psychologist*, 1981, *36*, 892–901.

Hyde, J. S. *Understanding human sexuality*. New York: McGraw-Hill, 1979.

Hyman, H. H., & Sheatsley, P. B. "The authoritarian personality"—A methodological critique. In R. Christian & M. Jahoda (Eds.), *Studies in the scope and method of "The Authoritarian Personality."* New York: Free Press, 1954.

Ickes, W. J., & Barnes, R. D. Boys and girls together—and alienated: On enacting stereotyped sex roles in mixed-sex dyads. *Journal of Personality and Social Psychology*, 1978, *36*, 669–683.

Ickes, W. J., & Barnes, R. D. The role of sex and self-monitoring in unstructured dyadic interactions. *Journal of Personality and Social Psychology*, 1977, *35*, 315–330.

Ickes, W., & Layden, M. A. Attributional styles. In J. Harvey, W. Ickes, & R. Kidd (Eds.), *New directions in attribution research* (Vol. 2). Hillsdale, N.J.: Lawrence Erlbaum & Associates, 1978.

Ickes, W., Wicklund, R., & Ferris, C. B. Objective self-awareness and self-esteem. *Journal of Experimental Social Psychology*, 1973, *9*, 202–219.

Insko, C. A., Arkoff, A., & Insko, V. M. Effects of high and low fear-arousing communications upon opinions toward smoking. *Journal of Experimental Social Psychology*, 1965, *1*, 256–266.

Insko, C. A., & Melson, W. H. Verbal reinforcement of attitude in laboratory and nonlaboratory contexts. *Journal of Personality*, 1969, *37*, 25–40.

Insko, C. A., & Wilson, M. Interpersonal attraction as a function of social interaction. *Journal of Personality and Social Psychology*, 1977, *35*, 903–911.

Isen, A. M., Clark, M., & Schwartz, M. F. Duration of the effect of good mood on helping: "Footprints on the sands of time." *Journal of Personality and Social Psychology*, 1976, *34*, 385–393.

Isen, A., and Levin, P. The effect of feeling good on helping: Cookies and kindness. *Journal of Personality and Social Psychology*, 1972, *21*, 384–388.

Izzett, R. Authoritarianism and attitudes toward the Vietnam War as reflected in behavioral and self-report measures. *Journal of Personality and Social Psychology*, 1971, *17*, 145–148.

Jacklin, E. N., & Maccoby, E. E. Social behavior at thirty-three months in same-sex and mixed-sex dyads. *Child Development*, 1978, *49*, 557–569.

Jackson-Beek, M., & Robinson, J. Television nonviewers: An endangered species? *Journal of Consumer Research*, 1981, *7*, 356–359.

Jackson, J. M., & Latane, B. All alone in front of all those people: Stage fright as a function of number and type of co-performers and audience. *Journal of Personality and Social Psychology*, 1981, *40*, 73–85.

Jacobs, R. C., & Campbell, D. T. The perpetuation of an arbitrary tradition through several generations of a laboratory microculture. *Journal of Abnormal and Social Psychology*, 1961, *62*, 649–658.

James, W. *The principles of psychology.* New York: Dover, 1950 (original 1890).

Janis, I. L. *Victims of groupthink: A psychological study of foreign-policy decisions and fiascos.* Boston: Houghton Mifflin, 1972.

Janis, I. L., & Feshbach, S. Effects of fear-arousing communications. *Journal of Abnormal and Social Psychology*, 1953, *48*, 78–92.

Janis, I. L., & Gilmore, B. The influence of incentive conditions on the sources of role playing in modifying attitudes. *Journal of Personality and Social Psychology*, 1965, *1*, 17–27.

Janoff-Bulman, R. Characterological versus behavioral self-blame: Inquiries into depression and rape. *Journal of Personality and Social Psychology*, 1979, *37*, 1798–1809.

Jellison, J., & Mills, J. Effects of public commitment upon opinions. *Journal of Experimental Social Psychology*, 1969, *5*, 340–346.

Jenkins, R. L. Contributions of theory to the study of family decision making. *Advances in Consumer Research*, 1980, *7*, 207–211.

Jennings, M. K., & Niemi, R. G. The transmission of political values from parent to child. In Jack Dennis (Ed.), *Socialization to politics: A reader.* New York: Wiley, 1973.

Jennings (Walstedt), J., Geis, F. L., & Brown, V. Difference of television commercials on women's self-confidence and independent judgment. *Journal of Personality and Social Psychology*, 1980, *38*, 203–210.

Johnson, C., & Scott, B. *Eyewitness testimony and suspect identification as a function of arousal, sex of witness, and scheduling of interrogation.* Paper presented at the meeting of the American Psychological Association, Washington, D.C., September 1976.

Johnson, T. J., Feigenbaum, R., & Weiby, M. Some determinants and consequences of the teacher's perception of causality. *Journal of Educational Psychology*, 1964, *55*, 237–246.

Johnson vs. Louisiana, *United States Reports*, 1972, *406*, 340–356.

Johnston, J., Ettema, J., & Davidson, T. *An evaluation of "Freestyle": A television series to reduce sex role stereotypes.* Ann Arbor: Institute for Social Research, University of Michigan, 1980.

Jones, C., & Aronson, E. Attributions of fault to a rape victim as a function of respectability of the victim. *Journal of Personality and Social Psychology*, 1973, *26*, 415–419.

Jones, E. E. The rocky road from acts to dispositions. *American Psychologist*, 1979, *34*, 107–117.

Jones, E. E., & Davis, K. E. A theory of correspondent inferences: From acts to dispositions. In L. Berkowitz (Ed.), *Advances in experimental and social psychology* (Vol. 2). New York: Academic Press, 1965.

Jones, E. E., Davis, K. E., & Gergen, K. J. Role playing variations and their informational value on person perception. *Journal of Abnormal and Social Psychology*, 1961, *63*, 302–310.

Jones, E. E., Gergen, K. J., & Davis, K. E. Some determinants of reactions to being approved or disapproved as a person. *Psychological Monographs*, 1962, 76 (2, Whole No. 521).

Jones, E. E., & Harris, V. A. The attribution of attitudes. *Journal of Experimental Social Psychology*, 1967, *3*, 1–24.

Jones, E. E., & Nisbett, R. E. *The actor and the observer: Divergent perceptions of behavior.* Morristown, N.J.: General Learning Press, 1971.

Jones, E. E., & Sigall, H. The bogus pipeline: A new paradigm for measuring affect and attitude. *Psychological Bulletin*, 1971, *76*, 349–364.

Jones, R. A., & Brehm, J. W. Persuasiveness of one- and two-sided communications as a function of awareness: There are two sides. *Journal of Experimental Social Psychology*, 1970, *6*, 47–56.

Jourard, S. *The transparent self: Self-disclosure and well-being.* Princeton, N.J.: Van Nostrand, 1964.

Jourard, S. M., & Lasakow, P. A research approach to self-disclosure. *Journal of Abnormal Psychology*, 1958, *56*.

Joy, L. A., Kimball, M., & Zabrack, M. L. Television exposure and children's aggressive behaviour. In T. M. Williams (Chair), *The impact of television: A natural experiment involving three communities.* A symposium presented at the annual meeting of the Canadian Psychological Association, Vancouver, June, 1977.

Judd, C. M., & Kenney, D. A. *Estimating the effects of social interventions.* Cambridge: Cambridge University Press, 1981.

Kagan, J. Emergent themes in human development. *American Scientist*, 1976, *64*, 186–196.

Kahneman, D., & Tversky, A. On the psychology of prediction. *Psychological Review*, 1973, *80*, 237–251.

Kalven, H., Jr., & Zeisel, H. *The American jury.* Boston: Little, Brown, 1966.

Kandel, D. B. Similarity in real-life adolescent friendship pairs. *Journal of Personality and Social Psychology*, 1978, *36*, 306–312.

Kaplan, M. F. Information integration in social judgment: Interaction of judge and informational components. In M. Kaplan & S. Schwartz (Ed.), *Human judgment and decision processes.* New York: Academic Press, 1975.

Karaz, V., & Perlman, D. Attribution at the wire: Consistency and outcome finish strong. *Journal of Experimental Social Psychology*, 1975, *11*, 470–477.

Karlin, R. A., Epstein, L. S., & Rosen, Y. M. Environmental psychology: A blueprint for the future. *APA Monitor*, 1978, *11* (8–9), 3; 47.

Karlin, R., et al. Normative mediation of reactions to crowding. *Environmental Psychology and Nonverbal Behavior*, 1976, *1*, 30–40.

Karlin, R. A., Rosen, L., & Epstein, Y. M. Three into two doesn't go: A follow-up on the effects of overcrowded dormitory rooms. *Personality and Social Psychology Bulletin*, 1979, *5*, 391–395.

Karlins, M., Coffman, T. L., & Walters, G. On the fading of social stereotypes: Studies in three generations of college students. *Journal of Personality and Social Psychology*, 1969, *13*, 1–16.

Kasarda, J. D. The use of census data in secondary analysis: The context of ecological discovery. In M. P. Golden (Ed.), *The research experience*, Itasca, Ill.: F. E. Peacock, 1976.

Kassarjian, H. H. Consumer psychology. *Annual Review of Psychology*, 1982, *33*, 619–649.

Kassin, S. M., & Wrightsman, L. S. On the requirements of proof: The timing of judicial instruction and mock juror verdicts. *Journal of Personality and Social Psychology*, 1979, *37*, 1877–1887.

Katz, D. The functional approach to the study of attitude. *The Public Opinion Quarterly*, 1960, *24*, 163–204.

Katz, D., & Braley, K. W. Racial stereotypes of 100 college students. *Journal of Abnormal and Social Psychology*, 1932, *28*, 280–290.

Katz, D., & Kahn, R. L. *The social psychology of organizations.* New York: Wiley, 1966.

Katzoff, P. Equal crime. *Boston Magazine*, December 1977, pp. 107–108; 206–210.

Keating, J. P., & Brock, T. C. Acceptance of persuasion and the inhibition of counter-argumentation under various distraction tasks. *Journal of Experimental Social Psychology*, 1974, *10*, 301–309.

Kehner, K. C. The Gary income maintenance experiment: Summary of initial findings. In T. Cook, et al. (Eds.), *Evaluation studies: Review annual* (Vol. 3). Beverly Hills: Sage, 1978.

Kelly, G. A. *The psychology of personal constructs.* New York: Norton, 1955.

Kelly, S., Jr., & Mirer, T. W. The simple act of voting. *American Political Science Review,* 1974, *68*(2), 571–591.

Kelley, H. H. Attribution theory in social psychology. In D. Levine (Ed.), *Nebraska symposium on motivation.* Lincoln, Neb.: University of Nebraska Press, 1967.

Kelley, H. H. Causal schemata and the attribution process. In E. E. Jones, D. Kanouse, H. H. Kelley, R. E. Nisbett, S. Valins, & B. Weiner (Eds.), *Attribution: Perceiving the causes of behavior.* Morristown, N.J.: General Learning Press, 1972.

Kelley, H. The warm-cold variable in first impressions of persons. *Journal of Personality,* 1950, *18*, 431–439.

Kelley, H. H., et al. Collective behavior in a simulated panic situation. *Journal of Experimental Social Psychology,* 1965, *1*, 20–54.

Kelley, H. H., & Thibaut, J. W. Group problem solving. In G. Lindzey & E. Aronson (Eds.), *Handbook of social psychology* (2nd ed.)(Vol. 4). Reading, Mass.: Addison-Wesley, 1969.

Kellogg, R., & Baron, R. S. Attribution theory, insomnia, and the reverse placebo effect: A reversal of Storm's and Nisbett's finding. *Journal of Personality and Social Psychology,* 1975, *32*, 231–236.

Kelman, H. C. Compliance, identification, and internalization. *Journal of Conflict Resolution,* 1958, *2*, 51–60.

Kelman, H. C. The role of the group in the induction of therapeutic change. *International Journal of Group Psychotherapy,* 1963, *13*, 399–432.

Kelman, H. C. (Ed.). *International behavior: A socio-psychological analysis.* New York: Holt, Rinehart & Winston, 1965.

Kelman, H. C., & Hovland, C. I. "Reinstatement" of the communicator in delayed measurement of opinion change. *Journal of Abnormal and Social Psychology,* 1953, *48*, 327–335.

Kennel, J. H., et al. Maternal behavior one year after early and extended post-partum contact. *Developmental Medicine and Child Neurology,* 1974, *16*, 172–179.

Kerr, N. L. Social transition schemes: Charting the group's road to agreement. *Journal of Personality and Social Psychology,* 1981, *41*, 684–702.

Kerr, N. L., et al. Guilt beyond a reasonable doubt: Effects of concept definition and assigned rule on judgments of mock jurors. *Journal of Personality and Social Psychology,* 1976, *34*, 282–294.

Kessler, R. C., & McRae, J. A. The effect of wives' employment on the mental health of married men and women. *American Sociological Review,* 1982, *47*, 216–227.

Keyes, R. *The height of your life.* Boston: Little, Brown, 1980.

Kidder, L. A. *Selltiz, Wrightsman, & Cook's research methods in social relations.* New York: Holt, Rinehart & Winston, 1981.

Kiesler, C. A. *The psychology of commitment.* New York: Academic Press, 1971.

Kiesler, C., Collins, B. E., & Miller, N. *Attitude change: A critical analysis of theoretical approaches.* New York: Wiley, 1969.

Kiesler, C., & Kiesler, S. *Conformity.* Reading, Mass.: Addison-Wesley, 1969.

Kiesler, C., et al. Commitment and the boomerang effect: A field study. Summarized in C. Keisler, *The psychology of commitment: Experiments linking behavior to belief.* New York: Academic Press, 1971.

Kilham, W., & Mann, L. Level of destructive obedience as a function of transmitter and executant roles in the Milgram obedience paradigm. *Journal of Personality and Social Psychology,* 1974, *29*, 696–702.

Kilman, H. C., & Cohen, S. P. Reduction of international conflict: An international approach. In W. G. Austin and S. Worchel (Eds.), *The social psychology of intergroup relations.* Monterey, Calif.: Brooks/Cole, 1979.

King, W. Youths' silence on murder victim leaves a California town baffled. *New York Times,* December 14, 1981.

Kipper, D. A., & Yinon, Y. The effect of modeling with expressed conflict on children's generosity. *Journal of Social Psychology,* 1978, 277–278.

Kitson, G. C., & Raschke, H. J. Divorce research: What we need to know. *Journal of Divorce,* 1981, *4*, 1–37.

Klapper, J. T. *The effects of mass communication.* Glencoe, Ill.: The Free Press, 1960.

Kleinke, C. L., Meeker, F. B., & LaFong, C. Effects of gaze, touch, and use of name on evaluation of "engaged" couples. *Journal of Research in Personality,* 1974, *7*, 368–373.

Klevorick, A. K., & Rothschild, M. A model of the jury decision process. *Journal of Legal Studies,* January 1979, 141–164.

Klopp, P., & MacDonald, M. Nutrition labels: An exploratory study of consumer reasons for nonuse. *Journal of Consumer Affairs,* Winter 1981, 301–316.

Knapp, M. L. *Nonverbal communication in human interaction* (2nd ed.). New York: Holt, Rinehart & Winston, 1978.

Knowles, E. S. Boundaries around group interaction: The effect of group size and member status on boundary permeability. *Journal of Personality and Social Psychology,* 1973, *26*, 327–331.

Knox, R. E., & Inkster, J. A. Postdecision dissonance at post-time. *Journal of Personality and Social Psychology,* 1968, *8*, 319–323.

Koeske, G. E., & Crano, W. D. The effects of congruous and incongruous source-statement combinations upon the judged credibility of a communication. *Journal of Experimental Social Psychology,* 1968, *4*, 384–399.

Kohlberg, L. The development of children's orientations toward a moral order: First sequence in the development of moral thought. *Vita Humana,* 1963, *6*, 11–33.

Kohlberg, L. Moral education for a society in moral transition. *Educational Leadership,* 1975, *33*, 46–54.

Kohlberg, L. *The philosophy of moral development.* New York: Harper & Row, 1981.

Kohlberg, L. Stage and sequence: The cognitive-developmental approach to socialization. In D. A. Goslin (Ed.), *Handbook of socialization: Theory and research.* Chicago: Rand McNally, 1969.

Kolbe, R., & LaVoie, J. C. Sex-role stereotyping in pre-school children's picture books. *Social Psychology Quarterly,* 1981, *44*, 369–374.

Komarovsky, M. Cultural contradictions and sex roles: The masculine case. *American Journal of Sociology,* 1973, *78*, 873–884.

Konecni, V. J. The mediation of aggressive behavior. Arousal level versus anger and cognitive labeling. *Journal of Personality and Social Psychology,* 1975, *32*, 706–712.

Koslin, S., Amarel, M., & Ames, N. A distance measure of racial attitudes in primary grade children: An explanatory study. *Psychology in the Schools,* 1969, *6*, 382–385.

Kotelchuk, M. The infant's relationship to the father: Experimental evidence. In M. Lamb (Ed.), *The role of the father in child development.* New York: Wiley, 1976.

Krafka, C., & Penrod, S. *The effects of witness and stimulus factors on eyewitness performance.* American Psychology-Law Society Biennial Convention, October 1981.

Krauss, R. M., et al. Verbal, vocal, and visible factors in judgments of another's effect. *Journal of Personality and Social Psychology,* 1981, *40*, 312–319.

Kraut, R. E., & Johnston, R. E. Social and emotional messages of smiling: An ethological approach. *Journal of Personality and Social Psychology,* 1979, *37*, 1539–1553.

Kraut, R. E., & Poe, D. Behavioral roots of person perception: The deception judgments of customs inspectors and laymen. *Journal of Personality and Social Psychology,* 1980, *39*, 784–798.

Krebs, D. Altruism—An examination of the concept and a review of the literature. *Psychological Bulletin,* 1970, *73*, 258–302.

Kroeber, T. *Ishi in two worlds*. Berkeley: University of California Press, 1961.

Kuhn, T. S. The structure of scientific revolutions. *International Encyclopedia of Unified Science* (Vol. 2). Chicago: University of Chicago Press, 1970.

Kulik, J., & Brown, R. Frustration, attribution of blame, and aggression. *Journal of Experimental Social Psychology*, 1979, *15*, 183–194.

Kulka, R. A., & Weingarten, H. The long-term effects of parental divorce in childhood on adult adjustment. *Journal of Social Issues*, 1979, *35*, 50–78.

Kurtines, W., & Grief, E. B. The development of moral thought: Review and evaluation of Kohlberg's approach. *Psychological Bulletin*, 1974, *81*, 453–470.

LaFrance, M., & Carmen, B. The nonverbal display of psychological androgyny. *Journal of Personality and Social Psychology*, 1980, *38*, 36–49.

Lamb, M. E., & Bronson, S. K. Fathers in the context of family influence: Past, present, and future. *School Psychology Review*, 1980, *9*, 336–353.

Lamm, H., & Myers, D. G. Group-induced polarization of attitudes and behavior. In L. Berkowitz (Ed.), *Advances in experimental social psychology* (Vol. 11). New York: Academic Press, 1978.

Lamm, H., & Ochsmann, R. Factors limiting the generality of the risky-shift phenomenon. *European Journal of Social Psychology*, 1972, *2*, 99–102.

Lamm, H., & Sauer, C. Discussion-induced shift toward higher demands in negotiation. *European Journal of Social Psychology*, 1974, *4*, 85–88.

Lamm, H., & Trommsdorf, G. Group versus individual performance on tasks requiring ideational proficiency (brainstorming): A review. *European Journal of Social Psychology*, 1973, *3*, 361–388.

Landy, D., & Aronson, E. The influence of the character of the criminal and his victim on the decisions of simulated jurors. *Journal of Experimental Social Psychology*, 1969, *5*, 141–152.

Landy, D., & Sigall, H. Beauty is talent: Task evaluation as a function of the performer's physical attractiveness. *Journal of Personality and Social Psychology*, 1974, *29*, 299–304.

Langer, E. J. The illusion of control. *Journal of Personality and Social Psychology*, 1975, *32*, 311–328.

Langer, E., & Aronson, R. R. The semantics of asking a favor: How to succeed in getting help without really dying. *Journal of Personality and Social Psychology*, 1972, *24*, 26–32.

Langer, E., Blank, A., & Chanowitz, B. The mindlessness of ostensibly thoughtful action: The role of "placebo" information in interpersonal interaction. *Journal of Personality and Social Psychology*, 1978, *36*, 335–342.

Langer, E., & Mulvey, A. Unpublished data. Cited in J. Rodin & E. Langer, Aging labels: The decline of control and the fall of self-esteem. *Journal of Social Issues*, 1980, *36*, 12–29.

Langer, E. J., & Rodin, J. The effects of choice and enhanced personal responsibility for the aged: A field experiment in an institutional setting. *Journal of Personality and Social Psychology*, 1976, *34*, 191–198.

Langer, E. J., & Roth, J. Heads I win, tails it's chance: The illusion of control as a function of the sequence of outcomes in a purely chance task. *Journal of Personality and Social Psychology*, 1975, *32*, 951–955.

Langer, E., & Weinman, C. When thinking disrupts intellectual performance: Mindfulness on an overlearned task. *Personality and Social Psychology Bulletin*, 1981, 7, 240–243.

Langley, R., & Levy, R. Wife abuse and the police response. *FBI Law Enforcement Bulletin*, 1978, *47*, 4–9.

LaPiere, R. T. Attitudes vs. action. *Social Forces*, 1934, *13*, 230–237.

LaPiere, R. T. *Collective behavior*. New York: McGraw-Hill, 1938.

Latané, B. The psychology of social impact. *American Psychologist*, 1981, *36*, 343–356.

Latané, B., & Bidwell, L. D. Sex & affiliation in college cafeterias. *Personality and Social Psychology Bulletin*, 1977, *3*, 571–574.

Latané, B., & Darley, J. M. *The unresponsive bystander: Why doesn't he help?* New York: Appleton-Century-Crofts, 1970.

Latané, B., Williams, K., & Harkins, S. Many hands make light the work: The causes and consequences of social loafing. *Journal of Personality and Social Psychology*, 1979, *37*, 822–832.

Lazarsfeld, P. F. The American soldier—An expository review. *Public Opinion Quarterly*, Fall 1949, pp. 377–404.

Leavitt, H. J. Some effects of certain communication patterns of group performances. *Journal of Abnormal and Social Psychology*, 1951, *46*, 38–50.

LeBon, G. *The crowd* (trans.). London: Allen & Unwin, 1903.

Leifer, A. D., Leiderman, P. H., Barnett, C. R., Williams, J. A. Effects of mother-infant separation on maternal attachment behavior. *Child Development*, 1972, *43*, 1203.

Lepper, M. R., Greene, D., & Nisbett, R. E. Undermining children's intrinsic interest with extrinsic reward: A test for the over-justification hypothesis. *Journal of Personality and Social Psychology*, 1973, *28*, 129–137.

Lerner, R. M. *Concepts and theories of human development*. Reading, Mass.: Addison-Wesley, 1976.

Lerner, M. J. The desire for justice and reactions to victims. In J. Macaulay & L. Berkowitz (Eds.), *Altruism & helping behavior*. New York: Academic Press, 1970.

Lerner, M. J., & Matthews, G. Reactions to the suffering of others under conditions of indirect responsibility. *Journal of Personality and Social Psychology*, 1967, *5*, 319–327.

Lesser, G. S., & Abelson, R. P. Personality correlates of persuasibility in children. In I. L. Janis & C. I. Hovland (Eds.), *Personality and persuasibility*. New Haven, Conn.: Yale University Press, 1959.

Lester, E., & Werbell, F. E. The lost hero of the holocaust. *The New York Times Magazine*, March 30, 1980, pp. 112–117; 128–131.

Leventhal, H. Findings and theory in the study of fear communications. In L. Berkowitz (Ed.), *Advances in experimental social psychology* (Vol. 5). New York: Academic Press, 1970.

Leventhal, H. Emotions: A basic problem for social psychology. In C. Nemeth (Ed.), *Social psychology: Classic and contemporary integrations*. Chicago: Rand McNally, 1974.

Leventhal, H., & Cleary, P. D. The smoking problem: A review of the research and theory in behavioral risk modification. *Psychological Bulletin*, 1980, *88*, 370–405.

Leventhal, H., & Niles, P. Persistence of influence for varying durations of exposure to threat stimuli. *Psychological Reports*, 1965, *16*, 223–233.

Leventhal, H., Safer, M. A., Cleary, P. D., & Gutmann, M. Cardiovascular risk modification by community-based programs for life-style change: Comments on the Stanford study. *Journal of Consulting and Clinical Psychology*, 1980, *48*, 150–158.

Leventhal, H., & Singer, R. D. Affect arousal and positioning of recommendations in persuasive communications. *Journal of Personality and Social Psychology*, 1966, *4*, 137–146.

Leventhal, H., Watts, J. C., & Pagano, F. Effects of fear and instructions on how to cope with danger. *Journal of Personality and Social Psychology*, 1967, *6*, 313–321.

Levin, I. P., Faraone, S. V., & Herring, R. D. Measuring personal satisfaction under varying economic conditions. *Bulletin of Psychonomic Society*, 1980, *16*, 356–358.

Levin, I. P., Faraone, S. V., & McGraw, J. A. The effects of income and inflation on personal satisfaction: Functional measurement in economic psychology. *Journal of Economic Psychology*, 1981, *1*, 303–318.

Levine, F. J., & Tapp, J. L. Eyewitness identification: Problems and pitfalls. In V. J. Konecni & E. B. Ebbesen (Eds.), *The criminal justice system*. San Francisco: W. H. Freeman, 1982.

Levinger, G. Marital cohesiveness and dissolution: An integrative review. *Journal of Marriage and the Family*, 1965, *27*, 19–28.

Levinger, G. A social psychological perspective on divorce. *Journal of Social Issues*, 1976, *32*, 21–47.

Levitt, E. E., & Klassen, A. D. Public attitudes toward homosexuality: Part of the 1970 National Survey by the Institute for Sex Research. *Journal of Homosexuality*, 1974, *1*, 29–45.

Lewin, K. *A dynamic theory of personality.* New York: McGraw-Hill, 1935.

Lewin, K. Forces behind food habits and methods of change. *Bulletin of the National Research Council*, 1943, *108*, 35–65.

Lewinson, D. J., & Huffman, P. E. Traditional family ideology and its relation to personality. *Journal of Personality*, 1955, *23*, 251–273.

Lewis, D. A., & Maxfield, M. G. Fear in the neighborhoods: An investigation of the impact of crime. *Journal of Research in Crime and Delinquency*, 1980, *17*, 160–189.

Leyens, J. P., & Parke, R. D. Aggressive slides can induce a weapons effect. *European Journal of Social Psychology*, 1975, *5*, 229–236.

Liang, J., & Sengstock, M. C. The risk of personal victimization among the aged. *Journal of Gerontology*, 1981, *36*, 463–471.

Likert, R. A technique for the measurement of attitudes. *Archives of Psychology*, 1932, No. 140.

Lindsay, R. C. L., Wells, G. L., & Rumpel, C. M. Can people detect eyewitness-identification accuracy within and across situations? *Journal of Applied Psychology*, 1981, *66*, 79–89.

Linz, D. *Assessing courtroom performance from the perspective of social science observer, the trial practice attorney, and the "jury box."* Annual Meeting of the Law and Society Association, Toronto, June, 1982.

Linz, D., & Penrod, S. *A meta-analysis of the influence of research methodology on the outcomes of jury simulation studies.* Annual Meeting, Academy of Criminal Justice Sciences, March, 1982.

Linz, D., et al. *The use of experts in the courtroom: Attorney judgments of expert witness credibility.* Annual Meeting, Academy of Criminal Justice Sciences, March, 1982.

Littlepage, G., & Pineault, T. Verbal, facial, and paralinguistic cues to the detection of truth and lying. *Personality and Social Psychology Bulletin*, 1978, *4*, 461–464.

Loftus, E. The incredible eyewitness. *Psychology Today*, July 1974, pp. 117–119.

Loftus, E. Leading questions and the eyewitness report. *Cognitive Psychology*, 1975, *6–7*, 160–172.

Loftus, E. F., & Palmer, J. C. Reconstruction of automobile destruction: An example of the interaction between language and memory. *Journal of Verbal Learning and Verbal Behavior*, 1974, *13*, 585–589.

Lohr, J. M., & Staats, A. W. Attitude conditioning in Sino-Tibetan languages. *Journal of Personality and Social Psychology*, 1973, *26*, 196–200.

Lord, C. G., Ross, L., & Lepper, M. R. Biased assimilation and attitude polarization: The effects of prior theories on subsequently considered evidence. *Journal of Personality and Social Psychology*, 1979, *37*, 2098–2109.

Lorenz, K. *On aggression.* New York: Harcourt Brace Jovanovich, 1966.

Lott, A. J., & Lott, B. E. Group cohesiveness, communication level, and conformity. *Journal of Abnormal and Social Psychology*, 1961, *62*, 408–412.

Lott, A. J., & Lott, B. E. Group cohesiveness as interpersonal attraction: A review of relationships with antecedent and consequent variables. *Psychological Bulletin*, 1965, *64*, 259–309.

Lott, D. F., & Sommer, R. Seating arrangements and status. *Journal of Personality and Social Psychology*, 1967, *7*, 90–95.

Loving, N. Responding to spouse abuse and wife beating: A guide for police. *Police Executive Research Forum*, 1980.

Lowry, D. T., Love, G., & Kirby, M. Sex on soap operas: Patterns of intimacy. *Journal of Communication*, Summer 1981, *31*, 90–96.

Loye, D. TV impact on adults—It's not all bad news. *Psychology Today*, 1978, *11*(12), 86.

Luchins, A. Primacy-recency in impression formation. In C. Hovland, W. Mandell, E. Campbell, T. Brock, A. Luchins, A. Cohen, W. McGuire, I. Janis, R. Feierabend, N. Anderson, *The order of presentation in persuasion.* New Haven: Yale University Press, 1957, pp. 33–61.

Lupri, E., & Frideres, J. The quality of marriage and the passage of time: Marital satisfaction over the family life cycle. *Canadian Journal of Sociology*, 1981, *6*, 283–305.

Lykken, D. T. The detection of deception. *Psychology Bulletin*, 1979, *86*(1), 47–53.

Lynch, K. *The image of the city.* Cambridge: MIT Press, 1960.

Maccoby, E. E. *Social development: Psychological growth and the parent-child relationship.* New York: Harcourt Brace Jovanovich, 1980.

Maccoby, E. F., & Jacklin, C. N. *The psychology of sex differences.* Stanford, Calif.: Stanford University Press, 1974.

Maccoby, N., & Alexander, J. Reducing heart disease risk using the mass media: Comparing the effects on three communities. In A. Baum & J. E. Singer (Eds.), *Advances in environmental psychology* (Vol. 3). Hillsdale, N.J.: Lawrence Erlbaum Associates, 1981.

Maccoby, N., et al. "Critical periods" in seeking and accepting information. In *Paris-Stanford Studies in Communication.* Stanford, Calif.: Institute of Communication Research, 1962.

MacDonald, W., & Oden, C. W., Jr. Effects of extreme crowding on the performance of five married couples during twelve weeks of intensive training. *Proceedings of the 81st Annual Convention of the American Psychological Association*, 1973, 209–210.

MacLacklan, J. What people really think of fast talkers. *Psychology Today*, 1979, *13*(6), 113–114, 116–117.

Major, B., Deaux, K., & Carnevale, P. J. D. A different perspective on androgyny: Evaluations of masculine and feminine personality characteristics. *Journal of Personality and Social Psychology*, 1981, *41*, 988–1001.

Malamuth, N. M., & Check, J. V. P. The effects of mass media exposure on acceptance of violence against women: A field experiment. *Journal of Research in Personality*, 1981, *15*, 436–446.

Malamuth, N. M., & Check, J. V. P. Attitudes facilitating violence and laboratory aggression against women. In preparation, 1982.

Malamuth, N. M., Haber, & Feshback, S. Testing hypotheses regarding rape: Exposure to sexual violence, sex differences, and the "normality" of rapists. *Journal of Research in Personality*, 1980, *14*, 121–137.

Malamuth, N. M., Heim, M., & Feshback, S. Sexual responsiveness of college students to rape depictions: Inhibitory and disinhibitory effects. *Journal of Personality and Social Psychology*, 1980, *38*, 399–408.

Malamuth, N. M., & Spinner, B. A longitudinal content analysis of sexual violence in the best-selling erotic magazines. *The Journal of Sex Research*, 1980, *16*, 3, 226–237.

Malof, M., & Lott, A. J. Ethnocentrism and the acceptance of Negro support in a group pressure situation. *Journal of Abnormal and Social Psychology*, 1962, *65*, 254–258.

Malpass, R. S., & Devine, P. G. *Eyewitness identification: Line-up instructions and the absence of the offender.* Unpublished manuscript, State University of New York at Plattsburgh, 1980.

Manis, M., et al. Base rates can affect individual predictions. *Journal of Personality and Social Psychology*, 1980, *38*, 231–248.

Mann, F., & Baumgartel, H. *Absences and employee attitudes in an electric power company.* Ann Arbor, Mich.: Institute for Social Research, 1952.

Mann, L., & Janis, I. A follow-up study on the long-term effects of emotional role-playing. *Journal of Personality and Social Psychology,* 1968, 8, 339–342.

Mann, R. D. A review of the relationship between personality and performance in small groups. *Psychological Bulletin,* 1959, 56, 241–270.

Mannheim, B. Reference groups, membership group, and the self image. *Sociometry,* 1966, 29, 265–279.

Mantell, D. M. The potential for violence in Germany. *Journal of Social Issues,* 1971, 27(4), 101–112.

Marcus, D. E., & Overton, W. F. The development of cognitive gender constancy and sex-role preferences. *Child Development,* 1978, 49, 434–444.

Margolick, D. Right to lawyer before lineups denied by court. *The New York Times,* April 9, 1982, p. 15.

Margolis, C. The black student in political strife. *Proceedings of the 79th Annual Convention of the American Psychological Association,* 1971, 6, 395–396.

Markus, H. The drive for integration: Some comments. *Journal of Experimental Social Psychology,* 1981, 17, 257–261.

Markus, H. Self-schemata and processing information about the self. *Journal of Personality and Social Psychology,* 1977, 35, 63–78.

Martin, J., & Westie, F. The tolerant personality. *American Sociological Review,* 1959, 24, 521–528.

Martindale, D. Territorial dominance behavior in dyadic verbal interactions. *Proceedings of the 79th Annual Convention of the A.P.A.,* 1971, 6, 305–306.

Marton, K. The Wallenberg mystery. *The Atlantic,* November 1980, pp. 33–40.

Maruyama, G., Fraser, S., & Miller, N. Personal responsibility and altruism in children. *Journal of Personality and Social Psychology,* 1982, 42(4), 658–664.

Masters, J. C., & Wilkinson, A. Consensual and discriminative stereotypes of sex-type judgments by parents and children. *Child Development,* 1976, 47, 208–217.

Masters, W. H., & Johnson, V. E. *Human sexual response.* Boston: Little, Brown, 1966.

Matarazzo, J. D. Behavioral health's challenge to academic, scientific, and professional psychology. *American Psychologist,* 1982, 37, 1–14.

Matthews, K. E., & Cannon, L. K. Environmental noise level as a determinant of helping behavior. *Journal of Personality and Social Psychology,* 1975, 32, 571–577.

Mayo, E. *The human problems of an industrial civilization.* New York: Macmillan, 1933.

Mazur-Hart, S. F., & Berman, J. J. Changing from fault to no-fault divorce: An interrupted time series analysis. *Evaluation Studies Review Annual,* 1979, 4, 586–599.

Mazur-Hart, S. F., & Berman, J. J. Changing from fault to no-fault divorce: An interrupted time series analysis. *Journal of Applied Psychology,* 1977, 7, 300–312.

MacAndrew, F. T. *Interpersonal attraction, arousal, and nonverbal immediacy behaviors: A correlational analysis.* Paper presented at the meeting of the Eastern Psychological Association, Hartford, 1980.

McArthur, L. A. The how and what of why: Some determinants and consequences of causal attribution. *Journal of Personality and Social Psychology,* 1972, 22, 171–193.

McArthur, L. A. The lesser influence of consensus than distinctiveness information on causal attributions: A test of the person-thing hypothesis. *Journal of Personality and Social Psychology,* 1976, 33, 733–742.

McArthur, L. A., & Eisen, S. V. Achievements of male and female storybook characters as determinants of achievement behavior by boys and girls. *Journal of Personality and Social Psychology,* 1976, 33, 467–473.

McArthur, L., & Post, D. Figural emphasis and person perception. *Journal of Experimental Social Psychology,* 1977, 13, 520–535.

McCain, G., Cox, V., & Paulus, P. The relationship between illness, complaints, and degree of crowding in a prison environment. *Environment and Behavior,* 1976, 8, 283–290.

McCarthy, D., & Saegert, S. Residential density, social overload, and social withdrawal. *Human Ecology,* 1978, 6, 253–272.

McCord, W., McCord, I., & Zola, I. K. *Origins of crime: A new evaluation of the Cambridge-Somerville Youth Study.* New York: Columbia University Press, 1959.

McCormick, N. Come-ons and put-offs: Unmarried students' strategies for having and avoiding sexual intercourse. *Psychology of Women Quarterly,* 1979, 4, 194–211.

McDougall, W. *Introduction to social psychology.* London: Methuen, 1908.

McDougall, W. *The group mind.* New York: Putnam, 1920.

McFatter, R. M. Sentencing strategies and justice: Effects of punishment philosophy on sentencing decisions. *Journal of Personality and Social Psychology,* 1978, 36, 1490–1500.

McGee, M. G., & Snyder, M. Attribution and behavior: Two field studies. *Journal of Personality and Social Psychology,* 1975, 32, 185–190.

McGinnies, E., & Ward, C. Persuasibility and locus of control: Five crosscultural experiments. *Journal of Personality,* 1974, 42, 360–371.

McGuire, W. The nature of attitudes and attitude change. In G. Lindzey and E. Aronson (Eds.), *The handbook of social psychology* (2nd ed.) (Vol. III). Reading, Mass.: Addison-Wesley, 1969, pp. 136–314.

McGuire, W. J. Personality and susceptibility to social influence. In E. F. Borgatta & W. W. Lambert (Eds.), *Handbook of personality theory and research.* Chicago: Rand McNally, 1968.

McGuire, W. J. The yin and yang of progress in social psychology: Seven Koan. *Journal of Personality and Social Psychology,* 1973, 26(3), 446–456.

McGuire, W. J., McGuire, C. V., & Winton, W. Effects of household sex composition on the salience of one's gender in the spontaneous self-concept. *Journal of Experimental Social Psychology,* 1979, 15, 77–90.

McGuire, W. J., & Millman, S. Anticipatory belief lowering following forewarning of a persuasive attack. *Journal of Personality and Social Psychology,* 1965, 2, 471–479.

McGuire, W. J., & Padawer-Singer, A. Trait salience in the spontaneous self-concept. *Joural of Personality and Social Psychology,* 1976, 33, 743–754.

McGuire, W. J., & Papageorgis, D. Effectiveness of forewarning in developing resistance to persuasion. *Public Opinion Quarterly,* 1962, 26, 24–34.

McGuire, W. J., & Papageorgis, D. The relative efficacy of various types of prior belief-defense in producing immunity against persuasion. *Journal of Abnormal and Social Psychology,* 1961, 62, 327–337.

McLuhan, M. *Understanding media.* New York: McGraw-Hill, 1964.

Mead, G. H. *Mind, self, and society.* Chicago: University of Chicago Press, 1934.

Mehrabian, A. Inference of attitude from the posture, orientation, and distance of a communicator. *Journal of Consulting and Clinical Psychology,* 1968, 32, 296–308.

Mehrabian, A. Relationship of attitude to seated posture, orientation, and distance. *Journal of Personality and Social Psychology,* 1968, 10, 26–30.

Mehrabian, A., & Diamond, S. The effects of furniture arrangement, props, and personality on social interactions. *Journal of Personality and Social Psychology,* 1971, 20, 18–30.

Mehrabian, A., & Ferris, S. R. Inference of attitudes from nonverbal communication in two channels. *Journal of Consulting Psychology,* 1967, 31, 248–252.

Mehrabian, A., & Wiener, M. Decoding of inconsistent communications. *Journal of Personality and Social Psychology*, 1967, *6*, 108–114.

Meiselman, K. C. *Incest*. San Francisco: Jossey-Bass, 1978.

Melbin, M. Night as frontier. *American Sociological Review*, 1978, *43*, 3–22.

Meyer, A. J., Nash, J. D., McAlister, A. L., Maccoby, N., & Farquhar, J. W. Skills training in a cardiovascular health education program. *Journal of Consulting and Clinical Psychology*, 1980, *48*, 129–142.

Michotte, A. *Perception of causality*. New York: Basic Books, 1963.

Midlarsky, E., Bryan, J. H., & Brickman, P. Aversive approval: Interactive effects of modeling and reinforcement on altruistic behavior. *Child Development*, 1973, *44*, 321–328.

Milgram, S. Nationality and conformity. *Scientific American*, 1961, *205*, 45–51.

Milgram, S. Behavioral study of obedience. *Journal of Abnormal and Social Psychology*, 1963, *67*, 371–378.

Milgram, S. The experience of living in cities. *Science*, 1970, *167*, 1461–1468.

Milgram, S. Liberating effects of group pressure. *Journal of Personality and Social Psychology*, 1965, *1*, 127–134.

Milgram, S. A psychological map of New York City. *American Scientist*, 1972, *60*, 194–200.

Milgram, S. *Obedience to authority: An experimental view*. New York: Harper & Row, 1974.

Milgram, S. Psychological maps of Paris. In H. M. Prochansky, W. H. Ittelson, and L. G. Rivein (Eds.), *Environmental psychology: People and their physical settings*. New York: Holt, Rinehart & Winston, 1976.

Milgram, S. *Texture of everyday urban experience*. Lecture given at the University of California, Berkeley, January 20, 1977.

Milgram, S., Bickman, L., & Berkowitz, L. Note on the drawing power of crowds of different sizes. *Journal of Personality and Social Psychology*, 1969, *13*, 79–82.

Milgram, S., & Toch, H. Collective behavior: Crowds and social movements. In G. Lindzey & E. Aronson (Eds.), *Handbook of social psychology* (2nd ed.), Vol. 4. Reading, Mass.: Addison-Wesley, 1969.

Miller, A. G. Constraint and target effects in the attribution of attitudes. *Journal of Experimental Social Psychology*, 1976, *12*, 325–329.

Miller, D. T., & Ross, M. Self-serving biases in the attribution of causality: Fact or fiction? *Psychological Bulletin*, 1975, *82*, 213–225.

Miller, G., Beaber, R., & Valone, K. Speed of speech and persuasion. *Journal of Personality and Social Psychology*, 1976, *34*, 615–624.

Miller, G. R., & Burgoon, J. K. Factors affecting assessments of witness credibility. In N. Kerr & R. Bray (Eds.), *The psychology of the courtroom*. New York: Academic Press, 1982, 176–177.

Miller, N., & Campbell, D. Recency and primacy in persuasion as a function of the timing of speeches and measurements. *Journal of Abnormal and Social Psychology*, 1959, *59*, 1–9.

Miller, N. E., & Dollard, J. *Social learning and imitation*. New Haven: Yale University Press, 1941.

Miller, N., & Zimbardo, P. Motives for fear induced affiliation: Emotional comparison of interpersonal similarity? *Journal of Personality*, 1966, *34*, 481–503.

Miller, R. Mere exposure, psychological reactance and attitude change. *Public Opinion Quarterly*, 1976, *40*, 229–233.

Mills, J. Opinion change as a function of the communicator's desire to influence and liking for the audience. *Journal of Experimental Social Psychology*, 1966, *2*, 152–159.

Mills, J., & Aronson, E. Opinion change as a function of communicator's attractiveness and desire to influence. *Journal of Personality and Social Psychology*, 1965, *1*, 173–177.

Mills, J., & Harvey, J. Opinion change as a function of when information about the communicator is received and whether he is attractive or expert. *Journal of Personality and Social Psychol-*

ogy, 1972, *21*, 52–55.

Mills, J., & Jellison, J. Effect on opinion change and how desirable the communication is to the audience the communicator addressed. *Journal of Personality and Social Psychology*, 1967, *6*, 98–101.

Mills, J., & Mintz, P. M. Effect of unexplained arousal or affiliation. *Journal of Personality and Social Psychology*, 1972, *24*, 11–13.

Milton, O. Presidential choice and performance on a scale of authoritarianism. *American Psychologist*, 1952, *7*, 597–598.

Mintz, A. Non-adaptive group behavior. *Journal of Abnormal and Social Psychology*, 1951, *46*, 150–159.

Mita, T. H., Dermer, M., & Knight, J. Reversed facial images and the mere-exposure hypothesis. *Journal of Personality and Social Psychology*, 1977, *35*, 597–601.

Mitchell, R. E. Some social implications of high density housing. *American Sociological Review*, 1971, *36*, 18–29.

Miyamoto, S., & Dornbusch, S. A test of interactionist hypotheses of self conception. *American Journal of Sociology*, 1956, *61*, 399–403.

Modigliani, A. Embarrassment and embarrassability. *Sociometry*, 1968, *31*, 313–326.

Moede, W. Die richtlinien der Leistungs-psychologie. *Industrielle Psychotechnik*, 1927, *4*, 193–207.

Money, J., Hampson, J. G., & Hampson, J. L. Imprinting and the establishment of gender role. *American Medical Association Archives of Neurological Psychiatry*, 1957, *77*, 333–336.

Monson, T. C., & Snuder, M. Actors, observers, and the attribution process. *Journal of Experimental Social Psychology*, 1977, *13*, 89–111.

Moreland, R. L., & Zajonc, R. B. Exposure effects may not depend on stimulus recognition. *Journal of Personality and Social Psychology*, 1979, *37*, 1085–1089.

Morgan, C. J. Bystander intervention: Experimental test of a formal model. *Journal of Personality and Social Psychology*, 1978, *36* (1), 43–55.

Morris, B. G., Gould, R. W., and Matthews, P. J. Toward prevention of child abuse. *Children*, 1964, *11*, 55–60.

Morris & Miller. The effects of consensus-breaking and consensus-preempting partners on reduction in conformity. *Journal of Experimental Social Psychology*, 1975, *11*, 215–223.

Moscovici, S. Toward a theory of conversion behavior. In L. Berkowitz (Ed.), *Advances in experimental social psychology*, 1980, *13*, 209–239.

Moscovici, S., & Faucheaux, C. Social influence, conformity bias, and the study of active minorities. In L. Berkowitz (Ed.), *Advances in experimental psychology* (Vol. 6). New York: Academic Press, 1972.

Moscovici, S., & Zavalloni, M. The group as a polarizer of attitudes. *Journal of Personality and Social Psychology*, 1969, *12*, 125–135.

Moss, M. K., & Page, R. A. Reinforcement and helping behavior. *Journal of Applied Social Psychology*, 1972, *2*, 360–371.

Moustakas, C. E. *Loneliness*. Englewood Cliffs, N.J.: Prentice-Hall, 1961, pp. 63–65.

Mueller, C. W., & Pope, H. Marital instability: A study of its transmission between generations. *Journal of Marriage and the Family*, 1977, *39*, 83–93.

Mueller, J. E. Choosing among 133 candidates. *Public Opinion Quarterly*, 1970, *34*, 395–402.

Mulder, M., & Stemerding, A. Threat, attraction to group and need for strong leadership: A laboratory experiment in a natural setting. *Human Relations*, 1963, *16*(4), 317–334.

Myers, D. G., & Kaplan, M. F. Group-induced polarization in simulated juries. *Personality and Social Psychology Bulletin*, 1976, *2*, 63–66.

Nadler, A. "Good looks do not help": Effects of helper's physical attractiveness and expectations for future interaction on help-seeking behavior. *Personality and Social Psychology Bulletin,* 1980, *6,* 378–383.

Nagel, S., & Neef, M. *Decision theory and the legal process.* Lexington, Mass.: Lexington, 1979.

Nahemow, L., & Lawton, M. P. Similarity and propinquity in friendship formation. *Journal of Personality and Social Psychology,* 1975, *32,* 205–213.

Nass, G. D., Libby, R. W., & Fisher, M. P. *Sexual choices: An introduction to human sexuality.* Belmont, Calif.: Wadsworth, Inc., 1981.

National Institute of Mental Health. *Television and behavior: Ten years of scientific progress and implications for the eighties* (Vol. 1). Washington, D.C.: U.S. Government Printing Office, 1982.

The National Study of Women's Correctional Programs. The women's movement and crime. *Target,* 1977, *6*(8).

Neisser, U. *Cognitive psychology.* New York: Appleton, 1967.

Nel, E., Helmreich, R., & Aronson, E. Opinion change in the advocate as a function of the persuasibility of his audience: A clarification of the meaning of dissonance. *Journal of Personality and Social Psychology,* 1969, *12,* 117–124.

Nelson, E. A., Grinder, R. E., & Mutterer, M. L. Sources of variance in behavioral measures of honesty in temptation situations: Methodological analyses. *Developmental Psychology,* 1969, *1,* 265–279.

Nemeth, C. Jury trials: Psychology and law. In L. Berkowitz (Ed.), *Advances in experimental social psychology* (Vol. 13). New York: Academic Press, 1981.

Nemeth, C., & Endicott, J. The midpoint as an anchor: Another look at discrepancy of position and attitude change. *Sociometry,* 1976, *39,* 11–18.

Nemeth, C., & Wachtler, J. Creating the perceptions of consistency and confidence: A necessary condition for minority influence. *Sociometry,* 1974, *37,* 529–540.

Nemeth, C., Wachtler, J., & Endicott, J. Increasing the size of the minority: Some gains and some losses. *European Journal of Social Psychology,* 1977, *7*(1), 15–27.

Newcomb, T. *The acquaintance process.* New York: Holt, Rinehart & Winston, 1961.

Newcomb, T. Dyadic balance as a source of clues about interpersonal attraction. In B. I. Murstein (Ed.), *Theories of attraction and love.* New York: Springer, 1971.

Newcomb, T. *Personality and social change.* New York: Dryden, 1943.

Newman, J., & McCauley, C. Eye contact with strangers in city, suburb, and small town. *Environment and Behavior,* 1977, *9,* 547–558.

Newsweek. Peacock's night to crow. November 17, 1980, p. 82.

Newtson, D. Dispositional inference from effects to actions: Effects chosen and effects foregone. *Journal of Experimental Social Psychology,* 1974, *10,* 489–496.

Newtson, D., & Czerlinsky, T. Adjustment of attitude communications for contrasts by extreme audiences. *Journal of Personality and Social Psychology,* 1974, *30,* 829–837.

The New York Times. Do the networks need violence? May 23, 1982, Section 2, pp. 1ff.

The New York Times. Living in the shadow of fear. September 21, 1980, p. E20.

The New York Times. When machines talk, business listens. May 9, 1982.

Nieva, V. F., & Gutek, B. A. *Women and work: A psychological perspective.* New York: Praeger, 1981.

Nisbett, R. E., & Bellows, N. Private access versus public theories. *Journal of Personality and Social Psychology,* 1977, *34,* 613–624.

Nisbett, R. E., & Borgida, E. Attribution and the psychology of prediction. *Journal of Personality and Social Psychology,* 1975, *32,* 932–943.

Nisbett, R. E., et al. Popular induction: Information is not necessarily informative. In J. S. Carroll and J. W. Payne (Eds.), *Cognition and social behavior.* Hillsdale, N. J.: Erlbaum, 1976.

Nisbett, R. E., Caputo, C., Legant, P., & Marecek, J. Behavior as seen by the actor and as seen by the observer. *Journal of Personality and Social Psychology,* 1973, *27,* 154–164.

Nisbett, R. E., & Ross, L. *Human inference: Strategies and shortcomings of social judgment.* Englewood Cliffs, N.J.: Prentice-Hall, 1980.

Nisbett, R., & Wilson, T. The halo effect: Evidence for unconscious alteration of judgments. *Journal of Personality and Social Psychology,* 1977, *35,* 250–256.

Nisbett, R. E., & Wilson, T. D. Telling more than we know: Verbal reports on mental processes. *Psychological Review,* 1977, *84,* 231–259.

Nogami, G. Y. Crowding effects of group size, room size, or density? *Journal of Applied Social Psychology,* 1976, *6,* 105–125.

Norman, R. Affective-cognitive consistency, attitudes, conformity, and behavior. *Journal of Personality and Social Psychology,* 1975, *32*(1), 83–91.

Norman, W. T. Toward an adequate taxonomy of personality attributes: Replicated factor structure in peer nomination personality ratings. *Journal of Abnormal and Social Psychology,* 1963, *66,* 574–583.

Nye, F. I. *Family relationships: Rewards and costs.* Beverly Hills, Calif.: Sage, 1982.

Oetzel, R. M. Classified summary of research in sex differences. In E. E. Maccoby (Ed.), *The development of sex differences.* Stanford, Calif.: Stanford University Press, 1966.

Olneck, M. R., & Bills, D. B. Family configuration and achievement. *Social Psychology Quarterly,* 1979, *42,* 135–148.

Olsen, M. E. Consumer's attitudes toward energy conservation. *Journal of Social Issues,* 1981, *37,* 108–131.

Omwake, E. B. Assessment of the Head Start Preschool Education Effort. In E. Zigler and J. Valentine (Eds.), *Project Head Start: A legacy of the war on poverty.* New York: The Free Press, 1979.

O'Neill, G., & O'Neill, N. *Open marriage.* New York: Avon, 1972.

Orlofsky, J. Sex-role orientation, identity formation, and self-esteem in college men and women. *Sex Roles,* 1977, *3*(6), 561–575.

Orne, M. T. Demand characteristics and quasi-controls. In R. Rosenthal, & R. L. Rosnow (Eds.), *Artifact in behavior research.* New York: Academic Press, 1969.

Orne, M. On the social psychology of the psychological experiment: With particular reference to demand characteristics and their implications. *American Psychologist,* 1962, *17,* 776–783.

Orne, M. T. The use and misuse of hypnosis in court. *The International Journal of Clinical and Experimental Hypnosis,* 1979, *27*(4), 311–341.

Osborn, A. F. *Applied imagination* (Rev. ed.). New York: Scribner's, 1957.

Osgood, C. E. Exploration in semantic space. *Journal of Social Issues,* 1971, *27*(4), 5–6A; 379–382.

Osgood, C. E., May, W. H., & Miron, M. S. *Cross-cultural universality of affective meaning systems.* Urbana: University of Illinois Press, 1975.

Osgood, C. E., Suci, G. J., & Tannenbaum, P. H. *The measurement of meaning.* Urbana: University of Illinois Press, 1957.

Osgood, C. E., & Tannenbaum, P. H. The principle of congruity in the prediction of attitude change. *Psychological Review,* 1955, *62,* 42–55.

Oskamp, S. *Attitudes and opinions.* Englewood Cliffs, N.J.: Prentice-Hall, 1977.

Osmond, H. Function as the basis of psychiatric ward design. *Mental Hospitals,* 1957, *8,* 23–30.

Overmeir, J. B., & Seligman, M. E. P. Effects of inescapable shock upon subsequent escape and avoidance responding. *Journal of Comparative and Physiological Psychology*, 1967, *63*, 28–33.

Packard, U. *A nation of strangers*. New York: David McKay Company, Inc., 1972.

Padawer-Singer, A. M., & Barton, A. H. The impact of pretrial publicity on jurors' verdicts. In R. J. Simon (Ed.), *The jury system in America: A critical overview*. Beverly Hills, Calif.: Sage, 1975.

Page, M. P., & Scheidt, R. J. The elusive weapons effect: Demand awareness, evaluation apprehension, and slightly sophisticated subjects. *Journal of Personality and Social Psychology*, 1971, *20*, 304–318.

Pailhous, J. *La representation de l'epace urbain: L'example du chauffeur de taxi*. Paris: Presses Universitaires de France, 1970.

Palmer, F. H., & Anderson, L. W. Long-term gains from early intervention: Findings from longitudinal studies. In E. Zigler and J. Valentine (Eds.), *Project Head Start: A legacy of the war on poverty*. New York: The Free Press, 1979.

Palmore, E. B. The introduction of Negroes into white departments. *Human Organization*, 1955, *14*, 27–28.

Parades, A., Ludwig, K. D., Hassenfeld, I. N., & Cornelison, F. S. A clinical study of alcoholics using audio-visual self-image feedback. *Journal of Nervous and Mental Disease*, 1969, *148*, 449–456.

Parke, R. D. Review of *Fathers. Contemporary Psychology*, 1982, 27, 151.

Parke, R. D., et al. Some effects of violent and nonviolent movies on the behavior of juvenile delinquents. In L. Berkowitz (Ed.), *Advances in experimental social psychology* (Vol. 10). New York: Academic Press, 1977.

Parke, R. D., & Collmer, D. A. Child abuse: An interdisciplinary analysis. In E. M. Hetherington (Ed.), *Review of Child Development Research* (Vol. 5). Chicago: University of Chicago Press, 1975.

Parsons, H. M. What happened at Hawthorne? *Science*, 1974, *183*, 922–932.

Parsons, T., & Bales, R. F. *Family, socialization and interaction process*. Glencoe, Ill.: Free Press, 1955.

Passini, F., & Norman, W. A universal conception of personality structure? *Journal of Personality and Social Psychology*, 1966, *4*, 44–49.

Patterson, A. Territorial behavior and fear of crime in the elderly. *Environmental Psychology and Nonverbal Behavior*, 1978, *2*, 131–144.

Patterson, M. L. An arousal model of interpersonal intimacy. *Psychological Review*, 1976, *83*, 235–245.

Patterson, M. L. Compensation in nonverbal immediacy behaviors: A review. *Sociometry*, 1973, *36*, 237–252.

Patterson, T. E., & McClure, R. D. *The unseeing eye: The myth of television power in national elections*. New York: Putnam, 1976.

Pendleton, M. G., & Batson, C. D. Self-presentation and the door-in-the-face technique for inducing compliance. *Personality and Social Psychology Bulletin*, 1979, *5*, 77–81.

Penrod, S. *Confidence, accuracy, and the eyewitness*. Unpublished manuscript, University of Wisconsin, 1980.

Penrod, S. Mathematical and computer models of jury decision making. In H. H. Blumberg and P. Hare (Eds.), *Small groups*. New York: Wiley, 1982.

Penrod, S., & Hastie, R. A computer simulation of jury decision making. *Psychological Review*, 1980, *87*, 113–159.

Penrod, S., & Hastie, R. Models of jury decision making: A critical review. *Psychological Bulletin*, 1979, *86*, 462–492.

Penrod, S., Loftus, E. F., & Winkler, J. The reliability of eyewitness testimony: A psychological perspective. In N. Kerr & R. M. Bray (Eds.), *The psychology of the courtroom*. New York: Academic Press, 1982.

Perlman, D., & Peplau, L. A. Toward a social psychology of loneliness. In S. Duck and R. Gilmur (Eds.), *Personal relationships*, Vol. 3: *Personal relationships in disorder*. New York: Academic Press, 1981.

Perloff, R., Perloff, E., & Sussna, E. Program evaluation. *Annual Review of Psychology*, 1976, *27*, 569–594.

Peterson, R. C., & Thurstone, L. L. *The effect of motion pictures on the social attitudes of high school children*. Chicago: University of Chicago Press, 1933.

Pettigrew, T. F. Social evaluation theory: Convergences and applications. In D. Levine (Ed.), *Nebraska symposium on motivation*. Lincoln, Neb.: University of Nebraska Press, 1967.

Petty, R. E., & Cacioppo, J. T. *Attitudes and persuasion: Classic and contemporary approaches*. Dubuque, Iowa: Brown, 1981.

Petty, R. E., & Cacioppo, J. T. Forewarning, cognitive responding, and resistance to persuasion. *Journal of Personality and Social Psychology*, 1973, *27*, 311–327.

Petty, R. E., Ostrow, T. M., & Brock, T. C. Historical foundations of the cognitive response approach to attitudes and persuasion. In R. E. Petty, T.M. Ostrow, & T. C. Brock (Eds.), *Cognitive responses in persuasion*. Hillsdale, N.J.: Erlbaum, 1981.

Petty, R., Wells, G., & Brock, T. Distraction can enhance or reduce yielding to propaganda: Thought disruption versus effort justification. *Journal of Personality and Social Psychology*, 1976, *34*, 874–884.

Piaget, J. *The language and thought of the child*. New York: Harcourt Brace, 1926.

Piaget, J. *The moral judgment of the child*. Boston: Routledge & Kegan Paul, 1932.

Piaget, J. *The origins of intelligence in children*. New York: Norton, 1952.

Pietropinto, A., & Simenauer, J. *Husbands and wives: A nationwide survey of marriage*. New York: Times Books, 1979.

Piliavin, I. M., Rodin, J., & Piliavin, J. A. Good Samaritanism: An underground phenomenon? *Journal of Personality and Social Psychology*, 1969, *13*, 289–299.

Pines, M. Recession is linked to far-reaching psychological harm. *The New York Times*, April 6, 1982, 21–23.

Pines, M. The civilizing of Genie. *Psychology Today*, September 1981, pp. 28–34.

Pittman, T. S., Cooper, E. E., & Smith, T. W. Attribution of causality and the overjustification effect. *Personality and Social Psychology Bulletin*, 1977, *3*, 280–283.

Pliner, P., et al. Compliance without pressure: Some further data on the foot-in-the-door technique. *Journal of Experimental Social Psychology*, 1974, *10*, 17–22.

Pomazal, R. J., & Clore, G. L. Helping on the highway: The effects of dependency and sex. *Journal of Applied Social Psychology*, 1973, *3*, 150–164.

Porter, L. W., & Miles, R. E. Motivation and management. In Joseph W. McGuire (Ed.), *Contemporary management: Issues and viewpoints*. Englewood Cliffs, N.J.: Prentice-Hall, 1974, 545–570.

Porter, L. W., & Steers, R. M. Organizational work, and personal factors in employee turnover and absenteeism. *Psychological Bulletin*, 1973, *80*, 151–176.

Premack, D., & Premack, A. J. Teaching language to an ape. *Scientific American*, 1972, *227*, 92–99.

Price, R. A., & Vandenberg, S. G. Matching for physical attractiveness in married couples. *Personality and Social Psychology Bulletin*, 1979, *5*, 398–400.

Pryor, J. B., & Kriss, M. The cognitive dynamics of salience in the attribution process. *Journal of Personality and Social Psychology*, 1977, *35*, 49–55.

Pruitt, D. G. Reciprocity and credit building in a laboratory dyad. *Journal of Personality and Social Psychology*, 1968, *8*, 143–147.

Quarles, R. C. Mass media use and voting behavior: The accuracy of political perceptions among first-time and experienced voters. *Communication Research*, 1979, *6*, 407–436.

Rabbie, J. M. Differential preference for companionship under threat. *Journal of Abnormal and Social Psychology*, 1963, *67*, 643–648.

Rabbie, J. M., & Wilkens, G. Intergroup competition and its effect on intragraoup and intergroup relations. *European Journal of Social Psychology*, 1971, *1*, 215–234.

Rada, J. B., & Rogers, R. W. *Obedience to authority: Presence of authority and command strength.* Paper presented at the meeting of the Southeastern Psychological Association, New Orleans, April, 1973.

Ramey, C. T. & Smith, B. J. Assessing the intellectual consequences of early intervention with high-risk infants, *It's the American Journal of Mental Deficiency*, 1977, *18*, 318–324.

Raskin, D.C., & Podelsny, J. A. Truth and deception: A reply to Lykken. *Psychological Bulletin*, 1979, *86*(1), 54–59.

Rasmussen, J. *Man in isolation and confinement.* Chicago: Aldine, 1973.

Raven, B. H., & French, J. R. P., Jr. Group support, legitimate power, and social influence. *Journal of Personality*, 1958, *26*, 400–409.

Raven, B. L., & Kruglanski, A. Conflict and power. In P. G. Swingle (Ed.), *The nature of conflict.* New York: Academic Press, 1970.

Ray, M. L., et al. Marketing communication and heirarchy-of-effects. In P. Clearke (Ed.), *New models for mass communication research* (Vol. 2). Beverly Hills, Calif.: Sage Publications, 1973.

Reeder, L., Donohue, G., & Biblarz, A. Conceptions of self and others. *American Journal of Sociology*, 1960, *66*, 153–159.

Regan, D. T., & Fazio, R. On the consistency between attitudes and behavior: Look to the method of attitude formation. *Journal of Experimental Social Psychology*, 1977, *13*, 28–45.

Regan, D. T., & Totten, J. Empathy and attribution: Turning observers into actors. *Journal of Personality and Social Psychology*, 1975, *32*, 850–856.

Rein, M., & White, S. Can policy research help policy? *The Public Interest*, Fall 1977, *49*, 119–136.

Reiss, I. L. *Family systems in America* (2nd ed.). Hinsdale, Ill.: The Dryden Press, 1976.

Rhine, R. I., & Severance, L. J. Ego involvement, discrepancy, source credibility and attitude change. *Journal of Personality and Social Psychology*, 1970, *16*, 175–190.

Rhyne, D. Bases of marital satisfaction among men and women. *Journal of Marriage and the Family*, 1981, *43*, 1948.

Rice, B. The Hawthorne defect: Persistence of a flawed theory. *Psychology Today*, February 1982, pp. 70–74.

Rich, W. C., et al. *Sentencing guidelines: An evaluation of the initial experiences.* Williamsburg, Virginia: National Center for State Courts, 1981.

Richardson, D. C., & Campbell, J. L. Alcohol & wife abuse: The effect of alcohol on attributions of blame for wife abuse. *Personality and Social Psychology Bulletin*, 1980, *6*, 51–56.

Riger, S. The impact of crime on women. In D. A. Lewis (Ed.), *Reactions to crime.* Beverly Hills, Calif.: Sage Publications, 1981.

Risser, D. T. A field study of behavioral congruence: Arm-crossing in dyads. Paper presented at the Eastern Psychological Association meetings, April 1979.

Rittle, R. H. Changes in self vs. situational perceptions as mediators of the foot-in-the-door effect. *Personality and Social Psychology Bulletin*, 1980, in press.

Roberts, D. F., Bachen, C. M., & Christenson, P. *Children's information processing: Perceptions of and cognitions about television commercials and supplemental consumer information.* Testimony to the Federal Trade Commission's Rulemaking Hearings on Television Advertising and Children,

San Francisco, Nov. 1978.

Robertson & Rossiter. Children and commercial persuasion: An attribution theory analysis. *Journal of Consumer Research*, 1974, *1*, 13–20.

Robertson & Rossiter. Development of sex-trait stereotypes among young children in the United States, England, and Ireland. *Child Development*, 1977, *48*, 1375–1384, 203–204, 205.

Robinson, J. P. Television and leisure time: A new scenario. *Journal of Communication*, 1981, *31*(1), 120–130.

Robinson, M. J. American political legitimacy in an era of electronic journalism: Reflections on the evening news. In D. Cater & R. Adler (Eds.), *Television as a social force: New approaches to TV criticism.* New York: Praeger, 1975.

Robinson, Paul. What liberated males do. *Psychology Today*, July 1981, *15*, 81–84.

Rodin, J. Managing the stress of aging: The role of control and coping. In S. Levine & H. Ursin (Eds.), *NATO conference on coping and health.* New York: Academic Press, 1980.

Rodin, J., & Langer, E. Aging labels: The decline of control and the fall of self-esteem. *Journal of Social Issues*, 1980, *36*, 12–29.

Rodin, J., & Langer, E. J. Long-term effects of a control-relevant intervention with the institutionalized aged. *Journal of Personality and Social Psychology*, 1977, *35*, 897–902.

Rodin, J., Solomon, S., & Metcalf, J. Role of control in mediating perceptions of density. *Journal of Personality and Social Psychology*, 1978, *36*, 988–999.

Roethlisberger, F. J., & Dickson, W. J. *Management and the worker.* Cambridge, Mass.: Harvard University Press, 1939.

Rogers, L. E., & Farace, R. V. Analysis of relational communication in dyads: New measurement procedures. *Human Communication Research*, 1975, *1*(3), 222–239.

Rogers, R. W., & Mewborn, C. R. Fear appeals and attitude change: Effects of a threat's noxiousness, probability of occurrence, and the efficacy of coping responses. *Journal of Personality and Social Psychology*, 1976, *34*, 54–61.

Rogers, T. B. Self reference in memory: Recognition of personality items. *Journal of Research in Personality*, 1977, *11*, 295–305.

Rokeach, M. Long-range experimental modification of values, attitudes, and behavior. *American Psychologist*, 1971, *26*, 453–459.

Rokeach, M., & Kliejunas, P. Behavior as a function of attitude-toward-object and attitude-toward-situation. *Journal of Personality and Social Psychology*, 1972, *22*, 194–201.

Rokeach, M., & Rothman, G. The principles of belief congruence and the congruity principle as models of cognitive interaction. *Psychological Review*, 1965, *72*, 128–142.

Rollins, B. C., & Cannon, K. L. Marital satisfaction over the family life cycle: A reevaluation. *Journal of Marriage and the Family*, 1974, *36*, 271–282.

Rollins, B. C., & Feldman, H. Marital satisfaction over the family life cycle. *Journal of Marriage and the Family*, 1970, *32*, 20–28.

Roper, R. T. Jury size and verdict consistency: A line has to be drawn somewhere. *Law and Society Review*, 1980, *14*(4), 977–995.

Rose, P. Student opinion on the 1956 presidential election. *The Public Opinion Quarterly*, 1957, *21*, 371–376.

Rosenbaum, L., & Rosenbaum, W. Persuasive impact of a communicator where groups differ in apparent co-orientation. *Journal of Psychology*, 1975, *89*(2), 189–194.

Rosenberg, L. A. Group size, prior experience, and conformity. *Journal of Abnormal and Social Psychology*, 1961, *63*, 436–437.

Rosenberg, M. *Society and the adolescent self-image.* Princeton, N.J.: Princeton University Press, 1965.

Rosenberg, S. New approaches to the analysis of personal constructs in person perception. In A. W. Landfield (Ed.), *Nebraska symposium on motivation.* Lincoln, Neb.: University of

Nebraska Press, 1976.

Rosenberg, S., & Jones, R. A. A method for investigating and representing a person's implicit theory of personality: Theodore Drieiser's view of people. *Journal of Personality and Social Psychology*, 1972, *30*, 372–386.

Rosenberg, S., Nelson, C., & Vivekananthan, P. S. A multidimensional approach to the structure of personality impressions. *Journal of Personality and Social Psychology*, 1968, *9*, 283–294.

Rosenberg, S., & Sedlak, A. Structural representations of implicit personality theory. In L. Berkowitz (Ed.), *Advances in experimental social psychology* (Vol. 6). New York: Academic Press, 1972.

Rosenfeld, P., Melburg, V., & Tedeschi, J. T. Self-serving attributions: Biased private perceptions and distorted public descriptions. *Journal of Personality and Social Psychology*, 1981, 224–231.

Rosenhan, D. L. On being sane in insane places. *Science*, 1973, *79*, 250–258.

Rosenkeotter, L. I. Resistance to temptation: Inhibitory and disinhibitory effects of models. *Developmental Psychology*, 1973, *8*, 80–84.

Rosenthal, R. *On the social psychology of the self-fulfilling prophesy: Further evidence for pygmalion effects and their mediating mechanisms.* Module 53, pp. 1–28. New York: MSS Modular Publications, Inc., 1973.

Rosenthal, R., & Rosnow, R. L. The volunteer subject. In R. Rosenthal and R. Rosnow (Eds.), *Artifact in behavioral research.* New York: Academic Press, 1969.

Rosenthal, R., & Rosnow, R. L. *The volunteer subject.* New York: Wiley, 1975.

Rosnow, R. L. Whatever happened to the "law of primacy"? *Journal of Communication*, 1966, *16*, 10–31.

Rosnow, R. L., Gitler, A. G., & Holz, R. F. Some determinants of post-decisional information preferencers. *Journal of Social Psychology*, 1969, *79*, 235–245.

Ross, L. The intuitive psychologist and his shortcomings: Distortions in the attribution process. In L. Berkowitz (Ed.), *Advances in experimental social psychology* (Vol. 10), New York: Academic Press, 1977.

Ross, L. D., Amabile, T. M., & Steinmetz, J. L. Social roles, social control, and biases in social-perception processes. *Journal of Personality and Social Psychology*, 1977, *35*, 485–494.

Ross, L., Bierbauer, G., & Polly, S. Attribution of educational outcomes by professional and non-professional instructors. *Journal of Personality and Social Psychology*, 1974, *29*, 609–618.

Ross, L., Greene, D., & House, P. The false consensus phenomenon: An attributional bias in self perception and social perception processes. *Journal of Experimental Social Psychology*, 1977.

Ross, L., Lepper, M., & Hubbard, M. Perseverance in self perception and social perception: Biased attributional processes in the debriefing paradigm. *Journal of Personality and Social Psychology*, 1975, *32*, 880–892.

Ross, M. Salience of reward and intrinsic motivation. *Journal of Personality and Social Psychology*, 1975, *32*, 245–254.

Ross, M., & Olson, J. M. *Standard and reverse placebo effects.* Unpublished manuscript, University of Waterloo, 1979.

Ross, M., & Olson, J. M. An expectancy-attribution model of the effects of placebos. *Psychological Review*, 1981, *88*, 408–457.

Ross, M., & Sicoly, F. Egocentric biases in availability and attribution. *Journal of Personality and Social Psychology*, 1979, *37*, 322–336.

Rothbart, M., et al. *Journal of Experimental Social Psychology*, 1978, *14*, 237–255.

Rothbart, M., et al. Recall for confirming events: Memory processes and the maintenance of social stereotypes. *Journal of Experimental Social Psychology*, 1979, *15*, 343–355.

Rothschild, M. L. Political advertising: A neglected policy issue in

marketing. *Journal of Marketing Research*, 1978, *15*, 58–71.

Rotter, J. B. Generalized expectancies for internal versus external control of reinforcement. *Psychological Monographs*, 1966, *80*(1, Whole No. 609).

Rotton, J., et al. Air pollution and interpersonal attraction. *Journal of Applied Social Psychology*, 1978, *8*, 57–71.

Rotton, J., et al. The air pollution experience and physical aggression. *Journal of Applied Social Psychology*, 1979, *9*, 397–412.

Rubenstein, C., Shaver, P., & Peplau, L. A. Loneliness. *Human Nature*, February 1979, 58–65.

Rubin, K. H., & Schneider, F. W. The relationship between moral judgment, egocentrism, and altrustic behavior. *Child Development*, 1973, *44*, 661–665.

Rubin, Z. From liking to loving: Patterns of attractions in dating relationships. In T. L. Huston (Ed.), *Foundations of interpersonal attraction.* New York: Academic Press, 1974.

Rubin, Z. Measurement of romantic love. *Journal of Personality and Social Psychology*, 1970, *16*, 265–273.

Rubin, Z., & Peplau, A. Belief in a just world and reactions to another's lot: A study of participants in the national draft lottery. *Journal of Social Issues*, 1973, *29*(4), 73–93.

Rule, B. G., & Ferguson, T. J. The attributional mediation of aggression. Paper presented at the meeting of Society of Experimental Social Psychology. Princeton, N.J., November 1978.

Rule, B. G., & Percival, E. The effects of frustration and attack on physical aggression. *Journal of Experimental Research in Personality*, 1971, *5*, 111–118.

Rushton, J. P. Generosity in children: Immediate and long-term effects of modeling, preaching and moral judgment. *Journal of Personality and Social Psychology*, 1975, *31*, 459–466.

Rushton, J. P., & Teachman, G. The effects of positive reinforcement, attributions, and punishment on model-induced altruism in children. *Personality and Social Psychology Bulletin*, 1978, *4*, 322–325.

Russell, J. A., & Mehrabian, A. Approach-avoidance and affiliation as functions of the emotion-eliciting quality of an environment. *Environment and Behavior*, 1978, *10*, 355–388.

Russo, N. F. Eye contact, interpersonal distance, and the equilibrium theory. *Journal of Personality and Social Psychology*, 1975, *31*, 497–502.

Rutter, M. Sex differences in children's response to family stress. In E. J. Anthony & C. Koupernik (Eds.), *The child and his family.* New York: Wiley, 1970.

Saario, T. N., Jacklin, C., & Tittle, C. K. Sex role stereotyping in the public schools. *Harvard Educational Review*, 1973, *43*, 386–416.

Sabol, B. All night with Jerry: Pitch with kitsch. *New York*, September 17, 1979, 98–99.

Seagert, S. C., Swap, W., & Zajonc, R. B. Exposure, context, and interpersonal attraction. *Journal of Personality and Social Psychology*, 1973, *25*, 234–242.

Sahakian, W. S. *Systematic social psychology.* New York:, 1974.

Saks M. J. Innovation and change in the courtroom. In N. Kerr & R. M. Bray (Eds.), *The psychology of the courtroom.* New York: Academic Press, 1982.

Saks, M., & Hastie, R. *Social psychology in court.* New York: Van Nostrand Reinhold, 1978.

Sales, B. D., Elwork, A., & Alfini, J. J. *Improving comprehension for jury instructions.* In B. D. Sales (Ed.), *Perspectives in law and psychology: The criminal justice system* (Vol. 1). New York: Plenum, 1977.

Sanders, G. S. Driven by distraction: An integrative review of social facilitation. *Journal of Experimental Social Psychology*, 1981, *17*, 227–251.

Santrock, J. W., & Warshak, R. A. Father custody and social development in boys and girls. *Journal of Social Issues*, 1979, *35*, 112–125.

Sarnoff, I., & Zimbardo, P. Anxiety, fear and social affilitation. *Journal of Abnormal and Social Psychology*, 1961, *62*, 356–363.

Saunders, D. The police response to battered women: Predictors of officers' use of arrest, counseling or minimal action. Doctoral dissertation, University of Wisconsin, 1979.

Scanzoni, J. Family organization and the probability of disorganization. *Journal of Marriage and the Family*, 1966, *28*, 407–411.

Scanzoni, J. A historical perspective on husband-wife bargaining power and marital dissolution. In G. Levinger & O. C. Moles (Eds.), *Divorce and separation: Context, causes, and consequences.* New York: Basic Books, 1979.

Schachter, S. Deviation, rejection, and communication. *Journal of Abnormal and Social Psychology*, 1951, *46*, 190–207.

Schachter, S. *The psychology of affiliation.* Stanford, Calif.: Stanford University Press, 1959.

Schachter, S. Recidivism and self-cure of smoking and obesity. *American Psychologist*, 1982, *37*, 436–444.

Schachter, S., & Singler J. Cognitive, social, and physiological determinants of emotional state. *Psychological Review*, 1962, *69*, 379–399.

Schaffer, R. *Mothering.* Cambridge, Mass.: Harvard University Press, 1977.

Schank, R., & Abelson, R. *Scripts, plans, goals, and understanding: An inquiry into human knowledge structures.* Hillsdale, N.J.: Erlbaum, 1977.

Schein, E. H. *Organizational psychology* (3rd ed.), Englewood Cliffs, N.J.: Prentice-Hall, 1980.

Scheffino, A. P., & Borden, R. J. Sex differences in response to naturalistic crowding: Affective reactions to group size and group density. *Personality and Social Psychology Bulletin*, 1976, *2*, 67–70.

Schenkel, R. Submission: Its features and functions in the wolf and dog. *American Zoologist*, 1967, *7*, 319–329.

Schneider, D. J. Implicit personality theory: A review. *Psychological Bulletin*, 1973, *79*, 294–309.

Schneider, D. J., Hastorf, A. H., & Ellsworth, P. C. *Person perception* (2nd ed.) Reading, Mass.: Addison-Wesley, 1979.

Schopler, J., & Layton, B. D. Determinants of the self-attribution of having infuenced another person. *Journal of Personality and Social Psychology*, 1972, *22*, 326–332.

Schorr, D. Hinckley: A media freak. *The New York Times*, May 10, 1982, A21.

Schulz, R. Effects of control and predictability on the physical and psychological well-being of the institutionalized aged. *Journal of Personality and Social Psychology*, 1976, *33*, 563–573.

Schuman, H., & Johnson, M. P. Attitudes and behavior. *Annual Review of Sociology*, 1976, *2*, 161–207.

Schwartz, E. Effects of sex guilt and sexual arousal on the retention of birth control information. *Journal of Consulting and Clinical Psychology*, 1973, *41*, 61–64.

Schwartz, S. Normative influences on altruism. In L. Berkowitz (Ed.), *Advances in experimental social psychology* (Vol. 10). New York: Academic Press, 1977.

Schwartz, S. H. Temporal instability as a moderator of the attitude behavior relationship. *Journal of Personality and Social Psychology*, 1978, *36*, 715–724.

Schwartz, S. Words, deeds, and the perception of consequences and responsibility in action situations. *Journal of Personality and Social Psychology*, 1968, *10*, 232–242.

Schwartz, S. H., & Calusen, G. T. Responsibility, norms, and helping in an emergency. *Journal of Personality and Social Psychology*, 1970, *16*, 299–310.

Schwartz, S. H., & Fleishman, J. A. Effects of negative personal norms on helping behavior. *Personality and Social Psychology Bulletin*, 1982, *8*(1), 81–86.

Sears, D., & Freedman, J. Effects of expected familiarity of argu-

ments upon opinion change and selective exposure. *Journal of Personality and Social Psychology*, 1965, *2*, 420–425.

Sears, D. O., & Riley, R. J. Positivity biases in evaluations of political candidates. Unpublished manuscript, University of California, L.A., 1969.

Sears, D. O., & Whitney, R. E. *Political persuasion.* Morristown, N.J.: Silver/Burdett/General Learning Press, 1973.

Sears, R., K., Maccoby, E. E., & Lewin, H. *Patterns of child rearing.* Evanston, Ill.: Row, Peterson, 1957.

Secord, P. F., & Backman, C. W. *Social psychology.* New York: McGraw-Hill, 1964.

Segal, M. W. Alphabet and attraction: An unobtrusive measure of the effect of propinquity in a field setting. *Journal of Personality and Social Psychology*, 1974, *30*, 654–657.

Seghers, C. Color in the office. *The Management Review*, 1948, *37*, 452–453.

Seligman, C., Becker, L. J., & Darley, J. M. Encouraging residential energy conservation through feedback. In A. Baum & J. E. Singer (Eds.), *Advances in environmental psychology* (Vol. 3). Hillsdale, N.J.: Erlbaum, 1981.

Seligman, C., et al. Predicting summer energy consumption from homeowner's attitudes. *Journal of Applied Social Psychology*, 1979, *9*, 70–90.

Seligman, M. E. P. *Helplessness.* San Francisco: Freeman, 1975.

Selznick, G., & Steinberg, S. *The tenacity of prejudice: Anti-Semitism in contemporary America.* New York: Harper Torchbooks, 1969.

Sensenig, J., & Brehm, J. W. Attitude change from an applied threat to attitudinal freedom. *Journal of Personality and Social Psychology*, 1968, *8*, 324, 330.

Seyfried, B. A. Complementarity in interpersonal attraction. In S. Duck (Ed.), *Theory and practice in interpersonal attraction.* London: Academic Press, 1977.

Shaffer, D. R., Rogel, M., & Hendrick, C. Intervention in the library: The effect of increased responsibility on bystanders' willingness to prevent theft. *Journal of Applied Social Psychology*, 1975, *5*, 303–319.

Shannon, C. E., & Weaver, W. *The mathematical theory of communication.* Urbana: University of Illinois Press, 1949.

Shaver, K. G. Defensive attribution: Effects of severity and relevance on the responsibilities assigned for an accident. *Journal of Personality and Social Psychology*, 1970, *14*, 101–113.

Shaw, J. I., & Skolnick, P. An investigation of relative preference for consistency motivation. *European Journal of Social Psychology.* 1973, *3*, 271–280.

Shaw, M. E. *Group Dynamics: The Psychology of Small Group Behavior* (2nd ed.) New York: McGraw-Hill, 1976.

Shepard, R. Recognition memory for words, sentences, and pictures. *Journal of Verbal Learning and Verbal Behavior*, 1967, *6*, 156–163.

Sherif, C. W., et al. Personal involvement, social judgment, and action. *Journal of Personality and Social Psychology*, 1973, *27*, 311–327.

Sherif, M. *The psychology of social norms.* New York: Harper, 1936.

Sherif, M., et al. *Intergroup conflicted cooperation: The robbers cave experiment.* University of Oklahoma: Norman Institute of Group Relations, 1961.

Sherif, M., & Hovland, C. I. *Social judgment: Assimilation and contrast effects in communication and attitude change.* New Haven, Conn.: Yale University Press, 1961.

Sherif, M., & Sherif, C. W. *Groups in harmony and tension.* New York: Harper & Row, 1953.

Sherif, M., & Sherif, C. W. Production of intergroup conflict and its resolution—Robbers Cave experiment. In J. W. Reich (Ed.), *Experimenting in society: Issues and examples in applied social psychology.* Glenview, Ill.: Scott, Foresman, & Co., 1982.

Sherif, M., & Sherif, C. W. *Social psychology.* New York: Harper &

Row, 1969.

Sherif, C. W., Sherif, M., & Nebergall, R. E. Attitude and attitude change: The social adjustment approach. Philadelphia: Saunders, 1965.

Sherif, M., Taub, D., & Hovland, C. I. Assimilation and contrast effects of anchoring stimuli on judgments. *Journal of Experimental Psychology*, 1958, *55*, 150–155.

Sherif, M., White, B. J., & Haney, O. J. Status in experimentally produced groups. *American Journal of Sociology*, 1955, *60*, 370–379.

Sherman. In Frieze, I., et al. (Eds.), *Women and sex roles: A social-psychological perspective.* New York: Norton, 1978.

Sherman, S. J., et al. Contrast effects and their relationship to subsequent behavior. *Journal of Experimental Social Psychology*, 1978, *14*, 340–350.

Sherrid, S., & Beech, R. Self-dissatisfaction as a determinant of charge in police values. *Journal of Applied Psychology*, 1976, *61*, 273–278.

Sherrod, D. R. Crowding, perceived control and behavioral aftereffects. *Journal of Applied Social Psychology*, 1974, *4*, 171–186.

Sherrod, D. R., et al. Environmental attention, affect, and altruism. *Journal of Applied Social Psychology*, 1977, 7, 359–371.

Sherrod, D. R., et al. Effects of personal causation and perceived control on responses to an aversive environment: The more control, the better. *Journal of Experimental Social Psychology*, 1977, *13*, 14–27.

Sherwood, J. J., Barron, J. W., & Fitch, H. G. Cognitive dissonance: Theory and research. In R. V. Wagner & J. J. Sherwood (Eds.), *The study of attitude change.* Monterey, Calif.: Brooks/Cole, 1969, 56–86.

Shiffrin, R. M., & Schneider, W. Controlled and automatic human information processing: II. Perceptual learning, automatic attending, and a general theory. *Psychological Review*, 1977, *84*, 127–190.

Shostak, A. B. Abortion as fatherhood lost: Problems and reforms. *Family Coordinator*, October 1979, *28*(4), 569–574.

Shultz, T. R., Wells, D., & Sarda, M. Development of the ability to distinguish intended actions from mistakes, reflexes, and passive movements. *British Journal of Clinical and Social Psychology*, 1980, *19*, 301–310.

Sicoly, F., & Ross, M. Facilitation of ego-biased attributions by means of self-serving observer feedback. *Journal of Personality and Social Psychology*, 1977, *35*, 734–741.

Siegel, A. E., & Siegel, S. Reference groups, membership groups, and attitude change. *Journal of Abnormal and Social Psychology*, 1957, *55*, 360–364.

Siegman, A. W. A cross-cultural investigation of the relationship between ethnic prejudice, authoritarian ideology, and personality. *Journal of Abnormal and Social Psychology*, 1961, *63*, 654–655.

Sigall, H., & Page, R. Current stereotypes: A little fading, a little faking. *Journal of Personality and Social Psychology*, 1971, *18*, 247–255.

Sigall, H., & Helmreich, R. Opinion change as a function of stress and communicator credibility. *Journal of Experimental Social Psychology*, 1969, *5*, 70–78.

Sigall, H., & Ostrove, N. Beautiful but dangerous: Effects of offender attractiveness and nature of the crime on juridic judgment. *Journal of Personality and Social Psychology*, 1975, *31*, 410–444.

Silverman, C. T., Sprofkin, J. N., & Rubinstein, E. A. Physical contact and sexual behavior on prime-time TV. *Journal of Communication*, 1979, *29*, 33–43.

Silverstein, C., & Stang, D. Seating position and interaction in triads: A field study. *Sociometry*, 1976, *39*, 166–170.

Siman, M. L. Application of a new model of peer group influence to naturally existing adolescent friendship groups. *Child Devel-*

opment, 1977, *48*, 270–274.

Simon, R. J., & Mahan, L. Quantifying burdens of proofs: A view from the bench, the jury and the classroom. *Law and Society Review*, 1971, *5*, 319–330.

Simons, H. W., Berkowitz, N. N., & Moyer, R. J. Similarity, credibility, and attitude change: A review and a theory. *Psychological Bulletin*, 1970, *73*, 1–16.

Simonton, D. K. Multiple discovery and intervention: Zeitgeist, genius, or change? *Journal of Personality and Social Psychology*, 1979, *37*, 1603–1616.

Simpson, E. Moral development research: A case study of scientific cultural bias. *Human Development*, 1974, *17*(2), 81–106.

Sistrunk, F., & McDavid, J. Sex variables in conforming behavior. *Journal of Personality and Social Psychology*, 1971, *17*, 200–207.

Skogan, W. G., & Maxfield, M. G. *Coping with crime: Individual and neighborhood reactions.* Beverly Hills, Calif.: Sage Publications, 1981.

Slaby, R. G., & Frey, K. S. Development of gender constancy and selective attention to same-sex models. *Child Development*, 1975, *46*, 849–856.

Slaby, R. G., Quaforth, G. R., & McConnachie, G. A. Television violence and its sponsors. *Journal of Communication*, 1976, *26*, 88–96.

Slater, P. E. Contrasting correlatives of group size. *Sociometry*, 1958, *25*, 129–139.

Slobin, D. I. *Psycholinguistics.* Glencoe, Ill.: Scott, Foresman, 1971.

Smith, E. A follow-up study of women who request abortion. *American Journal of Orthopsychiatry*, 1973, *43*, 574–585.

Smith, E. R., & Miller, F. D. Limits on perception of cognitive processes: A reply to Nisbett and Wilson. *Psychological Review*, 1978, *85*, 355–362.

Smith, G. F., & Dorfman, D. D. The effect of stimulus uncertainty on the relationship between frequency of exposure and liking. *Journal of Personality and Social Psychology*, 1975, *31*, 150–155.

Smith, J. R. Proxmire reenters the ring after scientist lands a hit. *Science*, April 1980, 156–157.

Smith, P. B. Social influence processes and the outcome of sensitivity training. *Journal of Personality and Social Psychology*, 1976, *34*, 1087–1094.

Smith, R. E., et al. Role and justice considerations in the attribution of responsibility to a rape victim. *Journal of Research in Personality*, 1976, *10*, 346–357.

Smith, S., & Haythorn, W. Effects of compatibility, crowding, group size, and leadership authority on stress, anxiety, hostility, and annoyance in isolated groups. *Journal of Personality and Social Psychology*, 1972, 22, 67–79.

Smith, S. S., Richardson, D., & Hendrick, C. Bibliography of journal articles in *Personality and social psychology:* 1979. *Personality and Social Psychology Bulletin*, December 1980, 606–636.

Snyder, M. Self-monitoring processes. In L. Berkowitz (Ed.), *Advances in experimental social psychology* (Vol. 12). New York: Academic Press, 1979.

Sbyder, M., Schultz, R., & Jones, E. E. Expectancy and apparent duration as determinants of fatigue. *Journal of Personality and Social Psychology*, 1974, *29*, 426–434.

Synder, M. & Swann, W. B., Jr. When actions reflect attitudes: The politics of impression management. *Journal of Personality and Social Psychology*, 1976, *34*, 1034–1042.

Synder, M., & Tanke, E. D. Behavior and attitude: Some people are more consistent than others. *Journal of Personality*, 1976, *44*, 501–517.

Synder, M., & Uranowitz, S. Reconstructing the past: Some cognitive consequences of person perception. *Journal of Personality and Social Psychology*, 1978, *36*, 941–950.

Sommer, R., & Becker, F. D. Territorial defense and the good neighbor. *Journal of Personality and Social Psychology*, 1969, *11*, 85–92.

Sommer, R., & Ross, H. Social interaction on a geriatric ward. *International Journal of Social Psychiatry*, 1958, *4*, 128–133.

Spence, J. T., & Helmreich, R. L. Masculine instrumentality and feminine expressiveness: Their relationships with sex role attitudes and behaviors. *Psychology of Women Quarterly*, 1980, *5*, 147–163.

Spence, J. T., Helmreich, R., & Stapp, J. Ratings of self and peers on sex role attributes and their relation to self-esteem and conceptions of masculinity and femininity. *Journal of Personality and Social Psychology*, 1975, *32*, 29–39.

Sperlich, P. W. Trial by jury: It may have a future. In P. Kurland & G. Casper (Eds.), *Supreme Court review*. University of Chicago Press, 1979, 191–224.

Spinetta, J. J., & Rigler, D. The child-abusing parent: A psychological review. In R. Kalmar (Ed.), *Child abuse: Perspectives on diagnosis, treatment, and prevention*. Dubuque, Iowa: Kendall/Hunt, 1977.

Sprofkin, J. N., Liebert, R. M., & Poulos, R. W. Effects of a prosocial televised example on children's helping. *Journal of Experimental Child Psychology*, 1975, *20*, 119–126.

Sprey, J. The family as a system in conflict. *Journal of Marriage and the Family*, 1969, *31*, 699–706.

Staats, A. W., & Staats, C. K. Attitudes established by classical conditioning. *Journal of Abnormal and Social Psychology*, 1958, *57*, 37–40.

Stang, D. Conformity, ability, and self-esteem. *Representative Research in Social Psychology*, 1972, *3*, 97–103.

Stapp, J., & Fulcher, R. The employment of APA members. *American Psychologist*, 1981, *36*, 1263–1314.

Stapp, J., et al., The employment of recent doctorate recipients in psychology: 1975 through 1978. *American Psychologist*, 1981, *36*, 1211–1254.

Stasser, G., & Davis, J. H. Group decision making and social influence: A social interaction sequence model. *Psychological Review*, 1981, *88*, 523–551.

Staub, E. Positive social behavior and morality. *Socialization and development* (Vol. 2). New York: Academic Press, 1979.

Staub, E., & Feinberg, H. K. Personality, socialization, and the development of prosocial behavior in children. In D. H. Smith & J. Macaulay (Eds.), *Voluntary action research*. San Francisco: Jossey-Bass, 1979.

Staub, E., & Sherk, L. Need approval, children's sharing behavior, and reciprocity in sharing. *Child Development*, 1970, *41*, 243–253.

Steele, R., Fuller, T., & Nater, T. Life in Jonestown. *Newsweek*, December 1978, 38–66.

Steenberger, B. N., & Alderman, D. Objective self-awareness as a non-aversive state: Effect of anticipating discrepancy reduction. *Journal of Personality*, 1979, *47*, 330–339.

Steiner, I. D. Group process and productivity. New York: Academic Press, 1972.

Steinmetz, S. K., & Straus, M. A. (Eds.), *Violence in the family*. New York: Dodd, Mead, 1974.

Stern, D. N. Mother and infant at play: The dyadic interaction involving facial, vocal, and gaze behaviors. In M. Lewis & L. A. Rosenblum, *The effect of the infant on its caretakers*. New York: Wiley, 1974.

Stern, P., & Gardner, G. T. Psychological research and energy policy. *American Psychologist*, 1981, *36*, 329–342.

Sternglanz, S. H., & Serbin. L. A. Sex-role stereotyping in children's television programs. *Developmental Psychology*, 1974, *10*, 710–715.

Sternthal, B., Dholakia, R., & Leavitt, C. The persuasive effect of source credibility: Tests of cognitive response. *Journal of Consumer Research*, 1978, *4*, 252–260.

Stever, F. B., Applefield, J. M., & Smith, R. Televised aggression and the interpersonal aggression of preschool children. *Journal of Experimental Child Psychology*, 1971, *11*, 440–447.

Stewart, R. H. Effect of continuous responding on the order effect in personality impression formation. *Journal of Personality and Social Psychology*, 1965, *1*, 161–165.

Stockdale, J. Crowding: Determinants and effects. In L. Berkowitz (Ed.), *Advances in experimental social psychology* (Vol. 11). New York: Academic Press, 1979.

Strodtbeck, F. L., James, R. M., & Hawkins. C. Social status in jury deliberations. In E. E. Maccoby, T. M. Newcomb, & E. L. Hartley (Eds.), *Readings in social psychology* (3rd ed). New York: Holt, Rinehart & Winston, 1958.

Stokols, D. On the distinction between density and crowding: Some implications for future research. *Psychological Review*, 1972, *79*, 275–277.

Stoner, J. A. F. *A comparison of individual and group decisions involving risk*. Unpublished master's thesis, Massachusetts Institute of Technology, School of Industrial Management, 1961.

Storms, M. D. Videotape and the attribution process: Reversing actors' and observers' points of view. *Journal of Personality and Social Psychology*, 1973, *27*(2), 165–175.

Storms, M. D., & Nisbett, R. E. Insomnia and the attribution process. *Journal of Personality and Social Psychology*, 1970, *16*, 319–328.

Straus, M. A. A general systems theory approach to a theory of violence between family members. *Social Science Information*, 1973, *12*, 105–125.

Straus, M. A. *Normative and behavioral aspects of violence between spouses: Preliminary data on a nationally representative USA sample*. Paper presented at the Symposium on Violence in Canadian Society, Simon Fraser University, March 1977.

Streeter, et al. Pitch changes during attempted deception. *Journal of Personality and Social Psychology*, 1977, *35*, 345–350.

Strickland, L. H., Lewicki, R. J., & Katz, A. M. Temporal orientation and perceived control as determinants of risk-taking. *Journal of Experimental Social Psychology*, 1966, *2*, 143–151.

Strodbeck, F., & Hook. H. The social dimensions of a 12-man jury table. *Sociometry*, 1961, *24*, 397–415.

Strom & Buck. Staring and participants' sex: Physiological and subjective reactions. *Personality and Social Psychology Bulletin*, 1979, *5*, 114–117.

Struening, E. Antidemocratic attitudes in a midwestern university. In H. Remmers (Ed.), *Antidemocratic attitudes in American schools*. Evanston: Northwestern University Press, 1963, ch. 9.

Sue, S., Smith, R. E., & Caldwell, C. Effects of inadmissible evidence on the decisions of simulated jurors: A moral dilemma. *Journal of Applied Social Psychology*, 1973, *3*, 344–353.

Suedfeld & Rank. Revolutionary leaders: Longterm success as a function of changes in conceptual complexity. *Journal of Personality and Social Psychology*, 1976, *34*, 196–178.

Suk, J., & Gastorf, J. In J. Suk & R. L. Miller (Eds.), *Social comparison processes*. Washington, D. C.: Hemisphere Halsted, 1977.

Sulloway, F. J. *Freud, biologist of the mind: Beyond the psychoanalytic legend*. New York: Basic Books, 1979.

Sundstrom, E., & Altman, I. Field study of dominance and territorial behavior. *Journal of Personality and Social Psychology*, 1974, *30*, 115–125.

Suomi, S. J., & Harlow, H. F. Social rehabilitation of isolate-reared monkeys. *Developmental Psychology*, 1972, *6*, 487–496.

Sutton-Smith, B., & Rosenberg, B. G. *The sibling*. New York: Holt, Rinehart & Winston, 1970.

Swann, W. B., Jr., & Hill, C. A. When our identities are mistaken: Reaffirming self-conceptions through social interaction. *Journal of Personality and Social Psychology*, in press.

Swann, W. B., Jr., & Read, S. J. Acquiring self-knowledge: The search for feedback that fits. *Journal of Personality and Social*

Psychology, 1981, *41*, 1119–1128.

Szucko, J. J., & Kleinmutz, B. Statistical versus clinial lie detection. *American Psychologist*, 1981, *36*, 488–496.

Tagiuri, R. Person perception. In G. Lindzey & E. Aronson (Eds.), *The handbook of social psychology*. Reading, Mass.: Addison-Wesley, 1969.

Tajfel, H. Experiments in intergroup discrimination. *Scientific American*, 1970, *223*, 96–102.

Tajfel, H., & Turner, J. An interpretive theory of intergroup conflict. In W. G. Austin & S. Worchel (Eds.), *The Social Psychology of Intergroup Relations*, Monterey, Calif.: Brooks/Cole, 1979.

Tan, A. S. TV beauty ads and role expectations of adolescent female viewers. *Journalism Quarterly*, 1979, *56*, 283–288.

Tan, A. S., & Vaughn, P. Mass media exposure, public affairs knowledge, and black militancy. *Journalism Quarterly*, 1976, *53*, 271–279.

Tanford, S., & Penrod, S. Biases in trials: Biases in trials involving defendants charged with multiple offenses. *Journal of Applied Social Psychology*, in press.

Taylor, D. W., Berry, P. C., & Block, C. H. Does group participation when using brainstorming facilitate or inhibit creative thinking? *Administrative Science Quarterly*, 1958, *3*, 23–47.

Taylor, S. E. A developing role for social psychology in medicine and medical practice. *Personality and Social Psychology Bulletin*, 1978, *4*, 515–523.

Taylor, S. P. Aggressive behavior and physiological arousal as a function of provocation and the tendency to inhibit aggression. *Journal of Personality*, 1967, *35*, 297–310.

Taylor, S. P., et al. The effects of alcohol + delta-9-tetra hydrocannabinal on human physical aggression. *Aggressive Behavior*, 1976, *2*, 153–161.

Taylor, S., & Crocker, J. Schematic bases of social information processing. In E. T. Higgins, P. Hermann, & M. P. Zanna (Eds.), *The Ontario symposium of personality and social psychology* (Vol. 1). Hillsdale, N.J.: Erlbaum, 1980.

Taylor, S. E., & Fiske, S. T. Point of view and perceptions of causality. *Journal of Personality and Social Psychology*, 1975, *32*, 439–445.

Taylor, S. E., & Fiske, S. T. Salience, attention, and attribution: Top of the head phenomena. In L. Berkowitz (Ed.), *Advances in experimental social psychology* (Vol. 11). New York: Academic Press, 1978.

Taylor, S. E., & Koivumaki, J. H. The perception of self and others: Acquaintanceship, affect, and actor observer differences. *Journal of Personality and Social Psychology*, 1976, *33*, 403–408.

Taylor, S. P., & Pisano, R. Physical aggression as a function of frustration and physical attack. *Journal of Social Psychology*, 1971, *84*, 261–267.

Tavris, C. Men and women report their views on masculinity. *Psychology Today*, 1977, *10*(8), 34–38, 82.

Tedin, K. L. The influence of parents on the political attitudes of adolescents. *American Political Science Review*, 1974, *68*, 1579–1592.

Teichman, Y. Emotional arousal and affiliation. *Journal of Experimental Social Psychology*, 1973, *9*, 591–605.

Terman, C. R. Pregnancy failure in female prairie deer mice related to parity and social environment. *Animal Behavior*, 1969, *17*, 104–108.

Terrace, H. S. *Nim: A chimpanzee who learned sign language*. New York: Knopf, 1979.

Thibaut, J. W., & Strickland, L. Psychological set and social conformity. *Journal of Personality and Social Psychology*, 1956, *25*, 115–129.

Thibaut, J., Walker, L., & Lind, E. A. Adversary presentation and bias in legal decisionmaking. *Harvard Law Review*, 1972, *86*, 386–401.

Thiessen, D. D. Population density, mouse genotype, and endo-crine function in behavior. *Journal of Comparative and Physiological Psychology*, 1964, *57*, 412–416.

Tilker, H. A. Socially responsible behavior as a function of observer responsibility and victim feedback. *Journal of Personality and Social Psychology*, 1970, *14*, 95–100.

Thistlethwaite, D., deHaan, H., & Kamenetzky, J. The effects of "directive" and "non-directive" communication procedures on attitudes. *Journal of Abnormal and Social Psychology*, 1955, *51*, 107–113.

Thomas, G. C., Batson, D. C., & Coke, J. S. Do Good Samaritans discourage helpfulness? Self-perceived altruism after exposure to highly helpful others. *Journal of Personality and Social Psychology*, 1981, *40*, 194–200.

Thompson, Fong, & Rosenhan. Inadmissible evidence and juror verdicts. *Journal of Personality and Social Psychology*, 1981, *40*(3), 453–463.

Thorndike, E. L. A constant error in psychological rating. *Journal of Applied Psychology*, 1920, *4*, 25–29.

Thornton, A., & Freedman, D. Change in the sex role attitudes of women, 1962–1977: Evidence from a panel study. *American Sociological Review*, 1979, *44*, 831–842.

Thurstone, L. L. Attitudes can be measured. *American Journal of Sociology*, 1928, *33*, 529–544.

The tragedy of Pruitt-Igoe, *Time*, December 27, 1971, 38.

Torrance, E. P. Some consequences of power differences on decision making in permanent and temporary three-man groups. In *Research Studies*, Washington State College, 1954, 22, 130–140.

Triandis, H. C. Attitude and attitude change. New York: Wiley, 1971.

Triplett, N. The dynamogenic factors in pacemaking and competition. *American Journal of Psychology*, 1898, *9*(4), 507–533.

Trist, E. L., & Banforth, K. W. Some social and psychological consequences of the Longwall method of coal-getting. *Human Relations*, February 1951, 3–38.

Tunnell, G. A. Three dimensions of naturalness: An expanded definition of field research. *Psychological Bulletin*, 1977, *84*, 426–437.

Turnbull, C. M. *The mountain people*. New York: Simon & Schuster, 1972.

Turner, C. W., & Simons, L. S. Effects of subject sophistication and evaluation apprehension on aggressive responses to weapons. *Journal of Personality and Social Psychology*, 1974, *30*, 341–348.

Turner, J. C. Social comparison and social identity: Some prospects for intergroup behaviour. *European Journal of Social Psychology*, 1975, *5*, 5–34.

Turner, J. C., Brown, R. J., & Tajfel, H. Social comparison and group interest in ingroup favoritism. *European Journal of Social Psychology*. 1979, *9*, 187–204.

Turner, R. H. The self-conception in social interaction. In C. P. Gordon & K. P. Gergen, *The self in social interaction*. New York: Wiley, 1968.

Tversky, A., & Kahneman, D. Causal schemas in judgments under uncertainty. In M. Fishbein (Ed.), *Progress in social psychology* (Vol. 1). Hillsdale, N.J.: Erlbaum, 1980.

Tversky, A., & Kahneman, D. Judgment under uncertainty: Heuristics and biases. *Science*, 1974, *815*, 1124–1131.

Underwood, B., & Moore, B. Perspective-taking and altruism. *Psychological Bulletin*, 1982, *91*, 143–173.

U.S. Department of Justice. Victims of crime. *Bureau of Justice Statistics Bulletin*, November, 1981.

Valenti, A., & Downing, L. Differential effects of jury size on verdicts following deliberation as a function of the apparent guilt of a defendant. *Journal of Personality and Social Psychology*, 1975, *32*, 655–663.

Valins, S. Cognitive effects of false heartrate feedback. *Journal of Personality and Social Psychology*, 1966, *4*, 400–408.

Vance, E. B., & Wagner, N. N. Written descriptions of orgasm: A study of sex differences. *Archives of Sexual Behavior*, 1976, *5*, 87–98.

Van Hoof, J. A. R. A. M. The facial displays of the catarrhine monkey and apes. In D. Morris (Ed.), *Primate ethology*. Chicago: Aldine, 1967.

Vaughan, E. D. Misconceptions about psychology among introductory psychology students. *Teaching of Psychology*, October 1977, pp. 138–141.

Vaughan, G. The trans-situational aspect of conforming behavior. *Journal of Personality*, 1964, *32*, 335–354.

Veitch, R., & Griffitt, W. Good news, bad news: Affective and interpersonal effects. *Journal of Applied Social Psychology*, 1976, *6*, 69–75.

Victor, J. S. *Human sexuality: A social psychological approach*. Englewood Cliffs, N.J.: Prentice-Hall, 1980.

Victor, J. The social psychology of sexual arousal. In N. K. Denzin (Ed.), *Studies in symbolic interaction*. Greenwich, Conn.: JAI Press, 1978.

Vidmar, N. Effects of decision alternatives on the verdicts and social perceptions of simulated jurors. *Journal of Personality and Social Psychology*, 1972, *22*, 211–218.

Vincour, J. G.I.s in West Germany meet rising wall of bias. *The New York Times*, June 25, 1982, A2.

von Baeyer, C. L., Sherk, D. L., & Zanna, M. P. Impression management: Female job applicants, male (chauvinist) interviewer. Paper presented at the Meeting of the APA, New York, 1979.

Waber, D. P. Sex differences in mental abilities, hemispheric lateralization, and rate of physical growth at adolescence. *Developmental Psychology*, 1976, *12*, 278–282; 1977, *13*, 29–38.

Wade, N. Shoot-out with Einstein in Arizona. *The New York Times*, April 19, 1982.

Walker, L., Thibaut, J., & Andreoli, V. Order of presentation at trial. *Yale Law Journal*, 1972, *82*, 216–226.

Wallach, M. A., Kogan, N., & Bem, D. J. Group influence on individual risk taking. *Journal of Abnormal and Social Psychology*, 1962, *65*, 75–86.

Wallin, Paul. Cultural contradictions and sex-roles: A repeat study. *American Sociological Review*, 1950, *15*, 288–293.

Walster, E. Assignment of responsibility for an accident. *Journal of Personality and Social Psychology*, 1966, *3*, 73–79.

Walster, E., Aronson, E., & Abrahams, D. On increasing the persuasiveness of a low prestige communicator. *Journal of Experimental Social Psychology*, 1966, *2*, 325–342.

Walster, E., Aronson, E., Abrahams, D., & Rottman, L. Importance of physical attractiveness in dating behavior. *Journal of Personality and Social Psychology*, 1966, *4*, 508–516.

Walster, E., Berscheid, E., & Barclay, A. A determinant of preference among modes of dissonance reduction. *Journal of Personality and Social Psychology*, 1967, *7*, 211–216.

Walster, E., & Walster, G. W. The matching hypothesis. *Journal of Personality and Social Psychology*, 1969, *6*, 248–253.

Walters, R. H., & Willows, D. Imitation behavior of disturbed children following exposure to aggressive and non-aggressive models. *Child Development*, 1968, *39*, 79–91.

Ward, D. A., Jackson, M., & Ward, R. E. Crimes of violence by women. In D. J. Mulvihill, & M. M. Tumin (Eds.), *Crimes of violence*. (National Commission on the Causes and Prevention of Violence.) Washington, D.C.: U.S. Government Printing Office, 1969.

Ward, W. C., & Jenkins, H. M. The display of information and the judgment of contingency. *Canadian Journal of Psychology*, 1965, *19*, 231–241.

Ward, S., Wackman, & Wartella, E. *How children learn to buy*. Beverly Hills, Calif.: Sage, 1977.

Warr, P., & Parry, G. Paid employment and women's psychological well-being. *Psychological Bulletin*, 1982, *91*, 498–516.

Watson, R. I., Jr. Investigation into deindividuation using a cross-cultural survey technique. *Journal of Personality and Social Psychology*, 1973, *25*, 342–345.

Watts, W. A. Relative persistence of opinion change induced by active compared to passive participation. *Journal of Personality and Social Psychology*, 1967, *5*, 4–15.

Watts, W. A., & Holt, L. E. Persistence of opinion change induced under conditions of forewarning and distraction. *Journal of Personality and Social Psychology*, 1979, *37*, 778–789.

Weary, G. Examination of affect and egotism as mediators of bias in causal attributions. *Journal of Personality and Social Psychology*, 1980, *38*, 348–357.

Waber, M. *Economy and society: An outline of interpretive sociology*. New York: Bedminster Press, 1968.

Weber, S. J., & Cook, T. D. Subject effects in laboratory research: An examination of subject roles, demand characteristics, and valid inference. *Psychological Bulletin*, 1972, *77*, 273–295.

Weigel, R. H., Loomis, J. W., & Soja, M. J. Race-relations on prime time television. *Journal of Personality and Social Psychology*, 1980, *39*, 884–893.

Weigel, R. H., & Newman, L. S. Increasing attitude-behavior correspondence by broadening the scope of the behavioral measure. *Journal of Personality and Social Psychology*, 1976, *33*, 793–802.

Weigel, R. H., Vernon, D. T. A., & Tognacci, L. N. Specificity of the attitude as a determinant of attitude-behavior congruence. *Journal of Personality and Social Psychology*, 1974, *30*, 724–728.

Weiner, B., et al. Perceiving the causes of success and failure. In E. E. Jones, et al. (Eds.), *Attribution: Perceiving the causes of behavior*. Morristown, N.J.: General Learning Press, 1972, 95–120.

Weiner, B., Heckhausen, H., Meyer, W. U., & Cook, R. E. Causal ascriptions and achievement behavior: A conceptual analysis of effort and reanalysis of locus of control. *Journal of Personality and Social Psychology*, 1972, *21*, 239–248.

Weiser, M. P. K., & Arbeiter, J. S. *Womanlist*. New York: Atheneum, 1981.

Weiss, R. S. *Loneliness: The experience of emotional and social isolation*. Cambridge, Mass.: MIT Press, 1973.

Weiss, R. S. *Marital separation*. New York: Basic Books, 1975.

Wells, G. L., Ferguson, T. J., & Lindsay, R. C. The tractibility of eyewitness confidence and its implications for triers of fact. *Journal of Applied Psychology*, 1981, *66*, 688–696.

Wells, G. L., Lindsay, R. C. L., & Ferguson, T. J. Accuracy, confidence, and juror perceptions in eyewitness identification. *Journal of Applied Psychology*, 1979, *64*, 440–448.

Wells, G. L., & Harvey, J. H. Do people use consensus information in making causal attributions? *Journal of Personality and Social Psychology*, 1977, *35*, 279–293.

Wells, G. L., & Harvey, J. H. Naive attributors' attributions and predictions. What is informative and when is an effect an effect? *Journal of Personality and Social Psychology*, 1978, *36*, 483–490.

Wells, G. L., & Petty, R. E. The effects of overt head-movements on persuasion, compatibility, and incompatibility of responses. *Journal of Basic and Applied Social Psychology*, 1980, *1*, 219–230.

Wells, L. E. Theories of deviance and the self-concept. *Social Psychology*, 1978, *41*, 189–204.

Werner, C. M., Brown, B. B., & Damron, G. Territorial marking in a game arcade. *Journal of Personality and Social Psychology*, 1981, *41*, 1094–1104.

West, S. G., & Brown, T. J. Physical attractiveness, the severity of the emergency and helping: A field experiment and interpersonal simulation. *Journal of Experimental Social Psychology*, 1975, *11*, 531–538.

Whitcher, S. J., & Fisher, J. D. Multidimensional reaction to therapeutic touch in a hospital setting. *Journal of Personality and Social Psychology*, 1979, *37*, 87–96.

Whiting, B. B., & Edwards, C. P. A cross-cultural analysis of sex differences in the behavior of children three through eleven. *Journal of Social Psychology*, 1973, *91*, 171–188.

Whyte, W. End of the exodus: The logic of headquarters city. *New York Magazine*, September 20, 1976, 80–94.

Wicker, A. W. Attitudes versus actions: The relationship of verbal and overt behavioral responses to attitude objects. *Journal of Social Issues*, 1969, *25*(4), 41–78.

Wicklund, R. A., & Brehm, J. W. *Perspectives on cognitive dissonance*. Hillsdale, N.J.: Lawrence Erlbaum, 1976.

Wilder, D. A. Homogeneity of jurors: The majority's influence depends upon their perceived independence. *Law and Human Behavior*, 1978, *2*, 363–376.

Wilder, D. A. Perception of groups, size of opposition, and social influence. *Journal of Experimental Social Psychology*, 1977, *13*, 253–268.

Wilder, D. Reduction of intergroup discrimination through individuation of the outgroup. *Journal of Personality and Social Psychology*, 1978, *36*, 1361–1374.

Wilder, D., & Allen, V. Veridical dissent, erroneous dissent, and conformity. Unpublished master's thesis, 1973.

Williams, E. Medium or message: Communications medium as a determinant of interpersonal evaluation. *Sociometry*, 1975, *38*, 119–130.

Williams, F., LaRose, R., & Frost, F. *Children, Television and Sex-Role Stereotyping*. New York: Praeger, 1981.

Williams v. Florida, *United States Reports*, 1970, *399*, 78–145.

Wilson, E. O. *Sociobiology: The new synthesis*. Cambridge, Mass.: Harvard University Press, 1975.

Wilson, E. O. *On human nature*. Cambridge, Mass.: Harvard University Press, 1978.

Wilson, D. W., & Donnerstein, E. Legal and ethical aspects of nonreactive social psychological research: An excursion into the public mind. *American Psychologist*, 1976, *31*, 765–773.

Wilson, R. D., & Muderrisoglu, A. An analysis of cognitive responses to comparative advertising. *Advances in Consumer Research*, 1980, *7*, 566–571.

Wilson, W. R. *Unobtrusive induction of positive attitudes*. Unpublished doctoral dissertation, University of Michigan, 1975.

Wilson, W., & Miller, H. Repetition, order of presentation, and timing of arguments and measures as determinants of opinion change. *Journal of Personality and Social Psychology*, 1968, *9*, 184–188.

Wiltz, C. Criminal victimization of minorities: A statistical profile. *The Urban League Review*, 1978.

Winch, R. F. Mate selection. *A study of complementary needs*. New York: Harper & Row, 1958.

Wispe, L. G. Positive forms of social behavior: An overview. *Journal of Social Issues*, 1972, *28*(3), 1–19.

Wispe, L., & Freshley, H. Race, sex, and sympathetic helping behavior: The broken leg caper. *Journal of Personality and Social Psychology*, 1971, *17*, 59–65.

Wolf, S. Behavioral style and group cohesiveness as sources of minority influence. *European Journal of Social Psychology*, 1979, *9*, 381–395.

Wolf, S., & Montgomery, D. A. Effects of inadmissible evidence and level of judicial admonishment to disregard on the judgments of mock jurors. *Journal of Applied Social Psychology*, 1977, *7*, 205–219.

Wolfgang, M. *Patterns in criminal homicide*. Philadelphia: University of Pennsylvania Press, 1958.

Wolfgang, M. E., & Strohm, R. B. The relationship between alcohol and criminal homicide. *Quarterly Journal of Studies on Alcohol*, 1956, *17*, 411–425.

Woman's Day Family Food Study on Nutrition. New York: Woman's Day Magazine, 1978.

Woodward, J. *Industrial organization: Theory and practice*. London: Oxford University Press, 1965.

Worchel, S. The effect of three types of arbitrary thwarting on the instigation to aggression. *Journal of Personality*, 1974, *42*, 300–318.

Worchel, S., & Teddlie, C. The experience of crowding: A two-factor theory. *Journal of Personality and Social Psychology*, 1976, *34*, 30–40.

Worchel, S., & Yohai, S. M. L. The role of attribution on the experience of crowding. *Journal of Experimental Social Psychology*, 1979, *15*, 91–104.

Worchel, S., & Brehm, J. W. Direct and implied social restoration of freedom. *Journal of Personality and Social Psychology*, 1971, *18*, 294–304.

Worthy, M., Gary, A., & Kahn, G. Self-disclosure as an exchange process. *Journal of Personality and Social Psychology*, 1969, *3*, 59–63.

Wortman, C. B. Causal attributions and personal control. In Harvey, J. H., Ickes, W., & Kidd, R. F. (Eds.), *New directions in attribution research* (Vol. 1). Hillsdale, N.J.: Erlbaum, 1976, 23–52.

Wortman, C. B., & Brehm, J. W. Responses to uncontrollable outcomes: An integration of reactance theory and the learned helplessness model. In L. Berkowitz (Ed.), *Advances in experimental social psychology* (Vol. 8). New York: Academic Press, 1975.

Wrightsman, L. Effects of waiting with others on changes in level of felt anxiety. *Journal of Abnormal and Social Psychology*, 1960, *61*, 216–222.

Yandell, B., & Insko, C. Attribution of attitudes to speakers and listeners under assigned-behavior conditions: Does behavior engulf the field? *Journal of Experimental Social Psychology*, 1977, *13*, 269–278.

Yankelovich, Skelly, & White, Inc. Highlights of a national survey of the general public, judges, lawyers, and community leaders. In T. Fetter (Ed.), *State courts: A blueprint for the future*. Williamsburg, Va.: National Center for State Courts, 1978.

Yankelovich, Skelly, & White, Inc., Judicial Reactions to sentencing guidelines 3–4. 1980. Cited in Clancy, K. et al., Sentence decisionmaking, *Journal of Criminal Law & Criminology*, 1981, *72*(3), 525.

Yerkes, R. M. & Dodson, J. D. The relation of strength of stimulus to rapidity of habit-formation. *Journal of Comparative and Neurological Psychology*, 1908, *18*, 459–482.

Youniss, J. *Parents and peers in social development*. Chicago: University of Chicago Press, 1980.

Yukl, G. *Leadership in organizations*. Englewood Cliffs, N.J.: Prentice-Hall, 1981.

Zadney, J., & Gerard, H. B. Attributed intentions and informational selectivity. *Journal of Experimental Social Psychology*, 1974, *10*, 34–52.

Zajonc, R. B., The concepts of balance, congruity, and dissonance. *Public Opinion Quarterly*, 1960, *24*, 280–296.

Zajonc, R. B. Attitudinal effects of mere exposure. *Journal of Personality and Social Psychology. Monograph Supplement*, 1968, *9*, 1–27.

Zajonc, R. B. Cognitive theories of social behavior. In G. Lindzey & E. Aronson (Eds.), *Handbook of Social Psychology* (Rev. ed.). Reading, Mass.: Addison-Wesley, 1968.

Zajonc, R. B. Social facilitation. *Science*, 1965, *149*, 269–274.

Zajonc, R. B., & Markus, G. B. Birth order and intellectual development. *Psychological Review*, 1975, *82*, 74–88.

Zajonc, R. B., Heingartner, A., & Herman, E. M. Social enhancement and impairment of performance in the cockroach. *Journal of Personality and Social Psychology*, 1969, *13*, 83–92.

Zanna, M. D., & Cooper, J. Dissonance and the pill: An attribution approach to studying the arousal properties of dissonance. *Journal of Personality and Social Psychology*, 1974, *29*, 703–709.

Zanna, M. P., Goethals, G. R., & Hill, J. F. Evaluating a sex-related ability: Social comparison with similar other and standard setters. *Journal of Experimental Social Psychology*, 1975, *11*, 86–93.

Zanna, M. P., & Hamilton, D. L. Further evidence for meaning change in impression formation. *Journal of Experimental Social Psychology*, 1977, *13*, 224–238.

Zanna, M. P., Kiesler, C. A., & Pilkonis, P. A. Positive and negative attitudinal affect established by classical conditioning. *Journal of Personality and Social Psychology*, 1970, *14*, 321–328.

Zanna, M. P., Olson, J. M., & Fazio, R. H. Attitude behavior consistency: An individual difference perspective. *Journal of Personality and Social Psychology*, 1980, *38*, 432–440.

Zanna, M. P., & Pack, S. J. On the self-fulfilling nature of apparent sex differences in behavior. *Journal of Experimental Social Psychology*, 1975, *11*, 583–591.

Zelnick, M., & Kantner, J. Sexual and contraceptive experience of young unmarried women in the United States, 1976 and 1971. *Family Planning Perspectives*, 1977, *9*, 55–71.

Zigler, E. Project Head Start: Success or failure? In E. Zigler and J. Valentine (Eds.), *Project Head Start: A legacy of the war on poverty.* New York: The Free Press, 1979.

Zilmann, D. Rhetorical elicitation of agreement, in persuasion. *Journal of Personality and Social Psychology*, 1972, *21*, 159–165.

Zillmann, D., & Bryant, J. Effect of residual excitation on the emotional response to provocation and delayed aggressive behav-ior. *Journal of Personality and Social Psychology*, 1974, *30*, 782–791.

Zimbardo, P. G. The human choice: Individuation, reason and order versus deindividuation, impulse, and chaos. In W. J. Arnold and D. Levine (Eds.), *Nebraska symposium on motivation* (Vol. 17). Lincoln: University of Nebraska Press, 1969.

Zimbardo, P. G. *Shyness: What it is, what you can do about it.* Reading, Mass.: Addison-Wesley, 1977.

Zimbardo, P. G., Banks, W. C., Haney, C., & Jaffe, D. A Pirandellian prison. *New York Times Magazine*, April 8, 1973.

Zimbardo, P. G., Ebbeson, E. B., & Maslach, C. *Influencing attitudes and changing behavior.* Reading, Mass.: Addison Wesley, 1977.

Zimbardo, P. G., & Formica, R. Emotional comparison and self-esteem as determinants of affiliation. *Journal of Personality*, 1963, *31*, 141–162.

Zimbardo, P., Snyder, M., Thomas, J., Gold, A., & Gurwitz, S. Modifying the impact of persuasive communications with external distractions. *Journal of Personality and Social Psychology*, 1970, *16*, 669–680.

Zimbardo, P., Weisenberg, M., Firestone, I., & Levy, B. Communicator effectiveness in producing public conformity and private attitude change. *Journal of Personality*, 1965, *33*, 233–255.

Zuckerman, M. Attribution of success and failure revisited, or: The motivational bias is alive and well in attribution theory. *Journal of Personality*, 1979, *47*, 245–287.

Zuckerman, M. Use of consensus information in prediction of behavior. *Journal of Experimental Social Psychology*, 1978, *14*, 163–171.

Zuckerman, M., Lazzano, M., & Waldgeir, D. Undermining effects of the foot-in-the-door technique with extrinsic rewards. *Journal of Applied Social Psychology*, 1979, *9*, 292–296.

NAME INDEX

McGuire, W. J., 134, 135, 136, 319, 321, 323
McKenna, R. J., 265
McLanahan, S., 608
McLuhan, M., 321
McMullan, S., 237
McPhee, W. N., 322
McPherson, J. M., 539
McRae, J. A., 605
Mead, G. H., 12, 24, 134
Mead, M., 430
Meeker, F. B., 227
Mehrabian, A., 228, 265, 268, 520, 521
Meiselman, K. C., 405
Melbin, M., 548
Melson, W. H., 298
Merton, R. D., 24
Mesmer, 9
Metcalf, J., 543
Meter, K., 459
Mewborn, C. R., 315
Midlarsky, E., 444
Miles, R. E., 507
Milgram, S., 13, 77, 367, 381, 384–87, 502, 548–49
Miller, A., 377
Miller, A. G., 187, 193
Miller, D. T., 192, 194
Miller, F. D., 137
Miller, G. B., 574
Miller, G. R., 271
Miller, J., 310
Miller, N., 24, 26, 220, 320, 457
Miller, R., 317
Miller, W., 322
Mills, J., 220, 311, 318
Mills, T., 146, 303, 483
Milton, O., 383
Mintz, Alexander, 502–3
Mintz, P. M., 220
Mirer, T. W., 347
Miron, 259
Mischel, W., 179, 205
Mita, T. H., 317
Mitchell, R. E., 537, 539
Miyamoto, S., 107
Modigliani, A., 153
Money, J., 115
Monson, T. C., 192
Montgomerey, D. A., 578
Moore, B., 444
Moreland, R. L., 222
Moreno, J. C., 11, 12
Morgan, C. J., 458
Morris, B., 377
Morris, M. G., 404
Moscovici, S., 375, 490, 491
Moss, M. K., 445
Mosteller, 55
Moustakas, C. E., 212
Mowen, J. L., 561
Muderrisoglu, A., 611
Mueller, C. W., 610
Mueller, J. E., 282
Mulder, M., 483
Mulvey, A., 627
Munsterberg, H., 22, 555

Murchison, C., 12
Myers, D. G., 490, 491, 581

Naccari, N., 309
Nadler, A., 464
Nagel, 577
Nahemow, L., 524
Nash, S. C., 110
Nass, G. D., 234, 235, 237–39
Nebergall, R. E., 306, 320
Neisser, V., 136
Nel, E., 144
Nelson, C., 172
Nelson, R. E., 311
Nemeth, C., 314, 375, 377, 567, 581
Newcomb, T., 224, 228, 229, 296, 297, 327
Newman, J., 549
Newman, L. S., 346
Newtson, D., 153
Nicassio, P., 149
Nicosia, G., 540
Niederehe, G., 260
Nieva, V. F., 602
Niles, P., 315
Nisbett, R. E., 137, 144, 148, 163, 173, 191, 192, 195, 199, 200, 201, 204, 299
Noble, A. M., 383
Nogami, G. Y., 540
Norman, R., 349
Norman, W. T., 171
Norton, A. J., 610
Nye, F. I., 610

Ochsmann, R., 491
Oden, C. W., Jr., 540
Oetzel, R. M., 112
Olneck, M. R., 101
Olsen, M. E., 621
Olson, J. M., 349
O'Neill, G., 235
O'Neill, N., 235
Orlofsky, J., 124
Orne, M., 387, 575
Ornstein, 70
Ortiz, V., 622
Orwell, George, 484
Osborn, Alex, 487
Osgood, C. E., 258, 259, 295, 301
Oskamp, S., 347
Osmond, H., 521
Oster, H., 263
Ostrom, T. M., 319
Ostrove, N., 226
Overmeier, J. B., 160

Pack, S. J., 153
Packard, V., 212
Padawer-Singer, A. M., 134, 135, 564–65, 566
Pagano, F., 316
Page, M. P., 414
Page, R., 343, 344
Page, R. A., 445
Pallak, M., 147

Palmer, J. C., 570
Palmore, E. B., 224
Papageorgis, D., 319, 323
Paradee, A., 199
Parke, P. D., 414
Parke, R. D., 103, 105, 221, 280
Parry, G., 604
Parsons, C., 431
Parsons, H. M., 509
Parsons, T., 485
Patterson, A., 533
Patterson, M. L., 269
Patterson, T. E., 280, 281
Paulus, P., 540, 542
Pavlov, 24, 297
Pawlby, 103
Payne, J. W., 589
Peck, R. F., 458
Pendleton, M. G., 379
Penrod, S., 489, 566, 567, 568, 570, 574, 579, 581, 582
Peplau, A., 464
Peplau, L. A., 211, 212, 214
Percival, E., 412
Perlman, D., 194, 211, 212, 214
Perloff, R., 69
Peterson, L., 192, 322
Petty, R. E., 319, 323, 324, 332, 333, 343, 380
Philips, 422
Phoenix, 111
Piaget, J., 87, 91–93, 96–97, 98, 443
Pietropinto, A., 239, 240
Piliavin, I. M., 42, 68, 458, 463
Piliavin, J. A., 42, 458, 463
Pilkonis, P. A., 297
Pineault, T., 273
Pines, M., 85, 600
Pisano, R., 413
Pittman, T. S., 145, 147
Plato, 9, 12, 86, 210
Podlesny, J. A., 563
Poe, D., 273
Pollak, H., 426
Pomazel, R. J., 464
Pomeroy, W. B., 237
Pope, H., 610
Porter, L., 506, 507
Porterfield, 262
Post, D., 203
Premack, A. J., 256
Premack, D., 256
Price, R. A., 227
Prince, M., 11, 12
Proxmire, William, 20, 233
Pruitt, D. G., 447

Quantz, M. B., 433
Quartles, R. C., 281

Rabbie, J. M., 220, 221, 389
Rada, J. B., 384
Ramchandra, V., 326
Ramey, C. T., 105
Ramirez, A., 316
Rank, A. D., 499

SUBJECT INDEX

STUDENT FEEDBACK QUESTIONNAIRE

When making revisions for the second edition of SOCIAL PSYCHOLOGY, I will find it helpful to have feedback from students who have actually used the book. This page is a tear-out questionnaire that can be sent, postage prepaid, to my publisher, who will then send it to me. Your assistance will help assure that the second edition is an improvement on the first.

1. First, tell me which three chapters of the book you liked best, and what you liked about them.

   chapter   *comment*

   _____   _____
   _____   _____
   _____   _____

2. Which three chapters did you like least, and what did you dislike about them?

   chapter   *comment*

   _____   _____
   _____   _____
   _____   _____

3. Which topics (from any chapter) were of the greatest interest to you, and why?

   topic   *comment*

   _____   _____
   _____   _____
   _____   _____

4. Which topics (from any chapter) interested you least, and why?

   topic   *comment*

   _____   _____
   _____   _____
   _____   _____

5. Overall, how would you rate this book on the following scales? (Circle the number that reflects your rating.)

a. easy to read	1	2	3	4	5	6	7	hard to read
b. hard to understand	1	2	3	4	5	6	7	easy to understand
c. interesting	1	2	3	4	5	6	7	boring
d. poorly organized	1	2	3	4	5	6	7	well organized
e. seemed to fit well with lectures	1	2	3	4	5	6	7	seemed mismatched to lectures

6. To what extent did each of the following features add to your understanding of the materials covered in the text? (Circle the number that reflects your rating.)

	Not helpful						*Very helpful*
a. research boxes	1	2	3	4	5	6	7
b. controversy boxes	1	2	3	4	5	6	7
c. application boxes	1	2	3	4	5	6	7
d. study questions	1	2	3	4	5	6	7
e. chapter summary	1	2	3	4	5	6	7

7. What was the approximate size of your social psychology class?_____students.

8. In which college year did you take this course?_____

FOLD ON LINE

9. What department was this course offered in?_____

10. What is your major?_____

11. How old are you?_____ years.

12. Name of your college. _____

THANK YOU!

FOLD ON LINE

537